2019
Year C-I

THE ALMANAC FOR PASTORAL LITURGY

SOURCEBOOK

FOR SUNDAYS, SEASONS, AND WEEKDAYS

Eric Bermani
Mary Birmingham
Charles A. Bobertz
Paul H. Colloton, OSFS
Donna M. Crilly
Joseph DeGrocco
Joyce Donahue
Mary A. Ehle
Christopher J. Ferraro

J. Philip Horrigan
Patricia J. Hughes
Corinna Laughlin
Timothy Matovino
Biagio Mazza
Jo-Ann Metzdorff
Jill Maria Murdy

Danielle A. Noe
Robert C. Rabe
Mary Patricia Storms
S. Anne Elizabeth Sweet, OSCO
Letitia Thornton
Paul Turner
Stephen Wilbricht, CSC
D. Todd Williamson
Daniella Zsupan-Jerome

LTP
LITURGY
TRAINING
PUBLICATIONS

Nihil Obstat
Reverend Mr. Daniel G. Welter, JD
Chancellor
Archdiocese of Chicago
October 26, 2017

Imprimatur
Most Reverend Francis J. Kane, DD
Vicar General
Archdiocese of Chicago
October 26, 2017

SOURCEBOOK FOR SUNDAYS, SEASONS, AND WEEKDAYS 2019: THE ALMANAC FOR PASTORAL LITURGY © 2018 Archdiocese of Chicago: Liturgy Training Publications, 3949 South Racine Avenue, Chicago, IL 60609; 800-933-1800; fax 800-933-7094; e-mail: orders@ltp.org; website: www.LTP.org. All rights reserved.

This book was edited by Danielle A. Noe, MDIV. Christian Rocha and Michael A. Dodd were the production editors. Ana M. Stephenson was the cover designer, Anna Manhart provided cover art direction, and Jane Kremsreiter was the interior designer. Kari Nicholls was the production artist.

Cover illustration © Steve Musgrave.

Illustrations for Sundays and solemnities by Corey Wilkinson; seasonal icons by Kari Nicholls © LTP.

Printed in the United States of America.

ISBN 978-1-61671-399-7

SSS19

CONTENTS

INTRODUCTION

About *Sourcebook*

SOURCEBOOK *for Sundays, Seasons, and Weekdays 2019: The Almanac for Pastoral Liturgy* provides guidance regarding the various liturgical elements (music, environment, prayers, readings, etc.) so that communities can prepare liturgies rooted in the vision of the Second Vatican Council.

Sourcebook is organized to help you follow liturgical time in sequence. It begins with Advent, which is the start of the liturgical year, and it continues with Christmas Time. Next begins Ordinary Time, so named because the Sundays are designated by their ordinal (counted) numbers. *Sourcebook* tags the Sundays in Ordinary Time after Christmas Time and up until Lent as "Ordinary Time (during Winter)." This is not an official description or designation, but merely a chapter heading *Sourcebook* uses to differentiate between the two parts in Ordinary Time.

Next you will find Lent, followed by the Sacred Paschal Triduum, and then Easter Time. After the Solemnity of Pentecost, Ordinary Time resumes. *Sourcebook* refers to this longer stretch as "Ordinary Time (during Summer and Fall)." When Ordinary Time concludes, the next liturgical year begins, so this chapter takes us through the end of the liturgical year.

Within each of the chapters of *Sourcebook*, you will find two sections: "The Liturgical Time" and "The Calendar." "The Liturgical Time" is organized into several parts:

◆ *The Meaning*: the theological meaning and history of the liturgical time or season (this year's edition combines "The Meaning" with "The Roman Missal" overview)

◆ *The Saints*: how the living witness of the saints can deepen and enrich liturgical time

◆ *The Liturgical Books*: what the *Lectionary for Mass*, *The Roman Missal*, and other ritual texts tell us about liturgical time

◆ *The Liturgical Environment*: ideas for the appearance of worship spaces

◆ *The Liturgical Music*: the musical expression of liturgical time and how to enhance it

◆ *Other Prayers, Rituals, and Devotions*: ideas to foster the parish's devotional life while emphasizing the primacy of the liturgy

◆ *Liturgical Ministers*: tips and formational notes for all liturgical ministers

◆ *Children's Liturgy of the Word*: how to prepare the Liturgy of the Word with children on Sunday

◆ *Evangelization*: opportunities for evangelizing through the liturgy and the liturgical year

- *The Parish and the Home*: how to carry liturgical time from the parish to the domestic Church (at home)

- *Reflections through the Year*: inspirational quotes that connect liturgy to life so that we may go forth and live as Christ's disciples

- *Mass Texts*: original prayers for the Order of Mass (where options are permitted)

"The Calendar" is a straightforward almanac for each day of the liturgical year. You can look up any day of the year and find basic liturgical information as well as ideas for how to celebrate it. The primary purpose of *Sourcebook*, however, is to help you celebrate Sundays, solemnities, feasts, and all of liturgical time. For this reason, you will find most of the material in "The Calendar" devoted to Sundays, solemnities, and feasts, which include the following three sections:

- *Lectionary for Mass*: an explanation of how the Scriptures of the day relate to what is being celebrated

- *The Roman Missal*: insights into the prayers and suggestions about options; particular notes are provided for the third edition of the Missal

- *Other Ideas*: Additional ideas for parishes, families, or liturgies

Other days include additional sections:

- *"About Today's . . ."*: what the Church is celebrating on this day (solemnities, feasts, and memorials) and why

- *Today's Saint*: Biographies of the saints celebrated on that day

Liturgical Calendar

The liturgical dates in Sourcebook follow those listed on the 2019 general calendar prepared by the Bishops of the United States of America. These dates do not take into consideration diocesan and parish feasts. Please consult your local ordo for these dates. Although the majority of the dates are similar, customers in Canada should also consult their local ordo.

How to Use *Sourcebook* on a Liturgical Ministers' / Parish Staff Retreat in Your Parish

◆ ONE OF THE BIGGEST STRUGGLES for a parish is sharing a common vision. St. Paul reminds us that there is "One Lord, one faith, one baptism" (Ephesians 4:5). Yet in reality we have varying gifts, ministries, and specializations and sometimes competing calendars and priorities. The Council Fathers set the standard in the *Constitution on the Sacred Liturgy*: "The liturgy is the summit toward which the activity of the Church is directed; at the same time it is the fount from which all the Church's power flows" (CSL, 10). Practically speaking, however, can this impact third-grade religious formation or the annual food drive in a meaningful way?

A community that is formed by staffs and active parishioners can become the foundation of this ideal. Our tradition reminds us to pray together, to speak honestly, and to listen to each other. We do this best on retreat. It is in this space that we can consciously allow the Spirit to move through us, create a common vision, and guide the practical decisions that will shape our parish's life rooted in Sunday worship.

For almost a decade this has been and continues to be the reality in our parish. We recognize it as sacred and draining time, but one to which we look forward. The work of the Spirit is clear and, like a pebble thrown into a lake, the experience fans out into the life of committees throughout the parish.

Who goes on this retreat? We are those with liturgical and pastoral responsibilities. We are the pastor, pastoral associate, directors of music, faith formation, RCIA, Christian service, and youth ministry. We are members of the art and environment committee, choir, readers, and Mass coordinators. So included are both parish staff and parish leaders, about twelve to fourteen in all.

When do we meet? We have found it best to meet in late August. It seems to be a quieter time in the parish, and those with families are freer than during the school year. Also, it give us space to take the ideas back to be fleshed out and integrated by our committees as we begin a new liturgical year. The days are spent in both reflection and practical preparation. Using a parishioner's home gives us freedom to share meals and space. The retreat takes about three days.

What do we bring? We bring our expertise, certainly. Just as important, however, is honesty and integrity. Everyone's area is up for discussion by everybody. We need to speak freely, disagree in charity, sometimes ask for forgiveness, and come to a consensus. All leadership must put aside any defensive posturing. This is one of the biggest hurdles to overcome for everyone. Trust is key.

We also bring work. Everyone is responsible to have already read the Gospel accounts for the upcoming year's cycle. Each person also brings a copy of *Workbook for Lectors, Gospel Readers, and Proclaimers of the Word* (LTP) and *Sourcebook for Sundays, Seasons, and Weekdays* for the coming year. One of the staff members packs up bins of hymnals, liturgical documents, the parish calendar, and other practical materials. (Use LTP's *Liturgy Documents* series, especially volumes 1, 2, and 4.)

We find the articles in *Sourcebook* to be extremely helpful—for example, by offering ideas on how one's ministry might dovetail with another, or simply by reminding us of how many resources the Church already provides—that there's no need to reinvent the wheel.

The plan for the retreat is simple, with plenty of room for the Spirit. First we begin with the Scriptures for the year. We may prayerfully read aloud together the entire Gospel (a *lectio* approach), stopping for group reflection and insights. (What did you hear? What images struck you?) Sometimes we've randomly chosen two to three Gospel accounts and reflected on them. Once we used just the First Readings. Everyone's ideas are recorded and posted on sheets of paper hung around the room. This usually takes a full day.

We also contemplate our parish. Where are we right now? What are our strengths, weaknesses, and challenges? What is going on in our larger Church? How does the Scripture challenge, shape, and influence us in this place at this time?

With all our ruminations echoing in our hearts, we begin preparing for the upcoming liturgical year. What themes of Advent need to have a special emphasis this year? What songs need to take forefront? How are we challenged today to embody the Gospel? What choices in *The Roman Missal* are best for the Introductory Rites? Shall we have a common Eucharistic Prayer for the season? Where will the Advent wreath be? How will it look, how does it get lit and by whom?

In the same way, we move through the year, season by season. The liturgical framework is slowly constructed. Maybe some images will stretch from season to season, perhaps a piece of the environment, or an acclamation. Perhaps the Palm Sunday procession will include families in sacramental preparation. Maybe people in the catechumenal process will speak of their experience to infant Baptism families. With everyone in the same room countless and new possibilities are generated.

Then, using the *Workbook*, the readings for the Easter Vigil are chosen. Sometimes the choices are obvious. At other times, we trust in the Spirit and select from a hat. With eyes on the Sacred Paschal Triduum as the high point in the parish's life, it is time to return to our regular programming. With "source and summit" in mind, we climb the mountain with interaction for all groups from everyone. How can faith formation and youth ministry embody this music, these themes? What will Christian service be like? Are there new areas to explore?

Finally it is time to return to *Sourcebook* and contemplate rites and sacraments within the context of parish life. For example, how can the rites of Christian initiation be embodied as we move through the seasons? What will be the dismissal songs given the other hymnody? Perhaps the faith formation program will use the same songs?

With all voices speaking and being heard, everyone feels empowered to live the liturgy and their specialized areas with a newness of purpose. Throughout the year we meet only sporadically because there is no need for monthly gatherings. E-mails and our committee minutes suffice. With a strong belief in the Spirit, and pledged integrity to the group's process, the parish moves forward in the same direction, to be formed in the Word and Sacrament we celebrate.

—Mary Dumm

Overview of the Gospel according to Luke

THE AUTHOR OF LUKE'S ACCOUNT of the Gospel also wrote the Acts of the Apostles. Both volumes are dedicated to an otherwise unknown patron of the early Christian Churches named Theophilus (Luke 1:3; Acts 1:1). Together the two volumes make up a substantial portion of the New Testament by telling the story of Jesus and then, following the Crucifixion, the story of the early Church as it rapidly spread throughout the Roman Empire. The Acts of the Apostles ends with Paul preaching openly in Rome itself (Acts 28:31), and so the two volumes point the reader to the ongoing mission of the Church for all time.

Ancient tradition in the Church attributes Luke-Acts to Luke, the beloved physician and companion of Paul (see Colossians 4:14; Philemon 24; 2 Timothy 4:11). There is scant information that modern scholars can use to either verify or discount such a tradition, though the argument that Luke-Acts contains specific medical terminology indicating a physician as the author has been largely disproved with better understanding of ancient Greek. The tradition that Luke was a companion of Paul is more controversial among scholars. In favor of the tradition is Luke's use of the so-called "we passages" in Acts (see 16:10–17, 20:5–15, 21:1–18, and 27:1—28:16) which appear to be a first-person account of part of Paul's missionary travels. Casting doubt on the tradition is the fact that the author admits to using written and oral sources already in existence when he wrote (see Luke 1:1–3) and that Luke-Acts portrays conditions in the life of the Church which reflect the early second century. For example, the issue of whether Jewish food laws should apply at the Lord's Supper (the ritual meal which over time became the Christian Eucharist that we know) is still unsettled in the letters of Paul (see Galatians 2:11–13) while in Acts there appears to be harmonious agreement (see Acts 15:22–29). Further, most modern scholars agree that Luke used both Mark's account and the source Q (an early source of the sayings of Jesus). Mark can be dated to around the time of the Roman-Jewish war (AD 66–73), so Luke must have been written sometime after Mark. Most scholars therefore date Luke to the latter part of the first century (AD 80–90) while important recent scholarship dates Acts separately to around AD 110–120.

Luke-Acts was probably written in the Greek city of Ephesus in Asia Minor (modern-day Turkey). The author is familiar with the area around the Aegean Sea there, and there is more activity in this area in the Acts of the Apostles than anywhere else. In addition we know that Ephesus was an important center of Pauline Christianity, and Acts is certainly centered on the leadership role played by Paul along with the Twelve Apostles of Jesus.

Our image of the beginning of a harmonious Christian Church under the leadership of Peter, Paul, and the Twelve Apostles owes more to Luke-Acts than any other text in the New Testament. There was undoubtedly more tension and disagreement in the early Churches than Luke-Acts suggests, but the two volumes do give us the important theological insight that the Church is in continuity with the Jewish tradition. Beginning with God's promises to Israel and their fulfillment in the life and mission of Jesus to the ongoing work of the Christian Church to bring these promises to the world, Luke gives the Church both its authentic history and its mission.

To turn now to just the Gospel according to Luke, it should be noted that the readings in Year C of the Lectionary give us a good sense of Luke's particular understanding of Jesus and his mission and his overall theological perspective. It is to these features of Luke that this introduction will now turn.

In most places in America, churches are filled to overflowing at Christmas. Many Catholic Christians will hear the Scriptures proclaimed only this one time a year. And every year the Gospel, whether at the Vigil or the morning Mass, will be Luke's story of the birth of Jesus (2:1–14; 2:15–20). What is at the heart of this story theologically?

First, Luke places the story of Jesus' birth squarely into the flow of history: Caesar Augustus was the emperor and Quirinius the governor (see 2:1–2). At a particular time and place God's Son comes into the world and into history to redeem the earth and all of the people in it. What might not be apparent to the people sitting in the pews at Christmas, however, is that this way of understanding Jesus and his mission was at odds with another, extremely popular, understanding of Jesus in some of the ancient Churches.

These Churches understood Jesus to be a divine, not human, revealer who suddenly appeared in the world as an adult in order to teach people the means by which they might escape from the world to a higher, more heavenly existence. Those who understood Jesus' teaching in this way would claim that this world was not worth saving and that only the heavenly or spiritual world mattered.

These Christians joined sectarian groups that would set themselves apart from the concerns of this world and their fellow Christians. Thus, when Luke tells the story of Jesus being born as a baby in a manger in a particular place (Bethlehem) and time (the reign of Augustus Caesar), he has in mind both the full humanity of Jesus and the fact that Jesus will care about, and ultimately redeem, creation and all the people in it (see 2:10).

These readings at Christmas also give us a characteristic part of Luke's theology that will appear again and again throughout his presentation of the story of Jesus and the early Church. God is especially concerned with the lives and suffering of the poor and marginalized within society. The almost adorable Christmas crèche does not actually appear in Luke. Mary, the pregnant teenager, is forced to give birth outside in the elements and has to use an animal feeding trough (manger) as the first crib for her child. There are shepherds nearby who also must live outside in the elements, among the most despised group in all of ancient society, and they are the first to be visited by the angel and see the glory of God (see 2:9). And even though they are poor and despised they have a great reverence for God and are privileged to have announced to them the Gospel (the word Gospel means "Good News") which is for everyone (see 2:10).

Every New Year's Day as well, on the Solemnity of Mary, the Holy Mother of God, we get another glimpse into Luke's basic theology. In the final sentence of the reading, "When eight days were completed for his circumcision, he was named Jesus, the name given him by the angel before he was conceived in the womb," Luke tells us that the life and mission of Jesus will take place in continuity with, and fulfillment of, the Jewish Scriptures and Tradition. Jesus is circumcised on the eighth day according to Jewish law just as his cousin John the Baptist had been earlier (see 1:59), and so both are incorporated into the Jewish people by the sign of the Covenant (see Genesis 17:1–12; Leviticus 12:3). In Luke, Jesus is presented as a law-abiding Jewish male who comes to bring the Covenant of God with Israel to its proper fulfillment. And so the name given to the baby is Jesus, the name given to Mary by the angel of God in the Annunciation (see 1:32), thus the readers and hearers of the Gospel know that all the events in the Gospel will unfold according to the unwavering plan of God.

The only other reading from Luke that Catholics hear every year is Luke 24:13–35 (Easter Sunday): the appearance of the resurrected Christ to two disciples on the road to Emmaus. For Catholic Christians, for whom the Eucharist is the source and summit of our faith, this story is perhaps the most important reading from Luke in the entire Lectionary. The story takes place on the first Easter Sunday (see 24:21). Two disciples, one named Cleopas and the other anonymous, are walking on the road to a village near Jerusalem called Emmaus and discussing the events of the Passion. While they were talking about these things, Jesus drew near and walked with them. Luke tells us that "their eyes were prevented from recognizing him" (24:16). Why? Some scholars suggest, as with the appearance to Mary Magdalene in John's account of the Gospel (see 20:14), that the Resurrection body was different enough that it was not immediately recognizable as Jesus. But Luke says the eyes of these disciples were actively prevented from recognizing Jesus (see 24:16). Then a bit later, these same two disciples tell of other disciples who had gone to the tomb that morning but also did not see him (see 24:24). In both cases the disciples are not able to "see" the resurrected Christ because they do not yet understand the Jewish Scriptures. For Luke the life, Death, and Resurrection of Jesus must be understood as the fulfillment of Scripture (Old Testament). Jesus must explain the Scriptures to them so that they understand him within God's Covenant with Israel and in continuity with Judaism. If they were to recognize Jesus without this explanation, even by having a vision of the resurrected Christ himself, then they might misunderstand the truth and purpose of Jesus' Resurrection. By shaping the story in this way Luke reminds those who listen to his account of the Gospel in any age that the Resurrection is not simply, or even at all, a divine wonder or apparition, but rather an event filled with purpose. As Israel first came to know God and to accept a relationship with him, so now in the resurrected Christ all people can come to know God and find a relationship with him.

Perhaps more important for the Catholics who hear this story every year, Luke forever establishes the relationship between the Scriptures and the Eucharist. The time of day is crucial. It is getting to be toward evening, yet the sun still has not set (see 24:29). In the Jewish tradition the actual setting of the sun marks a new day, so this day is still the day following the Sabbath, that is, Sunday. In the Jewish tradition the Sabbath day celebrates and enacts the perfect creation of the Garden of Eden which came about when God triumphed over the forces of chaos—water, darkness, and death (see Genesis 1:10).

In Luke's account, and in all of our accounts of the Gospel, the Resurrection of Jesus takes place sometime after sundown on the Sabbath day (Sunday). And so in this way the Resurrection of Jesus was understood by the earliest Jewish Christians to be an extension of the Sabbath day, God's triumph over darkness and death and the enactment of the original perfect creation, the Garden of Eden. For these Christians all of the laws, traditions, and prophecies in Jewish Scripture pointed toward the way back to this first creation, the Sabbath, now revealed in the Resurrection of Jesus on "the first day of the new week" (Sunday; see 24:1).

The early Christians, for whom Luke originally wrote this Gospel account, celebrated the Lord's Supper, the Eucharist, on Sunday. The liturgical gathering created sacred time and space out of the chaos of the Death and the Sacrifice of Jesus on the Cross. The Sabbath day was now extended into time itself (the new week) and the new creation was made present in the gathering of Jews and Gentiles around the one loaf, the Body of Christ (see 22:19).

So it is on this first Sunday that Jesus explains to the two disciples the meaning of the Scriptures. The messiah (Jesus) had to suffer these things (his Passion and Death on the Cross) because the restored creation, the Body of Christ, must again be God's victory over chaos (death). And when Jesus is persuaded to stay with these two disciples and, as the Greek text literally says, it was time to recline for the evening meal, Jesus himself performs the ritual of the Eucharist: he takes the loaf, blesses it, breaks it, and then gives it to these disciples (see 22:19; 34:30). Now in the Lord's Supper the eyes of these disciples are completely opened and they recognize Jesus as the resurrected Christ (see 24:31). In other words, Luke is teaching all who would listen to and read his account of the Gospel that the Eucharist, the Lord's Supper, is what gives meaning to the Scriptures: the Death and Resurrection of Jesus is the restoration of the original creation intended by God and now experienced in the Eucharist. All Scripture, rightly understood, brings us to this table and this time. So the story of the disciples on the road to Emmaus is the story of all the Lectionary readings in Year C. Each proclamation of Scripture points us directly to the Eucharist, for it is the Eucharist that reveals for us the meaning of the Scriptures. We are there at the table with Jesus and our eyes are fully opened.

—Charles A. Bobertz

New Ritual Book

THE CATHOLIC bishops of the United States have prepared a new supplement for the *Lectionary for Mass*. The *Lectionary for Mass Supplement*, available from LTP, Liturgical Press, and Catholic Book Publishing, includes updated citations, corrections, and new saints and blesseds that have been confirmed by the Holy See since the revisions made to the four-volume *Lectionary for Mass* between 1998 and 2002. This new supplement approved by the Congregation for Divine Worship and the Discipline of the Sacraments includes additional and amended readings for the Marriage rite, the Pentecost Vigil, saints' days, votive Masses, and Masses for Various Needs and Occasions.

The Order of Celebrating Matrimony

THROUGHOUT the seasonal introductions in this *Sourcebook*, you will find pastoral recommendations for celebrating form I (within Mass) of the revised Marriage rite (now called *The Order of Celebrating Matrimony*). This series of articles are not seasonal in focus, but rather, reflect on these aspects of the celebration.

◆ Advent: Entrance chant and procession

◆ Christmas Time: Gloria

◆ Ordinary Time during Winter: Liturgy of the Word

◆ Lent: Marriage Rite

◆ Sacred Paschal Triduum: Liturgy of the Eucharist

◆ Easter Time: Nuptial Blessing

◆ Ordinary Time during Summer and Fall: Concluding Rites

ADVENT

The Liturgical Time

The Calendar

The Roman Missal / The Meaning

ADVENIRE, the Latin from which *Advent* is derived, translates "to arrive" or "come to." Advent recalls God's first coming in Christ's birth and looks toward his return at the end of time, while we prepare to celebrate that first coming on Christmas. *Universal Norms on the Liturgical Year and the Calendar* (UNLY), 39 notes that:

Advent has a twofold character, for it is a time of preparation for the Solemnities of Christmas, in which the First Coming of the Son of God to humanity is remembered, and likewise a time when, by remembrance of this, minds and hearts are led to look forward to Christ's Second Coming at the end of time. For these two reasons, Advent is a period of devout and expectant delight.

The prayers in *The Roman Missal* reflect this. Preface I of Advent proclaims "For he assumed at his first coming / the lowliness of human flesh . . . that, when he comes again in glory and majesty . . . we who watch for that day / may inherit the great promise / in which now we dare to hope." Preface II of Advent, used from December 17 to 24, when we intensify our preparation for Christmas, prays: "It is by his gift that already we rejoice / at the mystery of his Nativity, / so that he may find us watchful in prayer / and exultant in his praise." To know what we believe about a feast or season, pray with the Preface(s) for that feast or season.

Remembering Christ's first coming, watching for his return, and living our faith in hope fill our Advent presidential prayers. In the Collects we pray for "the resolve to run forth to meet . . . Christ / with righteous deeds" (First Sunday); that "no earthly undertaking [will] hinder those / who set out in haste to meet [God's] Son" (Second Sunday); that God will enable us to "attain the joys of so great a salvation / . . . [and] celebrate them always / with solemn worship and glad rejoicing" (Third Sunday); and that God's grace may come into our hearts, so that we may "be brought to the glory of his Resurrection" (Fourth Sunday).

The Prayers after Communion call us to "press forward all the more eagerly" (Fourth Sunday), to prepare "for the coming feasts" (Third Sunday), to learn "to judge wisely the things of earth" and "hold firm to the things of heaven" (Second Sunday), "as we walk amid passing things" (First Sunday).

Advent is a time "of devout and expectant delight" (UNLY, 39). Because of the expectant delight, we do not sing the Gloria, except on the Solemnity of the Immaculate Conception (December 8) and the Feast of Our Lady of Guadalupe (December 12). We do profess the Creed on the Sundays of Advent and the Solemnity of the Immaculate Conception. Consider proclaiming the presidential prayers in a different manner. If you usually sing them, change the tone from solemn to simple, or recite them. Pray the Confiteor to reflect the repentance Advent invites. If you choose the third option for the Penitential Act, consider option I in the "Sample Invocations for the Penitential Act" in appendix VI. It reflects the twofold character of Advent. The Eucharistic Prayers for Reconciliation (EPR) are fitting for this season. EPRII speaks about Jesus coming as Word, hand extended to sinners, and way of peace. Its concluding section asks that we share with the heavenly family, "the unending banquet of unity / . . . where the fullness of your peace will shine forth," a clear reference to the Second Coming. EPRI refers to the Second Coming as

a time when, "freed at last from the wound of corruption / and made fully into a new creation, / we shall sing to you with gladness the thanksgiving of Christ, who lives for all eternity."

The Solemn Blessing for Advent, found as #1 in "The Order of Mass: Solemn Blessings," recalls Christ's first coming, our yearning for his return, and the fact that we now live in hope and charity. Among the various Prayers over the People which appear in the Missal after the solemn blessings, #1 seeks "consolation on earth" while we "strive for heaven"; #5 calls us to "[hold] fast to what is pleasing" to God and "accomplish all that is good." It sounds very similar to some of the Advent Prayers after Communion. The Prayer over the People #9 emphasizes the "mysteries of redemption" and their "effects." Number 19 asks God to "be near to us" as we "place [our] hope" in God's mercy. And #26 calls us to rejoice and progress "in the Christian life." Prayerful choice from the texts that *The Roman Missal* offers for Advent can "teach us to judge wisely the things of earth / and hold firm to the things of heaven" (Prayer after Communion, First Sunday of Advent), as we prepare to celebrate the Nativity of the Lord on the upcoming Christmas.

The Lectionary for Mass

THIS ADVENT, we journey with stories of a Messiah foretold and God's unbreakable covenant with Israel as well as the fulfilment of those promises in Jesus Christ. Luke's account of the Gospel presents us with a rich story of John the Baptist's ministry of proclamation and insight into the one whom he announces: the Messiah, Jesus Christ. Our Baptism—the one John knows Jesus will offer—is incorporation into the very life of God. In it, we share in the priestly, prophetic, and royal office of Jesus Christ.

In a season where listeners are preoccupied with preparing for Christmas, the readings draw us in to look at life as it is happening right now. Looking carefully, we see that the themes of love, hope, peace, and joy are present, but so are themes of destruction and restoration, exile and freedom, promise and fulfillment. We are reminded by the psalms that to wield power (whether as a king or as any sort of leader, be that parent, coach, teacher, or worker) is a responsibility that should be exercised in accordance with God's will. Wherever we are, whatever we are doing, we are to be God's agents—particularly to the poor and vulnerable.

In an age where people are gripped with uncertainty and even fear, remember that the God who comes intimately to us in human form is our source of solace and hope. God does not just promise the Messiah; God sends him into the world to reconcile all things to himself. Can we, like the figures we hear about this year, both recognize and marvel at this reality?

We are also reminded in this season that the human condition has always included suffering—many of the texts we hear point to brokenness and judgement. This is a moment to remember that ours is not the only age in which people have been captive to slavery, displaced from their homes, or unwelcomed as exiles. We are invited to ask ourselves where change of heart is needed, both individually and collectively. We remember that God sends us prophets to point the way to restoration of right relationship with God and each other. Are we each fulfilling our baptismal call to prophetically illuminate a path to justice and peace?

If we think we aren't up to that task, the stories of Zechariah, Elizabeth, Mary, and Joseph demonstrate to us that God will work with us despite our human frailty. We may be skeptical like Zechariah, eager to avoid like Joseph, startled in an unexpected season of life like Elizabeth, or the least likely expected agent of God like Mary, but God can and will work in and through us if we are open. Are we willing to learn from the patterns of the lives of these great figures and go with God to a new way of seeing and understanding the world? Are we willing to truly surrender and be God's agent in our time? These questions make our wonderment about the right present to buy pale in comparison and invite us to take our eyes off Christmas day and look into our world here and now.

Children's Liturgy of the Word

THE WEEKS before the opening of a new liturgical year are an ideal time to reassess the space used for children's Liturgy of the Word as well as your regular practices. Make sure that the prayer table or lectern you use to proclaim from the Lectionary is dignified and visible to all. Are some items looking worn and in need of replacing? Take time before the First Sunday of Advent to reflect on arrangements and furnishings, to speak with prayer leaders about what is working well and what needs improvement. Then, make any adjustments as Advent begins. A new year can be a new beginning.

For Advent, a dedicated prayer table draped in bluish violet, featuring a worthy Advent wreath, provides a focal point that helps sanctify the space—a symbol of the approaching dawn of Christ's birth. Have the appropriate candles lit before the children enter the space.

Even though it will most likely be daytime when you lead this liturgy, be sure to allow children to experience at least a hint of the darkness into which the light of Christ will appear. The frightening images in the Gospel of the First Sunday can be made less scary if you do a short catechesis on the light of Christ represented in the wreath and explain that the light will grow brighter as he comes near.

If you chose not to use the psalm of the day, use a simple musical setting of an approved seasonal psalm that can be sung or recited, such as Psalm 25.

John the Baptist is a key player in weeks two and three. Be sure to have a painting, icon, or other image of him present. As the herald of Christ's coming, he is an important figure who puts a face on expectation, just as Mary and Elizabeth do in the final week. They, too, should be shown to the children in some manner.

The Saints

THE SAINTS of Advent provide examples of spiritual light to encourage us through the winter darkness toward the hope of the Incarnation. Images and descriptions of the season's obligatory memorials are full of metaphors of light: St. Lucy, one of the virgin martyrs, is often depicted wearing a crown of glowing candles; Our Lady of Guadalupe is described as "a woman clothed with the sun" (Revelation 12:1).

The Memorial of St. Francis Xavier, one of the founders of the Society of Jesus, will be an especially important feast day for any community associated with foreign missions. His approach—to comprehend and build on the strengths and virtues of the cultures he was evangelizing—prefigured the Church's eventual approach to evangelization and inculturation in modern times. Other obligatory memorials include St. Ambrose—Bishop of Milan, and one of the first four great Doctors of the Church—and St. John of the Cross, known for his reformation of the Carmelite order and as the mystic-poet who authored *The Dark Night of the Soul*. Parish book groups could consider taking on a study of this beautiful, challenging meditation, to culminate on St. John's feast day.

The Advent sensibilities of hope, nascent joy, and waiting are highlighted in the season's two obligatory Marian observances: Our Lady of Guadalupe, Patroness of the Americas, and the Immaculate Conception (be sure to announce to the faithful in bulletins, on social media, and during announcements at prior liturgies that this is a Holyday of Obligation. Since Mary as the Immaculate Conception is Patroness of the United States, the Monday-Saturday rule for Holydays of Obligation does not apply.

Many parishes in the United States have congregations formed equally of Hispanics and Anglos; drawing connections (explicitly in preaching and printed resources, more subtly in environment and imagery) between these two feasts of Mary, just four days apart on the calendar, can reinforce unity and connectedness between the two communities.

The Liturgy of the Hours

IN THIS SEASON of secular distraction, gather a small group of friends, the parish staff, or Bible study folks and introduce yourselves to the Liturgy of the Hours. Find a time that's compatible with everyone, and catechize "as you go along" using either Morning Prayer or Evening Prayer. Your parish hymnal may have a setting of Morning or Evening Prayer that you can easily use. An accessible and helpful resource for beginning to pray the Liturgy of the Hours is Joyce Ann Zimmerman's *Morning and Evening: A Parish Celebration* (LTP). Use it as a guide to begin, and select a hymn or canticle that you can sing simply and without accompaniment. Also consider using the intercessions from Morning or Evening Prayer

as a family or meeting prayer during Advent, ending with the Lord's Prayer.

As the new liturgical year begins, look for other resources that are appealing, including electronic resources like Universalis.com. The Liturgy of the Hours is a liturgy that links our prayer with that of all Christians everywhere. There is abundant richness in observing an "hour" of the day with petition and praise to God in psalmody, enriched by readings. *Christian Prayer: The Liturgy of the Hours* includes music as well as a traditional format for prayer.

The Rite of Christian Initiation of Adults

THE *Rite of Christian Initiation of Adults* intends that the process attract interested inquirers to the parish. Intentional "taste and see" gatherings characterize the process of inquiry. There is a seasonal reason to welcome inquirers during Advent: the often over-romanticized version of Christmas stirs up deep yearnings in the unbaptized for a deeper and more authentic life of faith. These yearnings are hungers which often can't be named, but they draw the inquirer to search for something deeper and possibly more satisfying, not found in secular culture.

If a parish makes the effort to welcome inquirers throughout the year, one session could be scheduled for Advent. Welcome inquirers to the parish celebration of Advent, then mentor them gently throughout Christmas Time. Celebration of the Rite of Acceptance could be scheduled during Ordinary Time in winter. In Advent, there are usually parish members who have little or no family nearby, and they would be happy to informally share their faith and welcome inquirers if you schedule a session during Advent (don't forget the Christmas cookies). There are no specific official rites of Christian initiation that are mandated for Advent, but an atmosphere of hospitality, welcome, and joyful anticipation may be exactly the nudge of the Holy Spirit for those persons interested in becoming Catholic.

The Sacraments of Initiation

THE CELEBRATIONS of the sacraments of initiation are pivotal moments in the life of a parish. These are times when we welcome our children and young people into a deeper participation in the life of Christ as members of his Body, the Church. The celebrations of Baptism, First Communion, and Confirmation assure us that our faith tradition will continue. They are graced moments when the power of the Holy Spirit is at work in unique ways. When adults approach the sacraments of initiation, they do so based on an experience of personal conversion and an establishment of an adult relationship with Christ, which is fostered and enhanced through the process of the Rite of Christian Initiation Adults (RCIA). Children however, are typically brought to the sacraments by their parents, who may or may not have an intentional relationship with God. Some may be occasional participants in the life of the parish, and others may not be practicing their faith at all. Whatever their reason is for bringing their children to the sacraments, God is working within them. It is therefore essential that the celebration of the sacraments of initiation with children and young people be celebrated well. They are moments of an encounter with Christ, an immersion into the Paschal Mystery, not only for the children who are receiving the sacraments, but also for the parents and the entire parish community.

First Communion and Confirmation may be celebrated at Mass, with few exceptions for special circumstances. Baptism, too, may be celebrated at a Sunday Mass with the parish community. Many parishes, however, relegate the celebration of the Rite of Baptism to a liturgy outside of Mass on a Sunday afternoon or even on a Saturday to accommodate a larger number of families bringing children to Baptism. While this is certainly permissible, the connection to the wider parish community is lost. On the other hand, First Communion and Confirmation celebrations, as well as Baptisms celebrated at Sunday Mass can be overdone and filled with elements not called for in the rites that overburden the liturgy. Those preparing sacramental liturgies should keep in mind that the rites include every element that is needed for a valid celebration of the sacraments, and to be aware that adding elements can take away from the main symbols of the sacraments and often call attention to the participants and not to the sacramental action.

The beginning of the liturgical year is a time when we focus our attention on preparing for the commemoration of the birth of Christ and on his second coming at the end of time. It is a busy time in the parish and for families in general. When celebrating during Advent, remember that the Church prohibits ritual Masses on the Sundays of Advent. If the sacraments are celebrated at a Sunday Mass, the proper readings for the particular Sunday must be used. Baptisms can also be celebrated on a Sunday outside of Mass at which baptismal readings can be used. If Confirmation is celebrated on a weekday during Advent the Gloria can be sung, but is prohibited on a Sunday during Advent.

The Rite of Penance

THE CRY of the prophet to "prepare the way of the LORD" (Isaiah 40:3) echoes throughout the season of Advent. The same cry is taken up by John the Baptist, who with great urgency calls the people to repentance. The Church has long used this mantra as a call to the faithful to celebrate the Sacrament of Penance as a preparation for Christmas. The theology that underlines this annual practice states that the Lord desires to find a place in our lives. Our spiritual preparation is to remove any sin from our hearts that we might be ready to accept his presence worthily and gladly.

The great Hebrew prophets Jeremiah, Baruch, Zephaniah, and Micah proclaim the mighty works of God and announce that a new shepherd will arrive to bring peace to the people of God. Jesus is the fulfillment of that promise and his gift of peace is at the heart of the Sacrament of Reconciliation. As members of the new covenant we are beneficiaries of the One who "pardons all [our] sins / and heals all [our] ills" (Psalm 103:3).

Since the introduction of the reformed *Rite of Penance* (1973), most parishes have used what is known as form II (Reconciliation of Several Penitents with Individual Confession and Absolution; RP, chapter II) during Advent. The ritual text provides a number of options for the Scripture readings, though other readings can be chosen from the Lectionary readings for Advent.

There are sample outlines for the Examination of Conscience based on Scripture texts as well as various options for penitential intercessions. A complete outline is offered for Penitential Celebrations during Advent (RP, appendix II, 20).

Since these celebrations often involve extra confessors and parishioners from neighboring parishes, the host parish should make sure that suitable hospitality is provided. Parish greeters could be asked to be available and even some light refreshments could be offered after the celebration. Many parishes schedule extra times for individual confession during Advent to accommodate the many faithful who see Advent as a good time to prepare spiritually for Christmas. Consider setting aside several hours in one day, extending into the evening, instead of simply adding an hour to the usual Saturday schedule.

The Order of Celebrating Matrimony

The commentaries on Matrimony throughout this *Sourcebook* will guide readers through form I of the revised rite.

ENTRANCE CHANT AND PROCESSION: The purpose of the Introductory Rites is to "ensure that the faithful, who come together as one, establish communion and dispose themselves worthily to listen to the Word of God and to celebrate the Eucharist worthily" (GIRM, 46). During the Celebration of Matrimony, the Introductory Rites have a similar purpose in preparing and setting a tone for all those involved. Before the procession begins, the cantor or another suitable minister could welcome everyone to the celebration, if that has not been done before. The assembly should be invited to stand for the entire procession, not just when the bride begins to walk down the aisle.

The Order of Celebrating Matrimony offers two options for the procession. In the first option, which is preferred, the minister goes to the doors of the church, informally greets the wedding party, and then leads the procession into the church. In the second option, the minister does not participate in the procession, but rather greets the couple at their places. Whether the priest or deacon processes or not, there should be one liturgical procession which includes the altar servers, the presider, the witnesses, and the bridegroom and bride, either with each other or with their parents. Having both parents walk the bride and groom down the aisle helps to focus the attention on the joining of the two families rather than only on the entrance of the bride. The groom should be in the procession to reflect his complementary role as minister of the sacrament.

The archaic tradition of the groom not seeing the bride on the day of the wedding should be avoided. Its use comes from a time when the wedding was seen as a business transaction with the ownership of the bride being transferred from her father to the groom upon the exchange of the dowry.

Although singing a hymn during this point in the procession is possible, it is customary in most churches to have festive instrumental music played during the procession so that the assembly can watch the procession. There are many classical selections that are appropriate for the procession. The use of Wagner's Bridal Chorus should be discouraged as it was commissioned as part of a secular opera, *Lohengrin*, in which the bride is delivered to her husband as property and not of her own free will. A single piece of music for the entire procession is best. Many couples request a separate piece of music for the bride, however, that would not be respectful of the complementary roles of the bride and groom. It is possible, however, for the musicians to increase the volume and slow the tempo of the music when the procession culminates with the entrance of the groom and bride.

Once the procession is complete, *Sing to the Lord: Music in Divine Worship* (STL, 222) suggests a gathering song (although the rite itself notes that the song accompanies the procession). Psalm 20, Psalm 90, and Psalm 145 are the appointed entrance antiphons from *The Roman Missal* for weddings and could be sung. Alternatively, a strophic hymn with a beautiful and appropriate text set to a familiar hymn tune could be used. To foster participation, it is helpful to sing music that the assembly is familiar with and is easy to sing, particularly because there are often many guests from other parishes or even other faith traditions.

The Pastoral Care of the Sick

DESPITE OUR best efforts, Advent can take on a Christmas tone, thanks in part to the aggressive retail market. However, this need not and should not diminish our efforts as a faith community to bring the spiritual nature of the season into focus. The liturgy of the Church is decidedly about Advent in all its elements. The pastoral ministry of the parish needs to reflect this vision, especially for those who are not able to participate fully in the liturgies and other Advent activities.

Those who are homebound, in nursing homes, and in hospitals ought to receive our special attention during these days. One's spiritual well-being is intricately linked to one's physical well-being. It can be hard to pray or to focus on one's spiritual life when our bodies are weary or our minds distracted by loneliness, pain, or illness. Pastoral care visitors may need to spend a little extra time with those they visit, talking about the activities in the parish, even bringing them any prayer resources and bulletins.

Many people remember their deceased family members at this time with a certain sadness. There are wonderful prayers in the Rite for Anointing of the Sick that can be part of a pastoral visit that does not include sacramental anointing. Of course, if the person desires to be anointed then that should be arranged with a priest from the parish. Liturgy Training Publications offers these books of prayer that are excellent resources for the pastoral visitor: *Prayers during the Night, Prayers of the Sick,* and *Rites of the Sick.*

There can also be joyful aspects to this time of year for those who are ill or who cannot participate in the life of the parish. Arrange to have one or more choir members offer a concert of Advent and Christmas hymns at the nursing home or long-term care residence. If possible have a group of children bring homemade cards and messages to these parishioners, and, if appropriate, bring some Christmas cookies to share with them. Every gesture of care is a sign of Emmanuel, Christ among us.

The Order of Christian Funerals

THE CHURCH has a long and noble tradition of commending the dead to the Lord with suitable rites and gestures of pastoral concern. The Church acts as a tender mother for all her members, taking special care of those who suffer, those who mourn, and those who assist others when the fragments of life are close at hand. This important ministry belongs to the whole Church because "if [one] part suffers, all parts suffer with it; if one part is honored, all parts share its joy" (1 Corinthians 12:26).

The liturgical celebrations of the Church's sacraments have their own prayers, Scripture texts, musical selections, and particular characteristics and circumstances. But they are also celebrations of the whole Church and take place within a liturgical season that can influence the tone of the liturgy and some of the choices available in the ritual texts.

The themes of Advent, such as expectation, promise, hope, and waiting can be woven into the homily, the intercessions, and the music selections of the funeral liturgy. Although the *Order of Christian Funerals* offers a wonderful selection of Scripture texts from which to choose, the family members and/or the homilist are not restricted to those suggestions. Often family members are not very familiar with the texts of Scripture that can be appropriate for the funeral of a loved one. Those who prepare the liturgy can be especially helpful in assisting them to choose passages that are related to the Paschal Mystery rather than using a simple "like" or "dislike" criteria.

The liturgical environment of Advent can also be considered a text of the funeral liturgy. The candles of the Advent wreath announce the coming of the Messiah; the Eucharistic liturgy proclaims that Christ the Light has arrived in our midst, and those who have died are now embraced in the fullness of eternal light.

One of the celebrations in the *Order of Christian Funerals* is the Vigil for the Deceased. This prayer service is often held the evening before the funeral liturgy, either in the church or a chapel of the funeral home. The tradition of keeping vigil is an ancient gesture in religious communities. A reflection at the Vigil could note that the people of God in the Old Covenant kept vigil for generations waiting for the Messiah. Mary and Elizabeth kept vigil until the birth of their sons, and we keep vigil until we are called into the Kingdom of the Father. The universal nature of keeping vigil can help those who mourn to feel that they do not grieve alone and that the hope promised by God will indeed be their comfort.

The biblical characters of Advent can be companions for those who mourn and can be references for the homilist. Women can be remembered through Mary, as mother and nurturer; men can be remembered through Joseph, as protector and obedient servant to God' plan. An older person can be remembered through Elizabeth and Zechariah, wise in their ways and bearers of hope for the future. Children can be remembered through the delight of the shepherds who celebrate good news, and of course through the innocence and goodness of the child Jesus.

The Book of Blessings

The *Book of Blessings* (BB) is a rich treasury of prayers, Scripture readings, and intercessions that can be used for a wide variety of occasions throughout the liturgical year. This section in *Sourcebook* pertains to those blessings that are related to liturgical feasts and seasons. However, those who prepare the liturgy should be familiar with the many other blessings that can be celebrated at other times and for other reasons throughout the year.

THE MOST FREQUENTLY used blessing in Advent is the Blessing of the Advent Wreath (BB, chapter 47). There are two options: Within Mass and Within a Celebration of the Word of God. The pastoral notes (see BB, 1509–1516) provide helpful advice for this brief rite. The order of blessing does not replace the Penitential Act at the beginning of Mass, but rather replaces the concluding prayer of the Prayer of the Faithful. Usually the order of blessing takes place at the first Mass of Sunday (in most parishes the Mass on Saturday evening) and is not repeated at the other Masses. On the remaining Sundays of Advent the candles are lighted before Mass begins or just before the Collect. Prayers do not accompany this gesture.

The blessing and lighting of the Advent wreath is a worthy devotion; however, the placement of the wreath should not detract from the focus on the principal liturgical furnishings of the altar and the ambo. It could be placed in the area where the Nativity crèche will eventually be located, thus making a connection between the sign of waiting and the manger that holds the One for whom we have waited.

Many parishes provide a copy of the blessing for families to take home, thereby encouraging families to use an Advent wreath as a focus for family prayer throughout Advent.

The Liturgical Environment

DURING ADVENT we patiently await the birth of a child whose gender and name we already know. During this time of anticipation, our hearts and minds are filled with anticipation of the possibilities he will bring into our world. Indeed, the season itself is a long night of waiting for Christmas dawn. With this in mind, in early Advent streamline your environment, removing most plants and other decorations. Add a few simple, deep blue-violet accents such as banners near the nave entrance or fabric to accent the ambo and altar. Advent Scriptures speak of nature: mountains and valleys; stars and moons; roaring seas and the path of the sun from east to west. Incorporate stylized images of these elements into fabric banners, or drape supple fabric shot with metallic threads, bringing stars to mind.

Most parishes will mark the season with an Advent wreath. Like the Christmas crèche, an Advent wreath should not take a place of dominance nor compete with the view of the altar. Consider placing your Advent wreath in the same spot you will use for your crèche, mounting it vertically on a wall, or suspending it from the ceiling. Perhaps this year your parish will have a deconstructed Advent wreath, with the four candles set prominently in corners of the nave, nested in evergreens. Oversized glass cylinders can house candles safely or you might fill them with water and floating candles.

Advent includes several observances worthy of note. Observe the Solemnity of the Immaculate Conception on December 8 with the addition of a tasteful arrangement of white lilies and roses; alternatively, add the same flowers to your Advent wreath. Our Lady of Guadalupe is celebrated on December 12; if your parish has a statue or icon of this patron of the unborn and the Americas, place a vase of the red roses that are customarily associated with her nearby. Sts. Francis Xavier (December 3), Ambrose (December 7), Lucy (December 13), and John of the Cross (December 14) are also remembered during the Advent season. Moderately sized icons of these holy men and women could be arranged collectively or in rotation. Place them in areas designated for private prayer.

Outdoor wreaths can greet parishioners and visitors throughout Advent. Add a violet ribbon or floral picks that can be easily replaced with gold and white ones at Christmas. Wait until the fourth week before displaying outdoor Nativity sets or lighting lights on trees or wreaths.

During the weeks of Advent, advance progressively toward Christmas. Romans celebrate Bambinelli Sunday on the Third Sunday of Advent. On this day, the faithful bring their Christ-child figurine from their home Nativity set for a special blessing. The practice in your parish might include blessing the parish's Christ-child. Setting up the empty crèche within the church space this week, as well as undecorated evergreen trees or wreaths you may plan to use for Christmas, adds a heightened sense of anticipation, as well as spreading out the laborious work of decorating for Christmas. Share the blessing prayers for Christmas trees and for the crèche (available in *Catholic Household Blessings & Prayers*) in your bulletin, helping families remain in the Advent spirit while making Christmas preparations in their homes.

The Liturgical Music

THE PRIMARY object of this year's liturgical music commentary is to provide you with some resources which you may not know even exist and to provide some commentary from a different angle and perspective. A resource which is available to each of you is right in your own back yard: your local diocesan cathedral. The diocesan bishop is the "prime steward" of the liturgy in the given diocese (GIRM, 22) and therefore the cathedral should be "regarded as the center of the liturgical life of the diocese" (*Ceremonial of Bishops* [CB], 44) and "be a model for the other churches of the diocese" (CB, 46). What does this mean for you in parish ministry? On occasion, attend Mass at the cathedral and bring your fellow music ministers. Attending diocesan liturgies is a great opportunity for a pilgrimage. Observe what is being done, take it back to your parish community and adapt it to your particular circumstance. Cathedrals will often post their music and liturgical music selections online and this is an invaluable resource. Modeling and adapting what is being done at the cathedral is a good endeavor. Now, onwards towards Advent.

In some respects, Advent could be considered the "easiest" of the liturgical seasons, and keeping this in mind will be beneficial; this will enable you to do more during Christmas Time. Do things well, but prioritize and set realistic goals for both your assembly and your musicians. GIRM, 313 states:

> In Advent the use of the organ and other musical instruments should be marked by a moderation suited to the character of this time of year, without expressing in anticipation the full joy of the Nativity of the Lord.

Save using the festival trumpet and the pedal bassoon for Christmas Time. The use of the Gloria during Advent is restricted to the Solemnity of the Immaculate Conception and Feast of Our Lady of Guadalupe (and ritual Masses such as Confirmation). Utilizing the same setting of the Kyrie (Lord, Have Mercy), Gospel Acclamation, and Eucharistic Prayer settings will help to unite this brief season. This may be time to experiment using settings of the introit and Communion antiphon (using them is not as bad nor as frightening as you may think!). Some great resources are available: Columba Kelly's *Saint Meinrad Entrance and Communion Antiphons for the Church Year* (OCP, 30130174), Normand Gouin's "Entrance Antiphon for Advent" (GIA, G-7992), Paul Tate's *Radiant Light: Introits for Advent and Christmas* (GIA, 7994), Russell Weismann's *Advent Communion Antiphons* (GIA, G-8520), Richard J. Clark's *Communion Antiphons for Advent* (WLP, 005309) and James Biery's *Communion Antiphons for the Advent Season* (Morning Star Music, 80-005) are but a few of the gems available to us today. Starting in the middle of October, we are all bombarded with Christmas music, so give your assembly a break and avoid the temptation of using Christmas carols during the Advent season. This shouldn't be too difficult to avoid. In addition to the propers, we have plenty of excellent Advent chants ("Creator of the Stars of Night,"

"O Come, O Come, Emmanuel") and hymns ("People, Look East," "The King Shall Come When Morning Dawns," "On Jordan's Bank," "O Come, Divine Messiah," "Come, Thou Long-Expected Jesus," "Lift Up Your Heads, Ye Mighty Gates," "Lo, How a Rose E'er Blooming") from which to chose. Plenty of opportunities abound to use various choral music geared specifically toward Advent. Advanced choirs may use some of the choruses from Handel's *Messiah* ("And the Glory," "O Thou That Tellest Good Tidings to Zion") during the Preparation of the Gifts or as a prelude before Mass. Choral settings of the Ave Maria are appropriate especially around the Fourth Sunday of Advent. A little gem, which is easy for any choir to master, is Luigi Cherubini's "Veni Jesu." It can be found for free at www.CPDL.org. For more ideas in choosing choral anthems, check out NPM's choral planning project at http://www.npm.org/Choral_Anthem_Project/index.html and CanticaNOVA Publications at www.canticanova.com. In addition to whatever liturgical preparation aids you may subscribe to, these two websites contain a wealth of information which may be helpful over the course of the entire liturgical year.

The Liturgical Ministers

AT THE BEGINNING of a new liturgical year, the parish has a unique opportunity to gather all liturgical ministers to reflect on their respective ministries and prepare for the year ahead. This could take the form of a retreat or workshop. The first part of the session could be a time of formation, sharing prayer, and reflection on the call to ministry that is rooted in the model of Jesus Christ. In a follow up session each of the ministry groups could review the past year by sharing some of the challenges and graces they have experienced. A second consideration could be centered on what each ministry group, and individual, would focus on as ways to enhance their ministry in the year ahead. The focus might be on how each ministry enriches the liturgical experience of the whole assembly.

During Advent the liturgy offers rich fare for spiritual reflection for those in liturgical ministry. The great prophets of the Old Testament are wonderful examples for readers who proclaim the Word of the Lord to an expectant people. The prophets were bold and faithful and confident in their call as spokespersons for the Lord God. Readers and preachers can learn from their conviction and the way that they took their message to heart.

The example of hospitality in the story of Mary and Elizabeth can be a good reflection for greeters and ushers as they extend words and gestures to everyone who arrives to greet the Lord in word and sacrament.

Mary's ready and unconditional acceptance of her role in God's plan of salvation gives all of us a worthy model in our ministries that serve all God's people. In a sense, she could be regarded as the first liturgical minister who teaches us how to be both humble and courageous in our ministry. Like Mary we bear the light and love of God to all those we encounter both in liturgy and in life.

Other Prayers, Rituals, and Devotions

ADVENT ATTRACTS Christians throughout the world, and Catholics especially have many opportunities to celebrate and cherish the tradition of creating and lighting the Advent wreath.

St. Nicholas Day (December 6) sees children from the United States, Europe, South America, and Canada put handwritten notes on the windowsills, addressed to the Child Jesus. The children also put their shoes outside of a door and hope for an early Christmas treat. St. Nicholas in turn asks angels to take these requests to heaven, and a sweet treat appears in the children's shoes the next day. Although little is known about this saint, strong devotion is enacted by many cultures the world over.

The Solemnity of the Immaculate Conception (December 8) is celebrated with processions, Mass, and Marian music in many languages spoken in the United States of America. This is the patronal feast day of the United States, so be sure to highlight any shrine or statue of the Blessed Mother in the church. Fervent preparations for the celebration of the Feast of Our Lady of Guadalupe (December 12) include festive foods, drama, music, and dancing, and typically celebrating an all-night vigil.

It is interesting to note that St. Lucy's name (martyr, December 13) appears in Eucharistic

Prayer I. This memorial falls on Thursday this year, so schedule a school Mass and use EP I with special devotion to the saints.

Christmas novenas begin on December 16, on the Third Sunday of Advent this year. There are many opportunities to learn of and to celebrate Las Posadas, Simbang Gabi, and Las Parrandas. *Las Posadas* (meaning "lodging or inn") comes from Mexico and Central America, and narrates the story of the Holy Family seeking a place to stay and have their baby, in Bethlehem. Distinctive lyrics and antiphonal song characterize this nightly enactment, often carried out by an entire community throughout the community and ending with Mass and a piñata for the children. The last night of Las Posadas finds the Holy Family in the center aisle of the church before Mass begins at midnight, asking for lodging, and the congregation responds in song, "Enter, enter, holy pilgrims. . . . All I have please call your own." As the United States of America welcomes large numbers of Latino cultures, this devotion encourages hospitality to all migrants and refugees, while celebrating Hispanic culture with processions, prayer, music (and yes, hot chocolate) during Advent. Reading *The Night of Las Posadas* by Tomie dePaola is a worthy way to introduce children to Las Posadas.

The Christmas novena Simbang Gabi includes nine days of Masses and is part of the Catholic Filipino culture. Traditionally celebrated for the fisherman at the break of day (when the rooster crows and wakes them to go fishing), the novena's Masses are celebrated at times when many can easily attend. The last Mass of this novena is truly the "Mass of the Rooster" (Misa del Gallo), and a star-shaped lantern reminds the assembly of the star that led the Magi to the Blessed Infant. Processional movement with the lantern, plus feasting, are part of Simbang Gabi devotional celebration.

Las Parrandas has historical roots in Cuba and Puerto Rico. In eighteenth-century Cuba, a priest of the local cathedral sent children into the streets with plates, cups, and silverware to make noise and sing songs that would attract the townspeople to Midnight Mass during the week before Christmas. Such "noisemaking" evolved into elaborate street carnivals, new varieties of drums and noisemakers, and feasting during the week before Christmas. When Las Parrandas is celebrated as a novena, the street carnival ends on December 24 at 10 PM, and the *atambora* (drum) summons people in procession to the church for the Mass during the Night.

In addition to praying grace before meals (either at home or away), add an O Antiphon as Christmas approaches, and conclude with the Hail Mary. You will find that the O Antiphons are completely "portable" and found in Evening Prayer of the Liturgy of the Hours. The *Directory on Popular Piety and the Liturgy* is a helpful and valuable resource (see especially paragraphs 106–123) regarding popular devotions at Christmastide. The Jesse Tree is a Christian tradition that attracts many different age groups. Catechize with the Messianic story of Jesse (see Isaiah 11:10) and discover many age-appropriate, creative, tangible expressions of the Jesse Tree that families can create in their homes. Resources are available for youth, teens, and elders that reinforce the days of Advent and the approach of the Solemnity of the Nativity of the Lord.

Advent is the season to construct the crèche as a devotional shrine in the church, creating an inviting place to sit, kneel, or linger for private prayer (leave it empty until Christmas!). Reinforce your own creativity with a thorough reading of *The Sacristy Manual*, second edition (G. Thomas Ryan, LTP), chapter 15, "Shrines and Other Areas for Private Devotions." Study the norms for shrines and develop a plan for an annual crèche display that draws people to contemplation, rather than simply looking at the traditional "manger scene." Your crèche can become a place where a grandparent can bring a child and tell a Christmas story, or where a harried teen or parent can make a visit to church and find peace during the busy secular distractions of the Advent and Christmas seasons. A tip: begin to plan the Christmas crèche during the closing third of Ordinary Time, anticipating Advent and Christmas. Form a committee, read and pray the infancy narrative (see Luke 1:1–2:24), and make a plan to create a shrine in or near your worship space. Catechize the assembly during the first week of Advent regarding how to "use" the new shrine for devotion.

"Anticipate in advance of Advent" is the best mantra for preparing simple (or elaborate, depending on local culture) devotions, prayers, symbols (a shrine, Christmas trees, manger, wreaths), and novenas that stress joyful anticipation. This is a good time to form a multicultural commission that can plan and implement devotions for the parish to "taste and see." Catechize the parish community with bulletin inserts and website posts, appealing to their sense of the joyful expectation of the season.

Evangelization

Social media can also be platforms for observing Advent and witnessing our faith and traditions to others at the same time. One practice in recent years has been for parishes and ministry groups to capture and post daily photos that express or resonate with an Advent theme such as hope, joy, light, waiting, or preparing. Doing so creates a "Digital Advent Calendar." In response to the shared calendar, parishioners can be encouraged to post their own photos of their daily lives that communicate the common theme for the day. For example, if the theme for the day is *light*, one person may post a picture of the sunrise they saw that morning on their way to work, or perhaps the flame of the candle they lit in their home that evening as part of prayer. By using a hashtag, such as #light, to accompany the picture, these images can be connected to each other and gathered to reveal the community of people engaging in this practice together throughout the season.

Posting digital photos around daily Advent themes is a simple practice that can carry profound meaning. If a parish or ministry group generates a digital Advent calendar, people who belong to this community and participate in the sharing of photos can gain a sense of community from the experience by observing the faith and creativity of those who are otherwise unseen. It is also a way to witness to those outside of the community and to reveal the meaning of Advent in genuine, personal, and accessible ways. It can be an evangelizing practice both for those in and outside of the community.

The practice can also be tried in families, especially families who are separated by great geographical distance. As many such extended families gather for Christmas, preparing together during the season of Advent can be a beautiful way to share with one another about daily life and faith, and to enter into true encounter even before seeing one another face-to-face. Extended families do keep in touch with one another by posting photos on social media—why not turn this into a time of shared prayer in joyful anticipation of the Christmas gathering?

One important element of this Advent practice is simplicity. Using simple Advent words such as *light*, and giving people the freedom to genuinely discover and share where they come across this theme during their ordinary day is key to the success of this practice. The results will be beautiful moments of personal faith shared within a communal context, whether the parish, the ministry group, or the family.

The Parish and the Home

This year, the weekend before Advent is not part of the Thanksgiving holiday, which makes it ideal for preparing people of all ages for the upcoming season. Host an Advent-themed gathering at which evergreen wreaths and Advent candle sets are available for families and singles to build their own home wreaths. Be sure to include a copy of the blessing and lighting of an Advent wreath from *Catholic Household Blessings & Prayers* or the USCCB website at www.usccb .org. Encourage households to begin each evening meal by lighting the candle(s) of the week on the wreath each night and praying for the needs of the world, the community, and their loved ones, responding "Come, Lord Jesus!"

If your parish is multicultural, arrange an opportunity for sharing the Advent traditions of various ethnic groups by having families who practice them give a short demonstration and explanation (in costume if that is the tradition) during the pre-Advent parish gathering. Latino families could share traditions for Our Lady of Guadalupe, Pastorelas, and Las Posadas; Anglo-Europeans can share traditions associated with St. Nicholas and St. Lucy; Filipinos can explain Simbang Gabi, and so on. If these will be celebrated at your parish, be sure to put them on the parish Advent and Christmas Time event calendar, along with short explanations and an invitation to all.

Offer a session for adults in early Advent on living the liturgical year (with liturgical calendars available to take home). Teens can be encouraged to conduct a coat drive to provide warm clothing for those in need. Little ones could donate outgrown winter hats, mittens, gloves, and boots. A parish giving tree to collect Christmas gift donations for a local shelter is another idea.

Find ways to encourage people to celebrate Advent as an alternative to an all-December-long Christmas by offering CDs of music for Advent, holding an Advent concert, or by promoting online initiatives like the Advent Conspiracy (www.adventconspiracy.org/). Don't schedule parish Christmas-themed parties or dinners during December. Save them for the season. (Why not have people mark their calendar for Sunday afternoon, January 6, the Epiphany, for a parish gathering?)

An Advent communal Penance service is a great addition, allowing the community to gather and celebrate the sacrament together while preparing their hearts for Christmas. Be sure to announce the time and date at the beginning of Advent and to include it on the event calendar.

Reflections through the Year

O N THE SOLEMNITY of Pentecost, 2015, Pope Francis issued the encyclical letter, *Laudato si': On Care for Our Common Home* (LS). This letter presents a vital and firm plea for humanity to care for all that God has created. Noting significant problems—climate change, pollution, waste and materialism, the depletion of natural resources, global inequality, endangered species (plants and animals), and a decline in the respect given to the quality of human life (and many other concerns)—Pope Francis stresses the need to "take a frank look at the facts to see that our common home is falling into serious disrepair" (LS, 61): for Mother Earth now "cries out to us because of the harm we have inflicted on her by our irresponsible use and abuse of the goods with which God has endowed her" (LS, 2).

Francis' concerns do not present a radical new teaching, but reinforce a theological framework grounded in Catholic tradition. Citing Scripture, theologians, saints, former popes, and other Church documents, Francis emphasizes that creation is "a magnificent book in which God speaks to us and grants us a glimpse of his infinite beauty and goodness" (LS, 12). All creatures and life-forms are a reflection of God's great love! All of creation is sacred and majestic and gives God continuous praise, for he is the one whose hands fashioned and made all that is good. In his goodness, God created humanity in his image and likeness, granting us dominion over the world. Dominion requires that we continuously strive to seek the right relationship that was established through God's very act of creation. Sin disrupted this relationship, and this brokenness is reflected in the "destruction of creation" (LS, 8).

Even in our brokenness, God does not forsake us. He constantly seeks to embrace us and welcome us home to his Garden. It is through Christ that this relationship is restored and that our human state is redeemed. St. Irenaeus said, "Christ became human so that we may become divine." Through Christ, we are transformed to be ever more configured to his divine likeness—a likeness which we were created to be from the very beginning of God's creative acts. Through Christ, all of creation is restored; all of creation rejoices to give God thanks and praise. When we open ourselves to encounter Christ, we empty ourselves of all that separates us from God. This openness requires conversion and transformation of hearts and behavior.

In *Laudato si'*, Francis calls the Christian faithful to this conversion and transformation. It is through this conversion that we come to recognize that all of the created order—the seas and the sky, the birds and fish, mountains and plains, forests and farmland, plants, animals, and humankind—are imbued with God's presence.

Because of the many concerns and issues that face our world today, especially the environmental crisis, this edition of *Sourcebook* invites you to journey through the liturgical year with inspiring quotations from Pope Francis' encyclical letter, *Laudato si'*. Ask yourself how, as a Christian disciple, you are doing your part to protect God's precious gift in creation? How can your parish be proactive in environmental ministry? The few quotations noted in this *Sourcebook* barely scratch the surface of this prolific document. Invite parish staff and parishioners to study the document together. It is found here: http://w2.vatican.va/content /francesco/en/encyclicals/documents/papa -francesco_20150524_enciclica-laudato-si.html.

"LAUDATO SI', mi' Signore"—"Praise be to you, my Lord." In the words of this beautiful canticle, St. Francis of Assisi reminds us that our common home is like a sister with whom we share our life and a beautiful mother who opens her arms to embrace us. "Praise be to you, my Lord, through our Sister, Mother Earth, who sustains and governs us, and who produces various fruit with coloured flowers and herbs. (LS, 1)

This sister now cries out to us because of the harm we have inflicted on her by our irresponsible use and abuse of the goods with which God has endowed her. We have come to see ourselves as her lords and masters, entitled to plunder her at will. The violence present in our hearts, wounded by sin, is also reflected in the symptoms of sickness evident in the soil, in the water, in the air and in all forms of life. This is why the earth herself, burdened and laid waste, is among the most abandoned and maltreated of our poor; she "groans in travail" (Romans 8:22). We have forgotten that we ourselves are dust of the earth (cf. Genesis 2:7); our very bodies are made up of her elements, we breathe her air and we receive life and refreshment from her waters. (LS, 2)

Ways for a Parish to Become Eco-Friendly

The following websites provide excellent information for helping Catholic parishes to become more eco-friendly:

- https://www.trocaire.org/sites/default/files/pdfs/parishes/100-ways-to-implement-laudato-si.pdf
- http://ncrnews.org/documents/5%20Ways%20Eco_20160422_8.5x11.pdf
- https://catholicecology.net/blog/10-ways-catholics-can-protect-environment
- http://www.uscatholic.org/culture/environment/2011/10/think-outside-box-being-green-end-life

The following letter to Catholic families may be printed in your parish bulletin or posted on social media:

- http://www.pastoralliturgy.org/resources/Honor.pdf

Mass Texts

◆ INTRODUCTION TO THE MASS

We've begun a new liturgical year and recall that God became flesh in Jesus Christ, who promised to return. The world is busy shopping and decorating. We take time to remember that God is with us. We take time to ready ourselves for Christmas by standing erect, watching for the Lord's presence, discerning what is of value, and repenting or reorienting our lives to follow him, like John the Baptist preached. We ready ourselves to give birth to Christ in our lives like Mary did many years ago by asking Emmanuel, God-with-us, to come into our hearts.

◆ SEASONAL ALTERNATE TROPES FOR PENITENTIAL ACT FORM C

Lord Jesus, you came as Emmanuel, God-with-us: Lord, have mercy.

Christ Jesus, you come as Jesus, Jeshua, God-who-saves: Christ, have mercy.

Lord Jesus, you will come again in glory to shepherd your flock: Lord, have mercy.

◆ DISMISSAL FOR CHILDREN'S LITURGY OF THE WORD

Watching and waiting for someone or something we expect is not easy, but that is what we do during Advent. We watch and wait to celebrate the birth of Jesus at Christmas. Ask him to help you live like him, so that people can see him in the world by the way you live. Go and listen to the Word of God to discover how Jesus can come to you today. Go in peace.

◆ DISMISSAL OF CATECHUMENS

My sisters and brothers, as you learn the ways of the Lord Jesus Christ, listen carefully to the Word of God that we heard together. Watch for ways to open your hearts to Christ, to live his love clearly by deepening your relationship with him and with his living Body. May the Word of God help you to reorient your lives to live Jesus through your words, deeds, and attitudes. Go in peace.

◆ SEASONAL UNIVERSAL PRAYER (PRAYER OF THE FAITHFUL)

Invitation to Prayer

O come, Emmanuel, and open our minds and hearts to be attentive to the needs of our sisters and brothers throughout the world:

Intercessions

1. That all who follow Jesus Christ watch for ways to make his coming known in our world today, we pray to the Lord:

2. That world leaders seek ways to share our resources to make the justice of the Gospel concrete, we pray to the Lord:

3. That our sisters and brothers who are sick in body, mind, or spirit, might be visited by the healing Christ through the attentiveness and compassion of those who care for them, we pray to the Lord:

4. That during Advent we might take time to reflect on the gift of God's unconditional love made present in the birth of Jesus Christ and let that love abound more and more in us, we pray to the Lord:

5. That this worshipping community visit those who experience pain during the season with the loving presence of Emmanuel, God-with-us, we pray to the Lord:

6. That those who have died and know their time for Christ's return, might rejoice in seeing God face to face, and that the Prince of Peace might come to those who mourn their passing, we pray to the Lord:

Concluding Prayer

Bountiful and generous God,
make us turn to you and show us your face,
that we might prepare your way like
    John the Baptist
and visit others with your Son Jesus,
    like Mary visited Elizabeth,
for with Jesus and the Holy Spirit,
you are one God, for ever and ever.
Amen.

December 2018
Month of the Divine Infancy

Optional Memorials in Advent

The Roman Missal commentaries below pertain to the seasonal weekdays or other obligatory observances. As per the *General Instruction of the Roman Missal*, when celebrating optional memorials "on weekdays of Advent before December 17 . . . one of the following may be chosen: either the Mass of the weekday, or the Mass of the saint, or of one of the saints whose memorial is observed, or the Mass of any saint inscribed in the *Martyrology* for that day" (GIRM, 355b).

The GIRM also states that "on the weekdays of Advent from December 17 to December 24, . . . the Mass texts for the current liturgical day are used; but the Collect may be taken from a memorial which happens to be inscribed in the General Calendar for that day" (GIRM, 355a).

(#3C) violet
2 First Sunday of Advent

The Lectionary for Mass

◆ FIRST READING: As Advent commences, we hear from Isaiah, the mystic prophet of Israel. In an extended discourse, he speaks hopefully of the long anticipated new Davidic dynasty that has yet to be realized. This hoped-for Messiah will be the salvation of Israel.

◆ RESPONSORIAL PSALM 25: The psalm reminds us of the intimate connection between God and his people. God is available as teacher, guide, and savior, pointing the way for all who humbly seek his ways. Although these verses are optimistic, as a whole, Psalm 25 is a lament. This section affirms God's forgiveness of sinners.

◆ SECOND READING: Paul's powerful letter to the community at Thessalonica concludes with prayer and gratitude. His hope for the followers of Jesus is that they grow in love and persevere in right conduct as they continue to follow the Lord. Paul notes that he speaks not from his own authority; his instructions to them come "through the Lord Jesus."

◆ GOSPEL: Jesus speaks to his disciples about the cosmic occurrences at the time of the coming of the Son of Man. While others might be crushed with fear by the devastating reality of the end of the world, the followers of Jesus can stand with their heads held high, anticipating redemption. To be prepared for such a moment requires vigilance, however. They are called to watch and to pray, a foreshadowing of the instructions Jesus will give them in the Garden of Gethsemane as he faces the chaos and suffering of death on the Cross.

The Roman Missal

The Entrance Antiphon for the First Sunday of Advent, taken from Psalm 25:1–3, is a prayer for confidence. "To you, I lift up my soul, O my God / . . . let me not be put to shame . . . / let none who hope in you be put to shame." In the words of the old hymn, "'twas grace that taught my heart to fear, and grace my fears relieved." The Collect for the first Mass of Advent echoes the Last Judgment parables of Matthew 25. The first part of the prayer recalls the wise virgins (see Matthew 25:1–13). We pray for the resolve to be among those who "run forth" with eagerness to meet Christ at his coming, carrying, not lamps, but "righteous deeds." The second part echoes the parable of the sheep and the goats (Matthew 25:31–46). We hope to be gathered with the sheep at his right hand, and "possess the heavenly Kingdom." The Gloria is omitted, as it is for every Sunday of Advent. The Creed is said or sung. The Prayer over the Offerings expresses the divine exchange that takes place in the celebration of the Eucharist. We can only offer to God what God has already given to us; we pray that our devout celebration of the Eucharist "here below" will gain for us the eternal life of heaven. Preface I of Advent is the Preface prescribed for today (until December 16), and aptly so, as it lays out for us the two comings of Christ—namely, his first coming, when he assumed the lowliness of human flesh, and his Second Coming, the day that we watch for as we look forward to inheriting the "great promise," which is the foundation for our hopefulness. Our confidence in the future and our daring to hope are well founded, for they are grounded in Christ. Consider using Eucharistic Prayer III.

Other Ideas

At the beginning of this season it is customary to place an Advent wreath in the liturgical space. At the first liturgy of this weekend the wreath is blessed and the first candle is lighted. The *Book of Blessings* (BB, chapter 47) includes a blessing for this purpose. The blessing is done only once, but the first candle can be lighted at every Mass. Consider having a representative from one of the parish ministries or invite a family to do this. The blessing and lighting can be done before the entrance hymn; it does not replace the penitential act. Parishes should encourage families to set up an Advent wreath in their homes. A copy of the blessing could be included in the bulletin (be sure to secure proper copyright permission).

MON 3 (#175) white
Memorial of St. Francis Xavier, Priest

The Lectionary for Mass

◆ FIRST READING: Isaiah speaks to the revival of Judaism, where Judah and Jerusalem are restored. The renewal of religion is the renewal of the people and their moral code; they will stream to the mountain to learn how to follow God's ways. The effects of "true" religion will be seen in that age: peace and justice.

◆ RESPONSORIAL PSALM 122: The opening verses of this psalm of rejoicing depict the manner in which the faithful will stream to the house of the Lord. The restoration of the religious as well as the civil center of the community and the attending prosperity calls for celebration. Peace is the hallmark of the age.

◆ GOSPEL: The Centurion, a figure from outside the Jewish community, seeks out Jesus and appeals for healing for his suffering servant. Jesus offers to go to him, but the Centurion, a person aware of the power of an order given by someone in command, affirms that all Jesus needs to do is speak and the servant will be healed. Jesus extols the man's faith. Each time we pray at Mass, we echo the centurion's affirmation of trust and confidence. Do we stand in his conviction, as well?

The Roman Missal

Since today's memorial is obligatory, the orations from *The Roman Missal* are those found in the Proper of Saints, for December 3, and the color worn is white. However, on obligatory memorials, it is permissible to use the collect of the seasonal weekday as the concluding prayer to the Universal Prayer; this allows the sanctoral celebration to still maintain its context within the liturgical season, and it is strongly recommended that the priest take advantage of this option. Also, since there is no proper Preface assigned for today, Preface I of Advent may be used, and this would be another way of keeping a link with the season (although the Preface of Holy Pastors or Preface I or II of Saints could also be appropriate choices). The prayers refer to St. Francis Xavier's missionary work and ask that we too may have the same zeal for souls and bear witness to the Gospel as effectively as did this Jesuit priest. Consider using the Eucharistic Prayer for Various Needs and Occasions II.

Today's Saint

St. Francis Xavier (1506–1552), a native Spaniard, was one of the founding members of the Society of Jesus (the Jesuits). Francis Xavier felt called to be a "spiritual soldier" through missionary endeavors to Christianize foreign lands and convert the hearts of unbelievers. One of the many honors Francis received in his life was his appointment by the pope as apostolic nuncio (an ambassador of the Church) to the East. He traveled to many places, including India, the Philippines, and Japan. In his travels, Francis tended to the needs of the sick and infirm, revitalized the liturgical and sacramental life of already existing Christian populations, and drew people to faith in Jesus Christ.

TUE 4 (#176) violet
Advent Weekday

Optional Memorial of St. John Damascene, Priest and Doctor of the Church / white

The Lectionary for Mass

◆ FIRST READING: Isaiah's prophecy of the Messiah's coming continues with the image of the stump sprouting a shoot, an image that Christians cherish in Advent. What appears to be ruined in fact will produce life. The one sent by God will be empowered with God's spirit and display powerful graces. In his presence, the peaceable Kingdom on earth will be achieved.

◆ RESPONSORIAL PSALM 72: The King is the intercessor for the people with God. When the Messiah comes, righteousness and peace will flourish. The poor will be lifted up. For this, God's name is blessed forever.

◆ GOSPEL: Upon the return of the seventy-two from the ministry to which he has sent them, we hear that "Jesus rejoiced in the Holy Spirit"; in fact, the word is more akin to "exulted." He offers an extraordinary, passionate prayer to God that is both personal and communal, acknowledging what God has done for those who have trusted even beyond the capacity of prophets and kings. Here, Jesus reveals himself to be the path to the Father in language that is reminiscent of that used in the Gospel according to John.

The Roman Missal

The orations for today's liturgy remind the Church of God's great compassion and mercy. In the Collect, we ask God's "compassionate help" to meet the challenges of life, so that in all our trials we may be consoled by Christ's presence, and freed from "the corruption of former ways." Even as we are consoled by Christ's presence, we await his coming. Consider using the Eucharistic Prayer for Various Needs and Occasions I.

Today's Saint

St . John of Damascus (or Damascene/c. 657–749) was a Syrian monk and priest, the "last of the Fathers of the Church." Islam had taken root in Syria, and John worked for the caliph for a time but left to enter the monastery of St. Sabbas near Jerusalem. He is best known for his defense of the veneration of images and his summary of the teachings of the Greek Fathers, *The Fountain of Wisdom.*

W
E 5 (#177) violet
D **Advent Weekday**

The Lectionary for Mass

◆ FIRST READING: A hymn of thanksgiving is offered to God, who offers a spectacular banquet on his holy mountain. A feast for all God's people is described, held on his holy mountain, most likely Mount Zion. This is the triumph of God over the challenges that burden humanity. Even death is defeated. For this, all rejoice and extol God's greatness.

◆ RESPONSORIAL PSALM 23: The lyrical, image-filled Twenty-Third Psalm is beloved for expanding magnificently on the image of God as shepherd. To journey with God is to be steered to a rich oasis of sustenance, whether that be of water or food. This is the God of abundance and fidelity—a God who reinvigorates and refreshes those in need.

◆ GOSPEL: Jesus' fame is drawing enormous crowds, who bring with them all those who suffer (the lame, mute, blind, and more) for healing. Through his miraculous cures, Jesus both glorifies God and inspires believers. Jesus feels compassion for the hungry throng that has been listening to him and asks his disciples to feed them. They respond with less belief than the

crowd has displayed, expressing skepticism about food supplies. In an act foreshadowing the breaking and sharing of bread at the Last Supper, Jesus thanks God, blessing the meager food supply. It miraculously multiplies and all are fed. The pattern of taking, breaking, and giving remains the fundamental pattern of Christian communion.

The Roman Missal

We know that only God's power can "prepare our hearts" for the coming of the Lord (Collect). We pray that we may be found worthy to come to the banquet of life, where we will receive "heavenly nourishment" from the Lord's own hands. In the Eucharist, we have the foretaste of that heavenly banquet. Consider using the Eucharistic Prayer for Reconciliation I.

T
H 6 (#178) violet
U **Advent Weekday**

Optional Memorial of St. Nicholas, Bishop / white

The Lectionary for Mass

◆ FIRST READING: Isaiah offers a hymn evoking what people will sing when the Messianic promise is fulfilled. All lords have been defeated; God is triumphant, and in prevailing, the poor and lowly have been uplifted. This God who turns social standing on its head is a rock to be trusted eternally.

◆ RESPONSORIAL PSALM 118 reminds us that we must place our trust in God, not in frail and fallible humans. Even those who are highly placed, such as princes, cannot be given the fullness of trust that one can give to the Lord who is a rock. This trust can be extended because God is rich in mercy that endures always.

◆ GOSPEL: In these closing passages of the Sermon on the Mount, Jesus warns that it is not enough to call Jesus "Lord." True followers

will show a conversion of heart that produces an action consistent with what God wants of them. His simile of the man who builds his house on a rock remains relevant; the foundation is what will provide security. God is that rock and true foundation his listeners seek.

The Roman Missal

There is a sense of urgency in the air. This time of Advent preparation is nothing to take lightly. The prayers today are calling God to action, to get something started. The prayers are in direct correlation to the First Reading and the psalm. The Collect speaks of sins impeding and the Prayer over the Offerings emphasizes the word "devoutly." In all cases we are told what God asks of us, and just how we must respond. Consider using the Eucharistic Prayer for Various Needs and Occasions IV.

Today's Saint

Little is known about this saint, the "wonder-worker," other than the fact that he lived sometime during the fourth century and was bishop of the city of Myra in Asia Minor. There is some evidence that he was imprisoned during the Diocletian persecutions and later condemned Arianism, a heresy that denied the Son was coeternal with the Father. Many stories exist about St. Nicholas, but one most frequently passed down speaks of a poor man who could not feed or clothe his three daughters. Upon hearing of this man's dire situation, St. Nicholas tossed three bags of gold through his window one evening so the man could tend to his daughter's needs.

F
R 7 (#179) white
I **Memorial of**
St. Ambrose, Bishop and
Doctor of the Church

The Lectionary for Mass

FIRST READING: This optimistic prophecy speaks to the righting of everything that is "wrong" in the human condition. This includes healing physical infirmities and the elimination of those who abuse power. Note that some of what must be righted would be places of sin and darkness within the society Isaiah addresses.

◆ RESPONSORIAL PSALM 27 affirms the graciousness and protective power of God. Those who come to his house have no need to fear. Being strong of heart is called for. This psalm, like Psalm 23, is a powerful affirmation of the bounteous goodness and care of God.

◆ GOSPEL: Yet again we hear of Jesus providing healing to those who seek him in faith, in this case the two blind men. There are a number of incidents in which Jesus heals the blind; in John's account of the Gospel we have a vivid account of the discrimination and ostracizing that a blind person might experience. To be restored to physical wholeness is also to be restored to community. Blindness is often a metaphor for spiritual ignorance, a malady that Jesus cures with practically every encounter.

The Roman Missal

The prayers for today's memorial are found in the Proper of Saints for St. Ambrose. All the prayers are proper to the day. Consider using the Collect from the seasonal weekday to conclude the Universal Prayer. Consider using Eucharistic Prayer I.

Today's Saint

St. Ambrose (c. 340–397) was governor when he stopped the people's riot that erupted during the selection of a new bishop of Milan. The crowd cried, "Ambrose for bishop," and he was chosen, although he was just a catechumen. The Arian heresy—which denied the full divinity of Christ—divided the Church of his time. When Empress Justina

demanded that Ambrose give his basilica to the Arians, he and his congregation locked themselves in and sang in what was the first recorded instance of antiphonal singing.

(#689) white

Solemnity of the Immaculate Conception of the Blessed Virgin Mary

S A T **8**

Holyday of Obligation/Patronal Feastday of the United States of America

About Today's Solemnity

Today is the Patronal Feastday of the United States of America. Although our Gospel reading narrates the story of Jesus' conception, today's solemnity celebrates the Immaculate Conception of Mary, as she was conceived in her mother's womb. Prepared by God from the very first moment of her life to receive Jesus Christ, God's grace preserved Mary from sin from the womb to the end of her life because of her role in the mystery of salvation as the Mother of God. Today's solemnity praises God for the hope and possibility that Mary embodies as we turn to our Blessed Mother to learn from the first and most important relationship Jesus Christ experienced among us. Mary's freedom from the sin of Adam and Eve is shown in today's Gospel. In Mary's response to the angel, she shows her willingness to place herself fully in God's hands, even when

it promises to be difficult and requires great faith and trust.

The Lectionary for Mass

◆ FIRST READING: The readings for the Immaculate Conception begin with a reminder of where the stain of human sin originates. Adam is quick to cast blame on Eve for his transgression, even implicating God indirectly. Eve blames the serpent. This sinful pattern of casting blame rather than owning our sinfulness and repenting is part of the human condition.

◆ RESPONSORIAL PSALM 98: God has done amazing things, and is therefore worthy of human praise. The God of Israel is the God of triumph, displaying his power throughout the earth.

◆ SECOND READING: The opening benediction of this letter to the Ephesians echoes Hebrew prayer even as it embraces Christ as Lord. The emphasis here is on how God has acted through his Son, Jesus Christ, in whom believers have found the path to God. The relationship of believers is that of adoption, those who are chosen.

◆ GOSPEL: The vivid and poetic narrative of Mary being told that she, despite her lowly stature, will be the God bearer captivates both heart and mind. Overcome with fear at first, she nevertheless engages in conversation with the angelic emissary of the Most High. Her humble surrender—"I am the handmaid of the Lord. May it be done to me according to your word"— is filled with humility and trust. In that, she is in many ways the model for all disciples.

The Roman Missal

The texts for the Mass are found in the Proper of Saints. That Mary was preserved from the stain of Original Sin from the moment of her conception is the theme echoed throughout the prayers for the Mass. Mary is always seen within the context of the Church, as the model disciple, and hence the second part of the Collect asks for her intercession that we too "may be cleansed and admitted to your presence." The Preface is found right there along with the other texts for the day. As is common because it expresses the reasons we are giving thanks to God at this celebration, the Preface is a rich source for the meaning and theology of the solemnity we are celebrating, and it can be a splendid source for homiletic themes. Consider using Eucharistic Prayer II for Reconciliation. It is a good idea to use the Solemn Blessing at the end of Mass suggested for today, which is the one titled "The Blessed Virgin Mary," number 15, the first choice under the "For Celebrations of the Saints" section.

During Advent, the Gloria is sung (preferred) or said only twice: the Immaculate Conception (today) and Our Lady of Guadalupe (December 12 in the dioceses of the United States of America). Choose a musical setting in the style of a fixed response by the assembly or a call and response of cantor and assembly. By having the liturgical musicians sing the intervening parts, this fosters singing the hymn and has the assembly learn its smaller part by doing it. A well-chosen setting may require little assembly rehearsal.

Other Ideas

Even though Immaculate Conception falls on a Saturday, as the patronal feastday of the United States, it retains its obligatory status. Although the liturgical environment for Advent is in place, some decorative elements, such as a fresh flower arrangement, could be placed near an image of the Blessed Mother. Provide parishioners with additional ways they can pray or reflect together as a family. This could include at least one decade of the Rosary using the joyful myster-

ies, a reading from Luke's account of the Gospel (see 1:26–38), and a brief conversation on the meaning of Mary's gift to us as the mother of our Lord. Since today is a solemnity, it is appropriate to include more festive music (including the parish choir), incense, and a more formal Gospel procession (including candles and incense).

☀ **9** (#6C) violet
Second Sunday of Advent

The Lectionary for Mass

◆ FIRST READING: This passage in Baruch is a response to the destruction of Jerusalem. Written from the Babylonian captivity, the author directly addresses Jerusalem. It offers a vision of total restoration, in which the Holy City is raised back up and restored to glory.

◆ RESPONSORIAL PSALM 126: The Babylonian captivity was among the darkest eras in the life of the people of Israel, stripping them of their home and identity. Psalm 126 is a lament, but also offers tremendous affirmation of the power of God to intervene in desperate situations.

◆ SECOND READING: Here we experience Paul's deep and heartfelt gratitude for the faithful partnership of the community at Philippi. His prayer for the members is joyful and confident, grounded in God's promise. His desire that their love and discernment increase, along with their purity and blamelessness,

is as relevant a prayer for disciples today as it was in Paul's time.

◆ GOSPEL: Luke borrows the imagery from Isaiah as he introduces us to John the Baptist, the cousin of Jesus and the one who begins preparing people for the coming of the Prince of Peace. He is a pioneering figure, hearing God's word and springing into action, going out into the entire region to proclaim baptism for forgiveness of sins. The list of important persons of the day that starts this Gospel passage situates John within the culture and the age.

The Roman Missal

A sense of urgency continues to be conveyed in the Collect as we pray that nothing may "hinder those / who set out in haste to meet your Son." However, any progress we make in our Advent journey of running to meet Christ is not due to our own merits, as noted in the Prayer over the Offerings. In fact, since we can do nothing on our own, we recognize our need for rescue through God's mercy. Consider using Eucharistic Prayer III.

Other Ideas

Many parishes have the custom of a "Giving Tree" or a "Jesse Tree" festooned with gift tags with suggestions for gifts for children and others in the community who would otherwise find it difficult to afford Christmas presents. Be sure to remind parishioners of this opportunity, encouraging children to help select a gift tag and to actually assist with the shopping and wrapping of the presents. The Feast of Our Lady of Guadalupe is celebrated this Wednesday (December 12). Invite a member of the parish who is familiar with the traditions surrounding the devotion to the Virgin to say a few words about the importance of this feast at the end of the Sunday liturgies following the Prayer after Communion. An image of the Virgin Mary, the Patroness of the Americas, could be displayed in the church on the feast itself.

MON 10 (#181) violet
Advent Weekday

The Lectionary for Mass

◆ FIRST READING: This poetic passage from Isaiah describes the total transformation of a barren desert into a place teeming with water and blooming flowers. No longer will the sand burn or the jackal lay in wait, because the vindicating God has come with salvation. This is a profoundly beautiful narrative designed to inspire faith and rejoicing.

◆ RESPONSORIAL PSALM 85: Israel recalls the acts of God in the past. They become the source of solace and affirmation for the future. God is not distant, but near, and he will come to save. The posture of the psalmist is that of trust rather than that of making demands upon the Lord.

◆ GOSPEL: Once again, the scribes and Pharisees are caught focusing not on the miracle before their eyes, but on the legitimacy of the source of Jesus' power. In contrast we have the friends of the paralyzed man, who are not looking to challenge Jesus but to embrace him as healer. It is noteworthy that their faith is so vivid that even in their struggle to lower their friend, their faith can be seen by Jesus. Jesus acts in God's authority, to the amazement of those who are gathered.

The Roman Missal

Are you prepared to hope? The Entrance Antiphon from Jeremiah 31 and Isaiah 35 reminds us God is near and we have no reason to be afraid. The Prayer over the Offerings and the Prayer after Communion are the same as those used for the First Sunday of Advent, but we read, hear, and pray them differently because of the context of today's readings. All the prayers

allude to the mystery of God. Consider using the Eucharistic Prayer for Reconciliation I.

TUE 11 (#182) violet
Advent Weekday

Optional Memorial of St. Damasus I, Pope / white

The Lectionary for Mass

◆ FIRST READING: Here we experience Isaiah not only as a voice of warning but one of comfort. God's people are in deep need of tender words and reassurance that God has not forgotten her plight. The voice crying out is God's messenger who calls out to the barren places and straightens the path to God.

◆ RESPONSORIAL PSALM 96 exhorts all to sing a new song to the Lord, who comes with power. The power of God is to be announced not just to Israel, but to all nations, and creation will respond with rejoicing. The heavens, the sea, the plains, and the forest all join in this hymn of praise.

◆ GOSPEL: This parable must have seemed preposterous to the disciples—would a shepherd leave the ninety-nine for one? Here, Jesus underscores the value of every single individual to God. No person, no sheep, is disposable in the eyes of the Good Shepherd. And the work done by God in seeking the lost does not produce anger or retribution, but great rejoicing. The God of Jesus is one of love, fidelity, and protection.

The Roman Missal

We are progressing along in our Advent journey as evidenced by the first mention of the Nativity in the Collect; these days can be seen as a kind of movement slowly advancing from the first phase of Advent into the second phase. Consider using Eucharistic Prayer II.

Today's Saint

As pope, St. Damasus I (†384) commissioned his secretary, St. Jerome, to revise the Latin Bible in use at that time by translating the Old Testament from the Hebrew rather than the Greek version. The Vulgate remained the standard Latin translation until 1979. Damasus presided over the Council of Rome, at which the canon of Scripture, or recognized books in the Bible, was set. He fought to counteract Apollinarianism, an overcorrection to Arianism that de-emphasized Christ's humanity. He is also known for the verses he composed to adorn the tombs of the martyrs in Rome.

WED 12 (#690A) white
Feast of Our Lady of Guadalupe

About Today's Feast

Today the Church throughout America (North, Central, and South) celebrates Our Lady of Guadalupe, Patroness of the Americas. Today is a feast in the United States of America, but in many Hispanic countries, such as Mexico, it is raised to a solemnity. The story of the origins of the miraculous image of Our Lady of Guadalupe is well known. Juan Diego Cuauhtlatoatzin was a quiet, humble man, a poor peasant. When the Blessed Virgin Mary appeared to him and asked him to tell the local bishop to build a church in her honor, Juan Diego became a very reluctant messenger. The bishop would not believe him. So Mary filled Juan Diego's tilma, or cloak, with roses in December, and when he emptied out these beautiful flowers at the bishop's feet, there, imprinted on his tilma, was a wonderful image of the Virgin, dressed like a young Aztec woman.

The Lectionary for Mass

◆ FIRST READING, OPTION 1: Zechariah's vision promises abundance and restoration for Israel. The messenger speaks to the daughter of Zion, announcing that God will dwell among his people. Jerusalem will be restored.

◆ FIRST READING, OPTION 2: This vivid scene from the Book of Revelation evokes the birth and the rescue of the divine child. It offers a juxtaposition between those who are true to God and those who would literally devour God's plan. Later Christians began to identify the woman in this passage with Mary, thus its choice for the Feast of Our Lady of Guadalupe.

◆ CANTICLE: Today's psalmody is drawn from verses in the Book of Judith, the final book of the Old Testament as understood by Catholics. Written during the Maccabean revolt, it recounts the story of a valiant Hebrew woman who leads the people against the Assyrians. These words of blessing are spoken after her triumph over the invading general, Holofernes.

◆ GOSPEL, OPTION 1: The story of the Annunciation is one of tremendous surrender in faith. While initially incredulous at the proposal, once it is explained that "nothing will be impossible for God," Mary trusts in the will of God. This pattern is iconic for any Christian life, as every follower of Jesus will face moments where total surrender in faith will be needed.

◆ GOSPEL, OPTION 2: Luke's account of the Gospel most directly intertwines the story of John the Baptist and that of Jesus. Mary has been told that her kinswoman will conceive a child, despite Elizabeth's advanced age. Upon greeting Mary, the child in her womb—John—leaps in recognition of being in the presence of the God-bearer, a revered name for Mary in the Eastern Christian Tradition. We hear in this text many of the verses of the beloved prayer, "Hail Mary/ Ave Maria."

The Roman Missal

The orations for this Mass are found in the Proper of Saints. The Collect, Prayer over the Offerings, and Prayer after Communion are proper for today, so they replace the Advent texts. The Gloria is sung or said today. The Creed is not said or sung. You may use either Preface I or II of the Blessed Virgin Mary. Given the references in Preface II to God's extension of "abundant mercy from age to age," and that God looks upon "the lowliness of [his] handmaid," this Preface might be a more appropriate selection for today's celebration. Consider using the Eucharistic Prayer for Various Needs and Occasions I.

Other Ideas

The most widespread communal devotion for the Guadalupe feast is *las mañanitas* ("morning songs"), a tribute usually begun before dawn. In many parishes it leads into the feast-day Mass. Devotees' offering of flowers expresses their love and thanks to their mother. Accompanying the sung tributes are devotions such as the praying of the Rosary, Scripture readings, and testimonies or meditations about Guadalupe. Resounding in the song offerings are sentiments of joyful veneration, such as the beginning and ending of the traditional hymn *"Buenos Días, Paloma Blanca"* ("Good Morning, White Dove"): *"Buenos días, Paloma Blanca, hoy te vengo a saludar. . . . Recibe estas mañanitas, de mi humilde corazón"* (Good morning, White Dove, today I come to greet you. . . . Receive these *mañanitas* from my humble heart). Most of Guadalupe's faithful know these songs by heart and resonate with their emphases on thanking her, seeking her blessing and protection, and acclaiming her motherhood, purity, and miraculous apparitions to Juan Diego. Sacred dances called *matachines* are also offered to Guadalupe,

sometimes within the Eucharist itself during the entrance procession, the Preparation of the Gifts, or after Communion. Since there is no single order of worship for a *las mañanitas* celebration, liturgists can help prepare prayers, personal faith testimonies, Scripture readings, and/or meditations in a manner that complements the traditional songs. These enhancements should be brief so as to not detract from the song tribute that comprises the core faith expression of this event. But when done well, these additional worship elements help devotees deepen their appreciation of their traditions.

THU 13 (#184) red
Memorial of St. Lucy, Virgin and Martyr

The Lectionary for Mass

◆ FIRST READING: Isaiah's harsh description of the chosen people—a worm, a maggot—is jarring to hear. Jewish scholars interpret this positively in rabbinic commentary. A worm, with its small mouth, can destroy vegetation as powerfully as a saw or threshing sledge.

◆ RESPONSORIAL PSALM 145: The psalm reminds listeners that God is to be trusted. If one is faithful, keeping the law of God and blessing God's goodness, God will respond with grace and mercy in all generations.

◆ GOSPEL: Jesus affirms to the crowd the importance and role of John the Baptist as a great prophet. Jesus observes that the Messiah would be heralded as predicted by both Isaiah and Malachi. In John, Jesus sees one era coming into completion in John, whom he likens to the great prophet Elijah, and a new era that is commencing.

The Roman Missal

For today's obligatory memorial, the Collect is taken from the Proper of Saints for December 13.

The Prayer over the Offerings and the Prayer after Communion are taken from either the Common of Martyrs: For a Virgin Martyr or from the Common of Virgins: For One Virgin. It would be a good idea to use the Collect of the seasonal weekday, Friday of the Second Week of Advent, as the concluding prayer to the Universal Prayer to maintain the connection to the liturgical time. Also, since there is no proper Preface assigned for today, Preface I of Advent may be used, and this would be another way of keeping a link with the season, although certainly the Preface of Holy Virgins and Religious or one of the Prefaces for Holy Martyrs are also appropriate choices. Consider using Eucharistic Prayer I.

Today's Saint

St. Lucy (c. † 304), even from a young age, had a burning desire to serve God and a generous love for the poor. Living in Syracuse, a city in Sicily, she fell prey to the Diocletian persecutions, which eventually resulted in her martyrdom. She resisted a man, believed to be a Roman soldier, who tried to rape her. He, in turn, denounced her as a Christian and had her tortured and killed. Numerous legends revolve around her death, but one that has gained popularity is that she tore out her eyes in an act to resist her attacker. Her name in Latin, *Lucia*, comes from *lux, lucis,* meaning light; therefore, many northern countries honor her at this time of year when darkness is pervasive. Sweden celebrates the virginity and martyrdom of St. Lucy during a festival of light with a sacred procession of young girls clothed in white dresses with red sashes, and crowned with lit candles. She is the patron saint of those with eye troubles and those needing awareness.

((#185) white

FRI 14 Memorial of St. John of the Cross, Priest and Doctor of the Church

The Lectionary for Mass

◆ FIRST READING: Israel is reminded that their prosperity is directly tied to their willingness to honor God's commandments. It is as if God laments their stubborn resistance to following his ways. God awaits the people fulfilling their potential.

◆ RESPONSORIAL PSALM 1: For the people of Israel, a moral life depends on making right choices – something true to this day. This wisdom psalm recounts the importance of avoiding the wicked and following God's law. The contrast between those who follow God and those who don't is outlined in natural images (a tree, chaff) familiar then and now.

◆ GOSPEL: We continue to hear of the importance of the proclamation of John the Baptist and the unwillingness of people to hear him. Even in the time of Jesus, people were uncertain of what was before their eyes, and hesitant to choose rightly. The images of the flute and dirge point to the inner work required of believers, who can choose to believe or not. Jesus even mentions the manner in which his critics have been disparaging him, underlining that he will be vindicated.

The Roman Missal

All three of the orations are from the Proper of Saints. They echo the mystical theology associated with St. John of the Cross. The Collect references his "outstanding dedication to perfect self-denial / and love of the Cross," asking that we might imitate those spiritual virtues. The Prayer over the Offerings requests that "we, who celebrate / the mysteries of the Lord's Passion, / may imitate what we now enact." The

---

Prayer after Communion hails St. John as one through whom God has "wonderfully made known the mystery of the Cross" and prays that we may cling faithfully to Christ as we draw strength from participating in the offering of this Sacrifice. Consider using Eucharistic Prayer II.

Today's Saint

St. John of the Cross (1542–1591) grew up near Avila in poverty. His father died when he was young, and his widowed mother struggled to support the family. Shortly after his ordination in 1567, he met Teresa of Avila and was drawn into her reform of the Carmelites. The reform set Carmelite brother against brother, and John was even imprisoned but used the time to write the *Spiritual Canticle*. For this, and for his other great work, *Dark Night of the Soul*, he is considered one of the greatest poets to write in Spanish.

(#186) violet

SAT 15 Advent Weekday

The Lectionary for Mass

◆ FIRST READING: Ben Sira, author of this wisdom book, sings the praise of the Great Elijah, who was god-like in his ability to raise people back to life or to inflict death. The image of fire ties to incidents in the life of Elijah, including his being taken up into heaven on a fiery chariot.

◆ RESPONSORIAL PSALM 80: In this lament, the people cry out to God, reminding him that they are the vine that he has planted. They cry for help and promise that they will no longer turn from the Lord.

◆ GOSPEL: This passage in Matthew recounts the descent from the mountain after the Transfiguration. The scribes, consonant with the prediction of the prophet Malachi, believe that Elijah will return. Jesus affirms this, but points to John the Baptist as the promised one, who has done the work that was promised by the prophets.

The Roman Missal

Both the Entrance Antiphon and Responsorial use Psalm 80, and we see just how bold everything about this liturgy is today. To ask to see the face of God is a brave act of faith. Our readings speak of Elijah and flames, but that is exactly what our Collect promises as it speaks of the "splendor of your glory dawn in our hearts." We continue to pray with Advent Preface I. Consider using Eucharistic Prayer II. There is a simplicity and straightforwardness in these messages that speak of the coming Christ. Practice different vocal inflections to explore their full meaning. Then you too may experience the fire of those chariots burning within your heart. How will you express your faith today?

☀ 16 (#9C) violet or rose
Third Sunday of Advent

Gaudete Sunday

About Gaudete Sunday

The Third Sunday of Advent (like the Fourth Sunday of Lent) is a day of joy in the midst of our spiritual preparations for Christmas. It is traditionally called Gaudete Sunday, from the Latin of the Entrance Antiphon for today: *Gaudete in Domino semper,* "Rejoice in the Lord always; again I say, rejoice! The Lord is near" (Philippians 4:4–5). The antiphon captures the mood of the entire liturgy as we move into the second part of Advent: there is a sense of joyful expectation, an awareness that the fulfillment of God's great plan for us is near. That sense is strong in today's readings.

The Lectionary for Mass

◆ FIRST READING: Zephaniah prophesied fifty years before Isaiah, yet his message is similar. This joyous text hails the day of the Lord, which is on the horizon. Then, God as savior will be in the midst of the people. This passage is the perfect start for the readings of Gaudete Sunday.

◆ CANTICLE: In place of one of the psalms, we hear the cry of joy and praise for God found in the writings of the prophet Isaiah. The day of judgement and salvation is upon Israel, and it is time to exult in praise that the "Holy One of Israel" is in their midst.

◆ SECOND READING: This exquisite passage from Philippians reminds us that the path of the disciple of Christ is one of great rejoicing. Why? Because there is nothing of concern that we cannot place in the hands of God so that we may dwell in his peace—a peace that is beyond human comprehension.

◆ GOSPEL: The people see in John a mighty power, and ask him for direction on how to live their lives. Nothing in this would be startling news: share with each other, be fair, avoid the cruelty of extortion, practice being satisfied. However, his news that there is one even greater coming after him would have been attention getting. This will be a new baptism, not with water but with fire that would eliminate all the chaff—dividing the true from the false. This message, superficially frightening, is an affirmation of the Messiah and a therefore a cause for joy.

The Roman Missal

The Collect is a prayer for joy: we ask that we may reach the "joys of so great a salvation" and celebrate that salvation with "glad rejoicing" at Christmas Time. Even if the antiphon is not chanted, call attention to it or invite the congregation to recite it. The Gloria is once again omitted. The Creed is said or sung. Today's Prayer over the Offerings frequently reoccurs during Advent. In this prayer, we ask that the unceasing celebration of "the sacrifice of our worship," the celebration of the Eucharist, may accomplish God's saving work among us. Even though the rubrics seem to indicate that the priest celebrant has a choice between Prefaces I and II of Advent, only Preface I can be used today. Preface II is not used until December 17. Consider using Eucharistic Prayer III.

Other Ideas

The First Reading and the Responsorial Psalm for today are full of exhortations to rejoice, to sing joyfully, and to cry out with joy and gladness! The third candle in the Advent wreath may be rose, indicating this joyful tone as Advent prepares us for the celebration of the Nativity of the Messiah. Pastoral visitors of the parish might make a special effort to visit those who are confined to their homes or hospitals or who live in any of the long term care residences in the parish and to bring them Holy Communion (if that is a parish ministry), some small gifts, and a Christmas plant from the parish. Two or three members of the music ministry could accompany them and sing Christmas carols as a festive touch to the visit.

MON 17 (#193) violet
Advent Weekday

The Lectionary for Mass

The readings are proper to the day from December 17 through December 24.

◆ FIRST READING: Jacob, heir of Abraham and Isaac, calls his sons to pronounce a blessing upon each of them. Judah is the fourth to be praised. Although he has not been exemplary (he sold Joseph for profit and deals unfaithfully with Tamar) he has still shown character in interceding and offering himself for Joseph. This passage's blessing expresses, through Jacob, the grace and mercy of God.

◆ RESPONSORIAL PSALM 72 asks God to endow the king with all the qualities that will allow him to serve God in justice and peace. The king will be God's agent on earth and will follow God's precepts while leading.

◆ GOSPEL: The geneology of Jesus, spelled out here in detail, affirms him as the fulfillment of prophecy and as the expected Messiah of Israel. Notice how Matthew connects Jesus with all the greatest male figures of Israel, as well as some noteworthy women. This litany affirms Jesus' rightful claim to the throne of David.

The Roman Missal

Now we begin the special Mass formularies for the last days of Advent, leading to the celebration of the Nativity of the Lord. Skip the remainder of the Missal pages for the Third Week of Advent and go to the section titled "The Weekdays of Advent," using today the formularies for December 17. Begin to use Preface II of Advent. Consider using Eucharistic Prayer II.

TUE 18 (#194) violet
Advent Weekday

The Lectionary for Mass

◆ FIRST READING: It was foretold in 2 Samuel that the Messiah would spring from the line of David. Here, Jeremiah affirms this prediction. Although to all appearances David's line has been cut down, a new shoot will come forth from the Davidic tree who will restore the descendants of the house of Israel to their proper home.

◆ RESPONSORIAL PSALM 72: The king will be God's representative on earth. The reading of Psalm 72 which began yesterday continues, as more qualities of the just king are outlined.

◆ GOSPEL: Today we hear of the disturbed heart of Joseph, a righteous man facing a very troubling fact: his betrothed is with child. The angel comes to him in a dream to reassure him that all that is happening is the will and work of God. We are reminded of the prophecy of Isaiah, and the Gospel adds to our understanding of Jesus' origins and lineage.

The Roman Missal

The orations used are those specifically assigned for December 18. Preface II of Advent is used again. Consider using Eucharistic Prayer III.

WED 19 (#195) violet
Advent Weekday

The Lectionary for Mass

◆ FIRST READING: The recounting of the prediction of the conception of Samson reminds us that miraculous conceptions are part of the history of Israel. The angel explains that this much-wanted child will be consecrated to God from the womb, and that his hair is not to be cut.

◆ RESPONSORIAL PSALM 71: The voice in Psalm 71 is that of an elder who is seeking safety within the confines of the Temple. This holy person has followed God since his childhood—even from his mother's womb.

◆ GOSPEL: In contrast with Mary's trust in the words of the angel, Zechariah responds with skepticism—he and his wife are too old. This is reminiscent of Sarah literally laughing at the angel about the conception of Isaac. The righteous Zechariah remains dumb until the birth of his son, John, who will be consecrated to the Lord for his entire life as Samson should have been.

The Roman Missal

The prayers are those for December 19. The child born of Mary revealed God's glory to the world. In the Collect, we pray for right faith and due reverence as we prepare to celebrate the mystery of the Incarnation. In the Prayer over the Offerings, it is evident that we can offer so little, but we know that God's power is greater than our weakness. In the Eucharist, we receive a great gift from God, but the Eucharist is only a foretaste of the heavenly banquet. In the Prayer after Communion, we ask God to "arouse in us . . . the desire for those [gifts] yet to come." Consider using the Eucharistic Prayer for Reconciliation I.

THU 20 (#196) violet
Advent Weekday

The Lectionary for Mass

◆ FIRST READING: God invites Ahaz, the wicked King of Judah, to ask for a sign through the prophet Isaiah. Ahaz refuses God's invitation. In response to the stubbornness of Ahaz we receive one of the most famous prophecies: the virgin's conception of the Messiah.

◆ RESPONSORIAL PSALM 24: This psalm most likely was sung on special occasions as people entered the Temple. The ceremony is referenced in the first two (as well as later) verses. Once again, those praising God are reminded that only those who are true followers can ascend God's holy mountain.

◆ GOSPEL: The narrative of the annunciation of the angel Gabriel to Mary has beautiful poetic and narrative flow. Luke takes us on a vivid journey at Mary's side as the celestial apparition startles her with unexpected news—she, a virgin, will bear the Messiah. Her response is both logical (how can this be?) and also trusting (may it be done). She will be God's handmaid. The Greek word, *doulē*, is often translated as "slave," but it was also used at the time of Jesus to speak of a servant leader.

The Roman Missal

The prayers are those for December 20. The Collect extols Mary, who was filled with the Holy Spirit, and became "the dwelling-place of divinity" when the Word took flesh in her womb. We pray for the grace to imitate her by following her example of humble obedience to God's will. The Prayer over the Offerings reveals that Advent is about waiting in hope. Participating in the Eucharist, we have a pledge that one day we will possess fully the gifts for which faith teaches us to hope. In the Prayer after Communion, we ask for a share in the fruits of the Eucharist: "the joy of true peace." Consider using the Eucharistic Prayer for Various Needs and Occasions III.

F
R
I **21** (#197) violet
Advent Weekday

Optional Memorial of St. Peter Canisius, Priest and Doctor of the Church / violet

The Lectionary for Mass

◆ FIRST READING, OPTION 1: Song of Songs is unique to the books of the Bible in that it does not present history, prophetic teaching, or an illumination of Israel's covenant with the Almighty. Here, we hear the spectacular exclamation of the bride for her lover, and his invitation to her to come to him. It is both vivid and poetic.

◆ FIRST READING, OPTION 2: As the birth of the Messiah approaches, we hear a passage from Zephaniah that proclaims the joy that Zion feels with the arrival of the Messiah. God has kept his promise and the people are swept up in rejoicing.

◆ RESPONSORIAL PSALM 33 is a hymn of praise given to God. Notice that the musical accompaniment to praise, in this case harp and lyre, is mentioned. Praise of God, here, is fresh and new, and offered by the just ones who wait upon God's arrival.

◆ GOSPEL: After hearing that she will bear the Messiah and that her kinswoman will also have a child despite advanced age, Mary sets out to the hill country of Judah to see Elizabeth. This was a considerable distance from Galilee; between eighty and one hundred miles. We can imagine that Mary might hope that of all people, Elizabeth might understand what has happened. The spiritual attunement extends to the baby she carries, John, who leaps in his mother's womb with recognition of the presence of the Messiah growing within Mary.

The Roman Missal

The Mass formularies are taken from those specific to December 21. The Advent Collect makes reference to the two comings of Christ: it acknowledges our rejoicing "at the coming of your Only Begotten Son in our flesh," and it asks that "when at last he comes in glory," we may "gain the reward of eternal life." The Prayer over the Offerings speaks of the transformation of the offerings that is to occur; as they are transformed "into the mystery of our salvation," the implication is that we who receive those gifts will also be transformed—for example, saved. The Prayer after Communion prays that our "participation in this divine mystery" will result in protection and abundant health in mind and body. Consider using Eucharistic Prayer II.

Today's Saint

St. Peter Canisius (1521–1597) was the first Dutchman to join the Jesuits. He is known as the second apostle of Germany for his work restoring Catholicism after the Reformation, writing a "German catechism," which defined basic Catholic beliefs in German. Peter felt that it was more effective to clarify the teachings of Catholicism rather than engage in polemics with the reformers. His last twenty years were spent in Switzerland, where he founded the Jesuit College that is the core of the University of Fribourg. He is credited with adding "Holy Mary, Mother of God, pray for us sinners" to the Hail Mary. This appeared for the first time in his Catechism of 1555. He is also a Doctor of the Church.

S
A 22 (#198) violet
T **Advent Weekday**

The Lectionary for Mass

◆ FIRST READING: The recollection of other divinely supported conceptions continues as we hear of Samuel, who was conceived by Hannah after a long period of heartbreak and barrenness. Here, she dedicates him to the Temple in the presence of Eli, who was there when she pleaded with God for a child with such fervor that the priest believed her drunk.

◆ CANTICLE: Hannah's faithful prayer of thanksgiving to God is heard in lieu of a psalm today. She glorifies God and affirms that he raises up the lowly and humble. Although she is leaving her child to serve, she is filled with ecstatic gratitude to God.

◆ GOSPEL: The Magnificat, Mary's hymn of praise, shares many themes with the prayer of Hannah. Her words reflect a deep knowledge and understanding of Scripture. Her words celebrate the goodness, power, and faithfulness of the God of Israel. Her song of praise reflects convictions that are deep; she has not wavered in her yes to God.

The Roman Missal

The Mass texts are those for December 22. We hear the prayers of thanksgiving proclaimed by Hannah and Mary in their songs of praise, and both our Lectionary readings and the Missal texts speak of God's compassion and rejoicing. There is much to unpack in the Prayer over the Offerings: "through the purifying action of your grace, / we may be cleansed by the very mysteries we serve." We are brought low in humble adoration, sometimes through suffering and pain—all so that God may raise us again, in a purer, sacred form. This is the sense of wonder and awe that we must bring with

us to the liturgy, and that we pray about after we receive Communion. This is no small thing that the Lord is doing for us as we as we celebrate Eucharist and as we prepare for Christ's coming. Consider using the Eucharistic Prayer for Various Needs and Occasions IV.

☀ 23 (#12C) violet
Fourth Sunday of Advent

The Lectionary for Mass

◆ FIRST READING: Micah predicts that a great ruler will emerge from the lowliest of places: Bethlehem, the place of King David's birth (Ephrathah is the ancient name of Bethlehem). The word *Bethlehem* means "house of bread" in Hebrew; an apt birthplace for the one John will call "the bread of life."

◆ RESPONSORIAL PSALM 80: As Christmas nears, we are reminded by Psalm 80 that we, God's people, must turn to God once again and be saved. We are his vine, in need of protection and tending. The final stanza of the psalm is a prayer for the King, casting light on our welcome of the King of Kings.

◆ SECOND READING: The author of Hebrews builds, here, on the assertions of Psalm 40. A new kind of worship is now available; one not tied to sin offerings of burnt animal flesh. Jesus, the ultimate sacrifice, has offered his body as the once and final sacrifice to redeem all. In this passage, we are reminded that

the Incarnation is directly tied to redemption.

◆ GOSPEL: For the second time in Advent, we hear the story of Elizabeth and Mary encountering each other. We refer to the mother of Jesus as the "blessed" mother. Here, Elizabeth notes that reality when she cries out, in the Spirit, that her cousin is "blessed." Mary is blessed in two ways. First, because she has demonstrated a stunning faith in God, and second because she is the chosen one who will bring the Son of God into the world.

The Roman Missal

Use the presidential prayers for the Fourth Sunday of Advent rather than those for December 24. The Entrance Antiphon is the Rorate Coeli or "Drop down dew from above, you heavens" (Isaiah 45:8). There are exquisite chant settings of this Introit in English or Latin, as well as other beautiful choral arrangements. Just as the readings are shifting and leading us closer to the birth of Christ, so are our prayers. The theology presented in the Collect is a wonderful opportunity for liturgical preaching. It speaks of the angel proclaiming the Incarnation, but also connects the cradle to the Passion and the Cross. Similarly, the Prayer after Communion reminds us of "eternal redemption" and "salvation." The Gloria is omitted. The Creed is sung or said. On this Sunday, Preface II of Advent is used. Consider using Eucharistic Prayer III.

Other Ideas

With the last Sunday of Advent so close to Christmas there is the temptation to place some of the Christmas decorations in the church. Although this effort might make the work of decorating for Christmas a little easier it does take away from the liturgical nature of Advent which is understood as the Church's time of preparation for Christmas. A better solution is to recruit more volunteers to assist with the Christmas decorating, or consider downsizing the overall scheme of decorations. Some parishes set up the Nativity scene ahead of time, leaving the manger empty until Christmas Eve. However, placing Christmas trees and elaborate flower arrangements ahead of time seems to be less appropriate.

MON 24 (#200) violet
Advent Weekday

The Lectionary for Mass:
Morning Mass

◆ FIRST READING: Having heard many references to David and his line throughout Advent, we now hear God's message presented to David through the prophet Nathan. While Nathan thought that building a temple to God was reasonable, God does not want this. Instead, he reminds David of all that has been done for him, and speaks of the heir that will be raised up from David's line.

◆ RESPONSORIAL PSALM 89 is a lament about the defeat of the king, which is not obvious from today's verses. The affirmation of God's covenant opens the psalm, which circles back through grieving to the affirmation of God as rock and savior.

◆ GOSPEL: God has struck Zechariah mute due to his skepticism about God's power to bring Elizabeth a son. Having seen the promised miracle come to pass, and having named the child John as directed, Zechariah speaks once again. His words of praise are an affirmation of God's fidelity and the power of the covenant. Zechariah's song has been called the Benedictus from the first words of the hymn in Latin.

The Roman Missal:
Morning Mass

The texts for this Mass are taken from the assigned prayers for December 24, with Preface II of Advent being used again for the last time this year. The urgency of the Church's desire is unmistakable in the Collect, addressed directly to the Son: "Come quickly, we pray, Lord Jesus, / and do not delay." We trust in the compassion of Christ, and we long for the solace and relief his coming will bring. In the Prayer over the Offerings, we ask God to receive and make his own the offerings we bring, and to give them back to us for our purification as we await the coming of Christ. The Eucharist gives us "new vigor" to prepare for Christmas and hope to "possess in gladness" the reward of eternal life (Prayer after Communion). Consider using Eucharistic Prayer III.

The evening Masses are for the Solemnity of the Nativity of the Lord. Masses should not begin any earlier than 4 PM. The commentary for the Masses of Christmas are found on pages 41–43 in this *Sourcebook*.

CHRISTMAS TIME

The Roman Missal / The Meaning

PREFACE I of the Nativity of the Lord summarizes themes that recur throughout Christmas Time: "in the mystery of the Word made flesh [Incarnation] / a new light of your glory has shone upon the eyes of our mind [Christ the light], / so that, as we recognize in him God made visible, / we may be caught up through him in love of things invisible" [the holy exchange]. We celebrate God-incarnate, God-in-flesh. We recognize "the light of faith, which illumines our minds" (Collect, Mass at Dawn). We participate in the "glorious exchange, / that, by offering what you have given, / we may merit to receive your very self" (Prayer over the Offerings, Monday, Weekdays of Christmas Time). The *Universal Norms on the Liturgical Year and the Calendar* (UNLY) notes that: "After the annual celebration of the Paschal Mystery, the Church has no more ancient custom than celebrating the memorial of the Nativity of the Lord and of his first manifestations, and this takes place in Christmas Time" (32).

Christmas Time begins with the celebration of First Vespers (Evening Prayer I) of the Lord's Nativity and concludes with Second Vespers (Evening Prayer II) of the Baptism of the Lord, which, in the United States, is celebrated most often on the Sunday after Epiphany. In 2019 the Baptism of the Lord is celebrated on Sunday, January 13. Christmas Time in the Church continues long after secular society concludes the season. Most radio stations stop playing Christmas music on December 26. The Missal provides an embarrassment of riches to help us celebrate a time that bathes us "in the new radiance of [God's] incarnate Word" (Collect, Mass at Dawn), long past December 26. Just look at the Prefaces. We began this section with a quote from Preface I of the Nativity of the Lord. Preface II proclaims: "For on the feast of this awe-filled mystery, / though invisible in his own divine nature, / he has appeared visibly in ours; / and . . . / has begun to exist in time." And Preface III: "For through him the holy exchange that restores our life / has shone forth today in splendor: / when our frailty is assumed by your Word / . . . / by this wondrous union we, too, are made eternal." Remember, the Prefaces summarize our belief about a feast or season.

Like Easter, the Nativity of the Lord has its own Octave. The Octave of Christmas concludes on January 1, the Solemnity of Mary, the Holy Mother of God. On each day of the Octave we sing or say the Gloria, the Creed, and the proper form of the *Communicantes* ("In communion with those"), when the Roman Canon is prayed. Each day of the Octave is celebrated as another Christmas, so to speak. The Missal provides Mass texts for the Vigil, which may be celebrated either before or after First Vespers of the Nativity. Since priests may celebrate or concelebrate three Masses on Christmas Day, texts are provided for Mass during the Night, at Dawn, and during the Day. These Masses "are celebrated at their proper times" (rubric, At the Mass during the Night"). During the Octave we honor St. Stephen the Martyr (December 26), St. John the Apostle and Evangelist (December 27) and the Holy Innocents (December 28). Their Presidential Prayers are found in the "Proper of Saints" in the Missal. On the Solemnities of the Holy Family of Jesus, Mary, and Joseph; Mary, the Holy Mother of God; the Epiphany of the Lord; and the Baptism of the Lord, the Gloria and Creed are prayed, as on any Solemnity. The Missal provides Solemn Blessings

for the Nativity of the Lord, the Beginning of the Year, and the Epiphany of the Lord. These can be found in the section at the end of the "Order of Mass: Solemn Blessings."

There are also presidential prayers for the "Weekdays of Christmas Time." These are found in the "Proper of Time" section of the Missal after the Epiphany texts. The three Prefaces of the Nativity are used before the celebration of the Epiphany. In addition, the Preface of the Epiphany can be used on the weekdays that follow the Epiphany. Neither the Gloria nor the Creed is prescribed for these days. During this time we also celebrate the obligatory memorials for Sts. Basil the Great and Gregory Nazianzen (January 2), St. Elizabeth Ann Seton (January 4), and St. John Neumann (January 5). The texts for these memorials can be found in the "Proper of Saints." The Preface appropriate to each category of saint should be used.

We also celebrate the optional memorials of St. Thomas Becket (December 29), St. Sylvester (December 31), the Most Holy Name of Jesus (January 3), and St. Raymond of Penyafort (January 7). Presidential prayers are provided for each of these in the "Proper of Saints," and the appropriate Preface should be used.

If you choose the third form of the Penitential Act, praying the same tropes throughout the season offers some unity to it. Appendix VI of the Missal offers options for these tropes. Option I speaks of Jesus gathering the nations into God's Kingdom of peace; coming in Word and sacrament (an incarnational focus); and coming in glory, all of which reflect the various themes of the Christmas season mentioned earlier. Option II highlights the Incarnation: Jesus is Son of God and of Mary; the holy exchange: Jesus is Word made flesh and splendor of the Father; and Christ the light: Jesus is the Prince of Peace. Finally, when considering options for the Eucharistic Prayer: EPI (the Roman Canon) with its proper *Communicantes* ("In communion with those") connects this prayer to Christmas Time, and EPIII, by praying that God "give life to all things and make them holy," and by asking that Christ "may he make of us / an eternal offering to you," emphasizes the Incarnation and holy exchange.

The Lectionary for Mass

As MUCH AS WE ARE encouraging silence and hope in Advent, the weeks leading up to Christmas can be so busy, exhausting, or fraught with emotion that many people are ready to pack the season up with the ornaments and decorations! The season of Christmas reminds us to bask in the miracle of the Incarnation, dwelling in the stories of hope and promise this season brings. The Gospel according to John offers us the vivid, uplifting image of what has happened: the Word is now enfleshed, and dwells among us.

The Gospel accounts offer us few, and sometimes conflicting, stories of the birth of Jesus and his childhood. Each offers gems of insight into the reality that now surrounds us. The just king who was promised and about whom we heard a great deal in Advent, has come in a surprising form: a vulnerable infant born to a couple on the margins of society. The humble birth of Jesus is attended by contrasting figures.

First, we hear of the announcement of his birth to the shepherds, figures who lived, in many ways, on the margins of society. We also hear of learned astronomers, who travel from their homeland in search of a king who has been indicated by celestial activity. The Lord has come to the lowly and exalted alike. This is true to this day. No one among us is too high or too servile to not be of interest to our God.

In the weeks leading up to Christmas and after, we hear more stories of angelic presence than at any other time of the year. The angels, the messengers of the Almighty, always bear joyful if startling news. Unlike the early followers of Jesus, we may not feel like it is incumbent upon us to share the Good News of knowing Jesus. Isn't that the job of the professionals? But this birth is not a moment locked somewhere in the past; it is something happening over, and over, and over again—light that breaks into the darkness of our lives. Are we willing to be like the angels, and announce this astonishing news to those around us, so that others may come and see that God has fulfilled his promise in Jesus Christ?

Who will we all be? Will we be like the Magi and the shepherds, poised to worship, or like Herod, unwittingly participating in stamping out the Good News? In this "come and see" season, the choice is ours.

Children's Liturgy of the Word

Christmas FALLS on a Tuesday this year. If your parish has a children's Liturgy of the Word on Christmas Eve or Christmas Day, be sure your space has its own Nativity scene and use more candles than usual. This is the day on which the small tentative light of the Advent wreath becomes the bright light of Christ. Replace violet cloths with white ones to complete this transformation.

Check in advance with parish staff to learn which Gospel will be read during the evening and morning liturgies. Even though the Vigil Mass properly uses the genealogy of Jesus and the Mass during the Day uses the opening of the Gospel according to John, it has become a practice in some parishes to use the readings from the Mass during the Night at all Masses because it is sometimes felt that people want to hear the proclamation of the birth of baby Jesus, with angels and shepherds coming to the stable, rather than the long list of ancestors with difficult names or the more abstract description of Christ as the Word and the Light that overcame darkness. Whatever is used, make sure that children get an opportunity to know the key figures in the Nativity scene.

Choose a simple but lively musical setting of Psalm 98.

The Sunday after Christmas is the Feast of the Holy Family, a natural connection for children. Be sure to keep the Nativity scene in your celebration space and to refer to the figures of Jesus, Mary, and Joseph, emphasizing that Jesus was born into a human family just like theirs. If you did not have children's Liturgy of the Word on Christmas, make sure children know the story of Jesus' birth. Connect the joy of Hannah, who in the First Reading celebrates the birth of Samuel, as a foretaste of Mary's joy at the birth of Jesus.

On the Solemnity of the Epiphany of the Lord, January 6, celebrate the Three Kings in some way in the liturgy, especially if your parish does not ordinarily have costumed kings at Mass. Psalm 72 should be used. Help children understand that the kings represent nations of the world other than Israel coming to adore the King of Kings.

Christmas Time ends the following Sunday, January 13, with the Feast of the Baptism of the Lord. It is appropriate to feature a large bowl of water on a table with a white cloth as part of the environment that day.

The Saints

IN CHRISTMAS, the Church calls attention to Jesus as transcendent and immanent; born, and born to die for our salvation. The witness of the men and women highlighted during this season provides many examples of the Christian understanding of what it means to live within, and give expression to, that mysterious reality of the Incarnation.

The first saint memorialized during Christmas, St. Stephen, is mentioned in the Acts of the Apostles as one of the first deacons, a true servant of the Church. He was also the first disciple to join his fate to Christ's by dying in witness of his faith, thereby becoming the "protomartyr" of the Church. St. John, Evangelist and Apostle, was called "the one whom Jesus loved" (John 13:23). In his Gospel, more than in the other three, the natural, human affection between Jesus and his friends and family is emphasized—and John alone of the Apostles is mentioned as witnessing the Crucifixion. On the Feast of the Holy Family, our human families can be recognized by using the blessing from the *Book of Blessings* (BB, chapter 1).

The Memorial of the Holy Innocents—martyrs massacred as infants by Herod—may seem in strange proximity to the Nativity, until one considers that the birth of Jesus is inseparable from the birth of the Cross. Each of these celebrations offers parishes an opportunity to reflect on the human and divine nature of Jesus; on the bonds of love that bind us to each other and to all God's children; on what it means to be human, so vulnerable and yet partaking in the likeness of God.

Other obligatory celebrations for the season include the Memorial of Sts. Basil and Gregory—both bishops and Doctors of the Church, both known for their wisdom and learning. St. Elizabeth Ann Seton, next on the Church's calendar, was a mother of five who founded the Sisters of Charity, women dedicated to the education of the poor and to parish schools. St. John Neumann—bishop and a member of the Redemptorist Order of missionaries—was also a strong promoter of parochial schools. Both of these—St. Elizabeth Ann Seton and St. John Neumann—were American firsts: Elizabeth Ann Seton was the first native-born citizen of the United States, and John Neumann the first American bishop, to be canonized.

The Solemnity of Mary, the Holy Mother of God, brings an end to the Christmas octave and is a Holyday of Obligation. It is a fitting solemnity during Christmas, as we celebrate the "God-bearer" who gave birth to the Incarnation. This celebration of Mary, the mother of the Prince of Peace, is also designated the World Day of Peace. Communities should include intercessions for peace on this day.

The Liturgy of the Hours

MARKING THE TIME after Christmas can be a challenge for parish liturgy because there is a prevalent notion that "well, it's over for another year." Extending the season of Christmas can be perfectly accomplished by two well-planned potlucks for families, perhaps a brunch and a supper. Do a three-minute catechesis about the season, and then pray Midday Prayer, Evening Prayer, or light a candle and pray Night Prayer. Prepare a simple worship aid for everyone, and ask a parish musician to bring a guitar or keyboard and lead a song or two, in between reciting the psalms.

As parish groups gather to change the Christmas environment and other committees meet to evaluate hospitality and music of the season, suggest the use of Morning or Evening Prayer as a beginning to their meetings. The parish staff can begin the new calendar year by praying Morning or Midday prayer as they meet.

The minimal requirement for praying the Liturgy of the Hours is a structure of hymn, psalmody, reading, and prayers. Perhaps a parish New Year's resolution is in order: to learn more about this prayer of the Church through homily connections, bulletin inserts, and from the parish website or social media page. The starting point is that God should be praised always and everywhere. Select any tenet of chapter 2 of the *General Instruction of Liturgy of the Hours* as a starting point for catechesis.

The Rite of Christian Initiation of Adults

THE PROCESS of Christian initiation as found in the RCIA implicitly encourages a year-round process of inquiry, which currently seems to make parishes groan with anxiety. RCIA team leaders worry that it will be too much work to try and welcome inquirers to the faith during the summer months, relying on the beginning of a school year (surprisingly, even if the parish doesn't have a school) to have a "once-and-done" inquiry series, and place the catechumens on a single path to the Easter sacraments.

Christmas Time, albeit brief, can challenge the inquiry team to look at several other times during the liturgical year and schedule three informal sessions of inquiry during the coming liturgical year. In addition to August, inquirers could be welcomed with simple hospitality of a small group in early Advent, in May after Easter, and in July. It's easier than the calendar may indicate: if the inquiry team is trained to be responsible only for Christian hospitality, a bit of faithsharing, and basic information about becoming a Catholic, then the Christian initiation leaders can put their fears to rest. Also worth mentioning: the benefit to being a member of the inquiry team is that your presence is required only four times a year!

Between the liturgical celebrations of the Nativity of the Lord and the Baptism of the Lord, create some time to take a careful and sensitive look at the inquiry process in your parish. Gather for simple prayer with the Christmas candles lit, share and ponder the First Reading from the Mass during the Night, and review the *National Statutes for the Catechumenate* (NSC, 1 and 4). Revive your own catechesis regarding respect for those who inquire about becoming Catholic and have been baptized previously in another Christian religious denomination. Determine how to update your inquiry team, and make a commitment to move toward year-round inquiry. You may be surprised when the effect of this means that the parish community self-identifies as an evangelizing community!

The Sacraments of Initiation

CHRISTMAS IS a joy-filled time of the liturgical year when we commemorate the Nativity of the Lord. It is a time to put aside the secular hype that led up to Christmas and to focus on the Incarnation, the Word made flesh. The images of Christmas Time—light, joy, birth, family, and especially hope—are evident in the readings and prayers during this time. While the world has put the "holiday season" behind, we Catholics enter into the beauty of Christmas. We don't often see many parishes celebrating the sacraments of initiation, other than Baptism, during this season, but the celebration of the sacraments are permissible. The celebration of First Communion is appropriate, especially if the parish celebrates it whenever it is discerned that a child is ready, instead of following the school year model with the parish children receiving as a large group.

Ritual Masses are allowed on Sundays during Christmas unless a solemnity is being celebrated. Ritual Masses are not permitted on the Solemnity of the Nativity of the Lord (Christmas) on December 25; the Solemnity of Mary, the Holy Mother of God, on January 1; or the Solemnity of the Epiphany of the Lord on January 6. On these Sundays the proper readings for the day must be used. The Feasts of the Holy Family and the Baptism of the Lord are not solemnities, and ritual Masses may be celebrated; however, the readings for these feasts are quite appropriate for the celebration of the sacraments of initiation. Consider celebrating Baptism or First Communion on the Feast of the Holy Family.

The ancient Church, in addition to celebrating initiation at the Easter Vigil, also celebrated initiation on the Solemnity of Epiphany. Epiphany celebrates the manifestation of Christ to the Magi, but also the manifestations at Jesus' baptism and the performance of his first miracle at the wedding at Cana. Christ is certainly manifest in the sacraments of initiation conferred upon the children and young people. This might also be a good occasion to celebrate the Confirmation of Catholic adults, provided the priest receives the proper faculty to confirm them.

The Feast of the Baptism of the Lord is a perfect time to celebrate Baptism. The images of Baptism are so clear in the readings and the prayers of the Mass, and they encourage us all to remember our own Baptism, inspiring us to be continually transformed as we live out our baptismal promises. It is also an opportune time to schedule a reunion of all those families that have had children baptized during the previous year. This can be a festive occasion with the families invited to be recognized at a particular Mass on the feast, followed by hospitality. Include some opportunity for sharing time during the after-Mass gathering, and have information available about ministries and opportunities that your parish has for reaching out to families with young children. Look for moments to evangelize these young families throughout the year by initiating parent/child groups or prayer groups for parents. These type of opportunities with ample time for faith sharing help young parents to live out the promises they made at their child's Baptism.

The Rite of Penance

THE OVERFLOW CROWDS that gather in every parish church for the Christmas liturgies are a well-known phenomenon and can tax the ministerial resources of any parish. But one cannot but feel that the Spirit is at work in their hearts as they seek to mark this great feast of Light and Life by gathering with other believers. This is a good time to do some evangelizing, but not a time to judge or criticize motives and practices.

Parishes might consider spending a little more on some print materials to offer to everyone at the Christmas liturgies and during Christmas Time. Why not cut back on the amount spent on flowers; lavish displays of poinsettias don't bring folks back to the sacraments! These printed materials could be a synopsis of the parish activities, especially the times for liturgies, the programs for Catholics returning to Church, and an invitation to become initiated as a Catholic Christian by participation in the Rite of Christian Initiation of Adults. For many people who have faltered in the practice of their faith, going to confession is often a stumbling block. Perhaps an invitation could be included in the printed materials welcoming anyone seeking to return to Church to come to an open discussion on "how can I return to the practice of my faith?" Expecting people to begin by participating in the Sacrament of Reconciliation as a first step may not

be the most fruitful. Usually people "leave the Church" over a period of time. Coming back to Church may involve a similar journey. Every effort of hospitality and patience that can accompany them is worth offering. Perhaps the Sacrament of Reconciliation can be offered as part of their Lenten practice and the coming of Easter as a joyful return to full communion with the Lord and with the parish family.

The Order of Celebrating Matrimony

THE INCLUSION of the Gloria during the Celebration of Matrimony within Mass is not new to the second edition of *The Order of Celebrating Matrimony* (OCM). It appeared in the rubrics for the ritual Mass for the Celebration of Marriage in the third edition of *The Roman Missal* which was promulgated in 2011. It is even called for at wedding Masses during Lent and Advent, seasons when the Gloria is typically omitted. It would not be sung though on Sundays during Advent or Lent or other solemnities when ritual Masses are prohibited.

A simple setting of the Gloria will work best to facilitate participation at weddings. Even though a through-composed setting is preferable for Sunday Mass since it better respects the nature of the Gloria as a hymn, for weddings a setting with a refrain might be a more pastoral accommodation. Either way, it should be a setting that is accessible and familiar to the assembly.

It might be worthwhile to have the cantor verbally introduce the Gloria and direct the assembly to the appropriate page in the worship aid, hymnal, or other music resource before the wedding liturgy begins. At a Sunday Mass, the Gloria is preceded by the words of absolution of the Penitential Act or the Kyrie when the Confiteor is used. At the Celebration of Matrimony within Mass, the Penitential Act is omitted. After the Sign of the Cross and the ritual greeting from the Order of Mass, the priest addresses the couple and those present "to dispose them inwardly for the celebration of Marriage" (OCM, 52). The ritual gives two choices for this exhortation but also indicates that other similar words may be used. The cantor and organist will need to pay careful attention to the presider to know when to begin the Gloria.

The Pastoral Care of the Sick

MY SISTER DIED a few years ago two days before Christmas, and her funeral was two days after Christmas. I remember thinking that our family was the only family experiencing grief over Christmas. But I have since discovered that many families have had a similar experience, and we have shared stories of how that changes one's celebration during these days of festivity and family gatherings. Deep in our hearts we believe that the Lord was born to bring light and peace to the world, and we are included in his gift.

As the years have passed, we remember in a different way, yet it is always good when someone remembers with us and asks how we are. If you know someone who has experienced the death of a family member or close friend at Christmas Time, or during the past year, be sure to take a moment to remember with them. Ask how they are; ask if there is anything you could help with; share memories of other Christmases, and simply let them know you care about them.

Pastoral care visitors should schedule a time during the week after Christmas to visit those who were unable to come to church for Christmas. The Sunday between Christmas and New Year's Day is the Feast of the Holy Family (when Christmas doesn't fall on a Sunday). This is a good time to arrange with some family members to be present when the pastoral care minister is able to be there. A brief prayer service could be part of the visit, as well as a time to share stories and memories. This takes some effort to arrange but it will be well worth the effort and bring a measure of goodness and joy to everyone.

The Order of Christian Funerals

THE DEATH of a loved one can be especially difficult during Christmas Time. The Christmas Scripture passages and hymns can be a great source of comfort for grieving families as they emphasize the wondrous love of God and the salvific event of Christ's birth. The Scripture accounts of Christ's birth tell us that he was born not only into a human family but into the family of the whole world and his mission would lead him into the lives of many as a presence of grace and peace. Thoughts like this can be included in the funeral homily as the life of the deceased is seen through the eyes of faith and in the context of their own life of discipleship.

Because of the social events that accompany Christmas it is likely that most family members and friends of the deceased will be able to be present at the funeral rites. The parish liturgical ministers should be attentive to gestures of hospitality and make every effort to assist the immediate family with the options for readings and intercessions. *The Order of Christian Funerals* speaks about the ministry of consolation that belongs to the whole community (see OCF, 9); the task of the liturgical ministers is to make this ministry of consolation both visible and comforting.

The liturgical observances of the Holy Family; Mary, the Holy Mother of God; Epiphany; and the Baptism of the Lord all offer a rich selection of images and appropriate references for the homilist at a funeral liturgy. These events in the life of the Lord easily resonate with the life of God's beloved and assist us in understanding how our living and our dying are caught up in the mystery of the Lord's redeeming grace.

The Book of Blessings

TWO BLESSINGS are provided for Christmas Time: one for the Blessing of the Nativity Scene (BB, chapter 48) and one for the Blessing of a Christmas Tree (BB, chapter 49). The Blessing of the Nativity Scene can be done either within a Celebration of the Word of God or within Mass. The Blessing of the Christmas Tree can be celebrated within a Celebration of the Word of God or during Morning or Evening Prayer. A shorter rite is given for both options.

The pastoral notes indicate that the nativity scene should not be placed in the "presbyterium," that is, the sanctuary (BB, 1544).

There is no such restriction for the placement of a Christmas tree. However, the sanctuary should not be turned into a forest of trees that overpowers the primary liturgical furnishings or impedes the liturgical actions that take place there. Nor should the Christmas tree be put in place until after the Fourth Sunday of Advent.

Many parishes have introduced the custom of a "Giving Tree" or "Jesse Tree" as a way to collect gifts for families who would not otherwise be able to afford Christmas presents for their children. The Blessing of the Christmas Tree can easily be adapted for a blessing of these trees.

The blessings of the Christmas tree and the nativity scene can be given by a priest, deacon, or lay minister.

The Feast of the Holy Family is celebrated on Sunday, December 30, this year. The *Book of Blessings* includes an Order for the Blessing of a Family (BB, chapter 1). The blessing can be given either in a home or in the church. There are two options: one outside Mass and one within Mass. Since the feast falls on a Sunday it would seem likely that the latter form of the blessing be used. The order of blessing has two parts: the intercessions and the prayer of blessing. The intercessions are prayed in the usual place after the Creed. The prayer of blessing can be said as the closing prayer for the intercessions or as the blessing over the people prior to the dismissal.

The Solemnity of the Epiphany of the Lord has traditionally been the day for the blessing of homes. Although a priest or deacon could assist with this blessing, it would be impossible for them to bless all the homes in the parish. The Blessing of Homes provided in the *Book of Blessings* (BB, chapter 50) could be used by the family. It is appropriate and festive for other guests to be invited for this occasion. Securing proper copyright permissions, the parish staff could provide a take-home pamphlet with the blessings for the nativity scene, the Christmas tree, and the home for all parishioners. In this way, the prayers of families at home reflects the liturgical prayer of the parish.

The Liturgical Environment

CHRISTMAS MORNINGS during my childhood were the epitome of chaos: eighteen grandchildren and fourteen adults opening gifts resulting in a living room knee-deep in wrapping paper, boxes, and people. Afterwards, we scurried to dress and crammed ourselves into cars as preparation for the standing-room-only Masses in churches decorated with an over-abundance of poinsettias and evergreens. While crowded homes and churches are inevitable at Christmas, toning down the sense of bedlam with your Christmas decor complements the humble beginnings of our Savior's human life. Liturgically, the quiet of Advent joyfully gives way to Christmas peace. We join heaven's angels and earth's poor shepherds in greeting the newborn child, born in lowly circumstances. Art and environment joyfully reflects the announcement that God, born in a stable, is now and eternally with us!

Christmas celebrations often begin with Christmas Eve Masses, followed by Christmas Day creating the challenge of preparing an environment as pleasing during evening hours as it is at daybreak. If your space permits a large evergreen tree, liberally cover it with simple white lights and crystal garland that will reflect morning light. White is the color of Christmas; substitute—or at least intersperse—customary red flowers with white ones placed in gold-colored vases and pots. Integrate amaryllis or roses into your florals: roses are a traditional flower of Mary and amaryllis is also known as a Christmas lily. Large pots or arrangements atop tall stands provide noble grandeur while making it easier for ministers and assembly to navigate the space during the crowded vigil and Christmas day services. When the crowds disperse, fill in with more plants or arrangements to continue through the season.

Take a cue from the nave's architecture for greenery, symbolizing God's eternal love. Line your aisles with wreaths spaced along pillars; follow the curve of arches for swags of green. Use artificial greenery as a base, adding an assortment of live greens such as boxwood, seeded eucalyptus, wax flowers, white hypernicum, or pine along with natural elements like winterberry and pinecones. Placing floral orders several months in advance assures receiving the materials you want. Gold or pearl bead roping and wired ribbon adds seasonal color.

Nestle your Christmas crèche in a devotional niche where families bringing their children will have ready access. Place devotional candles nearby to provide light, or choose strands of lights that are a bit dimmer than those used elsewhere. Place the Magi at a distance until Epiphany.

Communicate the importance of the Christmas season to your neighborhood with outdoor decorations. Wreaths, banners wishing passersby

Christmas blessings, and well-lit Nativity sets announce the spiritual importance of the season, evangelizing in the process. Give your art and environment team oversight for the project, but delegate sections of the outdoor work to parish groups so that the team can focus on the interior.

The Christmas season includes the Solemnities of Mary, the Holy Mother of God (January 1), and the Epiphany (January 6), and the Feasts of the Holy Family (December 30) and Baptism of the Lord (January 13). It is appropriate to place a special floral arrangement or to drape fabric behind a statue of Mary for New Year's Day. Paintings of Mary as *Theotokos* or of the Holy Family could be displayed on easels in the narthex. Special floral arrangements can be placed around the font to highlight the Baptism of the Lord.

The Liturgical Music

BACK IN THE EARLY 1990s, when I was first diving into serious liturgical study and formation, I was blessed in having a great professor who was also a top-rate liturgist. Regarding Christmas, the gem he shared was that if we were using anything other than Christmas carols during the Christmas season we were definitely doing something wrong. His words of wisdom have stayed with me all of these years and I, too, share in his belief.

In terms of assembly hymns, utilize the vast Christmas carol treasury we have. This is for the entire season. Assemblies love singing these beloved annual favorites and will most certainly join in singing. It will also spare your musicians from learning new material. This is not the time to introduce new settings of the Gloria or Eucharistic Prayer acclamations. Rather, use something the assembly knows well and settings that visitors will be able to join in without too much difficulty. Beautiful settings based upon familiar carol melodies of the ordinaries exist. Some excellent examples are Daniel Laginya's "Christmas Gloria" (GIA, G–7800), Paul Gibson's "A Christmas Mass" (OCP, 30106749), James Chepponis' "Christmastime Alleluia" (GIA, G–4453), and Jennifer Pascual's "*Resonet in Laudibus* Eucharistic Acclamations" (WLP, 005337). Whatever settings you choose, maintain the same ordinaries since this, too, will act

to unify the season. For Christmas Eve and Day, communicate clearly with your priest to determine what Mass will be celebrated since various Mass options exist: Vigil Mass, Mass during the Night, Mass at Dawn, and Mass during the Day. Each Mass has its own Introit, Responsorial Psalm, Gospel versicle, and Communion antiphon. *The Roman Missal* includes *The Nativity of Our Lord Jesus Christ* from the *Roman Martyrology* (sung on December 24 during the celebration of the Liturgy of the Hours or, most commonly, sung before the beginning of Christmas Mass during the Night (note that it is not prescribed before the Vigil Mass) and *The Announcement of Easter and the Moveable Feasts* sung on the Solemnity of the Epiphany after the proclamation of the Gospel. Both may be sung by the cantor or deacon. The Missal gives direction that the Announcement of Easter is sung from the ambo while there is no indication in the Missal concerning the location of *The Nativity of Our Lord*. Music for both chants may be found in appendix I of *The Roman Missal*. Solos such as Adolph Adam's "*Cantique de Noël*," Handel's "Rejoice, Greatly," and Pietro Yon's "Gesu, Bambino" can certainly be utilized provided they are placed appropriately and do not cause an interruption to the flow of the liturgy.

The Liturgical Ministers

THE LITURGIES OF Christmas Time, especially those of Christmas Eve and Christmas Day, demand a lot from liturgical ministers, especially since the Christmas assembly is not the usual Sunday congregation. Readers need to be well-prepared. Additional extraordinary ministers of Holy Communion are needed, and the logistics can be different from the norm. Ushers and greeters need to be especially attentive to those who are visiting; many will be guests of parishioners, others will be visiting the community for the first time. Every gesture and word of welcome should be sincere and pleasant; this is not the time to lose one's patience or be judgmental. Most parishes have additional liturgies at Christmas, so extra assistance is always needed; be willing to volunteer for those occasions so the liturgical assembly is served joyfully and well. All ministry is part of the Church's mission of evangelization. What better time than Christmas to make that effort?

In the midst of the usual hectic family and social schedules of Christmas, liturgical ministers are not immune from such busyness(!), and those in ministry need to find some time and space to enter into the mystery of the Incarnation. It would be good to find a moment, or two or three, to read the Infancy Narrative from Luke's account of the Gospel and, like Mary, ponder the remarkable message of our salvation in the birth of the Christ child. What incredible Good News! What amazing reactions by shepherds and Magi! How might our ministry continue to portray the Good News in our demeanor, our proclamations, our facial communication as we extend the Body and Blood of Christ, our pleasant disposition as we greet others, and our many acts of service not only at Christmas but at each and every time we minister?

Other Prayers, Rites, and Devotions

THE ESSENTIAL FOCUS of all devotions during this brief season of Christmas is the indwelling of the Incarnation: God the Father sent his only Son, Jesus, who was made flesh and revealed the Father to us, and sent the Holy Spirit upon us. During the time of Christmas, devotions that reflect our discipleship will serve as reminders of the miracle of Incarnation. Sitting or kneeling before the manger scene (also known as a crèche) traces back to St. Francis of Assisi, around 1223 in Italy. His crèche was replete with real animals, intended to lead people to an encounter with Christ. In our churches today, there are replicas of the live manger scene, art forms of all kinds and from many cultures, that draw us to quiet reflection on the Gift that God sent to earth to redeem us. Gentle rejoicing is the best possible devotion at this time of the liturgical year, indeed, to reflectively calm our harried hearts at secular Christmastime.

Pray intentionally on December 26 for the men of the permanent diaconate, and also those who are deacon candidates, whose patron is St. Stephen, the First Martyr. The parish worship committee can remind pastors and others to use the *Book of Blessings* in a special way this season: the blessing of families (Holy Family on December 30), all mothers (on the Solemnity of Mary, the Mother of God), the crèche (when the Magi arrive, on Epiphany, January 6).

The Feast of the Baptism of the Lord closes the season, and what could be more appropriate than a sprinkling rite? This rite replaces the Penitential Act (at all Masses that day), and is a sacramental that carries blessing to the assembly as a tangible reminder of our Baptism in Christ (regardless of what age we received this sacrament).

A fitting close to the season of Christmas might be Solemn Exposition of the Blessed Sacrament, scheduled between the last two Masses on January 13, with Benediction preceding the final Mass of the day. This works particularly well when there is a long space of time between the last two Sunday celebrations, say 12:30 PM Mass and a 5 PM Sunday evening Mass. Use the ritual book *Order for the Solemn Exposition of the Blessed Sacrament* as a guide to celebrating this devotion worthily and well.

Evangelization

CHRISTMAS CELEBRATES the Incarnation, the birth of Christ, and it is perhaps the most recognizable Christian liturgical season for our greater culture. Although our greater culture is aware of Christmas, it focuses in on one aspect of it, the giving of gifts. While in this way most of our greater culture also celebrates Christmas, our liturgical calendars are increasingly in tension with the "secular" Christmas season which can begin as early as the fall, and ends promptly on December 26. It is always a challenge to sustain the spirit of Christmas through the proper Christmas season while the rest of the world around us has already thrown out the tree, returned and exchanged the gifts, and is now looking forward to New Year's Eve.

Pastors remind us each year from the pulpit that on the Nativity, Christmas has just begun. Social media can be an even further-reaching pulpit to convey to our greater culture the joy and celebration that endures in our homes and parishes these days. One approach for proclaiming Christmas in this context begins with discerning what it is that resonates with secular culture about the season and joyfully and creatively sharing the meaning of this time in a way that takes the conversation deeper. One point to begin the conversation is around the meaning of "gifts." The idea of gifts can be presented in simple, creative, and engaging ways to share the Good News about Christmas with the greater culture.

During the Christmas season, the gift of Christ in the Incarnation inspires us to give one another gifts to share in the joy of the coming of the Savior. While the greater culture may not be aware of the spiritual foundations of gift-giving, receiving gifts, and shopping for gifts are a quint-essential part of Christmas. Many are also con-scious of the strain on budgets or the excessive consumerism of this secular ritual and have grown to appreciate hand-made or home-grown expres-sions of gift-giving. Social media platforms such as Pinterest and market places such as Etsy are a testament to the appeal of a different kind of approach to gift-giving. Similarly on YouTube, creating how-to or demonstration videos are also abundant, and perhaps even more popular or trust-worthy than professionally produced "commer-cials" for a process or product.

This shift toward the appeal of the hand-made and home-grown is a great opportunity for evangelization around "gift." Part of the appeal of how-to videos and images is the sense that they are created by an amateur reviewer or hobbyist just like us, who usually feels free to bring their personalities to the process. In this vein, creative Catholics can compose a Pinterest board or make a YouTube video about how to make a home-made gift, a greeting card, an ornament, or a traditional seasonal recipe. It does not have to be perfect, only genuine and authentic, and demonstrate the joy and enthusiasm the person has for the process. In this is an opportunity to extend that joy not just to the process of making a gift but also to the joy of gift-giving and to the joy of Christ's coming that this honors.

The Parish and the Home

ENCOURAGE EVERYONE in the parish to help prepare the church for the celebration of Christmas. Announce times for decoration of indoor and outdoor spaces in advance, detailing the work that needs to be done, then plan to offer hot chocolate and cookies to helpers after the trees are up, the poinsettias and garlands are placed, and the Nativity scene is unpacked and arranged.

Let everyone know early in December about any parish gatherings during the seasons. Encourage teens and young adults to share the joy of the weeks after Christmas by caroling at local nursing homes or other venues. Christmas Time is long enough to provide plenty of opportunities.

Plan to celebrate a "Festival of Holy Families" on the weekend of December 29 and 30 with a potluck, games, some family conversations, and a blessing for families.

Throughout the season, encourage families to celebrate old and new traditions at home. As was done during Advent, find ways to share the practices of your ethnic groups. At the Epiphany gathering, have three costumed "kings" and be sure to hand out small bags containing a piece of chalk along with the Blessing of the Home and Household on Epiphany from *Catholic Household Blessings & Prayers* or the USCCB website at www.usccb.org.

Last, be sure to encourage people to return to help take down the church decorations after the last Mass on the Baptism of the Lord, again offering hot cocoa and cookies for the helpers and turning it into a community gathering.

Reflections through the Year

Human beings too are creatures of this world, enjoy-ing a right to life and happiness, and endowed with unique dignity. So we cannot fail to consider the effects on people's lives of environmental deteriora-tion, current models of development, and the throw-away culture. (LS, 43)

Mass Texts

◆ INTRODUCTION TO THE MASS

"Today a light will shine upon us, for the Lord is born for us." Today we bask in the light that no darkness can extinguish. Today the light of all nations removes the darkness of division and gathers all God's children together. Today the Word made flesh makes possible our reunion with God in a holy exchange between heaven and earth. Today and every day all the ends of the earth can see the saving power of God.

Rejoice, give thanks, and acclaim our God, who is generous in merciful love.

◆ SEASONAL ALTERNATE TROPES FOR PENITENTIAL ACT, FORM C

Lord Jesus, you became human that we might become divine: Lord, have mercy.

Christ Jesus, you dwell among us as the light of the world: Christ, have mercy.

Lord Jesus, you are Wondrous God and Prince of Peace: Lord, have mercy.

◆ DISMISSAL FOR CHILDREN'S LITURGY OF THE WORD

Today we remember the birth of Jesus, child of God and child of Mary, a child like you and me. The birth of a child helps us see God's love made visible in that new life. Christmas Time helps us remember that God loves us, is near to us, and is always with us. As you go to hear God's Word, listen carefully, God is speaking to you. Discover God is as near to you as you are to each other. Find the light that Jesus shares with us. Then be that light for everyone you meet. Go in peace.

◆ DISMISSAL OF CATECHUMENS

My sisters and brothers, during Christmas Time we remember that the Word became flesh and made his dwelling among us. Listen to the Word of God. Learn to live Jesus in your flesh. Invite the light of the world to lessen the darkness in your life and show you how to share the light of Christ each and every day. Your journey gives us light. We look forward to the time when we can gather as one around the Lord's Table. Go in peace.

◆ SEASONAL UNIVERSAL PRAYER (PRAYER OF THE FAITHFUL)

Invitation to Prayer

The people who walked in darkness have seen a great light. Darkness covers the earth and cries out for the light of Christ to shatter the power of sin and darkness. In prayer we hear where that light is needed and we discover how to be the light of Christ today:

Intercessions

1. That you will endow with right judgment those who lead us in faith, whether they are ordained, vowed, or lay leaders, we pray to the Lord:

2. That you endow world with your justice to bring peace where war, violence, abuse, and affliction abound, we pray to the Lord:

3. That our sisters and brothers who experience any kind of sickness, may find healing and hope in the Wondrous Counselor and Prince of Peace, we pray to the Lord:

4. That Jesus, the love of God-made-visible, may embrace all people who find these days to be difficult, we pray to the Lord:

5. That members of this faith community might pray with Simeon: "Now, Master, you may let your servant go in peace, for my eyes have seen your salvation, light, and glory," we pray to the Lord:

6. That those who have died may bask in the light of the One whose coming we celebrate and whose return we await, we pray to the Lord:

Concluding Prayer

We thank you, O God,
for your love become visible in the birth of
    Jesus Christ,
which we celebrate during this holy season.
Comfort your people,
fill us with your light,
and make us instruments of your Prince of Peace,
    Jesus Christ,
who with you and the Holy Spirit,
are one God, for ever and ever.
Amen.

December 2018
Month of the Divine Infancy

Optional Memorials during Christmas Time

The Missal commentaries below pertain to the seasonal weekdays or other obligatory observances. The *General Instruction of the Roman Missal* states that "on days within the Octave of the Nativity of the Lord . . . the Mass texts for the current liturgical day are used; but the Collect may be taken from a Memorial which happens to be inscribed in the General Calendar for that day" (GIRM, 355a). The GIRM also states that "on weekdays of Christmas Time from January 2 . . . one of the following may be chosen: either the Mass of the weekday, or the Mass of the Saint or one of the Saints whose Memorial is observed, or the Mass of any Saint inscribed in the *Martyrology* for that day" (GIRM, 355b).

(#13, 14, 15, 16ABC) white

TUE 25 **Solemnity of the Nativity of the Lord (Christmas)**

Holyday of Obligation

About Today's Solemnity

The Solemnity of the Nativity of the Lord (Christmas Day itself) celebrates the birth of our Lord Jesus Christ to Mary, his mother, and Joseph, her husband. Yet for Catholics, that is only the beginning. The Nativity of the Lord (Christmas Day) carries such importance within the life of the Church that it is an entire period of liturgical time lasting nearly three weeks. The celebration marks an event of the Lord and also expresses a part of Church doctrine. The doctrine of the Incarnation states a fundamental Christian belief that God's divine nature assumed a human nature. In other words, the unseen God became human. Both human and divine natures come together in the person of Jesus Christ. This became known as the "holy exchange," which tells us that the divine became a human being so that humans could become divine.

Parishes usually offer various opportunities to celebrate Christmas. Following the custom of our Jewish ancestors, a special feast day can begin the evening before, as soon as the sun sets. Thus, many parishes will begin Christmas Masses on the evening of December 24. These are known as the Vigil Masses. The Mass during the Night (previously called Mass at Midnight) is a great tradition for many Catholics. The Christmas story from Luke's account of the Gospel tells how the angel of the Lord came to the shepherds in the fields during their night watch. Some celebrate Christmas Mass at dawn, and others will attend Christmas morning or day. Catholic are expected to go to only one of these options to prayerfully celebrate the Christmas mystery.

The Lectionary for Mass: Vigil Mass

◆ FIRST READING: While Isaiah lived, Jerusalem still functioned as a city, but was profoundly corrupt. When God's chosen comes, the city will be so transformed as to have a new name. When the Gentiles see what God has done for Zion, all nations will sing of its glory.

◆ RESPONSORIAL PSALM 89 reminds us that God has made a binding covenant with Israel. His fidelity is not merely for a chosen few, but for all of Abraham's descendants. Knowing that God is rock, father, and savior, the people are filled with the impulse to sing of God's goodness.

◆ SECOND READING: Paul addresses the community gathered at the synagogue in Antioch. He opens his remarks by placing himself, and the story he is about to share, squarely in relationship with Judaism. Reminding listeners of God's fulfillment of the covenant, he affirms that Jesus is the promised savior.

◆ GOSPEL: The first twenty-five verses of the Gospel according to Matthew affirm to his Jewish readers the lineage of Jesus. The Messiah is promised in prophecy, and described as descending from the House of David. Here, Jesus is connected in his birthright to the greatest figures in the history of Israel. The transition following is to the story of upright Joseph, who is inclined to sever his relationship with his betrothed as is his right by law. The angel assures him that this wondrous child is, indeed, the promised Savior.

The Lectionary for Mass: Mass during the Night

◆ FIRST READING: Having explored many beautiful passages of Isaiah, we now hear what is probably the most famous of all his prophecies. The child is born and he is hailed by a rush of exalted titles: "Wonder-Counselor, God-Hero, Father-Forever, Prince of Peace." In faith we embrace these titles as descriptions of Jesus who was born this day as God incarnate.

◆ RESPONSORIAL PSALM 96 proclaims joy at the enthronement of the King and celebrates God's kingship over all. Interspersed as the refrain is our profession, captured from Luke, that on this day our savior, Christ the Lord is born.

◆ Second Reading: Here, Titus reminds the community that Christ has come, in this moment of birth into the human family, and that he will also come again. Like the disciples of his time, we are invited to live lives that reflect our deep relationship with Christ and to hope for his coming, again.

◆ Gospel: Luke's story of the birth of Jesus offers historical details, but most are, as noted in the *Jerome Biblical Commentary*, symbolic and tied to the Biblical narrative that precedes them. The world is dominated by Rome, with all its power and might. The true king is born in the most modest of circumstances, placed in a manger, not a cradle. He is attended by angels, the traditional signifiers of miraculous occurrences, and the marginalized—shepherds, who were usually poor and often dishonest. The simplicity of the story contrasts the magnitude of its message.

The Lectionary for Mass: Mass at Dawn

◆ First Reading: With the way prepared before him, the Savior will come. Those who receive him will be called holy, and the city that once appeared abandoned is now called "Frequented." These themes reflect the joy believers experience upon welcoming the birth of the savior.

◆ Responsorial Psalm 97: The verses of this psalm, which speak of light shining in darkness, are appropriate for Christmas. We think of the people who have walked in darkness, for example, who now experience a great light. The theme of light overcoming darkness is central to the season of Advent into Christmas Time.

◆ Second Reading: As with the readings from the Mass during the Night, the words from Titus remind us that the Savior truly was among us. This happened not by our collective virtue, but through God's

generosity. Baptism is referenced, reminding that every one of us has experienced new birth in Christ Jesus.

◆ Gospel: We now hear how the shepherds responded to the exhortation of the angels. They are willing to go see this "thing" that has taken place. The Greek word *rhēma* means something akin to a pronouncement made by a living voice. It is interesting to note who these first witnesses were: shepherds, like prostitutes and tax collectors, were considered sinners, and their testimony was not considered legally admissible. Still, they share what they experience in such a compelling way that "all who heard it were amazed."

The Lectionary for Mass: Mass during the Day

◆ First Reading: Isaiah extols the beautiful feet of those who are willing to proclaim the Good News of God—peace and salvation. These are glad tidings that are worthy of being cried out to the people. Salvation will not only be seen by Israel, but the whole world.

◆ Responsorial Psalm 98: Themes pertinent to the nativity of Jesus abound. A new song is now sung because God has done what he promised; he has saved humanity. This wondrous work is seen throughout the land, and the people respond with the fullest musical joy.

◆ Second Reading: The letter to the Hebrews addresses a community of Jewish Christians and, in a series of sermon-like passages, may have served as a corrective to misguided ideas. Here, it is explained that Christ is not one among many angelic beings; he is the true Son of God.

◆ Gospel: The opening of the Gospel according to John is the great hymn to the *Logos*, the Word, now made man in Jesus. The prologue is a lyrical, poetic discourse

about life and light in Christ Jesus. A few of the great images for the Messiah—the light that shines in the darkness, the Word become flesh, the true light—appear here. God speaks creation into existence, and speaks Jesus into that creation as the ultimate self-communication.

The Roman Missal

The Gloria is sung or said; given the festivity of the occasion, the musical setting used should be a magnificent one indeed, as the text echoes the words of the heavenly host praising God's glory. During the recitation or singing of the Creed, all are to kneel at the words "and by the Holy Spirit was incarnate," up to and including the words "and became man." Don't let the assembly be caught by surprise by this such that very few kneel or such that it winds up being awkward and haphazard. After leaving a silent pause after the homily, the priest may offer a spontaneous introduction to the Creed that explains how and when the kneeling is to take place, so that all might properly participate in this gesture that highlights the Incarnation. Note that if Eucharistic Prayer I, the Roman Canon, is used, there is a proper form of the *Communicantes* that is used. Use the Solemn Blessing at the end of Mass, form #2, "The Nativity of the Lord."

The prayers for the Vigil Mass very much maintain the sense of vigiling as they speak of waiting and looking forward. There is a choice from among three for the Preface at this Vigil Mass—Preface I, II, or III of the Nativity of the Lord. These can be found immediately following the two Advent Prefaces. Note that if Eucharistic Prayer I, the Roman Canon, is used, there is a proper form of the *Communicantes* that is used.

Preface III is a good choice for the Mass during the Night; its mention of "the holy exchange" would echo the Prayer over the Offerings as explained above. The Prayer after Communion gives voice to our joy at participating in the Nativity and asks that we "through an honorable way of life [may] become worthy of union with him."

At the Mass at Dawn, Preface I of the Nativity, with its emphasis on light, shining glory, and the divine being made visible, is the most appropriate choice among the three possible Prefaces.

While any of the three Prefaces are appropriate, there may be a particular fittingness to using Preface III of the Nativity at the Mass during the Day insofar as it echoes the Collect with its mention of "the holy exchange."

The Christmas Proclamation should be done before the Mass during the Night. The rubrics state that it should be sung or recited "*before the beginning* of Christmas Mass during the Night. It may not replace any part of the Mass" (emphasis added). Before the Mass begins—perhaps following a prelude or "carol service," sung by choir and congregation—a cantor could process to the ambo and chant the Proclamation, after which the opening notes of the Entrance Hymn or Introit would follow.

Pull out the stops for today's solemnity—use incense when appropriate and have a more formal Gospel procession.

Other Ideas

The social and family events that surround Christmas, as well as a variety of parish customs can sometimes overpower the primacy of the liturgy, which celebrates the Nativity of the Lord as the astonishing intervention of God in human history. Surely this is not the time to be cynical or critical toward those who might be "visiting" the church on Christmas. All liturgical ministers will want to put forth their best effort so everyone can participate in this holy evening/day. If members of the assembly are

to have worship aids that include the music selections, please make sure that enough, even more than enough, are available. If all are welcome, then extra efforts are needed to be hospitable.

WED 26 (#696) red
Feast of St. Stephen, The First Martyr

The Lectionary for Mass

◆ FIRST READING: In this account of the first follower martyred for proclaiming Christ, we hear of Stephen's faithfulness, wisdom, and grace. He has been a channel for the power of God and has debated with those who have yet to believe. A long discourse of teaching and challenge to the people is excised from this reading, and it leads to the fury that ends in Stephen's stoning.

◆ RESPONSORIAL PSALM 31: We are familiar with Psalm 31 as the source of the final words uttered by Jesus as he dies on the Cross: "Into your hands, O Lord, I commend my spirit." Stephen also exhorts God to receive his Spirit as he is crushed to death by rocks flung by an angry mob.

◆ GOSPEL: In the tenth chapter of the Gospel according to Matthew, the disciples are sent out to preach that the Kingdom is at hand. But here they are warned that not all will receive them with open arms. They will be handed over and persecuted. To follow Jesus, then and now, is to embrace his Cross. The promise, though, is eternal salvation for those who endure.

The Roman Missal

The texts for this Mass are found in the Proper of Saints at December 26; all the orations are proper to the day. Since today is within the Octave of Christmas, the Gloria is sung or said at this Mass. One of the three Prefaces of the Nativity is used today. Be sure to use the proper form of the *Communicantes*, if

Eucharistic Prayer I, the Roman Canon, is used.

Today's Saint

St. Stephen (c. † 34) is the protomartyr, the first martyr. Stephen was arrested and tried by the Sanhedrin for blasphemy. His fate was sealed when he had a vision during his trial and cried out, "I see the heavens opened and the Son of Man standing at the right hand of God" (Acts of the Apostles 7:56). He was taken out to be stoned to death by a mob, which included Saul of Tarsus. Stephen is shown in art with three stones and a martyr's palm, sometimes wearing a dalmatic, a deacon's vestment.

THU 27 (#697) white
Feast of St. John, Apostle and Evangelist

The Lectionary for Mass

◆ FIRST READING: The prologue of the first letter of John parallels, in a number of ways, the prologue of John's account of the Gospel—and this day is John's feast. It is similar stylistically, with its poetic vision of the experience of the community in encountering Jesus—the Word of life. In him, their joy is complete.

◆ RESPONSORIAL PSALM 97: The psalm underscores the call for rejoicing. Those who have been true followers of the Lord will see his might and power. The images are all those of a God with power over creation, a sign of his might.

◆ GOSPEL: Still remembering the evangelist, we now hear John's account of the Resurrection. Mary has gone to the tomb, found it empty, and has rushed to get Peter and the "other" disciple to come with her to investigate. This anonymous figure, which appears only in John's account of the Gospel may be a model for all disciples, or he may be a particular person. His identity is debated by scholars.

Some think he may be Lazarus, James the brother of Jesus, or John the Apostle, as asserted by Eusebius in the fourth century.

The Roman Missal

The texts for today's feast are found in the Proper of the Saints. The prayers from today's liturgy all include Johannine themes, including the Word of God brought to the Church from the Apostle John, which has "so marvelously [been] brought to our ears" (see the Collect); the "hidden wisdom of the eternal Word" revealed through John (see the Prayer over the Offerings), and the image of the "Word made flesh" in the Prayer after Communion. Preface I, II, or III of the Nativity of the Lord may be used and the Gloria is said or sung throughout the Octave of Christmas. Since we are within the Octave of the Nativity, be sure to use the proper form of the *Communicantes* if Eucharistic Prayer I, the Roman Canon, is used.

Today's Saint

St. John (first century), Apostle and fourth Evangelist, is called the "beloved disciple" because of his close relationship with Jesus. Throughout his account of the Gospel, St. John, named as the son of Zebedee and brother of St. James the Greater, makes an appearance at significant moments in Jesus' life, specifically, at the Last Supper, the Garden of Gethsemane, the foot of the Cross, and the upper room. These appearances point to the intimate relationship he had with our Lord. His account of the Gospel is quite different from the synoptic accounts (Matthew, Mark, and Luke) due to his high Christology (divine emphasis), which is proclaimed through symbolic language and poetic form. The eagle is the chosen symbol for John's account, ultimately representing the depth and height to which the human

spirit must soar in order to grasp the meaning of John's text. Among his many important contributions to the Church, other scriptural writings are attributed to his name, including three epistles and the Book of Revelation.

FRI 28 (#698) red
Feast of the Holy Innocents, Martyrs

The Lectionary for Mass

◆ **First Reading:** The Johannine themes of light and darkness are unpacked further in this section of the letter. To be in right relationship with God, we must recognize that we are sinners, and do our utmost to live upright lives. We can do this because of the mercy and forgiveness of God, and because Christ died for our sins.

◆ **Responsorial Psalm 124:** The images of the psalm are those of rescue. Israel is compared to a bird that was captured but is now freed from the snare, while the enemies of Israel are compared to a flood that might have overcome them.

◆ **Gospel:** After the visit by the Magi, wise astronomers, an angel warns Joseph of Herod's threat to the infant's life. They depart for Egypt—now a place in which to gain safety, not a place of enslavement as in the time of Moses. It is not Pharoah who murders the innocents now; rather, it is the murderous Herod. In the passage from Jeremiah, Rachel is presented as a voice for the bereaved mothers of Bethlehem.

The Roman Missal

The Mass formularies for today are found in the Proper of Saints for December 28; all the orations are proper to the day. Since today is a day within the Octave of Christmas, the Gloria is sung or said at this Mass. One of the three Prefaces of the Nativity is used today. Since we are within the Octave of the Nativity,

be sure to use the proper form of the *Communicantes* if Eucharistic Prayer I, the Roman Canon, is used.

Today's Saints

Herod the Great, fearing for his throne after the Magi told him about the birth of Jesus, ordered the execution of all male children in Bethlehem, hoping that Jesus would be among those killed (see Matthew 2:16–18). According to Matthew, this fulfilled the prophecy of Jeremiah (31:15): "A voice is heard in Ramah, lamentation and bitter weeping. Rachel is weeping for her children." The haunting Coventry Carol refers to this episode as it asks, "O sisters too, how may we do, / For to preserve this day / This poor youngling for whom we do sing / By, by, lully, lullay."

SAT 29 (#202) white
Fifth Day within the Octave of the Nativity of the Lord

Optional Memorial of St. Thomas Becket, Bishop and Martyr / white

The Lectionary for Mass

◆ **First Reading:** The evidence of one truly knowing Jesus is not empty talk, but a life lived consonant with the commandments of God. There is no new Decalogue offered; instead the commandments can be lived in a new fullness. To be "perfected" is to reach a fullness and maturity not before seen.

◆ **Responsorial Psalm 96:** Israel has sung many songs to God, but there are times in which something so startlingly new is occurring that a new song must be sung. This psalm extols the Kingship of God, and in this Christmas season, Christians pray it to extol the presence of Jesus Christ, born among us.

◆ **Gospel:** When Joseph and Mary bring Jesus to the Temple in keeping with the law, they encounter the devout and righteous Simeon. From his beautiful proclamation to

God, we surmise that he was quite elderly but had pleaded with God to live long enough to see the Messiah born. We can only guess at the blend of surprise, joy, and even trepidation in Mary and Joseph as they hear what Simeon observes—including the reality that Mary will experience both delight and pain in being the Mother of the Lord.

The Roman Missal

The prayers for the Octave Mass are found in the Proper of Time. Preface I, II, or III of the Nativity of the Lord may be used. Consider using Eucharistic Prayer III. The Gloria is said or sung throughout the Octave of Christmas. Since we are within the Octave of the Nativity, be sure to use the proper form of the *Communicantes* if Eucharistic Prayer I, the Roman Canon, is used.

Today's Saint

St. Thomas Becket (1118–1170) was born in London as the son of Norman parents. He received a good education at Merton Abbey, and later in Paris. When he left school, he became a secretary, a position of some prestige in a society with limited literacy. Eventually, he became assistant to Theobald, Archbishop of Canterbury. Recognizing his talent, Theobald sent him to the court of King Henry II, and eventually Thomas was named Lord Chancellor of England. In 1162, hoping to gain control over the Church, Henry had him installed as archbishop of Canterbury, but Thomas had a conversion, resigned as Chancellor, and thus began a conflict between king and archbishop. When Thomas returned from exile in France and excommunicated Henry's followers, Henry said in a rage, "Will no one rid me of this meddlesome priest?" Four knights took this as a command and killed Thomas as he went to join the monks for vespers in the abbey church. The story is retold in T. S. Eliot's play *Murder in the Cathedral* and Jean Anouilh's play *Becket*.

(#17C) white
30 Feast of the Holy Family of Jesus, Mary, and Joseph

About Today's Feast

The Feast of the Holy Family of Jesus, Mary, and Joseph, which is usually observed on the Sunday in the Octave of Christmas, is quite a new feast, added to the calendar by Pope Leo XIII in 1893. The pope wanted to highlight the importance of the Christian family and to point to the Holy Family as a model for all families to follow. Mary and Joseph could not surround the newborn Jesus with material things: he was born in poverty, with, as we sing in the carol, "no crib for his bed" ("Away in a Manger"). Yet, what they had, they lavished on Jesus: love, tenderness, and care. Love transformed the stable, making it a source of light and hope, just as love can transform every home, even the poorest, and make it a place where children can grow as Jesus did, in wisdom, love, and grace. This feast urges us to see in the Holy Family, a "shining example" for all family life (Collect). In their mutual love and forbearance, in their patience in times of trial, and in their total obedience to God's will for them, the Holy Family shows us how to live together in peace. For further reading on the Holy Family and the nature of the Christian family refer to Pope Francis' encyclical letter, *Amoris laetitia*.

The Lectionary for Mass

The First Reading, Responsorial Psalm, and Second Reading from Year A may also be used.

◆ First Reading: Hannah's fervent prayer is rewarded with the birth of a son, Samuel. She and her husband Elkanah take him to the Temple to dedicate him. There she encounters Eli, who overheard her desperate plea to God for a child, and true to her promise, dedicates him in service to the Temple.

◆ Responsorial Psalm 84: As we encounter stories involving the Temple, literally the place where God resided, we are invited to remember that to dwell with God is to be in a place that is lovely and filled with blessing. We are reminded that those who live with God, the angels, praise constantly.

◆ Second Reading: This section of the first letter of John addresses the pain of the community in the wake of losing members in a split. John is reassuring those he writes to that they are the children of God, not those who have departed. They keep God's commandments and remain in Christ.

◆ Gospel: Jesus' adolescent escapade of hanging behind his community and remaining at the Temple is resonant for countless people who have misplaced a child or dealt with a rebellious adolescent. Jesus is nearing manhood, but not yet a man. We are reminded of Samuel's life as a servant of God in the Temple. The story illuminates for us the already developed relationship between Jesus and his Father, and places him within the Jewish story.

The Roman Missal

The Collect holds in great esteem the Holy Family as a shining example to model our lives after. The Gloria and the Creed are said or sung today. The Prayer over the Offerings also looks to the Virgin Mary and St. Joseph to intercede for all families to live "firmly in [God's] grace and [his] peace." Preface I, II, or III of the Nativity of the Lord may be used. Consider using Preface II since it declares Christ restoring unity to all creation and calling humanity back to himself, a theme to be embraced by all families. Consider using Eucharistic Prayer III. Since we are within the Octave of the Nativity, be sure to use the proper form of the *Communicantes* if Eucharistic Prayer I, the Roman Canon, is used. The Prayer after Communion calls on the Church "to imitate constantly the example of the Holy Family." Pull out the stops for today's feast—incense when appropriate, continue to sing Christmas hymns, and include a more formal Gospel procession.

Other Ideas

On this feast it seems only natural to be especially attentive to the families of the parish and to the parish family. The *Book of Blessings* includes an Order for the Blessing of Families (BB, chapter 1). There are several well-worded options for the Universal Prayer that can be used at the liturgies this weekend. The parish might consider making a small prayer card with a blessing of the family that could be used at home. Consider writing a short historical note in the bulletin describing how the parish family got its name; for example, why is it named after the saint or the event in the life of Jesus or the Blessed Mother? Encourage parishioners to visit family members who were unable to join them at church on this weekend.

(#204) white

MON 31 Seventh Day within the Octave of the Nativity of the Lord

Optional Memorial of St. Sylvester I, Pope / white

The Lectionary for Mass

◆ FIRST READING: Once again, we hear John address the split in the community. This rupture must have been deeply wounding. John reassures the community that those who left were not truly counted among their number. The antichrist appears only in the Gospel according to John, and the identity of this figure has been the subject of speculation. It may simply mean a false teacher.

◆ RESPONSORIAL PSALM 96: The power of the Lord of Israel is revealed in the fact that the entirety of creation responds to his presence. Not only are humans called to sing a new song, but every aspect of creation—heavens, seas, plains, trees, and forest—will extol God's rule of justice.

◆ GOSPEL: The prologue of John places the Word, Jesus Christ, at the founding of creation, and upholds him as a light for all of humanity. John the Baptist, who preached of the coming of the Messiah, was his herald. Here the text distinguishes between the one who is the light—Jesus—and the messenger who was witnessing to the light, John. John the Baptist (and John the evangelist) has definitely named Jesus for who he is: the Word made flesh, God's self-revelation.

The Roman Missal

The texts for December 31 are found in the Proper of Time. Since today is within the Octave of Christmas, the Gloria is sung or said at this Mass. One of the three Prefaces of the Nativity is used today. Since we are within the Octave of the Nativity, be sure to use the proper form of the *Communicantes* if Eucharistic

---

Prayer I is used. Pull out the stops for today's solemnity—use incense when appropriate and have a more formal Gospel procession.

Today's Saint

Very little is known about St. Sylvester I. He was pope from 314 to 335 during the era of Constantine, when the Church was able to come out of hiding after years of persecution. During his pontificate some of the great churches in Rome were built, such as the original Lateran Basilica and St. Peter's Basilica.

January 2019
Month of the Holy Name

(#18ABC) white

TUE 1 Solemnity of Mary, the Holy Mother of God / The Octave Day of the Nativity of the Lord

Holyday of Obligation

About Today's Solemnity

We are still in the midst of Christmas Time, and today the Church celebrates the Solemnity of Mary, the Holy Mother of God. This solemnity is the most ancient liturgical observance of Mary in the Church's calendar. It honors Mary as *theotokos* or "Mother of God," the title accorded her at the Council of Ephesus in 431. Mary is not just the Mother of Jesus: she is the Mother of God, because Jesus is both God and man, divine and human. As other Marian feasts entered the calendar, January 1 acquired a different focus. The eighth day after birth was the traditional day for the circumcision and naming of a child, and so this became the Feast of the Circumcision of the Lord (and the naming of Jesus). It was only in 1969 that the Marian character of this ancient feast was restored.

The Lectionary for Mass

◆ First Reading: Today we hear the magnificent Aaronic blessing, deeply loved by both the Jewish and Christian communities to this day. Moses is assured that when this blessing is evoked by the priestly class (Aaron and his sons), God will confer this mighty blessing.

◆ Responsorial Psalm 67 was most likely used in a liturgy of the Temple, and echoes the Aaronic blessing of the Book of Numbers. The response of the people is exultation and praise.

◆ Second Reading: Paul speaks of what has been achieved by Christ. In sending the Son, all who believe have effectively been incorporated into the Sonship. No longer is the relationship with God distant, but one of close and intimate connection —he is Abba, the loving name given to a father by a small, devoted, and trusting child.

◆ Gospel: Here we have a contrast. In experiencing God's wondrous deeds, Mary moves in humility to ponder what has happened in her heart. The shepherds, however, are so overcome that despite their marginal stature, they start telling what has happened to all whom they encounter. Both of these responses are to God's glory. Recounting the circumcision and naming underscores how truly devout were both Mary and Joseph.

The Roman Missal

The texts for this Mass are found in the Proper of Time section (the be-

ginning of the Missal). The Gloria is sung or said, since it is the Octave of the Nativity and a solemnity. The Creed is said or sung. The Preface assigned for today is Preface I of the Blessed Virgin Mary. For the last time this year, the proper form of the *Communicantes* for the Nativity of the Lord and its Octave is to be used if Eucharistic Prayer I, the Roman Canon, is chosen. Consider also using Eucharistic Prayer III. Interestingly, the formula of Solemn Blessing that is suggested at the end of Mass is the one for "The Beginning of the Year." Certainly the fact that this Mass is celebrated on New Year's Day (or New Year's Eve) makes this an appropriate choice, as the beginning of the new calendar year is an event that should be recognized, and one might argue it is therefore the preferred choice. Other possible Solemn Blessings, however, could be the one for "The Nativity of the Lord" (since it is the Octave of Christmas) and "The Blessed Virgin Mary" (since it is a Marian feast). Pull out the stops for today's solemnity—use incense when appropriate and have a more formal Gospel procession.

Other Ideas

January 1 is also the World Day of Prayer for Peace. The intercessions in the Prayer of the Faithful should include one for peace in the world. Note that the Mass for the Preservation of Peace and Justice (see Masses for Various Needs, 30) cannot be used on this day (the solemnity takes precedence). In keeping with the honor given to Mary as the Holy Mother of God, it is appropriate to offer a blessing over all mothers today. The *Book of Blessings* (BB, 236–278) includes blessings for mothers; however, the prayers need to be modified in order to include all mothers (honorary mothers, birth mothers, stepmothers). The blessing over the mother

in the *Rite of Baptism for Children* might also be adapted for this purpose. One or more intercessions in the Prayer of the Faithful could be directed to mothers. On this first day of the New Year consider listing some "spiritual resolutions" in the bulletin.

(#205) white

WED 2 Memorial of Sts. Basil the Great and Gregory, Bishops and Doctors of the Church

The Lectionary for Mass

◆ First Reading: John directly addresses truth and falsehood. To deny Jesus is to deny the Father (consider the many times Jesus speaks of his followers coming to the Father through him). Likewise, the converse is true. The community is exhorted to remember the teaching they have received from the time of the Apostles.

◆ Responsorial Psalm 98: God has acted, and his power has been revealed not only to Israel but to all the nations. The victory is God's, and the people break into songs of praise.

◆ Gospel: John the Baptist is interrogated by the priests and Levites. They want to determine his identity. Is he Elijah? A prophet? John responds with the words of Isaiah, indicating that he is the one who has come to announce the coming of the Messiah. Pharisees join the mix. Still, John stands firm that his baptism is pale in power compared to the one the Lord is sending— Jesus Christ.

The Roman Missal

The prayers for this Mass, all proper for the day, are found in the Proper of Saints at January 2. Since we are now outside the Octave, the Gloria is no longer sung or said on weekdays. The Collect asks that we may follow the example and teaching of bishops Sts. Basil and Gregory, putting it into practice in charity; the Prayer after Communion echoes that, asking that through our partaking of the Eucharist, "we may preserve in integrity the gift of faith / and walk in the path of salvation you trace for us." Consider Eucharistic Prayer IV.

Today's Saints

Sts. Basil and Gregory became close friends as students in Athens. Together they fought against the Arian heresy, which denied the full divinity of Christ. Their writings also aided the Church's understanding of the Holy Spirit and the Trinity. With Basil's brothers, Gregory of Nyssa and Peter of Sebaste, they are among the Capadocian Fathers. Gregory is known as "the Theologian" by the Eastern Churches. Basil is known as the father of Eastern monasticism and had a great influence on the development of liturgy, East and West.

THU 3 (#206) white
Christmas Weekday

Optional Memorial of the Most Holy Name of Jesus / white

The Lectionary for Mass

◆ First Reading: John underlines the new relationship obtained with God for all who follow Jesus: they are now the children of God. Everyone who believes in Jesus Christ seeks to live purely, rejecting sin. One cannot be in Christ and sin, nor sin and be in Christ.

◆ Responsorial Psalm 98: We continue with the joyful verses of Psalm 98 today. In this season of recognizing the wonder of a God incarnate, we cannot be sufficiently reminded to praise God and laud his saving power.

◆ Gospel: As Jesus approaches the Baptist, John announces who is before them. John was born before Jesus, but recognizes him as the Messiah who was with God from the beginning of time. The alighting dove is a sign to John that this person is truly the one anticipated by Israel. This sign of the Spirit is the place in which the reality of the Trinity is revealed scripturally.

The Roman Missal

Preface I, II, or III of the Nativity of the Lord may be used. If you are using the texts from the Proper of Time for Tuesday of the Weekday of Christmas, be sure to use the first Collect, "Before the Solemnity of the Epiphany," since two options are provided. Consider Eucharistic Prayer II.

About Today's Memorial

The name of Jesus is important. It means "God saves." His family does not choose the name of Jesus; rather, God gives it to him before his birth: "You are to name him Jesus," the angel tells Joseph in a dream, "because he will save his people from their sins" (Matthew 1:21). Jesus' name is both his identity and his mission. Jesus' name is powerful: "Whatever you ask in my name, I will do," he tells his disciples (John 14:13). In the letter to the Philippians, St. Paul sings a hymn to the power of Jesus' name: "God greatly exalted him and bestowed on him the name that is above every name, / that at the name of Jesus every knee should bend, of those in heaven and on earth and under the earth, / and every tongue confess that Jesus Christ is Lord, to the glory of God the Father" (Philippians 2:9–11).

FRI 4 (#207) white
Memorial of St. Elizabeth Ann Seton, Religious

The Lectionary for Mass

◆ First Reading: John's instructions on the path to holiness continue, now exhorting listeners to not be deceived but to live in righteousness. John makes the choice clear: One can abide in sin, and in doing so align with the devil, or abide in love and righteousness and belong to Christ.

◆ Responsorial Psalm 98: Still more verses of exultant Psalm 98 are heard this morning. Creation is made to glorify God, and now the sea and all who dwell in it, the rivers and the mountains raise their voices—literally shouting for joy.

◆ Gospel: We meet Andrew, the brother of Simon Peter in this passage, and an unnamed disciple that many speculate is John the evangelist. Although they are disciples of the Baptist, he points to Jesus as the Lamb of God, and they follow. The theme "come and see" occurs in multiple places in this Gospel, and the two go with Jesus. Andrew's recognition is immediate; this is the Messiah. When Andrew brings Simon, Jesus renames him—Cephas, who will be the "rock" upon which the Church is built.

The Roman Missal

All of the prayers are proper for today and are found in the Proper of Saints at January 4. Although one of the two Prefaces of the Saints could be used, the preferred choice would be to use one of the Nativity Prefaces, in order to maintain the sense of Christmas Time. Consider using the Eucharistic Prayer for Various Needs and Occasions IV.

Today's Saint

St. Elizabeth Ann Seton was born into an Episcopalian family and later in life joined the Catholic Church. She was married, a mother of five, and a founder of a religious order, the Sisters of Charity. At the invitation of the archbishop of Baltimore, Elizabeth founded a girls' school which gave rise to the parochial school system in the United States. She was canonized by Paul VI in 1975.

S A T 5 (#208) white
Memorial of St. John Neumann, Bishop

The Lectionary for Mass

◆ FIRST READING: John continues to illustrate the difference between good and evil. Love is a central element; loving one another is, to this day, a core precept of the Christian life. John warns, though, that this love may be met by hate. We must remain confident in God.

◆ RESPONSORIAL PSALM 100: Similar to Psalm 98, Psalm 100 invites the world to rejoice as the arrival of the king is celebrated and the people enter the Temple with joy. These hymns remind us that the God of Israel, often considered a punishing God by Christians, was a God of love, faithfulness, and goodness—to all generations.

◆ GOSPEL: Jesus continues to call the disciples. Philip joins him, and entreats his friend Nathanael to come, noting that he is convinced he has found the Messiah. Nathanael's honest response may have been more of a jest than a slam, but it still reeks of prejudice. Jesus responds favorably, appreciating the candor. "Under the fig tree" referenced a place at which devout young rabbinic students might have been found studying or in prayer. Nathanael may have been praying for the Messiah, a fact that Jesus recognized and which inspires Nathanael's ready belief.

The Roman Missal

All of the prayers are proper for today and are found in the Proper of Saints at January 5. Although one of the two Prefaces of the Saints could be used, the preferred choice would be to use one of the Nativity Prefaces, in order to maintain the sense of Christmas Time. Consider using the Eucharistic Prayer for Various Needs and Occasions IV.

Today's Saint

St. John Neumann (1811–1868) came to the United States from what is now called the Czech Republic with the dream of being a priest and missionary. Received with open arms by the bishop of New York, he was ordained and immediately asked to help build churches and schools for German immigrants and Native Americans. Needing spiritual support and companionship, he eventually entered a religious order, the Redemptorists, where he was made novice master and eventually vicar of all the Redemptorists in the United States. The larger Church recognized his holiness and affinity for leadership by appointing him bishop of Philadelphia, the largest diocese at the time. While bishop, he was an avid supporter of the work of religious orders, a proponent of Catholic education, and an advocate for the needs of immigrants.

6 (#20ABC) white
Solemnity of the Epiphany of the Lord

About Today's Solemnity

Today we celebrate that the child born in the darkness of night in a lowly manger is revealed as the manifestation (the meaning of *epiphany*) of God. Christ is revealed in many ways: as Lord, as King, as the one in whom God is present and acts. All of these manifestations are "lights" that shine on Christ, revealing a deeper understanding of who he is. All the readings for today reveal, in a way, a different manifestation of who Christ is for all who believe. Traditionally, three events in the life of Christ are remembered today as manifestations of God's presence and action through Christ: the visit of the Magi, the wedding feast of Cana, and the baptism of Jesus in the Jordan River. Lights have played an important role in today's solemnity. Parishes might follow this tradition by increasing the number of candles in church. They might be carried in the opening procession, or placed in the sanctuary, around the altar before Mass begins.

The Lectionary for Mass

◆ FIRST READING: Isaiah poetically describes the light that has shone on Jerusalem. The exiles have returned, and they must not be downcast, but walk with eyes raised. There has been a total transformation. The heart of the text is a reminder of the glory of God in Israel's—and our—midst.

◆ RESPONSORIAL PSALM 72: This psalm was composed for the coronation of the King and was sung for all those who reigned during the Davidic dynasty. Notice that the people pray that God will endow the king with right judgement, allowing him to be just and care for those who are afflicted.

◆ SECOND READING: The author of Ephesians reminds the community that God has made mystery known to him by revelation. He was not a companion of Jesus; the Spirit has brought him the grace to speak of Christ to the community and to proclaim that Jesus is not just the Savior of the Jewish people but of all—gentiles included.

◆ GOSPEL: The story of the visit by the Magi appears only in the Gospel according to Matthew. Here we see wise figures, most likely astronomers, seeking out the newly born king to pay him homage. The number three is a late interpretation, as are names for these mysterious figures. The gifts acknowledge the infants regal stature, and hint at the anointing that will await him in death. This story underscores the universality of the Messiah, who has come to redeem all.

The Roman Missal

The Gloria and the Creed are sung or said today. The Preface assigned for today is the Preface of the Epiphany of the Lord, which can be found after Preface III of the Nativity of the Lord. Consider using Euchairstic Prayer I. For the Final Blessing, be sure to use the Solemn Blessing for the Epiphany of the Lord (#4).

Other Ideas

Announcing on Epiphany the moveable feasts for the coming year is an ancient liturgical custom. See the proclamation in *The Roman Missal*, appendix I: "The Announcement of Easter and the Moveable Feasts." It can be sung, making it more solemn and festive, after the Gospel and before the homily. A deacon or cantor chants the Proclamation. No allowance seems to be made for the priest to do so. While *The Roman Missal* indicates that the Christmas and Easter Proclamations may be recited if no competent minister is available to sing them, and even includes the text without music, no such rubric is included for the Epiphany Proclamation, suggesting that if it is not chanted, it should be omitted.

Another popular custom is to bless homes and inscribe the numerals of the New Year over the main door of one's home using white chalk. The numerals are separated by the letters CMB which represent the legendary names of the three Magi: Caspar, Melchior, and Balthasar. This act symbolizes the hospitality offered to guests. The parish could provide chalk sticks to every household as a symbolic

gift on this feast of gift giving. An abbreviated text of a house blessing could be wrapped around each piece of chalk. The house blessing is found in *Catholic Household Blessings & Prayers* (USCCB).

MON 7 (#212) white
Christmas Weekday

Optional Memorial of St. Raymond of Penyafort, Priest / white

The Lectionary for Mass

◆ FIRST READING: John invites the community into a deep form of obedience to the commandments, most notably to love one another. Through this, they will be in a position to have their prayer answered. We are reminded to test our spiritual experience to ensure that they are from God and not from false prophets.

◆ RESPONSORIAL PSALM 2: God speaks to the King, assuring him that he is God's son and will give him an abundant inheritance of all nations. The Lord's anointed will lead consonant with God's ways. All earthly kings are called to see this and follow suit.

◆ GOSPEL: Upon John's arrest, Jesus withdraws to Galilee. This was a highly populated area, and Jesus begins his ministry of itinerant preaching. He gains renown as a healer, and the people are drawn to him from throughout the region. Distinguished visitors were often asked to speak in the local synagogues. Clearly the fame of Jesus was spreading.

The Roman Missal

The texts are found in the Proper of Time at the beginning of the Missal, after the Epiphany Mass during the Day, for Monday during the Weekdays of Christmas Time. Be sure you use the proper Collect—the correct one to use is the second one, for "After the Solemnity of the Epiphany." For the Preface, you may use either the

Preface of the Epiphany ("after the Epiphany") or one of the Prefaces of the Nativity. It might be advantageous to use the Preface of the Epiphany in order to highlight these last days of Christmas Time. This option will be the same for each Christmas weekday between now and Saturday. Consider using the Eucharistic Prayer for Various Needs and Occasions IV.

Today's Saint

St. Raymond traveled far and wide to convert nonbelievers, change the hearts of heretics, and infuse the great universities of Europe with solid theological instruction, resulting in a presence of the Dominicans at the universities of Oxford and Cambridge. Recognized as a visionary leader, St. Raymond was elected third master general of the Dominican order, following in the footsteps of Blessed Jordan of Saxony. His spiritual aptitude and theological literacy reached beyond the walls of the Dominicans to other areas: he served as spiritual director to the pope, archbishop of Tarragona, and compiler and reviser of Church laws (canon law).

TUE 8 (#213) white
Christmas Weekday

The Lectionary for Mass

◆ FIRST READING: John continues to expound upon love and how it is central to the lives of the followers of Jesus. Disciples love not because a command is issued to them, but because it is the only response possible in light of how much they themselves are loved by God.

◆ RESPONSORIAL PSALM 72: We return to additional verses of Psalm 72, which presents the king as God's agent on earth. Notice that primary among the tasks of the king is to care for the poor, the afflicted, and the vulnerable (children). These are the ones in whom God has great interest.

◆ GOSPEL: Jesus and his disciples have tried to escape from the crowd, but the people follow them in throngs. Moved to pity, Jesus begins teaching. Both the disciples and Jesus see the need before them: Physical as well as spiritual sustenance is needed. The disciples are quick to throw their hands up in the air at the impossibility of this challenge. Jesus blessed the loaves and fishes, but holds the disciples to the task of feeding the hungry masses with the miraculously multiplied food.

The Roman Missal

The texts are found in the Proper of Time at the beginning of the Missal, after the Epiphany Mass during the Day, for Tuesday during the Weekdays of Christmas Time. Be sure you use the proper Collect—the correct one to use is the second one, for "After the Solemnity of the Epiphany." For the Preface, you may use either the Preface of the Epiphany ("after the Epiphany") or one of the Prefaces of the Nativity. It might be advantageous to use the Preface of the Epiphany in order to highlight these last days of Christmas Time. Consider using Eucharistic Prayer III.

WED 9 (#214) white
Christmas Weekday

The Lectionary for Mass

◆ FIRST READING: John reminds us of the mingled reality of God and love. When we remain in love, God remains in us. To embrace this extravagant idea of a God who is perfect, almost incomprehensible love can challenge the human mind, which may prefer a god of retribution or punishment.

◆ RESPONSORIAL PSALM 72: The king, given the blessing of judgment, acts justly on behalf of those who are afflicted. The kings of all other nations will see this and offer tribute and gifts. Most important of all is the task of having pity on the lowly and helping the lives of the poor.

◆ GOSPEL: After the feeding of the multitude, Jesus has the disciples leave by boat while he goes to the mountain to pray. A storm arises, tossing the boat. Jesus comes to the terrified men, walking on the water. Although they see this, and they have just experienced that multiplication of the loaves and fishes, they don't seem to understand who is before them—the Son of God. Their hearts are hardened. This cluelessness is a theme throughout the Gospel according to Mark.

The Roman Missal

The texts are found in the Proper of Time at the beginning of the Missal, after the Epiphany Mass during the Day, for Wednesday during the Weekdays of Christmas Time. Be sure you use the proper Collect—the correct one to use is the second one, for "After the Solemnity of the Epiphany." For the Preface, you may use either the Preface of the Epiphany ("after the Epiphany") or one of the Prefaces of the Nativity. It might be advantageous to use the Preface of the Epiphany, in order to highlight these last days of Christmas Time. Consider using Eucharistic Prayer II.

THU 10 (#215) white
Christmas Weekday

The Lectionary for Mass

◆ FIRST READING: John emphasizes that there is a difference between the Christian life as a nice idea and the Christian life fully lived. His example is love of one's brother. If one hates one's brother, one cannot love God. This text is reminiscent of Jesus' instruction to leave one's gift at the altar if there is ill will with another.

◆ RESPONSORIAL PSALM 72: The final verses of this prayer for the king—which extols his righteousness—highlights the action he will take. As the agent of God, he will save people from fraud and violence. Each one will be precious to him. The name of the king will be forever blessed, for in him all the tribes and nations find happiness fulfilled.

◆ GOSPEL: The fame of Jesus is expanding throughout the region, and he is being welcomed into the synagogues to teach. When he returns to his home town, he opens the scroll of Isaiah and reads the words that will be spoken by the Messiah. The entire community is awed by the grace with which he spoke, probably words that expounded on the meaning of the text.

The Roman Missal

The texts are found in the Proper of Time at the beginning of the Missal, after the Epiphany Mass during the Day, for Thursday during the Weekdays of Christmas Time. Be sure you use the proper Collect—the correct one to use is the second one, for "After the Solemnity of the Epiphany." For the Preface, you may use either the Preface of the Epiphany ("after the Epiphany") or one of the Prefaces of the Nativity. It might be advantageous to use the Preface of the Epiphany in order to highlight these last days of Christmas Time. Consider using Eucharistic Prayer I.

FRI 11 (#216) white
Christmas Weekday

The Lectionary for Mass

◆ FIRST READING: John's conviction is that those who believe in Jesus Christ will be the victors over the world, overcoming all challenges. Nothing that is empowered by God can be overcome. John is also making clear that Jesus Christ is and was real, not a gnostic phantom figure.

◆ RESPONSORIAL PSALM 147 has three parts, all focused on praise. Jerusalem is reminded that God has been the source of strength and security. God also has entered into a unique and preferred relationship with Israel: one of covenant.

◆ GOSPEL: The leper, who entreats Jesus for healing, stands out for his faith. He knows that Jesus can heal him, and Jesus responds to his faith. Leprosy was considered a particularly vile disease, and Jews were expected to keep at least six feet from those suffering with it—it was contagious, and also a sign of sinfulness. The man says, "if you are willing," recognizing that a devout Jew would not come near him. That Jesus heals him with a touch, not a word, is particularly poignant.

The Roman Missal

The texts are found in the Proper of Time at the beginning of the Missal, after the Epiphany Mass during the Day, for Friday during the Weekdays of Christmas Time. Be sure you use the proper Collect—the correct one to use is the second one, for "After the Solemnity of the Epiphany." For the Preface, you may use either the Preface of the Epiphany ("after the Epiphany") or one of the Prefaces of the Nativity. It might be advantageous to use the Preface of the Epiphany in order to highlight these last days of Christmas Time. Consider using Eucharistic Prayer I.

SAT 12 (#217) white
Christmas Weekday

The Lectionary for Mass

◆ FIRST READING: John affirms the confidence that the followers of Jesus Christ have in God. Clearly, there will be sin but not all sin will be deadly. People are exhorted to pray for each other, and to invite God's healing power.

◆ RESPONSORIAL PSALM 149 is voiced by the lowly who have sought sanctuary in the Temple. In this powerful dwelling, they will be secure. They call out in affirmation, inviting the praise of God and rejoicing. In God they will have their victory.

◆ GOSPEL: This passage recounts an overlap of time in the ministries of John the Baptist and Jesus. Some of John's followers are concerned about the crowds flocking to Jesus. John is not perturbed. He has always known that the one who follows him is the Messiah—the Christ. His humility is seen in the joy he feels in knowing that as his ministry decreases, so increases the ministry of Jesus, the Son of God.

The Roman Missal

The texts are found in the Proper of Time at the beginning of the Missal, after the Epiphany Mass during the Day, for Saturday during the Weekdays of Christmas Time. Be sure you use the proper Collect—the correct one to use is the second one, for "After the Solemnity of the Epiphany." For the Preface, you may use either the Preface of the Epiphany ("after the Epiphany") or one of the Prefaces of the Nativity. It might be advantageous to use the Preface of the Epiphany in order to highlight these last days of Christmas Time. Consider using the Eucharistic Prayer for Reconciliation II.

13 (#21C) white
Feast of the Baptism of the Lord

About Today's Feast

Christmas Time always ends with a feast in honor of the baptism of the Lord. This feast is celebrated on the Sunday after Epiphany, except when the Nativity of the Lord (Christmas) falls on a Sunday; then, in the United States of America, the Baptism of the Lord is transferred to a Monday. The Feast of the Baptism of the Lord proclaims a theophany, a revelation or manifestation of the divine Sonship of Jesus by his anointing and appointment to his messianic office. It is the feast that proclaims the Baptism that elevates believers to the status of sons and daughters of God. When Jesus came to the Jordan to be baptized, John the Baptist exclaimed: "I need to be baptized by you, and yet you are coming to me?" (Matthew 3:14). We might want to ask the same question. Why does Jesus come to be baptized? He is sinless; why does he need to receive John's baptism of repentance? Jesus answers, "It is fitting for us to fulfill all righteousness" (Matthew 3:15). In other words, Jesus is baptized because this is God's plan for him—and for us. Jesus is baptized because we need Baptism. He opens the way for us, sanctifying the water, to wash away our sins.

The Lectionary for Mass

The First Reading, Responsorial Psalm, and Second Reading from Year A may also be used.

◆ First Reading: We return to the prophet Isaiah and one of his best-known prophecies. The prophet of whom he speaks is crying out in the desert, exhorting all to make ready for the Lord. This magnificent depiction of a passionate voice became the framework for understanding the role of John the Baptist in announcing Jesus as the Messiah of God.

◆ Responsorial Psalm 104 speaks to the wondrous works of God. The images are vivid and spark the imagination: God's palace is constructed on the waters, the clouds are a chariot, the wind is God's wings. God also provides abundantly, and in praise we respond, "O bless the Lord, my soul."

◆ Second Reading: The letter to Titus affirms that it is not through their merit that the followers of Jesus have been saved but by grace. This, along with training in right living (temperance, justice, devotion), empowers the community to "await in blessed hope" the second coming of Jesus.

◆ Gospel: John had clearly developed a following and many people were wondering if he, in fact, was the Messiah. John says no; his baptism is with water and one will come behind him who is more powerful. This account differs in significant ways from the account in Matthew. Note that there is no reference to John baptizing Jesus. Still we again see the presence of the Holy Spirit, and hear the affirmation by God the Father of his Son, affirming the Sonship spoken of in Luke's account of the Annunciation.

The Roman Missal

Two options for the Collect are offered in the Missal. The first Collect includes three important components of Christ's baptism: water, the Holy Spirit, and the declaration that he is the "beloved Son." The Collect shows God's great love for all of his beloved sons and daughters. The alternative Collect focuses on the title "Son" and on Christ's humanity: he "appeared in our very flesh." Consider the Rite for the Blessing and Sprinkling of Water. Sing or say the Gloria and the Creed.

The Prayer over the Offerings calls to our attention that the Holy Spirit is always the active transforming agent at work in the Church, changing bread and wine and people into the Body and Blood of Christ. Again, this oration calls us to faithful listening, not just to what we have heard in the Mass, but to what we will do in the world. The Preface is given right there along with the other Mass formularies for the day as it recapitulates not only scriptural references to the baptism of the Lord, but also the meaning of that baptism in understanding who Christ is as the Servant who "has been anointed with the oil of gladness / and sent to bring the good news to the poor." Consider using Eucharistic Prayer III. The Prayer after Communion reminds us that, having been nourished with the sacred gifts, we must be God's children "in name and in truth" by "faithfully listening to your Only Begotten Son." Pull out the stops for today's feast—sprinkling rite, incense when appropriate, and include a more formal Gospel procession.

Other Ideas

Today a celebration of Baptism at one or more of the Sunday liturgies is appropriate. If no one is to be baptized, the assembly could be invited to renew their baptismal promises in place of the Creed. Today's feast represents the end of Christmas Time celebrating the birth of the Christ the Light. It would be appropriate to have every one hold a lighted taper for the renewal of baptismal promises. A better idea would be to invite parishioners, especially children, who have a baptismal candle of their own to bring those to church this Sunday. Obviously this announcement needs to have been made last weekend! If tapers are to be distributed and collected, be sure to let the ushers know ahead of time. The presider might lead the renewal of baptismal promises from the font.

ORDINARY TIME DURING WINTER

The Roman Missal / The Meaning

THE WORD *ordinary* is related to the Latin *ordinalis*, which gives us the English *ordinal*, which in turn is defined as "of or relating to order, rank, or position in a series" (dictionary.com). Ordinary Time is that span of thirty-three or thirty-four weeks "in which no particular aspect of the mystery of Christ is celebrated, but rather the mystery of Christ itself is honored in its fullness, especially on Sunday" (UNLY, 43). Preface VI of the Sundays in Ordinary Time summarizes the focus of Ordinary Time well: "For in you we live and move and have our being, /and while in this body / we not only experience the daily effects of your care, / but even now possess the pledge of life eternal." During Ordinary Time in winter, our focus is the beginning of Jesus' public ministry and our call to live, move, and have our being in him, to follow his example, and to make him known in our lives. The Collect for the Third Sunday in Ordinary Time expresses this call: "Direct our actions according to your good pleasure, / that in the name of your beloved Son / we may abound in good works."

Ordinary Time in winter "begins on the Monday which follows the Sunday occurring after January 6 and extends up to and including the Tuesday before the beginning of Lent" (UNLY, 44). We celebrate the Baptism of the Lord on the Sunday after the Epiphany, January 13, which means that in 2019, Ordinary Time begins on Monday, January 14. Since Ash Wednesday is on March 6 in 2019, this part of Ordinary Time ends on Tuesday, March 5. It will resume on the Monday after Pentecost (June 10), with Monday of the Tenth Week in Ordinary Time. That section concludes on the Saturday before the First Sunday of Advent (November 30). In 2019, there are seven Sundays in Ordinary Time (second through eighth) before Lent begins.

The Mass texts for Ordinary Time can be found in *The Roman Missal* titled "Ordinary Time." It follows the texts for Easter Time, which concludes with the Mass for Pentecost. Since Ordinary Time begins on a Monday, a set of texts is provided for the First Week in Ordinary Time. The Sundays in Ordinary Time begin with the Second Sunday. You will find these texts after those provided for the first week. While priests usually choose to use the Sunday texts in the week that follows it, unless the day is a particular feast or obligatory memorial, "any of the thirty-four Masses may be used [on weekdays], provided the pastoral needs of the faithful are taken into consideration" (Ordinary Time, rubric 3b). This can be a good time to utilize texts found near the end of *The Roman Missal* titled "Masses and Prayers for Various Needs and Occasions" and "Votive Masses."

If you use the third form of the Penitential Act, consider options VI and VII in appendix VI of *The Roman Missal*, "Sample Invocations for the Penitential Act." They reflect how we live, move, and have our being in Christ. They also offer guidance about how to "carry out in both word and deed / that which is pleasing to [God]" (Collect, Seventh Sunday in Ordinary Time). In "The Order of Mass: Solemn Blessings," six options are provided for use during Ordinary Time. Consider using these on Sundays only, so as to reflect progressive solemnity by making a distinction between Sunday and weekday Masses. Since Lent provides "Prayers over the People" for each day, required on Lenten Sundays and optional on Lenten weekdays, using Solemn Blessings in Ordinary Time is another way to distinguish between Ordinary Time and Lent. Of course the Liturgy asks us to sing or recite the Gloria and the Creed on the Sundays in Ordinary Time, since the Gloria is only omitted on the Sundays of Advent and Lent.

The Roman Missal offers eight Prefaces for the Sundays in Ordinary Time and six Common Prefaces for the weekdays. Read and pray with them carefully, in light of the readings, to choose texts that will highlight the various aspects of Christ's public ministry and his teachings that call us to serve after his example. If you choose one of the Eucharistic Prayers for Uses in Masses for Various Needs, remember that each of these four prayers has its own Preface.

Finally, during Ordinary Time in winter be aware of these noteworthy celebrations: January 22, Day of Prayer for the Legal Protection of Unborn Children; January 25, the Conversion of St. Paul the Apostle; February 2, the Presentation of the Lord with the blessing of candles; and February 22, the Chair of St. Peter the Apostle. Other feasts or memorials during this time may have particular value in your pastoral setting. Take time to reflect on these celebrations and what the Missal, and thus, the Church, asks us to consider in celebrating them.

The Lectionary for Mass

THIS YEAR, seven and a half weeks in Ordinary Time mark the time between the conclusion of the Christmas season and the beginning of Lent. The counted Sundays go from the Second Sunday in Ordinary Time through the Eighth Sunday in Ordinary Time. Year C in the Lectionary cycle of readings serves as our guide for the Sundays, while Year I in the weekday Lectionary helps us journey Mondays through Saturdays. The first week in Ordinary Time begins immediately after the Feast of the Baptism of the Lord, which is why there is no "First Sunday in Ordinary Time."

The Old Testament readings for the Sundays of this segment of Ordinary Time come from the major prophets Isaiah (Second and Fifth Sunday in Ordinary Time), Nehemiah (Third), and Jeremiah (Fourth and Sixth), the historical book of 1 Samuel (Seventh Sunday), and the wisdom literature of Sirach (Eighth Sunday). From these readings, we renew our trust that God will remain faithful to his promise to restore his people. We hear God's call of the prophets to their challenging ministry and reflect on our own, and we acknowledge the reality that the words that we speak reflect what we believe in our hearts about God and how we are to extend God's mercy to others.

On these seven Sundays in Ordinary Time, the Second Readings all come from Paul's first letter to the Corinthians. At the time of Paul's writing, the Corinthian community was divided into many factions—rich and poor, those who strictly followed Jewish laws and those who wanted to more openly welcome followers of Christ who did not observe those laws. They were divided with respect to whose spiritual gift was the most important. The selections we proclaim from 1 Corinthians show how Paul based his teaching in the kerygma. The Gospel of Jesus Christ who suffered, died, and rose is the basis for our life together. There is only one God and one Lord Jesus Christ, so our communities of faith must be one. The Corinthians and we today are and must live as one Body of Christ. The person of Jesus Christ and his love for us is our foundation. Paul's letter culminates when he acclaims to the Corinthians Christ has taken away death's victory. We will share in Christ's Resurrection.

The Gospel readings for each of the Sundays, except the Second Sunday in Ordinary Time, come from Luke. On the Second Sunday we proclaim the first of the signs of Jesus' glory in John, the miracle of Jesus turning water into wine at the wedding feast of Cana. At the beginning of Ordinary Time this Gospel text reminds us once again who this Jesus is that we will follow throughout Ordinary Time into Lent and Easter, and again when the season of Ordinary Time resumes after Pentecost. Early on in Luke (Third Sunday in Ordinary Time), we hear Jesus announce on a Sabbath in his hometown synagogue that Isaiah's prophecy is fulfilled here and now. Jesus, who himself fulfills the prophecy, knows the people of his hometown will not accept him (Fourth Sunday), so he moves on to call disciples (Fifth Sunday), and to teach them extensively in the Sermon on the Plain

on what it means to follow him (Sixth, Seventh, and Eighth Sundays). We are his disciples today. Blessed are we when we follow his ways and let ours hearts speak his compassion for others.

The weekday Lectionary provides us with First Readings from Hebrews (first through fourth weeks), Genesis (fifth and sixth weeks), and Sirach (seventh week and the two days prior to Ash Wednesday). Twice during Ordinary Time, for the Conversion of St. Paul and Feast of Sts. Timothy and Titus, do the First Readings come from different sources: Acts of the Apostles and 2 Timothy or 2 Titus, on the respective days. This is the case because these days have proper readings assigned to them to reflect the nature of the celebration.

The Gospel readings come from Mark. We begin in the opening chapter of Mark with the call of Jesus' first disciples to fish for other followers and progress through Mark to hear Peter reveal Jesus' identity as the Christ, and also to tell him that indeed the disciples have given up everything to follow him. Having heard two predictions of Jesus' ensuing suffering and Death, and that disciples, too, will experience suffering, Jesus teaches us that those who follow him will know eternal life in the age to come. Those the world deems to be last will indeed be first in the Kingdom of God (see Mark 10:28–31).

The Responsorial Psalms during Ordinary Time in winter emphasize the praise and thanks due to God for his wondrous deeds (Psalms 1, 92, and 138). They also focus us on God's kindness and mercy in the face of our sin (Psalm 103). Throughout this holy time of counted Sundays and weekdays, we hear and take to heart again and again the message that the Lord's words are Spirit and life as reflected in the psalm refrain taken from the Gospel according to John (John 6:63c) for the Third Sunday in Ordinary Time. Indeed, the Lord's word brings life to his disciples!

Children's Liturgy of the Word

WHEN YOU NEXT see the children on the weekend of January 20, it will be Ordinary Time. Dress your prayer area with darker green fabric and whatever natural vegetation you can find this time of year—dried reeds or pine cones, perhaps. Greet the children the first week by asking them what green means to them. In your prefatory remarks, explain that they have now entered Ordinary Time—a time to grow by listening closely to important stories about Jesus over the next seven weeks.

If the psalm of the day will not be used, choose one of the common psalms of Ordinary Time from "Common Texts for Sung Responsorial Psalms" in the Lectionary. There are many fine, child-friendly musical settings. The advantage of repeating the same psalm is that children learn it well, so it can become a theme for their prayer lives.

On January 20, the second Sunday, we hear of the wedding at Cana. During reflection time, note that Jesus is the bridegroom and the Church is his bride. An icon or other image of the wedding at Cana would be a nice addition to the prayer space.

On January 27, the third Sunday, we hear about Ezra reading the scrolls of the law and Jesus reading the scroll of the text from Isaiah in the Temple—both taking the role of teacher. Incorporate into your liturgical environment a rolled up scroll to show the children. As they prepare to return to their parents in the main worship space, remind them that their parents are their first teachers of the faith—and ask them to thank them for teaching them about God.

On February 10, Isaiah says, "Here I am, send me," and we hear the Gospel of the calling of the disciples. Fishnets and seashells would be nice additions to the prayer space that day. The reflection could include asking how children think Jesus talks to them.

The next Sunday, February 17, we encounter Jesus preaching the Beatitudes. This is an opportunity to display an icon of Christ the Teacher in the space.

On March 3, the last Sunday before Lent, we hear about bad fruit and good fruit in the First Reading and the Gospel. Bring a bowl of fruit to enhance the prayer space. Help the children understand that a person can bear spiritual fruit—and it, too, can be good or it can be spoiled if there is sin in the person's life. Tell them that on Ash Wednesday, we will receive a cross of ashes on our foreheads as a sign that we are asking God to help us bear better spiritual fruit.

The Saints

PLACED AS IT IS between the more prominent seasons of Christmas and Lent, Ordinary Time in winter is associated for many with quiet, everyday sacredness. In fact, the Church teaches that the days of Ordinary Time, especially the Sundays, are devoted to the "entire mystery of Christ" in all its aspects (UNLY, 1). Beginning the Monday after the Baptism of the Lord on January 14, and running to the Tuesday before Ash Wednesday on March 5, this season's feasts celebrate the saints whose varied, holy lives also reflect the mystery of Christ in all its aspects.

The Memorial of St. Anthony, Abbot, recognizes one of the first and most influential of the Desert Fathers. As a hermit in Egypt, Antony is considered the "Patriarch of the Monks" and the founder of religious life. The ascetic, desert sensibility of Antony is in some ways a contrast to St. Agnes, whose short life ended in the chaos of political and social violence. *Agnes* means "lamb," and on her feast day, two lambs are blessed whose wool will then be used to make the pallia given by the pope to metropolitan archbishops as a symbol of their jurisdiction. In one story is an aspect of Christ in the desert; in the other story, an aspect of Christ who established and sustains a faith community founded on St. Peter, the rock.

There are several other martyrs whose memorials are observed during this period of Ordinary Time. St. Agatha is one of the most highly venerated virgin martyrs of the Church, a third-century believer who was tortured because of her Christian faith and put to death. St. Paul Miki, a Jesuit scholastic, suffered the same fate of martyrdom in a much different setting, crucified in Japan along with twenty-five companions; these are the protomartyrs of the Far East. And St Polycarp, disciple of St. John the Evangelist and one of the most revered of the Apostolic fathers, is arguably one of the oldest of the Christian martyrs: he was burned at the stake at the advanced age of eighty-six, after many years of service as bishop of Smyrna.

On the Feast of the Conversion of St. Paul, the Church celebrates the singular event by which a persecutor of Christians became the Apostle who proclaimed the Gospel of Christ to all the nations. And on the Memorial of Sts. Timothy and Titus, bishops in Asia Minor and Greece, we recognize two companions of St. Paul, recipients of his letters (epistles), whose stories serve as reminders of spirit and mission.

St. Francis de Sales is a Doctor of the Church whose book, *An Introduction to the Devout Life*, was one of the first of its kind written for everyday people rather than clerics and religious in cloister. He was the bishop of Geneva when it was a Protestant stronghold, and his voice of love, tolerance, and understanding helped to re-establish the credibility and vitality of the Catholic Church during the tumultuous time of the Reformation. "The measure of love, is to love without measure," he has said, and lived his life by that dictum.

Another Doctor of the Church, medieval priest and Dominican St. Thomas Aquinas, was a theologian whose profound ideas and brilliant writings continue to engage philosophers and theologians nearly eight hundred years later. His attempts to reconcile faith with reason greatly influenced both Church and intellectual authorities of his time and formed the basis for contemporary theology and philosophic thought. St. Thomas Aquinas is the patron saint of Catholic academics and places of learning; of philosophers, theologians, and scholars.

St. John Bosco was also dedicated to education of the young, particularly those from disadvantaged backgrounds. This founder of the Salesian order (named for St. Francis de Sales) was given the title "Father and Teacher of Youth" upon his canonization.

Sibling saints Cyril and Methodius were brothers who followed different routes (Cyril was a monk, while Methodius became a bishop) but together brought Christianity to the Slavic people; they are considered to be a bridge between the traditions of the East and West.

From bishops to martyred missionaries, hermits to close, loving siblings, the men and women recognized in Ordinary Time in winter model many different pathways to sainthood. As well, these days offer opportunities to reflect on a number of aspects of discipleship: What does it mean to be persecuted in this day and age? To be faithful? Who is our family, and whom do we count as brother or sister? Who will help us on our own path to sainthood, and who can we help along the way? What is the path we are called to follow as we follow Christ?

The Liturgy of the Hours

THERE ARE FIFTEEN FEASTS and memorials in the Proper of the Saints that can be designated days in a parish for praying Morning or Evening Prayer. These days are both weekdays and some Saturdays, so there would be a convenient day for everyone to pray together. Use this liturgical time to begin to pray the Liturgy of the Hours. It will mark a saint's day, as well as provide ample opportunity to introduce a new type of prayer for people. The overview to the *General Instruction of the Liturgy of the Hours*, written by Joyce Ann Zimmerman and found in *The Liturgy Documents, Volume II*, second edition (LTP), has great value as parish liturgy leaders learn to unearth the treasures of the Liturgy of the Hours. It is important to keep in mind S. Zimmerman's guidance that any reasonably competent minister can not only adapt but also craft a setting of the Liturgy of the Hours for parish celebration.

An issue that seems to create resistance to the idea of praying an hour of the day is general confusion about options and adaptations for this type of liturgical prayer. The parish worship committee, or several people interested in praying the Liturgy of the Hours, can easily discover how to make simple accommodations for this prayer after discussing S. Zimmerman's overview as a guide for preparing.

The Rite of Christian Initiation of Adults

IT'S TIME TO UPDATE, catechize, organize, and energize the initiation catechists and team members. Invite a speaker from a parish that does the initiation process well, and facilitate a morning or evening of renewal for your parish team. Welcome newcomers as catechists. Anticipating the Lenten season means reviewing Mass schedules for the Scrutinies; highlighting opportunities for catechizing the assembly regarding Baptism, Confirmation, and Eucharist; and scheduling the Rite of Acceptance for the unbaptized and the Rite of Welcome for the baptized (again and soon). Calendar and team catechesis aside, consider investing in a (bilingual if needed) resource that will help your congregation better understand the Christian initiation process. *Disciples Making Disciples* (LTP) is an excellent way to put something into the hands of every parishioner. There is also a Christian Initiation Series: virtual workshops that are easily accessible before a parish meeting or intentional gathering, created by LTP in collaboration with the Federation of Diocesan Liturgical Commissions, plus various e-resources that can captivate and inform the congregation.

Review the Gospel accounts for the Second through the Eighth Sundays in Ordinary Time, and invite the homilists for those Sundays to make an initiation connection for the congregation. The Lukan Gospel accounts in Year C emphasize our participation in Jesus' ministry and living a life of discipleship. Direct the homilist to use *Scripture Backgrounds for the Sunday Lectionary, Year C: A Resource for Homilists* (LTP) for scholarly yet accessible literary-liturgical insights on the Sunday Lectionary readings. *The Living Word: Leading RCIA Dismissals, Year C* is most helpful for RCIA catechists who break open the Word each week with the catechumens. Steep yourselves in resources and anticipate Lent.

and even from parish to parish. However, it is important to remember that in preparing these liturgies, innovations and elements not contained in the rite are to be avoided. The rites speak for themselves, and additions only take away from the primary symbols of the sacraments. All the Church's liturgies, including sacramental celebrations with children, are not private. The focus of these celebrations is not solely on the children; we are not celebrating the children, but are participating with them in the awesome gift of grace that is poured out by God upon the children, their families, and the people of the parish.

When celebrating First Communion or Baptism at a Sunday Mass, the readings we hear proclaimed during this season are quite appropriate. The Second Readings proclaimed on Sundays during these weeks are from St. Paul's first letter to the Corinthians, and speak of how we are to live our Christian life. The Gospel tells us of Jesus' early ministry, the call to discipleship and his teachings. Although they are not specifically Eucharistic in theme, they do help us to understand our responsibilities as baptized Christians and how to move forward in living our faith by following Christ's call and teachings.

The Sacraments of Initiation

THE LATE DATE of Easter this year makes this winter section of Ordinary Time quite lengthy. This time between Christmas and Lent helps us to focus on our life as Christians and the ministry and mission of Jesus.

Ritual Masses can be celebrated any day (that does not otherwise have restrictions, such as a solemnity), including Sunday, depending on the parish schedule. Unlike the RCIA, which is usually celebrated with adults once a year at the Easter Vigil for those receiving all three sacraments of initiation, these same sacraments for infants, children, and young people are celebrated throughout the year. Although the sacramental rites must be adhered to, the guidelines regarding some details on how the sacraments of Baptism, First Communion, and Confirmation are celebrated may vary slightly from diocese to diocese,

The Rite of Penance

THE SECOND READING from these Sundays in Ordinary Time offer rich fare for preaching on Reconciliation and encouraging people to begin the New Year with the grace of the Sacrament of Penance. The passages are taken from St. Paul's first letter to the Corinthians:

◆ "For in one Spirit we were all baptized into one body" (Third Sunday).

◆ "So faith, hope and love remain, these three; but the greatest of these is love" (Fourth Sunday).

◆ "For I handed on to you as of first importance . . . that Christ died for our sins" (Fifth Sunday).

◆ "If Christ has not been raised, your faith is vain . . . you are still in your sins" (Sixth Sunday).

◆ "The sting of death is sin; but thanks be to God who gives us the victory through our Lord Jesus Christ" (Eighth Sunday).

Note that the Gospel for the eighth Sunday recounts Jesus' teaching on attending to the "wooden beam" in our own eye before drawing attention to the "splinter" in the eye of another. Preaching on these texts can make allusions to the Sacrament of Reconciliation and begin to prepare the faithful for the impending season of Lent.

The World Day of the Sick (see section on Pastoral Care of the Sick) occurs during this time. Parishes should consider scheduling a communal celebration for both sacraments on or close to this day (February 11) as a time to gather all those who seek the healing grace of the sacraments. Given the complexities of life and the many and various challenges to our health and well-being there is always a need for the assurance of the Lord's compassion and mercy. The power of just being together in prayer is in itself both healing and comforting.

The Order of Celebrating Matrimony

THE PROCLAMATION of the Word of God is central to our liturgical gatherings and celebrations of the Sacraments. *The Order of Celebrating Matrimony* is no exception. Marriage has its roots in the Bible and Christ's command to love God and one another is well documented on the pages of Sacred Scripture.

Engaged couples have a plethora of Scripture readings to choose from. *The Order of Celebrating Matrimony* offers nine Old Testament readings, seven Responsorial Psalms, fourteen New Testament readings, five Alleluia verses, and ten Gospel readings to choose from. At least one reading that is chosen must explicitly speak of Marriage. These readings are designated with an asterisk (*) in the ritual. The LTP book *United in Christ: Preparing the Liturgy of the Word at Catholic Weddings* is an excellent resource for engaged couples to use in selecting the readings. In addition to commentary on the readings, it offers suggestions for pairing one reading or psalm with others with similar themes. Engaged couples need to be aware of guidelines for particular seasons when choosing readings for their wedding. For example, the Old Testament is not read during

Easter Time, so a couple getting married during that time must choose Revelation 19:1, 5–9a as their First Reading. Also, if a couple gets married on Sundays or other days where ritual Masses are prohibited, they may have to choose the readings of the day if they elect to marry within Mass.

The Responsorial Psalm should be sung, not recited. It is preferable to use musical settings that match what is in the *Lectionary for Mass* even though *Sing to the Lord* gives the option for psalm paraphrases. "Songs or hymns that do not at least paraphrase a Psalm may never be used in place of the Responsorial Psalm" (STL, 159). Just as at Sunday Mass, the psalmist or cantor should proclaim the psalm from the ambo or another suitable place. If it is not sung from the ambo, it should at least be sung from a place where the cantor is visible to the assembly.

The Gospel Acclamation is always sung. The Alleluia is the appropriate acclamation, except during Lent when another appropriate acclamation is sung. A Lenten acclamation is provided in *The Order of Celebrating Matrimony*.

Whoever proclaims the readings needs to be a good reader, be comfortable speaking in public and be a person of deep faith. As a practice, readers should be fully initiated Catholics, however the local bishop can make an exception for a Christian baptized in another tradition to proclaim a reading. Often couples choose close family members or friends, but parish readers can also be used. Time should be spent at the wedding rehearsal with those doing the readings going over the text, learning when and how to approach the ambo and getting used to the sound system. It is helpful if a member of the parish wedding host ministry is present at the rehearsal and at the wedding itself to assist with guest readers. Readings should be proclaimed from the *Lectionary for Mass* or from a carefully prepared and dignified liturgical binder. Reading from loose sheets should be avoided. It is essential that the readings be proclaimed with dignity and grace for the benefit of those gathered for the celebration.

The Pastoral Care of the Sick

THE OPTIONAL MEMORIAL of St. Blaise (February 3) is the traditional day for the blessing of throats. This year, the optional memorial does not take place because it falls on a Sunday. However, the blessing of throats may still be done at the end or after Sunday Masses. Among the stories associated with the saint is one where he saved a young boy from choking on a fish bone; hence the origin of the blessing on this day. The rite itself has two options: the blessing of individuals or a communal blessing, both done with two blessed candles in a cross arrangement. The blessing prayer is found in the *Book of Blessings*. Usually the blessing is directed to all ailments of the throat and in a more general way to all those who are sick. Refer also to the *Book of Blessings* overview in this chapter.

The optional Memorial of Lady of Lourdes (February 11) was designated as the World Day of the Sick by Pope John Paul II in 1992. The pope noted that it was a "special time of prayer and sharing, of offering one's suffering for the good of the Church, and of reminding us to see in our sick brother and sister the face of Christ who, by suffering, dying, and rising, achieved the salvation of humankind" (*Letter Instituting the Day of the Sick*, May 13, 1992).

The parish could consider scheduling a communal Anointing of the Sick on or close to this day as an opportunity to gather all who seek the healing grace of the sacrament and for all members of the parish to join in prayerful support of those who are sick. Plans for this celebration need to be done well in advance. Parish ministries need to prepare both the liturgy and the logistics of inviting, accompanying, and providing transportation for those who desire to participate. In some parts of the country winter weather may be a factor; appropriate contingencies need to be put in place for the comfort and safety of all participants. Consider inviting those who are involved with the medical care of the sick; their awareness of the spiritual needs of the sick can be a great benefit in their treatment of the physical needs of their patients.

The Order of Christian Funerals

A REFERENCE WAS made in the Christmas section to the ministry of consolation that belongs to the whole faith community when one of its members dies. Here are some further thoughts on that important ministry.

Many parishes have either staff persons or volunteers who carry out this ministry in various ways. A liturgy coordinator meets with the family to go over the funeral liturgy and assists them with choosing passages of Scripture and intercessions. Sometimes family members have requests for certain additions during the liturgy, and parish representatives need to be both accommodating to such requests and at the same time firm in denying requests that might be contrary to the spirit of the Church's liturgy. This often occurs around music selections and the inclusion and placement of mementos of the deceased. It is helpful if the parish has a policy in this regard that is applied to every situation.

The ministry of consolation also applies to the larger community. Many parishes post the day and time of a funeral on a parish website or social media page, or on a designated announcement board in the gathering area of the church. Perhaps an announcement can be made at the Sunday liturgies inviting members of the parish to participate in the funeral liturgy. In large congregations it is impossible to know everyone by name, yet we are all brothers and sisters in the household of faith and our prayerful participation is a sign of that communion in faith. Providing worship aids for everyone is another way to involve everyone, especially those who are not members of the Church to engage in the prayers and gestures of the liturgy.

The OCF (10) suggests that members of the community can assist the bereaved family in other ways. In my home parish, a small farming community, it is common for neighbors and parishioners to bring food items to the home of the deceased and to volunteer to take care of any chores or daily tasks that need to be done. These expressions of concern are examples of faith in action and of true marks of Christian discipleship.

Some parishes have a team of volunteers who form a grief committee and whose ministry is to assist with the Vigil liturgy, perhaps being trained to lead it. These good people also do follow up with the immediate family members after the funeral. Perhaps they can offer to visit from time to time; or offer an older person a ride to church if they need it; or assist with any other daily tasks as the person adjusts to being on their own.

In most places funeral directors are very attentive to every detail surrounding the funeral rites, though sometimes to the exclusion of the parish. The time of death has a social impact on family members, but it is also a faith-based event within the community of believers. Every baptized person has a right to the Church's rituals of comfort and farewell. The ministry of the Church is one of consolation as well as the assurance that their life and death is a participation in the life, Death, and Resurrection of the Lord.

The Book of Blessings

AS NOTED EARLIER, the blessing of throats associated with St. Blaise may still take place on Sunday, February 3, even though the optional memorial itself is not celebrated. Since the eighth century, St. Blaise has been regarded as the patron of those who are sick, especially those who suffer from ailments of the throat. It is customary to bless throats on this day. The Order for the Blessing of Throats (BB, chapter 51) is related to the Church's ministry to all those who are sick and expresses the Church's intercession to the Lord who had special care in his own ministry for those who were sick. This blessing can be given either during Mass or within a Celebration of the Word of God. The gesture of blessing is to touch the throat of each person with two candles that have been joined together in the form of a cross. The pastoral notes indicate that when large numbers are present and it is not possible to bless each person, a general blessing without using candles can be bestowed on the assembly.

Many parishes maintain the custom of blessing candles on the Feast of the Presentation of the Lord on February 2. The prayer of blessing for the candles on this day is found in *The Roman Missal* among the rubrics for the Mass for this feast. The blessed candles are given to parishioners to take home; they may also bring their own candles to have them blessed. Another option is to adapt the Blessing of Religious Articles found in the *Book of Blessings* (BB, chapter 44).

The Liturgical Environment

FROM THE VANTAGE point of a third-generation immigrant, time has tempered the stories of the hardships my relatives endured. Epiphany reminds us that Jesus was forced to flee with his family to Egypt to avoid probable death in his homeland. In the week following, the Church observes National Migration Week. Consider using the theme of welcoming immigrants and refugees throughout the eight weeks of winter Ordinary Time. Acquire woven Guatemalan fabrics, embroidered banners from El Salvador, West African batiks, silks from India, or tapestries from China. Be sure the fabric patterns are consistent with our beliefs; search for small, repetitive patterns that are predominately green. Pool fabrics underneath green plants left from your Christmas decor, perhaps adding some peace lilies or other green houseplants. Hang lengths as banners near the nave entrances or suspend from pillars.

Ordinary Time immerses the followers of Jesus into the day-to-day rhythms of Christian life. We join the Apostles in Jesus' early ministry, responding to his call to follow him. During Catholic Schools Week, invite students enrolled in Catholic schools your parish supports to add their thumb or handprints to simple fabric runners. Alternately, have the students sign their names using permanent markers. Incorporate the fabric into your decor, using them atop tables in the narthex where bulletins are kept, or over a credence table.

The Day of Prayer for the Legal Protection of Unborn Children is observed on January 22. Coordinate with the parish's respect life team, using a niche inside the church or a devotional chapel as a place to encourage prayer for this occasion.

The Feast of the Presentation of the Lord on February 2 is the traditional day for blessing candles for home use. Step up your use of candles this weekend: bring in candelabras for use near the altar. Situate groupings of large white pillars in prominent places such as near the ambo or the presider's chair. Adding white flowers to your plants further accents the feast. Near the entrances to your building, fill large pots with sand or rock to anchor tapers of varying heights. For evening Masses, lining the pathways with luminaries both welcomes and sends worshipers to bring Christ's light to the world.

As Valentine's Day approaches, the Church highlights the witness of married couples on World Marriage Day. Avoid a schmaltzy display of hearts and cupids, but if your parish hosts a renewal of marriage vows or blessings for couples, place a few floral arrangements within the sanctuary.

Winter Ordinary Time gives way to Lent. In preparation for Ash Wednesday, practice good stewardship by maintaining a simple environment, using modest groupings of green plants that will prosper in office windows throughout the Lenten and Easter seasons, returning to the church space for Ordinary Time in the spring.

The Liturgical Music

ONE COULD ARGUE that the celebration of Ordinary Time is, perhaps, more important than other seasons. "What? More important?! How can that be?" you might query. Perhaps in some situations (that is, places where the propers are not used and one is searching for appropriate hymns), Ordinary Time runs the chance of being sidestepped and underacknowledged due to its length and that it is not a "high season." When preparing music for liturgies during Ordinary Time, here is a good rule of thumb to keep in mind: "When we approach the preparation of the Fourth Sunday in Ordinary Time with as much diligence as we do with Midnight Mass, we're on track." This is not to suggest that the Fourth Sunday in Ordinary Time should be celebrated with the same degree of solemnity as that of Midnight Mass, following the principle of progressive solemnity. However, Sundays in Ordinary Time do deserve the same time in preparation as that of any other solemnity. Despite the time of year, good principles of liturgy remain in place for all celebrations. This is why I would suggest that Ordinary Time might be more important since adequate preparation and practice time—not to mention resources—are typically always given to the seasons of Advent, Christmas, Lent, Triduum, and Easter. Even today, in some parishes, music stops completely during Ordinary Time especially over the summer months (thank goodness Christmas or Easter is not celebrated in July!). Preparations for Ordinary Time should not be met with angst and trepidation but rather with a sense of joy. There is a wealth of appropriate music ranging from the propers to hymns to choral anthems. Everything used should be grounded in the liturgy of the day so do take time to pray with the readings and the ritual texts. Take adequate notes as to what music you are using so that you don't reinvent the wheel next time liturgical year C rolls around.

This year, Ash Wednesday falls on March 6, so we have seven and a half of Ordinary Time. These winter months present a good opportunity to introduce new music to your parish community, such as a new setting of the Kyrie, Gloria, or Eucharistic Prayer acclamations. Maintain using these new pieces throughout the weeks until we reach Lent. Music for the Triduum comes up later but begin to practice chanting the Exsultet and other important chants of the Triduum now. These are important elements of the liturgy which must be sung well and should be looked at before the beginning of Holy Week. Develop a game plan before Ash Wednesday because time has a habit of moving quickly.

The Liturgical Ministers

THE GOSPEL ACCOUNTS for the first few Sundays in Ordinary Time present Jesus in the early stages of his public ministry. He is a guest at the wedding feast of Cana; he teaches in the synagogue of Nazareth; he joins his first disciples in their fishing boat. In each of these encounters he portrays characteristics of ministry that offer a model for all of us to follow. His gracious hospitality, his compassion for those who seek the wisdom of the Word of God, and his desire to include others in the work of the Father can be seen as markers that help us to shape our own ministry.

Following the liturgical celebration of the Baptism of the Lord (the feast which concluded the Christmas season), the Church proclaims these stories as indicative of the call to discipleship that Jesus announces. Our ministry, which is rooted in the grace and mandate of Baptism, is always in response to that call. Our respective ministries are expressions of our enthusiasm for and our willingness to embrace our ministry as our vocation. The image in Jeremiah (First Reading, Sixth Sunday) is a good one for liturgical ministers to reflect upon.

We are like trees planted beside the flowing waters of Baptism; our roots, our whole being stretches out with life-giving service to others.

Other Prayers, Rites, and Devotions

THIS SEASON surely presents as a reprieve from the bustle of the Christmas holidays, and the extra obligatory Masses of the season (December 25 and January 1). We must acknowledge, too, that there are persons who find the season of Christmas to be a sad reminder of "what used to be" or possibly the death of a loved one during Christmas past. Some seek an antidote to the (possibly gloomy) weather patterns and continuing darkness of the season in the northern hemisphere. There are rich opportunities for intentional prayer, if we consult the internet or even an old missal from home, retrieving some of the gems of prayer in our Catholic heritage: the Angelus, the prayer to St. Michael the Archangel, the Apostles' Creed, and the prayer to the Guardian Angels. Discover how to pray the Rosary or Divine Mercy Chaplet, rediscover the Luminous Mysteries of the Rosary, or recite the Morning Offering or the Divine Praises. Introduce a new prayer to someone from another generation.

Join parents and parishes in prayer for unborn children (January 22 is the National Day of Prayer for the Legal Protection of Unborn Children in the United States). Attend Mass that day, and listen especially to the proper prayers, "For Giving Thanks to God for the Gift of Human Life" (from the Mass for Various Needs and Occasions as found in the third edition of *The Roman Missal*). Candlemas Day (February 2) used to be celebrated as the Feast of the Purification of the Blessed Virgin Mary, now the liturgical calendar's Feast of the Presentation of the Lord. Combining a blessing of candles, procession with candles, and the celebration of the feast of "moving into the house of the Lord" (Jesus and Simeon), the Presentation of the Lord falls on a Saturday this year. Invite parish members to bring candles for blessing, and offer each person a lighted candle to carry in procession, if only during the entrance song at Mass.

Evangelization

ORDINARY TIME in the winter begins after Jesus' baptism and invites us along as he begins his public ministry and preaching. This presents a mission focus to the season, reminding us that as baptized disciples we are called to share the Good News in word, deed, and witness of life. Along these lines, Ordinary Time in winter also has a series of commemorative events that recognize certain themes important for the Church, such as the Day of Prayer for the Legal Protection of Unborn Children (January 22) or the Week of Prayer for Christian Unity (January 18–25). For these weeks it is an especially fitting response to use social media to raise awareness or to connect with people in support of the focus of these days. Especially the Day of Prayer for the Legal Protection of Unborn Children, which generally corresponds with the annual March for Life, social media is a readily available channel to foster a sense of unity around the important issue of human life and dignity from womb to tomb. Social media in this case is a way to lend support and convey a sense of presence and solidarity from far and wide, to share resources, and to join our voices together to demonstrate that protecting human life and dignity is of paramount importance to the Church's mission.

Using social media to raise awareness about the Week of Christian Unity has similar potential. In our local communities, some Christians organize and participate in ecumenical gatherings. Along these lines, creating ways of joining together through social media can extend a much broader invitation to Christians from all denominations to support Christian unity, and offer a powerful, hopeful witness to the world that we are members of one Body in Christ. Social media, and digital culture as a whole, offers the great gift of connecting us to one another, and these connections can become a profound symbol toward community and communion to some extent. While not in Eucharistic communion with our separated brothers and sisters in Christ, we can move toward another sense of communion with them through the authentic sharing of our words in the digital context.

Through these means, we can enter into Ordinary Time responding to the mission we are all called to from our Baptism, and proclaim the Good News in prophetic ways, following the example of Christ. The themes of these weeks give us an opportunity to bring this sense of mission to specific causes. Social media is one important place where we can share our voices and connect with others in support and solidarity.

The Parish and the Home

AS WEATHER becomes inclement, encourage people not to forget the homeless, hungry, and homebound. Find opportunities for ministry and service, such as organizing a canned food drive, visits, or making homemade cards for those in nursing homes and the homebound during the dark days of winter, sharing the love of the community with those unable to get to weekend Mass. Offer opportunities as often as possible for younger parishioners to visit older adults, as this can be a lonely and depressing season especially for those who live alone. Encourage families whose grandparents are gone or live far away to "adopt a grandparent" who has no family nearby.

Special opportunities in February include the Presentation of the Lord (Saturday, February 2) when blessed candles for homes can be made available for purchase after a morning Mass and blessing. Be sure to offer the traditional blessing of throats for the optional memorial of St. Blaise after weekend Masses on February 2 and 3. Other opportunities for communal celebrations include World Day of the Sick (Monday, February 11) which could spark a communal celebration of Anointing of the Sick at weekend Masses on the ninth and tenth. This is a chance to catechize the parish about the sacrament. World Marriage Day, on February 10, is another opportunity to honor, bless, and celebrate married couples.

The weekend of March 3, the final Sunday in Ordinary Time before Lent, is a great time to offer an intergenerational Mardi Gras event. Invite people to your parish gym or other large gathering space to prepare for Lent as a community, with family reflections and projects to enhance home

prayer and reflection. As they arrive, collect last year's blessed palms in a receptacle. Include an option to make masks or hats, play Cajun music in the background, and conclude the event with a Mardi Gras–style parade. ("We Are Marching in the Light of God" would be a great processional song for the parade.) Finish outside, gathered around a brazier in which your priest or deacon solemnly burns the palms people brought back to make ashes for Ash Wednesday. An outline of a paraliturgy for burning the palms is found in LTP's *Guide for Celebrating Holy Week and the Triduum*.

Reflections through the Year

On Sunday, our participation in the Eucharist has special importance. Sunday, like the Jewish Sabbath, is meant to be a day which heals our relationships with God, with ourselves, with others and with the world. Sunday is the day of the Resurrection, the "first day" of the new creation, whose first fruits are the Lord's risen humanity, the pledge of the final transfiguration of all created reality. It also proclaims "man's eternal rest in God." In this way, Christian spirituality incorporates the value of relaxation and festivity. We tend to demean contemplative rest as something unproductive and unnecessary, but this is to do away with the very thing which is most important about work: its meaning. We are called to include in our work a dimension of receptivity and gratuity, which is quite different from mere inactivity. Rather, it is another way of working, which forms part of our very essence. It protects human action from becoming empty activism; it also prevents that unfettered greed and sense of isolation which make us seek personal gain to the detriment of all else. The law of weekly rest forbade work on the seventh day, "so that your ox and your donkey may have rest, and the son of your maidservant, and the stranger, may be refreshed" (Exodus 23:12). Rest opens our eyes to the larger picture and gives us renewed sensitivity to the rights of others. And so the day of rest, centered on the Eucharist, sheds it light on the whole week, and motivates us to greater concern for nature and the poor. (LS, 237)

Mass Texts

◆ INTRODUCTION TO THE MASS

We gather during the time we call ordinary, not because there is nothing special about this time, but because we order the weeks by counting them. *Ordinary* is related to the Latin word *ordinalis,* denoting an order of succession. Every day is filled with the extraordinary presence of God. We gather as members of the Body of Christ. So we participate in this liturgy fully, actively, and consciously, to glorify God and grow in holiness.

◆ SEASONAL ALTERNATE TROPES FOR PENITENTIAL ACT FORM C

Lord Jesus, the Spirit of God rests upon you: Lord, have mercy.

Christ Jesus, the healing touch of God flows out from you: Christ, have mercy.

Lord Jesus, the Word of God is made flesh in you: Lord, have mercy.

◆ DISMISSAL FOR CHILDREN'S LITURGY OF THE WORD

Jesus brought healing to people who were sick, joy to people gathered at a wedding, and hope to people who needed it. Go and listen carefully to the Word of God. Discover how you can heal people by the way you treat them, bring joy to people by being with them, and hope to people by caring for them in little ways that can mean a lot. When you rejoin us, we hope to see Jesus in you. Go in peace.

◆ DISMISSAL OF CATECHUMENS

Jesus rose up in the synagogue and proclaimed: "The Spirit of the Lord is upon me" to bring glad tidings, liberty, sight, and freedom. As you go forth from us to reflect on the Word we heard today, ask the Spirit of the Lord to come upon you. Deepen your relationship with God, through Jesus. Then live in ways that bring the Good News of Jesus Christ to all you meet. You can remind us how to follow the example of Jesus today. Go in peace.

◆ SEASONAL UNIVERSAL PRAYER (PRAYER OF THE FAITHFUL)

Invitation to Prayer

Almighty God, in you we live, and move, and have our being. Open our ears to hear how we can help people see you in our world and where the touch of Jesus is needed in our world.

Intercessions

1. For the Church, help us dedicate ourselves to serve all people in your name, like Jesus taught us, we pray to the Lord:

2. For the planet we share with all creation, fill us with the same concern for reconciliation and restoration that Jesus exemplified, we pray to the Lord:

3. For those in need of joy, hope, freedom, healing, and sight, empower us to live in ways that help all people find what they need, we pray to the Lord:

4. For the people we can ignore or take for granted, may we see them with the same attention Jesus offered to the people he met, we pray to the Lord:

5. For this community of faith, deepen our resolve to carry Jesus in our words, deeds, and attitudes, so others may see him and be attracted to him, we pray to the Lord:

6. For those who have died, give them eternal light and peace, we pray to the Lord:

Concluding Prayer

Abundant God,
you are the center of our lives.
Deepen our connection with you.
Make us aware of your Spirit within us,
and empower us to be witnesses of our hope and
      trust in your Son, Jesus Christ,
who lives and reigns with you and the Holy Spirit,
one God, for ever and ever.
Amen.

January 2019
Month of the Holy Name

Weekdays during Ordinary Time

Except for the days of the First and Thirty-Fourth Weeks in Ordinary Time. The Roman Missal does not provide prayer texts for the weekdays in Ordinary Time. Instead, priest celebrants and those who prepare the liturgy may select from among the prayers provided for the Sundays in Ordinary Time.

Optional Memorials during Ordinary Time

On all Saturdays during Ordinary Time that do not have an obligatory memorial, a memorial to the Blessed Virgin Mary may be celebrated. The prayers may be selected from the Common of the Blessed Virgin Mary. Commentary below is only provided for Sundays, solemnities, feasts, and obligatory memorials. The *General Instruction of the Roman Missal* states that when celebrating optional memorials on "weekdays in Ordinary Time, there may be chosen either the Mass of the weekday, or the Mass of an Optional Memorial which happens to occur on that day, or the Mass of any Saint inscribed in the Martyrology for that day, or a Mass for Various Needs, or a Votive Mass" (GIRM, 355c).

MON 14 (#305) green
Weekday

First Week in Ordinary Time

The Lectionary for Mass

◆ First Reading: Jesus is the fulfillment of the prophets. He reflects God's glory and is God's Son. All God's angels will worship him. So begins the letter to the Hebrews, which emphasizes Jesus' high priesthood. His divinity makes him higher than the angels. Let us listen to the Son through whom God the Father continues to speak.

◆ Responsorial Psalm 97: The refrain for today's Psalm is also the last line of the First Reading and calls on God's angels to worship the Lord. Christians believe Jesus to be the Lord, the King, the One in whom God's justice is fulfilled. He is exalted above all gods. Together with the angels, let us to offer our worship to the Lord.

◆ Gospel: The plain truth is this: The Kingdom of God is present in Jesus. Now is the time to change our lives and follow the Gospel. Such is Jesus' message to the people of Galilee. Such is the message Jesus invites Simon, Andrew, James, and John to embrace when he calls them to leave their ordinary lives and follow him. Such is the message that is also ours to accept.

TUE 15 (#306) green
Weekday

The Lectionary for Mass

◆ First Reading: The author of Hebrews uses Psalm 8 to speak of Jesus' humanity, but also to emphasize how God crowned him with the glory and honor of all of creation—even the angels are now subject to him. We exist as Jesus' brothers and sisters for our origin, too, lies in God. We are united to God for Jesus shares in our humanity, and so, we praise God.

◆ Responsorial Psalm 8 summons us to reflect on our place in the universe. We, whom God created "little less than the angels," are stewards of all creation. Christians see in Jesus the fulfillment of this verse quoted in our First Reading. He is the One to whom all creation bows down and worships. Praise be to God for his Son who rules over creation and empowers us to be faithful stewards of its beauty and abundance.

◆ Gospel: Little did the fledgling disciples know what one of the first experiences with Jesus would entail! A man with an unclean spirit acclaims Jesus as the Holy One of God. Jesus exorcises the man's evil spirit and amazement fills the synagogue in Capernaum that Sabbath day. How does amazement at Jesus' teaching and authority fill us this day?

WED 16 (#307) green
Weekday

The Lectionary for Mass

◆ First Reading: It was necessary that Jesus become fully human in order to destroy death and free us from sin. He had to become completely like us to know our suffering. We know the freedom and grace that comes through the forgiveness of our sins only because Jesus truly suffered. And what a freedom it is! Through the fullness of his humanity and divinity, he is a high priest like no other.

◆ Responsorial Psalm 105: We sing our praise and thanks to God in the words of Psalm 105. The psalm refrain (see verse 8a) reminds us that God will never forget his covenant. We see in Jesus the everlasting fulfillment of God's promise of life for his people. We proclaim God's wondrous deeds done through his Son. May our thanks to God last forever.

◆ Gospel: The four disciples accompany Jesus as he enters the house of Simon and Andrew. Once inside, Jesus' healing touch frees Simon's mother-in-law of her fever. She does not take any time to recover from her illness, but instead immediately begins to wait on Jesus and the disciples. Word spreads and many others come to Jesus seeking healing. After taking time for a short respite to center himself through prayer, Jesus' mission continues in the neighboring synagogues and villages. The life of discipleship continues too.

THU 17 (#308) white
Memorial of
St. Anthony, Abbot

The Lectionary for Mass

◆ FIRST READING: Using a citation from Psalm 95, the author of Hebrews encourages us to remain faithful. Each day we strengthen our resolve to resist the hardening of our hearts that comes from sin. Christ is our partner, just as we are his. This is the truth of faith that leads us forward from this day until the end of earthly lives and the end of time.

◆ RESPONSORIAL PSALM 95: Let us hear God's voice. Let us not harden our hearts, and instead worship the Lord, our Creator, the Creator of all living things. God guides and shepherds us along our journey. Psalm 95 helps us give voice to God's desire that we not become like the people of Israel who turned from God at Meribah and Massah in the desert. May we listen to God's Word and may our hearts remain centered on God.

◆ GOSPEL: Jesus healed Simon's mother-in-law in yesterday's Gospel reading. Today, Jesus heals again—and this time the recipient of his healing power is the man with leprosy who begged Jesus to make him clean. In Jesus, the man with leprosy is no less than anyone else even though he felt the weight of society's stigma upon him. Unconditional love and grace is ours in Jesus. How can we keep quiet about that? We cannot—just like the man could not and had to publicize his new life in Jesus!

The Roman Missal

The Mass texts are proper for today and can be found in the Proper of Saints at January 17. The orations all echo the virtues of St. Anthony's

life: his "wondrous way of life in the desert" and the need for self-denial in order to love God above all things (Collect), being free from "earthly attachments" so that "we may have our riches in you alone" (Prayer over the Offerings), and the saint's "glorious victories / over the powers of darkness" (Prayer after Communion). Although no particular Preface is indicated in the rubrics for today, certainly one should be chosen from among the two Prefaces of Saints or the Preface of Holy Virgins and Religious. Consider using Eucharistic Prayer II.

Today's Saint

Early in his life, St. Anthony of Egypt (251–356) discovered the grace of solitude. He journeyed to the desert, and for nearly thirty years he lived a life of solitary prayer and self-discipline—a life of utter dependence on God. After his time in the desert, he emerged as a man of balance, ready to share all he learned regarding the human thirst for God. Realizing that the spiritual life takes root within a community of believers, he founded a group of monks. While serving as abbot, a spiritual father, to the monks, Saint Anthony mentored them in the ways of contemplative prayer and helped them overcome illusory thinking. His dynamic personality continued to attract others. As a result, he counseled a steady stream of pilgrims and laid the foundation for many monasteries.

FRI 18 (#309) green
Weekday

The Lectionary for Mass

◆ FIRST READING: In the Old Testament, entering into God's rest referred to coming into the Promised Land. In the reading from Hebrews, we come to know that Jesus fulfills God's promise of rest. Each day of our lives when we believe in him and listen to the Good

News, we know God's rest. We seek the peace that comes from resting in God each time we do not harden our hearts to God's Word in Jesus Christ.

◆ RESPONSORIAL PSALM 78: The refrain reminds us to never forget the Lord's works. All that we have heard and all that we have seen—everything our ancestors in faith have communicated to us—are the wondrous deeds of the Lord. In gratitude, we strive to keep our heart centered in God and our spirit faithful to him. This we do in contrast to those who turn away from God and choose sin.

◆ GOSPEL: How far would our friends go to bring us to Jesus for healing? To what extent would we go for a friend to experience Jesus' healing? Many had gathered and carried a paralytic to Jesus. We do not even know that these people knew each other. All we know is that these men saw a person in need of healing and we know the circumstances which prompted these men to bring him to Jesus. Jesus responds by forgiving the paralytic's sins and commanding him to rise and go home. He had found his home—his rest—in Jesus.

Other Ideas

Today begins the Week of Prayer for Christian Unity. Each year, Christians from many denominations observe a special week of prayer for Christian unity. Coming together in a variety of ways, through joint prayer and meetings, we remember how much we share, and we look honestly at the issues that still keep us apart. It is a time to reflect on Christ's prayer the night before he died: "The glory that you have given me I have given them, so that they may be one, as we are one, I in them and you in me, that they may become completely one, so that the world may know that you have sent me and have loved them even as you have loved me" (John 17:22–23). For Catholics, the unity of all Christian believers is more than just one more dream; it is central to the Church's mission.

S A T 19 (#310) green
Weekday

Optional Memorial of the Blessed Virgin Mary / white

The Lectionary for Mass

◆ FIRST READING: The Word of God is so sharp it can pierce everything. Even when we try to hide what we think, God penetrates our hearts. Jesus, the Son of God, sympathizes with us because he is fully human. He completely understands and shares our humanity. Ours, then, is the confidence to come near to God for grace and mercy.

◆ RESPONSORIAL PSALM 19: Spirit and life come from the Lord's words, as today's psalm refrain from John 6:63 tells us. The verses from Psalm 19 speak of the beauty and wisdom of the Lord's Word. This connection with the First Reading's reference to the power of God's Word compels us to reflect on how the divine Word helps us discern God's wisdom for our own lives.

◆ GOSPEL: The first disciples Jesus called have witnessed the One they follow exorcise demons and heal the sick. Jesus now calls Levi from his station where he was collecting custom taxes. Those in Levi's role extorted many for their own profit. The scribes who professed to be Pharisees were not pleased to see Jesus dining with sinners and tax collectors. Jesus makes his mission clear: he comes to call sinners. Do you hear him calling you?

☀ 20 (#66C) green
Second Sunday in Ordinary Time

The Lectionary for Mass

◆ FIRST READING: The prophet's words, from one of the last chapters of Isaiah, set the stage for our journey during Ordinary Time. These words give us confidence that the Lord delights in his people and will intimately accompany us on the journey of faith as a bridegroom rejoices in his bride. Restoration will be ours in God as it was Zion's.

◆ RESPONSORIAL PSALM 96: The joyful verses, which compose our response to the good news from Isaiah, call us as a community to announce the Lord's salvation and proclaim his glory to all people. In so doing, we give back to the Lord the glory the Lord rightly deserves.

◆ SECOND READING: God is one and the same, and from him comes the myriad of diverse gifts and works. The same Spirit—the Spirit of the Lord—produces these gifts. From the ability to communicate wisdom, to faith, to gifts of healing, to prophecy, and discernment of spirits and interpretation of tongues, these marvelous gifts come from one and the same Spirit. The Corinthians struggled to maintain the unity of their community of faith in light of these gifts. The Corinthians wanted to prioritize these gifts in order of importance and set people against each other in light of which gift they received.

This would only serve to divide the one God, the Lord, and the one Spirit.

◆ GOSPEL: Jesus turns water into wine as the first of the signs that reveal his glory in the Gospel according to John. The signs help us to see Jesus as the fulfillment of the restoration of Jerusalem. We know from the beginning of his ministry that the one who will call his disciples and us to follow him fulfills God's covenant to Israel. On this initial Sunday of Ordinary Time, we begin to believe anew in him as the disciples began to believe for the first time.

The Roman Missal

The Mass texts for today are found in the "Ordinary Time" section of the Proper of Time. The Gloria and the Creed are sung or said today. The Collect acknowledges God as the one who governs "all things," and so asks him to "bestow [his] peace on our times." The Prayer over the Offerings reiterates how "whenever the memorial of this sacrifice is celebrated / the work of our redemption is accomplished." The Prayer after Communion highlights the unity of the faithful that is a constitutive element in the meaning of the Eucharist. It asks God to pour the Spirit of love on us so that those who have been nourished by the "one heavenly Bread" may become "one in mind and heart." Any one of the eight Prefaces of the Sundays in Ordinary Time may be selected for today. Consider using Eucharistic Prayer III.

Other Ideas

The Gospel account of the wedding feast at Cana is a suitable context for the blessing of married couples and the blessing of newly engaged couples (an event that often occurs at Christmas!). *The Order of Celebrating Matrimony* includes a blessing that may be used with engaged couples (outside Mass) and married couples on particularly significant anniversaries (may be done within Mass). Since Ordinary Time began last Monday consider placing a short description about Ordinary Time in the bulletin. A good text is found in LTP's *Companion to the Calendar, Second Edition* (be sure to secure copyright permission). For the next several weeks, until the First Sunday of Lent (March 10) the Second Reading for Sunday is from the first Letter of St. Paul to the Corinthians. A good family prayer exercise is to read through Paul's letter over the course of these weeks and talk about them together.

(#311) red

MON 21 Memorial of St. Agnes, Virgin and Martyr

The Lectionary for Mass

◆ FIRST READING: The prayers of Jesus communicated to the Father through his cries and tears on the Cross were heard. Jesus' obedience —even to the point of death—led to our salvation. He is a high priest unlike any other high priest because he knows our humanity. In his suffering and Resurrection, God glorified him once, for the salvation of all. Jesus is an eternal priest, a priest forever.

◆ RESPONSORIAL PSALM 110: The refrain echoes the First Reading's reference to Jesus as an eternal priest like Melchizedek, the ancient king of Jerusalem. The verses of this royal psalm attest to how the Lord will rule over his enemies. God's splendor in Jesus Christ will forever reign over all enemies. His priesthood is everlasting. We acclaim our confidence in God's power in the words of Psalm 110 and in our life of faith.

◆ GOSPEL: People ask Jesus why his disciples do not fast, but the disciples of John and the Pharisees do. Jesus responds in a mini-parable. He teaches the people that it is the

relationship between God and his people that is important. This relationship began in Jesus, the bridegroom. Outward acts, such as fasting, are no longer necessary with Jesus present in their midst. Would that we, too, focus on pouring ourselves into our relationship with Jesus as he pours himself out for us.

The Roman Missal

The Collect is the only oration proper for today, and it is found at January 21 in the Proper of Saints. The prayer has Pauline echoes in its assertion that God chooses "what is weak in the world to confound the strong." The other orations are taken either from the Common of Martyrs: For a Virgin Martyr, or from the Common of Virgins: For One Virgin. Although no particular Preface is indicated in the rubrics for today, certainly one of the two Prefaces of Holy Martyrs should be considered as likely choices, although the Preface of Holy Virgins and Religious could be another candidate. Consider using Eucharistic Prayer I.

Today's Saint

St. Agnes (c. 292–305) is one of the women whose name is mentioned in Eucharistic Prayer I. She is thought to have been a member of Roman nobility, and was martyred at the age of twelve under Diocletian on January 21, 304, for refusing to marry a prefect's son. She is the patron saint of Christian virtue and is often represented with a martyr's palm and a lamb (a translation of her name in Latin). This gave rise to the tradition of blessing lambs at the Roman Basilica of St. Agnes on this day. The wool from these lambs is then used to weave the pallia worn by archbishops and others of metropolitan rank.

(#312, #947A–947E, or #887–891)
white or violet

TUE 22 Day of Prayer for the Legal Protection of Unborn Children

About Today's Day of Prayer

On January 22, 1973, the United States Supreme Court handed down a decision known as Roe versus Wade, which made abortion legal throughout the United States, and struck down many states' laws restricting abortion. Since that decision, more than 50 million abortions have been performed in the United States. In all the dioceses of the United States, today is observed as a day of penance for violations to the dignity of the human person committed through acts of abortion, and for the full restoration of the legal guarantee to the right to life. We pray not only for the innocent children who are not able to be born, but for all mothers and fathers who are considering abortion and those who have had abortions. On this day, hundreds of thousands will participate in pro-life marches across the nation. The largest of these takes place in Washington, DC, where some 400,000 gather on the Mall and march up Capitol Hill to witness to the Gospel of life.

The Lectionary for Mass

For the Day of Prayer, any of the following readings may be chosen: Genesis 1:1—2:2 (41) or 2 Maccabees 7:1, 20–31 (vol. II, 499) or Isaiah 49:1–6 (587) or Romans 11:33–36 (121) or Ephesians 1:3–14 (104) or Ephesians 3:14–21 (vol. III, 476) or Colossians 1:12–20 (162) or 1 John 3:11–21 (208); Matthew 18:1–5, 10, 12–14 (414) or Mark 9:30–37 (134) or Luke 1:39–56 (622) or Luke 17:11–19 (144) or Luke 23:35–43 (162) or John 1:1–5, 9–14, 16–18 (755) or John 6:24–35 (113), or the Lectionary for ritual Masses (vol. IV), the Mass "For Peace and Justice," 887–891. The commentary below pertains to the Ordinary Time weekday.

◆ FIRST READING: Our hope is in Jesus Christ, the eternal high priest. We encourage each other to be eager to share in the fulfillment of God's promise to Abraham. Others can be encouraged in their own journey by the way we imitate our predecessors in faith. God sees our work and love we do in his name.

◆ RESPONSORIAL PSALM 111: We sing a psalm of thanks to the Lord with our whole heart for all the Lord has done for us. For the Lord's grace and mercy, and the food he provides, we acclaim his name. In the words of the psalm refrain taken from verse 5, we profess our faith that the Lord indeed will remember his covenantal promises forever.

◆ GOSPEL: Not only do Jesus' disciples not follow the ritual purity laws to which the Pharisees behold themselves to, but they also work on the Sabbath. Jesus responds to the Pharisees' inquiry into this violation of their law by referring them back to David's action of eating the offering bread in God's house and then sharing it with his hungry companions. Jesus is Lord of the Sabbath, a holy observance made for people of faith who nourish each other.

The Roman Missal

According to GIRM, 373: "In all the Dioceses of the United States of America, January 22 . . . shall be observed as a particular day of prayer for the full restoration of the legal guarantee of the right to life and of penance for violations to the dignity of the human person committed through acts of abortion. The liturgical celebrations for this day may be the Mass 'For Giving Thanks to God for the Gift of Human Life' (no. 48/1 of the Masses and Prayers for Various Needs and Occasions), celebrated with white vestments, or the Mass 'For the Preservation of Peace and Justice' (number 30 of the Masses

and Prayers for Various Needs and Occasions), celebrated with violet vestments." In the Mass for Peace and Justice, we pray that all governments, especially our own, seek a truly just society, one in which the common good of all people, including the most vulnerable, is sought. In a very real way, we pray for the end of this genocide, the victims of which we remember with our violet vestments and mournful hymns. This Mass celebrates their brief lives, reminding us also of the beauty and sacredness of the lives around us, who have not yet been lost. We remember, we intercede, we hope—and the Church leads us in all three.

Other Ideas

As well as remembering the unborn, make parish members aware of opportunities to serve women facing crisis pregnancies. This is also a good day to catechize that as Catholics, we honor the dignity of all life—from conception to natural death. As such, we are committed to helping the poor and the hungry, the homeless, prisoners, immigrants, and refugees. We must be committed to living lives of justice helping all those in need, for all people are children of God. Pray for the sanctity of all life—of all creation!—in today's Universal Prayer.

Be mindful of those who have had abortions and are seeking reconciliation. Refrain from judgment, but welcome them with loving hospitality. Although memorials to the unborn are certainly acceptable, it's not best practice to place them in front of a church building as a constant reminder to those who are remorseful—doing so can harm reconciliation efforts. Instead, place memorials in a prayer garden or the parish cemetery. In a document that ended the Year of Mercy in 2016, Pope Francis gave all priests permission to absolve women and others involved in abortion. For more ideas

consult the USCCB website: http://www.usccb.org/about/pro-life-activities/respect-life-program/.

WED 23 (#313) green
Weekday

Optional Memorials of St. Vincent, Deacon and Martyr / red; St. Marianne Cope, Virgin / white

The Lectionary for Mass

◆ FIRST READING: This passage refers to a meeting between Abram and Melchizedek (see Genesis 14:17–20). Melchizedek brings bread and wine to celebrate Abram's victory over Chedorlaomer and the kings who sided with him. Melchizedek was the righteous king of Salem (Jerusalem) and as such is seen as a type of Christ in this passage from Hebrews.

◆ RESPONSORIAL PSALM 110: We sang this psalm on Monday, January 21, 2019. Refer to that commentary for more background. The psalm refrain, which comes from verse 4 of Psalm 110, echoes the final verse of the First Reading.

◆ GOSPEL: A man with a withered hand and in need of healing stood before the Pharisees. Jesus turns the tables on the Pharisees and asks them a question about the legality of doing good on the Sabbath. The question reduces the Pharisees to silence. Jesus chooses compassion and life over the letter of the law, hardness of heart, and death, and heals the man. The Pharisees who have witnessed Jesus teach, feed, and heal on the Sabbath fashion their plot to put Jesus to death. Do our choices resemble more Jesus' choice or that of the Pharisees?

Today's Saints

St. Vincent was from Saragossa in third-century Spain. He is also known as Vincent the Deacon and served under St. Valerius, bishop of Saragossa. He was martyred in 304 in the persecution of the emperor

Diocletian. Just before he was killed on a gridiron or grill, he was offered his freedom if he would throw a copy of the Scriptures on the fire that was prepared for him, but he refused. After witnessing Vincent's faith and heroism, his executioner converted to Christianity.

St. Marianne Cope (1838–1918) was born in West Germany, but a year after her birth the Cope family emigrated to the United States of America to seek work and educational opportunities. From a young age, she felt the call to enter religious life, which led to her decision to enter the Sisters of St. Francis in Syracuse, New York. She had a deep affection for the suffering and sick. St. Marianne was instrumental in the establishment of two of the first hospitals in the central New York area—hospitals that were open to all people regardless of ethnicity, religion, or race. While serving as superior general of her religious community, she accepted an invitation to care for the sick, especially those afflicted with leprosy, in Hawaii. St. Marianne joined the mission to Hawaii where she helped establish homes for leprosy patients and cared for St. Damien De Veuster of Moloka'i who contracted leprosy because of his ministry to the sick. Following the death of St. Damien, St. Marianne continued his compassionate ministry of care for leprosy patients.

(#314) white
THU 24 Memorial of St. Francis de Sales, Bishop and Doctor of the Church

The Lectionary for Mass

◆ FIRST READING: Jesus lives forever as our eternal high priest. When we come to God through him, he has the ability to save us. Other high priests had to offer continuous sacrifices day after day, but Jesus' sacrifice of his own life is a once for all sacrifice. Because of Jesus'

self-emptying gift, we need not perform additional sacrifices. Jesus has brought about a new covenant that surpasses the old covenant.

◆ RESPONSORIAL PSALM 40 helps us both to thank God for the justice shown to us and to lament upon those who turn their backs to God. Each time we pray the refrain, we present ourselves to the Lord with readiness to do the Lord's will. When we align our desire with the Lord's will, we glorify the Lord.

◆ GOSPEL: Jesus taught, fed the hungry, and healed the sick. His mission angered the Pharisees, but clearly the people desired to know him. Crowds from throughout Galilee and Judea, from diverse neighborhoods and towns make it almost impossible for Jesus to make his way to a waiting boat. Who could resist experiencing the power of the One whom even unclean spirits worship and acclaim as the Son of God!

The Roman Missal

The orations are proper for today and are found in the Proper of Saints at January 24. The prayers include mention of St. Francis de Sales by way of his gentleness, his meekness, his charity, and his being inflamed with the Holy Spirit. Although no particular Preface is indicated in the rubrics for today, the Preface of Holy Pastors would make sense, since St. Francis was a bishop. Consider using Eucharistic Prayer II.

Today's Saint

St. Francis de Sales (1567–1622), bishop of Geneva, contributed immensely to the development of spirituality through the publication of his book *An Introduction to the Devout Life*. Living during a time when most manuals on spirituality were written primarily for clerics and members of religious orders, St. Francis' book provided a practical path to holiness for people

from all states of life. He challenged the prevailing belief that only a select few could attain sanctity. Along with his accomplishments in the area of an "everyday" or "lay" spirituality, he cofounded with St. Jane Frances de Chantal the Order of the Visitation of Holy Mary—a religious community of nuns that move beyond traditional enclosure to a blend of prayer and service to the poor. Together, Sts. Francis and Jane, with their close friends Sts. Vincent de Paul and Louise de Marillac, transformed the face of the Church in France. St. Francis has been named a Doctor of the Church.

(#519) white
FRI 25 Feast of the Conversion of St. Paul the Apostle

About Today's Feast

Today's feast celebrates God's triumph, even in the most unlikely circumstances. Before Paul meets the Risen Lord on the Road to Damascus, he is dedicated to viciously persecuting the followers of Jesus Christ. Imagine yourself among those early Christians, and hearing that Saul, one of the most feared enemies of your community, has encountered the Lord and changed his life entirely to serve him from then on. Although certainly astonishing, the conversion of Paul is also deeply inspiring, for it tells us that God does not hold our mistakes against us, but rather calls us to turn our minds and hearts to follow his Son instead. The conversion of Paul is proof that no one is too far beyond the call of the Lord to follow, and that in Christ, change for the better is always possible.

The Lectionary for Mass

◆ FIRST READING, OPTION 1: Paul defends himself in front of the crowds in Jerusalem. He presents an autobiographical account of his faith journey from his days as a strict follower of Jewish ancestral law, to the times when he persecuted the disciples of the Way, to his conversion to Jesus the Nazorean. His testimony ends with his call to the people to have themselves baptized and their sins forgiven in the name of Jesus Christ. Paul's story invites us to chronicle our own story of conversion.

◆ FIRST READING: Two options are given for the First Reading. Both are Paul's account (as reported by St. Luke) of his experience of the Risen Christ on the road to Damascus and the important identification of Jesus with believers. In the first option, we hear of Paul's Jewish heritage, particularly that of a Pharisee. The second option focuses on Ananias's, understandable fear and hesitancy about going to Saul. He is obedient, nonetheless. Both readings speak of Paul's experience of the bright light (identified with the Lord) and his hearing the Lord's voice (note the discrepancy though, in Acts of the Apostles 22, where Paul's companions hear the voice as well). Both readings contrast Paul, the zealous and aggressive defender of Judaism, with the blinded man who needed to be led by the hand. Paul's blindness is the result of his experience of the Risen Christ manifest in light so bright that he was left unable to see. Paul is led by the hand literally by his companions and figuratively by Ananias whose word led Saul to Baptism and an understanding of his call and mission from Jesus.

◆ RESPONSORIAL PSALM 117: The antiphon for the Responsorial Psalm comes from Mark 16:15 and is the Risen Christ's commission to the remaining eleven disciples to go into the world and proclaim the Gospel. The verses of praise come from the shortest psalm—only two verses—in the psalter.

◆ GOSPEL: The Gospel reading begins with the commission of the eleven disciples. This was the same text used as the Responsorial Psalm's refrain. Ours is the choice, like Paul's was, to go out and preach the Good News or not. Should we choose to believe and proclaim Jesus' name, we will have the power to drive away evil and heal the sick, bringing life to the world.

The Roman Missal

Notice that the prayers have a very fervent nature to them, and this should be reflected throughout the liturgy. The Gloria is sung or said. Use Preface I of the Apostles. Consider using Eucharistic Prayer I. You may select from two options for the Solemn Blessing: Peter and Paul (#16) or the general one for Apostles (#17). The prayers clearly explain we are celebrating Paul's conversion and they ask us to follow his example and draw nearer to Our Lord. It is interesting to note that it speaks of stirring fire but that the fire is one of charity. We must use our fervor for the Lord in a kind fashion. The Spirit will fill us with wisdom and enlighten us on the path we must go. May we follow this wisdom, to be better witnesses in our prayer and in our life.

(#520; Gospel #316) white
S A T 26 Memorial of Sts. Timothy and Titus, Bishops

The Lectionary for Mass

◆ FIRST READING, OPTION 1: Paul writes to Timothy of his gratitude to God for their friendship and his desire to see Timothy again. Paul offers words of encouragement to Timothy to continue to testify to others about the Lord even in the face of hardship and persecution. Paul reminds Timothy to remember the power, love, and self-control God gives him in order to fulfill his mission. This is a good reminder for us as well as we turn away from fear and choose courage to live the life of a disciple.

◆ FIRST READING, OPTION 2: The second option for the First Reading comes from the letter to Titus, the third of the three pastoral letters. These first four of these verses are Paul's lengthy greeting to his co-worker, Titus. Paul affirms the faith they share in Christ Jesus, the Savior. Paul reminds Titus of the charge he has in Crete. As part of organizing the Church there, Titus needs to appoint presbyters in every town. The faith Paul and Titus share is our faith, too. We are heirs to the organization and tradition of the Church that stems from the early first century.

◆ FIRST READING, OPTION 2: A very lengthy sentence serves as Paul's opening greeting to Titus. Paul left Titus in Crete to appoint leadership for the Church there. Common faith in Jesus Christ unites Paul and Titus as it has united Apostles and disciples from the time of Jesus forward.

◆ RESPONSORIAL PSALM 96: A marvelous hymn of praise, Psalm 96 focuses us on the wonders of the Lord's salvation. May this Psalm buoy us to proclaim God's wonders inside and outside the walls of the church building.

◆ GOSPEL: The two brief verses that are today's Gospel serve as an introduction to the rest of Mark 3. We know this from the Gospel reading: Jesus and his disciples enter a house. They have arrived home, but the crowd is still with them. Presumably it is the size of the crowd that makes it impossible for them to eat. Because of this Jesus' relatives accuse him of being "out of his mind" and want to apprehend him. As we will find out in the coming days, it is not really the size of the crowd and the inability to eat which is the reason for Jesus' relatives thinking he is not altogether of sound mind.

The Roman Missal

The prayers are found in the Proper of Saints. Appropriately on this memorial, the Collect echoes the words of St. Paul's letter to Timothy (2:12). We pray that we may live "justly and devoutly in this present age" and so come to our "heavenly homeland." In the Prayer over the Offerings, we ask for "sincerity of heart," that we may be acceptable to God. We pray that the sacrament we receive may nourish us in the faith that was taught and "kept safe" by Sts. Timothy and Titus (Prayer after Communion). The Preface of Pastors is used. Consider using Eucharistic Prayer II.

Today's Saints

Sts. Timothy and Titus, first century bishops and martyrs, are celebrated together because of their joint association with St. Paul. Timothy is first mentioned in Acts of the Apostles 16:1–2, when Paul visits Lystra, in what is now Turkey. Timothy's mother was Jewish; Paul circumcised him so he would be accepted by the Jewish Christians. Timothy accompanied Paul on some of his journeys, and he is the one addressed in the Letters to Timothy in the New Testament. Tradition says that Paul made him bishop of Ephesus in 65. He was martyred by stoning in either the year 65 or 80 for preaching against the worship of idols.

St. Titus was also a disciple and companion of St. Paul. He was probably a Gentile, and Paul refused to have him circumcised because the Gospel freed Gentiles from the Law of Moses. Although he is not mentioned in the Acts of the Apostles, he is mentioned several times in Paul's letters and was probably commissioned to preach to the Gentiles. According to Paul, Titus was with Paul and Timothy at Ephesus and was sent to Macedonia to collect alms for the Christians in Jerusalem. He also spent time in Macedonia, Crete, and Dalmatia in modern-day Croatia. Tradition says that he was a bishop in Crete and died in the year 107.

27 (#69C) green
Third Sunday in Ordinary Time

The Lectionary for Mass

◆ FIRST READING: Ezra the scribe and priest, brings the book of the law before the intergenerational assembly and proclaims clearly and audibly from it as gifted readers do in our assemblies today. The law was to serve as the basis for the community's life together. Its demands do not go unacknowledged by the community as they respond with tears to its proclamation. Nehemiah admonishes the community to replace their tears with joy, for the Lord is their strength, and to feast abundantly because the day is holy for the Lord. May we heed this advice when the demands of discipleship cause us to feel overburdened.

◆ RESPONSORIAL PSALM 19 emphasizes the refreshment that comes to our souls from the Lord's law. Clear and right are the words of the Lord, so much so that Wisdom herself is present in them. And, from the Lord's words come Spirit and life. The refrain taken from Jesus words in John 6:63 tells us this.

◆ SECOND READING: For the Corinthian community that struggled to understand that they were to value each member equally and affirm the diversity of gifts present among them, Paul's teaching about the unity of the many parts of the body was not easy to accept or enact. God designed the body as such—so if one part suffers, all do, and if one part succeeds, all can experience joy. Paul tells the Corinthians that they together are Christ's Body. There can be no division among them since there is only one Christ. There is a longer and shorter form of today's reading.

◆ GOSPEL: The first half of today's Gospel reading is from the prologue to the Gospel in which Luke informs us that he writes to provide an orderly and accurate of account of the events that have occurred in their midst. The second half of the reading reveals to us how, early on in his account, Luke identifies Jesus as the fulfillment of God's covenantal promises in the Old Testament. On the Sabbath and in his hometown synagogue in Nazareth, Jesus proclaims Isaiah 61:1–2 and announces the fulfillment of this Scripture passage here and now.

The Roman Missal

The Mass texts for this Sunday are found in the "Ordinary Time" section of the Proper of Time. The Gloria is sung or said today. The Creed is said or sung. The Collect asks that God may direct our actions so that "in the name of your beloved Son / we may abound in good works." In the Prayer over the Offerings we are asking God to accept our offerings so that, in sanctifying them, "they may profit us for salvation." The Prayer after Communion asks that, as a result of receiving the grace of being brought to new life (for example, in the Eucharist), "we may always glory in your gift." Any one of the eight Prefaces of the Sundays in Ordinary Time may be selected for today. Consider Eucharistic Prayer II.

Other Ideas

Note in the parish bulletin that we are in Year C of the Sunday Lectionary and that Luke is the primary evangelist. Encourage individuals and families to use the Gospel according to Luke as their source of prayer during the year. Many parishes publish the notations for the Sunday Scriptures in the bulletin; if your parish does not do this consider asking if that could be done. LTP's *The Daily Mass Readings 2019: A Simple Reference Guide* could be cheaply purchased in bulk and given to parishioners to use as a guide for praying with the readings each day. Likewise, LTP's *Daily Prayer 2019* provides a short order of prayer loosely based on the Liturgy of the Hours which includes an excerpt of the daily Mass readings.

Some parishes place the *Book of the Gospels* on a lectern near the main doorway of the church; it is kept there during the week. Considering doing so if your parish does not already practice this custom. Keep in mind that this should not done at the ambo for it is intended as a place for proclamation and not as a place to enshrine either the Lectionary or the *Book of the Gospels.*

(#317) white

MON 28
Memorial of St. Thomas Aquinas, Priest and Doctor of the Church

The Lectionary for Mass

◆ FIRST READING: Some of the major truths of our faith come from this passage from Hebrews. Christ mediates a new covenant. He entered the sanctuary as a high priest, not many times, but once for all. The sacrifice he offered was the sacrifice of his blood. Because of this, no other sacrifices are necessary. Sin is forgiven! Christ, who died to bring life, will come again bringing salvation, wholeness, and everlast-ing life to those of us who willingly prepare ourselves as we wait for his Second Coming.

◆ RESPONSORIAL PSALM 98: The Lectionary provides us with the psalm of the Christmas season for today's Responsorial Psalm. Psalm 98 exudes praise for the Lord for his amazing deeds and the victory he has won. In the words of the refrain, we sing a "new song" to the Lord for his salvation is indeed known to us and seen to the ends of the earth.

◆ GOSPEL: The truth comes out. Not only have the Pharisees begun to plot Jesus' death, but now the scribes declare Jesus is possessed by Beelzebul, the prince of demons. Jesus offers harsh words to them in the form of a parable. Kingdoms and houses divided will not stand. Those who speak words against the Holy Spirit will not know forgiveness. The scribes claimed Jesus had an unclean spirit, but whose spirit really is unclean?

The Roman Missal

The Collect is proper for today and is to be found in the Proper of Saints at January 28. The first part of the oration recognizes St. Thomas Aquinas' zeal for holiness and study of sacred doctrine; the second part asks God to grant "that we may understand what he taught / and imitate what he accomplished." The other prayers are taken either from the Common of Doctors of the Church or from the Common of Pastors: For One Pastor. The Preface to use is either the Preface of Holy Pastors or one of the two Prefaces of Saints. Consider using Eucharistic Prayer II.

Today's Saint

St. Thomas Aquinas (1225–1274), called the "Angelic Doctor" for his writings, was born near Naples. Against his family's wishes, he joined the newly established Dominicans and went to study under Albert the Great in Paris. Thomas' theological writings, especially the *Summa Theologiae*, remain preeminent texts to this day. For all his brilliance, Thomas was also a man of deep prayer who realized that the mysteries of God cannot fully be expressed by words. He contributed the liturgical texts for the Solemnity of the Most Holy Body and Blood of Christ, including the Tantum Ergo, which is still sung at Benediction of the Blessed Sacrament.

(#318) green

TUE 29
Weekday

The Lectionary for Mass

◆ FIRST READING: The law never makes perfect. Perfection comes through Jesus Christ who offered his Body once for all. He came to do God's will. He came to draw us closer to God through the forgiveness of our sins by his sacrifice. No longer are annual offerings necessary for Jesus fulfilled God's will.

◆ RESPONSORIAL PSALM 40: The verses of the psalm connect with the emphasis of the passage from Hebrews on Jesus' sacrifice. God did not seek burnt offerings or sin offerings. In Jesus' obedience is the example for us of what it means to present ourselves to the Lord as ready and willing to do the Lord's will.

◆ GOSPEL: The short Gospel passage repeats the theme of doing God's will found in the refrain of the Responsorial Psalm. We are part of Jesus' immediate family if we choose to align our hearts and lives with God's will. Those who choose not to do so will remain outside of God's house. Would that we accept the call to imitate Jesus' example of doing God's will detailed in the First Reading, from Hebrews. And, as we do so, may we remember Jesus accompanies us on the journey to the Cross.

W E D **30** (#319) green
Weekday

The Lectionary for Mass

◆ FIRST READING: PSALM 110 provides the reference for the author of Hebrews when he speaks about Jesus sitting forever at God's right hand and awaiting his enemies as his footstool. God's law of forgiveness remains forever implanted on our hearts through Jesus' sacrifice. This is why the need for other sacrifices no longer exists. We worship in gratitude for the one offering through which Jesus made perfect those—including us—whom God makes holy.

◆ RESPONSORIAL PSALM 110: Again, Psalm 110 follows upon a First Reading from Hebrews which emphasizes Jesus' everlasting priesthood. We root our acclamation of Jesus as a priest forever in Melchizedek's blessing of Abram found in Genesis 14:18–20. May our repeated use of this psalm empower us to see anew our share in Christ's priesthood through Baptism.

◆ GOSPEL: Large crowds hungry to hear Jesus' message again surround him. Jesus teaches them about the Kingdom of God through the parable of the sower. We, perhaps, understand this parable all too well, for we know we do neither want to be like the seed that fell on rocky ground nor among thorns. We desire to fall on the path. We want to have ears to hear so that we might indeed bear fruit.

T H U **31** (#320) white
Memorial of St. John Bosco, Priest

The Lectionary for Mass

◆ FIRST READING: Jesus' sacrifice must compel us who believe to "love and good works." Our con-

fession is not just words about the One who forgave our sins by the sacrifice of his own Blood. No, it is much more than words. It gives us hope—hope in the promise of God in Christ. Jesus made our hearts clean through his sacrifice and the waters of Baptism have washed us clean. We must respond with sincerity and trust on our journey to God.

◆ RESPONSORIAL PSALM 24: Today's refrain emphasizes our desire to see God's face and connects with the words from Hebrews about our journey to God. Ours is the call to climb the Lord's mountain and stand in his presence. In faith, we encourage one another as the day dawns when we will come face to face with the Lord.

◆ GOSPEL: Will we hide our lamp under a bushel basket? Will we measure out to others from our lack or from our abundance? All depends on how we hear and understand Jesus' message about the Kingdom of God that he enacts in his very person and mission. The Gospel leaves us with the question about how much God will give to us.

The Roman Missal

The Collect for St. John Bosco is proper. The remaining prayers may be taken from the Common of Pastors: For One Pastor, or from the Common of Holy Men and Women: For Educators. Consider using the Eucharistic Prayer for Various Needs and Occasions IV.

Today's Saint

God gifted St. John Bosco (1815–1888) with the ability to read and interpret the signs of the times. Living during rapid industrialization and growing anticlericalism, he became very concerned about the emotional and spiritual livelihood of people, especially the plight of the young. He worked to provide positive and affirming environments, including

orphanages and oratories, where the young could learn and recognize their infinite potential. In the spirit of his favorite hero, St. Francis de Sales, he founded the Salesians, a religious congregation devoted to works of charity, with an emphasis on empowering young people to become strong pillars of faith in a culture of instability. His work among young men living in the slums proved to be a worthy endeavor.

February 2019
Month of the Passion of Our Lord

F R I **1** (#321) green
Weekday

The Lectionary for Mass

◆ FIRST READING: Followers of Jesus must take the long view of the journey. Persecution and suffering will meet us along the way, so the author of Hebrews tells us, and we must not let our confidence abate. We must not pull back and stand on the sidelines of faith. We must embrace endurance, and we have the ability to do so because Jesus fully embraced his own suffering, even to the point of death. In him, we will not perish, but will have life!

◆ RESPONSORIAL PSALM 37 reminds us of the reality of evil in the world and connects us with the First Reading's words about suffering, persecution, and the endurance of the faithful. As we pray the refrain, we acknowledge that the salvation of those who are just comes from the Lord. The Lord will bring justice to those of us who commit to him, trust in him, and take delight in him. We could not ask for more.

◆ GOSPEL: Jesus again speaks to the crowds about the Kingdom of God with nature parables. The Gospel begins with a general parable reflecting on the wonder of nature's harvest. Seed gets scattered and the land amazingly yields fruit that needs to be harvested. We learn in the second and more specific parable that the tiniest of seeds—the mustard seed—grows into the largest of plants and becomes a home for others. So it is with God's Kingdom. God plants seeds, they grow and are harvested. The Kingdom grows exponentially. God's home is a home large enough for all.

SAT 2 (#524) white
Feast of the Presentation of the Lord

About Today's Feast

Forty days after Christmas, we celebrate the Feast of the Presentation of the Lord, which recalls the event described in the Gospel according to Luke: "When the time came for their purification according to the law of Moses, they brought him up to the Lord (as it is written in the law of the Lord, 'Every firstborn male shall be designated as holy to the Lord')" (Luke 2:22). Joseph and Mary bring Jesus to the Temple, and while they are there, they meet two extraordinary people. First they meet Simeon, who, taking Jesus in his arms, recognizes him as the long-awaited Messiah. Not only that, Simeon knows that this Messiah has come not only to the Jewish people, but to all. He is "a light for revelation to the Gentiles" (Luke 2:32). There is a note of sorrow in this joyful encounter: Simeon prophesies over the child, telling Mary that Jesus will encounter great opposition, while her own heart is pierced by a sword. They also meet Anna, a widow, 84 years old, who prays and fasts in the Temple night and day, and who also recognizes who Jesus is, and begins to proclaim him: "At that moment she came, and began to praise God and to speak about the child to all who were looking for the redemption of Jerusalem" (Luke 2:38). Jesus is the light to the nations, and from the moment of his birth, people are drawn to his light. That is why on this Feast of the Presentation of the Lord, we carry lit candles, and the priest blesses the candles to be used in the celebration of the liturgy during the coming year. Because of this, today's Mass is often called Candlemas.

The Lectionary for Mass

◆ FIRST READING: The Lord will come to the Temple to refine and purify. The Lord will cleanse us and make us new. A messenger will prepare the way for the Lord. For Christians, Jesus is the Lord who comes into the Temple and whom Simeon and Anna recognize as the One who will redeem Israel. The Lord continues to come into our presence today and we are his messengers in the world continuously preparing the way for him.

◆ RESPONSORIAL PSALM 24: Multiple times Psalm 24 asks "Who is the king of glory?" and each time the psalmist responds, "the LORD!" We give pause today on the Feast of the Presentation of the Lord to wonder if we, too, can confidently respond with the same answer. Psalm 24 invites us to join with those in the past who sang this psalm as they welcomed the Ark of the Covenant into the Temple. May we welcome the Lord into our hearts and community.

◆ SECOND READING: In the context of today's feast, we draw out from these verses the fact that Jesus shares in our flesh and blood. He is fully human like us in all ways but sin. He endured suffering and experienced the ordinariness of human life in its fullness, and, because of this he can forgive our sins. We are all brothers and sisters in Christ.

◆ GOSPEL: The long form of the Gospel reading includes the experiences of both Simeon and Anna when Mary and Joseph presented the child Jesus in the Temple. We know Simeon's canticle as the *Nunc Dimittis*, which we sing at Compline. Simeon and Anna recognized in Jesus the hope for the people of Israel. On this feast, their example and that of Mary and Joseph, faithful Jews, give us pause to reflect on Jesus as our salvation and a light for revelation to the whole world.

The Roman Missal

Everything is proper to today's feast, so all texts and rubrics are found at February 2 in the Proper of Saints.

The Blessing of Candles and the Procession

The Missal calls for this Mass to begin with the blessing of candles and a procession, in one form or another. Two possibilities are given in the Missal: "The Procession" and "The Solemn Entrance."

◆ FIRST FORM: The Procession: All should gather in a place apart from the worship space where the procession will go to — for example, a smaller church, or perhaps a space in the parish hall, or perhaps even the gathering space of the church. The gathered faithful are to be already holding candles, so either the people bring candles with them or candles are handed to them as they gather. The priest, wearing white Mass vestments (although he may wear a cope at this point instead of a chasuble), and the ministers enter. There is no mention of a procession or of any singing, so the priest and the ministers just informally take their places. First, light everyone's candles and while this is done the antiphon suggested in the Missal (*Ecce Dominus noster* — "Behold, our Lord will come with power, to enlighten the eyes of his servants, alleluia") or some other appropriate song is sung. If another song or chant is used, the words should speak of the imagery of light.

After the candles are lit and the singing is concluded, the priest begins with the Sign of the Cross and one of the usual forms of the Greeting for Mass. Then he gives an introductory address; he may use the exact words as provided in the Missal at #4 for the Feast of the Presentation of the Lord, or he may use similar words. The address as given in the Missal notes the passing of forty days since the celebration of the Nativity and recalls how "Today is the blessed day / when Jesus was presented in the Temple by Mary and Joseph." It goes on to speak of the meaning of this feast as Jesus "coming to meet his believing people" and how Simeon and Anna, enlightened by the Holy Spirit, recognized him. It ends with the exhortation that we should "proceed to the house of God to encounter Christ," particularly as we shall recognize him in the breaking of bread until he comes again. Whether the priest uses the exact words in the Missal or similar words, the point of the address is to encourage the faithful "to celebrate the rite of this feast day actively and consciously."

After the address, the priest extends his hands and blesses the candles using the exact words of one of the two prayers of blessing given at #5 in the Missal (Feast of the Presentation of the Lord). In the first prayer, which specifically recalls Simeon and which refers to "the Light for revelation to the Gentiles," the priest makes the gesture of blessing with the Sign of the Cross where indicated; there is no such gesture in the second prayer, which speaks more generally about light and God's glory.

Next the priest sprinkles the candles with holy water without saying anything. Then he puts incense into the thurible for the procession, receives his lighted candle from the deacon or another minister, and the procession begins with the words of invitation from the Missal, given by the deacon, or, if there is no deacon, by the priest himself.

With everyone carrying lighted candles, the procession, in the usual order (that is, thurifer, crossbearer, candlebearers, and so on), moves into the worship space while an appropriate antiphon or song is sung. This Missal offers two suggestions for antiphons: "A light for revelation to the Gentiles and the glory of your people Israel" or "For my eyes have seen your salvation, which you have prepared in the sight of all the peoples." The Latin text for the first option is provided in the Missal.

When the priest arrives at the altar in the church, he venerates it and incenses it, if incense is being used. He then goes to the chair where he changes from the cope into the chasuble, if he wore a cope for the procession. The Gloria is then sung, after which the priest prays the Collect and Mass continues as usual.

◆ SECOND FORM: The Solemn Entrance: When the procession as described above is not going to take place, then the assembly gathers in the church as they usually do, holding candles. The priest, along with the ministers and a representative group of the faithful, goes to a place in the church that is visible to the rest of the assembly. They can be at the doors of the church or even somewhere inside the church itself. Notice that it is presumed that more than just the priest and ministers will gather and move in procession; a certain number of the faithful are expected to participate in this. The priest wears white Mass vestments; no mention is made of using a cope in this form of the entrance.

The priest and the others arrive at the place for the blessing of candles, without any music or formal procession. Once they are in place, everyone's candles are lit, with an antiphon or song being sung, as described above (this may take a little bit of thinking through ahead of time, so that it is not done haphazardly; ushers can be of assistance here). Once everyone's candles are lit, the priest begins in the same way as in the first form above, with the Sign of the Cross, Greeting, introductory address, and blessing of candles and sprinkling, followed by the procession, accompanied by singing; he uses the same texts as designated for the first form of procession. As in the first form, the priest incenses the altar when arriving there, if incense is being used, and then he goes to the chair, at which point the Gloria is sung and Mass continues in the usual manner.

◆ AT THE MASS: The Collect makes a connection between Christ's being presented "on this day in the Temple / in the substance of our flesh" and the request that, by God's grace, "we may be presented to you with minds made pure."

The Prayer over the Offerings draws a parallel between the offering of the Son, offered as the Lamb without blemish for the life of the world, and the offering we make now with exultation, asking that our offering here and now be pleasing to God, as was the offering of the Son.

The Preface, found right along with the other texts for this Mass in the Proper of Saints, is a brief one, succinctly stating that the "coeternal Son was presented on this day in the Temple / and revealed by the Spirit / as the glory of Israel and the Light of the nations." Because of this, "we, too, go forth, rejoicing to encounter your Salvation." This going forth to encounter salvation occurs on many levels: certainly in the journey of our life, but also as we continue forth with the offering of this sacrifice, where we will encounter Christ in the salvific power of the Paschal Mystery made present in the Church's anamnesis of the Eucharistic Prayer and in Christ's Real Presence in the Eucharist. This would be a good occasion to chant the introductory dialogue and Preface, in order to highlight the festivity of this liturgy.

Simeon is mentioned again, this time in the Prayer after Communion, as we pray that just as his expectation was fulfilled "that he would not see death / until he had been privileged to welcome the Christ," so too may we meet the Lord in the gift of eternal life.

Other Ideas

On the Feast of the Presentation of the Lord, we also observe the World Day for Consecrated Life. The Gospel today tells the story of Mary and Joseph taking Jesus to the Temple "to present him to the Lord." Simeon and Anna recognize in this little child the Savior whom they have awaited with eager expectation. It's the perfect feast to take some time to give thanks to God for the gift of consecrated life—for all the men and women who have dedicated their lives to the Lord and to service in his Church. Men and women religious throughout the world renew their commitment to the consecrated life this day. It's also a time to encourage young men and women to consider whether God might be calling them to this mode of life. "What would become of the world if there were no religious?" St. Teresa of Avila once asked. "This is a question which brings us to give unceasing thanks to the Lord, who by this singular gift of the Spirit continues to enliven and sustain the Church in its demanding journey through this world" (Pope John Paul II, Message for the First World Day for Consecrated Life, 1997).

3 (#72C) green
Fourth Sunday in Ordinary Time

The Lectionary for Mass

◆ FIRST READING: A sixth- and seventh-century prophet of Judah, Jeremiah detested the idolatry to which the people and their leaders would fall victim. In today's verses Jeremiah recounts how the Word of the Lord came to him and called him to be a prophet. Even before he was formed in the womb, the Lord chose him for this important role. Jeremiah would have to stand up to Judah's corrupt kings, princes, priests, and people. They would fight against Jeremiah and try to discredit the Word of the Lord he spoke, but the Lord would stand by him and deliver him.

◆ RESPONSORIAL PSALM 71: Like many laments in the Psalter, Psalm 71 recounts the struggles the psalmist experienced throughout his life, but in the end turns to convey hope in the Lord. The hope and confidence of the psalmist in the face of affliction links to Jeremiah's perseverance in his prophetic call despite the push back he receives. We, too, sing of the Lord's salvation in the refrain taken from the latter half of the psalm.

◆ SECOND READING: The longer form is a continuous reading from last Sunday and serves as a preface to Paul's beautiful and well-known words about love. The shorter form of the reading begins with the description of what love is and is not. The triad of faith, hope, and love, which concludes the reading, is part of the early history of Christian communities and appears, for example, in 1 Thessalonians 1:3. All three will last, but love is the greatest. Would that the Corinthians bond together in love modeled on Christ's love for them, and we do the same in our communities of faith today.

◆ GOSPEL: The Gospel reading opens with a repetition of the closing verse from last Sunday, in which Jesus announces the fulfillment of the passage he read from Isaiah to the people in Nazareth's synagogue. People already begin to wonder about his identity, but their amazement at his "gracious words" quickly turns into fury as Jesus draws the connection between himself and the prophets Elijah and Elisha. Perhaps the people were not ready for Jesus' prophetic words and the extension of his ministry to the Gentiles. Prophets are not accepted in their place of origin, a reality of which Jesus is well aware.

The Roman Missal

The simple Collect echoes the words of Christ to the scribe who asked him which Commandment was most important: we are to "honor [God] with all our mind, / and love everyone in truth of heart." In the Prayer over the Offerings, we ask God to transform the "offerings of our service" and make them "the Sacrament of our redemption." In the Prayer after Communion, we pray that the "redeeming gifts" we receive may help the faith to spread. The sacrifice is offered not just for our own salvation, but for that of the whole world. Consider using Eucharistic Prayer III. The Gloria and the Creed are sung or said today.

Other Ideas

When February 3 falls on Sunday, the optional Memorial of St. Blaise is not observed. However, the blessing of throats, which is associated with the patronage of the saint, may be given at the Sunday liturgies. The formula of the blessing is found in the *Book of Blessings* (chapter 51). It may be given after the Prayer of the Faithful. Lay ministers and deacons and lay ministers may assist the priest. However, for pastoral reasons it may be given as a general blessing over all.

Some parishes bless and distribute candles to each household on the Feast of the Presentation. Parishioners can be invited to bring their own candles to be blessed. Lighting the candle during family prayer is a good way to center the attention and thoughts of those who gather to prayer.

Today is also the National Day of Prayer for the African American Family. On the first Sunday of February, which is Black History Month, the United States Conference of Catholic Bishops invites us to observe a National Day of Prayer for the African American Family. This observance was instituted by Father James Goode, OFM, in 1989, as an opportunity to give thanks for our families, and to entrust every family to the loving care of Jesus.

MON 4 (#323) green
Weekday

The Lectionary for Mass

◆ FIRST READING: Our faith has a long history in the kings and prophets who came before Jesus. They, too, endured suffering and persecution. Yet, they remained faithful. Some families even knew the resurrection of their dead. The kings and prophets, however, did not fulfill God's promise of someone who would perfect us. By their faith and witness, they prepared the way for

Jesus. By our faith and witness, we lead others to see their salvation in Jesus.

◆ RESPONSORIAL PSALM 31 is a lament in which the psalmist grieves because of the suffering he experiences. As with many laments, the psalmist's trust and confidence in the Lord remain palpable. The Lord's goodness stays in the forefront of his mind for the Lord has touched him personally with his mercy. Despite his distress, he will continue to love the Lord and take comfort in him. Will we?

◆ GOSPEL: Immediately upon arriving in the territory of the Gerasenes, known to be pagan territory, a man with an unclean spirit greets Jesus and his disciples. Shackles and chains, and even tombs could no longer hold this man down. Jesus releases the evil spirit from within him and exorcises the evil spirits from throughout the people of the area and sends them into the herd of swine. New life comes to the man who wishes to remain with Jesus, and who would not want to do so? Jesus, however, sends him out to witness to his own family about the Lord's merciful deed. The man did not wait to announce God's glory until he arrived at his home, but began proclaiming it en route.

TUE 5 (#324) red
Memorial of St. Agatha, Virgin and Martyr

The Lectionary for Mass

◆ FIRST READING: We persevere in faith together. We run the race together. How do we do this? We have tunnel vision, keeping our eyes fixed on Jesus who himself endured the Cross for us. We know we struggle with sin, and at times we do not opt for the best choice—the choice of justice, love, and peace. Yet we know Jesus overcame our sin on the Cross, shedding his own Blood for us.

◆ RESPONSORIAL PSALM 22: Today's Responsorial Psalm comes from the latter part of Psalm 22, a psalm also sung on Palm Sunday. In this lament, we see how the psalmist continues to trust that his soul will live in the Lord. We join our voices in praise to the Lord, for we believe when we remain in the race, we will live. The Lord's justice will prevail.

◆ GOSPEL: Two healing stories in one Gospel mark today's Good News! Sandwiched between the beginning and end of the story of Jesus' healing of Jairus' daughter, is the healing of the woman who suffered with hemorrhages for twelve years. She endured the race, and now she reaches out in confidence to touch Jesus clothes. Her faith in Jesus' healing power bears fruit as Jesus heals her and makes her whole. The twelve-year-old daughter of the synagogue official rises on Jesus' command. New life is also her gift. Whether we run the race twelve years or more, or even less, Jesus' healing power extends to us.

The Roman Missal

The Mass text that is proper for today is the Collect, and it is found in the Proper of Saints at February 5. The prayer highlights St. Agatha's courage in martyrdom and her chastity. The Prayer over the Offerings and the Prayer after Communion will come either from the Common of Martyrs: For a Virgin Martyr, or from the Common of Virgins: For One Virgin. For the Preface, one of the two Prefaces of Holy Martyrs is a good choice. Use Eucharistic Prayer I since St. Agatha is included in the Canon.

Today's Saint

St. Agatha was born in Sicily, probably around the year 231, and is one of the women mentioned by name in Eucharistic Prayer I. According to legend, she was the daughter of a prominent family and was very beautiful. The Roman senator Quintianus wished to marry her, but when Agatha spurned him, he had her put in a brothel. In spite of this, Agatha held to her Christian faith. Quintianus then had her tortured by having her breasts cut off. She eventually died in prison in 253. Because her breasts were cut off as part of her torture, she is considered the patron saint of breast cancer patients.

WED 6 — (#325) red
Memorial of St. Paul Miki and Companions, Martyrs

The Lectionary for Mass

◆ FIRST READING: The author of Hebrews encourages us to endure all the difficulties we face as part of the *discipline* of following the Lord. We are God's sons and daughters and God is our Father. Parents do discipline their children, which is why God disciplines us. The two verses from Proverbs quoted within the passage from Hebrews draw our attention to this, but also remind us how God lovingly cares for those he disciplines.

◆ RESPONSORIAL PSALM 103: God only wants the best for his sons and daughters. Psalm 103 prompts us to remember God's everlasting kindness. God's compassion and justice for us who are his sons and daughters, and the children who will remain faithful to the covenant after us, will endure forever.

◆ GOSPEL: His wisdom and mighty deeds caused those in the synagogue on that Sabbath day to wonder about the identity of the one they thought to be the son of Mary and the brother of James, Joseph, Judas, and Simon. They thought his sisters were among them in the synagogue. Dismay filled everyone present. Belief in who Jesus truly was did not exist among them in that place, at that time. Amazement filled Jesus, yet he was also pragmatic, noting that a prophet will find honor everywhere but in his home and among his own people.

The Roman Missal

The Collect, which is proper for today, is found in the Proper of Saints at February 6. The prayer refers to God as "the strength of all the Saints," and asks that through the intercession of St. Paul Miki and companions, "we may hold with courage even until death / to the faith that we profess," just as they did. The Prayer over the Offerings and the Prayer after Communion are taken from the Common of Martyrs: For Several Martyrs. Use one of the two Prefaces of Holy Martyrs. Consider using Eucharistic Prayer II.

Today's Saints

St. Paul Miki (c. 1562–1597), a Jesuit priest, was one of the twenty-six martyrs of Japan. The local governor felt threatened by the growing influence of the Jesuits and had members of the Christian community arrested and thrown in jail. They were forced to walk six hundred miles from Kyoto to Nagasaki as a deterrent to other Christians, but they sang the Te Deum as they went. At Nagasaki, they were crucified. When Christian missionaries returned to Japan in the nineteenth century, they found that a secret Christian community had survived by transmitting the beliefs and prayers from generation to generation.

THU 7 — (#326) green
Weekday

The Lectionary for Mass

◆ FIRST READING: The new covenant in Christ allows Christians to approach the heavenly Jerusalem, God's city, without fear and trepidation. Through Jesus, who mediates the new covenant through his sacrifice on the Cross, we know the depth of God's love and mercy for his children. What unbounded mercy this is that welcomes us into communion with God and allows us to directly approach him with confidence instead of worry about the judgment we will face.

◆ RESPONSORIAL PSALM 48 offers praise to the holy city of Jerusalem, God's dwelling place. This provides a direct link to the First Reading, from Hebrews, in which we are reminded how we are part of the assembly who journeys toward the lasting home of God. How great is the dwelling place filled with mercy and justice. How wondrous it is that we have the opportunity to take the journey to God's home.

◆ GOSPEL: Jesus sent the Twelve out in six pairs, two disciples each. One pair of shoes and one tunic was all they had with them. Yet they had so much more than their meager material possessions. They had the power of life given them by Jesus. Unclean spirits would perish and meet death. Healing would replace sickness and disease. Sin would come to know the power of repentance and forgiveness. They would preach the message of life in the Kingdom of God, and should people not receive the Good News, they would follow Jesus' example and continue the journey.

FRI 8 — (#327) green
Weekday

Optional Memorials of St. Jerome Emiliani / white; St. Josephine Bakhita, Virgin / white

The Lectionary for Mass

◆ FIRST READING: We hear instructions for how we are to live as followers of Jesus Christ. In following the instructions presented, we imitate him who is, who was, and who ever shall be. Our love for each other is the center of our relationships. Hospitality and care for prisoners, the honor we give to Marriage, and the way we do not make money the center of our lives, show how we imitate those who have gone before us in faith and Jesus Christ, himself.

◆ RESPONSORIAL PSALM 27 helps us affirm that the Lord is our light and salvation. The Lord is the One whom we seek as we journey forward. We need not fear, even when we face difficulties or others question us for our faith. The Lord will always help us. This is why the author of Hebrews quoted Psalm 27 in the First Reading, for imitating Christ is not always easy, but in faith we can and will endure as Christ did.

◆ GOSPEL: Herod is perplexed and confused. He thought he had John the Baptist beheaded, and now John appears to be raised in Jesus. This not being the case, Herod fulfills the wish of Herodias' daughter to have the head of John on a platter. John's disciples remain faithful to the end, retrieving his body and laying it in a tomb, a precursor to how Joseph of Arimathea will care for Jesus' body after the Crucifixion.

Today's Saints

St. Jerome was born into a wealthy family, and before being led to study for the priesthood he was a soldier in Venice. As a priest, Jerome was greatly devoted to helping the poor and the disadvantaged. He founded hospitals, orphanages, and an order of priests whose apostolate it was to care for the orphans.

St. Josephine was born in Sudan and at the age of nine was taken into slavery. Bought by an Italian diplomat, she was taken to Italy where she converted to Christianity at the age of 25. Three years later, after having been freed from slavery, she joined the Institute of the Canossian Daughters of Charity.

SAT 9 (#328) green
Weekday

Optional Memorial of the Blessed Virgin Mary / white

The Lectionary for Mass

◆ FIRST READING: We hear instructions to do good and to share our possessions with others. Obedience to our leaders should mark our relationships with those who guide us in faith. A sacrifice of praise coming from our lips, which confess Jesus as Lord, stands as our offering of thanks to God. We pray in the words of the author of Hebrews that God accompany us as we seek to do his will.

◆ RESPONSORIAL PSALM 23: The beautiful imagery of Psalm 23 helps us to ponder how God is present as we live as faithful disciples. God provides green pastures upon which we can graze and fresh waters for us to quench our thirst. God grants protection from harm when we experience despair and courage to take the next step in finding our way. Table provisions together with goodness and love God offers us. The Lord is our shepherd.

◆ GOSPEL: The Twelve return from mission to give report to Jesus. Weary from their travels and the work they accomplished, Jesus invites them to go away to a deserted place and rest. If we read the text closely, we will notice Jesus retreats with the Apostles. They would know their rest is in him. They will know, too, that the work of the Kingdom never ceases as large crowds await them as they disembark. Jesus does not ask the Apostles to respond, but rather he exudes compassion toward those in need.

☀ 10 (#75C) green
Fifth Sunday in Ordinary Time

The Lectionary for Mass

◆ FIRST READING: Isaiah's prophetic call is dramatic theatre! Angels acclaim the Lord's glory so intensely that the door to Isaiah's house shakes, and smoke enters. He thinks death will come to him because he is not without sin. But the opposite is the case. One of the seraphim approaches Isaiah with an ember from the altar, a sign of the Lord's offer of forgiveness. "Whom shall I send?" is the Lord question to Isaiah and the Lord's question to us on this Fifth Sunday in Ordinary Time. Will we present ourselves for mission once again?

◆ RESPONSORIAL PSALM 138: In the words of Psalm 138, a hymn of thanksgiving, we sing our praise and thanks to the Lord for all he has done for us. The Lord answers our call. The Lord's fidelity to his promises is beyond compare. The reference to angels in the refrain from verse 1c provides a direct connection the seraphim in the First Reading. May our song of gratitude arise from our assemblies this day in the presence of the angels.

◆ SECOND READING: Paul's testimony begins with a statement of the kerygma that he received. All that Paul has handed on to the Corinthians was the faith others gave to him: Christ died, was buried, rose from the dead, and appeared to many after his Resurrection. In humility, Paul notes that the Risen Christ appeared to him last of all for he had persecuted Christians. Grace made Paul the preacher of the Gospel to the Corinthians. Grace will do the same for the Corinthians—and for us as we proclaim and live the Gospel. There are longer and shorter forms of the reading.

◆ GOSPEL: Simon struggles to trust that any catch will come to the fishermen should they follow Jesus' command to lower their nets. They had worked hard all day, but caught nothing. Much to their surprise an abundant supply of fish filled their nets to the point of tearing and the boat of sinking. Simon's humble reply mirrors Isaiah's as he confesses his sinfulness. Instead of leaving him as Simon requested, Jesus turns the tables and invites Simon to fish for followers with him. Jesus will never depart from us, but will only draw closer.

The Roman Missal

The Mass texts for today are found in the "Ordinary Time" section of the Proper of Time. The Gloria and the Creed are sung or said today. The Collect asks that the Lord will keep us safe as we rely "solely on the help of heavenly grace." The Prayer over the Offerings prays for the transformation of the created realities we offer, that is, bread and wine, so that just as they are material sustenance for us, so too may they become "the Sacrament of eternal life." The Prayer after Communion highlights the unity of the faithful that is to be the result of their participation in the Eucharist. Being united in the one Body of Christ through "the one Bread and the one Chalice" (a presumption that the chalice is offered to the assembly at all Masses?) is the way that we "joyfully bear fruit / for the salvation of the world." Any one of the eight

Prefaces of the Sundays in Ordinary Time may be selected for today. Consider using the Eucharistic Prayer for Reconciliation I.

Other Ideas

Tomorrow, February 11, is the World Day of the Sick. Pope John Paul II gave this designation to coincide with the optional Memorial of Our Lady of Lourdes. Consider adding to the Universal Prayer petitions for those who are sick, both in the parish and in the world. Encourage families to make an extra effort to visit family members who are sick on this day. Be sure to take time to pray with them and take along a parish bulletin. If the parish celebrates the Sacrament of the Anointing of the Sick at the liturgies this weekend, volunteer to assist. Ask if there is a need to provide transportation to and from church for those who have mobility challenges; it's a great way to meet other parishioners and to do a good deed.

MON 11 (#329) green
Weekday

Optional Memorial of Our Lady of Lourdes / white

The Lectionary for Mass

◆ FIRST READING: Light, sky, earth and seas, vegetation, sun and moon—all these are gifts of the first four days of creation. The opening chapter of Genesis provides us with a creation account that emphasizes the goodness of God's creation. The rhythms of evening and morning become clear to us. We rest in the beauty of God's creation and wait to hear our charge to be stewards of all God gives us.

◆ RESPONSORIAL PSALM 104 praises God for the wonders of his creation and fittingly serves as a response to the passage from Genesis. The references in today's verses to life-giving springs of water directly link to the third day of cre-

ation. Our souls bless the Lord for the beauty of creation which surrounds us from morning to evening each day.

◆ GOSPEL: Jesus' reputation has spread so much that people immediately recognize him. They know he comes to offer healing to the sick, so they go to the countryside to retrieve the sick and bring them to Jesus. The Gospel text does not tell us if the people only retrieved their friends and neighbors, which leads us to think that they brought all who were sick, even those they did not know. Those who had faith to touch even the tassel on Jesus' cloak experienced healing. May their faith be ours this day.

About Today's Optional Memorial

It was on this day in 1858 that the fourteen-year-old Bernadette Soubirous, a peasant girl in Lourdes, saw a lady in a grotto near the river Gave, at the foot of the Pyrenees Mountains in France. Over the next several months, Bernadette encountered the Lady many times. During one of these apparitions, the Lady directed Bernadette to drink from the fountain. But there was no fountain there—only the river. At the Lady's command, Bernadette began to dig in the ground near the grotto, and a spring of water began to flow. Immediately, numerous miraculous healings took place for those who bathed in or drank the water of the spring. Only later did the Lady reveal to Bernadette who she was: "I am the Immaculate Conception." Today, Lourdes is one of the most popular pilgrimage places in the world. Every year, hundreds of thousands of people make the pilgrimage to the little town, to drink of the water and to feel close to the Virgin and to her Son, Jesus Christ, healer of body and soul (see the Lourdes website: https://en.lourdes-france.org/).

T U E 12 (#330) green Weekday

The Lectionary for Mass

◆ FIRST READING: We claim again the wonder of the fifth, sixth, and seventh days of creation for our faith. Living creatures in the water, and birds in the sky, coupled with their ability to reproduce, belong to God's good acts of creation on day five. Day six brings the creation of seed-bearing plants and mammals, including the human being—created by God, male and female in his own image. Goodness surrounds us in abundance. There exists so much goodness in the heavens and earth we can hardly take it all in. We rest with God on the holy seventh day. We breathe in God's creation.

◆ RESPONSORIAL PSALM 8: Like Psalm 104, today's psalm announces the beauty of God's creation. We sing these verses with the same humility in which the psalmist penned them as he reflected on the place of the human person in relation to the magnificence of creation. May we take pause to reflect on the amazing gift God has given us—in the heavens we look up to and on the earth, on which we accept the privilege to step gently.

◆ GOSPEL: What is the relationship between human tradition and God's commandment? Jesus teaches the Pharisees how to align this relationship aright after they ask him why his disciples do not follow traditional purity laws. Lip service will never suffice for a disciple of Jesus, but rather hearts of love attuned to God's matter most. Disciples hear and follow the Word of God present and active in Jesus Christ. No room exists for the hypocrisy of lip service in living God's word.

W E D 13 (#331) green Weekday

The Lectionary for Mass

◆ FIRST READING: Our origin is in the earth's clay and God's breath, so the second creation story in Genesis tells us. God's creative, divine hand forms us. God places the first human persons in the Garden of Eden, the garden of life, to tend the garden and to feast on its abundance. One boundary only does God give: do not eat of the tree of knowledge of good and evil. Our story, like that of the first human persons, is rooted in whether we will choose life or death. Each day, each moment, we live in God's earthly paradise, we must choose.

◆ RESPONSORIAL PSALM 104: Today's verses connect with the First Reading from Genesis in their focus on the creation of human beings and the food and breath God provides them. Without breath, we die. With breath, we participate in God's creative action in the world. For this opportunity we bless the Lord in the words of the psalm refrain.

◆ GOSPEL: What comes into us from the outside world—even its negativity, pollution, and evil—cannot harm us. Only what comes out from within us causes harm. In this short parable, Jesus directs us to reflect on the condition of our hearts. Are they filled with the vices he names such as greed and malice and deceit? Are they filled with the healing love and compassion he has graciously offered to others? The disciples witnessed this love. We heard it proclaimed. Will we align our hearts with his?

T H U 14 (#332) white Memorial of Sts. Cyril, Monk, and Methodius, Bishop

The Liturgy of the Word

◆ FIRST READING: Man and woman share a common humanity and a common origin in God. They are partners in God's creative work in the world. In our humanity, there is no shame—only the divine image and likeness. Domination and power over each other does not exist. Rather, together they love all that God gives and serve as faithful stewards of creation, tending to the well-being of all living creatures he has made.

◆ RESPONSORIAL PSALM 128: What goodness God provides us! How blessed are we indeed! Our journey of faith leads us to walk in God's ways and to bear fruit in our homes and around our tables. The psalm reminds us twice that those who "fear the LORD" are blessed. Fear does not mean that we are to be anxious or afraid of the Lord, but rather that we stand in awe of the Lord and the life the Lord gives us and respond in praise and action accordingly.

◆ GOSPEL: Just as Jesus tried to get away on a boat with his disciples for some respite, he enters a house in the district of Tyre and hopes that no one will notice. But a Greek Syrophoenician woman begs Jesus to heal her daughter possessed by a demon. The woman fell at Jesus' feet. Her posture not only reveals how desperate she is, but also acknowledges her trust and faith in Jesus. On the faith of this Gentile woman, Jesus heals her daughter. Life seems always to be Jesus' choice.

The Roman Missal

All the texts for this Mass are proper for this day, and they are found in the Proper of Saints at February 14. The Collect makes explicit reference to Sts. Cyril's and Methodius' mission to the Slavic peoples. The Prayer over the Offerings speaks of the transformation that we pray will occur as a result of entering into the Sacrifice: "grant that these gifts may become the sign of a new humanity, / reconciled to you in loving charity." It's a reminder that at the heart of all Christian missionary work is the belief that the sharing in the life of Christ makes all things new, and that one of the fruits of living in Christ's love is reconciliation. The Prayer after Communion refers to the universality of the Eucharist: God is the "Father of all nations," the one who makes us "sharers in the one Bread and the one Spirit." As a result of our one sharing in the Eucharist, we pray that "the multitude of your children, / persevering in the same faith, / may be united in building up the Kingdom of justice and peace." No rubric assigns a particular Preface for this Mass; since the two saints are honored together and one is a monk while the other one is a bishop, one of the two general Prefaces of Saints would probably be the best choice. Consider using Eucharistic Prayer II.

Today's Saints

Sts. Cyril (827–869) and Methodius (815–884) were brothers born in Thessalonica (Greece), in the ninth century and are known as the "apostles to the Slavs." Cyril was a scholar and linguist, and Methodius was a monk. As part of their work, they translated some of the Scriptures into Old Slavonic and devised a liturgy in that language. Shortly before his death, Cyril became a monk; Methodius continued the mission alone and later was made an archbishop.

F R I 15 (#333) green Weekday

The Lectionary for Mass

◆ First Reading: The serpent connives and deceives. The woman and the man are both complicit in choosing evil. Passing the blame around for the evil choice of disobedience serves no purpose. Rather, we learn from the progression of the story of humanity's relationship with God, that we must own our shame when we choose death over life. This is not the choice God desires us to make, but in our humanity, sometimes we do not make the best choice.

◆ Responsorial Psalm 32: The Lord does not intend our confession of sin to induce guilt. In our confession we recognize we have chosen death, not life, and humbly seek God's forgiveness and mercy. This penitential psalm leads us to see how blessed we are when God forgives our sins. God is always our shelter. God is always our protection from distress. In the words of the psalmist, we acknowledge the joy that is ours when the Lord delivers us.

◆ Gospel: Jesus moves on in his journey through Sidon to the district of the Decapolis where he encounters a deaf man with a speech impediment. In a very human, personal, and intimate encounter, Jesus, with his own touch and spit, heals the man. Again, Jesus' multiple orders to the man to remain silent about the healing do no good. Who could keep quiet about this life that comes from heaven?

S A T 16 (#334) green Weekday

Optional Memorial of the Blessed Virgin Mary / white

The Lectionary for Mass

◆ First Reading: Relationships will never again be ideal. We have the proclivity to sin, and because of the choices of the first humans to disobey God, a distance exists in our relationship with God. Ours is now the work on earth to grow in love for God and others. In eternity, God will restore our relationships. Christians believe this happens through the saving work of Jesus Christ.

◆ Responsorial Psalm 90: The Lord is our refuge. Throughout the saving history of humankind, God protects his people, even when they stray from him. The psalmist recognizes this and acclaims the newness that comes into our lives each time God calls us back to him. We pray that God continue to teach us how to live in right relationship with him and that we might know divine wisdom.

◆ Gospel: With only seven loaves and a few fish, Jesus feeds the large crowd of about four thousand that had followed him for three days. It was such an abundant feast that there were even leftovers. Never shall God's people go hungry on the journey of faith. And on this lengthy journey we will continually learn that our true satisfaction lies in God alone.

☀ 17 (#78C) green Sixth Sunday in Ordinary Time

The Lectionary for Mass

◆ First Reading: Jeremiah speaks the Lord's words about who is cursed and who is blessed. The nature images of a barren bush and a tree rooted near water describe the two types of people. The bush bears no fruit, and the tree is eternally green, even during times of drought. Where one's heart resides makes the difference. May our heart be in the Lord and our strength be in him.

◆ RESPONSORIAL PSALM 1: The psalm includes the imagery of the tree planted beside running water as found in the passage from Isaiah and contrasts the yield of this tree with the wicked, whom the wind blows away like chaff. The psalmist's words encourage us to follow the law of the Lord rather than take counsel with the wicked. Why? Because the blessed are those who place their hope in the Lord.

◆ THE SECOND READING comes from the climactic chapter of 1 Corinthians, chapter 15, in which Paul responds to those who do not believe in the resurrection of the dead. With a teacher-like conditional statement Paul simply states that if there is no resurrection of the dead, then Christ himself has not been raised. If Christ has not been raised, then the dead have perished. Let us place our hope in Christ, whose Resurrection is the hope of our own resurrection.

◆ GOSPEL: Today we begin to proclaim the Gospel reading from Jesus' Sermon on the Plain in Luke 6. Both Jesus' disciples and a large crowd gather to hear him teach, but in Luke it seems that Jesus directs the Beatitudes most immediately towards his disciples, raising his eyes toward them before he begins stating blessings and woes. Today he teaches us the Beatitudes, and we have the opportunity to hear them anew, connecting them to our earthly life of discipleship.

The Roman Missal

The Gloria and the Creed are sung or said today. The Collect asks that our lives "may be so fashioned by your grace / as to become a dwelling pleasing to you." The Prayer over the Offerings reiterates that such transformation should be the heart of the oblation we make; as we make our offering at Mass in union with Christ's. In the Prayer after Communion we pray that,

"having fed upon these heavenly delights" of the Eucharist, "we may always / long for that food by which we truly live. Consider using Eucharistic Prayer II.

Other Ideas

The Gospel account for today gives us Luke's version of the Beatitudes. Unlike the eight beatitudes found in Matthew, Luke lists only four. At religious education classes, ask the children to list other actions that might be considered "Blessed." This could also be a good exercise for parents with children at home. If the parish has a bulletin board in the gathering area some of the newly created Beatitudes could be placed there. Invite the children who have composed them to draw a picture that depicts their Beatitude. The Beatitudes offer a good source of reflection on our discipleship.

M O N 18 (#335) green
Weekday

The Lectionary for Mass

◆ FIRST READING: Jealousy gets the best of Cain as he responds with violence to the favor the Lord showed Abel in response to his offering of one of the firstborn of his flock. Before Cain acts out in violence, the Lord tries to reason with him, asking him to do well lest evil make its way into his house. Cain chooses against obeying the Lord's advice and chooses instead to murder his brother. Even in the face of death, the Lord gifts the first human persons with more children. Life triumphs anew.

◆ RESPONSORIAL PSALM 50 invites us to offer God a "sacrifice of praise," as Abel did in the First Reading by choosing the first offspring of his flock. In the psalm, God asks why the people say one thing and do another. How often do we profess God while our actions contradict his word. God will

correct us and lead us to right action should we choose to follow.

◆ GOSPEL: The Pharisees neither understand Jesus nor his mission as they ask him for a sign from heaven. Frustrated with their desire for a sign, Jesus sighs a deeply human sigh, tells them no sign will be given, and immediately departs to the other shore of the Sea of Galilee. He leaves the Pharisees to ponder what they have asked of him. Do they not see who is before them and God's power present and active in him?

T U E 19 (#336) green
Weekday

The Lectionary for Mass

◆ FIRST READING: Grief so overtakes the Lord because of the evil choices human persons have made that he regrets having created them. The Lord's words communicate his desire to destroy human persons and the other living creatures he made. Yet all is not lost, for the Lord approves of Noah and commissions him to build and populate an ark. In the story of the flood, we experience a story of God rebuilding and blessing our relationship with him.

◆ RESPONSORIAL PSALM 29: The psalmist's words invite us to acclaim the Lord with the glory due the divine name. The references to the power of the Lord's voice over the water prompts us to remember that despite the flood and the many times the Israelites faced off with their enemies, the Lord will bring victory to his people. Sin stands no chance to come out victorious over the Lord—the King whose throne is above the flood.

◆ GOSPEL: The disciples think Jesus orders them to watch out for the Pharisees' leaven because the Pharisees have no bread. How the disciples misunderstand Jesus again! Their misunderstanding causes Jesus to remind them how, with only a five loaves he fed five thousand and with only seven loaves he fed four thousand. It is not that the Pharisees go hungry, but that they do not hear and understand the message of the Kingdom of God. They refuse to have faith in Jesus and follow him.

W E D **20** (#337) green
Weekday

The Lectionary for Mass

◆ FIRST READING: The reference to Noah opening the hatch of the ark and sending out a raven after forty (plus) days at sea in the flood points us to the fact that the Church's forty-day penitential season of Lent arrives in only a few weeks. Noah patiently waits to see if the flood waters have receded, sending a raven out once and a dove out three times within that span of time. The second time the dove returns with an olive branch—a symbol of peace—and the third time the dove does not return. God covenants with Moses that the earth and its people will never know doom again. Despite human persons choosing sin, God will continue to draw us back again and again.

◆ RESPONSORIAL PSALM 116: Noah offered a sacrifice of praise to God for all God had done to save his people and his creation. In the psalm refrain, we acknowledge our own willingness to offer the Lord a sacrifice of praise for everything the Lord does in our lives and in creation. We make this vow to the Lord as the psalmist did in times past to thank the Lord for rescuing him from danger.

◆ GOSPEL: He exorcises demons. He heals the sick. He makes the deaf hear and the mute speak. Still there is more to come. People now lead a blind man to Jesus with hopes that Jesus can help him to see. With a personal and organic gesture in which he places spittle on the blind man's eyes, Jesus enables him to see a blurred vision of people looking like trees. With a second, personal touch of the man's eyes, Jesus clarifies his vision and fully restores his sight. Like others whom he healed before, Jesus sends this man home ordering him not to stop in the village. The evangelist Mark leaves it to us to surmise what the man did. Do you think he publicized Jesus' name as others did, or kept his new vision to himself?

T H U **21** (#338) green
Weekday

Optional Memorial of St. Peter Damian, Bishop and Doctor of the Church / white

The Lectionary for Mass

◆ FIRST READING: Before God establishes his covenant with Noah and his sons, God blesses them with the instructions to be fertile and multiply and be stewards of the earth. God's words to Noah and his sons also contain important words of accountability for life. God imprinted the divine image on human life and because of this, God would hold Noah and his descendants—including us—accountable for upholding the sanctity of life. The bow in the sky serves as a visual reminder of God's covenant with humanity and the earth from the time of Noah forward.

◆ RESPONSORIAL PSALM 102: The antiphon helps us visualize the connection between heaven and earth. This also assists us in seeing the covenant between the Lord and Noah bridging the distance between heaven and earth. The Lord knew how much his people needed him to overcome their sin. We now know that the Lord will look down on his creation and care for his people forever. May we in turn praise and serve the Lord.

◆ GOSPEL: As part of an ordinary conversation between Jesus and his disciples on the way to the villages of Caesarea Philippi, Jesus inquires of his followers who people are saying that he is. The disciples give a variety of answers, to which Jesus responds by personalizing the question. Peter's response, in which he identifies Jesus as the Christ, reveals Jesus' identity and serves as a turning point in Mark's account of the Gospel. Suffering and death will come to him, Jesus tells his disciples, but so, too, will Resurrection. Peter does not like what he hears and we probably would not have either. Certainly it needs clarification as the journey to Jerusalem continues.

Today's Saint

St. Peter Damian (1007–1072), born to a large Italian family, entered a Camaldolese Benedictine monastery comprising hermit monks who followed an austere life of fasting and prayer. Dedicating himself to the study of Scripture and the Fathers of the Church, he gained a reputation among the hermits as being both a gifted scholar and spiritual guru. Although he lived in a monastery, removed from the world, St. Peter was a powerful voice of reform in the Church. He spoke out against clerical abuses, challenged bishops to recommit themselves to their vocation, and announced the need for a reformed papacy. Recognized for his ability to lead, he was made abbot of his monastery and later installed as bishop of Ostia. As bishop, he never lost sight of his calling to be a monk. He was so influential in the Church that Pope Leo XII declared him a Doctor of the Church.

FRI 22 (#535) white
Feast of the Chair of St. Peter the Apostle

About Today's Feast

The chair of a bishop, called the cathedra, is the symbol of his foundational ministry to be a teacher of faith to his Church community. What then can we learn from Peter, the rock of our Church? His extraordinary confession of faith teaches us courage to confess truth, even if it may sound far-fetched by everyday standards. Peter listened to the Spirit of God in his heart and proclaimed Jesus as Christ, Son of the living God. When Jesus asks "Who do you say that I am?" each of us is presented with the same question. What is the Spirit of God prompting us to proclaim? Today's feast, attested to as early as the mid-fourth century, has its roots in the Parentalia, or commemoration of dead relatives and friends celebrated between February 13 and 22. At this commemoration, a chair, or cathedra, was left empty for particular deceased persons. Since the actual date of Peter's death was unknown, it came to be remembered on February 22, eventually becoming a celebration of his taking over the pastoral responsibility of the Church of Rome.

The Lectionary for Mass

◆ FIRST READING: How fitting, but ironic, that in this passage from Peter's first letter, he identifies himself as one who witnesses to the sufferings of Christ the day after we heard him identify Jesus as the Christ but wanted nothing to do with Jesus' message that he must suffer and die. Peter reminds his fellow presbyters that they also give witness to Christ's sufferings and will share in his glory. They shepherd their flock not with arrogance and power, but with humility, imitating Jesus' own example.

◆ RESPONSORIAL PSALM 23: The beautiful poetry of the beloved psalm of the shepherd helps us acknowledge in song that it is the Lord who is our Shepherd. In him, all our desires are met; the Lord leaves us with nothing to want. In suffering, the Lord accompanies us. We trust that one day we will dwell in the Lord's house having faithfully followed the true Shepherd.

◆ GOSPEL: Matthew's account of the Gospel includes the most developed understanding of what would be the basis for the institutional Church, the head of which is the Petrine office. Today's passage is Matthew's account of Simon Peter's confession of Jesus' identity. Matthew develops Peter's confession from Mark's account (proclaimed yesterday) by adding the words "Son of the living God." Because of the faith exhibited in his confession, Peter receives the keys to the Kingdom. His confession, on Jesus' pronouncement, forever remains the rock of the Church.

The Roman Missal

Everything is proper to today's feast—all texts are found at February 22 in the Proper of Saints. All of the orations include mention of St. Peter, as might be expected, focusing on his teaching and on our need to hold fast with integrity to the faith that has been both confessed and taught by Peter. In fact, this idea of the Church's faith being built upon the faith of Peter is expressed in the liturgy even before the orations: in the Entrance Antiphon, taken from Luke's account of the Gospel, we hear, "The Lord says to Simon Peter: / I have prayed for you that your faith may not fail, / and, once you have turned back, strengthen your brothers." The Gloria is sung or said today. There is no Creed. The Collect presents an image of the surety and strong foundation that we can have when we rely on the faith con-

fessed by Peter, as particularly evidenced by the role that Jesus gave to Peter after the Apostle's confession of faith in the Lord: we ask that "no tempests may disturb us" because we have been set "fast / on the rock of the Apostle Peter's confession of faith." Again acknowledging that it is only through Peter's teaching that the Church can hold the faith in all its integrity, the Prayer over the Offerings also recognizes St. Peter as the shepherd of the Church. The Preface assigned for today is Preface I of the Apostles, which expresses how through the blessed Apostles God continues to watch over the Church to protect his flock always. Consider using Eucharistic Prayer I. The Prayer after Communion speaks of the Eucharistic celebration as "this redeeming exchange," asking that our nourishment "by communion in the Body and Blood of Christ . . . may be for us a Sacrament of unity and peace." Thus, the prayer brings to the fore the importance of unity that is at the heart of both the Petrine ministry, even down to our day in the role of the pope, and the celebration of the Eucharist. It is suggested in the Missal to use a Solemn Blessing at the end of Mass, the formula of blessing titled "The Apostles." It would be a good idea to use this today.

SAT 23 (#340) red
Memorial of St. Polycarp, Bishop and Martyr

The Lectionary for Mass

◆ FIRST READING: For one weekday we return to Hebrews for our First Reading. Faith is everything. Our ancestors in faith have shown us this. Through them, we have learned the importance of listening and living the Word of God. Their faith has taught us to believe how God orders the universe rightly. Our faith attests to our understanding of this. Even though there are things yet to come that we do not see now, by faith and in trust we walk forward in confidence that God's order includes a share in his eternal life for us.

◆ RESPONSORIAL PSALM 145: A hymn of praise, Psalm 145 invites us to join our voices in praise of God, the king of the universe. Many generations praise God for the multitude of his amazing works. The words of the psalmist encourage us to discourse about the glory of God's Kingdom. We should do this not just today, but forever we should praise the Lord.

◆ GOSPEL: Three select disciples —Peter, James, and John—now go up the mountain with Jesus and witness the glory of his Transfiguration. They hear a voice from a cloud identify Jesus as his "beloved Son" and command them to listen to him. All this they should keep to themselves until Jesus rises from the dead. They did not know what we know because of faith—the meaning of rising from the dead.

Today's Saint

St. Polycarp, an esteemed Christian leader, lived during the first half of the second century and was a friend to many who personally knew Jesus. He converted to the Christian faith under the influence of St. John the Evangelist. St. Polycarp later became bishop of Smyrna, in Turkey, around the year 96. He fought many of the gnostic heresies that were beginning to overtake the early Church. When there was a controversy over the celebration of Easter, the Churches in Asia Minor sent Polycarp as their representative to discuss the issue with Pope Anicetus. The Romans tried to burn Polycarp at the stake (when he was in his late 80s), but when he survived that, they finally stabbed him to death with a dagger.

24 (#81C) green
Seventh Sunday in Ordinary Time

The Lectionary for Mass

◆ FIRST READING: The Lord saves Saul's life as he went into the desert with three thousand Israelites to search for David. David finds Saul asleep with weapons nearby. Abishai, who accompanied David in the desert, wants to use the weapons against Saul, but David recognizes him as God's anointed one and refuses to inflict harm on him for fear of divine retribution. David's words at the end of the reading proclaim that the Lord will reward the just and faithful.

◆ RESPONSORIAL PSALM 103 is a common psalm for Ordinary Time. The refrain from verse 8 makes us mindful of the Lord's kindness and mercy. In the verses, the psalmist blesses and thanks the Lord for all his benefits, especially forgiveness for sins. The Lord has put significant distance between us and our sins. What fatherly compassion we have experienced!

◆ SECOND READING: We continue a proclamation from the next to last chapter of 1 Corinthians as Paul continues to develop his teaching on Jesus' Resurrection. Paul uses the Adam-Christ typology as he speaks about the first man, *adam*, as a "living being" and the last *adam* as a "life-giving spirit." The first man was earthly and the second was from heaven. When we live

we bear the image of the earthly man, but in the future we will bear that of the heavenly one. We *will* share in Jesus' Resurrection. Our eternal home will be in him.

◆ GOSPEL: Jesus' Sermon on the Mount continues as he teaches his disciples to love their enemies and bless those who curse them. His wisdom turns the way the disciples are used to relating to people upside down. In conveying his wisdom, Jesus attempts to distinguish what is required of his followers from the way sinners live. Jesus' disciples are to extend mercy in the same manner in which the Father does.

The Roman Missal

We pray that we may fix our hearts on "spiritual things," so that we may follow God's will in word and deed (Collect). The Eucharist is our pledge of salvation, our taste of eternal glory (Prayer over the Offerings, Prayer after Communion). The Gloria and the Creed are sung or said today. Consider using Eucharistic Prayer IV.

Other Ideas

The Gospel for today leads to a reflection on how we share our love and our resources with others. The so called "Golden Rule" that is in today's Gospel ("Do to others as you would have them do to you") presents a good opportunity to highlight the charitable efforts of the parish on behalf of the larger community. The work of the St. Vincent de Paul Society is a good example. Perhaps one of the members could give a brief presentation about their work. If there are other groups that do similar works of charity they might arrange a display in the gathering area and invite other parishioners to chat with them or to consider signing up as volunteers. The entire Gospel text works well as a personal spiritual reflection, helping us to critique our efforts at being faithful disciples.

MON 25 (#341) green Weekday

The Lectionary for Mass

◆ FIRST READING: The Lord, the Creator of all, is the source of Wisdom. The Lord created Wisdom through the Holy Spirit. Through the Lord's Word, Wisdom came to be and was sent forth upon everything. The author of Sirach poses a series of questions to which the answer always is "the LORD." Would that we come to know the Lord's wisdom active and present in our own lives and in creation around us, for God created us to share in divine Wisdom.

◆ RESPONSORIAL PSALM 93 acclaims the Lord's kingship over the world. These few verses from Psalm 93 solidify that the Lord has charge over all of creation, for his Wisdom permeates life. The authority of the divine Word governs all that came into being through it.

◆ GOSPEL: The disciples fail to drive out an evil spirit from a father's son who was possessed since childhood. Jesus succeeds in exorcising the demonic spirit because of prayer. He does not ask the father to believe, but merely informs him that everything is possible when a person has faith. The father professes his faith in an "I do," similar to the "I do" we proclaim when we renew our baptismal promises. Yet, humility fills the father's affirmation of faith as he recognizes his faith might be tinged with unbelief. Through prayer, may our unbelief turn into faith as we experience how Jesus heals and raises us as he did the father's son.

TUE 26 (#342) green Weekday

The Lectionary for Mass

◆ FIRST READING: The author of Sirach encourages us to hope in the Lord, for when we do, the Lord will not disappoint us. Though at times the journey will be long and arduous, a child of God who has patience and continues to serve will know the Lord's compassion and mercy. The sage advice in this passage helps us be realistic about daily life. Every day will not be easy and joyful, but our patience, trust and hope in the Lord, and ultimately our love of the Lord, will lead to lasting joy.

◆ RESPONSORIAL PSALM 37: When we commit to the Lord, he will be there for us. The psalm refrain declares this truth. In the verses from Psalm 37, we hear again the theme of trust from the First Reading. God's justice and righteousness will prevail. Those who trust, in the Lord believe nothing less than this.

◆ GOSPEL: Jesus' second prediction of his Passion, Death, and Resurrection begins this Gospel reading. Part of the reason why Jesus will suffer and die is because he turned the world's wisdom upside down, particularly in relation to his teaching about who is the greatest—the very question the disciples themselves argued about on the way to Capernaum.

WED 27 (#343) green Weekday

The Lectionary for Mass

◆ FIRST READING: God breathed the breath of life into the first human person. The passage from Sirach connects God with divine Wisdom as it opens by stating it was Wisdom who "breathes life into her children." As Wisdom's children, ours is the call to love her and serve her, to trust and obey her. In doing this, we love and serve God and trust and obey God. Our faithfulness to divine Wisdom will yield happiness and a share in Wisdom's knowledge.

◆ RESPONSORIAL PSALM 119: The verses sung today emphasize the gift of "great peace" that comes from loving the Lord's law, the law of wisdom. In these verses we pledge to keep the Lord's decrees, to sing of the Lord's promise of justice for the faithful, and to praise the Lord for all that his Word teaches us.

◆ GOSPEL: The disciples always try to act in Jesus' best interest, but sometimes they just misunderstand a bit of what Jesus is about. This is the case with John in today's passage. John confesses to Jesus that he and the other disciples saw someone exorcising demons in Jesus' name. This person was not part of the community of disciples who intentionally followed Jesus. Since life reigns over death in Jesus himself and in his mission, Jesus tells John not to prevent the life-giving actions of this person. Choosing life means one is on the side of Jesus.

THU 28 (#344) green Weekday

The Lectionary for Mass

◆ FIRST READING: Wisdom's practical advice is for us not to put off until tomorrow what we can do today. Today is the day we should turn our hearts to the Lord and convert to him. No longer should we rely on wealth or our own power or strength. And, surely our anger will be no help to us, but will only deceive us and lead us astray. God will triumph over our enemies and his mercy will prevail over our sin. What reasons, then, could we possibly have to procrastinate in turning our hearts to the Lord each day?

◆ RESPONSORIAL PSALM 1: The opening psalm of the psalter contrasts the wise with the wicked. The person who chooses to follow the Lord's Word is like a tree planted near water that produces abundant

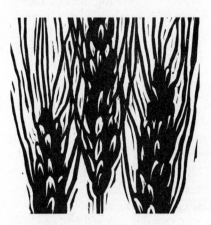

fruit. Rooted in God's Word, this tree never dies. The wicked face a different fate.

◆ GOSPEL: Let not the salt in you lose its ability to enhance flavor. Such is the moral of the short parable that ends today's Gospel. When we keep God's Word alive in us and act on it accordingly, we remain faithful disciples. When sin takes root in us and we even tempt others with sin, the stark consequences of Gehenna await. Let us refine ourselves as we journey toward God's Kingdom.

March 2019
Month of St. Joseph

FRI 1 (#345) green
Weekday

The Lectionary for Mass

◆ FIRST READING: This passage includes practical advice on what it means to be a faithful friend. In a series of proverbs from the wisdom teacher who authored Sirach, we learn that if we fear God we will act cautiously with respect to those we choose as our friends. Faithful friends will accompany each other and provide shelter in times of need. We cannot put a price on a God-fearing friend, but we can recognize what a treasure one is.

◆ RESPONSORIAL PSALM 119: Wednesday of this week, verses from the latter part of Psalm 119 served as the Responsorial Psalm. Seen in the light of the words from the book of Sirach on friendship, today's verses from the earlier part of the psalm draw our attention to the wonder of the Lord's Word. We express our desire to grow in understanding of the divine commands. This helps us to become a better friend to others.

◆ GOSPEL: Jesus arrives in the district of Judea where he again en-

counters crowds of people who gather to hear him teach. Among the crowds are Pharisees who attempt to entrap Jesus with a question about the legality of divorce. Jesus responds by pointing out the hardness of the Pharisees' hearts. Relationships between God-fearing people ideally never end if they both strive to grow in their knowledge of God and God's precepts, becoming the best of friends. Perhaps the Pharisees need to address the lack of openness in their hearts to Jesus' message.

SAT 2 (#346) green
Weekday

Optional Memorial of the Blessed Virgin Mary / white

The Lectionary for Mass

◆ FIRST READING: In short statements, the author of Sirach details God's creation of the human person and the history of God's covenant with us. God created us in his image and likeness from the earth to which we will return. God fills our creative hearts with wisdom to understand and act in line with God's will. God watches over us and knows all that we do—his covenant with us lasts forever. Our charge is the acceptance of Wisdom's knowledge.

◆ RESPONSORIAL PSALM 103: In the words of Psalm 103, we praise the Lord for his kindness toward us that lasts forever. The verses from the middle of the psalm emphasize the Lord's compassion toward his children. We know that we will return to the dust from where we came and that our days on earth are numbered. We try to remain faithful to Wisdom, yet sometimes we choose sin. Even faced with our sin, the Lord's kindness and mercy prevail.

◆ GOSPEL: The hard-hearted, misunderstanding disciples tried to hold people back from bringing children to Jesus. Although Jesus

was frustrated and angry with the disciples, he used this time as a teachable moment. Allow the children to come to me, he teaches them, for God's kingdom avails itself to those who are like children. With humility and a child's curiosity and openness to growing in understanding, let us seek the Kingdom. And let us hold each other accountable when hardness of our hearts takes over.

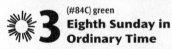

3 (#84C) green
Eighth Sunday in Ordinary Time

The Lectionary for Mass

◆ FIRST READING: Stubborn, wicked, and immoral speech gain a person nothing. Rather, this type of speech contrasts with the wisdom of the Lord's Word. In a few pithy proverbs, the author of Sirach instructs us about how our words reveal both our faults and our goodness (the fruits we bear). Only after people speak can we praise them, for only then will we know if their speech has reflected the Lord's word.

◆ RESPONSORIAL PSALM 92: The refrain from Psalm 92:2a states a simple, but profound truth about how good it is to give thanks to the Lord. Psalm 92 in its entirety is a psalm of thanksgiving. The verses use the nature image of a tree flourishing and thereby connect directly with the passage from Sirach. Those who praise and thank the Lord and plant themselves firmly in him will bear fruit throughout their lives.

◆ SECOND READING: Paul draws the connection between death and sin and acclaims that victory over death comes from God through our Lord Jesus Christ. Paul solidifies for the Corinthians and for us that death's sting is no more in Jesus Christ. Paul's words urge the community of believers to remain devoted to following the Lord for it leads to a share in Christ's Resurrection. This is a tall order for a community as divided as the Corinthians, but Paul knows they can succeed when they remain in the Lord.

◆ GOSPEL: Jesus turns to short parables as he continues to teach the disciples on the plain. The disciples hear how their teacher will train them in his ways; how they should not judge another person when sin remains in them; and how trees are known by the fruit they bear—a direct connection to the First Reading from Sirach. The Gospel reading concludes as we hear Jesus speak what we could consider an obvious tautology: good comes from good and evil from evil. We speak what is in our heart—let that be goodness!

The Roman Missal

The Mass texts for today are found in the "Ordinary Time" section of the Proper of Time. The Gloria is sung or said today. The Collect asks that God's peaceful rule may direct the course of our world, and that under such protection the Church "may rejoice, / untroubled in her devotion." The Prayer over the Offerings recognizes that the outward gifts we offer (bread and wine) are meant to be signs of the inward, spiritual sacrifice we bring to the Sacrifice of the Mass, which, of course, must be the sacrifice of "our desire to serve you with devotion." The prayer then goes on

to ask that what is granted to us in the offering "as the source of merit / may also help us to attain merit's reward"—in other words, we pray that our participation in the offering will itself be the source of our transformation. The Prayer after Communion connects the nourishment we have received through the Sacrament here and now with the heavenly liturgy, asking that having been fed now "in the present age, / you may make us partakers of life eternal." Preface VI of the Sundays in Ordinary Time, "The pledge of the eternal Passover," might be a good choice today insofar as it speaks of our closeness to God—"in you we live and move and have our being"—and of our experiencing God's care as a daily effect; this could connect with the Gospel theme of not being anxious, and trusting in God's care for us. This is the last Sunday we will hear the Alleluia until Easter Time, and (except on two weekday solemnities) this will be our last Gloria, too. Make the most of them today. Pull out all the stops on the organ. Open up the beauty of these prayers. In this way, their absence during Lent will help us to long for Easter all the more. The Creed may be said or sung. Consider using Eucharistic Prayer III.

Other Ideas

This last Sunday in the winter section of Ordinary Time means that the season of Lent is at hand. Today would be a good time for the parish to publish a separate bulletin that would list all the parish activities and liturgies for the Lenten season. It might also include events like committee meetings that have been canceled; sometimes it's a good thing for the parish calendar to "fast"! The agendas of people today get filled well in advance, so scheduled penance services, Lenten devotions, a parish mission, soup suppers, and so on,

need to be advertised well ahead of time. Encourage every parishioner and every family to review these offerings and decide which ones will help them observe Lent in a way that will be spiritually enriching.

MON 4 (#347) green
Weekday

Optional Memorial of St. Casimir / white

The Lectionary for Mass

◆ FIRST READING: The first two verses of this four-verse reading provide guidance on how we should act when we sin. We should act confidently in returning to God because God always leads us back to him. The concluding two verses remind us that those in the depths of the nether world cannot glorify God, but we who live here and now can! We can we experience God's boundless mercy and forgiveness when we return to God from our sin!

◆ RESPONSORIAL PSALM 32 expresses the joy of the just who have experienced the Lord's forgiveness. This psalm, like the six other penitential psalms, also is a psalm of thanksgiving for God's mercy. The psalmist's words help us thank the Lord for his presence with us in times of distress. The Lord hears our prayers and leads us away from danger—including the distress of sin.

◆ GOSPEL: Today a man of unknown background asks Jesus what he needs to do to gain eternal life. The conversation between Jesus and the man clarifies for us that observing the commandments is not enough. We must divest ourselves of material possessions and take care of the poor. How difficult, if not seemingly impossible this is for the man, for Jesus' disciples, and for us. A camel could more readily pass through the eye of a needle! All is not lost—for God, not you or me, saves.

Today's Saint

St. Casimir was a prince of Poland and of the Grand Duchy of Lithuania. Born in the royal palace in Krakow, he was heir apparent to the throne. When the king went to Lithuania, Casimir was left in charge of Poland from 1481 to 1483, and it is said that he ruled with great justice and prudence. Casimir was known for his piety and devotion. Weakened by fasting, he developed a lung disease that was probably tuberculosis, and died. St. Casimir is buried in the cathedral of Vilnius, in Lithuania.

TUE **5** (#348) green
Weekday

The Lectionary for Mass

◆ FIRST READING: What does it mean to be a just one? This is the topic of today's passage that comes from about two-thirds of the way through the book of Sirach. Our nonparticipation in evil means we follow the commandments and avoid injustice. The generosity of our spirit should stand out to God and others. Joy should mark our giving. Our generous spirit and joy reflect God's very own generosity from which God will give abundantly in return to us, for God is just.

◆ RESPONSORIAL PSALM 50: The sacrifice God requires is praise, not burnt offerings. God requires justice of his people and that they uphold the covenant. The psalm refrain taken from the final verse of Psalm 50 communicates that those who follow God's ways of justice and obey him will know God's salvation.

◆ GOSPEL: Peter speaks for the disciples and responds to Jesus' teaching about giving up material possessions and caring for the poor, by stating that the disciples have indeed "given up everything" to follow him. Jesus' words are meant to reassure Peter and the disciples: those who have given up everything —including their families—will know a reward in the age to come that far exceeds anything they can benefit from in the here and now. Yet those who see themselves above everyone else now will be last.

LENT AND HOLY WEEK

The Roman Missal / The Meaning

IN THE COLLECT for the First Sunday of Lent we pray: "Grant, almighty God, through the yearly observances of holy Lent, that we may grow in understanding of the riches hidden in Christ and by worthy conduct pursue their effects." The *Universal Norms on the Liturgical Year and the Calendar* (27) states.

Lent is ordered to preparing for the celebration of Easter, since the Lenten liturgy prepares for celebration of the Paschal Mystery both catechumens, by the various stages of Christian Initiation, and the faithful, who recall their own Baptism and do penance.

The catechumens grow in understanding the riches hidden in Christ by entering fully into the RCIA process. The baptized grow in understanding these riches by doing penance to repent or reorient their lives to live those riches more clearly. Catechumens, the elect, and the baptized give evidence of their union with Christ by conduct that shows that union. During Lent the Church prepares for and renews the initiation of the members of the Body of Christ.

The section of *The Roman Missal* entitled "Lent," is found immediately following the texts for Christmas Time. The section begins with the texts for Ash Wednesday (March 6), includes the texts for Holy Week, and concludes with the texts of the Chrism Mass. An Entrance Antiphon, Collect, Prayer over the Offerings, Communion Antiphon, Prayer after Communion, and Prayer over the People (optional on weekdays, required on Sundays) are provided for each day during Lent and Holy Week. The Sundays include Prefaces that fit the Gospel accounts of Year A. Two Communion Antiphons are provided for the first and second Sundays. Three are provided for the third, fourth, and fifth Sundays, which correspond to the various Gospel accounts in each of the three-year Sunday cycle of readings.

Use form 3 of the Penitential Act and tropes found in options III and IV within appendix VI: Sample Invocations for the Penitential Act. These tropes reflect the healing, reconciling, and pardoning focus of the season (option III) and the transformative and enlightening process that the elect experience during their final weeks of preparation for initiation at the Vigil (option IV). One way to highlight the penitential aspect of Lent is to sing the Penitential Act. Use the chants provided in appendix I: Various Chants for the Order of Mass. Especially if you do not sing the Penitential Act at other times during the liturgical year, this simple practice can add a progressive solemnity to this season. Another way to highlight the season's penitential focus is to recite the Confiteor. If you do not normally use the second form of the Penitential Act, praying it during Lent can highlight our need for repentance: "Have mercy on us, O Lord. / For we have sinned against you. / Show us, O Lord, your mercy. / And grant us your salvation." You can sing this form by using the notation provided in appendix I of the Missal.

There are four Prefaces provided for use during the first four weeks of Lent. Any of the four can be used on the weekdays of Lent or the Sundays where the included preface does not fit the readings that Year. Ash Wednesday directs us to use either Preface III ("The fruits of abstinence"), or Preface IV ("The fruits of fasting"). During the Fifth Week of Lent "Preface I of the Passion of the Lord" is to be used and during Holy Week "Preface II of the Passion of the Lord." These two

weeks move us to direct our attention on the passion and death of the Lord.

Either Eucharistic Prayer for Reconciliation (EPR) is fitting during this season. They can be used without their proper Prefaces, thus they can be prayed beginning with one of the Lenten or Passion prefaces. EPR I asks God to pour out the power of the Holy Spirit on the human race "that they may become the Body and Blood / of your beloved Son, Jesus Christ, / in whom we, too, are your sons and daughters," certainly a connection with the Sacraments of Initiation. EPR II seeks reconciliation with God through Jesus Christ:

> When we ourselves had turned away from you
> on account of our sins,
> you brought us back to be reconciled, O Lord,
> so that, converted at last to you,
> we might love one another
> through your Son,
> whom for our sake you handed over to death.

Loving one another is expressed in our worthy conduct.

The Gloria is not sung or recited during Lent, with the exception of the Solemnity of St. Joseph, March 19, and the Annunciation of the Lord, March 25. Neither is the Alleluia sung or recited from Ash Wednesday until the Easter Vigil in the Holy Night, when it returns with great delight.

Many dioceses celebrate the Rite of Election on the First Sunday of Lent. While this rite is often celebrated within a Liturgy of the Word, if it is celebrated during Mass on that Sunday, the texts for the day are used. If it is celebrated during Mass on another day, use the texts "For the Election or Enrollment of Names" within the "Ritual Masses" section of the Missal. You will also find Ritual Masses for the celebration of the scrutinies in that section. Become familiar with these texts and rubrics to celebrate the scrutinies on the Third, Fourth, and Fifth Sundays of Lent, with all the resources that the Church has to offer.

The Lectionary for Mass

LENT IS ALSO known as the Period of Purification and Enlightenment for those catechumens (now called the elect following the Rite of Election on the First Sunday of Lent) preparing for the Easter sacraments. On the Third, Fourth, and Fifth Sundays of Lent, parishes may choose to use the readings from the Year A cycle of readings or the readings from the current cycle—in this case, Year C. The Year A readings highlight baptismal themes and are especially appropriate for the catechumens who will be initiated at the Easter Vigil. The information below applies to the Year C readings, although commentary for both sets of readings is included in this resource.

◆ FIRST READINGS: The First Readings for Lent in Year C recount various events in the religious life and history of ancient Israel and God's covenant with the Chosen People. Selections from Deuteronomy, Genesis, Exodus, Joshua, and Isaiah illustrate God's loving care for the Chosen People, even in the midst of slavery in Egypt and exile in Babylon. It is God who always brings them home and reestablishes his covenant. Even when they turn away from God, God does not forget them and offers them new beginnings. These are wonderful stories of reconciliation. The Isaiah reading assigned for Palm Sunday as well as the other readings for Palm Sunday are designed to prepare us for the Holy Week that follows.

◆ RESPONSORIAL PSALMS: The Responsorial Psalm is part of the Liturgy of the Word. God speaks to us, and we provide our prayerful assent to that Word. For the first two Sundays of Lent, we pray psalms of trust (Psalms 91 and 27). For the third and fourth Sundays, the psalms are prayers of thanksgiving (Psalms 103 and 34). For the fifth Sunday, Psalm 126 is a prayer of confidence, and on Palm Sunday, we pray Psalm 22, a psalm of lament.

◆ SECOND READINGS: All of the Second Readings are from the letters of St. Paul. In various ways, these selections stress the central role of Christ in all of salvation. Christ has reconciled us with God, and therefore Christ is to be the center of our own life and the source of all meaning and consolation.

◆ GOSPEL READINGS: The Gospel readings for the first two Sundays of Lent follow the same pattern each year: the Gospel reading on the First Sunday of Lent recounts Jesus' temptation in the desert, and the Gospel reading on the Second Sunday of Lent is the Transfiguration. The first is a narrative of struggle and temptation, the second a passage of glorification. This year, Year C, the accounts are taken from the Gospel according to Luke. On the Third Sunday of Lent we hear the parable of the fig tree and are reminded of the necessity of being prepared for death at all times.

On the fourth and fifth Sundays, we encounter two Gospel readings of sin and forgiveness: the prodigal son and the woman caught in adultery. Both stories are instructive of the tremendous mercy and compassion of God. To summarize, the Gospel selections for Lent in Year C show us suffering and glory, sin and reconciliation with God. The Gospel reading for Palm Sunday is the Passion according to Luke.

If a parish has elect preparing for the Easter sacraments, the readings for the Third, Fourth, and Fifth Sundays of Lent are taken from Year A and the Gospel according to John to coincide with the scrutiny rites that are celebrated on these Sundays. These three accounts, the woman at the well, the man born blind, and the raising of Lazarus, are three of the most ancient texts used for preparing the elect for Baptism. They are instructions on the power of Christ over sin, darkness, and death for both the elect and the faithful.

Children's Liturgy of the Word

WHEN CHILDREN enter on the First Sunday of Lent, they should notice an immediate difference. Like the church, everything should be as spare and stripped down as possible. A hint of reddish violet fabric on the lectern, a simple suggestion of the desert on the prayer table, featuring rocks, an overturned empty pottery jar, a cactus "skeleton." Keep it very simple for the next five Sundays. Musical accompaniment, if any, should be simple, and the Gospel Acclamation is no longer Alleluia, but one of the many Lenten options, such as "Praise to you, Lord Jesus Christ, King of endless glory."

If not using the psalms of the day, consider using a common Lenten psalm. The choices are Psalms 51, 91, and 130.

When preparing for Lent, check ahead with your pastoral staff to learn whether there are adults who will be baptized at the Easter Vigil. If so, this may mean that Year A Lent readings will be used on the third, fourth, and fifth Sundays instead of the Year C readings at some or possibly all Masses. This is because the parish will celebrate the scrutinies on those days, which require those readings to match the prayers. It is very important that children and their parents hear the same readings.

On the First Sunday of Lent, March 10, we hear the story of Jesus' forty days in the desert, tempted by Satan. First, however, we hear from Moses in the desert, recalling the deliverance of God's people from slavery in Egypt—a reminder that Jesus will deliver us all from sin and death. Children may need a brief review about the story of Moses to make this dynamic of desert and deliverance more accessible.

On the Second Sunday of Lent, March 17, we encounter the Transfiguration. During the reflection, have children recall the candles of Advent and the lights of Christmas, reminding them that Christ is our light. Today, in the Gospel story, he shows his disciples how brightly he shines. Light a single white candle as you explain this. Remember that St. Patrick takes a back seat that day to Jesus (saint's days are not celebrated on Sundays of Lent). There should be no shamrocks, or other symbols of the saint present during the liturgy. Yes, this is still his feast day, but Patrick would certainly understand that Jesus' Transfiguration takes precedence.

On the Third Sunday of Lent, March 24, in the Year C readings (if used; see the note above) we encounter with Moses the burning bush and hear Jesus speak about a second chance for a fruitless fig tree. (Remember that spiritual fruit a few weeks ago?) Keep the environment simple for the Year C reading, but if your parish is using the Year A reading, the woman at the well, you may want to add a bowl of water and ask what is the "living water" which Jesus offers.

On the Fourth Sunday of Lent, March 31, Year C the stories are about God's mercy—forgiving the Jews for lack of faith in the desert and the loving welcome of the returning prodigal son. If the Year A reading, the man born blind, is used, the focus is on healing and sight. What is it in our own lives that we refuse to "see." What does Jesus need to heal in us?

On the Fifth Sunday of Lent, April 7, the Year C reading is again about forgiveness: the woman caught in adultery. If the Year A reading, the raising of Lazarus, is used, the theme is Jesus freeing us from death. Do we, like Martha, believe Jesus is the Messiah, who will free us from death?

Palm Sunday, April 14, finds us in Jerusalem for Jesus' triumphal entry and Passion. If you have Liturgy of the Word that day, help the children accompany Jesus to the Cross, emphasizing that he

needed to die so that he could send us to heaven to be with the Father forever. Be sure to display red fabric and palms in your prayer environment today to show that the day is very different from Lent.

The Saints

DURING LENT, all commemorations of the saints are more limited than during other liturgical seasons, as the Church reserves this space and time to focus primarily on the daily Lenten discipleship of prayer, fasting, and almsgiving. But while parishes should maintain the environment and observances of Lent, there are two solemnities that are the exception: the Solemnity of St. Joseph and the Solemnity of the Annunciation, two days that direct our attention to the unique and salvific consequences of saying yes to God. St. Joseph, spouse of the Blessed Virgin Mary and patron of the universal Church, overcame his doubts and fears to accept the role of protector and nurturer of both Mary and the child Jesus. Mary's yes to the Archangel Gabriel gave birth to the salvation of the world.

St. Joseph should be celebrated with the appropriate liturgical color (white); the Gloria should be sung. Parishes may wish to consider the blessing of bread traditionally done on this day, found in the *Book of Blessings* (chapter 53). St. Joseph, a silent figure throughout most of the Gospel, is a man in whom the goodness of work and absolute faith in God are embodied.

For the Solemnity of the Annunciation, there are countless beautiful and inspiring depictions of the angel Gabriel appearing to Mary and numerous beloved hymns that extol the joy and gratitude with which Mary accepted God's will for her. During Lent, many parishes introduce a regular schedule of Liturgy of the Hours; Evening Prayer, with its Marian Gospel canticle, can be especially meaningful on this day.

Several of the saints whose memorials are optional during Lent are nonetheless cherished, especially in certain communities, and each generation can gain new or different insight by learning these saints' stories. For example, millennials may find in the ancient story of Sts. Felicity and Perpetua a decidedly modern strand of female self-determination. Hagiography movingly describes these two young women, both new mothers, whose strength through God allows them to claim their own identity as Christians in defiance of society and family in order that, as St. Perpetua declared, "our liberty not be obscured."

The Liturgy of the Hours

EVERY FRIDAY in the Church's official Morning Prayer, Psalm 51 urges God to have mercy on us. Lent, as a season for renewal, has a distinctly penitential character that is emphasized especially on Friday. Gather every Lenten Friday for Morning Prayer, and steep the parish in Psalm 51. Morning Prayer can be recited completely or interspersed with a hymn or two. It can be more fully experienced with a cantor and accompaniment, but an elaborate celebration is secondary to learning the rhythm and flow of the prayer itself. It is important to observe the postures for liturgical prayer, which adds to the devotional aspect and underscores the fact that it is, truly, liturgy. To begin, stand and make the Sign of the Cross. Sit for the psalmody, and stand for the psalm-prayer. Stand for the canticle and include any particular intentions from the congregation in the intercessions. On an occasion when you are praying Morning or Evening prayer alone, make the effort to sing aloud the hymns and notice how this improves the quality of your prayer.

During Lent, we give our complete attention to doing penance, reconciling ourselves to God's unconditional love, and renewing our commitment to professing the Paschal Mystery each day of our lives. We don't need to find a desert and wait for temptation to happen. We know that it happens as a typical part of our daily lives. This is where Lent comes in: Lent is God's time, given to us to learn through the prophets and through the Gospel accounts about Jesus' life. Lenten prayer is a good start for examining how we can participate more fully in God's time. Through the prayer and psalmody especially in the Liturgy of the Hours, we make intentional connections with living the Paschal Mystery.

The Rite of Christian Initiation of Adults

THE SEASON OF LENT is essentially an act of "re-membering," for those who have experienced Lent before. For the elect, Lent is a time to prepare for celebrating the Paschal Mystery, and a time to prepare intensely to receive the sacraments of Christian initiation. For both groups, the Christian initiation process puts forward a new freedom "from the power of darkness" and being "joined to Christ's death, burial, and resurrection" (*Christian Initiation*, General Introduction, 1). Increased prayer, fasting, and almsgiving are certainly part of the Lenten observance, but there is a more vital reason that moves a congregation, along with their elect and catechumens, to conversion: to plunge all of us into a deeper relationship with the Paschal Mystery.

The catechumens are firmly enmeshed in the "first step" according to the *Rite of Christian Initiation of Adults*, having reached the point of initial conversion and now "having progressed in faith and nearly completed the catechumenate, they are accepted into a more intense preparation for the sacraments of initiation" (RCIA, 6.2). It is important at this point for team members to work together to develop and assimilate the (often-overlooked) understanding that the Rite of Acceptance begins this second period, a period that "may last for several years" (see RCIA, 7.2). Often, the school-year model prevails in a parish and fails to allow the catechumens sufficient time to grow through a period of conversion into deep faith. It is important, especially during Lent, to accommodate Christ's message and begin to live as a Catholic Christian. The *National Statutes on the Catechumenate* are clear (NSC, 6): "The period of catechumenate, beginning at acceptance into the order of catechumens and including both the catechumenate proper and period of purification and enlightenment after election or enrollment of names, should extend for at least one year of formation, instruction, and probation." And further, from the NSC, 6: "Ordinarily this period should go from at least the Easter season of one year until the next; preferably it should begin before Lent in one year and extend until Easter of the following year." Regarding the catechumens, we must accept and believe that "they're ready when they're ready" and truly "it takes as long as it takes."

The enrollment of names and the Rite of Election with the bishop anticipate receipt of the Easter sacraments on Holy Saturday, and represent God's election and choosing of the catechumens. From now on, they will be known as the elect. The twofold character of Lent is embodied in this election by the bishop: the elect are accepting their nomination to Christian life for the first time, just as the faithful are renewing their commitment to living a Christian life. Guided by their leaders and sponsors, and supported by the prayer of the congregation, the elect are becoming secure in their commitment to turn away from things that are "displeasing to Christ," as is evidenced through participation in the upcoming scrutinies. It is important to recall RCIA, 121, which states, "Before the rite of election the bishop, priests, deacons, catechists, godparents, and the entire community, in accord with their respective responsibilities and in their own way, should, after considering the matter carefully, arrive at a judgment about the catechumens' state of formation and progress."

The question needs to be raised and answered: are they ready to move forward with election? With careful anticipation, prepare the liturgical events at which the catechumens will be anointed with the oil that has been blessed at the Chrism Mass, and presented with the Creed and with the Lord's Prayer. Be intentional also about the Ephphetha Rite, using the words that the rite provides. There is flexibility in the initiation process to accomplish the optional anointing and presentations even outside of Lent, and team wisdom indicates that these events need to be "spaced out" in the course of Lent (or at another time) for maximum impact.

On the Third, Fourth, and Fifth Sundays of Lent, the celebration of each scrutiny occurs. Catechize your congregation in advance, because there exists a cultural perception of the word *scrutiny* that is somewhat difficult to relate to the holy movement of becoming Catholic. To *scrutinize* means "to examine closely and minutely," according to Merriam-Webster.com. For some in the parish community, it can truly sound harsh. For the Church, the scrutinies positively intend "to enlighten the minds and hearts of the elect with a deeper knowledge of Christ the Savior" (RCIA, 139) during the period of Purification and Enlightenment. There is an embedded theme of repentance in the language of each scrutiny, and

a reminder of "baptism already received" for the worshiping assembly (RCIA, 138). More than placing the elect under a microscope for observation, each scrutiny and its accompanying exorcism offers abundant encouragement for the elect to turn intensely to the God who loves them. Always shift the Gospel readings to Year A at the Mass that celebrates each scrutiny; each set of intercessions in the rite will intersect meaningfully with the message of each Gospel.

As the Lenten observance winds down, the assembly will begin to anticipate the special opportunities for growth and rebirth that the Triduum brings. There may be parish Reconciliation services during Lent, which should embody all the love and hospitality that a parish can muster. The liturgy, especially the music of the season, should be prepared with tender care, and a sufficient number of confessors should be available to give absolution. Remember that a Reconciliation service can be the point of welcoming back those who have been away for varying amounts of time and for many reasons. It is important that the church environment, hospitality, and music reflect welcome without judgement. Authentic welcome equals an explicit invitation to return, especially to those who search for reconciliation. Your mission statement: "We're not complete unless you're here with us." Have packets ready, and put your best foot forward regarding information about the parish and its mission, vision, and activities. Non-Catholics who may accompany reconciling Catholics to a Reconciliation service may even become inquirers if there is an inquiry event advertised at this time.

The Sacraments of Initiation

THE SEASON OF LENT is the Church's annual retreat. It is a time for us to prepare ourselves through prayer, fasting, and almsgiving for the great celebration of Easter. As we delve deeper into the Paschal Mystery, we take the time to look at our own lives and uncover all that keep us from a relationship with Christ and his Church. While it is a penitential season during which our liturgical celebrations take on a more sober character, the sacraments of initiation can be celebrated during this season. When they are celebrated during Lent, keep in mind the liturgical directives with regard to music and the church environment. While the celebration of sacraments of initiation are joyous occasions, it is still a season that is subdued liturgically. Keep in mind that ritual Masses cannot be celebrated on the Sundays of Lent, but if one of the sacraments is celebrated, even outside of the regularly scheduled parish liturgies, the Sunday readings must be used and the Gloria and Alleluia is omitted, as it is on all Sundays of Lent. If a ritual Mass is celebrated during the week, the Gloria may be sung, but the Lenten Gospel Acclamation must be used. It is prudent to avoid celebrating the sacraments of initiation at those liturgies where the scrutinies are being celebrated, in order not to overshadow the importance of those rites for the elect and indeed for the whole community.

Most parishes will probably avoid celebrating these sacraments during Lent, but it is a good time to schedule a First Communion or Confirmation retreat. Be sure to include the parents and sponsors. Using the Lenten readings for reflection and discussion helps to prepare young people for the sacraments they will soon receive. Parishes that schedule Confirmation of adults during Easter Time can also use this time to begin preparation sessions, remembering that adult Catholics preparing for Confirmation are not part of the RCIA. Reconciliation services can also be scheduled for those preparing for the sacraments of First Communion and Confirmation.

There was a time, and it still might be practiced in some parishes, where Baptism was not celebrated during Lent, and parishes refrained from the use of Holy Water to keep the focus off Baptism until Easter. This was never an approved practice, as infant Baptisms are to be celebrated within a short time following birth, as long as the parents are sufficiently prepared. Parishes that usually celebrate Baptism within the Sunday assembly may want to consider celebrating Baptism outside of Mass during Lent.

The Rite of Penance

J ESUS BEGAN his public ministry with the words "Repent, and believe the gospel" (Mark 1:15). Since that time the Church has never failed to call people from sin to conversion and through the celebration of Penance to show the victory of Christ over sin.

During Lent the whole Church responds to the call of the Lord to be reconciled with each other and with Christ Jesus. The very tone of the Lenten liturgies is penitential. The practices of prayer, fasting, and almsgiving offer opportunities to all the faithful to make Jesus' call to repentance a personal journey in these forty days. But the journey of conversion is part of the communal nature of the Church. Just as our failings affect the whole community of believers, so our efforts at Penance and Reconciliation involve and affect all members of the Church.

This is brought home so clearly in the communal celebration of the Sacrament of Penance. Most parishes schedule at least one such celebration during Lent. Confessors from neighboring parishes are always happy to assist with these liturgies. Usually one of the visiting confessors is willing to give a brief homily, which is a welcome break both for the pastor and the members of the host parish! The *Rite of Penance* offers numerous options for the prayers, intercessions, and Scripture readings (see chapter II), and appendix II provides an example of a penitential celebration during Lent. Liturgy coordinators should become familiar with the great resources in the ritual text and not recycle the same choices from the previous year.

Of course parishes also schedule times for individual confession throughout Lent and these times should be well publicized in the bulletin and on the parish website. Other related rituals during Lent include the scrutinies for the elect. Although these rites are directed to the elect during their final stage of preparation for the sacraments of Easter, all the baptized are encouraged to offer signs of their own repentance to the elect.

Pastors will need to set aside time to visit those who are unable to come to church. Those who have been faithful when they were able continue to need the grace of the sacraments for their spiritual well-being.

If the parish has continued to offer pastoral guidance to those who might be returning to Church as a result of the invitation extended at Christmas, then Lent is an ideal time to encourage these persons to complete their journey of reconciliation through the sacrament. At the same time an invitation to others to come home to the Lord can be extended through homilies and bulletin announcements. Lent is a time for all to know again the tender mercy of the Father.

The Order of Celebrating Matrimony

IT WOULD BE DIFFICULT to offer commentary on the *Order of Celebrating Matrimony* without highlighting the active role of the assembly. The Celebration of Matrimony begins with an important rubric "with all standing" (OCM, 59) and later on calls for the assembly to make an acclamation of praise after the reception of consent. The assembly may then sing a hymn of thanksgiving and practice their baptismal priesthood by offering the Universal Prayer. The assembly does not sit and simply observe what is happening but rather, by their posture and responses, participate in the important ritual action that is taking place and witness the external expression of Christ's love for his Church.

The priest questions the bride and bridegroom about "their freedom of choice, fidelity to each other, and the acceptance and upbringing of children" (OCM, 60). The couple responds affirmatively to each question before exchanging consent. Whether the couple chooses to declare their consent using the first option in the ritual, or the second option from the older Sarum Rite, the assembly should hear the words coming from the couple, not from the priest. A judicious use of the microphone here is important.

The acclamation "Let us bless the Lord" and its response "Thanks be to God," or another acclamation is sung or said (OCM, 65). It is preferable to sing this acclamation and response since it follows the climactic moment in the rite and singing helps to highlight the text. This could be rehearsed with the assembly ahead of time and should be included in the worship aid. Because this dialogue is not within the liturgical vocabulary of most Catholics, even though it is a familiar response to those who pray the Liturgy of the Hours, it is possible to sing or say another acclamation. An Alleluia response could be used outside of the Lenten season. One of the short acclamations from 1 John could also be used.

The outward sign of the Sacrament of Matrimony follows in the blessing and giving of rings. A member of the wedding party or a server can stand next to the minister with the rings on a small tray. After the blessing, the priest sprinkles the rings with holy water before he gives the rings to the bridegroom and then the bride. When the bridegroom and then the bride give their ring to their respective spouse, their words should be clearly heard by all. If the option of the cultural expression of the blessing and giving of the *Arras* is chosen, it takes place after the Giving of Rings. The *Order of Celebrating Matrimony* states: "Then a hymn or canticle of praise may be sung by the whole community" (OCM, 102). It is clear by the phrase "may be sung" that this is optional, however this is not a time for a solo or instrumental music. This hymn or canticle ritually expresses the thoughts and emotions of the assembly who has just witnessed the profound moment of two lives becoming one in Christ.

The Celebration of Matrimony concludes with the Universal Prayer. Several samples are provided in the ritual; however, the couple can be encouraged, with careful guidance from the priest or deacon, to write their own petitions or to adapt the ones provided. The OCM indicates that if the rubrics require the Creed, for example on Sundays or solemnities, it is said after the Universal Prayer, not before it, as is the usual custom during Mass.

The Pastoral Care of the Sick

AS THE WHOLE Church enters Lent to walk with the Lord toward the memorial of his suffering, Death, and Resurrection, those who suffer and are ill accompany the Lord in a special way. Through their own experience of suffering they share in the very Passion of Christ knowing that he had a special compassion for those who suffer. This is a powerful witness that those who suffer and are sick give to the Church at all times, and in a particular manner during Lent.

There are a number of ways that those in pastoral care ministries can minister to the sick during Lent. Any printed materials that the parish provides should be taken to those who are unable to come to church. If the parish has a website that includes podcasts of homilies these can be made accessible to parishioners at home. Often parishes have the technical ability to produce CDs or MP3s of their Sunday music selections which can be made available to people at home (be sure to secure proper copyright permission from the various Catholic music publishers). If the parish sponsors a Lenten mission, ask the guest homilist to visit those who are in nursing homes or long term care residences. The Sacrament of Reconciliation and the Sacrament of the Anointing of the Sick should be offered to those unable to come to church.

Many parishes schedule a communal celebration of both these sacraments of healing during Lent. Arrangements can be made to see that those who might otherwise not be able to be at church are present for these celebrations. The Lectionary readings for Lent and the respective ritual texts for these sacraments offer a wide variety of readings and prayers for these liturgies. Even if the celebrations are specifically directed to those who are sick, the entire parish should be invited. Suffering and illness are part of the human condition and all are caught up in the mystery of Christ's Passion and receive the benefits of his redeeming grace.

Those who enjoy good health, or who have recovered from illness of any kind, can be a sign of hope for those who suffer. These persons may be encouraged to reach out to the sick and homebound with the promise of prayers and words of compassion.

Those who are not usually involved in the pastoral care ministry of the parish could seek out ways to visit the sick and homebound during Lent as part of their own spiritual exercises. The whole Church is called to the spiritual works of mercy; when we reach out in compassion to those who suffer we reach out to Christ himself.

The Order of Christian Funerals

THERE ARE A NUMBER of contrasting scenes and spiritual encounters as we follow the Lord through Lent—from the temptations in the desert to the Transfiguration on the mountain; from the pronouncement of victory over death in the raising of Lazarus to the awareness of his own impending death; from the joyous shouts of the crowd as he enters Jerusalem to the shouts of derision on his way to the Cross. These Lenten events are made real for us at the time of death and find their counterpart in the liturgy of the funeral. Often there is a sense of peace when a person dies after much suffering; but there is always the sense of loss in their absence. There can be a feeling of gratitude for all the gifts and memories that someone has left

us; but there can be an accompanying desire to still have physical access to his or her presence with us. We can express our faith in the Resurrection, but we can have difficulty trusting in that faith.

As Jesus reminds us, sometimes his teaching can be a stumbling block and sometimes it is the cornerstone for moving forward in hope.

The Christian funeral liturgy does not intend to ignore or deny the human side of death, its pain of loss, its sense of disruption, or its feelings of helplessness. These honest emotions are rather lifted up to the tender gaze of the Father, to the redeeming grace of the Risen Lord. The prayers and readings of the funeral rightfully place our earthly journey alongside that of Jesus Christ and invite us to enter into his suffering and death with the assurance that we will also share in his glory with the Father. The process of grieving can take some time. The presence and support of others can help; but the Church's rituals, symbols, and ministries are profound forms of pastoral care. As a liturgical minister, preaching and presiding at funerals, and as one who has been the recipient of the loving ministry of others in my own grief, I know this to be true.

The Book of Blessings

LENT BEGINS with the blessing and distribution of ashes. Although the blessing of ashes normally takes place during Mass on Ash Wednesday, they can be blessed at another time within a Celebration of the Word of God. If the blessing takes place during Mass it follows the homily. If ashes are distributed at other liturgical celebrations during the day the blessing is not repeated. The blessing of ashes is reserved to a priest or deacon; lay ministers may assist with the distribution.

The *Book of Blessings* has not been updated since its publication, and there have been recent changes in the language of the prayers for the blessing of ashes. The most recent version of the Order of Blessing of Ashes can be found in *The Roman Missal*; this translation should be used for the order of blessing.

The St. Joseph's Table is a festive custom in many parishes during Lent and it is often celebrated either on the Solemnity of St. Joseph on March 19 or on the Sunday closest to this day.

The order for the blessing of St. Joseph's table is found in the *Book of Blessings* (see BB, chapter 53). Usually the blessing takes place outside of Mass in the venue where the food is made available. A priest, deacon, or lay minister may lead the order of blessing. A shorter rite is offered (see BB, 1697).

The Liturgical Environment

WHEN ASKED to name Holydays of Obligation, most people will include the high-attendance but nonobligatory observance of Ash Wednesday. Moving from Ordinary Time to the start of Lent invites each of us to examine our lives and engage in the Lenten practices of prayer, fasting, and almsgiving. We are summoned—individually and communally—to distance ourselves from the distractions of the world. An austere environment reinforces and reminds us of this call, standing in stark contrast to our world. Remove all plants from the worship space as well as any unnecessary furnishings. The purple used during Lent favors the red end of the spectrum, foreshadowing the Passion to come. Coordinate your choice of purple with the vesture of your priests so that there is not a drastic contrast. Use the color sparingly; it serves to mark the season rather than decorate it. Simple strips of fabric may be draped vertically on the ambo, altar and credence table.

The crucifix is the dominant symbol of Lent. Drawing attention to it may be achieved by removing any nearby plants and banners. If this is not sufficient, you may wish to drape a single piece of purple at the foot of a free-standing crucifix or behind the head and over the arms of a wall-mounted one.

During Lent we are especially reminded of our baptismal promises to reject Satan and believe in Christ. Because of this, leave holy water in its usual places where it reminds those gathered of the promises they have made and the graces God has bestowed upon us.

Outdoors, place a single large urn near the entrance. Fill it with soil and lay a grapevine wreath horizontally on top. Insert a cross of wood or metal that is large enough to be seen by

passersby without overwhelming the space. Secure the base with small stones.

With the Annunciation, Mary surrenders herself completely to God's plan with a simple yes. Her fiat serves as a model for Christians to follow God's will for each of us. For the solemnity, you may want to bring in a noble, yet simple arrangement of white flowers, symbolizing her purity.

Palm Sunday ushers in Holy Week. Obtain plenty of palm plants and fronds to decorate the worship space and also the place where the first Gospel will be read and the procession begins. Lash large fronds with red ribbon onto a lectern. Add red ribbon and proportionate fronds to the processional cross. Outside, add more palm fronds and red ribbon to welcome the assembly. If you know someone skilled in weaving palm branches, have a large, ornamental palm prepared for the presider to carry in procession. Add several large palm plants behind or on either side of the altar. You may choose to leave purple fabric in place, remove it altogether, or replace it with simple red runners or banners. Anticipate Triduum by mobilizing your team this week for a seamless transition.

The Liturgical Music

WE ARE BLESSED in having a rich, beautiful heritage of Lenten music from which to draw. We are also fortunate to have newer, high quality gems to add to the sacred music repertoire.

It is important to avoid associating chant solely with Lent because its usage is important throughout the course of the liturgical year. Nonetheless, some of the most beautiful chant melodies can be found in the Lenten repertoire. "Attende Domine," "Ubi Caritas," and "Parce, Domine" are annual favorites with simple refrains encouraging assembly participation. Though longer, "Vexilla Regis" and "Pange Lingua" are also appropriate. Shorter, Latin based refrains from Taizé, such as "Domine Deus," "Salvator Mundi," and "Benedictus Qui Venit" have proven useful in many parishes. The Kyrie from the "Missa Orbis Factor" is as much associated to Lent as "Silent Night" is to Christmas. It might look a bit long and intimidating but assemblies do pick it up quickly (and, remember, there is no Gloria, so for some who might be under the "time watch," it will all work out evenly). If you use it, keep it flowing and the phrases arched nicely to avoid stagnation. To further the chant theme, perhaps consider using a setting of the Eucharistic Acclamations based on chant. The one in *The Roman Missal* would be first but if your assembly sings it during other times of the year, you may want to consider one of the Latin Masses ("Cantus Missae") or other English options such as "Mass in Honor of St. Ignatius" (Russell Weismann), "Missa Simplex" (Richard Proulx), "Corpus Christi Mass" (Richard Proulx), "Missa Ubi Caritas" (Bob Hurd), "Siena Chant Mass" (Michael Dominic O'Connor) or "Mass of Charity and Love" (Paul Benoit and Steven Warner).

Many parishes use Lent as the time to employ the introit and Communion antiphons. Numerous options abound from the Latin *Graduale Simplex* to English chant settings by Columba Kelly (OCP), Bruce Ford (*By Flowing Waters*, Liturgical Press), Adam Bartlett (www.musicsacra.com), or Richard Clark (www.ccwatershed.org/blog/2016/jan/8/communion-antiphons-lent-rcia-scripture-clark/), to more contemporary settings such as those by Paul Tate ("In the Shadow of God," GIA).

There are many classic Lenten hymns from traditional to contemporary. Whatever resources you are using, look to the back of the book and take advantage of the "Liturgical Index." This index lists each piece and classifies it according to the liturgical year. Every hymnal and accompaniment book includes this section. Regardless of the musical genres of the parish, you must have in your library as many hymnals as you can get your hands on. The organ and other musical instruments are to be used in "moderation" and to support the singing of the assembly (GIRM, 313). In some places this is taken to the extreme but it is best to balance the approach. Definitely save the festive hymn accompaniments and reed stops for Easter and use instrumental music wisely, carefully, and sporadically. An important note is that the Gloria, mostly suspended during Lent, is prescribed for ritual Masses celebrated during Lent. Keep the setting simple and not overly festive.

The Liturgical Ministers

LITURGICAL MINISTERS, along with the whole Church, enter the season of Lent as though going on a retreat. It is a time for spiritual reflection, prayer, works of charity, and acts of penitence. Each of the liturgical ministries in a parish can find its own inspiration in the very tasks of their ministry. Can those in hospitality go out of their way to welcome those who seem distant or difficult to engage? Can readers spend a little more time praying with the Word that they will proclaim? Can ministers of Communion support efforts to bring food to those in the larger community? Can preachers make the Scriptures of Lent their own source of spiritual enrichment with lectio divina for everyday? Can those in music ministry take a different Lenten hymn each week as their prayer for meditating on the mysteries that they sing? These are only a few suggestions. They are meant to stir up the imagination of liturgical ministers as they explore other ways to enter into this great season using its rich tapestry of prayers, readings, and traditional practices to renew their relationship with the Lord.

Other Prayers, Rites, and Devotions

THE SEASON of Lent brings forward some of the most tangible, popular, and historically grounded devotions of Catholic Christianity: ashes on the forehead on Ash Wednesday, the Way of the Cross, devotion to Mary in the Sorrowful Mysteries of the Rosary, blessed palm branches on Passion Sunday, and the blessing of food at St. Joseph's Day to be given to the poor (see the *Book of Blessings*, chapter 53). The Litany of St. Joseph can also be found in the *Book of Blessings* (BB, 1691), and can be reprinted in the parish bulletin or on the website or social media page. Receiving blessed ashes has morphed into an unofficial "Holyday of Obligation" for Catholics and non-Catholics alike. Even non-Christians come to churches for ashes, and these ashes are worn back to work and at home and school throughout the day. The inherent power of sacramental ashes can represent a type of first aid for some, a reminder of mortality for others, or a time for transformation to living a good (or better) life, for many. Regardless of the motive of the recipient, receiving ashes can easily be regarded as the most widespread and widely-used sacramental in history.

There are abundant and diverse ways to celebrate the devotion of the Way of the Cross: moving around praying the Stations of the Cross in a church, praying the stations out of doors at a shrine or on a retreat, observing the stations as liturgical drama in many cultural expressions on Good Friday, and even quiet contemplation of the stations during the season of Lent. Many publishers have created booklets that guide us in praying the Stations of the Cross. With care and concern, ask the parish worship committee to select several formats that can become part of the devotional life of the parish. Remember to provide bi- or multi-lingual resources, and locate appropriate musical accompaniment for a communal service. The optional veiling of crosses during the last week of Lent guides the assembly to contemplate the notions of emptiness and absence of the approaching Holy Week.

Remind your congregation of the Lenten blessings and prayers in *Catholic Household Blessings & Prayers* (USCCB Publishing, Inc.). Lent might be a good time to acquire a copy. It is rich in sacramentals for Catholics. Prayer, fasting, and almsgiving have the combined character of being sacramental and often devotional, particularly during the season of Lent. Among the best resources to assist in feeding hungry and weary souls, discover LTP's *Keeping the Seasons* (bilingual Spanish/English reproducible resource) and *What Am I Doing for Lent This Year?* (second edition, by Paul Turner, in English and Spanish, a resource that supports Lenten devotion with self-guidance and the author's wisdom).

Evangelization

W**HAT ARE** you giving up for Lent? This is a popular question we hear in the beginning of the season, and often the reply is chocolate, desserts, soda, or, nowadays, Facebook. These are a good start, but our Catholic tradition offers us a deeper way to think about Lenten disciplines. The traditional Lenten practices that we inherit from the early centuries of the Church are actually

threefold: prayer, fasting, and almsgiving. One interesting idea is to think about how all these three might be incorporated into our presence on social media during the season of Lent.

There are many ways to offer prayers on social media. Some people like to post an inspirational quote, a short reflection based on their daily prayer practice, or a Scripture verse. Others will share an existing prayer resource, such as an image or brief video reflection they have come across or have found to be inspiring. Others still will invite prayers from or offer prayers to others through comments, creating a virtual prayer space in the midst of one's circle of friends.

When it comes to social media, many people think about fasting from it entirely as a Lenten discipline. This can be an especially holy practice especially for those who otherwise spend an excessive amount of time on these platforms. But one does not need to disengage entirely from social media in order to fast. Questions to discern about social media can be: What sort of activities online do I want to decrease? What kinds of things do I engage in there that keep me from holiness of life? Perhaps it is mocking others through comments, reposting mean-spirited memes or falsehoods, or lacking in charity when it comes to sharing theological or political opinions. The fruits of the Holy Spirit are: love, joy, peace, patience, kindness, goodness, faithfulness, gentleness, and self-control. We may fast from any words or actions online that do not demonstrate these fruits.

The practice of almsgiving is rooted in the call to be generous and self-giving toward others, especially those in need. One straightforward way to give alms through social media of course is to contribute funds and to raise awareness about worthwhile causes, projects, or ministries that are serving those in need. But there are also ways for us to engage in the spirit of almsgiving, and to think about what we can do to be generous and self-giving toward others in and through our social media presence itself. The way we communicate with and reach out to support and encourage others can demonstrate this almsgiving spirit. In order to do this, we must first listen, and become attentive to the needs, the brokenness, and the sufferingthat others may be expressing online, sometimes in subtle ways. Many people seek attention, support, a sense of community, and a sense that their presence matters to someone else. When we see this, we can extend our time, attention, and good words to them as a gift.

The Parish and the Home

TRADITIONALLY a time punctuated at parishes by Friday Stations of the Cross and fish fries, the celebration of Lent in the community can be much more. Lent is a communal journey of penance and prayer, so there should be an emphasis on doing things together as well as individually. In the announcement of Lenten disciplines this year, why not emphasize that there are three, and fasting is only one of them. Inform them of upcoming parish opportunities for prayer and charitable giving.

To encourage Lenten prayer and spirituality, add a weekly Bible study or small group experience open to all adults in the parish (a good resource to use is *At Home with the Word* published by LTP). Gather on an evening each week to celebrate Evening Prayer or a Taizé-style sung prayer. Be sure to schedule a communal Penance service, along with ample times for individual confession. And do include communal Stations of the Cross and fish fries (be sure to provide vegetarian/vegan options). Most importantly, if there are catechumens in the parish preparing for Baptism, make prayer for and with them a parish-wide priority. Be sure to publicize when the scrutinies will be celebrated and to explain their purpose and importance to those already baptized.

Other gathering opportunities should involve service and charity. Promote the Catholic Relief Services Rice Bowl (www.crsricebowl.org/), but also find ways to feed the hungry locally and to serve others in your own community. A food drive, a day of parish service assisting the elderly with yard clean-up, serving a meal at a homeless shelter, or a group visit to provide conversation and prayer for the elderly homebound or in nursing homes gives the parish community a chance to express its identity.

For busy families with children, home prayer and charitable activities they can do as a family might be a better option. One of the projects they might make at the end of Ordinary Time could be a "good deeds jar," filled with slips of paper describing actions they can take the next day to help others, which are drawn from the jar each day at dinner time. An at-home child-friendly version of the Stations of the Cross can be distributed so that families may pray this devotion in their homes.

As Lent comes to an end, be sure to prepare the community for Holy Week and the Easter Triduum by inviting all to be present for the solemn celebrations to come.

Reflections through the Year

A sense of deep communion with the rest of nature cannot be real if our hearts lack tenderness, compassion, and concern for our fellow human beings. It is clearly inconsistent to combat trafficking in endangered species while remaining completely indifferent to human trafficking, unconcerned about the poor, or undertaking to destroy another human being deemed unwanted. This compromises the very meaning of our struggle for the sake of the environment. It is no coincidence that, in the canticle in which Saint Francis praises God for his creatures, he goes on to say: "Praised be you my Lord, through those who give pardon for your love." Everything is connected. Concern for the environment thus needs to be joined to a sincere love for our fellow human beings and an unwavering commitment to resolving the problems of society. (LI, 91)

Moreover, when our hearts are authentically open to universal communion, this sense of fraternity excludes nothing and no one. It follows that our indifference or cruelty towards fellow creatures of this world sooner or later affects the treatment we mete out to other human beings. We have only one heart, and the same wretchedness which leads us to mistreat an animal will not be long in showing itself in our relationships with other people. Every act of cruelty towards any creature is "contrary to human dignity." We can hardly consider ourselves to be fully loving if we disregard any aspect of reality: "Peace, justice and the preservation of creation are three absolutely interconnected themes, which cannot be separated and treated individually without once again falling into reductionism." Everything is related, and we human beings are united as brothers and sisters on a wonderful pilgrimage, woven together by the love God has for each of his creatures and which also unites us in fond affection with brother sun, sister moon, brother river, and mother earth. (*Laudato si'*, 92)

Mass Texts

◆ Introduction to the Mass

During Lent we walk with our elect as they prepare for their Christian initiation at the Easter Vigil and we recall our baptismal promise to live Jesus clearly. Through prayer, fasting, and almsgiving, we do penance and grow in charity, to reorient our lives after the example of the Lord who revealed the face of God's mercy, which we now acclaim.

◆ Seasonal Alternate Tropes for Penitential Act Form C

Lord Jesus, you came to reconcile us with God and with each other: Lord, have mercy.

Christ Jesus, you emptied yourself to become one with us: Christ, have mercy.

Lord Jesus, by dying you destroyed our death: Lord, have mercy.

◆ Dismissal for Children's Liturgy of the Word

When we were baptized we promised to live Jesus so that all we say, do, and are might show people that we belong to him. We need the Word of God to show us how to live Jesus. Since we don't always live like Jesus, we also need the Word of God to help us say "I'm sorry" and learn how to make up for any wrong we have done. Go, listen to the Word of God and ask Jesus to show you how to live like him more clearly.

◆ Dismissal of Catechumens and Elect

On Ash Wednesday we were marked in ashes with the Sign of the Cross that reminds us that we were claimed for Christ during the Rite of Acceptance. Each week of Lent helps us discover what difference wearing the cross makes. Listen to the Word of God. Believe what you hear. And live what you believe. We look forward to the time when you will join us at the Table of the Lord, fully one with us as members of the Body of Christ. Go in peace.

◆ Seasonal Universal Prayer (Prayer of the Faithful)

Invitation to Prayer

The Holy Spirit sent Jesus to the desert for forty days. Lent is a time like that desert retreat. Open our hearts to discover what you ask of us, and our world, as we offer these prayers.

Intercessions

1. May Christians everywhere be guided this Lent to live the promises we made when we were baptized into the Body of Christ, we pray to the Lord:

2. May world leaders fast from greater concern for themselves or their own countries, and make available whatever is needed to care for the physical, spiritual, and emotional needs of all people, we pray to the Lord:

3. May our prayer, fasting, and almsgiving make us more aware of our utter dependence upon God, our interdependence with one another, and the hungers of those who go without food, shelter, faith, or love, we pray to the Lord:

4. May our catechumens and elect find credible witnesses in all the baptized as they make their final preparations for full initiation, we pray to the Lord:

5. May we abstain from arrogance and pride and grow in humility to empty ourselves like Jesus, who became one with us that we might be one with God, we pray to the Lord:

6. May our beloved dead rejoice in the light of God's face and may those who are dying find hope in our faith in the Resurrection we prepare to celebrate, we pray to the Lord:

Concluding Prayer

God of mercy,
hear the prayers of your adopted daughters
    and sons.
May our prayer deepen our closeness with you,
our fasting deepen our hunger for you,
and our almsgiving unite us more closely with our
    sisters, brothers, and all creation.
Through Christ our Lord.
Amen.

March 2019
Month of St. Joseph

Optional Memorials during Lent

The Missal commentaries below pertain to seasonal weekdays or other obligatory observances. The following should be consulted when celebrating optional memorials during Lent (please note that all obligatory memorials become optional during Lent): "If an obligatory memorial falls during Lent, it becomes optional. On the weekdays of Lent, except Ash Wednesday and during Holy Week, the Mass texts for the current liturgical day are used; but the Collect may be taken from a Memorial which happens to be inscribed in the General Calendar for that day, except on Ash Wednesday and during Holy Week" (GIRM, 355a).

WED 6 (#219) violet
Ash Wednesday

About Ash Wednesday

In the early Church, when Lent was a time for the reconciliation of public penitents, the penitents would come to the church at the beginning of Lent, that is, on Ash Wednesday. They would wear a penitential garment, suggesting sackcloth, and be sprinkled with ashes. Then they would be ritually expelled from the assembly to do their penance for forty days, returning to the church on Holy Thursday, when they would be readmitted to the sacraments. With time, the expulsion of penitents disappeared, but the ashes remained and became a call to penance for all the faithful. In the Scriptures, sackcloth and ashes are the signs of penance. The practice of using ashes from the palms of the previous year's Palm Sunday is a relatively new element of the liturgy, first appearing in the twelfth century. It adds another layer of meaning to this rich rite, reminding us of where we are headed—to the glory of Easter.

The Lectionary for Mass

◆ FIRST READING: Locusts had overrun Judah and the prophet Joel saw in their attack a sign that the Lord's day would soon arrive. His prophetic words encourage the people to turn their hearts back to the Lord and experience the Lord's mercy. With the sound of a trumpet and the proclamation of a fast, the people gather together in assembly as we do each Lent to plead with the Lord to save them.

◆ RESPONSORIAL PSALM 51: A common penitential psalm for Lent, Psalm 51 follows upon the people's request for the Lord's mercy in the First Reading, with similar appeals to the Lord for forgiveness and compassion. The psalmist asks the Lord to cleanse his heart and renew his spirit for he has lost the joy that comes with knowing the Lord's salvation. Would that our Lenten journey this year enable us to discover a newfound joy in the Lord!

◆ SECOND READING: The emphasis in Paul's words lies in reconciliation—our reconciliation to God. Christ became our righteousness and because of him, our responsibility rests in becoming the righteousness of God. When do we fulfill our responsibility? Paul cites the prophet Isaiah to inform us that there is no other time than the present, acceptable time, to undertake the journey toward reconciliation with God and others.

◆ GOSPEL: The Gospel reading comes from the Sermon on the Mount in Matthew. In it, we find Jesus cautioning the disciples not to do righteous deeds with the hubris of having other people see them. Only hypocrites need others to acknowledge their good works. When disciples fast, give alms, and pray, their focus should remain on growing in their relationship with God.

The Roman Missal

The prayers for the day can be found at Ash Wednesday in the Lent section of the Proper of Time toward the beginning of the Missal. There is no Penitential Act today, since it is replaced by the distribution of ashes. There is no singing of the Gloria, and the Alleluia is omitted until the Easter Vigil. The rite for the blessing and distribution of ashes takes place after the homily. The priest celebrant, with any necessary ministers (for example, the bookbearer, and someone to hold the vessel with water, if needed), goes to the place where the vessel(s) with ashes is (are). His hands remain joined for the introduction (the rubric for which does *not* indicate "these or similar words"), and then he leaves a brief period for silent prayer. Then, with hands extended, he prays one of the two prayers of blessing. While both prayers include the gesture of making the Sign of the Cross over the ashes, the gesture has a somewhat different focus in each of the two prayers: in the first, the priest is asking the grace of God's blessing on those "who are marked with these ashes," and in the second, the blessing is invoked more specifically on the ashes themselves. Consequently, the gesture should match the action according to the words of the prayer. After the prayer, the priest sprinkles the ashes with water, but this is done in silence, without his saying anything. Either one of two formulas is used to impose ashes: "Repent, and believe in the Gospel" or "Remember that you are dust, and to dust you shall return." The rubric states simply that ashes are placed on the head of all those present who come up, as the formula is said. Customarily, this is done by the priest (or deacon or minister) dipping his (or her) thumb in the ashes, and then tracing the ashes on the person's forehead in the Sign of the Cross, although, technically, there is nothing that requires this. (Interestingly, we know, for example, that historically ashes have also been sprinkled on the top of people's heads.)

Singing is to take place during the imposition of ashes, and several possibilities are spelled out in the Missal. There are three suggested antiphons that can be used in connection with the verses of Psalm 51; a responsory is also suggested, or another appropriate song may be sung.

Be sure to provide the means for priests and other ministers to wash their hands after the distribution of ashes. Premoistened towelettes sometimes work better than plain water, although water and towels should also be available.

After the imposition of ashes (and the ministers' washing their hands), the Universal Prayer takes place; the Creed is not said. After the Universal Prayer, Mass continues as usual.

If the blessing and distribution of ashes takes place outside Mass, then everything proceeds as described above, including all the readings and their chants as at Mass, but then, after the Universal Prayer, the priest simply blesses and dismisses the faithful, using the Prayer over the People given at the end of the Mass formularies. Interestingly, there is no specific mention in the rubrics that the Our Father is prayed when the blessing and distribution of ashes occurs outside Mass; they simply direct that the rite is concluded with the Universal Prayer, the blessing, and the dismissal of the faithful.

Use either Preface III or Preface IV of Lent. Both Prefaces are short and to the point, in keeping with the starkness of this day's liturgy. Consider using the Eucharistic Prayer for Reconciliation I.

For the dismissal, the priest is to use the Prayer over the People. There is no indication that this dismissal text is optional. The prayer is prayed with the priest's hands extended over the people. The prayer asks that God will pour out on us "a spirit of compunction" as a result of our doing penance, again pointing to the inward, spiritual conversion that should take place as a result of the outward actions.

Other Ideas

On Ash Wednesday and every Friday during Lent, Catholics are asked to fast from eating meat. In the dioceses of the United States, Catholics are obliged to refrain from eating meat on every Friday of the year unless he or she substitutes this practice with another act of penance (see the 1966 USCCB document, *Pastoral Statement on Penance and Abstinence*). Let's consider a new practice to implement that is rooted in both an act of penance and care for the environment. In his encyclical *Laudato si'*, Pope Francis challenges all peoples to protect our environment from climate change and other destructions caused by humanity. In 2016, Pope Francis also added Care for Creation to the traditional Corporal Works of Mercy. Dorothy Day once said, "Everything a baptized person does each day should be directly or indirectly related to the corporal and spiritual works of mercy." Simple things, such as not eating meat once a week, have great implications for the environment, and many environmentalist groups advocate for meatless Mondays (this includes fish). These groups argue that if everyone fasts from eating meat, just one day a week, we will minimize water usage, reduce greenhouse gases, and reduce fuel dependence. As a way of living our baptismal call to care for creation, encourage parishioners to take on the habit of meatless

Fridays throughout the year. Refer to this practice as "Fruit and Veggie Friday." This website explores the scientific connection between going meatless and protecting the environment (www.downtoearth.org /go-veggie/environment/top-10 -reasons).

T H U **7** (#220) violet
Thursday after Ash Wednesday

Optional Memorial of Sts. Perpetua and Felicity, Martyrs / violet

The Lectionary for Mass

◆ FIRST READING: Moses clearly presents the two options available to the people: life or death. If the people choose life, this means they choose to obey the Lord's commandments. If they choose death, they choose to turn their hearts away from God. The choice of God's people in Moses' time is our choice today. Will we choose God's blessing or curse?

◆ RESPONSORIAL PSALM 1: The opening hymn of the psalter, which sets before us the contrast between the good and the wicked, also served as the Responsorial Psalm for Friday of the Second Week of Advent, December 14, 2018, with a different refrain. Today's refrain expresses the blessedness of those who place their hope in the Lord. How blessed are we who choose life, not death. We, who follow the Lord's law, will surely be happy!

◆ GOSPEL: Jesus' first prediction of his Passion, Death, and Resurrection forms the heart of the Gospel reading. His prediction emphasizes the role the religious leaders—the elders, chief priests, and scribes—will have in his coming suffering. Immediately following his prediction, Jesus lays out the primary condition of discipleship: taking up one's cross each and every day and following him. On the journey of the cross, disciples will find their life for God will save them in Jesus.

The Roman Missal

The Collect is the perfect prayer for the beginning of Lent. We ask that God may be with us in all we do: inspiring our actions, helping them along, and bringing them to completion. Consider using the Eucharistic Prayer for Reconciliation II. In the Prayer over the Offerings, we ask God to give us his forgiveness, so that the offerings we make may give him honor. One of the four Prefaces of Lent is used today, and any one of the four is appropriate. In the Prayer after Communion, we ask that the "heavenly gifts" we have received may bring us both forgiveness and salvation. The Prayer over the People is a prayer that God, who made known the "ways of eternal life," will also guide his people along those ways.

Today's Saints

In the year 203, Sts. Perpetua and Felicity were martyred in the amphitheater at Carthage. Their crime was professing faith in Jesus Christ. Perpetua was a wealthy noblewoman, the mother of a young son; Felicity was a humble slave girl, who gave birth to a daughter just a few days before she died. These women, so different in their circumstances, were united in their death. The names of these heroic women are included in Eucharistic Prayer I, alongside the names of Apostles and martyrs. They lived today's Gospel, praying for their persecutors.

F R I 8 (#221) violet
Friday after
Ash Wednesday

Optional Memorial of St. John of God, Religious / violet

The Lectionary for Mass

◆ FIRST READING: The Lord presents a challenging word to the people through the prophet Isaiah. The word requires of them a paradigm

shift around their understanding of a "fast." On the day that is found acceptable to the Lord, the image of a proper fast is no longer a person lying in sackcloth and ashes, but rather people working to set the oppressed free, feeding the hungry, providing shelter for the homeless, and clothing the naked.

◆ RESPONSORIAL PSALM 51: A different refrain and verses of the penitential Psalm 51 than those used on Ash Wednesday, make up today's Responsorial Psalm. While the emphasis remains on our prayer for God's mercy, in the refrain we humbly approach God with penitent hearts, trusting that God will not turn us away. Verses 18-19 connect with the First Reading in their acknowledgment that the Lord no longer wants burnt offerings and sacrifices, but a repentant spirit from his people. This, too, is a paradigm shift.

◆ GOSPEL: The question about fasting posed by the disciples of John the Baptist links the Gospel reading directly to Isaiah's prophetic words about fasting in the First Reading. John's disciples and the Pharisees fast on many occasions, but Jesus' disciples do not. Jesus explains in short, parable-like language to John's disciples that this is the case because the bridegroom is still with them. A new fast will begin when the bridegroom leaves them.

The Roman Missal

The Collect is a prayer for the strength to complete the "bodily observances" we have undertaken this Lent. Our Lenten observance is a sacrifice that we offer to God. We pray that it will be acceptable to God, and strengthen "our powers of self-restraint" (Prayer over the Offerings). We do not fast from enjoyable things because they are inherently bad. We fast because it shows us the way to self-control.

One of the four Prefaces of Lent is used today, and any one of the four is appropriate. Consider using the Eucharistic Prayer for Reconciliation II. In the Prayer after Communion, we pray for the fruits of the Eucharist, that we may be forgiven, and made ready for "the remedies of [God's] compassion." We are a people on a "pilgrim journey," and the disciplines we undertake during Lent are "age-old." In the Prayer over the People, we pray that, always giving God thanks, we may deserve to come into God's presence forever. Even though the Prayer over the People is optional on weekdays, it would be good to use it, to highlight the liturgical time.

Today's Saint

St. John of God was a Portuguese friar who became a leading religious figure. After a period in the army in Spain, he began to distribute religious books, using the new Gutenberg printing press. At one point, John had an intense religious experience that resulted in temporary insanity. He was thrown into a mental institution, and while there, he realized how badly the sick and the poor were treated. Once he recovered, he spent the rest of his life caring for them. In Granada he gathered a circle of disciples around him who felt the same call and founded what is now known as the Brothers Hospitallers of St. John of God.

S A T 9 (#222) violet
Saturday after
Ash Wednesday

Optional Memorial of St. Frances of Rome, Religious / violet

The Lectionary for Mass

◆ FIRST READING: Today we hear Isaiah elaborate on the new paradigm of fasting. The removal of oppression and false charges coupled with putting an end to hateful speech and feeding the hungry are some of the requirements.

Honoring the Sabbath as the Lord's day rather than our own brings delight to those who fast. Those who undertake the new fast will experience the Lord's providential care in abundance.

◆ RESPONSORIAL PSALM 86: The author of Psalm 86 laments to the Lord for he is in distress. In a prayer that has a gentle flow to it, the psalmist asks the Lord for mercy in return for his devotion. He wants to learn the Lord's way so that his soul can rejoice.

◆ GOSPEL: In Jesus' time, many saw tax collectors as corrupt and selfish. Regardless of what others thought, Jesus personally reaches out to a tax collector named Levi while he is at work and invites Levi to follow him. Without any questions, Levi follows Jesus and throws a banquet for him at his [Levi's] house where many other tax collectors and sinners join them. The Pharisees and scribes fail to understand why Jesus chooses to dine with these people. If only the Pharisees and scribes would grasp their own need for repentance.

The Roman Missal

We are weak, but we ask God to look with compassion on us, and protect us with the "right hand" of his majesty (Collect). In the Prayer over the Offerings, we ask God to receive the sacrifice we offer, which is a "sacrifice of conciliation and praise." The Eucharist we celebrate can cleanse us and make our minds "well pleasing" to God. The Eucharist we receive is a mystery and will always remain a mystery "in this present life," but it has power to help us toward eternity. One of the four Prefaces of Lent is used today, and any one of the four is appropriate. Consider using the Eucharistic Prayer for Various Needs and Occasions IV. The Prayer after Communion prays for the protection of all "who have

touched the sacred mysteries" in the celebration of the Eucharist. Even though the Prayer over the People is optional on weekdays, it would be good to use it, to highlight the liturgical time.

Today's Saint

St. Frances of Rome was born in Rome to wealthy parents. Although she wanted to enter a monastery, her parents married her off to Lorenzo Ponziano, commander of the papal troops in Rome. It was a happy marriage that lasted forty years. Her husband was often away at war, and Frances spent her time praying, visiting the poor, and caring for the sick. Eventually, her example inspired other wealthy women to do the same. Frances founded a lay congregation of Benedictine Oblates now known as Oblates of St. Frances of Rome.

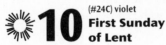
☀ 10 (#24C) violet
First Sunday of Lent

The Lectionary for Mass

◆ FIRST READING: When the ancient Israelites talked about God, they recounted what God had done for them. They told about God's call to their ancestor Abraham and of their deliverance from Egypt. Both signified God's grace, power, and covenant faithfulness. The Israelites reminded themselves of God's presence by giving offerings and regularly reciting God's mighty deeds in history. The harvest ritu-

al described in this passage bridges the border between the Hebrews' experience in the wilderness and their experience as a settled people. The offering of the first fruits of the harvest links with a recitation about where they came from. Always remembering their former lives as slaves and wanderers, our ancestors celebrated the gift of a sustaining land in which to live. Like all celebrations of God's saving activities, thanksgiving to God and generosity to others mark the ritual.

◆ RESPONSORIAL PSALM 91: It is easier to enter new territory or situations when we know God is with us. The psalmist intimately knows God's saving presence. God is the one who saves, protects, and rescues. In this week's Gospel, the devil quotes this psalm to Jesus during his time in the wilderness. He urges Jesus to test whether God truly protects him. Like the psalmist, however, Jesus knows a relationship with God is not about avoiding difficulty but about trusting God in the midst of difficulty.

◆ SECOND READING: The early Church found itself entering unexpected territory. Some Jews and a large number of Gentiles were willing to follow Jesus as God's Christ. If all of the early converts were Jews, it would have been simple to welcome them into the community. How to include gentile believers who were not first converts to Judaism was more difficult. By what basic standard of belief would they judge conversion? The early confessional statement, "Jesus is Lord," was one essential. It meant giving allegiance to Jesus rather than to Caesar. It meant believing that God, who raised Jesus from death, continued to work in the lives of all believers. On that basis, Jews and gentiles could work together to create a new community in which race, nation, gender, and economic status mattered less than one's confession of faith.

◆ GOSPEL: The story of Jesus' temptations in the wilderness is always told on this First Sunday of Lent. This year is Luke's turn to tell the story. Luke's temptation story follows Jesus' baptism. Jesus goes into the wilderness led by the Spirit, whom Jesus experienced so vividly in his baptism. Jesus experiences trials like those his ancestors faced in their forty years in the wilderness. They, too, struggled to remain faithful to God when faced with hunger, the gods of other nations, and risky situations. It is important to recognize the temptations as real options that Jesus could reasonably have accepted. The devil tempts Jesus with good things. It is good to eat when you are hungry. It is good to have the authority to bring about change. It is good to be protected from danger. Yet, for Jesus to accept these good things from the devil would mean giving up his allegiance to God and abusing God's promise to care for him. Because he was grounded in Jewish faith and Scripture, Jesus had the resources to meet these temptations with integrity and confidence. He refuses to doubt or test his relationship with God, refuses to bypass the Cross. Lent is a perfect time for questioning, sorting our priorities, and recommitting ourselves to God. We remember that temptations are not aberrations or glitches in the Christian life. As in Jesus' case, temptations are part of that life, forcing us to focus on what is really important.

The Roman Missal

The Gloria is omitted today. The Creed is said or sung. The Preface to be used for this Mass is given on the pages right there along with the other texts for the Mass. The reason this Preface, "The Temptation of the Lord," is used today is obvious, since the Gospel reading for

the First Sunday of Lent is always the account of the temptation of Jesus from one of the Gospel accounts. Consider chanting the introductory dialogue and the Preface today; if this is not the regular practice of your community, this can be a way of powerfully drawing attention to the solemnity of Lenten time (but be sure to prepare and rehearse your assembly as needed, especially if your people are not familiar with the responses!). Consider using the Eucharistic Prayer for Reconciliation II. The Prayer over the People is required, not optional, on the Sundays of Lent, and the text is given right after the Prayer after Communion.

The *Rite of Christian Initiation of Adults* includes an optional Rite of Sending of the Catechumens for Election. If your diocese celebrates the Rite of Election on the First Sunday of Lent, as suggested by the RCIA, then consider celebrating this Rite of Sending in your parish. Celebrating the rite is yet another way to catechize the entire parish about the meaning of RCIA and the journey the catechumens (soon to be elect) undertake. Also, the rite provides yet another opportunity for the catechumens to be supported in prayer by, and to receive the good wishes of, those who will soon be their brothers and sisters in Baptism. The rite takes place after the homily at Mass and is described in numbers 106–117 in the RCIA.

Other Ideas

On this First Sunday of Lent the elements of the liturgy, the environment, the music, the readings, and the tone of the various prayers speak of the nature Lent as a call to *metanoia*, a change of heart. This tone is like a thread that weaves its way through Lent. Consider creating a symbol, a signature image, in today's language an emoji, that appears on all parish literature, including bulletins, handouts and

posters that announce parish activities for Lent. Lent calls for a more somber tone than that of other liturgical seasons; but this does not mean that it is dull or weary. On the other hand, be careful not to burden the Sunday liturgies with too much "stuff"—like unnecessary announcements, presentations, or pious rituals. The Lenten liturgies are very powerful, let them speak clearly and keep the focus on the call to repentance.

M O N **11** (#224) violet
Lenten Weekday

The Lectionary for Mass

◆ FIRST READING: The Lord gives Moses the commandments he is to speak to the entire assembly of the children of Israel. In the passage from Leviticus, the book of the Law, we find the commandments situated within God's call to holiness. Each day we live the commandments, we embrace more deeply God's summons to us to be holy as he is holy.

◆ RESPONSORIAL PSALM 19 reminds us that we come to know the Lord's wisdom through the commandments. The refrain comes from John 6:63b and helps us to open ourselves to the life that comes from the Lord's words.

◆ GOSPEL: Jesus teaches his disciples that when the Son of Man comes in glory, he will base the final judgment on the works of mercy we have performed. Whenever we have done a merciful, life-giving deed on behalf of those society considers the least, we have done the deed for Jesus. Our actions on behalf of justice have nothing to do with the self-righteousness of those who fail to see when Jesus is hungry and thirsty and in need of a warm welcome.

The Roman Missal

Only by conversion and understanding of "heavenly teaching" can we benefit from the good works we offer to God this Lent (see the Collect). In the Prayer over the Offerings, we pray that the offering we make to God may change our lives, reconcile us to the Father, and bring us forgiveness. In the Prayer after Communion, we pray that the power of the sacrament we receive may bring us "help in mind and body" and "the fullness of heavenly healing." The Eucharist is food for body and soul. The Prayer over the People is a simple prayer that asks that God's people may receive the grace to see what needs to be done—and the strength to do it.

T U E 12 (#225) violet
Lenten Weekday

The Lectionary for Mass

◆ FIRST READING: The brief two verses from Isaiah speak of all that the Lord will fulfill through his Word. Like the earth receives moisture from rain and snow, like the sower receives seed, and the hungry, bread, we receive God's Word. May we accept the invitation to welcome the Word in our hearts this Lent as a guide for our journey.

◆ RESPONSORIAL PSALM 34 is a common psalm for Ordinary Time, although with different refrains. Today's refrain, from verse 18b, acknowledges how God saves the just from pain and anguish. In verses 4–5 and 6–7 the psalmist extends an invitation to us to glorify the Lord and to turn to the Lord for our joy. In the latter two stanzas, verses 16–17 and 18–19, the psalmist communicates his faith that the Lord indeed looks out for the just and hears their cries.

◆ GOSPEL: When Jesus teaches his disciples how to pray, he differentiates their prayer from that of

pagans, rather than that of the Pharisees and scribes—those whom he has previously criticized as self-righteous hypocrites. God does not decide whose prayer to hear based on the number of words in it as the pagans think, because God knows what we must ask him for even before we pray. Although, note that Jesus does not say God refuses to hear the prayers of the pagans. Through prayer, we develop our relationship with God who knows our innermost thoughts. This is why Jesus teaches his disciples to pray beginning with the words "Our Father" and that less is more in prayer.

The Roman Missal

We do not undertake "bodily discipline" in Lent for its own sake, like athletes or dieters. Rather, through this observance, we grow in "yearning" for God (Collect). In the Eucharist, we bring "temporal sustenance," bread and wine, and in his goodness God transforms them into food for eternal life (Prayer over the Offerings). Consider using the Eucharistic Prayer for Various Needs and Occasions III. Controlling our desires can help us to correct our priorities—to "love the things of heaven" (Prayer after Communion). Any one of the four Prefaces of Lent can be used today. Even though the Prayer over the People is optional on weekdays, it would be good to use it, to highlight the liturgical time. In this prayer, we pray that God may be with us in all the trials of life—our consolation in grief, our perseverance in times of trial, our protection in danger.

W E D 13 (#226) violet
Lenten Weekday

The Lectionary for Mass

◆ FIRST READING: On the Lord's direction, Jonah makes his way to the city of Nineveh where he warns the people that God would destroy

Nineveh in forty days. The prophet's words lead not only the people to believe in God, but the king to join in their fast. Their confidence that God would reconsider and not destroy the city and its people, was far from bold, but their actions were audacious enough that God did not bring evil upon Nineveh.

◆ RESPONSORIAL PSALM 51: For the third time already this Lent, our Responsorial Psalm comes from Psalm 51. Today's verses are a combination of those from Ash Wednesday and last Friday. In the psalm, we see an individual experience the conversion of his heart and spirit to the Lord. We join our voices with his as we express our belief that the Lord will not turn us away when we humbly approach him.

◆ GOSPEL: Jesus refers to the prophet Jonah as a sign to the Ninevites of their need for conversion. The Son of Man will be a similar sign to the people of Jesus' generation—and by extension—our own generation and generations to come. At the final judgment, will the people of Nineveh condemn the generations because their peoples failed to embrace change and see the Wisdom of God present among them?

The Roman Missal

We pray that the Lord may "look kindly" on us, so that our bodily self-restraint may lead to renewal in mind (Collect). For our sake God makes our gifts into the Sacrament of Christ's Body and Blood. We pray that this same sacrament may be for us "an eternal remedy," food for everlasting life. Any one of the four Prefaces of Lent can be used today. Consider using the Eucharistic Prayer II. Even though the Prayer over the People is optional on weekdays, it would be good to use it, to highlight the liturgical time. In the Prayer after Communion, we pray that the sacrament we have received may bring us "unending life."

T H U 14 (#227) violet
Lenten Weekday

The Lectionary for Mass

◆ FIRST READING: A pained Queen Esther gives herself up to the Lord in prayer as she lies prostrate and cries out to him. Three times she asks for God's help because she is alone. As part of her prayer, she acknowledges how God has freed his people in the past. Her request is nothing less than for God to do the same now and make his people whole once again.

◆ RESPONSORIAL PSALM 138: In this psalm of thanksgiving, the psalmist recognizes that nothing he does will cause the Lord to save him. Rather, the Lord rescues him out of his own unconditional kindness and mercy. So it is with us, too. When we call to God for help, God answers us. We give thanks with our whole hearts for God's loving responses to our prayers that lead us to wholeness.

◆ GOSPEL: What we know as the Golden Rule concludes the Gospel reading from Matthew in which Jesus teaches his disciples to ask, seek, and knock and God will give to them, they will find God, and God will open the door for them. God will provide good for his children even more than we can ever provide for our children on earth.

The Roman Missal

Consider using the Eucharistic Prayer III.

F R I 15 (#228) violet
Lenten Weekday

The Lectionary for Mass

◆ FIRST READING: Virtuous human persons can become wicked and the wicked can convert to a life of virtue. The prophet Ezekiel presents the Lord's words about the consequences for both conversions in today's First Reading. Ezekiel knows the people view the Lord's way as unfair. We do not know if they had anyone ever tell them that life is not always fair. We can, however, wonder why they would consider life in God for the virtuous and punishment for the wicked unfair even as Ezekiel attests to the fact that God's pleasure comes from life, not the death of the wicked.

◆ RESPONSORIAL PSALM 130 is one of the Penitential Psalms. We are familiar with it as the *De profundis*. From the depths of sorrow, the psalmist cries out to the Lord to hear his voice. His trust is palpable; his patience notable; and his selfishness evident. In the end, it is not solely about his personal experience of forgiveness, but of the redemption God will bring to Israel.

◆ GOSPEL: From Jesus' words to the disciples, we can surmise that the scribes and Pharisees do not know how to build community with their brothers and sisters through reconciliation. Their self-righteousness does not permit this. For disciples, however, entering the Kingdom of heaven requires a righteousness whereby we enact the process of reconciliation among members of our communities.

The Roman Missal

Any one of the four Prefaces of Lent can be used today. Consideration might also be given, in light of the Gospel's call for us to be reconciled with one another (especially before bringing our gifts to the altar), to using Eucharistic Prayer for Reconciliation II, as it describes in its Preface how it is through the power of the Spirit "that enemies may speak to each other again, / adversaries join hands, / and peoples seek to meet together" and how the Spirit "takes away everything that estranges us from one another."

S A T 16 (#229) violet
Lenten Weekday

The Lectionary for Mass

◆ FIRST READING: Moses has presented the people with many and various statutes and laws for how they are to live together in harmony and to honor the Lord their God. As Moses addresses the people in today's passage from Deuteronomy, he makes known to them that on "this day" they are to observe all God's commandments with their whole heart and soul. This is the day of covenant. On this day, the people covenant with the Lord and the Lord with them. Going forward, each and every day is the day we keep covenant with the Lord and observe the commandments.

◆ RESPONSORIAL PSALM 119: The opening verses of Psalm 119, the longest hymn in the psalter, speak to how happy the people are who follow the Lord's commandments. We give thanks to the Lord in the words of the psalmist for we have learned the Lord's laws and we pray in his words that we might remain committed to them.

◆ GOSPEL: We skip ahead over the sections in Matthew 5 on adultery, divorce, and vengeance to find Jesus instructing the disciples on how to be perfect like the heavenly Father is perfect. In God's eyes, perfection lies in being merciful. Living mercy entails a wisdom the world does not know. This wisdom teaches us as Jesus' disciples to love our enemies and pray for those who oppress us. It is relatively easy to love those who love us. Living mercifully, on the other hand, requires a lifetime commitment to discipleship.

The Roman Missal

In the Collect we pray that we may seek "always the one thing necessary" so that while we undertake works of love, we may worship the Lord. The Eucharist is the reward of saints and food for sinners. We pray that these "blessed mysteries" may restore us and make us worthy to receive them (Prayer over the Offerings). We have been refreshed by a "divine mystery," "imbued with heavenly teaching." We ask that God may accompany us on our way with his consolations (Prayer after Communion). We long for God's blessing. We ask that his benediction may strengthen us to follow his will and rejoice in his gifts (Prayer over the People). Any one of the four Prefaces of Lent can be used today.

17 (#27C) violet
Second Sunday of Lent

The Lectionary for Mass

◆ FIRST READING: In chapter 12 of Genesis, God came to Abram and promised to bless him with descendants. Through those descendants the world would also be blessed. God comes to Abram again and twice repeats the earlier promise, but Abram is skeptical at first. He had no children and a wife who was long past her childbearing years. How would God give him descendants? Abram's questions are really questions about God's reliability. Can God be trusted to do what he promised? God's dramatic response is to make a covenant with Abram. While Abram sleeps, God performs an ancient covenant ceremony. God passes through the pieces of a sacrifice, saying in effect, "May I

end up like this sacrifice if I do not fulfill my promise to Abram." The relationship between Abram and God binds both of them. Abram is not the only one to greet God's messages of hope with skepticism. Many of us may find such messages hard to believe. Lent, however, is a time when we remember that hope does not depend on us. Our hope is in God's covenant faithfulness shown to us in Jesus Christ.

◆ RESPONSORIAL PSALM 27: In the midst of false accusations and plotting adversaries, the psalmist turns to God for shelter. Through an awareness of God's ongoing faithfulness and goodness, the psalmist finds courage and confidence to face the surrounding turmoil and trouble. God is the light that guides, the stronghold that gives shelter.

◆ SECOND READING: Paul wrote his letters to communities such as the Philippians after the early believers' experience of Jesus' Death and Resurrection. He preached the hope of salvation through the Cross and by belief in the Gospel of Jesus Christ. Paul invited believers to imitate his own path to righteousness and reject the lure of evil. It is the profession of faith in Christ crucified and raised from the dead that separated those who awaited the Second Coming. Paul saw all others as enemies of the Cross of Christ. Paul's final instructions say stand firm in the Lord. Listen to what you have been taught. Be faithful as others have been faithful before you. Remain steadfast, for in doing so you will remain grounded in God who offers a citizenship not of this world but of heaven. Like the disciples in today's Gospel who experience how different following Jesus will be from their expectations, if we listen to God through the words of Paul, we too will encounter God as our ancestor Abram did.

◆ GOSPEL: Luke's version of the Transfiguration emphasizes hope.

While Mark connected the Transfiguration to Jesus' death, Luke deliberately tied it to the Resurrection. Hence, Luke refers to the "eighth day," to the Exodus, and to Jesus' glory—all symbols of the Resurrection and Easter (reference to the eight days is omitted in the Lectionary text; see Luke 9:28). Through these symbols the readers of Peter, James, John, and Luke receive a glimpse of the Resurrection, a taste of the glory that waits on the other side of the Cross. It is a beautiful vision, filled with light, white robes, Old Testament luminaries, and even a voice from heaven. No wonder Peter wanted to stay. Most of us would have too. The key, however, is not to hold on to the vision but to listen to Jesus, the crucified and now Risen Savior.

The Roman Missal

"Of you my heart has spoken: Seek his face" (Psalm 27:8/Entrance Antiphon). The second option for the Entrance Antiphon is from Psalm 25 (24). The Collect shows us the way to see God. God has commanded us to listen to the Word of his Son. We pray that, fed by his divine Word, our sight may be "made pure" so that we too may "behold your glory." It clearly connects with the Gospel reading of the Transfiguration. The imagery in the prayer all but puts us in the Transfiguration scene. The Gloria is omitted today. The Creed is sung or said.

In the Prayer over the Offerings, we ask that our sacrifice may cleanse and sanctify us for the celebration of Easter. The Preface to be used for this Mass is given on the pages right there along with the other texts for this Mass. Titled "The Transfiguration of the Lord," the Preface clearly recalls and gives the meaning of the Transfiguration: "to show, even by the testimony of the law and the prophets, / that the Passion leads to the glory of the Resurrection." Consider chanting the introductory dialogue and the Preface today; if this is not the regular practice of your community, this can be a way of powerfully drawing attention to the solemnity of Lenten time (but be sure to prepare and rehearse your assembly as needed, especially if your people are not familiar with the responses!). The Prayer after Communion is a simple prayer of thanksgiving for the grace of being "partakers . . . of the things of heaven" while still on earth. The Eucharist is our everyday Transfiguration! Consider using Eucharistic Prayer II.

The Prayer over the People also echoes the Gospel account of the Transfiguration, with its prayer that we may be faithful to the Gospel of the Son of God and one day attain "that glory whose beauty he showed in his own Body." The Prayer over the People is required, not optional, on the Sundays of Lent, and the text is given right after the Prayer after Communion.

The RCIA offers the option of celebrating the Penitential Rite for the baptized candidates. It is designed to be celebrated on the Second Sunday of Lent, but it may be celebrated on a Lenten weekday or at another suitable time. If the Penitential Rite is celebrated on the Second Sunday of Lent, the Mass and the readings are from that day; if it is celebrated on another day, appropriate readings from the Lectionary are used, and the Collect provided in the rite is prayed. This rite follows a pattern similar to the scrutinies; instead of focusing on preparation for Baptism, however, the texts and prayers look to preparation for Reconciliation. The candidates will receive the Sacrament of Reconciliation before they are confirmed, share in the Eucharist and, if appropriate, are received into the full Communion of the Catholic Church.

There is no ritual Mass for the Penitential Rite as there are for the scrutinies. There is no combined rite for the scrutinies and the Penitential Rite. The prayers and other texts of the scrutinies are specific to the elect; they include prebaptismal exorcisms, which are not appropriate to the baptized (see RCIA, 445–472).

Other Ideas

If the parish hosts the "St. Joseph Table" it will likely be scheduled on this weekend. Use this opportunity to encourage everyone to support those parish projects that provide assistance for those not as blessed with food or shelter. A good counterpoint to the usually lavish St. Joseph Table is a soup supper on one or more evenings during Lent. One parish auctions the donations of bread and pans of Italian pasta at the St. Joseph Table event and donates the money to a Lenten alms project. Involve the children of the parish in this exercise by having them bid on smaller offerings of food items and adding their contributions to a fund that will go toward buying some favors, like toiletries, for those who are in health care residences. The blessing is found in chapter 53 of the *Book of Blessings.*

MON 18 (#230) violet
Lenten Weekday

Optional Memorial of St. Cyril of Jerusalem, Bishop and Doctor of the Church / violet

The Lectionary for Mass

◆ FIRST READING: Daniel attempts to understand the Word of the Lord that came to the prophet Jeremiah, who spoke about the coming Babylonian captivity of seventy years. Daniel also lived during a time of persecution. His words give us a model confession of the people's infidelity that, at the time, he considered responsible for their suffering. His confidence in the Lord's compassion and forgiveness parallels the trust of generations of people of faith up to our day.

◆ RESPONSORIAL PSALM 79: The refrain for our Responsorial Psalm comes from Psalm 103:10a, a psalm of praise for God's mercy. In the refrain, we express that the Lord does not base his relationship with us on our sins and impart the punishment due to us for them. The verses come from Psalm 79, a lament in which the people plead with the Lord to deliver them from their sins and free the prisoners from death. We will give thanks to God forever for his mercy!

◆ GOSPEL: Jesus calls his disciples to extend mercy just as the Father does. The disciples are not to give judgment and condemnation. The extension of forgiveness to those in need will, however, bring the same to the disciples.

The Roman Missal

In the Collect, God teaches us to undertake physical penances for the good of our souls. We ask for the strength to "abstain from all sins," and to carry out God's loving commands. In the Prayer over the Offerings, we pray that all whom God allows to participate in these sacred mysteries may be "set free from worldly attractions." In the Prayer after Communion, we pray that the Communion we receive may cleanse us of our faults, and "make us heirs to the joy of heaven." In the Prayer over the People, we pray that with God's grace, we may be faithful in prayer to God, and truly love one another. Consider using the Eucharistic Prayer for Reconciliation I.

Today's Saint

St. Cyril of Jerusalem (c. 315–386), bishop of Jerusalem and Doctor of the Church, is venerated as one of the great theologians of the early Church. Like his contemporaries, he was embroiled in the Arian controversy and was exiled three times for teaching that the Son is fully divine. Cyril is best known for twenty-three lectures to catechumens, encompassing introductory teachings through postbaptismal mystagogy. From them we learn much about catechetical methods and liturgical practices in the early Church, as well as the development of teaching on the Eucharist: "Since then He Himself declared and said of the Bread, This is My Body, who shall dare to doubt any longer? And since He has Himself affirmed and said, This is My Blood, who shall ever hesitate, saying, that it is not His blood?" (*Catechetical Lecture* 22:1). He was much loved by the people of Jerusalem during his lifetime for his charitable works and generosity—he even sold gifts from the emperor to raise money for the poor. Cyril is one of the Greek Fathers of the Church and is venerated by Catholics, Anglicans, and the Orthodox alike. He was named a Doctor of the Church by Pope Leo XIII in 1883.

(#543) white

TUE 19 Solemnity of St. Joseph, Spouse of the Blessed Virgin Mary

The Lectionary for Mass

◆ FIRST READING: The words of the Lord that Nathan is to communicate to David reveal the Lord's promise that he will raise up a son. Through this son David's kingdom will remain forever. Christians see in Jesus, Son of God and Son of Man, whose earthly father is Joseph, the fulfillment of this prophecy.

◆ RESPONSORIAL PSALM 89 reflects God's promise to David heard in the First Reading. The emphasis in the psalm lies on the everlasting nature of the Lord's covenant with David. For God's kindness toward David and his ancestors in faith, we sing our gratitude today in the words of the psalmist.

◆ SECOND READING: Paul recounts to the Romans how Abraham, our father in faith, trusted in God's promise that God would make him a father to the nations. Abraham's faith serves as a lasting example of trusting in God for people of all generations. When Joseph accepted his role as the earthly father of Jesus who was to be born of Mary, a virgin, Joseph took his special place in the line of the faithful ones who followed Abraham's example.

◆ GOSPEL: The opening verse of the Gospel reading is the concluding verse of the genealogy in Matthew's account of the Gospel. This verse names Jacob as Joseph's father and Joseph as Mary's husband and by relation the father of Jesus whom Mary bore. The other verses that make up the reading come from Matthew's infancy narrative and emphasize Joseph's righteousness and obedience in following the angel's command to take Mary as his wife and accompany her in the birth of Jesus, son of David, who will bring salvation to a sinful people.

The Roman Missal

The Entrance Antiphon, based on Luke 12:42, speaks of Joseph as the "faithful and prudent steward, / whom the Lord set over his household." The Collect presents Joseph as a model for the Church. Just as Joseph watched over Christ in his infancy, so the Church must "watch over / the unfolding of the mysteries of human salvation." Since today is a solemnity, the Gloria and the Creed are said or sung today. We pray that we may imitate the "loving care" of St. Joseph's service of the infant Christ (Prayer over the Offerings). The Preface is subtitled "The mission of Saint Joseph," and, like the Entrance Antiphon, speaks of Joseph as the steward of God's household, watching "like a father" over the Son of God. The Prayer after Communion is a prayer for

the protection of the Church on this Solemnity of St. Joseph. Consider using Eucharistic Prayer III. Even though it is Lent, you can pull out the stops (moderately) for today's solemnity. Use festive music (possibly inviting the choir to sing), incense, and a longer, more formal Gospel procession.

Other Ideas

The Blessing of the St. Joseph's Table can take place on March 19, the Solemnity of St. Joseph, husband of the Blessed Virgin Mary. It is also well suited to the Lenten season. The introduction to the order of blessing explains that "we rejoice at this table, which is a sign of God's generous blessings and of our call to serve the poor and hungry" (BB, 1685). It is traditional to share most of the food blessed on this day with the poor. The order of blessing (which takes place outside of the Mass) includes the Litany of Saint Joseph (see BB, 1691). On March 14, the Sunday before the Solemnity of St. Joseph, the parish could prepare prayer cards (separate from a prayer in the weekly bulletin) to be distributed after Mass. For the Solemnity of St. Joseph, include a part of the Litany of St. Joseph, which names the various ways in which he is a model and patron. See also page 116.

Today's Saint

Joseph was the foster father of Jesus, the man entrusted with his care and upbringing. We know that Joseph was a "righteous man" who protected Mary from disgrace after she was found to be pregnant with Jesus (Matthew 1:19). Like the earlier Joseph in Genesis, he received instruction and reassurance from God through dreams. The Gospel gives little information about him, save that he was an artisan who lived in Nazareth, was a descendant of David, and went to Bethlehem for a census, causing Jesus to be born there in fulfillment of the prophecies. When warned in a dream that Jesus was in danger because of the evil intentions of King Herod, Joseph took Jesus and Mary to live in exile in Egypt until he learned that Herod had died (see Matthew 2:12–15). As a result, Jesus was spared the fate of the Holy Innocents. After the account of Jesus' being lost and found in the Temple during a pilgrimage, Joseph is not mentioned again. We can infer that he had died before Jesus began his ministry; he was certainly not alive at the time of the Crucifixion, because he would have been the one to claim Jesus' body, not Joseph of Arimathea. Catholic tradition describes him as dying in the arms of Jesus and Mary, and so he is invoked as the patron of a happy death. Because he was a man who worked with his hands, he is the patron of workers and especially carpenters. Devotion to St. Joseph developed rather late, and was popularized by St. Bernardine of Siena during the fifteenth century.

WED 20 (#232) violet
Lenten Weekday

The Lectionary for Mass

◆ FIRST READING: Their hatred for Jeremiah's teaching against idolatry was so strong that the people of Judah engineered a plot to kill the great prophet. At the heart of the plot was the people's desire to bring Jeremiah down using the words he himself spoke. In response, Jeremiah prays to the Lord that vengeance come upon the people.

◆ RESPONSORIAL PSALM 31 correlates to Jeremiah's experience in the First Reading. In Psalm 31, the author addresses the Lord with confidence, noting how the Lord will save him from the traps his enemies have set. The psalmist commends his spirit to the Lord in verse 6 of this psalm, a verse that the evange-

list Luke places on Jesus' lips as he dies on the Cross.

◆ GOSPEL: En route to Jerusalem, Jesus speaks words to his inner circle of the Twelve about the fate the Son of Man will face. Will the Twelve be able to drink of the same cup as the Son of Man? Will we? The mother of Zebedee's sons wants to ensure the destiny of her sons is at the Father's side, but Jesus assures her that the decision is not his to make. Surely, though, their willingness to drink of the same cup as the Son of Man sets them on the way to greatness.

The Roman Missal

In the Collect, we ask God to keep his "family," the Church, "schooled always in good works," to surround us with his protection, and to lead us to heaven. Lent is this school for our souls. The Eucharist is a "holy exchange" (Prayer over the Offerings). We offer to God the sacrifice his Son offered for us, and in return, God gives us forgiveness. The Communion we have received is our "pledge of immortality." We pray that it may "work for our eternal salvation" (Prayer after Communion). The Prayer over the People asks God for everything we need to live the Christian life: grace and protection, health, love, and devotion. Consider using the Eucharistic Prayer for Various Needs and Occasions II.

THU 21 (#233) violet
Lenten Weekday

The Lectionary for Mass

◆ FIRST READING: We step back a chapter in Jeremiah from yesterday's First Reading to hear the Lord's reflection on the blessedness of those who trust in him and the curse that will come upon those who trust only in themselves. The former will flourish as a tree planted by water and the latter will exist

as a barren desert bush. Even in times of trials, the tree will survive and bear fruit.

◆ RESPONSORIAL PSALM 1: The opening psalm of the psalter is also the Responsorial Psalm for Friday of the Second Week of Advent although with a different refrain. Today's refrain comes from the thanksgiving portion of Psalm 40. In the psalmist's assertion of the blessedness of those who hope in the Lord, we find a direct connection to the First Reading. The nature imagery that the author of Psalm 1 employs to contrast the blessed and the wicked also provides an obvious link to the Lord's words in the First Reading.

◆ GOSPEL: At his death, Lazarus, scarred by poverty and the sores on his body, receives life in Abraham's bosom. Upon his death, the rich man cries out to Abraham for pity, but to no avail. Those who have chosen not to heed the words of Moses and the prophets surely will not change their ways based on someone who rises from the dead, Abraham tells the rich man. Would the Pharisees, to whom Jesus addresses this parable, change and live out the Kingdom's wisdom of greatness?

The Roman Missal

Today's Collect brings to mind how the purification we undergo during Lent can restore us to innocence, as it asks that being caught up in the fire of the Holy Spirit, "we may be found steadfast in faith / and effective in works." The Prayer over the Offerings again highlights the necessary connection between our exterior behaviors of Lenten disciplines and our interior dispositions and conversion: those disciplines are supposed to both be a sign of and bring about the inward, spiritual realities. The Prayer after Communion prays that the sacrifice we have just celebrated may truly be active and strong within us. Consider using the Eucharistic Prayer III.

F R I 22 (#234) violet
Lenten Weekday

The Lectionary for Mass

◆ FIRST READING: We hear another story from the Old Testament about a plot to kill the innocent person. Our First Reading, from Genesis, describes how Joseph's brothers conspire to put him to death because he is their father's favorite. The brothers, though, remain conflicted and decide not to kill Joseph, but rather sell him to the Ishmaelites.

◆ RESPONSORIAL PSALM 105 calls upon the people to praise the Lord who promises the land of Canaan to them. The verses from the psalm we use today recount how the Lord worked through Joseph for the good of the people. Even though his brothers sold him into slavery, Joseph would experience freedom. His freedom stands as a symbol of the marvels the Lord performs for his people from age to age.

◆ GOSPEL: Jesus instructs the chief priests and scribes to hear another parable about the Kingdom of God. This parable of the tenants, to whom the landowner leased his land while he was away, and their servants foreshadows how those in authority will put Jesus to death. In his explanation of the parable, Jesus cites Psalm 118:22–23 to teach the chief priests and elders how the rejected servant put to death will, in the end, by the Lord's doing, become the cornerstone. Therefore the Kingdom will not belong to those who bring suffering upon God's servants, but rather to those who produce the Kingdom's fruit. Finally, the religious leaders realize their place in Jesus' words about the Kingdom and they do not take well to it. Their plot to arrest Jesus in-

tensifies, but they fear the people who are enthralled by the person and teaching of Jesus.

The Roman Missal

The Collect asks that our penance may purify us, and lead us "to attain the holy things to come." In the Prayer over the Offerings, we ask for God's "merciful grace" to prepare us to celebrate these mysteries, and to lead us to "a devout way of life." Prefaces I–IV are the choices once again today. While any one is appropriate, perhaps Eucharistic Prayer for Reconciliation I, with its own Preface, would be a good choice for today, insofar as that Preface tells how God is rich in mercy, offering constant pardon, how he never turned away despite how humanity broke the covenant again and again, and how now is a time for turning back. In the Eucharist, we receive a "pledge of eternal salvation" (Prayer after Communion). We pray that we may "set our course" toward the redemption God has promised. In the Prayer over the People, we ask for "health of mind and body," so that we may use these precious gifts for "good deeds." Consider using the Eucharistic Prayer II.

S A T 23 (#235) violet
Lenten Weekday

Optional Memorial of St. Turibius of Mogrovejo, Bishop / violet

The Lectionary for Mass

◆ FIRST READING: Micah's prayer from the final verses of the prophetic book expresses his confidence that the Lord will forgive the people's sins burying them in the deep waters of the sea. There is none other like the one God who remains faithful to his people after they have returned from exile. Thus, the prophet prays that God will continue to shepherd his people and feed them as God has done in former days.

◆ RESPONSORIAL PSALM 103: The psalmist moves from speaking his praise of the Lord in the first person, to recognizing how the Lord forgives the people's sins spoken in the second person, to an acknowledgment in the first person plural that the Lord will not deal with "us," his people, always according to our sins. In the final stanza, the psalmist depicts the expansiveness of the Lord's kindness in terms of the geographical directions of east and west and heaven's heights.

◆ GOSPEL: Jesus welcomes sinners and eats with them because his focus is the life they can experience in him, not death that comes from a life lived in hypocrisy as the Pharisees and scribes choose. We have the choice to respond in jealousy as the older son did to the return of his lost, wayward brother and the ensuing celebration their father threw him, or to respond with forgiveness, compassion, and joy as the father did. Ours is to choose a Pharisaic way or the way of the Father, which leads onward to his Kingdom.

The Roman Missal

Prefaces I–IV are the choices once again today. While any one is appropriate, perhaps Eucharistic Prayer for Reconciliation I, with its own Preface, would be a good choice for today, insofar as that Preface tells how God is rich in mercy, offering constant pardon, how he never turned away despite how humanity broke the covenant again and again, and how now is a time for turning back.

Today's Saint

St. Turibius of Mogrovejo (1538–1606) was born into the Spanish nobility and dedicated his life to bringing Christianity to the native peoples of Peru as the missionary archbishop of Lima. He traveled the whole of his enormous diocese, usually on foot, evangelizing and baptizing as he went. Among those he baptized and confirmed were St. Rose of Lima and St. Martin de Porres. St. Turibius also founded the first seminary in the Western hemisphere and built roads, schools, chapels, hospitals, and convents. He is remembered for his defense of the native peoples against the injustices of the Spanish government.

24 (#30C or #28A) violet
Third Sunday of Lent

The Lectionary for Mass: Year C

◆ FIRST READING: This passage includes two pivotal events in the life of the Israelites: the call of Moses and the revelation of God's name. A conversation with God was probably the last thing on Moses' mind when he spotted the mysterious burning bush. After all, Moses was in hiding after killing an Egyptian for beating an Israelite slave. He was hardly the person one might expect to witness an appearance of the divine. Moses' call follows the pattern of prophetic calls in the Scriptures. God appears to the prophet-to-be in a spectacular fashion and gives the new prophet a commission to "rescue them from the hands of the Egyptians." The prophet objects, citing unworthiness: "Who am I to tell them?" God then reassures the prophet, often giving

the prophet a sign: in this case, God's own name. God's personal name is clearly meant to be a verb, most likely a form of "to be." Unlike most gods, who are defined by things, the God of Israel is a being that cannot be imaged. This story tells us about God's will and way. God does not wait until we are ready before calling us, and God calls those whom others might consider unworthy. The story also reveals that God is compassionate, wills justice for the oppressed, and is greater than any of our descriptions.

◆ RESPONSORIAL PSALM 103: The psalmist begins by calling on his own soul to give praise. He then goes through an exhaustive list of God's benefits: God heals diseases, vindicates the oppressed, keeps promises, and deals compassionately with sinners. God removes sin, bestows mercy, loves the righteous, and extends love to their descendants.

◆ SECOND READING: Paul writes to those who see themselves transformed by Christ. They converted from worship of the Roman gods to faith in Christ, and they revel in the freedom that brings. From Paul's perspective, they may be too certain of their salvation and cannot, therefore, know when they need correction. Paul challenges their overconfidence with a story from Israel's sojourn in the wilderness. The Israelites went through their own baptism, passing through the waters of the sea, and were sustained by manna and water in the wilderness. For Paul that experience was like the Corinthians' experience of Christ's presence in Baptism and the Eucharist. Yet despite the richness of their experience with God, the Israelites still sinned. Because of their hardness of heart, none of them ever saw the Promised Land. The Corinthians are also in danger of assuming that their

participation in the Christian community exempts them from wrongdoing. Paul asks them to learn from their forebears' experience and turn to God for the strength that will help them resist temptation. With God's help they can stand firmly as examples of faithfulness to others.

◆ Gospel: People come to Jesus with a question about the Galileans killed by Pilate and eighteen citizens killed by a falling tower. Were their deaths punishments for being sinners? No, says Jesus, they did not die because of their sinfulness any more than we live because of our righteousness. While Jesus assures them that those deaths were not punishment, he also warns them, "Unless you repent, you will all perish." As an illustration Jesus tells a parable about an unproductive fig tree. In the Bible the spiritual health of a country was measured by the health of its fig trees, which normally take three years to reach maturity. The fig tree in Jesus' story passed the three-year mark and still does not produce any fruit. Its owner wants to destroy it, but the gardener bargains for another year of fertilizing care to allow the tree time to produce. It seems that for us and for the fig tree, there is still time to change and, with God's help, a possibility of bearing fruit.

The Lectionary for Mass: Year A

◆ FIRST READING: In the reading from Exodus, the Israelites have just escaped Egypt, passing through the waters of the Red Sea to safety. They have been fed with food from heaven, manna by day, quail by night. Now they complain that they have no water to drink. They are testing God, demanding to know whether he is still with them. At God's command, Moses strikes the rock, and water flows from it. God can bring forth life from nothing, water from a stone.

◆ RESPONSORIAL PSALM 95, which is prayed at the beginning of each day in the Liturgy of the Hours, recounts the same story of the doubt of the chosen people at Meribah and Massah—names which mean "the place where the Israelites quarreled with God" or "the place they put God to the trial" (*The Catholic Study Bible*, 752, footnote, 1).

◆ SECOND READING: Paul urges the Romans to trust in God. Christians have nothing to fear because Christ died for us "while we were still helpless," "while we were still sinners"; God's love is given to us not because we had earned it or because we can somehow earn it now. God's love is total gift.

◆ GOSPEL: The story of the Samaritan woman is rich and multilayered. Here are just a few reflections, focusing on the aspects of the story which are echoed in the prayers for the first scrutiny. The woman is thirsty; she has always been thirsty—"'Sir, give me this water, so that I may not be thirsty or have to keep coming here to draw water.'" All of us sometimes try to satisfy our thirst at other wells; Jesus, the living water, can alone satisfy the thirsting spirit. The woman, responding to Jesus, acknowledges the truth about herself: "'I do not have a husband.'" In the scrutinies, we pray that the elect also listen to the voice of Jesus, acknowledging their sins and weaknesses. Her conversation with Jesus leads the Samaritan woman to faith and hope; it turns a sinner into a disciple. The scrutiny prayer likewise prays that Jesus "give them peace" (RCIA, 154A), even as he heals them and sets them free from the spirit of evil. Baptism is like this conversation between Jesus and the Samaritan woman, this conversation over the font. In Baptism, we speak to God, saying, "I believe in you," and God responds, as he did at the baptism of Jesus: "You are my beloved, in whom I am well pleased."

The Roman Missal

There are two options for today's Entrance Antiphon. The second, taken from Ezekiel 36:23–26, is especially appropriate when the scrutiny of the elect is celebrated: "I will pour clean water upon you." We are burdened by sin, but God has given us a remedy in the Lenten disciplines of prayer, fasting, and almsgiving. The Gloria is omitted today. The Creed is sung or said. We pray in the Collect that we, who are weighed down by a heavy conscience, may be lifted up by God's forgiving mercy. With the sacrifice we make, we ask God for forgiveness and reconciliation. We who ask these blessings must "take care to forgive our neighbor," as Jesus taught (Prayer over the Offerings).

When the Gospel about the Samaritan woman is read, the proper Preface for the Third Sunday of Lent is used. It is found in the Proper of Time. It reflects beautifully on the encounter at the well. Jesus asks the Samaritan woman for water, and gives living water. Jesus is on fire for her faith, and he gives "the fire of divine love." Consider chanting the introductory dialogue and the Preface today; if this is not the regular practice of your community, this can be a way of powerfully drawing attention to the solemnity of Lenten time (but be sure to prepare and rehearse your assembly as needed, especially if your people are not familiar with the responses!). Consider using Eucharistic Prayer II. The Prayer after Communion expresses the mystery of Holy Communion: "we receive the pledge" of what is "hidden in heaven," and are fed on earth with "Bread that comes from on high." We pray that we may come to the "true completion" of this mystery which is already at work in us.

The Prayer over the People echoes the golden rule: we ask this one grace, to abide in love of God and neighbor, and thus to fulfill the whole of God's commandments. The Prayer over the People is required, not optional, on the Sundays of Lent, and the text is given right after the Prayer after Communion.

If your parish is celebrating the First Scrutiny with the elect, then according to a rubric in the Missal, the proper prayers should be used; these Mass formularies are found in the "Ritual Masses" section of the Missal, under segment I—For the Conferral of the Sacraments of Initiation; #2—For the Celebration of the Scrutinies; A—For the First Scrutiny. For the actual ritual of the scrutiny itself, consult RCIA, 150–156. The scrutiny takes place after the homily.

Other Ideas

Consider putting a notice in the parish bulletin titled "It's not too late to start!" which encourages people to review their Lenten resolutions and initiate them if they have yet to do so. If the parish has decreased, hopefully, the number of regular meetings, then the next three weeks would be a good time to schedule spiritual "meetings." For example, an evening of Lenten music and poetry, a holy hour, one or more penitential liturgies with one being sacramental and the other being for the reconciliation of divisions in our world.

(#545) white

MON 25 — Solemnity of the Annunciation of the Lord

About Today's Solemnity

On this solemnity, we remember when the angel brought to Mary the amazing news that she would be the mother of God's Son. On this day, as in Christmas Time, we contemplate the wonder of the Incarnation: in Jesus, God took on our flesh, becoming like us in all things but sin. The Annunciation is a Solemnity of the Lord, but it is also a day to give thanks to and for Mary. The Gospel account of the Annunciation in Luke reveals a great wonder: God sought the free consent of a young girl to carry out his plan for us. God asked for help! No wonder so many artists throughout the ages have chosen to depict this moment of decision that changed the world for ever. The Solemnity of the Annunciation of the Lord reminds us of the supple heart of Mary who welcomed the gift of God's indwelling and new life in Christ. In Mary we behold our capacity for hospitality for God and humankind.

The Lectionary for Mass

◆ First Reading: King Ahaz encounters the Lord who instructs him to ask for a sign that the Lord stands with the house of David against its oppressors. Ahaz refuses to ask for a sign from the Lord not wanting to tempt the Lord. But Isaiah responds with words that tell of the generous sign the Lord will provide even without being asked: Emmanuel will be born of a virgin and come to dwell among God's people.

◆ Responsorial Psalm 40: The emphasis of this psalm lies in what God asks of us. God asks neither sacrifice nor oblation, but rather obedience to his Word. God desires that we discern and follow his will. On this feast of the Annunciation, we look to Mary and her son as examples of how we align our lives with God's will.

◆ Second Reading: The author of Hebrews has Christ speak verses from Psalm 40:7–9, verses also a part of today's Responsorial Psalm. Christ also affirms that he has come to do God's will. Because Christ

fulfilled God's will in his own sacrifice on the cross, God no longer desires other sacrifices and sin-offerings. We have been made holy through this once for all offering of Christ's own Body so that our earthly sacrifices are unnecessary.

◆ Gospel: Mary responds to the angel Gabriel's announcement to her that she will bear Jesus first with a question about how this could possibly be because she is a virgin and then with a statement of faith and openness to God's will, her fiat. We wonder this Lent how God calls us to open ourselves to God's will and the new life that Easter will bring.

The Roman Missal

All the Mass texts for this solemnity are proper for the day and can be found in the Proper of Saints at March 25. The Gloria is sung or said. The theology underlying the words of the Collect reflects the understanding that as a result of the Incarnation, humanity is given a share in divinity. Not unlike the prayer the priest prays at the mixing of a little water into the wine ("By the mystery of this water and wine / may we come to share in the divinity of Christ / who humbled himself to share in our humanity"), this Collect asks, insofar as God willed that his Word should take on human flesh, that we "may merit to become partakers even in his divine nature."

The Creed is said today in observance of the solemnity. Today is one of two times (the other being at the Masses on the Nativity) when all genuflect, instead of bow, at the words "and by the Holy Spirit was incarnate of the Virgin Mary and became man." Be sure your assembly is prepared for this; the priest can give a brief explanation of this in his introduction to the Creed.

The Prayer over the Offerings highlights that it is the Church that is making this offering (notice what this means in terms of

liturgical theology—the entire assembly makes the offering, not just the priest), and in so doing, she (the Church) is recognizing that her life began with the Incarnation of the Son. In God's acceptance of this offering, we pray that the Church "may rejoice to celebrate his mysteries on this Solemnity." The Preface assigned for today is given right there along with the other Mass texts for the Solemnity of the Annunciation of the Lord in the Proper of Saints. Titled "The Mystery of the Incarnation," it relates Mary's hearing "with faith" about the Christ who was to be born "by the overshadowing power of the Holy Spirit." The text goes on to relate how, by bearing the child in her "immaculate womb" the promises made to the children of Israel were fulfilled and the hope of the world was realized. Consider using Eucharistic Prayer II. The Prayer after Communion expresses our confession in Jesus as "true God and true man" as among the "mysteries of the true faith," and asks that we may attain eternal joy "through the saving power of his Resurrection."

No Solemn Blessing or Prayer over the People is designated for the end of Mass, but if you desired to use one, certainly Solemn Blessing #15, "The Blessed Virgin Mary," would be appropriate for today.

Even though it is Lent, you can pull out the stops (moderately) for today's solemnity. Use festive music (possibly inviting the choir to sing), incense, and a longer, more formal Gospel procession.

Other Ideas

The Annunciation has been the subject of many artistic interpretations throughout the centuries, resulting in great works of beauty. For an extraordinary interpretation of the human elements of this story, see two paintings: *Ecce Ancilla Domini* by Dante Gabriel Rossetti (1850), and the painting *Annunciation* by the Catholic contemporary painter and sculptor John Collier. These are quite a departure from the frequent depictions of Mary in an Italian noblewoman's finery. For something different during Lent, invite an art expert to talk about and reflect on the iconography of Mary, particularly the representations of the Annunciation.

Many religious orders celebrate this special day with festivity. Remember to keep them in your prayers as you pray the Rosary for their charism of service under Mary's patronage. Tour a convent or rectory as part of a vocation fair or event to have young people know more about the religious orders that serve our country. Dedicate a special Rosary or walk for vocations on this day, or plan one now for later in the year. Some dioceses have pilgrimages or walks from religious order house to religious order house (a "nun-run"). Check out your local diocesan vocation office or vicar for religious for information.

If the parish has a Marian image, especially of the Annunciation, see how it can be decorated this week with some flowers and candles. The image can be reverenced with incense at the beginning of Mass.

TUE 26 (#238) violet
Lenten Weekday

The Lectionary for Mass

◆ FIRST READING: On behalf of Shadrach and Meshach, Azariah (Abednego) prays to the Lord in the fiery furnace to have mercy on them and the entire people. He does not want the Lord to cancel the covenant made with Abraham, Isaac, and Jacob, their ancestors in faith. As Azariah's prayer draws to a conclusion, he offers the Lord a contrite heart and humble spirit and commits to follow the Lord with his whole heart.

◆ RESPONSORIAL PSALM 25: We join with the psalmist as he pleads with the Lord to remember his mercies. We ask the Lord to show his ways to us and teach us his path. We profess our faith that the Lord does indeed lead sinners on the right path and those with humility to justice.

◆ GOSPEL: How many times must we forgive our brother or sister? A sincere Peter wants Jesus to respond honestly to this question, but the answer Peter receives is probably not the one he wanted to hear. Through the parable of the king who settles accounts with his indebted servants, Jesus teaches Peter that our infinite forgiveness of one another or our inability to forgive will be reflected in the Father's response to us as we seek the Kingdom of heaven.

The Roman Missal

We pray in the Collect for God's continued grace, that we may dedicate ourselves to his "holy service," and receive his help in our need. We pray in the Prayer over the Offerings that the sacrifice we offer may cleanse us of sin, and be pleasing to God. In the Prayer after Communion, we ask for "pardon and protection" through our sharing in the Eucharist. In the Prayer over the People, we ask God to drive sin away from us, so that we may remain safely under his protection. Consider using Eucharistic Prayer III.

WED 27 (#239) violet
Lenten Weekday

The Lectionary for Mass

◆ FIRST READING: Moses instructs the people of Israel to hear the statutes and decrees that the Lord has commanded him to teach them. Their observance of the laws will lead them to enter the land the Lord is giving them and to continue to occupy it. The people should live in fidelity to the Lord's statutes and decrees for generations to come. Doing so allows their wisdom to shine forth and others to see that Israel is indeed a great nation.

◆ RESPONSORIAL PSALM 147: Today's Responsorial Psalm comes from the latter third of Psalm 147, a hymn of praise to God in celebration of God's wisdom, goodness, and power. In today's verses, the psalmist calls upon the people of Jerusalem to glorify the Lord for the Lord has restored them through his Word. What strength we gain from the Lord's Word to live in the world today as God's people.

◆ GOSPEL: Jesus teaches his disciples that he comes to fulfill the law, not to abolish it. Further, he instructs them that those who will be the greatest in the Kingdom of heaven will observe and teach the commandments. And, on the other hand, those who will be least in the Kingdom, will have not only broken them commandments themselves, but will have taught others to do so. A disciple must possess awareness of how his or her actions influence others, for ours is the mission to teach Jesus' ways through the example of our obedience to his commands.

The Roman Missal

Lent is a school in which we learn "holy restraint" (Collect). We pray that we may learn from our Lenten observance and from God's Word to be devoted to the Lord and united in prayer. The Prayer over the Offerings is a prayer for the protection of all those who "celebrate your mysteries." In the Prayer after Communion, we pray that our sharing in the heavenly banquet may make us holy and cleanse us from "all errors," so that we may see the fulfillment of God's promises in heaven. In the Prayer over the People, we ask for "a resolve that is pleasing" to God, for we know that those who are conformed to God's Word will experience his favor. Consider using the Eucharistic Prayer II.

THU 28 (#240) violet
Lenten Weekday

The Lectionary for Mass

◆ FIRST READING: The Lord commanded his people to listen to him and walk step by step according to his law. Should they choose to do this, they will flourish. But the Lord's people decided otherwise. Even with the encouragement and the warnings of the prophets the Lord sent their way, the people still chose evil. At the end of today's passage, then, the Lord seems resigned to the fact that his people will not listen as he sends Jeremiah to inform them that their infidelity shows how God's Word no longer finds itself in their words.

◆ RESPONSORIAL PSALM 95: The words of Psalm 95 both invite us to glorify the Lord in worship and to not harden our hearts as God's people had done at Massa and Meribah. Instead, the psalmist pleads with us to hear God's voice. It is God's voice that shepherds us and guides us to lands of abundance.

◆ GOSPEL: Do we see that Jesus drives out demons by the power of God present within him? Are we with Jesus or against him with the powers of the world that exist to bring death and not life? Disciples journey to the Kingdom of God together with Jesus. They stand united with him and do not seek to divide his house.

The Roman Missal

At the midpoint of Lent, there is somewhat of a sense of urgency in today's Collect, which takes note of the journey we are on toward the celebration of Easter. Referring to that upcoming feast as "the worthy celebration of the Paschal Mystery," the prayer asks that as that feast draws closer, "we may press forward all the more eagerly" toward it. Thus we are again reminded of the ultimate purpose of our Lenten journey, which is to share in the risen life of Christ celebrated at Easter. The Prayer over the Offerings is a prayer for cleansing. We must be cleansed "from every taint of wickedness," and freed from "false joys," if we are to bring our gifts to God and receive "the rewards" of his truth. In the Prayer after Communion, we pray that the sacrament which renews us may bring us salvation. We will know this salvation "in mystery" through the sacraments, but it must also be expressed "in the manner of our life." God is the source of everything, "all that we are." We ask his grace, that we may "seek what is right" and "do the good we desire" (Prayer over the People). Consider using the Eucharistic Prayer for Reconciliation I.

FRI 29 (#241) violet
Lenten Weekday

The Lectionary for Mass

◆ FIRST READING: The Lord's words spoken through the prophet Hosea invite Israel to return to the Lord for only the Lord can save her; Assyria will not. In the first person "I" the Lord states beautifully that he will heal and love Israel, gently watering Israel with dew so Israel might blossom. The Lord will also make Ephraim flourish. Truly all those who understand the Lord's wisdom walk as just ones in his paths.

◆ RESPONSORIAL PSALM 81: The people gathered in assembly hear the Lord speak in the first person "I" about how the Lord has rescued them and saved them throughout their history. The Lord questions the people as to whether they will hear him or not for he desperately desires that they follow in his ways and feast on the luscious food he provides.

◆ GOSPEL: We switch to the Gospel according to Mark today to hear Jesus respond to a question from one of the scribes about which commandment is the first of all by connecting the commandment to love God with our whole soul, mind, and strength with the commandment to love our neighbor as we love ourselves. The scribe shows his understanding of Jesus' words by restating the two commandments, but then adding the note that following those commandments achieves more than any sacrifice or burnt offering could. Jesus lets the scribe know just how close he is to the Kingdom of God. How close are we?

The Roman Missal

In the Collect, we ask God to pour his grace into our hearts, for it is only by his grace that we can observe "heavenly teaching," and be "drawn away from unruly desires." It specifies what we want God's grace to do for us: we ask that "we may be constantly drawn away from unruly desires" and more closely obey the "heavenly teaching," which has been given to us as a gift. In the Prayer over the Offerings, we ask God to "look with favor" upon the sacrifice we offer, that these gifts may be pleasing to him and bring salvation to us. In the Prayer after Communion we pray that as a result of sharing in the sacrament, God's strength will be at work in us completely, "pervading our minds and bodies" and bringing us "the fullness of redemption." God has given us gifts, but not for ourselves alone. We need to spread these gifts, "far and wide" (Prayer over the People). Consider using the Eucharistic Prayer II.

S A T 30 (#242) violet
Lenten Weekday

The Lectionary for Mass

◆ FIRST READING: The Lord desires love, not sacrifice. Knowledge of God, the Lord prefers over burnt offerings. Hosea speaks of God's Word of longing to Israel as the Lord again invites Israel to return to him. When Israel returns, new life will come to Israel. This, the prophet tells them as he conveys the Lord's words of promise that Israel will be raised up on the third day. Christians see Christ's Resurrection prefigured in these words of promise.

◆ RESPONSORIAL PSALM 51, a common penitential psalm for Lent, is today's Responsorial Psalm. The refrain comes from Hosea 6:6, the final verse of the First Reading. In our repetition of the refrain, we remind ourselves that God desires mercy, not sacrifice. We owe God nothing. God only wants us to love. May we approach God with hearts contrite and humble, for God will never reject us.

◆ GOSPEL: When we convince ourselves of our own self-righteousness, we need to hear the parable of Pharisee and the tax collector that Jesus addresses to those holier-than-thou who despised everyone but themselves. What a surprise the conclusion of the parable must have been to them! The contrite tax collector who humbled himself before God, God would exalt, but the superficial, pretentious Pharisee, God would humble.

The Roman Missal

The Collect connects our observance of Lent with what they are oriented toward, namely, celebrating with joy the Paschal Mystery at Easter; that is the focus our hearts should be set on. The Prayer over the Offerings prays simply that it is by God's grace that we can approach the celebration of the mysteries, and

so we ask that our minds may be made pure. The prayer includes an interesting phrase about the mysteries, as it asks that we may offer God "fitting homage . . . in reverently handing them on." The phrase can remind us of how our celebrations of the Eucharist are not isolated actions, but instead should be seen as actualizations that perpetuate the one offering made by Christ, that offering made present in our space and time through the Spirit. The Prayer after Communion asks for heavenly assistance so that we might seek God with all our hearts and be granted what we request. Perhaps we can hear the phrases "minds made pure" and "fitting homage" in light of the virtue of humility that is emphasized in the Gospel. While any one of the four Prefaces of Lent can be used today, perhaps Preface III with its reference to God's will that we "humble our sinful pride" would echo the Gospel reading. Even though the Prayer over the People is optional on weekdays, it would again be good to use it. Consider using the Eucharistic Prayer for Reconciliation II.

☀ 31 (#33C or #31A) violet or rose
Fourth Sunday of Lent

The Lectionary for Mass: Year C

◆ FIRST READING: Crossing the Jordan River, the Israelites return to a home they have never seen. It has been generations since Jacob

and his family left Canaan during a famine for the plenty of Egypt. It has been forty years since the Hebrew slaves fled the Egyptian army through the Red Sea. Their wilderness wanderings saw a new generation born not into slavery but into freedom. Now those born in nomadic freedom have passed through the waters of the Jordan into the land they shall reclaim as their own. The Passover at Gilgal was possibly the first Passover celebrated since the original Passover in Egypt, and it was the first Passover celebrated in Canaan. The covenant is renewed, this time with the second generation. God promises again to remove the disgrace of their slavery in Egypt. Just as in the wilderness, God provides a source of food. In place of manna, the people have the produce of their own land to eat. God, who cared for the wilderness generation, pledges to care for their children. At Gilgal the people themselves confirm and renew their relationship to God. They celebrate that relationship at the Passover, and they demonstrate it by changing their diet and their lifestyles.

◆ RESPONSORIAL PSALM 34: One of seven penitential psalms used in the early Church, this psalm is imbued with an awareness of God's salvation. The psalmist knew illness and recovery, confession and forgiveness, and estrangement and reconciliation with God. This powerful experience taught the psalmist that steadfast love surrounds those who trust in God. Knowing God's love and forgiveness is a cause for celebration. Today the Church uses this psalm to remind us of God's care for us as we continue on our Lenten journeys.

◆ SECOND READING: God's love in Christ is at the heart of Paul's message to the Corinthians. In love God seeks reconciliation, not punishment; therefore, God does not count our sins against us. God instead reconciles with humanity through Christ by making "him to be sin who did not know sin." Paul does not explain this but rather focuses on the result. We are new creations, reconciled with God and given a message and ministry of reconciliation. Using a political term, Paul calls Christians "ambassadors for Christ," entrusted with representing God's reconciling love to the world in which they live.

◆ GOSPEL: For Luke, God's reconciling love is the core of Jesus' teaching. When the Pharisees and scribes criticize him for eating with sinners, Jesus tells a parable found only in Luke's account of the Gospel, a parable about love, reconciliation, and resentment. The father is the central figure in this parable. He gives his younger son part of his estate, even though the father still has legal rights to it and might need it in his old age. He lets the son take the money and run, with no assurance that he will ever see him again. When the son wastes the entire fortune, the father not only welcomes him back home, but he also throws the son an expensive party. We are clearly meant to identify this father with God. But why would God let his son squander his inheritance and then welcome the wastrel back home? Anyone else who acted like that would be thought crazy, at best a soft touch and at worst an old fool. For years the older brother was the dutiful son, yet he never received a party. Instead, his no-good brother receives the fatted calf. It does not seem fair. The older brother, the Pharisees, and the rest of us who live by the rules may not like it, but God is exactly like the prodigal father. When it comes to mercy and compassion, God is very extravagant. When it comes to relationships, God spares no expense. God wants to be friends with everyone, even wayward sons and tax collec-

tors as well as dutiful grown children and Pharisees.

The Lectionary for Mass: Year A

◆ FIRST READING: In the reading from 1 Samuel, God and Samuel, his prophet, see the sons of Jesse quite differently. Samuel sees Eliab, the eldest son, and is impressed at his appearance, his "lofty stature." God, however, tells him, "I have rejected him." In David—the youngest and least of the brothers, the one who is not even important enough to be invited to meet this great prophet—God sees something special: a shepherd becoming a king. Being chosen by God changes a person. "From that day on, the spirit of the Lord rushed upon David."

◆ RESPONSORIAL PSALM 23: This is one of the best known of the psalms. It is full of vivid and comforting images, two of which stand out. The first portrays God as a loving and faithful shepherd, leading the flock into safe pastures, caring for them, feeding them, and pouring healing oil over their wounds. The second image pictures God as a host setting a table for guests and seeing to their every need.

◆ SECOND READING: The reading from Ephesians uses imagery of darkness and light. We have all been in the darkness; but in Christ we have become "light in the Lord" and are called to live in the light. The reading ends with a passage from what is thought to have been a baptismal song: "Awake, O sleeper, / and arise from the dead, / and Christ will give you light." In these lines we hear an echo of the earliest Christian worship.

◆ GOSPEL: Today's reading proclaims the story of the man born blind. Like the Gospel according to John as a whole, this pericope exists on two levels. On one level, the story is very simple. The sentences are short, the vocabulary and

syntax are easy to understand. The reading consists largely of questions and answers, the most basic format for teaching, as witnessed by the Catechism. At the same time, the narrative is complex, a kind of crescendo of meaning, in which every word matters. The healing of the man's physical blindness occupies only a few lines: the rest of the long reading has to do with spiritual blindness, especially the blindness of the Pharisees. After the opening of his eyes, the man born blind gradually transforms: He becomes a witness to Christ. He does not say a word before Jesus heals him, in a sacramental way, by anointing his eyes with clay and saliva, but after his healing, we see his responses growing gradually more sophisticated. Though he begins by saying "I don't know," the man gradually comes to an understanding of who Jesus is. At the end of the story, he comes face to face with Jesus—whom he has not yet seen with his physical eyes—and worships him.

The Roman Missal

Traditionally, this Fourth Sunday of Lent marks a joyful relief amidst the seriousness and somberness of the many weeks of preparation for Easter. Hence, today is called Laetare Sunday, a name that comes from the Entrance Antiphon for this Mass: "Rejoice, Jerusalem, and all who love her. / Be joyful, all who were in mourning; / exult and be satisfied at her consoling breast" (Isaiah 66:10–11). Even in Lent, a time of fasting and repentance, we rejoice because we know that God is love, and our loving God will provide for all our needs. Rose-colored vestments may be worn, and the altar may be decorated with flowers. However, the Gloria is still omitted today. The Creed is still sung or said.

In the Collect, we ask for "prompt devotion and eager faith" as we hasten toward the "solemn celebrations" to come—the Paschal Triduum of the Lord. "With joy" on this Laetare Sunday, we bring our offerings to God and ask that they may be received "for the salvation of all the world" (Prayer over the Offerings). The Preface that is given on the pages right there along with the other texts for this Mass, "The Man Born Blind," is to be used today. Do not use Preface I or II of Lent; that is meant for other years when that Gospel is not read. Using the motif of humanity's being led out of darkness into "the radiance of the faith," the Preface relates how being "born in slavery to ancient sin" (that is, original sin) is to be in darkness, and how we are led out of that darkness "through the waters of regeneration." The theme of the Sacrament of Baptism as enlightenment could not be clearer here, a reference so appropriate as the Church approaches the Easter Vigil, when the elect will be baptized and the faithful will renew their baptismal promises. Consider chanting the introductory dialogue and the Preface today; if this is not the regular practice of your community, this can be a way of powerfully drawing attention to the solemnity of Lenten time. Be sure to prepare and rehearse your assembly as needed, especially if your people are not familiar with the responses! Consider using the Eucharistic Prayer for Reconciliation II. The Prayer over the People is required, not optional, on the Sundays of Lent, and the text is given right after the Prayer after Communion.

If your parish is celebrating the Second Scrutiny with the elect, then according to a rubric in the Missal, the proper prayers should be used; these Mass formularies are found in the "Ritual Masses" section of the Missal, under segment I—For the Conferral of the Sacraments of Initiation; #2—For the Celebration of the Scrutinies; B—For the Second Scrutiny. For the actual ritual of the scrutiny itself, consult RCIA, 164–170. The scrutiny takes place after the homily.

Other Ideas

Today Luke's account of the Gospel account gives us the wonderful and familiar story of the Prodigal Son. This story can be a great discussion topic for a family as it gathers for Evening Prayer. More creative children could even do a skit and lead the conversation. Many families experience difficulties in their relationships; include an intercession for healing within families in the Prayer of the Faithful. This Sunday is a good time to emphasize the opportunities for the Sacrament of Penance as preparation for Easter. There are many inexpensive resources on the sacrament of penance, from simple prayer cards to small pamphlets that can be made available for parishioners. These can be especially helpful for those who have been away from the sacrament for some time.

April 2019
Month of the Holy Eucharist

MON 1 (#243 or #244) violet
Lenten Weekday

The Lectionary for Mass: #243

The readings from Lectionary #243 may be used on any day of the week when the Year A readings are not proclaimed on Sunday.

◆ FIRST READING: The prophet Micah puts his trust in the Lord in contrast to those who have betrayed the Lord. Micah's words express his confidence that even though he has fallen in sin, in the Lord, he will arise. The Lord will bring him to justice and he will see the light.

◆ RESPONSORIAL PSALM 27: Psalm 27:1, which serves as the refrain, picks up mention of light in the First Reading. In the words of this verse, we proclaim with confidence our belief that the Lord is our light and salvation. The verses from the second half of the psalm were originally a separate hymn in themselves. They, too, show forth the writer's confidence in the Lord. The Lord will hear his call and he will one day see the Lord's abundance together with others who have chosen to live in the Lord.

◆ GOSPEL: The blind man's neighbors, the Pharisees, and his parents do not know how the blind man is now able to see and who is responsible for restoring his sight. But, the once-blind-man knows for he is now a disciple of Jesus. Would that the others do God's will and have faith in the God of Jesus as the healed man advised. Then, they would see. Yet the Pharisees choose to think their vision needs no correction. Sin, not the light of Christ, remains their choice.

The Lectionary for Mass: #244

The readings from Lectionary #244 are the assigned readings for the Monday Lenten weekday.

◆ FIRST READING: The author known as Third Isaiah announces the Lord's vision for a new heavens and a new earth, where the Lord will forget the people's past. Joy rather than weeping will prevail in the new Jerusalem. Life—life in abundance—life in all its richness—will be the norm.

◆ RESPONSORIAL PSALM 30: Our voices move together with the voice of the psalmist as we first praise the Lord for the Lord's rescue of us and then invite others in the assembly to join in our praise. The psalmist's words also allow us to recall how the Lord has helped us in the past changing our sadness into dancing.

◆ GOSPEL: Jesus' proclamation to the royal official that his son would live coincided with the time that his son began to recover. Upon recognizing this coincidence, which became to the official much more than mere coincidence or chance, he and his entire family believed in Jesus. This is the second sign revealing Jesus' power and glory in the Gospel according to John, the first being the turning of water into wine.

The Roman Missal

Only God can see the big picture. We pray that God guide the Church according to his "eternal design," and come to our aid in "this present age." God is present, now and for ever (Collect). By the sacrifice we offer, we pray that we may leave behind "earthly ways" and grow in "heavenly life" (Prayer over the Offerings). In the Prayer after Communion we ask God to renew us, sanctify us, and lead us to eternal life. Any one of the four Prefaces of Lent is equally appropriate today. The Prayer over the People continues the theme of renewal present in all today's prayers. We ask God to renew his people "within and without" so that they may not be hindered by the pleasures of the flesh, but persevere in their "spiritual intent"—hope for the life to come. Consider using the Eucharistic Prayer for Various Needs and Occasions IV.

TUE 2 (#245) violet
Lenten Weekday

Optional Memorial of St. Francis of Paola, Hermit / violet

The Lectionary for Mass

◆ FIRST READING: The Lord's angel escorts Ezekiel around the Temple where he encounters water flowing in every direction. As they walked a thousand cubits and another thousand cubits (roughly eighteen inches for each cubit), they came upon waters that eventually pooled into a river. The area around the river teemed with life as creation originally did. Its vegetation would serve as food for all living creatures. God would restore paradise to his people.

◆ RESPONSORIAL PSALM 46: The refrain proclaims God's presence among us and around us. We need not fear, for the God of Jacob will always be our strength. The reference in stanza 2, Psalm 46:5, to the river's streams that gladden God's city links to the imagery of water in the First Reading. God is present in the life-giving waters.

◆ GOSPEL: Near a pool of water known for its healing power, Jesus heals a man who had been ill for thirty-eight years. The words of Jesus' command to the man are words of healing. On that Sabbath day, Jesus needed no water to heal. He only needed to speak and life came to the man through his words. The man whom Jesus healed came to know his identity, but some of the Jewish leaders harassed him merely because he showed his glory in this third sign on a Sabbath performing a work that violated their law.

The Roman Missal

We pray that the ancient Lenten practices we observe—"the venerable exercises of holy devotion"—may "shape" our hearts, so that we may come "worthily" to the celebration of the Paschal Mystery (Collect). We give to God what God has given to us, and we pray for awareness of the Creator's loving care for us, and for the spiritual "healing / that brings us immortality." God cares for us, body and soul (Prayer over the Offerings). We ask God to purify and renew our minds with the sacrament we share, both now and in the future. Any one of the four Prefaces of Lent is equally appropriate today. Consider using Eucharistic Prayer III.

Today's Saint

Although St. Francis of Paola (1416–1507) was attracted to the Franciscan friars, he longed for a more contemplative life grounded in solitude and asceticism. Building upon the Franciscan tradition, he founded the hermits of Brother Francis of Assisi, which eventually became known as the Minim Friars, meaning "the least" of all God's servants. The community had a strong devotion to the five wounds of Christ and the Virgin Mary. Due to his reputation for holiness and the miraculous, King Louis XI of France requested St. Francis' spiritual guidance as he was preparing for death. Saint Francis spent the last twenty-five years of his life advising kings and restoring peace between France and its neighboring countries. Many miracles connected to the sea have been attributed to him; therefore, he is the patron saint of navigators and naval officers.

WED 3 (#246) violet
Lenten Weekday

The Lectionary for Mass

◆ FIRST READING: The Lord will restore Zion. Prisoners will experience freedom. Those who suffer in darkness will see the light. No one will hunger or thirst. Despite Zion's words that the Lord has forsaken her and left her for naught, these will serve as signs that the Lord cares for his people as a mother comforts the child in her womb.

◆ RESPONSORIAL PSALM 145: The context for the verses taken from Psalm 145 for today's Responsorial Psalm is the psalmist's praise of the Lord who is God and King. The Lord reigns with the grace and mercy he extends to all. His faithfulness and holiness together with the justice he brings to the oppressed, characterize his kingship.

◆ GOSPEL: After his cure of the sick man by the pool on a sabbath, Jesus responds to those Jews who persecuted him with a lengthy statement of how the Son performs what he has seen the Father do. The fact that Jesus refers to God as his own Father further angers those who questioned Jesus' authority and identity.

The Roman Missal

In the Collect, we call on God, who rewards the just and forgives the repentant. We pray that we who acknowledge our sinfulness may receive God's pardon. The Prayer over the Offerings is a prayer for renewal. We ask God to wipe away the old, and increase the "grace of salvation" and new life within us. One of the four Prefaces of Lent is used today. While any one of the four is appropriate, perhaps, in light of the Collect's focus on repentance, either Preface III, with its direct reference to self-denial and humbling our sinful pride, or Preface IV, with its mention of how bodily fasting restrains our faults, would be good options. The Prayer after Communion echoes St. Paul: "A person should examine himself, and so eat the bread and drink the cup. For anyone who eats and drinks without discerning the body, eats and drinks judgment on himself" (1 Corinthians 11:28–29). We pray that the sacrament which God gives us as a "heavenly remedy" may not bring us judgment. We ask God's protection so that we may do "what is good in this world," and so reach God, our "highest good" (Prayer over the People). Consider using the Eucharistic Prayer for Reconciliation I.

Lenten Weekday

Optional Memorial of St. Isidore, Bishop and Doctor of the Church / violet

The Lectionary for Mass

◆ FIRST READING: The Lord sends Moses to the people who have built a molten calf and are worshiping this idol as the one that has delivered them from slavery in Egypt. Before Moses confronts the people with the Lord's wrath and their impending destruction at his hands, Moses pleads with the Lord for his mercy reminding him of all that he has done for his people to this day. Through the intercession of Moses, the Lord's chosen servant, the Lord's mercy prevails and he will not destroy his unfaithful people.

◆ RESPONSORIAL PSALM 106 carries forward the theme of God's mercy from the First Reading. In the refrain, the people ask God to remember them with his mercy. The verses reference the molten calf the Israelites worship in Horeb and how Moses interceded on their behalf so that God would not destroy them. God's mercy prevails despite the depths of his people's sinfulness.

◆ GOSPEL: Jesus continues to explain to those among the Jews who question his authority and identity that his works testify that the Father has sent him. Even the Scriptures show that life comes through Jesus, for those who believed in Moses would also believe in Jesus. Those who struggle to believe in the words of Moses will certainly have difficulty believing in Jesus' words. In whom will we place our hope?

The Roman Missal

The Collect for today sets a tone of humility and it reminds us of the purpose of our Lenten penance: it should correct us and school us in doing good works. The prayer

also asks for perseverance so that we might "come safely to the paschal festivities." Again there is the undertone in this prayer of calling on the Lord for help as we continue through the long haul of Lent. The Prayer after Communion again points to the purification that comes to us through the sacrament, as it asks that we be granted "freedom from all blame." The sense of how participation in the Eucharist brings new life and heals us from our burdens is highlighted as the prayer asks "that those bound by a guilty conscience / may glory in the fullness of heavenly remedy." The Prayer over the Offerings asks for cleansing and protection through the offering we make in sacrifice. Although any one of the four Prefaces of Lent is equally appropriate today, perhaps Preface I of Lent would work particularly well to echo the orations, with that Preface's mention of "minds made pure," being reborn, and being led to "the fullness of grace." Although the Prayer over the People continues to be optional on weekdays, its consistent use would mark the daily liturgies of Lent in a significant way. Consider using Eucharistic Prayer II.

Today's Saint

What do an archbishop of Seville, an avid writer, a systematic and liturgical theologian, an evangelizer to the skeptic, a minister to the poor, and an establisher of schools have in common? They encapsulate the life and work of St. Isidore of Seville (c. 565–636). He is credited with organizing the Church of Spain through various councils and synods. His theology of the Trinity and Incarnation were the basis for a Creed that was approved at the Fourth Council of Toledo (AD 633). Along with these two noteworthy accomplishments, he also revised the Mozarabic Rite—the accepted liturgy of Spain—and opened cathedral schools for the training of priests. Saint Isidore was named a Doctor of the Church due to his extensive writing, including doctrinal summaries, etymological studies, and rules for religious communities.

FRI 5 (#248) violet
Lenten Weekday

Optional Memorial of St. Vincent Ferrer, Priest / violet

The Lectionary for Mass

◆ FIRST READING: The passage from Wisdom 2:1a, 12–22 describes how the wicked plan to torment the just one who has named their sin to them. In their persecution of him, they believe that if the just one is the son of God, God will come to his aid and take care of him. These verses from Wisdom stand as prophetic words about Jesus' Passion and Death.

◆ RESPONSORIAL PSALM 34 is a testament to our faith that the Lord destroys evildoers and sides with the just. The just will not have an easy road in life, but the Lord will accompany them and deliver them from their trials. Redemption will come to the just servants of the Lord. This the psalmist knows from his own personal experience of the Lord rescuing him.

◆ GOSPEL: The Jewish feast of Tabernacles nears and Jesus and some of his relatives (not necessarily disciples) make their way to Jerusalem. Some of Jerusalem's citizens question Jesus' identity, asking if he is the one some of the authorities sought to kill. Perhaps Jesus overheard their discussion for from inside of the Temple where he was teaching, Jesus tells them they know him and from where he comes. Anger at Jesus' words which linked his identity to the Father, caused some of the people to attempt his arrest; however, the appropriate time had not yet come, but the growing intensity reveals its approach.

The Roman Missal

The Collect for the Lenten Weekday reminds us that the penances we undertake during Lent are gifts that have been given to us from God as "helps for us in our weakness." As a result, those helps have healing effects on us, effects that we should receive with joy and reflect in the way we live daily "a holy way of life." The Prayer over the Offerings asks for cleansing so that we might approach the source of this sacrifice with purity; thus, the prayer reminds us that our worship can never be mere outward ritual, but must always draw us more deeply into the mystery being celebrated. The Prayer after Communion for the weekday uses the contrast between old and new to ask that we leave former ways behind and "be renewed in holiness of mind." The prayer reminds us that reception of the sacrament is never a passive reception but must represent the offering of self and the openness to transformation of a life that is continually being renewed in Christ. Consider using Eucharistic Prayer III.

Today's Saint

St. Vincent Ferrer was born around 1350, the son of an English immigrant to Spain. He entered the Order of Preachers (Dominicans) at the age of 18, and was eventually sent to study theology, earning a doctorate at Lleida. Vincent traveled widely, preaching the Gospel as he went. The saints are human and prone to mistakes as anyone, and, unfortunately, Vincent is an example: he is said to have been responsible for the forced conversion of many Spanish Jews to Catholicism. He was also a supporter of the Avignon pope, Benedict XIII, during the Great Schism, a period during which three men each claimed to be the true pope. Eventually, after Benedict did nothing to end the schism, Vincent withdrew his support. Vincent Ferrer died on April 5, 1419, in Brittany (France) and is buried in Vannes Cathedral. He was an eloquent speaker, and he lived a life of great asceticism and imposed severe penances on himself such as sleeping on the floor, and fasting continuously. Vincent firmly believed that the end times were near and that he had been sent to prepare humanity. Known as the "Angel of the Apocalypse," he is the patron saint of construction workers because of his work to "build" the Church.

SAT 6 (#249) violet
Lenten Weekday

The Lectionary for Mass

◆ FIRST READING: The Lord advised Jeremiah of those who conspired to kill him, for the prophet had not realized on his own that he faced impending doom at the hands of the wicked. Jeremiah describes himself as an innocent lamb led to slaughter. His trust in people is, perhaps, naive, but his confidence that the Lord's vengeance will come upon those who seek his death, signifies a mature faith.

◆ RESPONSORIAL PSALM 7: The psalmist mirrors Jeremiah's experience as he seeks refuge from his enemies in the Lord. His innocence is similar to Jeremiah; his desire for the Lord to act justly for him and against the wicked reflects Jeremiah's. As a people of faith, we approach God for sanctuary through the words of Psalm 7.

◆ GOSPEL: The topic at hand is from where the Christ will come. After hearing Jesus speak the crowds became divided with some people identifying him as the Christ and others disputing this based on scriptural evidence in support of the Davidic lineage of the Christ. The chain of command from the guards to the chief priests and the Pharisees also do not agree about Jesus, yet the Pharisees show their true colors with a rhetorical question that reveals they and the authorities do not believe Jesus is the Christ. It is Nicodemus, the Pharisee and ruler of the Jews who previously had come to Jesus in the night and asked him about being born from above, who steps forward saying the law requires hearing before a person is condemned.

The Roman Missal

The Lenten Collect once again reminds us that without God we can do nothing: "without your grace / we cannot find favor in your sight." The Prayer over the Offerings points out that even in bringing our oblations we are not yet perfected, and we may in some way be defiant of God's will; nonetheless, in our offering to God, we pray that he will assist us in conforming our will to his own. This prayer, then, reminds us of the willingness to have our will transformed. This must be an inherent part of participating in the offering of the sacrifice. The Prayer after Communion for the Lenten Weekday again asks for purification so that we may be pleasing to God. Consider using the Eucharistic Prayer for Reconciliation II.

☀ **7** (#36C or #34A) violet
Fifth Sunday of Lent

The Lectionary for Mass: Year C

◆ FIRST READING: During the Babylonian Exile, our Judean ancestors struggled with despair. Forced exportation from their homeland and the destruction of the Temple left them feeling without identity, land, or God. Many of them longingly looked back to the Exodus, when God freed them from landless slavery in Egypt and brought them to the promised land. Would they ever experience God's care again? Would they ever again be a nation? Isaiah answers their questions with this prophecy. God does not want them looking to the past and yearning for what was lost. Rather, God wants them to see the future as God-filled. God will bring them through a new Exodus from Babylon to their homeland. The wilderness that stretches between Babylon and Judah will not prove a barrier for them. The story also lives for us today. Like Israel, God continues to be with us; we are still God's people. What matters most is that we look to the future with hope knowing that God goes before us.

◆ RESPONSORIAL PSALM 126: Pilgrims probably sang this psalm as they made their way to the Temple for the festivals. Their thoughts immediately turn to God and to the many times God delivered their ancestors out of trouble. In their minds flash pictures of the Exodus and, more recently, the return from the Exile in Babylon. As the pilgrims sing, the thought crosses their minds that perhaps God will return to save them. At that, the tone of the psalm shifts. "Restore our fortunes, O LORD," the pilgrims pray. "Those who sow in tears / shall reap rejoicing." This Lent we join those pilgrims as we recall God's mighty deeds in the Death and Resurrection of Jesus.

◆ SECOND READING: From prison Paul writes to the Philippians about what he values most. He reminds them that he was raised as a Jew with education and privilege. He became a devoted follower of God and strove to please the Almighty One he loved by zealously keeping the Law and persecuting those he thought strayed from God's way. In the midst of persecuting the church, he encountered the Risen Christ in an intimate and life-changing experience. What he previously valued no longer mattered, and Paul left it all "because of the surpassing value of knowing Christ Jesus." Knowing Christ and "the power of his resurrection" enables Paul to look to the future with hope, whether or not it brings release from prison or further suffering and death.

◆ GOSPEL: The plot of John's story is deceptively simple. The Pharisees ask Jesus his opinion on a case concerning a woman who was caught committing adultery, a capital offense in Israel. The real action is in the plot beneath the plot. Those Pharisees are not interested in the woman or her alleged crime. They are more interested in trapping Jesus. They know that because Rome rules Galilee, they have no power to invoke the death penalty, even if Jesus agreed to it. They also know that the Law had stringent requirements for a capital case, and their case against the woman met none of those requirements. The evidence against her simply was not enough to convict her. Jesus, however, is not interested in legal machinations. He wants instead to demonstrate God's forgiving love and the new life that love offers to all willing to receive it. He begins with the Pharisees. He very gently but firmly holds a mirror before their faces, hoping that when they see themselves, they will have more compassion for others just like them. And it works, to a degree. Each of the Pharisees ends up leaving quietly. Jesus then turns to the woman. She, too, sees herself in Jesus' eyes, but instead of walking away, she turns to Jesus and hears those beautiful words, "Neither do I condemn you."

The Lectionary for Mass: Year A

◆ First Reading: This reading includes a promise of resurrection. God tells his people that he will bring them out of their graves, fill them with his spirit, and restore them to their land. In its context in the Book of Ezekiel, the death spoken of is not physical death; rather, this death is the loss of hope, a separation from God through sin, exile, and despair.

◆ Responsorial Psalm 130: The psalm praises the God who lifts us from "the depths," the God of mercy and redemption.

◆ Second Reading: The reading from Romans contrasts the body and the spirit. It is not the body that gives life, but the Spirit of God. This is not to say that the body does not matter. Rather, through Christ, the body comes to life, as a dwelling place for the very Spirit of God.

◆ Gospel: The story of the raising of Lazarus speaks frankly about death and everything that goes with it: sickness; terrible grief of those who remain; even the stench of

death is mentioned. This reading is really about Resurrection. The mourning of women; the tomb hewn in the rock and sealed with a stone; the burial bands and the face cloth—all these details will re-emerge in the account of Christ's Resurrection. In this Gospel, we see Jesus at his most divine—he has power over death itself. We also see him at his most human. Again and again John tells us what Jesus was feeling: he "loved Martha and her sister and Lazarus" (John 11:5), he was "perturbed and deeply troubled," he "wept," he was "perturbed again." When God became human in Jesus Christ, he did not just take on a human form, but a human heart as well.

The Roman Missal

The Fifth Sunday of Lent can be seen as a turning point in the Lenten journey as we enter the final days of this season with less than two weeks left before we begin the Sacred Paschal Triduum. The Missal includes a rubric pointing to a practice that can serve as a visual reminder to the assembly that we have reached this point in Lent: the practice of covering crosses and images in the church may be observed beginning with this Sunday. Images and statues are covered until the beginning of the Easter Vigil; crosses, however, are uncovered sooner, remaining covered only until the end of the Celebration of the Lord's Passion on Good Friday. Consider doing this in your church so that the faithful continue to be engaged in the somberness and tone of Lent through the visible environment of the worship space. Also, as with the previous two Sundays, there are two sets of Mass formularies from which to choose today. Use either the Mass for the Fifth Sunday of Lent if you are not celebrating the Third Scrutiny or the Mass for the Third Scrutiny if you are celebrating that ritual. The Gloria contin-

ues to be omitted today. The Creed is sung or said.

The Preface that is given on the pages right there along with the other texts for this Mass, titled simply "Lazarus," is the Preface that is to be used today if the Year A readings are done for RCIA, and the Gospel account of Jesus raising Lazarus is the text assigned for the day. Consider chanting the introductory dialogue and the Preface today. If this is not the regular practice of your community, this can be a way of powerfully drawing attention to the solemnity of Lent (but be sure to prepare and rehearse your assembly as needed, especially if your people are not familiar with the responses!). The Prayer over the People is required, not optional, on the Sundays of Lent, and the text is given right after the Prayer after Communion. Consider using the Eucharistic Prayer for Reconciliation I.

If your parish is celebrating the Third Scrutiny with the elect, then according to a rubric in the Missal, the proper prayers should be used; these Mass formularies are found in the section "Ritual Masses," under segment I—For the Conferral of the Sacraments of Initiation; #2—For the Celebration of the Scrutinies; C—For the Third Scrutiny. For the actual ritual of the scrutiny itself, consult RCIA, 164–170. The scrutiny takes place after the homily.

Other Ideas

In these closing days of Lent we should encourage ourselves, and each other, to remain faithful to our Lenten resolutions. Prayer, fasting, and almsgiving are still worthy spiritual exercises and the parish most certainly will have a number of options for each of them. Our own personal initiatives are always a good idea. Make extra time in your daily schedule for prayer; consider participating in one or more weekday Masses. Fasting can be practiced on any day and in a variety of ways; choose one that will be doable but that also represents a personal sacrifice. Ask another member of your family or a friend or a colleague at work to join you. Almsgiving can be a personal act or invite others to join you in supporting a particular cause. The work of the Lord needs many hands and many hearts!

M O N **8** (#250 or #251) violet
Lenten Weekday

The Lectionary for Mass: #250

The readings from the Lectionary #250 may be used on any day of the week when the Year A readings are not proclaimed on Sunday.

◆ FIRST READING: Elisha arrived at the home of a Shunammite woman only to find her son lying deceased on the bed of the man of God. Through prayer and a healing touch, Elisha brings the boy back to life. Death is not the end of this story for either the mother or father, who most certainly deeply mourned the loss of their son, or for the boy himself. Life has the final word for a child of God.

◆ RESPONSORIAL PSALM 17: The psalmist who most likely has spent the night sleeping in the Temple's sanctuary, speaks of awakening at peace in God's presence. Like the psalmist, the Lord protects us in the shadow of his wings. We experience the Lord's glory in the life he brings to us. We know that death does not have the final say. Those who seek to do us harm will not succeed. What joy we find in him!

◆ GOSPEL: The Gospel reading for the optional Mass on this Monday of the Fifth Week of Lent is the raising of Lazarus from the Gospel according to John. The story in which we come to know Jesus as the Resurrection and the Life is the Gospel reading for Year A on the Fifth Sunday of Lent and when the Third Scrutiny is celebrated with the elect.

The Lectionary for Mass: #251

The readings from the Lectionary #251 are the assigned readings for the Lenten Monday weekday.

◆ FIRST READING: The longer form of the First Reading sets the context for Susanna's prayer to God stating her innocence against the charges the elders brought against her. The shorter form of the reading begins with Susanna's prayer after she has been falsely condemned to death. In the end, God's justice triumphs as the young boy, Daniel, whom God fills with the Holy Spirit, acts to adjudicate the truth. In the responses of the two elders to Daniel's questions, the elders perjure themselves. They, instead of the innocent Susanna, would be put to death according to the law of Moses.

◆ RESPONSORIAL PSALM 23: The refrain from verse 4b connects with Susanna's experience in the First Reading. Susanna herself must have gone through the dark valley of despair after being wrongly condemned, but yet she trusted that the Lord was by her side. We share in the hope of the psalmist and Susanna as we trust that the goodness of the Shepherd will follow us forever.

◆ GOSPEL: The Pharisees are unhappy with Jesus' claim to be the Light of the World because he appears to be testifying on his own behalf without evidence for his claim. What the Pharisees do not understand (or want to believe) is that the Father has sent Jesus. This is evidence enough for his claim to be the Light of the World. Still, no one arrests Jesus, because the hour of his Passion has not come.

The Roman Missal

As we begin the last days of Lent, the Collect for the Lenten Weekday invites us to more and more deeply focus on entering into the Paschal Mystery and to dying and rising with Christ, particularly as that mystery will be celebrated during the Sacred Paschal Triduum, which is rapidly approaching. Thus, the prayer asks that Christ's passage will be ours: "grant us so to pass from former ways to newness of life, / that we may be made ready for the glory of the heavenly Kingdom."

In keeping with the shift to the period of late Lenten time, starting today there is no longer a choice among Prefaces; rather, Preface I of the Passion of the Lord is the Preface assigned for today. It speaks explicitly of the Passion of Christ and of the "wondrous power of the Cross" that reveals both God's judgment on the world and the "authority of Christ crucified." Consider using this Preface even if you are using one of the Eucharistic Prayers for Reconciliation (you are not required to use the Preface that goes with the Eucharistic Prayer for Reconciliation). Consider using Eucharistic Prayer II.

Use the suggested Prayer over the People at the end of Mass, even though it is optional, especially in these final days of Lent.

T U E **9** (#252) violet
Lenten Weekday

The Lectionary for Mass

◆ FIRST READING: Hungry and thirsty in the desert, the children of Israel complained against both God and Moses. It was not until the Lord sent seraph serpents to bite the people so they perished, that others repented of their sin and requested Moses pray to the Lord to remove the serpents from their midst. In what Christians now interpret as a symbol of the life that comes through Jesus' Death on the Cross, Moses, according to the Lord's instructions, mounts a seraph on a pole. Those bitten by a serpent, but who look to the bronze serpent on the pole, will live. Once again, death is not the end of the story. Life is.

◆ RESPONSORIAL PSALM 102 is one of the penitential psalms, in which the psalmist cries out to the Lord to hear his prayer in time of distress. Like the people cried out to Moses and the Lord in the desert, and like Moses approaches the Lord in prayer on behalf of the repentant people, the psalmist yearns for the Lord to listen to him. The final verse acknowledges the Lord does hear him. Praise is the response due back to God for generations to come.

◆ GOSPEL: When people understand Jesus as "I AM," a designation reserved for God alone, then they will understand his unique relationship with the Father and believe. They will lift up the Son of Man as Moses lifted up the serpent on the pole to bring life to the people. Many already believed in Jesus, but John leaves open how many among the believers at this point were Pharisees who were willing to see the world through the lens of life, not death.

The Roman Missal

The Collect today includes an important petition—namely, that we may persevere in obeying God's will. Again, the prayer seems to recognize our need for encouragement and strength to maintain the long discipline of Lent. There is an interesting result of that perseverance that is mentioned: so that "the people dedicated to your service / may grow in both merit and number." Perhaps this phrase could remind us of the importance of giving good example to those preparing for initiation; our witness as we persevere through Lent can have a direct

effect on their coming into the faith. The Prayer over the Offerings recognizes the reconciliation that is brought about between God and humanity as a result of our participation in the sacrifice; through it, we can ask God, who is full of compassion, to pardon our offenses. The Preface assigned for today is Preface I of the Passion of the Lord, as it will be every day this week. Use this Preface even if you are using one of the two Eucharistic Prayers for Reconciliation (it is not required to use the Preface that goes with the Eucharistic Prayers for Reconciliation). The Prayer after Communion notes how a constitutive dimension of being human is to seek what is divine. Although the Prayer over the People continues to be optional on weekdays, its continued use would mark this late Lenten Weekday in a significant way. Consider using Eucharistic Prayer III.

WED 10 (#253) violet
Lenten Weekday

The Lectionary for Mass

◆ FIRST READING: Shadrach, Meshach, and Abednego remain staunchly faithful to God in their encounter with King Nebuchadnezzar who wants them to serve his god. The fiery furnace awaits them as Nebuchadnezzar takes revenge on them for their trust in the God they serve. Much to the king's surprise, he sees a fourth man—one like a son of God—in the furnace with the three. All are alive and walking about. Nebuchadnezzar experiences his own conversion to the God of Shadrach, Meshach, and Abednego. The God of life can bring even the unbelieving to faith.

◆ CANTICLE: Today's canticle comes from the song of the three who lived in the fiery furnace. In the midst of the flames, they glorified the Lord to whom they had

remained faithful. They sang of the Lord's blessedness over and over again. Our voices join in their praise of the Lord whose glory the vast heavens and earth reflect.

◆ GOSPEL: Even those among the Jews who believed in Jesus, become perplexed with Jesus' words that the truth will set them free. They claim Abraham as their father, but Jesus points out if that is the case, they would be engaged in doing Abraham's works, not plotting to put Jesus to death. Abraham and Jesus both stand on the side of life, not death.

The Roman Missal

God himself awakens devotion in us. We ask him to enlighten those who have been "sanctified by penance" this Lent and to hear us when we cry out to him (Collect). We ask God to "receive back" the sacrifice he has given us, that it may be "for our healing" (Prayer over the Offerings). The Preface assigned for today is Preface I of the Passion of the Lord, as it will be every day this week. Use this Preface even if you are using one of the two Eucharistic Prayers for Reconciliation (it is not required to use the Preface that goes with the Eucharistic Prayers for Reconciliation). The sacrament we receive is "heavenly medicine," purging evil and strengthening us with God's protection (Prayer after Communion). God has given us our hope in his compassion. In the Prayer over the People, we ask him to let us feel his mercy as well. Consider using the Eucharistic Prayer for Reconciliation I.

THU 11 (#254) violet
Lenten Weekday

Optional Memorial of St. Stanislaus, Bishop and Martyr / violet

The Lectionary for Mass

◆ FIRST READING: God covenants with Abram and, as a sign of their covenant, changes Abram's name to Abraham. As part of the covenant God makes three promises to Abraham—prosperity, progeny, and land. The requirement God places on Abraham and his descendants is to remain faithful forever.

◆ RESPONSORIAL PSALM 105: The references in Psalm 105 to the covenant the Lord made with Abraham allude to the First Reading. Ongoing faithfulness characterizes the Lord's commitment to the covenant. For our part, the words of the psalmist remind us to look to the Lord as our strength, to recall his wondrous deeds, and to serve him continuously. In doing these things, we uphold our end of the covenant.

◆ GOSPEL: The tension between Jesus and some of the Jews escalates such that by the end of the Gospel passage they pick up stones to hurl at him, but Jesus escapes out of the Temple area. Jesus' claim that those who adhere to his words would never know death heightened the drama between him and some of the Jews to the point of violence. Not even Abraham claimed this. But even as Jesus asserts his identity as "I AM" once again, anxiety and fury takes over.

The Roman Missal

In the Collect, we ask for the grace of perseverance "in holy living," so that we may be "full heirs" of God's promises. We offer the holy sacrifice not only for our own conversion, but for "the salvation of all the world" (Prayer over the Offerings). As with the other days this week, the Preface assigned for today is Preface I of the Passion of the Lord, and it should be used even if you are using one of the Eucharistic Prayers for Reconciliation (it is not required to use the Preface that goes with the Eucharistic Prayer for Reconciliation). Through the sacrament of which we partake here and now, we pray to be "partakers

of life eternal" (Prayer after Communion). In the Prayer over the People, we ask that we may reject those things that displease God, and instead be filled "with delight" in God's commandments. Consider using the Eucharistic Prayer for Reconciliation II.

Today's Saint

Noted for his compassionate concern for the poor and wise counsel, St. Stanislaus (c. 1030–1079) was appointed bishop of Krakow. His consecration as bishop was met with great joy on the part of the people. While serving as bishop he spoke out against King Boleslaus, an unjust and cruel man who incited fear in the people of Poland. Saint Stanislaus, outraged by the oppressive behavior of the monarch, declared that an unjust king has no place in the Church. In response, the king defamed his reputation, eventually ordering guards to kill him, but they refused. The king took matters into his own hands by stabbing him with a sword. Saint Stanislaus, the martyr, is the patron saint of Poland and the city of Krakow.

F R I 12 (#255) violet
Lenten Weekday

The Lectionary for Mass

◆ FIRST READING: Jeremiah's words to the Lord reflect his confidence in the Lord despite feeling trapped by his enemies—even people who were his friends—on all sides. He trusts the Lord will put them to shame and rescue him from his distress, even though at other points, the prophet is close to despair. Yet Jeremiah will praise the Lord should he witness the Lord take revenge on those who persecute him.

◆ RESPONSORIAL PSALM 18: Perhaps Jeremiah could have sung his thanks to the Lord in words

similar to that of Psalm 18. In this psalm, the author sings his gratitude to the Lord for hearing his voice when he was in distress. The psalmist's words reflect a profound love for the Lord who delivered him from death.

◆ GOSPEL: We move ahead two chapters in John's account of the Gospel only to find some of the Jews once again picking up rocks to stone Jesus. The stoning is not a result of the good works Jesus has performed. Rather, blasphemy is their charge against him. Jesus made himself "I AM" and spoke of himself as the Son of God. These were received as absurd and dishonest claims by Jesus, and caused some of the Jews to try and arrest him again, but to no avail. Across the Jordan, many others believed in Jesus and accepted the truth of the divine power active in him.

The Roman Missal

There are two options for the Collect today. The first prayer is a prayer for pardon, asking that we be set free from "the bonds of the sins / we have committed in our weakness." The second option notes how in this liturgical time the Church imitates the Blessed Virgin Mary "in contemplating the Passion of Christ," and therefore the prayer goes on to ask that through her intercession "we may cling more firmly each day / to your Only Begotten Son / and come at last to the fullness of his grace." Thus, in a certain sense, this second prayer puts us at the foot of the Cross along with Mary, clinging to Jesus even throughout his Passion and Death, and prepares us well to enter into the celebration of Holy Week. The Preface assigned for today is Preface I of the Passion of the Lord; remember to use it even if you are using one of the Eucharistic Prayers for Reconciliation (it is not required to use the Preface that goes with the Eucharistic Prayer for

SAT **13** (#256) violet

Lenten Weekday

Optional Memorial of St. Martin I, Pope and Martyr / violet

The Lectionary for Mass

◆ FIRST READING: God promises to make of the children of Israel one nation. A divided kingdom will never again exist. Through the eternal and everlasting Davidic covenant of peace, God will forever dwell with his people. God consecrates Israel as his people and becomes their God. Forever God knits himself in relationship to his holy people

◆ CANTICLE: Today's Canticle comes from the Lord's words spoken through the prophet in Jeremiah 31. These words describe the act of the Lord gathering his people together and protecting and guarding them as a shepherd tends his sheep. Redemption comes to the Lord's people and they will respond with joyful shouts and lively dances.

◆ GOSPEL: The Jewish people remain divided over Jesus even after he brought Lazarus back from the dead. Some believed, but others went directly to the authorities and reported Jesus for his glorious life-giving sign. The authorities had to choose between leaving Jesus alone and risk everyone believing in him, or putting him to death. On the words of Caiaphas, who prophesied that Jesus was going to die for all the children of God, the authorities expedited their plan to kill Jesus as Passover neared. Would Jesus come to the Passover feast?

The Roman Missal

The Collect prays for those who have already been called to eternal life. There is much emphasis on forgiveness of sins, as if the prayers themselves are cajoling us one last time to seek the Sacrament of Reconciliation before Holy Week starts, or to implore Christ in his mercy to take on whatever is lacking in our penance. As we share in both the suffering of the Lord and the table of the Lord, may we truly become "sharers of his divine nature" as the Prayer after Communion suggests. Consider using Eucharistic Prayer III.

Today's Saint

St. Martin I was a Roman of noble birth and had a reputation for intelligence, learning, and charity. He fought against the Monothelite heresy, which claimed that Jesus had two natures—human and divine—but only one will. At that time, the government was deeply involved in theological controversies. If the Church was torn by doctrinal conflicts, the emperors felt it threatened public order. They sought peace at all costs, even sacrificing orthodoxy. Martin was tried by Emperor Constans II in Constantinople and was imprisoned and exiled. He died from mistreatment at the hands of fellow Christians in 655.

14 (#37C, #38ABC) red
Palm Sunday of the Passion of the Lord

About Today's Liturgy

Branches of palm, olive, or sometimes even budding willow are ancient symbols of victory and hope, as well as of new life. The procession celebrating Jesus' entry into Jerusalem overflowed with praise and excitement, as onlookers waved these triumphant branches and proclaimed their blessings. Yet, in a few days, they will cry "Crucify him!" The crowd's change of heart illustrates the problem of holding God to our expectations. The crowd expected a liberating leader, the Messiah, to free them from Roman oppression. Jesus instead takes up his Cross and invites us to do the same. Through his Death and Resurrection he is indeed a liberator, but from death and sin, not from Rome. But unable to see past their need, the crowd's disappointment turns into anger and a death order. As we enter Holy Week, Palm Sunday teaches us to let God be God and to trust in God's wisdom not only to meet but shatter and exceed our expectations.

The Lectionary for Mass

◆ GOSPEL AT THE BLESSING of the Palms: As disciples of Jesus, today we imitate his first followers by accompanying him into Jerusalem. Jesus completes his journey to Jerusalem, where he is greeted with great joy as the long-awaited Messiah. A colt never ridden, willing acquiescence to Jesus' directives, cloaks spread out on the road, praise and acclamation boldly proclaimed—all these details affirm his followers' acknowledgment of Jesus as God's Messiah and prophet. How many will be ready to suffer with him as the authorities challenge his person and teachings? This perennial question confronts his followers in every age.

◆ FIRST READING: This passage depicts a servant whom God called to strengthen the weary. Like many prophets, he encounters rejection, insult, and violence. Confident that God will ultimately vindicate him, the servant sets his face "like flint" in endurance. Although this song comes from the time of the Babylonian Exile, it gave the early Church a way of speaking about Christ's suffering. The Servant Songs are not direct predictions about Jesus but a means for his followers to understand his suffering and death.

◆ RESPONSORIAL PSALM 22: This psalm is the lament of a person who endures great suffering. Some people ridicule him, convinced that his troubles are caused by great sin. His enemies gloat, his friends desert him, and his family members divide up his belongings as if he were already dead. Even so, the psalmist still expresses confidence that he will eventually be vindicated. He weaves such expressions into his cries of despair until at last he manages a vow: If God will save him, he will sing a song of praise to God in the midst of all the people. Jesus will quote the psalm's opening line from the Cross, and the early Church will rely heavily on this psalm for understanding Jesus' death. The psalm's vivid imagery and profound insights into the suffering of the innocent make it a natural choice for explaining how the Messiah could have met such an ignoble end.

◆ SECOND READING: This early creedal hymn, which Paul quotes, provides Christians with a framework for understanding the life, death, and exaltation of Jesus Christ. Like Isaiah's prophet, Jesus is seen as God's servant—one who did not regard being made in God's image as something about which to boast. Rather, Jesus chose the path of self-emptying as the way to remain faithful to his calling. "He humbled himself, becoming obedient to the point of death, even death on a cross. Because of this, God greatly exalted him." The early Christians who sang this hymn knew that the agony and disgrace of Jesus' Crucifixion were to be under-

stood only in light of his vindication by God through the Resurrection. For Paul this creed is all one needs to know about Jesus' life. Paul, however, is not only concerned that the Philippians intellectually know this passionate way, but he also wants them, and us, to know it in our hearts. We are to be imitators of the passionate Christ just as Paul is.

◆ GOSPEL: From Jesus' Last Supper with his disciples to his final breath on the Cross, the picture of Jesus in Luke's Gospel is of one who is a servant faithful to God in the face of evil. The power of darkness, which left Jesus after the temptations "until an opportune time" (Luke 4:13), now returns to attack Jesus. Yet throughout the story we encounter Jesus' deep compassion as he experiences Judas' betrayal, his arrest by armed soldiers, Peter's denial, his followers' abandonment, his opponents' mockery, and the crowd's vilification. When one of the slaves in the arresting party has his ear cut off, Jesus heals him. When he is shuttled back and forth from the Sanhedrin to Herod to Pilate, his faithful obedience to the demands of the moment does not waiver. When one of the criminals being crucified with him asks to be remembered, Jesus offers him the blessing of paradise. Never does he betray his understanding of himself as "one who serves," whose life is being "given" and "poured out" for his disciples. The cry of the soldier at the Cross, "Certainly this man was innocent," completes the picture of Jesus' innocence in the midst of evil. While his murder was a political act that satisfied military and religious leaders whose authority he challenged, Jesus' revolutionary work for God's reign had just begun.

The Roman Missal

A careful reading of the Missal by all those involved in the preparation of today's liturgy will help ensure a smooth flow to the ritual. All the

texts are found in the "Holy Week" section of the Missal that follows Saturday of the Fifth Week of Lent in the Proper of Time.

All Masses today take place with the Commemoration of the Lord's Entrance into Jerusalem, "to accomplish his Paschal Mystery," in the words of the Missal; that Commemoration takes place using one of three forms: the Procession, the Solemn Entrance, or the Simple Entrance. The Missal indicates that the Procession (the first form) or the Solemn Entrance (the second form) take place before the principal Mass and that the Solemn Entrance, but not the Procession, may be celebrated with a large gathering of people (note, therefore, that the Missal envisions the first form, the Procession, taking place only once, whereas the Solemn Entrance may be used at as many Masses as is deemed pastorally advantageous in light of the gathering of the people).

First Form: The Procession

This form of the commemoration takes place with all gathering at a place other than inside the church to which the procession will go — either a smaller church, or perhaps a parish center room, or perhaps even outside. The faithful already hold palm branches.

The priest and the deacon wear red vestments; the priest may wear a chasuble, or he may wear a cope and then change into a chasuble when the procession is over. At the appointed time, the priest, deacon, and other ministers go to the place where everyone is gathered. The Missal does not indicate that this is any kind of a formal procession per se, so it can be an informal gathering of the clergy and ministers as they arrive at the place of beginning. The Missal does state, however, that "meanwhile" (while the ministers are assembling, or perhaps even while all are gathering, not just the ministers, to create a prayerful environment as all arrive) an antiphon or an appropriate song is sung; the antiphon suggested is from chapter 21 of Matthew's account of the Gospel: "Hosanna to the Son of David; blessed is he who comes in the name of the Lord, the King of Israel. Hosanna in the highest."

After this singing and when all have arrived, the priest begins with the Sign of the Cross and the usual liturgical greeting for Mass, followed by an introductory address. For this introduction, he may use the words given in the Missal (#5, at Palm Sunday of the Passion of the Lord); if he uses his own words, it is important that he convey the invitation for the faithful to participate actively and consciously in the celebration this day.

After the address, the priest says one of the two prayers of blessing. Only the first option includes the gesture of making the Sign of the Cross by the priest; the second one does not. The first prayer specifically asks God to bless the branches, and then goes on to ask that we "who follow Christ the King in exultation, may reach the eternal Jerusalem through him." The second option focuses more on the people "who today hold high these branches to hail Christ in his triumph," asking for their faith to be increased and their prayers to be held, so that they "may bear fruit for you by good works accomplished in him." Whichever prayer is used, however, the branches are next sprinkled after the prayer, in silence.

Then the deacon, or the priest if there is no deacon, proclaims the Gospel account of the Lord's entrance according to the proper cycle of Lectionary readings in the liturgical year; the Missal states this is done "in the usual way," meaning that there should be the greeting "The Lord be with you" and the announcement "A reading from

the holy Gospel according to . . ." as is always done. Incense may also be used here. The third edition of *The Roman Missal* has the texts for this first Gospel reading right there in the Missal, which makes things much easier.

The Missal notes that after the Gospel, a brief homily may be given. The key word concerning this homily would seem to be "brief," if one were to be given at all—it's optional. Then an invitation is given by either a priest, deacon, or lay minister, using the words in the Missal or similar ones, to invite the people to begin the procession.

The procession is led by the thurifer, if incense is used, followed by a crossbearer. The Missal specifically points out that the cross that is carried should be "decorated with palm branches according to local custom." The cross is carried between two ministers with lighted candles. Behind this follow the deacon with the *Book of the Gospels*, the priest, the ministers, and then the faithful (note that the priest celebrant is not at the end of the procession, but rather walks before the people). Singing takes place during this procession, with various options suggested in the Missal; other appropriate songs may of course be chosen.

Keep in mind in your preparations that it will be important to choose music that will be able to be sung easily by the choir and the people as they move along in procession. Think through the route that will be used and how the movement will affect people's ability to sing. Think of ways to maintain the singing. *Sing to the Lord: Music in Divine Worship* (STL, 93–94) points out that while recorded music should not normally be used in liturgy, the use of recorded music to accompany communal singing during a procession outside is an exception. Therefore, if necessary, look into resources for

having prerecorded music broadcast. For example, your choir could record the singing ahead of time, and then that recording could be broadcast outside via a bell tower or some other external speaker system, and that music would support and enhance the assembly's singing while they are processing to the church.

The Missal notes that a second song or a responsory is sung as the procession enters the church; thus, the music should change.

Then, as the procession enters the church, the priest goes to the altar, venerates it, and, if appropriate, incenses it. The people, meanwhile, continue to process into the church. He then goes to his chair, changes from cope to chasuble if necessary, and, when all are in the church, the singing ends. The priest goes right into the Collect of the Mass, and then Mass continues in the usual way; the other Introductory Rites are omitted.

Second Form: The Solemn Entrance

This form of the entrance is used at Mass when the first form, the procession, is taking place or has taken place at another Mass, or when a procession outside the church cannot otherwise take place for some reason.

In this case, the priest, ministers, and, if possible, a small group of the faithful gather somewhere other than the sanctuary, but preferably at a place where the people can see the rite. All are already holding branches in their hands.

An antiphon or another song is sung while the priest approaches the place where the rite is to begin, and then the Sign of the Cross, liturgical greeting, introduction, blessing and sprinkling, and proclamation of the Gospel all occur as described above. After the Gospel, the priest, ministers, and small group of the faithful process solemnly through the church to the sanctuary while an appropriate song is sung. Then, arriving at the altar, the priest venerates it and then goes to the chair, where, omitting the Introductory Rites, he says the Collect of the Mass after the singing ends. Mass then continues in the usual way. The Missal makes no provision for the priest to wear a cope in this form of entrance; he wears the chasuble.

Third Form:
The Simple Entrance

Essentially, this form of entrance is the same as any other Sunday: the priest proceeds to the altar while the Entrance Antiphon with its psalm or some other suitable song is sung; he arrives at the altar, venerates it, and then goes to his chair; and then he begins Mass with the Sign of the Cross, greets the people as usual, and Mass continues. In this form, the usual Introductory Rites would occur.

At the Mass

There are special instructions for the proclamation of the Lord's Passion: it is to be read without candles and without incense, and there is to be no greeting before the proclamation and no signing of the book. It is customary in many places to have several people participate in the reading of the Passion, not just the priest and deacon. However, the part of Christ should, if possible, be read by the priest. Only a deacon asks for the blessing of the priest before reading the Passion, as he does before reading the Gospel. Your community may wish to consider chanting the Gospel; this is a wonderful way of highlighting the solemnity of the day. The Missal notes that there should be a homily after the narrative of the Passion, but interestingly the adjective "brief" is used again. The Creed and the Universal Prayer take place as usual. The Preface assigned for today, "The Passion of the Lord," is given right there in the Missal along with the other texts for this Mass. The Preface is a very succinct proclamation of how Christ, though innocent, "suffered willingly for sinners" in order to save the guilty. Consider using the Eucharistic Prayer for Reconciliation I.

Other Ideas

Today the parish will want to emphasize the various times for the liturgies of Holy Week. Print a special card with the necessary information as a handy reference for everyone. If at all possible use the first form of the procession and blessing of palms in *The Roman Missal*. This ancient celebration of the Church should be afforded the solemnity it deserves. Taking blessed palms home provides a good opportunity for a family conversation on the importance of the different celebrations of Holy Week. If you live alone reread the passion narrative later today, pausing over each scene of Jesus' journey to the cross and reflecting on the grace that is ours in our own journey. If you know someone who is not able to be at Church, consider doing this with them and sharing in the power of the Word.

M O N 15 (#257) violet
Monday of Holy Week

The Lectionary for Mass

◆ FIRST READING: During these first three days of Holy Week, we will hear three of the "servant songs" of Isaiah. Today, we hear God speaking to his beloved servant, "my chosen one with whom I am pleased." Though the servant suffers greatly, this reading is suffused with hope. The Lord has "grasped you by the hand" and made the servant a light to the nations.

◆ RESPONSORIAL PSALM 27: we hear the voice of God's faithful servant, who trusts in the Lord even when surrounded by "evildoers," "foes," and "enemies."

◆ GOSPEL: On this Monday of Holy Week, we read the story of Mary anointing Jesus' feet with oil. It is "six days before Passover." Judas objects, but Jesus tells them, "Leave her alone." This anointing—perhaps Mary's way of thanking Jesus for what he has done for her in raising her brother Lazarus from the dead—takes on another meaning. By it, Mary prepares Jesus' body "for the day of my burial." At the end of the reading, we find that not only Jesus, but Lazarus is in danger. To be a friend of Jesus is to share his fate.

The Roman Missal

The fact that we are now in Holy Week is marked by the assignment of a new Preface—Preface II of the Passion of the Lord is assigned for today. The Preface makes specific mention that "the days of his saving Passion and glorious Resurrection are approaching." In view of this, it might be better to use this Preface and not replace it with the proper Preface if one of the Eucharistic Prayers for Reconciliation is used (it is not required to use the Preface that goes with the Eucharistic Prayers for Reconciliation). In fact, it might be advantageous to highlight a certain starkness of these days of Holy Week through using an economy of words; along those lines, perhaps Eucharistic Prayer II would be a good choice for these last three days before the Sacred Paschal Triduum. Its direct statement of "At the time he was betrayed and entered willingly into his Passion" makes it perhaps especially appropriate for these three days.

T U E 16 (#258) violet
Tuesday of Holy Week

The Lectionary for Mass

◆ FIRST READING: Today we hear the Second Oracle of the Servant of the Lord. This one is spoken in the voice of the servant. Though he seemed to toil "in vain, / and for nothing, uselessly," God changes loss into gain, failure into triumph. Jesus, too, emptied himself, becoming obedient to the point of death; in letting go of everything, he gained everything for us.

◆ RESPONSORIAL PSALM 71 is the song of a faithful servant of God, who in the midst of danger and difficulty remembers that the Lord is a "rock" and a "fortress."

◆ GOSPEL: The Gospel according to John does not include an account of the institution of the Eucharist; rather, he tells of Christ's self-gift on the night before he died through the account of the washing of the feet. But John does include a Last Supper, and we read this account today. Jesus is "deeply troubled," for he knows that one of his disciples will betray him. They are surprised to see Judas get up and leave—the others do not understand that he is going to betray Jesus. Peter boldly promises to follow Jesus wherever he goes—"I will lay down my life for you." Even this faithful disciple will deny Jesus before cockcrow. Notice the short and telling line just after Judas' departure: "And it was night." Jesus' hour is near.

The Roman Missal

Today's Collect prays that we may receive pardon through our celebration of "the mysteries of the Lord's Passion." The Prayer over the Offerings asks that we may be given a share in the fullness of the sacred gifts in which we have been made partakers. The Prayer after Communion makes a connection between the earthly liturgy and the heavenly liturgy as it asks that having been nourished by the saving gifts in this present age, we may be made "partakers of life eternal." Preface II of the Passion of the Lord, first used yesterday, is again as-

signed for today. Consider using the Eucharistic Prayer II.

WED 17 (#259) violet
Wednesday of Holy Week

The Lectionary for Mass

◆ FIRST READING: We continue to read the oracles of the suffering servant. The servant speaks with sublime confidence: "I have not rebelled, / have not turned back." He knows that God is with him, and so he speaks God's word to rouse the weary, and he submits to insults and beatings from his enemies.

◆ RESPONSORIAL PSALM 69: The Church has long heard the voice of Jesus in this psalm, saying that "zeal for your house consumes me, / and the insults of those who blaspheme you fall upon me."

◆ GOSPEL: This Wednesday of Holy Week is sometimes called "Spy Wednesday," because we read Matthew's account of Judas' betrayal on this day. In John's account of the same episode, Judas never speaks a word; but in Matthew's version, we see him as a consummate hypocrite, plotting with Jesus' enemies one moment, eating with him the next. Judas has known Jesus for a long time and has been an apostle, entrusted by Jesus with a mission to heal others and preach the kingdom; yet he dares to ask Jesus, "Surely it is not I, Rabbi?" Jesus does not accuse him before the others; he only answers, "You have said so."

The Roman Missal

Preface II of the Passion of the Lord, used on the previous two days, is once more assigned for today, and the connection throughout these last three days of Lent can be maintained if, having used Eucharistic Prayer II on Monday and Tuesday, it is used again today.

THU 18 violet
Thursday of Holy Week

About Holy Thursday (morning)

Today no Mass is celebrated before the Mass of the Lord's Supper except for the diocesan celebration of the Chrism Mass. However, the norms allow for this liturgy to be celebrated earlier in Holy Week (see *Paschale solemnitatis*, 35). This is because the presence of the diocesan presbyterate and of the faithful, gathered around the bishop, is of key importance to this liturgy. The demands of Holy Thursday often make it difficult for priests and the faithful to go to the cathedral. Because of this, many dioceses celebrate the Chrism Mass earlier in the week. Tuesday is a common day for celebration.

During this Mass, the holy oils that will be used throughout the coming year are blessed by the bishop: oil of catechumens, used to anoint those preparing for Baptism (infants, children, and adults); oil of the sick, used to anoint those who are suffering from mental and physical illnesses and handicaps; sacred chrism, used to anoint during Confirmation and Ordination, and to bless and consecrate every new altar. At the conclusion of the Chrism Mass, the oils are distributed to representatives of every parish of the diocese. This one Mass touches the sacramental and worship life of every parish in the diocese. Because of this, all the faithful should be informed of the purpose, meaning, and time/location of the celebration.

Opportunities should be provided to ensure that the faithful can attend this Mass. In most dioceses there is no general invitation, because of the lack of space in any cathedral. For example, in the Archdiocese of Chicago, there is no general invitation. Tickets are given to each parish. You might include a notice in the bulletin throughout Lent, or include short announcements before a Lenten Mass or following the Prayer after Communion. You might even solicit volunteers to organize car pools, especially in areas that are quite far from the cathedral. Because no morning Mass is celebrated today (save the Chrism Mass at the cathedral), the celebration of Morning Prayer in the place of the usual daily Mass is most appropriate. Because the celebration of the Chrism Mass is a diocesan or cathedral liturgy, and does not take place in the parish, specifics about this liturgy are not discussed in this *Sourcebook*.

Many parishes are discovering the role of Morning Prayer during these days of the Triduum. If your parish is not yet accustomed to celebrating the Hours during these days, this year would be the perfect time to start. There is no better way to keep the faithful connected to the liturgical life of the Church, while at the same time introducing an alternative form of their daily offering of thanks and praise to God. If your parish has a school, the students could take part in this celebration of Morning Prayer. Each of the major Catholic music companies offers a format of sung prayer for the Liturgy of the Hours that is accessible and easy to follow in prayer. Familiar settings of the prescribed Psalms (selected from the parish's existing repertoire) can be used. Simple chant tones are available for easy singing of the Psalms and Canticles.

Holy Communion may be given to the sick and homebound. Both *The Roman Missal* and *Paschale solemnitatis* note that for pastoral reasons the diocesan bishop may allow another celebration of the Mass of the Lord's Supper earlier in the day: "Where pastoral considerations require it, the local ordinary may permit another Mass to be celebrated in churches and oratories in the evening, and in the case of true necessity, even in the morning, but only for those faithful who cannot otherwise participate in the evening Mass" (*Paschale solemnitatis*, 47; see also the rubrics for the Mass of the Lord's Supper under Holy Thursday in *The Roman Missal*).

SACRED PASCHAL TRIDUUM

The Liturgical Time

The Roman Missal / The Meaning

IN THE FIRST RUBRIC for the Sacred Paschal Triduum, *The Roman Missal* states our focus for these three days: "In the Sacred Triduum, the Church solemnly celebrates the greatest mysteries of our redemption, keeping by means of special celebrations the memorial of her Lord, crucified, buried, and risen" (Triduum, #1). This section is located between the sections for Holy Week and Easter Time, although the liturgies for Easter Sunday of the Resurrection of the Lord: "The Easter Vigil" and "At the Mass during the Day," conclude the Triduum texts in the Missal.

"The Paschal Triduum of the Passion and Resurrection of the Lord begins with the evening Mass of the Lord's Supper, has its center in the Easter Vigil, and closes with Vespers (Evening Prayer) of the Sunday of the Resurrection"

(UNLY, 19). When the Mass of the Lord's Supper starts, Lent is over and the Triduum has begun. As the rubric quoted above states, these days celebrate the memorial of the Last Supper, Passion, Death, Burial, and Resurrection of the Lord. They are anamnetic, which means that we remember the events that we celebrate, to make them present now, in order to effect how we live into the future. These liturgies are not play-acting. We do not repeat the events remembered during these days like we might reenact events in a play. We remember to celebrate the importance of these events in our life of faith, to deepen our belief so as to live what we believe. Our lives are different because of the washing of the feet, institution of the Eucharist, priestly orders, and the Passion, Death, and Resurrection of the Lord Jesus. Keep this distinction in mind when planning these liturgies. Following what the Missal asks will help us do just that.

Because "the sacred Paschal Triduum of the Passion and Resurrection of the Lord shines forth as the high point of the entire liturgical year" (UNLY, 18), *The Roman Missal* is very specific about the need for "a sufficient number of lay ministers . . . who must be carefully instructed as to what they are to do" (Triduum, 2). Singing by "the people, the ministers, and the Priest Celebrant has a special importance in the celebration of these days, for when texts are sung, they have their proper impact" (Triduum, 2). These celebrations "are to be carried out in cathedral and parochial churches and only in those churches in which they can be performed with dignity, that is, with a good attendance of the faithful, an appropriate number of ministers, and the means to sing at least some of the parts" (Triduum, 3). This means that smaller communities are to join together in these churches "to carry out the sacred celebrations in a more noble manner" (Triduum, 3). Take these directions to heart so that the Triduum can be celebrated with the noble dignity it deserves, and with all that each liturgy of these three days requires.

Many parishes have incorporated the Reception of the Holy Oils into the beginning of the Mass of the Lord's Supper. However, rubric 15 at the end of the Chrism Mass tells us that the reception of the Holy Oils may take place in local communities "either before the celebration of the Evening Mass of the Lord's Supper or at another time that seems more appropriate," which means a change of practice for many parishes. There are creative ways to accomplish what this rubric asks.

Work with your liturgy committee and pastor to develop a practice that respects the rubric and the worthy practice of receiving the Holy Oils in local communities. Rubric 7 for "At the Evening Mass," asks for bells to be rung during the Gloria and that musical instruments, including the organ, only be used to support singing after the Gloria is sung. "The Washing of Feet," while optional (10), is a central act of this liturgy (see rubric 9 and the emphasis on the call to charity). Permission is now given for women and girls to be included in the Mandatum (decreed on January 6, 2016). Prepare carefully so that the "suitable place" for carrying out this part of the liturgy (11) is visible to the entire assembly, invites the participation of all in ways appropriate to your pastoral setting, and reflects the full diversity of the Church gathered. The call to wash feet, to be charitable, is reinforced: "At the beginning of the Liturgy of the Eucharist, there may be a procession of the faithful in which gifts for the poor may be presented with the bread and wine" (14). If you have not tried this collection, this is the year to do so. It gives people a direct connection between the Eucharistic table and the tables of those in need. The Preface given for this night emphasizes the institution of the priestly order and offers a fine summary of the ordained priesthood and the common priesthood of the faithful. The Roman Canon (EPI) is printed within the texts for this night, an indication of the importance the Church gives to this Canon. If you do not use it on any other occasion, tonight would be the night to consider it. On this of all nights, consider offering Communion under both kinds, if that is not your parish's common practice. Finally, pay close attention to the directions for the conclusion of the Communion Rite and the Transfer of the Most Blessed Sacrament. Following these rubrics will invite reverence and noble simplicity to this part of the rite.

Remember that the liturgy on Friday of the Passion of the Lord is not a Mass. It is a celebration of the Word of God, with an extended Prayer of the Faithful, that includes Adoration of the Cross and a Communion service. Each section deserves its own attention. We begin and end in silence (Good Friday, 5 and 32). The Prayer that follows is prayed without "Let us Pray" (6). We are not performing a play about the Passion and Death of the Lord. The proclamation of the Passion is anamnetic. The Solemn Intercessions are powerful on this day. Pray them in ways that follow what the Missal directs. Consider the options given and choose that which will help your assembly enter into the rhythm of contemplation and action that ritual repetition over ten prayers can elicit.

Next we adore the Cross. Adoration implies more than veneration. It is about deep reverence and worship. Prepare to follow the rubrics with your particular worshipping community in mind. This takes time. Let it. The Missal offers great resources for music during this action. The Communion service that follow the Adoration of the Cross is very simple. Let the simplicity speak. The prayer that concludes the liturgy begins with "Let us pray" (30), unlike the Collect. Lastly there is a "Prayer over the People." Then "all, after genuflecting to the Cross, depart in silence" (32). We genuflect to the Cross today. People are encouraged to stay and adore it like the adoration of the Blessed Sacrament the night before. Those who celebrate the Good Friday Liturgy do not celebrate Vespers (34). And the Church is encouraged to fast into Holy Saturday, with a fast different from that of Lent. In Lent w,e fast to do penance. Today we fast with the elect, in anticipation of what we will celebrate during the Easter Vigil in the Holy Night.

The Easter Vigil in the Holy Night is "the greatest and most noble of all solemnities" (Vigil, 2). There can only be one celebration of the Vigil and it "must take place during the night, so that it begins after nightfall and ends before daybreak on the Sunday" (3). There is so much to emphasize here that I will make only a few statements. First and foremost, plan with *The Roman Missal* in one hand and the *Rite of Christian Initiation of Adults* in the other. The Missal does not contain everything needed to celebrate Christian initiation with the elect. Distinctions are made between baptizing infants, and older children and adults. There are differences if you are receiving already baptized Christians into the Roman Catholic Church. And if there is no one to initiate at the Vigil, the rubrics call for a different outline. Be aware of your situation. Plan accordingly and consider developing your own "Missal" for this night so that a priest celebrant, MC, musicians, and RCIA director do not need to juggle two books.

Because this is the "mother of all holy Vigils" (UNLY, 21), consider reception of Communion under both species, especially if people are partaking of Communion for the first time. After all, symbols speak loudly.

Create a bonfire. Rubric 8 says that "A blazing fire is prepared in a suitable place outside the church." A little dab will not do you tonight. Plan

how to spread the light of Christ reverently, yet quickly, after the second singing of "The Light of Christ" (Vigil, 16). Note that the lights in the Church, excepting the altar candles, are now lit before the Exsultet is proclaimed (Vigil, 17). While hearing the readings in candlelight had become customary in many places, the light of Christ even has power over electricity. Regarding the readings, all nine readings "should be read whenever this can be done, so that the character of the Vigil, which demands an extended period of time, may be preserved" (Vigil, 20). This is not a night to cut corners, although you can lessen the number for "serious pastoral reasons" (Vigil, 21). People are there because they want to be there and/or to support someone who is being initiated tonight. The singing of the Gloria returns us to full instrumental use and the bells are rung (Vigil, 11). The Alleluia returns in all its glory.

At the Vigil and on Easter Morning, we renew baptismal promises and are sprinkled with the newly blessed water. In the Eucharistic Prayer "a commemoration is made of the baptized and their godparents in accord with the formulas which are found in the Roman Missal and the Roman Ritual for each of the Eucharistic Prayers" (Vigil, 63). You will find these in the Ritual Masses section of the Missal: "For the Conferral of Baptism" and "For the Conferral of Confirmation."

There is much to consider. Make the Missal a friend and foundation and the liturgies of the Sacred Paschal Triduum will reflect the preeminence that these days hold in our liturgical calendar and ecclesial life.

The Lectionary for Mass

WE HEAR A LOT of Scripture during the Paschal Triduum. There are 15 Scripture readings and 9 psalms, and that's not counting Easter Sunday (the day that concludes the Triduum)! All of them are important; in fact, we need them all. The readings—especially the nine readings of the Vigil—build in a remarkable way, leading us through the story of salvation history from the very dawn of time straight to the Resurrection of Jesus Christ. Resist the temptation to save time by cutting the readings short.

The readings for the Triduum carry us into the very heart of the Old and New Testaments.

There are great narratives—the sacrifice of Isaac, the crossing of the Red Sea, the Passion according to John, the Resurrection narrative according to Mark. There are rich prophetic readings from Isaiah, Baruch, and Ezekiel. There is wonderful poetry, like the song of the suffering servant from Isaiah, and the song of the Israelites after the crossing of the Red Sea. There are also key readings from the letters of St. Paul, readings that teach us about the Eucharist, readings that proclaim with utter confidence the truth we celebrate at Easter—that Christ is risen, and that we have risen with him through our Baptism.

In scheduling and training readers for the Paschal Triduum, this variety of readings should be considered. If possible, have a different person do each reading during the Triduum. Work with the readers on the special demands of the reading they are assigned. A prophetic reading should not be read in exactly the same way as a narrative; and a poem demands different pacing, a different style of proclamation, than does an intricate passage from St. Paul.

The reading or chanting of the Passion according to John has challenges of its own. It is not a Passion play, yet it certainly is dramatic. Careful preparation on the part of the readers (and cantors) can help the assembly hear the rich and wonderful variety in the readings to which we are treated during these three days.

Children's Liturgy of the Word

THE LOGISTICS OF THE TRIDUUM make it unlikely—and indeed undesirable—that most parishes will have children's Liturgy of the Word. These three days are so important and so based in communal experience, we should be together. The washing of the feet and adoration of the Eucharist on Holy Thursday, the Adoration of the Cross, the Passion and the Communion Procession on Good Friday, and the gathering around the fire followed by sharing of the light of the candle on Holy Saturday evening, are so elemental to our identity as the Body of Christ that no child should be segregated from his or her parents. Parish staff should encourage families to attend with their children.

The Saints

DURING THESE THREE DAYS, we celebrate all saints and no saints. The liturgies of the Triduum take precedence over all saints' days, no matter how significant. And yet, during the Paschal Triduum, we are constantly aware of the great company of witnesses who have gone before us, who have witnessed to the mystery of Christ's Passion, Death, and Resurrection by the holiness of their lives. "May your face thus be our vision, bright in glory, / Christ our God," we sing in the Holy Thursday hymn "Ubi caritas," "with all the blessed Saints in heaven" (*The Roman Missal*). At the Easter Vigil, we beg the prayers of all the holy men and women throughout the ages in the great Litany of Saints. And the saints are invoked in the Eucharistic Prayer: the "blessed Apostles and Martyrs" (Eucharistic Prayer I), "all the Saints who have pleased you throughout the ages" (Eucharistic Prayer II), the saints "on whose constant intercession in your presence / we rely for unfailing help" (Eucharistic Prayer III). Yes, the saints are with us during the Paschal Triduum!

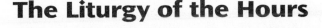

The Liturgy of the Hours

SINCE THE CELEBRATION of the Eucharist is only allowed on Holy Thursday (with the exception of the Chrism Mass being held in a few dioceses), and no Mass is allowed on Good Friday, Morning Prayer is a worthy way to engage the congregation in praying throughout the Triduum. Alert people that the usual morning Mass time will be the time for the Morning Prayer of the Church, and catechize several weeks in advance regarding the beauty of praying these prayers together on Holy Thursday, Good Friday, and Holy Saturday morning. Prepare a simple worship aid, alternate singing the psalms with recitation of the psalms. Go gently into calling people from private prayer to communal prayer, but suggest that the Liturgy of the Hours is welcome alternative to the busyness of preparing homes and hearts for the solemnity of Easter. Encourage school families to participate in Morning Prayer, particularly if there are no classes during the Triduum.

On Holy Thursday, following the Mass of the Lord's Supper, the Blessed Sacrament is removed from the church and placed on an altar of repose. In many parishes, Eucharistic adoration occurs late into the evening or throughout the night, until celebrating the Office of Readings before Morning Prayer the next day. Following the rubric in the GILOH, invite those who could not participate in Holy Thursday's Mass to come for Evening Prayer (note the rubric that those who participated in the evening Mass do not participate in Evening Prayer on that day). Evening Prayer before the Blessed Sacrament provides a special opportunity for those who work a middle- or late-shift, or who lack a dinner time babysitter for a child or an aging parent, to participate importantly in the parish observance of the Triduum. Designate a person to prepare and lead Evening Prayer; the Church has already planned it for us.

On Good Friday, celebrate the Office of Readings before Morning Prayer. Evening Prayer may be celebrated only by those who have not attended the celebration of the Lord's Passion, earlier in the day. Again, there are persons who will attend if the importance and beauty of the Church's Evening Prayer is emphasized. The physical, environmental emptiness of the parish church will contrast with the richness of the psalmody in Evening Prayer. Allow sufficient lighting for reading the worship aids and for safety, but not so much as to indicate that "it's almost the Easter Vigil."

The GILOH tells us that "on Good Friday and Holy Saturday, the office of readings should be celebrated publicly with the people before morning prayer, as far as this is possible." (GILOH, 210). Include the elect in this prayer, emphasizing the quiet and prayerfulness of anticipating the Vigil of all Vigils (rehearse them the week before, and intentionally plan some time for reflection and rest). The Canticle for Holy Saturday's Morning prayer (Isaiah 38:10–14, 17–20) sets the liturgical tone for the approaching Easter Vigil. Bask in the power of the intercessions of that day, and in the baptismal images that will resonate with the baptized and the soon-to-be baptized alike.

It may take more than liturgical ambition, or living in an intentional religious house of prayer, to enact Morning and Evening Prayer on Easter Sunday. Certainly the various cultures and ethnicities in the United States participate actively in the Easter Sunday Mass, but the notion of praying the "hinge" Hours has been difficult to implement. Even with careful preparation and Lenten catechesis, plus a sincere invitation to the congregation, the reason for a lack of interest in the Hours on Easter Sunday seems to be "exhaustion." The ministers, the musicians, the parish staff, the neophytes, and yes, the congregation, resist making one more trip back to the church for prayer. Why not craft a prayer card or put a prayer-page in the Easter bulletin, and mention that a fitting beginning to celebrate the season of Easter (another catechetical moment) would be to pray Evening Prayer on Easter Sunday. Perhaps liturgists aim too high when they attempt to prepare yet another worship service on Easter Sunday: maybe a smaller, more intimate celebration of Evening Prayer is required. Even if both Hours cannot frame Easter Sunday, a gentle celebration of Evening Prayer (or even abbreviate with Psalm 114, the intercessions, and the prayer at closing) would be a wondrous beginning to the season of Easter.

The Rite of Christian Initiation of Adults

THE SACRED PASCHAL TRIDUUM liturgies are already well planned by the Church, and the parish liturgical ministers and music staff rehearse with intensity and devotion to prepare. Catechizing the parish on the meaning of these three wondrous days that serve as one, continuous celebration is absolutely essential. Catechesis can contribute to increased participation in the celebration of each liturgy of the Triduum. Catechesis as "encounter" is an important goal.

The Chrism Mass is celebrated during Holy Week in every diocese, and some dioceses welcome the elect to attend, dismissing them to break open the Word. Often, the cathedral is only accessible, in terms of distance, for some. Other cathedrals may lack an auxiliary space for breaking open the Word. This gesture of welcoming the elect, if possible, sends a positive message regarding how much the diocese values the initiation process. Perhaps a small "cluster" of parishes could be invited each year to bring their elect and participate in the Chrism Mass.

The elect should fully participate in the Mass of the Lord's Supper and be immersed in the three "movements" of the celebration of the Passion of the Lord on Good Friday. Although *The Roman Missal* makes no mention of the elect participating (or not) in the Washing of the Feet on Holy Thursday, many initiation catechists consider it best that the elect not participate in this rite until they are fully initiated. This is a reminder that Baptism is the powerful, sacramental entry rite for membership in the Church.

On Holy Saturday, it may be helpful to draw those receiving the Easter sacraments together for a rehearsal. Choosing a baptismal name is also important on or by Holy Saturday.

Better than an extended walk-through, however, would be a pared-down description of where to process, bow, sit, stand, and what to say—allowing most of the details of the Easter Vigil to be experienced first-hand. The point of a rehearsal should be to allow the elect to be comfortable as they ritually move to experience the Vigil Mass and receive the Easter sacraments. Sometimes we walk and talk to excess: the challenge for the team is to let the Vigil speak for itself, in its many beautiful "languages" of ritual. Be sure that the movement involved in receiving Holy Communion has been taught, so that the newly baptized can receive seamlessly and comfortably.

Sometimes a simple prayer-retreat or a nature walk and praying Morning Prayer (from the Liturgy of the Hours) is all that's needed on Holy Saturday, after a brief rehearsal. What better time to give yourself over to the promise of the Easter sacraments?

It is important to revisit some essentials prior to the Easter Vigil:

◆ Make certain that the music director has the information about inserting the saints' names of those to be baptized into the Litany of the Saints.

◆ Make a plan and offer a choice of Easter season Masses so that those seeking Full Communion can be received into the Church. The Easter Vigil is truly not the occasion to confirm baptized adults, recalling that the age of seven constitutes an adult in the Church's understanding. (Although a combined rite is available for the Easter Vigil, the distinction of honoring a person's previous Baptism becomes blurred for those concerned, and especially for the congregation.)

◆ Remember to relight the congregation's candles (deacon or servers with a taper, from the paschal candle) for their own Renewal of Baptismal Promises; these are the same candles that have been lit previously during the Service of Light.

◆ Order the baptismal candles that are to be presented to the newly baptized, and make arrangements for

an alb or gown to be worn (the "white garment") after Baptism. (A stole is never appropriate for the newly baptized, since it is the symbol reserved for the ordained.)

◆ The weeks immediately prior to the Easter Vigil are not the time to unearth previous marriage bonds or seek to dissolve a previous bond "at the last minute." Diocesan tribunals are typically working as fast as they can manage regarding the annulment process. The pastor should be the first and prime mover regarding situations of prior bonds, with the goal being not to raise false (although probably temporary) hope for the unbaptized in the RCIA process. The entrance interview with the pastor or deacon goes a long way in creating a realistic timeline for those in irregular marriages.

The Sacraments of Initiation

DURING THE TRIDUUM, the sacred three days, the Church does not celebrate Sacraments of Initiation before the Vigil. If there is a danger of death however, these sacraments may be celebrated privately, not in the context of a Mass. Some might suggest that the Mass of the Lord's Supper on Holy Thursday, is a fitting time to celebrate first Communion, however the Church does not deem it appropriate for first Communion to be celebrated at this Mass (see *Redemptionis sacramentum*, 87). While the Easter Vigil is the time to celebrate the sacraments of initiation with the elect, infant Baptisms might also be celebrated. However, given that the Lucernarium begins this Mass, the rite of receiving the children, which is usually done at the doors of the church at the beginning of the Rite of Baptism, can be done earlier in the day at Morning Prayer or at a more convenient time. The prayer of exorcism and anointing with the Oil of Catechumens follows.

Baptisms and first Communion can also be celebrated on Easter Sunday at a regular parish Mass. Taking into consideration the larger number of people attending Easter Masses, parishes may not deem it suitable to include a Baptism or first Communion. Even so, it is quite appropriate and is a beautiful witness to the community of the faith of young families who may choose the Church's greatest feast day to celebrate a Baptism or first Communion, two of her most important sacraments.

The Rite of Penance

THE SACRAMENT of Reconciliation may be celebrated in all liturgical seasons and on any day. In actual practice most parishes would have already scheduled times for the sacrament during Lent, including additional opportunities for individual confession as well as a communal celebration. The full schedule of liturgical celebrations during Holy Week makes it difficult for priests to set aside additional times for confession. However, no priest should refuse to make himself available if there is an obvious pastoral need.

The focus of Lent has been to prepare the faithful to enter into the liturgies of Holy Week with ready spirits and contrite hearts. The Triduum celebrates the gift of salvation won for all God's people through the death of the Lord. We have been reconciled by the outpouring of his blood on the Cross; our response in the great liturgy of the Triduum is one of unconditional gratitude and joy.

The Order of Celebrating Matrimony

"The celebration of Marriage on Friday of the Passion of the Lord and Holy Saturday is to be avoided altogether" (*Order of Celebrating Matrimony*, 32). Technically, a Marriage could potentially take place outside of the Evening Mass of the Lord's Supper or on Easter Sunday; however, because of the importance of these high holy days, it would be best to advise ccouples against selecting these dates. What follows is commentary concerning the regular practice of Marriage outside of the Triduum.

AT THE TIME of the Preparation of the Gifts, the bride and bridegroom may bring the bread and wine to the altar. Alternatively, other family members or friends may bring the gifts forward. Because this action is so intimately linked to the Eucharistic Prayer and ultimately the reception of Holy Communion, those bringing the gifts forward should receive Holy Communion at Mass. It would be inhospitable to invite someone to bring forward the bread or wine in procession if they will not be in the later procession to receive the

Body and Blood of Christ. Enough hosts should be brought up in procession so that everyone can receive hosts consecrated at the Mass. Enough wine should also be placed in the carafe. The priest can ascertain from the couple the number of people attending the wedding. This will assist the sacristan in putting the proper amount of bread and wine out for the procession. While not mentioned in the rite, gifts for the poor may be brought up in procession as well.

During the time of the Preparation of the Gifts, instrumental music may be played or a hymn may be sung by the assembly. If a solo is chosen for the wedding, this would be the time to do it in the liturgy. The part of the rite is usually brief since there is no collection.

Just as on Sundays, the acclamations during the Eucharistic Prayer and the Lamb of God should be sung. The setting should be familiar to the assembly. Interpolations of prayers for the husband and wife during Eucharistic Prayers I, II, and III are included in the *Order of Celebrating Matrimony*.

The Nuptial Blessing is prayed during the Communion Rite after the Lord's Prayer. The embolism and doxology are omitted. After the Nuptial Blessing, the prayer "Lord Jesus Christ" is omitted and "The peace of the Lord" is said followed by the sign of peace, a ritual that expresses "peace and charity" (OCM, 75).

Often extraordinary ministers of Holy Communion are needed at the Celebration of Matrimony within Mass, especially if the laudable custom of distributing Communion under both species is done. The parish may assign extraordinary ministers or the bride and groom may select family members or friends who are commissioned ministers. Before the wedding begins, the ministers should meet with the priest to discuss their stations and the local procedures for the reception of Holy Communion.

The Communion procession is one of the major processions of the Mass. During this time, we sing as a sign of our unity on our journey to the altar to receive the sacrament of unity. The singing begins at the moment the priest first partakes of Holy Communion and continues until the last person receives. Depending on the size of the assembly, one or more hymns may be required. Music during the Communion procession at weddings should always be appropriate to the action and should be Christocentric. Devotional hymns that are best for Adoration of the Blessed

Sacrament are usually not appropriate for the Communion procession. The Communion song, or at least the refrain, should be something that the assembly can sing. Solos and pieces that can't be sung by the assembly are better suited at the Preparation of the Gifts or as a prelude.

A responsorial form of singing, similar to the way the Responsorial Psalm is sung, is appropriate during the Communion procession since the assembly is moving and singing at the same time. When sung outside the Liturgy of the Word, psalms may be arranged in a hymn setting. For example, Psalm 34 ("Taste and see the goodness of the Lord") is a Communion psalm par excellence and is one of the Communion antiphons prescribed in *The Roman Missal*. The other Communion antiphons are Ephesians 5:25, 27 and John 13:34.

As at every celebration of Mass, a time for reflective silence before the Prayer after Communion is appropriate. This will likely be one of the few silent moments the newly married couple will have on their wedding day.

Pastoral Care of the Sick

Parish ministers need to be aware of these pastoral norms related to pastoral care of the sick during the Sacred Triduum:

- Holy Communion may be brought to the sick at any time during Thursday and Friday of Holy Week. Holy Communion may not be distributed to the sick outside of Mass on the Saturday of Holy Week unless it is Viaticum.

- A communal celebration of Anointing of the Sick within Mass is not permitted during the Sacred Paschal Triduum.

- If Holy Communion is taken to the sick on Holy Thursday it is most appropriate that it be taken from the liturgy of the Lord's Supper. Since this liturgy is intended to be celebrated in the evening it may be difficult to schedule visits to the sick at this time. The consecrated hosts cannot be kept overnight by the pastoral minister.

- The Sacrament of the Anointing of the Sick may be celebrated for individuals at any time during the Sacred Paschal Triduum if there is a pastoral need.

The liturgies of Holy Week and the Sacred Paschal Triduum are important for all the faithful. Every effort should be made to help those who are unable to be present to somehow connect with the communal gatherings. Pastoral visitors could pray with the sick, as they are able, using some of the prayers from the liturgies. The Lectionary offers some of the most familiar and moving texts of Scripture; one or more passages could be read and even be the source of a shared reflection with the sick person, if they have sufficient energy.

Prayer booklets of the Stations of the Cross could be shared with those who are sick, and if they are able, to join with them in this devotion. Praying the Rosary with them, using the mysteries particular to the day, is especially comforting for those who have practiced that prayer throughout their life.

The life of the parish is always hectic during Holy Week and those who are involved in pastoral ministries may well have a lot on their plate. But any time that can be spent with those who are sick will be truly appreciated by them, and will be a sign that the ministry of the Risen Lord is at work in the world around us.

The Order of Christian Funerals

The celebration of the liturgies of the Sacred Triduum take precedence over all ritual Masses. The Order of Christian Funerals may be celebrated during the Triduum, but only with a Liturgy of Word with the usual prayers of the commendation. Communion may be given at these liturgies.

However the same attention should be given to the preparations for the liturgy and pastoral care extended to the family as at other times in the liturgical year. The fact that a funeral Mass is not celebrated during these days should not be a reason to have the funeral liturgy in the funeral home. The church is the proper and appropriate place for the Church's liturgy. A celebration of the Word of God with the accompanying blessings and prayers proper to the funeral rite can be a powerful source of comfort for the family and friends of the deceased. At the same time, it is, like all of the Church's liturgical celebrations, an act of faith in the Paschal Mystery and a celebration of hope in the resurrection for all believers.

The last days of Jesus' life that are commemorated in the liturgical celebrations of the Triduum offer a ready source of reflections for homilists. At the time of death "the Church confidently proclaims that God has created each person for eternal life and that Jesus, the Son of God, by his death and resurrection has broken the chains of sin and death that bound humanity" (OCF, 1). This is the message the Church boldly proclaims in every liturgy, and does so with all compassion and trust at the funeral of one of its faithful members.

The Book of Blessings

BECAUSE THE celebrations during the Triduum comprise the great liturgy of the Church, secondary blessings and devotions are kept to a minimum. However, there are some traditional blessings that can be celebrated in the parish, such as the blessing of food for the "first meal of Easter." This blessing usually takes place in a brief celebration of the Word of God on Holy Saturday. It is a more popular custom in some cultures than others, but everyone in the parish can be invited to bring baskets of food for the blessing. The blessing is also a celebration of the end of the practice of fasting during Lent. A priest, deacon, or lay minister may lead the order of blessing.

When parishes purchase new items for liturgical celebrations they often inaugurate them at special times of the year, for example at Christmas or Easter. Such items might include Communion vessels, art work, vestments, or other objects that are worthy and suitable for the liturgy. The blessing for these items can be taken from the Order of Blessing of Articles for Liturgical Use (chapter 39). These blessings should be done outside the liturgies of the Triduum.

The Liturgical Environment

WHILE IN COLLEGE, my children would bring friends home for Easter break, many of whom had never before participated in the three most sacred days of the year: the Sacred Paschal Triduum. The emotional and spiritual responses of these young people to the rituals together with my own children's shared stories of Triduums past cemented my belief that every ounce of liturgical energy used observing this special "day" is vital.

Begin preparing with a session for your team during which they learn the rhythms of the Triduum. Although chronologically three days, the Triduum is celebrated as one ongoing day of prayer. Bringing the pastor and RCIA team leader into the conversation avoids miscommunication and stress later. Review what has been done in the past, what has worked, what needs adjusting. Evaluate new ideas. Make a list for each day that spells out in detail the materials needed—sacred oils for Holy Thursday, fabric to veil the Cross used for adoration, towels for the washing of the feet and Baptisms, among others. Build a list of tasks that will need to be completed, organizing them by deadlines. (Save both of these lists for future use.) Secure a room near the nave where materials can be staged and ready a week or more in advance; ask for help carrying items from storage.

The Mass of the Lord's Supper includes presenting the sacred oils, the Mandatum, and a procession of the Blessed Sacrament to the chapel of reservation. The color for today is white. Obtain simple yet colorful flowering plants that will be used in the church, moved to the chapel, and then incorporated into the Easter decor. Recruiting separate team leaders for each part of the evening allows all of your team dedicated prayer time this night. Ask families to carry flowers in procession. A parish group might create a candlelight corridor for the procession, particularly if the path leads outdoors. Invite choir members to stay a few minutes afterwards to help strip the altar and remove remaining plants and fabric while another group cleanses and packs the foot washing bowls and pitchers and arranges for towels to be laundered and returned.

Good Friday's color is red, except for the veiling of the Cross, which is violet. Aside from the presider's chasuble, there is no need to decorate anything but the cross. A volunteer who specializes in knots can make easy the task of securing strips of fabric that will be ritually removed during the unveiling. While it is tempting to begin adding Easter decor tonight, instead spend the evening in prayer and reflection. With advance preparation and plenty of helpers, the Easter Vigil environment can be completed in a few hours the next day.

The Great Easter Vigil begins with a fire, preferably outdoors. Recruit a skilled camper to build and tend the fire. Invite family members of the elect to distribute individual candles for the Service of Light. Inside, the color white leads the glorious celebration. Flowering plants and floral arrangements announce the extraordinary occasion. The stand for the Paschal candle may be decorated with flowers or ribbon. Near the font, towels, pitchers, and candles await Baptisms; the chrism is in place. With thoughtful organization and preparation, your team can actively participate in the Vigil.

The Liturgical Music

THE EASTER TRIDUUM is celebrated as one liturgy, so if you have different ensembles serving the community, try to gather everyone together to form one ensemble. *Sing to the Lord* (110–114) stresses the importance of observing the principle of "progressive solemnity," and it doesn't get any more solemn ("solemn" is not synonymous with gloomy, sullen or dreary but rather marked with sanctity and gravity) than the Triduum.

◆ HOLY THURSDAY: Consider using a setting of the entrance antiphon for Holy Thursday: "We should glory in the cross of our Lord, Jesus Christ." Many settings exist of this text which sums up our faith by utilizing few words. If you have sung the Penitential Act during Lent, sing it tonight followed by the Gloria. Save your festive setting for the Gloria for the Easter Vigil and utilize a simpler setting this evening. To add to the solemnity, consider having your readers chant the introductions ("A reading from . . .") and conclusions ("The word of the Lord") to the readings. The cantor can assist if the reader is not

able to do this. For formulas, refer to appendix I in *The Roman Missal* ("Tones for the Readings"). Chanting the Gospel is also very appropriate. Check out "Sung Gospels for Major Solemnities in Multiple Voices" (Liturgical Press) by Anthony Ruff or "Book of Sung Gospels" by Gary Penkala (www.canticanova.com). Whatever you do along these lines tonight, strongly consider repeating it throughout the Triduum. Luke Mayernik's collection "Responsorial Psalms for Holy Week" (Morning Star 80–406) is good resource to have on your shelf.

Albeit optional, a beautiful ritual, often overlooked due to the Mandatum and the Transfer of the Most Blessed Sacrament, is the Rite of Reception of the Blessed Oils. Effective when celebrated, this rite has the power to beautifully connect, and highlight, the important and vital presence of the blessed oils (which took place at the Chrism Mass) and the unique role of the bishop as shepherd of the church in each parish community. The ritual text is found at the USCCB website: www.usccb.org/prayer-and-worship /liturgical-year/triduum/reception-of-holy-oils. cfm. Recommended music would be Schiavone's "Rite for Receiving the Holy Oils" (OCP, 9120) or Inwood's "Rite of Reception of the Blessed Oils" (OCP, 30102947).

The Transfer of the Most Blessed Sacrament is a unique and beautiful moment which has the power to leave a lasting imprint on the minds and hearts of the assembly. Admittedly, it can be challenging due to the unavoidable dimensions of singing and walking often in the dark. If the transfer is taking place within two different locations, it might be best to split your choral ensemble up into three: have some at the beginning, middle, and end of the procession in order to maintain the assembly song. While many options are available, ranging from litanies to Taizé-style ostinato refrains to strophic hymns, traditionally the ancient *Pange lingua* is sung at this point in time. It could be sung in Latin or English or even a combination. The last two verses (*Tantum ergo*) are not sung until the procession reaches the altar of repose and the presider, kneeling, incenses the Blessed Sacrament. After a time of silent adoration, many parishes end the day with compline.

◆ GOOD FRIDAY: The Triduum is but one celebration and, as such, today's celebration begins in silence while the priest and concelebrants process and prostrate themselves at the foot of the altar. The Collect follows without the customary greeting. The music today should be simple and, wherever possible, completely a cappella. In a situation where this is not possible, consider softly accompanying just the assembly part with the choir or cantor singing verses a cappella. The use of a cappella music will heighten and deepen the liturgical and ritual action unlike anything which is accompanied. Music during the Adoration of the Holy Cross should be a good balance between assembly song and choral music.

◆ EASTER VIGIL: Similar to Good Friday, the Vigil begins with a silent procession to where the fire pit is prepared for the blessing of the fire and preparation of the candle. Following the solemn entrance (deacons may sing either "The Light of Christ" or "Lumen Christi"), the Exsultet (Easter Proclamation) is chanted. Many consider the Exsultet to be the most beautiful prayer in the life of the Church as well as the most challenging. The Exsultet deserves proper respect and is not a chant which is to be looked at a week prior. Many people begin practicing this before Lent begins. While there may be numerous settings available, many consider the chant in *The Roman Missal* to be the best option.

Regarding the Responsorial Psalms, it is noteworthy to use psalms having the same tone, or character, as the earlier Triduum celebrations. If the music at Good Friday was a cappella, try having the psalms a cappella and the instruments return in splendor with the singing of the Gloria. After forty days of abstention, the Alleluia returns with solemnity. Tonight, the only time in the course of the year, it is sung with three versicles drawn from Psalm 118. Traditionally, the Alleluia itself is sung three times, each time with the repeat a half step higher.

When the rites of initiation are celebrated, it is important to incorporate the various acclamations and responses. When celebrated fully, we have the Litany of the Saints, the acclamation during the blessing of the water, acclamation during the Rite of Sprinkling, and even an "Alleluia" following each Baptism. Usage of these acclamations involve the entire assembly, not just the catechumens.

◆ EASTER DAY: The music for Easter Sunday should be splendid and glorious, thus mirroring the great solemnity itself. Draw out all of the stops: engage full, combined choral ensembles (combined choral ensembles throughout the Triduum is preferable over "assignment" approach), utilize the beautiful blended sonorities of brass and timpani and plan for full instrumental ensembles. This day should be full of joy and grandeur!

Easter Sunday often brings about more visitors to church than Christmas, so this is a wonderfully important opportunity for each community to be as hospitable, charitable, and welcoming as possible while simultaneously celebrating this solemnity in all its fullness. Utilize familiar hymns such as "Jesus Christ Is Risen Today" (EASTER HYMN), "Christ, the Lord Is Risen Today" (LLANFAIR) and various Easter texts combined with the tune LASST UNS ERFREUEN. These are hymns that people know well and love to sing.

The great sequence, *Victimae Paschali Laudes*, is sung (preferably) today after the Second Reading. There are numerous settings of this and the beautiful Gregorian melody is found in both Latin and English in many worship resources.

For the Renewal of Baptismal Promises, utilize whatever settings were used at the great Easter Vigil and continue using these settings for the Rite of Sprinkling throughout the fifty days of Easter. Great treasures of choral music abound whether it be choral settings of the Mozart or Thompson "Alleluia" to Handel's "Hallelujah Chorus" (MESSIAH) or "Hallelujah, Amen" (JUDAS MACCABAEUS) to Byrd's "Haec Dies" to Angotti's "He Is Risen" or Mahler's "We Arise." Choose choral repertoire wisely and always maintain an accessible level for your singers.

The Liturgical Ministers

THE VERY HEART of the Church's liturgical year unfolds in the liturgies of the Sacred Paschal Triduum. If God is in the details, then surely the details of the liturgies of the Triduum reveal the profound and glorious mystery of God. Every liturgical ministry places its full attention at the service of the liturgies in these days. The assembly of the faithful deserve the very best celebration of the Triduum. The ministers of hospitality need to be especially attentive to those who are visitors; readers are presented with some of the most important texts of Scripture; the music ministry moves from the call to serve on Holy Thursday, to the somber tones of Good Friday, to the joyous Alleluias of Easter; the liturgy coordinators have a hundred and one details to care for; and priest celebrants and deacons must lead the assembly so that the liturgy is a seamless and beautiful act of praise of the God of our salvation. What an awesome task! What a great experience of communal worship! This is not the time for turf wars or performances or shoddy preparations; it is the time for a deep spiritual engagement in each one's ministry so that all can participate with the full, active, and conscious participation that is called for by the liturgy.

Other Prayers, Rites, and Devotions

TENEBRAE, THE COMBINATION of the Office of Readings with Morning Prayer, may take place as a kind of prelude to the Triduum. This service is more devotional than liturgical. *The Sacristy Manual*, second edition (by G. Thomas Ryan, LTP), outlines carefully how this devotional service can take place. Since the Second Vatican Council reformed rites, Tenebrae has a strong devotional aspect during the dark hours of the morning when the Office of Readings is recited, Morning Prayer happens very early, and candles are gradually extinguished as dawn breaks.

The most common devotions during this time are Adoration of the Blessed Sacrament, on Holy Thursday after the Mass of the Lord's Supper and throughout the night in many churches, the Way of the Cross, prayed in recitation or as drama on Good Friday, and visits to other churches on Holy Thursday during the time of Adoration. Good Friday has inspired the most devotions among every culture in the world, many of which are enacted in local ways: youth, teen, and young adult characterizations of the Way of the Cross, "Station Walks" through a city, neighborhood, or park to observe the Way of the Cross, the *Tre Ore* (three hours) of keeping company with Jesus as he hung on the cross and even musical and poetic performance of the "Seven Last Words" of the Jesus, in many churches.

Evangelization

FROM HOLY THURSDAY through the Easter Vigil, we arrive at the high point of the liturgical year, and we celebrate the continuity of one liturgy, over three days, as we enter the heart of the Paschal Mystery. When it comes to extending the celebration of this in and through social media, the Triduum is a time to share abundantly from the wealth of the tradition about the meaning of these holy days. Here is a chance to inform, inspire, and celebrate with others, with the hope of inviting them ever more deeply into the profound mystery unfolding over these days.

From a practical standpoint, we can begin with informing people about the basics. Many people are "Christmas and Easter Catholics," visiting our churches only on rare occasions and usually on these major feast days. The liturgical moments of the Triduum are unique and replete with specific symbolism—someone who rarely attends church might be a bit confused, a bit overwhelmed, and after a three-hour Easter Vigil, a bit antsy to go home. Social media can be a place to share easily accessible information about what to expect at church over the Triduum, whether in the form of an infographic or a short animation. For those who are interested to go deeper, short articles or videos through Catholic media can take people deeper into the meaning of the symbols, rituals, and traditions of these days.

The Triduum is also a time for sharing inspiration. Because we are called into the Paschal Mystery, sometimes the best path is one of symbol, metaphor, and the creative space that the arts are able to offer to lead us toward beauty and inspiration. The Triduum liturgy itself is conscious of this, as we are invited to engage with symbols such as the Adoration of the Cross, or witness and participate in profound performative elements such as the washing of the feet, the sharing of the light from the Easter candle, or the shared narrative reading of the Passion. These all work upon us deeply and differently than an informative text. Through social media, we can invite people to engage in similar meaning-making through sharing with them works of art, recordings of music, or videos that portray some moment of Christ's journey from the Last Supper through Calvary to the empty tomb.

Finally, the Triduum is a time for sharing a sense of celebration. Many families, dressed in their Easter best, pose for a photo in front of the lilies decorating the church at Easter. Many still post this picture to wish people in their social networks a happy Easter. Others capture and share the moments of Christian initiation at the Easter Vigil and post these to welcome and celebrate the new members of the church. Others still use the whimsical tools that social media itself provides—special frames, backgrounds, hashtags, or emoji to sing a joyful Alleluia to the digital world. Whether through text or image, we celebrate and let the world know that Christ is risen, risen indeed.

The Parish and the Home

IT IS A SAD REALITY that only the most dedicated people in our communities attend the liturgies of the Sacred Paschal Triduum. For some, the issue is work and family schedules, while for others it may be that they are not aware of the true importance of the Three Days. Many of our families will come for Palm Sunday and Easter Sunday without experiencing the full Triduum. Many Catholics, at this time, are not just Sunday Christians.

Begin educating and preparing the community during the final weeks of Lent, explaining that these are far more than just long and complicated "services," but part of one continuous, glorious liturgical celebration during which we accompany Christ to his death and celebrate his return from the dead. If people only attend Mass on Easter Sunday, they will find the tomb already empty.

For those whose work schedule does not permit them to attend an afternoon Good Friday celebration, offer an alternative service at a later time, if the need is great. Alternately, you can offer evening Taizé prayer around the Cross or a celebration of Tenebrae as appropriate ways to include the community.

For families with young children unable to sit through the lengthy celebrations, send home a ritual for family foot-washing, a child-friendly Stations of the Cross for Friday, and instructions for making, blessing, and lighting a family Paschal candle at sunset on Saturday.

Reflections through the Year

It is in the Eucharist that all that has been created finds its greatest exaltation. Grace, which tends to manifest itself tangibly, found unsurpassable expression when God himself became man and gave himself as food for his creatures. The Lord, in the culmination of the mystery of the Incarnation, chose to reach our intimate depths through a fragment of matter. He comes not from above, but from within, he comes that we might find him in this world of ours. In the Eucharist, fullness is already achieved; it is the living center of the universe, the overflowing core of love and of inexhaustible life. Joined to the incarnate Son, present in the Eucharist, the whole cosmos gives thanks to God. Indeed the Eucharist is itself an act of cosmic love: "Yes, cosmic! Because even when it is celebrated on the humble altar of a country church, the Eucharist is always in some way celebrated on the altar of the world." The Eucharist joins heaven and earth; it embraces and penetrates all creation. The world which came forth from God's hands returns to him in blessed and undivided adoration: in the bread of the Eucharist, "creation is projected towards divinization, towards the holy wedding feast, towards unification with the Creator himself." Thus, the Eucharist is also a source of light and motivation for our concerns for the environment, directing us to be stewards of all creation. (LI, 236)

Mass Texts

◆ INTRODUCTION TO THE TRIDUUM

Lent is over. The Great Three Days of the Paschal Triduum now begin. We gather to remember the institution of the Eucharist, the priestly order, the command to wash feet as Jesus did, and to join him on his journey through suffering and death to resurrection and new life. Our liturgies these days are intimately connected. Throughout these days we celebrate the mystery of faith, the death and resurrection of the Lord. We glory in the Cross of our Lord Jesus Christ, filled with the gamut of feelings to become what we profess to be, people saved and delivered by the mysteries we remember and celebrate.

◆ Seasonal Alternate Tropes for Penitential Act Form C (Holy Thursday)

Lord Jesus, you call us to do what you did, serve others by washing feet: Lord, have mercy.

Christ Jesus, you call us to worship and fulfill our baptismal priesthood: Christ, have mercy.

Lord Jesus, you call us to celebrate the Eucharist in memory of you: Lord, have mercy.

◆ Dismissal of Catechumens and Elect

We gather these three days to recall the great mystery of faith, the Death and Resurrection of Jesus Christ. We remember these events to be conscious of the saving love that still frees us so that the unconditional and merciful love these days celebrate can continue to renew us. Reflect on what you have heard and seen tonight. Discover how Jesus invites you to live. We look forward to the day when you will join us at the Eucharistic Table. Go in peace.

◆ Universal Prayer (Prayer of the Faithful) for Holy Thursday

Invitation to Prayer

Jesus gives us a new commandment, to love one another as he has loved us. We live that command and exercise our baptismal priesthood by praying as the faithful, aware that our world needs the love of Christ today:

Intercessions

1. That all members of the Church may model how to be attentive to the needs of our sisters, brothers, and all creation, so that we wash each other's feet and serve as Jesus did, we pray to the Lord:

2. That, as we celebrate the New Covenant in Christ, we recall the People of the First Covenant, as they gather to celebrate Passover, we pray to the Lord:

3. That the nations of the world become more concerned with the needs of the entire global family than with the needs of their own countries, we pray to the Lord:

4. That those unable to join us because they are sick or homebound may experience our love and concern in concrete ways, we pray to the Lord:

5. That our elect and all preparing for Baptism may deepen their union with Christ in ways that lead them to the baptismal pool, we pray to the Lord:

6. That those who have died may share in the Resurrection we will celebrate this Triduum, and that those who are dying may embrace their Cross, we pray to the Lord:

Concluding Prayer

How holy is this feast, O God,
when Christ is our food.
How holy are these days, O God,
when his Passion is recalled
and we celebrate this pledge of future glory.
Hear our prayers.
Make us servants who learn how to love and live
by celebrating this Sacred Triduum.
We ask this through Christ, our Lord,
who lives and reigns with you and the Holy Spirit,
one God, for ever and ever.
Amen.

◆ Universal Prayer (Prayer of the Faithful) for Easter Vigil

Introduction

Christ has triumphed over death. In the fullness of Easter joy, let us pray to the God of life.

Intercessions

1. For the holy Church of God, that she may be filled with grace and light on this most blessed [night/day], we pray:

2. For the world, that peace and justice may transform the darkness of its pain into the life and joy of Easter, we pray:

3. For all who struggle with pain, doubt, or temptation, that they may experience the joy of Christ's victory over death, we pray:

4. For the newly baptized, here and throughout the world, that they may persevere in faith and love to the end of their days, we pray:

5. For all who have died in Christ, especially N. _____, that they may share in his Resurrection, we pray:

6. For all of us gathered in this holy place, that we may die to sin and live for God in Christ Jesus, we pray:

Concluding Prayer

God of life,
you have made all things new in Christ.
May we who have died with Christ in Baptism
rise with him to lives of love and joyful service.
Who lives and reigns for ever and ever.
Amen.

April 2019
Month of the Holy Eucharist

(#39)   white

Thursday of Holy Week (Holy Thursday) Evening Mass of the Lord's Supper

THU **18**

About the Evening Mass of the Lord's Supper

This evening Lent ends and the Church enters the Sacred Paschal Triduum, gathering to pray, building toward the prolonged vigiling of Saturday night. This evening's celebration, the Mass of the Lord's Supper, is the threshold liturgy of the Triduum. It commemorates the institution of Eucharist and the priesthood, as well as Jesus' command of love and service. It should be the only parish Mass today, even if varied language groups make up the parish community. Another Mass is celebrated only with permission of the bishop, and it should not dissuade people from attending the principal Mass. Aside from the possibility of the Chrism Mass, no other Masses are celebrated today.

Preparing this liturgy and the others of the Triduum can be enormously stressful if not reviewed well in advance. Avoid scheduling rehearsals during Holy Week; conduct them instead during the last few weeks of Lent. While there should be one overall coordinator for the Triduum liturgies, it helps greatly to have people responsible for each ministry and willing to rehearse each group. Rehearsals calm anxiety and ministers will be able to identify the processional routes, the stations for the washing of the feet, musical cues for movement, the location of readings and petitions, as well as the placement of needed liturgical items.

It is interesting to note that the Missal gives a series of instructions for the whole Sacred Paschal Triduum; these are listed before the rubrics for Thursday of the Lord's Supper. Liturgy committees would do well to take note of these important instructions and reflect on how they can best be implemented in their parish celebrations.

First, the centrality of these days as the preeminent days for celebrating the Paschal Mystery is noted, since on these three days the Church solemnly celebrates "the greatest mysteries of our redemption, keeping by means of special celebrations the memorial of her Lord, crucified, buried, and risen" (rubric for Triduum, 1).

The Paschal fast is also mentioned. The fast is to be kept everywhere on the Friday of the Lord's Passion, but the Missal goes on to recommend that it be prolonged through Holy Saturday. Catechesis about this Paschal fast might be useful for parishioners, because its meaning differs from that of the Lenten fast. While the Lenten fast is centered on penance, conversion, and renewal, the Paschal fast is more focused on preparation and anticipation (in a sense, almost being too excited to eat!); it is a way of preparing to come, "with spirit uplifted, to the joys of the Lord's Resurrection" (Triduum, 1). The Paschal fast helps us to enter into *kairos*, the "time outside of time" that characterizes the continual anamnesis of the Three Days, which, in some sense, are actually one.

A second rubric cautions that a sufficient number of lay ministers is required in order to fittingly celebrate the Sacred Paschal Triduum. Thus, what is true all year long must be especially in evidence during the Church's most sacred days, namely, that liturgical celebrations are diversified actions celebrated by the entire Body, and that a variety of ministers is needed, in proper number, so that the fullness of the Church's liturgical ministries may be in evidence. While "good enough is never good enough" is a maxim that should always apply to the Church's liturgical celebrations, the necessity of allowing the rites to be celebrated in all their fullness, which includes an adequate number of lay ministers, is heightened during these days.

In actuality, the point about lay ministers simply underscores the importance of the full, conscious, and active participation of the faithful during the celebrations, and this is the point that is highlighted next. The Missal points out that "the singing of the people, the ministers, and the Priest Celebrant has a special importance in the celebrations of these days, for when texts are sung, they have their proper impact" (Triduum, 2). Thus, the Missal is calling on communities to sing the rites during these days, and indeed these are the days to sing as many of the texts as possible—maybe even all of them! Furthermore, the full participation of the faithful is so important that the Missal makes a special reminder to pastors to catechize their people about the meaning and order of the celebrations. If we take this seriously, then we understand that catechesis about the Sacred Paschal Triduum through bulletin articles, preaching, workshop sessions, and adult education courses is as important a part of liturgical preparation as are the flow charts, gathering of necessary items, and sprucing up of the environment and the vestments.

A third notation specifies that the liturgies of the Sacred Paschal Triduum "are to be carried out in cathedral and parochial churches and only in those chosen churches in which they can be performed with dignity, that is, with a good attendance of the faithful, an appropriate number of ministers, and the means to sing at least some of the parts" (Triduum, 3). For some, this might be a challenge to a radically new understanding of the rites. The liturgies of these days are not formalities or simple prayer experiences that can be performed perfunctorily just for the sake of giving people a nice experience; they are liturgies that are supposed to be powerful expressions of the very heart of what we believe and who we are. Thus, it is essential that these liturgies be celebrated with the dignity and fullness of expression that their nature demands. Small communities and other groupings of the faithful — small communities of religious, nursing homes or other institutions, schools, and even mission parishes — may need to ask some very difficult questions about their ability to celebrate these liturgies properly, and perhaps consider joining with larger communities.

The Lectionary for Mass

◆ First Reading: The profound story of the final acts of God that produce Israel's freedom from captivity in Egypt are now recounted. Moses has demanded their release, and Pharaoh's obstinacy has resulted in nine horrifying plagues. Water has become blood; frogs, lice, flies, and locusts have been sent; disasters of hail, fire, and darkness have been unleashed; and the people have been afflicted with boils. Now, God sends the devastating death of the firstborn. Israel will be spared by following the directions offered here. An unblemished male lamb will be

sacrificed, and the doorposts marked with its blood. The flesh of the lamb will be consumed by people who stand ready to leave — "loins girt," sandals on, and a walking staff held in the ready for departure. This done, God will "pass over" the homes of the chosen people. God instructs the people through Moses to memorialize this moment every year. To this day, observant Jews recount and remember this powerful moment of deliverance in the Seder, the festive meal of Passover, by telling this story in the liturgy contained in the Passover.

◆ Responsorial Psalm 116 offers thanksgiving to God, who has delivered his people. The God of the covenant has done great things. Having escaped trials and suffering, the response is to extol the greatness of God in thanksgiving. To "call upon the name of the Lord" is to pray in gratitude. The lives of those who love God are precious, including those who have died. The "cup of salvation" mentioned in the first stanza is a reference to an offering made to God upon deliverance from death; the "blessing cup" in the antiphon evokes the third ritual cup of wine in the Passover celebration. This night of Holy Thursday, the cup that is shared is the blessing cup that contains the Blood of Christ — a cup that represents our salvation. The antiphon is drawn not from the psalm but from the reading from 1 Corinthians that is about to be proclaimed.

◆ The Second Reading is from Paul's letter to the growing community in Corinth, an important city of commerce in Greece. It is believed that Paul stayed in Corinth longer than he stayed in any other city, and his letters reflect an intimacy and familiarity with the life and concerns of people to whom he writes. Here, in the midst of a narrative addressing issues in the

liturgical assemblies in Corinth, Paul offers us the earliest description of how the Eucharist was instituted. In the account, he first establishes himself as an authoritative recipient of the Lord's instructions. Paul did not know Jesus in life, and his conversion en route to Damascus as described in the Acts of the Apostles does not mention the Eucharist. Rather, the authority that has passed on the Lord's direction is most likely the early Christian community, the Church — which speaks with authority. The description here, which ties past, present, and future together, recounts our Eucharistic practice to this day. It is fitting that on the day we celebrate the Last Supper, we are reminded of this core belief.

◆ Gospel: The exquisite, poetic narrative from the Gospel according to John describes the actions of Jesus Christ at the Passover meal we now call the Last Supper. John's telling focuses on washing the feet of the disciples rather than the institution of the Eucharist. While foot washing was a common task in the time of Jesus, it was also a menial task. Listeners in the life of the early Church would have found this account almost shocking; for the one who is Lord to take on a task relegated to slaves. Here, an everyday task become a ritual that totally upends social convention. From the first letter to Timothy, which mentions washing the "feet of the holy ones," we know that this practice became a part of Christian hospitality. This practice demonstrated the reality that while Christians might have to accommodate the dominant social conventions of their day, within their own communities a new world order was established that was consistent with the reign of God. In this passage, we experience yet again the enthusiasm and grandiosity of Peter, who at first resists the Lord and then offers his entire body for cleansing. The foot washing of the Holy Thursday liturgy is more than a quaint custom; it is a direct access to an embodied experience of what Jesus Christ asks of all his followers: self-forgetting, humble service, and radical hospitality. To use the categories of cultural anthropologist Victor Turner, this ritual—then and now—is a transformation of roles and status with a horizon from the present to the future, unlike a ceremony, where the horizon is past-to-present and where status is confirmed and often elevated.

The Roman Missal

Before the Mass texts are given, the Missal lists special instructions that pertain to the celebration of the Evening Mass of the Lord's Supper, some of which are worth highlighting here. First to be noted is that the Mass is celebrated in the evening, "with the full participation of the whole local community and with all the Priests and ministers exercising their office" (*The Roman Missal*, Thursday of the Lord's Supper, 1). Thus, once again the importance of the community gathering as the one body with a variety of roles and ministries in evidence is affirmed; in fact, it is ancient tradition that all Masses without the participation of the people are forbidden on this day (see PS, 47). Another rubric mentions that flowers are permitted as decorations, but there should be moderation; we are not yet at Easter. This moderation applies to the place where the Blessed Sacrament will be reserved after Mass; *Paschale solemnitatis* specifies that this space must be conducive to prayer and meditation, and therefore demands sobriety, and abuses are to be suppressed (see PS, 49). Nor is the place of reservation to be made to resemble a tomb, because the chapel of repose is not representing the Lord's burial; rather, it is for the custody of the Eucharistic bread that will be dis-

tributed in Communion on the next day (see PS, 55).

There is no mention in the Missal about the reception of the Holy Oils. However, it has become an accepted practice in the dioceses of the United States to present the oils to the community, who in turn receives these oils to be used throughout the year. This rite is included in *Sourcebook* on page 170.

The Entrance Antiphon, taken from Galatians 6:14, sums up the mystery we are celebrating throughout the days of the Sacred Paschal Triduum. It's a mystery that can only be understood by living in its truth: "We should glory in the Cross of our Lord Jesus Christ." How is it possible to find glory in the midst of suffering and death? It's possible because through Christ's suffering and Death "we are saved and delivered." That's the mystery that is the heart of the Christian faith, the mystery that is celebrated in every liturgy, and the mystery that is the raison d'être of the Christian life — it is the Paschal Mystery that through Christ, with him, and in him, death becomes life and self-emptying leads to fullness.

The Gloria returns this evening, and it should be sung with joy and fullness; the Missal mentions that bells are rung. Outdoor bells could be rung in the carillon; bells inside the church may be rung by choir members, or altar servers and other ministers, perhaps even by members of the assembly. After this joyous ringing out of the glory of God, the bells are to remain silent until the Gloria of the Easter Vigil. To further highlight the seriousness and uniqueness of the days of the Triduum, a rubric notes that "during this same period [between the Gloria of the evening Mass on Holy Thursday and the Gloria at the Easter Vigil], the organ and other musical instruments may be used only so as to support the singing."

The Collect for this Mass draws our attention to this night's Eucharist being linked to the Last Supper, which is referred to in the Second Reading, with the meaning of the supper being clear: it is the meal Jesus "entrusted to the Church" as "the banquet of his love," "a sacrifice new for all eternity." The effects of participating in that sacrificial banquet are also made clear: we are to draw "from so great a mystery the fullness of charity and of life."

This evening is one of the rare occasions when the Missal specifies for the homilist the themes he is to touch on. The priest's homily is to shed light on "the principal mysteries that are commemorated in this Mass, namely, the institution of the Holy Eucharist and of the priestly Order, and the commandment of the Lord concerning charity." As will be noted several times below, the connection between participation in the Eucharist and living a life of love cannot be overlooked, and that connection should be at the core of the meaning of this Mass. The institution of the ministerial priesthood is commemorated because of the close connection between priesthood and the Eucharist; it is the priest who acts in the person of Christ the Head (*in persona Christi capitis*) within the liturgical assembly and without whom the Eucharist cannot be celebrated. Notice, however, that there is nothing in the ritual for this evening about priests renewing their promises; the place for that is at the Chrism Mass and it has no place in this liturgy. It is something that is meant to be led by the bishop; there are no texts for it at the evening Mass, and it should not be added.

Sacrificial charity and sacrificial living are ritualized in the washing of feet, which, as the Missal notes, follows the homily. Although technically optional, the ritual has such power that one might rightly question why a community would not celebrate it. The unique power of this startling gesture should be allowed to stand on its own and should not be obscured by gimmicks or adaptations. Yes, it is uncomfortable, especially (and ironically), not for the one doing the foot washing, but for the one having his or her feet washed (it's not unusual for people to be shy and reticent about doing this); yes, it is countercultural; yes, it can be awkward. However, all three can also be said about Christian humility and sacrificial love. Resist the temptation to weaken the gesture by changing it to a washing of hands. Nor is there any foundation in the Missal for anyone other than the priest celebrant to wash feet; he functions as the sacramental image of Christ the Head at all other parts of the Eucharist, so why should there be the need to mute this representation during this rite, which is part of the Eucharist? True, all are called to wash one another's feet, that is, serve one another, but the same call to service (and unity) is true of every Eucharist, and the priest exercising his liturgical function alone at other times does not negate or lessen the assembly's participation in the mystery; the same is true here. Therefore, also to be avoided is diminishing the power of the gesture by having others, whether they be clergy or laity, join the priest celebrant in washing feet.

As you prepare for the Sacred Paschal Triduum, parishes should be aware that a decree issued on January 6, 2016, changed the rubrics of *The Roman Missal* to allow for washing the feet of women and girls during the liturgy on Holy Thursday. At the direction of Pope Francis, the Congregation for Divine Worship and the Discipline of the Sacraments has decreed that rubric 11 on Holy Thursday read: "Those chosen from among the People of God are accompa-

nied by the ministers. . . ." (In the *Ceremonial of Bishops*, the wording will change in nos. 299b and 301.) The "Decree concerning the Rite of the 'Washing of Feet'" can be found at www.vatican.va. Pope Francis notes, "After careful consideration I have decided to make a change to *The Roman Missal*. I therefore decree that the section according to which those persons chosen for the Washing of the feet must be men or boys, so that from now on the Pastors of the Church may choose the participants in the rite from among all the members of the People of God. I also recommend that an adequate explanation of the rite itself be provided to those who are chosen." This means parishes may choose men, women, the young and the old, the healthy and the sick, clerics, and consecrated persons and laypeople.

Also, no specific number is mentioned, and therefore it need not be limited to twelve. While twelve is a customary number, any number can be used, and the people chosen should adequately reflect the makeup of the community. People of all ages, including young children, may be asked to have their feet washed; people of different races and language groups may be included; at least one of the elect, preparing for initiation at this year's Easter Vigil, may be included.

Next, the only location mentioned is "a suitable place." Therefore, there is no need for this rite to take place exclusively in the sanctuary; in fact, there are several reasons that would argue against that practice. Certainly, the visibility of the rite would be an important factor. Having multiple stations throughout the church would allow for a maximum number of people to be up close to the action as it is taking place. (This is also one way of reinforcing what is true for all liturgy — that the liturgical action takes place in the entire worship

space, not just in the sanctuary.) Additionally, there can be something very touching — part of the meaning of humble service — to have the priest celebrant move throughout the assembly, going to those before whom he will kneel, rather than having them come to him. However, the suitability of various locations must be carefully considered: how will chairs be placed and then removed in such a way that this action does not draw undue attention to itself? Will the priest be able to kneel easily enough, and will the necessary ministers have access to assist him? What about numbers of pitchers, basins, and towels — how will they be made available, taken away, and who will see to this? None of these details are insurmountable; they need only be thought through in advance so that specific needs can be prepared for and the action can be carried out smoothly, with a minimum of distraction.

Also of interest is the statement that the priest removes his chasuble if necessary; given the action to be performed, one would think it is necessary, for ease of movement. However, there is no mention of the priest tying a towel around his waist, which is nonetheless a custom that many priest celebrants do; the Gospel for the Mass mentions that Jesus did so before he washed the disciples' feet. The rubric goes on to mention that the priest goes to each person and, assisted by ministers, pours water over each one's feet and then dries them. The plural "feet" is used, which would seem to indicate that both feet of each person are to be washed, not just one. (Many priest celebrants have the custom of kissing the feet of the people as well, after washing them.)

While the rite should not be unduly prolonged, neither should it be hurried; the fact that several examples of antiphons are given in the Missal indicate this. The meaning of the rite is revealed in the antiphons: it is all about Jesus' example of love, humble service, and sharing in Jesus' life by following him.

After the washing of feet, the priest washes and dries his hands, puts the chasuble back on, and the Mass continues with the Universal Prayer as usual. The Creed is not said. After the Universal Prayer, Mass continues with the preparation of the altar and the presentation of the gifts.

Rarely does one find in the Missal a specific rubric about the procession with the gifts, but there is one given here: it is mentioned that gifts for the poor may be presented along with the bread and wine, with those gifts being carried in procession by the faithful. This hearkens back to the ancient practice of the Church, where everyone brought something for the offering, and some of the offerings would be set aside for the poor. Such a procession would be a stark reminder of the practical charity that must be a consequence of our participation in the Eucharist — we cannot truly share bread at the Eucharistic table unless we are also sharing bread with the hungry outside the Eucharist. Perhaps these offerings on Holy Thursday can be an impetus for catechizing the faithful at other times about the offering of self that is the heart of our participation in the Eucharistic sacrifice. Certainly the sight of everyone processing forward to bring their gifts to the altar, with the gifts of bread and wine that will be transformed through the power of the Spirit being carried last, would be a powerful sign of the participation of all the faithful. The Missal's suggestion of the antiphon to be chanted, *Ubi caritas*, "Where true charity is dwelling, God is present there" highlights the unity of meaning between the foot washing, which was just completed, and the bringing

forward of the offerings for the celebration of the Eucharist.

The Prayer over the Offerings offers a succinct summary of the very essence of liturgical theology: "whenever the memorial of this sacrifice is celebrated / the work of our redemption is accomplished" (one suspects that the homilist could well include this theme in his preaching). To the degree that we are aware of and appreciate what is taking place in our midst here and now (the work of our redemption), that is the degree to which we can be said to be participating worthily in the mysteries.

The Preface assigned for this Mass is Preface I of the Most Holy Eucharist, and the text, with musical notation, is given along with the other texts for this Mass; one could argue that this is revealing the Church's preference for the priest celebrant to chant the Preface. The text itself zeros in on the core of Eucharistic theology. As it recalls Christ offering himself "as the saving Victim," it also notes how the Eucharist was instituted as the pattern of his sacrifice, and therefore the offering of the Eucharist is the memorial of his offering and sacrifice. Participation in the Eucharist means to join one's own offering with the self-offering of Christ that is made present through anamnesis. This is further emphasized as the Preface goes on to note, "As we eat his flesh that was sacrificed for us, we are made strong, and, as we drink his Blood that was poured out for us, we are washed clean."

The complete text for Eucharistic Prayer I, the Roman Canon, is given along with the other texts for this Mass. This allows for an easy use of the special inserts for the *Communicantes* ("In communion with those"), the *Hanc igitur* ("therefore, Lord, we pray"), and the *Qui pridie* ("On the day before he was to suffer"), which are used at this Mass. However, while it might

be argued that, given these special inserts, there is a certain preference for using the Roman Canon, it is not required (as indicated by the rubric at number 17, "When the Roman Canon is used . . ."), and so Eucharistic Prayer III could also be used. (Eucharistic Prayer II because of its brevity would not be appropriate, and Eucharistic Prayer IV is disqualified because of its proper Preface.)

There is a special rubric concerning Holy Communion: after distribution, a ciborium with hosts for Communion tomorrow is left on the altar. The Prayer after Communion makes an eschatological reference as it asks that "just as we are renewed by the Supper of your Son in this present age, so we may enjoy his banquet for all eternity." This is the last prayer that will be proclaimed at this liturgy; the transfer of the Blessed Sacrament follows immediately.

The transfer of the Blessed Sacrament is rather simple and direct. After the Prayer after Communion, the priest, after putting incense in the thurible, goes to the Blessed Sacrament and incenses it three times. He puts on a white humeral veil, rises, takes the ciborium, and uses the ends of the humeral veil to cover it.

A procession is then formed, led by a minister with a cross, flanked by ministers with lighted candles; although the people are not mentioned, if the place of repose is in another location, the assembly will join the procession, following these ministers. Other ministers with lighted candles may follow the assembly, preceding the minister carrying the smoking thurible, who is directly in front of the priest carrying the Blessed Sacrament. During the procession, a suitable Eucharistic chant is sung; the Missal suggests *Pange, lingua*, excluding the last two verses (the *Tantum ergo*), and it might be argued there is a certain fondness for using this chant.

Upon reaching the place of repose, the priest places the ciborium in the tabernacle, but leaves the door open. Placing incense in the thurible, he incenses the Blessed Sacrament while kneeling and while the *Tantum ergo* or another Eucharistic chant is sung. After this, the tabernacle door is closed.

Next comes a period of adoration in silence (note that the door is to be closed before the period of adoration). After a period of silence, the priest and ministers rise, genuflect, and then depart, but with no formal procession—this is simply a functional leaving of the ministers, not a ritual departure. Adoration by the faithful before the Blessed Sacrament continues, but the Missal notes that midnight is a demarcation point for adoration: "after midnight the adoration should take place without solemnity" (rubric, 43). However, there is no requirement to continue adoration past midnight, but only "for a suitable length of time during the night." Thus, there is nothing to prevent a parish closing the period of adoration at midnight.

Notice that there is no formal or specific dismissal to this liturgy, thus emphasizing that the liturgies of the Sacred Paschal Triduum are, in some sense, one continuous liturgy. After the liturgy, at an appropriate time, the altar is stripped and crosses are removed from the church, if they can be; if not, they should be veiled (number 57 of *Paschale solemnitatis* notes that the veil should be red or purple, unless they have already been veiled on the Saturday before the Fifth Sunday of Lent). This stripping is done without any ritual or solemnity.

The Missal makes a final note that if for some reason the Passion of the Lord is not celebrated in the same church on the next day, then Mass ends in the usual way, and the Blessed Sacrament is reserved in the tabernacle as usual, without any procession or adoration.

A good resource which discusses the procession with the Blessed Sacrament is *Guide for Celebrating Worship of the Eucharist outside Mass* by John Thomas Lane, sss (LTP).

The Reception of the Holy Oils

The holy oils are blessed and consecrated at the Chrism Mass, celebrated by the bishop with the priests of the diocese in the cathedral on the morning of Holy Thursday, or on a more convenient day before Easter. Following the Chrism Mass, the pastor or his delegate then brings the fresh oils back to the parish in time for the celebration of the Triduum.

The Chrism Mass wonderfully highlights the importance and meaning of the holy oils. However, most of the faithful never participate in this liturgy, and may not even be aware that the oils are renewed each year in preparation for Easter. Thus, the Church provides an optional rite for the Reception of the Holy Oils in the parish community: "The reception of the Holy Oils may take place in individual parishes either before the celebration of the Evening Mass of the Lord's supper or at another time that seems more appropriate" (*Roman Missal*, Thursday of Holy Week, 15).

The rubric in the Missal does not provide much guidance about how this reception is actually to take place. For that, we need to go to the supplemental materials prepared for the dioceses of the United States, available at www.usccb.org/prayer-and-worship/liturgical-year/triduum/reception-of-holy-oils.cfm and printed in this *Sourcebook* on page 176. This short rite engages the whole assembly, with acclamations for the people, texts that express the purpose of each of the oils, and individual parishioners designated as presenters. (It would be especially powerful if these representatives joined the pastor at the diocesan Chrism Mass.)

Note that with the third edition of *The Roman Missal*, the time for the reception has changed. The oils are no longer received as part of the gifts procession; instead, they are presented before Mass begins. This timing can be challenging. If the ambry is located near the entrance of the church, it could work well to receive the oils near the doors just before the entrance procession of the Holy Thursday Mass. As he receives each of the oils, the priest could place it directly in the ambry. The rubrics suggest that the oils can also be placed on a table in the sanctuary, but this could be awkward before Mass begins, since the priest would then have to make his way to the doors of the church for the entrance procession. If your church's "geography" does not make for a graceful reception of the oils, you might consider doing this optional rite at a different time, for example before or after a weekday Mass shortly following the Chrism Mass.

If your community gathers for Night Prayer, invite them (with readers and musicians) earlier for additional Eucharistic adoration. Prepare a time of interwoven Scripture and song using some excerpts from the Gospel according to John, chapters 13–17 (see *Paschale solemnitatis*, 56).

Other Ideas

The challenge for ministers is to prepare the rites so that the symbols are fully expressed. Mystagogical reflection on the Triduum symbols can offer those who prepare and serve at the Triduum liturgies a renewed understanding from which to work. Such a gathering could be conducted around a single symbol or a group of several. Let's imagine a mystagogical reflection on the symbol of oil. A flagon or bowl of oil, a crucifix, and a Bible might be placed in the environment. The group could begin with the sign of the cross and an opening prayer. Because oil is the sacramental symbol by which the Holy Spirit is conferred, the opening prayer for Pentecost would be especially appropriate. Scriptures might then be proclaimed. Participants might then encounter the oil experientially, dipping their fingers into the bowl, rubbing it into their skin, and responding to the following questions: What does this oil evoke in you? What are its properties? How does it feel, taste, smell, look? In what way do those properties speak to us about the Holy Spirit? How do the properties of oil, the sacramental symbol of oil, and the inherent gift of the Holy Spirit invite us deeper into the mystery of Christ's Death and Resurrection?

Such a reflection process might lead to questions about transformation and discipleship: in what way does anointing with Chrism invite us to become what we receive—to go out into the world, to lay down our lives for others, and to offer the Spirit of Christ to those who hunger and thirst for meaning? Questions like this are appropriate, not only for those who are recently anointed but also for those who anamnetically remember (a remembering that makes the event present) or even imagine their own anointing through their participation in the celebration of the sacraments of initiation. This sort of mystagogical reflection process could be presented around any of the Triduum symbols.

(#40)   red

F R I 19 Friday of the Passion of the Lord (Good Friday)

About Good Friday

On this day, the parish community gathers to prayerfully recall the Death of Jesus "in the hope of their resurrection" (Prayer over the People, Good Friday). Because his Resurrection is inseparable from his Death, the Lord's Passion is truly celebrated. We remember last night's words from St. Paul, "We should glory in the Cross of our Lord Jesus Christ, / in whom is our salvation, life and resurrection, / through whom we are saved and delivered."

A rubric in the Missal describes how the environment in the church expresses the somber mood of the day: the altar should be completely bare, without cross, candles, or cloths. The liturgy is to begin at three o'clock in the afternoon or later; a time before then is not envisioned. It is a liturgy consisting of three parts: the Liturgy of the Word; the Adoration of the Cross; and Holy Communion.

The liturgy may be repeated later with the permission of the diocesan bishop, and this is important. For people who work and/or who would otherwise be unable to attend the afternoon liturgy but who are looking to attend a service to mark the day, it would be preferable for them to be able to experience the liturgy of the Church.

Certainly devotional celebrations such as Stations of the Cross can be scheduled on this day, but as much as possible we should be encouraging people to pray the official liturgies of the Church. Finally, there is a specific rubric mentioning that this liturgy "by its very nature" may not be celebrated in the absence of a priest; therefore, a deacon may not preside.

The Lectionary for Mass

◆ First Reading: Isaiah, the great prophet, speaks to his age and ours in the First Reading as he describes the experiences of the servant of the Lord. This famed passage is one of four "servant songs" in this book of Israel's prophetic literature. Many Christian and most Jewish scholars assert that at the time of its writing, the "servant" of whom Isaiah speaks is the nation of Israel. Christians have a long history of reading the narrative as a prediction of the Passion of Jesus. It is referenced in the narratives of all four Gospel writers. Isaiah, whose name means "salvation of the Lord," addresses the people as Assyria is rising as a cruel and destructive power. This remarkable passage can be divided into three parts. The opening lines speak of the appearance of God's servant. Listeners are warned that how things appear is not necessarily how they are; while the servant's appearance is battered beyond recognition, his suffering will be transformed into glory. Next we hear about the purpose of the servant's suffering. His suffering is like that of Job; misunderstood by onlookers. In fact, his suffering is not the result of his own actions; rather, he has taken on the sins of the people, the onlookers who scoff. The servant's death atones for them all—through his actions, he has restored their right relationship with God. Finally, we hear of the triumph of the servant as God's exalted one. God's work has been done in and through him.

His trust and surrender are rewarded profusely; his endurance and faith are vindicated by God.

◆ RESPONSORIAL PSALM 31 is a lament and also a statement of trust. The psalmist calls out to God for rescue in the face of total degradation. The vivid descriptions ("an object of reproach," "A laughing-stock," "a dread to my friends," "like the unremembered dead," and "a dish that is broken") all describe the devastation of being an outcast. This is a picture of human suffering in the most vivid terms. Still, the psalmist asserts a depth of trust in God that transcends the horrific circumstances. He affirms his faith in God, in rescue, and in blessing. On Good Friday, this psalm recalls for us the context of the words "into your hands I commend my spirit," uttered in faith by Jesus as he dies on the Cross.

◆ SECOND READING: Jesus Christ the High Priest has been given by God. No longer are ongoing sin offerings needed; unlike the human high priest of the Temple, Christ has offered himself up, once and for all people. Christ, God entering into human flesh and experience, understands all the joys and trials of human life. His followers can come to him "confidently," knowing that he sees our lives for everything that they are, and that we will receive grace and mercy. Like us in every way except for sin, Christ is now the path to salvation for those who listen to him and follow him. Jesus has become one with human struggle, and has seen human sin in its most extreme in the actions of those who have crucified him unjustly. His response is sympathy, and our response is boldness—to take ourselves to him fully, in love and obedience.

◆ GOSPEL: John's depiction of the Passion has a number of qualities that make it unique. It begins in the garden with the arrest of Jesus.

Under cover of darkness, Judas leads the soldiers and guards of the Temple to seize Jesus. Jesus, completely in control of the situation, steps forward. From the very start of the Gospel, Jesus has been aware of his divine destiny; he is the Word made flesh that came to dwell with humankind. His words to his captors are "I AM," a divine revelation that causes them to recoil from him. The protective posture he takes toward the disciples around him remind us that he is the Good Shepherd, an image used by Jesus earlier in the Gospel. He is brought to the Jewish authorities: first to Annas, who then sends him to the high priest Caiaphas, for questioning. Jesus is composed throughout; he is at peace despite the fact that the charge against him—blasphemy—carries the death penalty.

Placed between the descriptions of his interrogation are two of the three episodes in which Peter denies that he knows Jesus. This story appears in all the Gospel accounts; here we see the effusive, grandiose personality displayed in the foot washing reduce to fear and equivocation. Fear and frailty have overcome his commitment to witnessing, the heart of discipleship.

Jesus is then escorted to Pilate, the Roman governor of Judea. The responses of Jesus to Pilate's questioning (a dialogue unique to this Gospel) make clear the crime of which he is accused: claims to kingship (albeit not earthly), a political offense against the empire. However, Pilate is aware that Jesus has not led a rebellion, and falls back on his privilege of releasing a convicted criminal at Passover. The crowd chooses Barabbas; boldly threatening Pilate himself—if he does not do as they demand, Pilate is "no friend of Caesar." Jesus is scourged, crowned with thorns, and taken away to be crucified.

Throughout all, Jesus is dignified. In this Gospel account, Jesus,

the Lamb of God, moves through persecution to a fate that he accepts. Embracing the Cross, he accomplishes God's plan for salvation.

Many images are juxtaposed in this Gospel: darkness versus light, belief versus unbelief; earthly kingdom versus heavenly kingdom. Probably the greatest of all is the contrast between life and death, the triumph of goodness over evil.

The Roman Missal

Just as last night's liturgy had no formal ending, so today's has no formal beginning—one liturgy flows into the next in the unity of these days. Wearing red Mass vestments, the priest and deacon simply go to the altar in silence and, after reverencing it, prostrate themselves; all others in the assembly kneel. Then, after a period of silence, the priest rises and goes to the chair. He should take care to make sure that the period of silence is noticeable. It has been said that true silence begins only when the shuffling, rustling, and other noises end, and so the priest should allow for a prolonged period of true silence on this particular day.

At the chair, the priest prays the prayer. This prayer is not a Collect, and the invitation "Let us pray" is omitted, further showing both the stark nature of this liturgy and the way this liturgy flows from the previous one. The priest has a choice from among two prayers. The first option asks God to remember his mercies and to protect his servants, because they are the ones for whom Christ shed his blood and established the Paschal Mystery. The overt use of the phrase "Paschal Mystery" is striking, and it reminds us of the total mystery we are celebrating through the Sacred Paschal Triduum. The second option asks that just as we have borne "the image of the man of earth," that is, Adam, so too, "by the sanctification of grace," may we "bear the image of the Man of heaven." Bearing the image of Christ is possible because by his Passion he "abolished the death inherited from ancient sin."

The Liturgy of the Word takes place, with the Lord's Passion read in the same way as it was read on Palm Sunday of the Lord's Passion. After the reading of the Passion, a brief homily is preached; the rubric goes on to mention that at the end of the homily "the faithful may be invited to spend a short time in prayer" (rubric 10). Certainly this day above all others calls for noticeable periods of silence.

The Solemn Intercessions follow. A deacon or lay minister sings or says the invitation while standing at the ambo. Then all pray in silence for a while, followed by the priest saying or singing the prayer with his hands extended. A rubric mentions that it is traditional for all to kneel for silent prayer after each invitation to prayer, as the deacon may add "Let us kneel" and "Let us stand." While technically optional, one could argue a certain preference for following this tradition on this day: it highlights the solemnity of the intercessions, and the unusual gesture serves to further mark off the rites of the Sacred Paschal Triduum as rites that occur only once a year to mark our central and holiest days. A key element, however, would be to make sure the people are left to kneel silently for a long enough period of time, lest the kneeling and standing become simply a distracting (and perhaps unintentionally comical) series of down-and-up, down-and-up movements.

There are ten intercessions provided by the Missal: for the Holy Church; for the pope; for all orders and degrees of the faithful; for catechumens; for the unity of Christians; for the Jewish people; for those who do not believe in Christ; for those who do not believe in God; for those in public

office; and for those in tribulation. The titles reveal the universality of these prayers as the Church expresses her concern and intercedes for the whole world. It is significant that on one of her most solemn days, the Church spends so much time pleading for the well-being of the entire world.

After the Solemn Intercessions, which conclude the Liturgy of the Word, comes the second part of the liturgy, the Adoration of the Holy Cross. The Holy Cross is first shown, and then it is adored; there are two forms for the showing, and there are two ways that the adoration may take place.

In the first form of the showing, the deacon, accompanied by one or more ministers, goes to the sacristy and then returns in procession, accompanied by two ministers carrying lighted candles, carrying the Cross, which is covered with a violet veil, through the church to the middle of the sanctuary. There the priest receives the Cross and, after uncovering a little of its upper part, elevates it while singing "Behold the wood of the Cross . . ." After responding, "Come, let us adore," the people kneel and adore the Cross in silence for a brief period while the priest stands and holds the Cross up. Then the priest uncovers the right arm of the Cross, again raising it, and then singing "Behold the wood of the Cross . . ." and the rest taking place as the first time. Lastly, he uncovers the Cross completely and the same sequence of events occurs. In the second form of showing, the priest or the deacon, accompanied by one or more ministers, goes to the door of the church and takes up the unveiled Cross as the ministers take up lighted candles. Then, in procession, they move through the church to the sanctuary, stopping in three locations—just inside the entrance to the church, in the middle of the church, and in front of the entrance to the sanctuary—at

which times the priest or deacon elevates the Cross, sings "Behold the wood of the Cross . . ." with all responding "Come, let us adore." A rubric states that also in this second form the people are to kneel and adore the Cross in silence for a brief moment, as in the first form.

For the Adoration of the Cross, one option is to have the priest or deacon, after carrying in the Cross, hand over the Cross to ministers to hold at the entrance to the sanctuary, or at some other suitable place, with candles placed to the right and left of the Cross. At that location, the priest celebrant, possibly with chasuble and shoes removed, approaches the Cross, followed by the clergy, lay ministers, and the faithful, all coming in procession. The sign of reverence to the Cross can be varied: a simple genuflection, a kiss, or some other meaningful gesture. Consider inviting everyone to remove their shoes before approaching the Cross; there is nothing that forbids this, and the strangeness of this gesture not only reinforces the uniqueness of the days of the Triduum, but also makes a statement about the holiness of the ground we walk on in adoring the instrument of our salvation.

It is clearly stated that only one Cross should be used for adoration, so parishes should avoid using multiple crosses. When the assembly is so large that approaching individually is not feasible, a second option is given for the adoration. (It should be noted, however, that several people can approach the Cross and venerate it at the same time, to accommodate a larger number of participants. There is no need to rush this part of the liturgy, and the music that is suggested would seem to indicate that more than just a brief time should be accorded to the adoration.) In this second option, the priest, "after some of the clergy and faithful have adored" (the Missal does not specify who these "some" are) takes the Cross and invites the people in a few words (of his own choosing — no text is given) to adore the Holy Cross, after which he holds the Cross high for a brief time while the faithful adore it in silence. The Missal suggests and gives the texts for an antiphon, the Reproaches, and/or the hymn *Crux fidelis* to be sung during the adoration; other suitable songs may be used as well, and a rubric mentions the *Stabat Mater* as another possibility, in addition to some other "suitable chant in memory of the compassion of the Blessed Virgin Mary."

When adoration is finished, the Cross is carried to its place at the altar, where it stands with lighted candles, which are placed either around the altar, on it, or near the Cross. The third part of the liturgy, Holy Communion, now begins with the altar being prepared with a cloth, a corporal, and the Missal being placed on it. While this is being done, the deacon, or, in his absence, the priest, wearing a humeral veil, brings the Blessed Sacrament from the place of repose to the altar while the assembly stands in silence. The Missal specifically notes that the deacon or priest uses "a shorter route," indicating that this is not in any way to be an elaborate procession; it is simply more of a functional bringing of the Blessed Sacrament to the altar for Holy Communion, although appropriate marks of honor for the Real Presence are nonetheless used — the humeral veil, and two ministers with lighted candles accompanying the Blessed Sacrament. As the Blessed Sacrament is placed on the altar, candlesticks are placed on or around the altar.

If the deacon brought the Blessed Sacrament to the altar, the priest goes to the altar once the ciborium is uncovered, and he genuflects upon arriving there. He then introduces the Lord's Prayer, which is prayed with its embolism and doxology, followed by a private prayer of the priest, his genuflection, and then the "Behold the Lamb of God . . ." with the response "Lord, I am not worthy. . . ." Communion is then distributed, during which Psalm 22 or another appropriate song may be sung.

When the distribution of Holy Communion is completed, the Blessed Sacrament is taken by the deacon or another minister to a place prepared outside the church. Of note here is that there seems to be a preference for the priest not to do this; if a deacon is not present, then perhaps another minister would be a more appropriate choice. No mention is made of candles accompanying the Blessed Sacrament, so this too is a simple action of returning the sacrament to its place of repose, and is in no way a procession or movement with a great deal of solemnity; this is in keeping with the tone of the day. If required, the Blessed Sacrament may be placed in the tabernacle, although it would appear the preference is to use a place outside the church.

The liturgy ends as starkly as it began. After the Blessed Sacrament has been removed, the priest prays the Prayer after Communion. Then follows a simple dismissal: the deacon or priest invites the people to bow down for the blessing, the priest extends his hands over the people and prays the prayer; and then they simply depart after genuflecting to the Cross. There is no procession by the ministers or the faithful; it is a simple dispersing.

After the liturgy, the altar is stripped, but the Cross remains with two or four candlesticks; people should be encouraged to pray before the Cross.

Other Ideas

The Stations of the Cross are of course a beloved devotion that takes place throughout Lent and on Good Friday. Consider a new form of the Stations for your parish. *A Light for My Path: Praying the Psalms on the Way of the Cross*, composed and written by Michael Ruzicki, provides a unique opportunity to pray the traditional fourteen Stations of the Cross.

This resource incorporates the Book of Psalms with the Gospel accounts of Jesus' Passion and Death. Praying the psalms helps us to become more familiar with the prayer of Jesus and to be united with his suffering and Death. In addition to the Scripture readings and psalmody, pastoral reflections, art, and original music are provided for each station for further participation and meditation. Assembly and leader's editions are available from LTP.

Today is the special collection for the Holy Land. In the words of Paul VI, it is "not only for the Holy Places, but above all for those pastoral, charitable, educational, and social works which the Church supports in the Holy Land for the welfare of their Christian brethren and of the local communities" (available from: http://www.usccb.org/nationalcollections/ncdescriptions.shtml). Rather than interrupt the flow of the liturgy, the collection could be taken up at the door, either by an usher or with a well-marked basket placed in a prominent place. A note regarding this collection could be placed in the Triduum worship aid.

(#41)   white

Easter Sunday of the Resurrection of the Lord: The Easter Vigil in the Holy Night

SAT 20

In the Morning

Christ was in the tomb; he lay in darkness in the womb of the whole world. Holy Saturday commemorates that day and has a character all its own. It is a quiet day of meditation, reflection, and anticipation, especially for the elect preparing for Baptism. Although there is much to do, don't let it just be a day for decorating the church. During the day, invite people to pray Morning Prayer and keep vigil in front of the crucifix in the barren church.

There is no Mass during the day, and Holy Communion may be given before the Vigil only as viaticum. Reconciliation and Anointing of the Sick may be celebrated today. Ministers to the sick should make every effort to visit the sick during Good Friday and Holy Saturday, sharing with them some of the readings and bringing the prayers of the community. During the day today we continue the Paschal fast. The elect should be fasting in preparation for their Baptism, and the faithful may join them in solidarity of spirit. This recommendation dates back to about the year 100, where it appeared in the *Didache*. Linked to the past, we continue this discipline in a prayerful spirit. The climax of the Sacred Paschal Triduum, the Easter Vigil, begins after darkness has fallen, officially forty-five minutes after dark. You can find the exact time for the setting of the sun in your area by consulting the Navy website (http://aa.usno.navy.mil/data/docs/RS_OneYear.php). The Easter Vigil launches us into Easter Time, and it should not be confused with Holy Saturday itself. The color for the morning is violet.

About the Easter Vigil

Shattering the darkness, the great Paschal candle is lit with the Easter fire, five wax nails of incense are embedded, and it becomes the symbol of the crucified Christ. The Paschal Mystery, already celebrated in various ways since the Evening Mass of the Lord's Supper, is clearly and joyfully announced from the very beginning of the Vigil liturgy. It is in the light of the Paschal candle that the liturgy continues to unfold. The Easter Vigil is the most beautiful of all liturgies. Ranking highest among the celebrations of the liturgical year, it should rank highest in the spiritual life of the parish community, not a small task in places where Christmas is considered the high point. Encourage all parishioners to take part by offering good, solid catechesis and invitations in advance. If the community has been involved in the journey of the catechumens, they will want to be present and surround them for this celebration.

The four parts of the Easter Vigil move us through a gradual unfolding of the Paschal Mystery of Christ. The great fire immediately dispels the gathering gloom. The Liturgy of the Word reveals the path of God's plan throughout salvation history. The Liturgy of Baptism draws the elect through the baptismal waters into the promise of eternal life and renews the baptismal belief of the faithful. The Liturgy of the Eucharist brings the celebration to the climax of the banquet of the Lamb, as we experience the presence of the Risen Christ in our midst.

The Missal gives several introductory and explanatory rubrics for the celebration of the Easter Vigil. Some comments about them are noted here.

This night's Vigil is explicitly described as "the greatest and most noble of all solemnities." The importance and grandeur of this evening's celebration cannot be emphasized too strongly, and parishes must resist any temptation to abbreviate the rites or to enact them in a perfunctory way. Feeble excuses such as "it's too long for the people" are in fact insulting to the people of God—their spiritual wherewithal when the rites are done in all their fullness is quite hearty; let's not shortchange the people of God on "this most sacred night."

The Vigil is to take place "during the night," so that it begins after nightfall and ends before daybreak on the Sunday. This is an absolutely crucial and nonnegotiable point, as strongly stated by PS, 78: "This rule is to be taken according to its strictest sense. Reprehensible are those abuses and practices that have crept into many places in violation of this ruling whereby the Easter Vigil is celebrated at the time of day that it is customary to celebrate anticipated Sunday Masses." The starting time, then, is to be after nightfall: thus, depending on the date of Easter and in what part of the country you live, the time will vary.

The Easter Vigil is made up of four parts: the Solemn Beginning of the Vigil or Lucernarium; the Liturgy of the Word; the Baptismal Liturgy; and the Liturgy of the Eucharist.

First Part: The Solemn Beginning of the Vigil or Lucernarium

The Vigil begins with the church in darkness. The Missal states that "a blazing fire is prepared in a suitable place outside the church," and that the people gather around the fire. The intent is clear that this is to be a bonfire, more than just a few small flames flickering from a table-top hibachi. As a later rubric describes, the blessing of fire may be adapted if difficulties arise constructing a bonfire. In such cases, the people may gather in the church as usual, and at the door of the church the rites of blessing the fire and preparing the candle take place.

The liturgy begins with the Sign of the Cross and the priest offering a greeting to the people "in the usual way"—presumably, using one of the liturgical greetings for Mass; unlike the Good Friday liturgy, the Easter Vigil is a Mass. The priest then instructs the people about the meaning of this night, "in which our Lord Jesus Christ / passed over from death to life," and that we keep this memorial in "the sure hope / of sharing his triumph over death / and living with him in God." The instruction may be given using the exact words in the Missal or similar words of the priest's own choosing.

The priest then blesses the fire, after which the candle is prepared. The rubric simply states that one of the ministers brings the Paschal candle to the priest; while therefore any minister may do this, perhaps it is fitting, if a deacon is carrying the candle into the church, for him to be the one to do this, in a sense taking custody of the candle. The lines of the cross, the alpha and omega, and the numerals of the current year are cut into the candle; this preparation of the candle is not optional. Thus the rite presumes that a real candle that is actually prepared in this way is used; *Paschale solemnitatis* clearly states that it "must be made of wax, never be artificial, be renewed each year, be only one in number, and be of sufficiently large size so that it may evoke the truth that Christ is the light of the world" (PS, 82).

Plastic tubes that hold oil canisters and have permanent symbols, where only the last numeral changes from year to year, should be avoided at all costs!

After the cutting of the cross and other signs have been made on the candle, five grains of incense may be inserted in the form of a cross, with the accompanying words. This part is optional.

Next the priest lights the Paschal candle from the new fire with the accompanying words sung or said. A little careful preparation and rehearsal will ensure that all goes smoothly at the beginning of the Vigil; it can become rather awkward managing the various items needed and matching the gestures to the words, and making sure all the necessary things are handy, so think this through ahead of time.

Once the candle has been lit, the procession forms. Ministers take burning coals from the fire and place them in the thurible, and the priest puts incense into the thurible in the usual way. A deacon, if present (otherwise, any other suitable minister), carries the candle. The order of procession is: first the thurifer with the smoking thurible, then the deacon or other minister with the candle, followed by the priest with other ministers, and finally the people, all carrying unlit candles. Note that the priest precedes the people, and that candles are not yet lit.

The same three stations used for carrying in the cross on Good Friday are used again: the door of the church, the middle of the church, and in front of the altar. At each station the candle is lifted high and "The Light of Christ" is sung, with the people's response. Only the priest's candle is lit after the first "Light of Christ" and its response; then, after the second, the people's candles are lit; after the third, the Paschal candle is placed in its stand

that is located next to the ambo or in the middle of the sanctuary.

The Missal is clear that it is at this time that the lights are turned on in the church, although the altar candles are not yet lit. Although there has arisen the custom of not turning the church lights on until later, usually during the Gloria, it is clear that the rubrics do not call for this. The powerful symbol of the light of the Paschal candle is being emphasized in that once it is brought into church, its brightness completely illumines everything.

With the Paschal candle in its stand, the priest goes to his chair, and after handing his candle to a minister so his hands are free, he puts incense in the thurible and blesses the incense as at Mass. The deacon asks for and receives the blessing from the priest in preparation for singing the Easter Proclamation (Exsultet). The blessing is the same one given before the Gospel at Mass, except that the words "paschal praise" are used instead of the word "Gospel." After receiving the blessing, the deacon incenses the book and the candle, and then proclaims the Easter Proclamation at the ambo or at some other lectern; the assembly remains standing and holds lighted candles. The choice as to whether to use the ambo or some other lectern can be made based on the arrangement of your church; presumably, if the ambo were some significant distance from the Paschal candle, it might be advantageous to use a lectern that is right next to the candle.

It is possible for someone other than the deacon to sing the Exsultet, with the Missal specifically mentioning the priest celebrant or a concelebrating priest, although a lay cantor is another possibility. One presumes the decision will be made according to which person will be able to proclaim such an important piece best. Note the omission of certain lines in the case of a layperson singing the Proclamation. Immediately after the Proclamation, all extinguish their candles.

Second Part: The Liturgy of the Word

This Vigil is referred to as "the mother of all holy Vigils," and so nine readings are provided, seven from the Old Testament and two from the New, an Epistle and a Gospel reading. Considering the importance of this liturgy, all nine readings should be considered, "so that the character of the Vigil, which demands an extended period of time, may be preserved." Liturgy committees and preparers, and indeed all parishioners, should understand that the solemn Easter Vigil is not just another Mass, nor is it even just "a long Mass"; it is a Vigil, and a Vigil takes time. It is part of the experience of "time outside of time," the sacred time of the Triduum that was begun on Holy Thursday night and is reaching its climax this night. Any attempts to truncate or abbreviate the experience should be avoided. The Missal is clear that using all nine readings is the norm and is preferred. Nonetheless, the Missal does admit of the possibility of reducing the number of readings "where more serious pastoral circumstances demand it." One might take special note of the deliberate use of the word "serious," which is weightier than just preference, impatience or, as noted above, a misguided sense that the people cannot handle it. In the case of a shortened Liturgy of the Word, at least three readings should be read from the Old Testament, both from the Law and the Prophets, and the accompanying Responsorial Psalms should be used; additionally, the reading of chapter 14 of Exodus and its canticle is always to be used—it cannot be omitted.

The priest gives an instruction, using the words of the Missal or his own words, to invite the people to listen to the Word of God "with quiet hearts" and reminding them to meditate on how God has saved his people throughout history and especially by sending his Son as Redeemer.

The Missal gives prayers to follow each of the Scripture readings; in some cases, the priest has a choice between two prayers.

After the last Old Testament reading followed by its Responsorial Psalm and prayer, the altar candles are lit and the priest intones the Gloria. Since the Missal gives the notation for the priest to sing, there would seem to be indicated a preference that the priest do this. After he intones the Gloria, the assembly then takes up the hymn. Bells are rung during the hymn, but no further specification of this is given; it simply says "according to local custom," so this can be left open to the creativity of the parish — perhaps the choir rings bells, or servers, or even members of the assembly who have brought their own, or any combination or all of these! When the Gloria is concluded, the priest prays the Collect.

After the Collect, the Epistle is proclaimed. After the Epistle, all rise and the priest solemnly intones the triple Alleluia, with the Missal specifically noting that he raises the tone by a step each time, and all repeat after him. However, if the priest is not capable of singing this properly, it is possible for a cantor to do so. Incense is placed in the thurible as usual, and the deacon receives the blessing as usual. Only incense is carried in procession with the *Book of Gospels*; the Missal explicitly states that candles are not used. Finally, there is a rubric stating that the homily is not to be omitted. The importance of preaching on this holiest of nights is underscored by this rubric.

On "this night," the Christian community tells the story that attempts to answer the query: who are you, O God, you who create, redeem, and promise future glory? Out of the evening shadows, the Church quietly listens and makes its pilgrim way in confidence and faith that "Christ our Passover" (from the prayer after the First Reading) is the incarnate answer to the question we pose to our God.

The Lectionary for Mass

◆ FIRST READING: It is logical indeed to begin the telling of the story of salvation "in the beginning, when God created the heavens and the earth" (Genesis 1:1) In this reading, God's goodness is revealed in the creation of the cosmos, with its waters, its light, the sky, the earth, the sea, vegetation, animals, and finally humans. The Church hears in this reading that every step of creation was sealed with God seeing "how good it was." The Church is led to contemplate that God's goodness is revealed in the creation of order out of chaos. In distinguishing light from darkness and day from night, God is able to bestow upon creation an inherent dignity that mirrors God's very likeness. Thus, the purpose of creation is to return the love God has bestowed in his gift, by reflecting God's word—"how good it was"—and by working to restore the harmony and the oneness that is the blueprint of God's design.

◆ RESPONSORIAL PSALM 104 follows this reading and echoes the story of creation as a blessing of God's glory: "Bless the Lord, O my soul! O Lord, my God, you are great indeed! . . . The earth is full of your creatures. Bless the Lord, O my soul!" God's love is revealed in the oneness of creation, and the Church recognizes in Christ such oneness restored. The psalmist praises what God has produced in creation. The first seven strophes of the psalm are in harmony with the seven days of creation recounted in the Book of Genesis. After the psalmist blesses God, speaking of God as clothed in a garment of light, he offers descriptors of the wonders that surround him: the mountains, the waters, the birds, the grasses that feed cattle, and more. Witnessing the indescribable wonders of the natural world, the psalmist cannot refrain from again extolling God's "manifold" works and joining in a cry of praise and blessing with all of creation.

◆ RESPONSORIAL PSALM 33: As an alternative to Psalm 104, a different song of creation may follow the First Reading: Psalm 33. It, too, praises God for the wonders of nature. This psalm envisions that the waters of the ocean are contained as in a flask, confined as though in cellars in the deep. Notably, Psalm 33 includes morality among God's creations.

God's word is "upright," all God's works are "trustworthy," God loves "justice and right," and the earth is full of God's "kindness." Here is echoed the belief from the First Reading that what God made is "good." We praise God not just for the things that are, but for the goodness of things that are. Christians interpret one of the verses of this psalm as a prophecy for our belief in the Holy Trinity: "By the word of the Lord the heavens were made; / by the breath of his mouth all their host." In one verse we find references to the Lord, the Word, and the breath, images of the Triune God, preexisting all that is.

◆ SECOND READING: The Second Reading of the Easter Vigil tells the dramatic story of God putting Abraham to the test by asking him to sacrifice his son, Isaac. This story represents so much more than the horror of one man willing to kill his son; rather, it signals the potential destruction of a relationship with God and the loss of an entire nation. Quite simply, if Isaac dies,

so too does the covenant, for God had promised to Abraham: "With him (Isaac) I will establish my Covenant, a Covenant in perpetuity, to be his God and the God of his descendants after him" (Genesis 17:19). Thus, the test of Abraham's faith tells us more about God's unconditional love for his people. It is the story of God's desire to fulfill what he has promised. The human response to God's fidelity is ongoing obedience, which the Church sees in the perfect obedience of Christ's sacrifice. With those awaiting the waters of Baptism, the attitude of obedience in response to God's ongoing fidelity is made apparent in the Church "this night."

◆ RESPONSORIAL PSALM 16: This psalm speaks to the trust the psalmist places in his God. No other gods will be worshipped; only the Lord, who will be set "ever before" him. The whole body is swept up in this experience. The heart is glad and the body confident.

◆ THIRD READING: The night of Passover, in which God came to rescue Israel from the clutches of Pharaoh and forced slavery in Egypt, is the backdrop for the Third Reading of the Vigil. In the Book of Exodus, God calls Moses and orders him to say to Pharaoh in God's name: "Israel is my firstborn son. I ordered you to let my son go to offer me worship. You refuse to let him go. So be it! I shall put your firstborn to death" (Exodus 4:23). In the account from Exodus proclaimed here, we picture the Egyptians in hot pursuit of the Israelites after the angel of death has passed through all of Egypt, putting to death all the firstborn in the land. While the Israelites follow Moses and his outstretched hand through the sea "with the water like a wall to their right and to their left" (Exodus 14:22), the focus of this reading is upon God's mighty power. Not only will Israel come to faith because of God's mar-

velous display of might, but so too will all of Egypt be awe-struck: "The Egyptians shall know that I am the Lord, when I receive glory through Pharaoh and his chariots and charioteers" (Exodus 14:17).

◆ CANTICLE: Having been saved from attack, the people—filled with gratitude and joy—sing to God in this passage commonly referred to as the Song at the Sea. Not surprisingly, given the 430 years of captivity, the structure of this song reflects the Egyptian poetry of the time. The themes, however, are reminiscent of those found in the Wisdom literature, particularly the Book of Deuteronomy. This poem is believed to be one of the Bible's oldest compositions and very likely was an independent work at some point. God's love is steadfast, as demonstrated in this salvific miracle. Our reading of the Exodus story of God's victory at the sea concludes with our joining Moses, Miriam, and all the Israelites in their song of praise for what God has accomplished: "I will sing to the Lord, for he is gloriously triumphant: horse and chariot he has cast into the sea." Furthermore, the Church sees in this reading the foreshadowing of Baptism, where God's power is revealed in the "waters of rebirth."

◆ FOURTH READING: The prophecy of Isaiah constitutes the fourth installment in our Paschal account of salvation history, and here Isaiah calls the Lord the "husband" of Israel: "The Lord calls you back, like a wife forsaken and grieved in spirit, a wife married in youth and then cast off" (Isaiah 54:6). Although God's people may have behaved as an immature spouse, not ready for the responsibilities of a serious and demanding relationship, God's wrath will not last, and redemption will be close at hand. While God's might may be shown in his ability to move the Israelites through the Red Sea, an even greater demonstration of God's power is shown here in the gift of mercy: "Though the mountains leave their place and the hills be shaken, my love shall never leave you nor my covenant of peace be shaken, says the Lord, who has mercy on you" (Isaiah 54:10). These words from the prophecy of Isaiah are brought into the immediate life of the Church, and we are reminded that, even though we have sinned and wandered far from God, mercy and redemption are always his to give.

◆ RESPONSORIAL PSALM 30 offers a song of thanksgiving for being delivered from death. The voice is that of an individual who has been cured of illness. Restored to health, the psalmist bears witness to the mercy of God. The name of God, LORD, appears six times in the verses used at the Easter Vigil. The speaker is not content to praise God alone; all are invited to join in the hymn. The "faithful," or *hasidim*, are the keepers of *hesed*, the mutual covenant of love with God. The pains of life, such as weeping or anger, are momentary. The psalmist cries out in closing, asking for God's pity and help in the fight against complacency. The psalm ends as it opens, with praise and gratitude.

◆ FIFTH READING: If the first four readings of the Easter Vigil may be seen as weaving a thread from God's goodness in creation through the fidelity he shows in keeping the covenant through his great and mighty power to his ability to show the limitlessness of his mercy, the Fifth Reading, again from the prophet Isaiah, begins to allude more precisely to the work of salvation accomplished by Jesus Christ and to the sacramental response of the Church. Now is the time to turn to the Lord: "come, without paying and without cost. . . . Seek the Lord while he may be found, call him while he is near"

(Isaiah 55:1, 6). The prophet Isaiah consoles Israel with the promise that God's ways are not the ways of the world; God is generous and loving without end. This reading falls at this moment in our retelling of salvation history because it is a reminder that the search for God is always worth undertaking. The Church accepts the invitation to "come" to the Lord in the Sacrament of Baptism, and continues to celebrate the source of all life in the Eucharist. Thus, the declaration made in the accompanying canticle certainly turns our contemplation to what will take place shortly in the baptismal font.

◆ CANTICLE: The words of Isaiah are now presented antiphonally, an appropriate response to the passage that was just proclaimed. In the face of the abundance of God's gifts, the answer is to burst forth joyfully in song with words of thanks and praise. The third verse features the phrase, "the holy one of Israel," a term used in a number of places in Isaiah. This name for God stands out among the prophets, and echoes the experience the prophet had in his vision, where the Seraphim sing to God, "Holy, Holy, Holy!"

◆ SIXTH READING: In a similar way, the prophet Baruch, in the Sixth Reading chosen for the Easter Vigil, reminds Israel of old and the Church of today that wisdom is the greatest of all treasures. God alone knows wisdom, but he has given her to Israel to cherish. Baruch calls Israel to accountability with this gift bestowed by God: "She (wisdom) is the book of the precepts of God, the law that endures forever; all who cling to her will live, but those will die who forsake her" (Baruch 4:1). We know that the history of the Jewish people, like our own history in Christianity, is a long pilgrimage of straying from the path and finding the right way again, all by the goodness of God's

mercy and grace. The prophetic words of Baruch serve as a reminder of what is truly enduring in this world, namely the wisdom of God that never fails.

◆ RESPONSORIAL PSALM 19: This beautiful prayer extols the life-giving Word of God. God's law is perfect, refreshing. It is just and fair, a source of rejoicing and enlightenment. Fear of the Lord, awe and wonder before him, is the natural response to the goodness and generosity of God. Knowing God's law and receiving it is the greatest possible gift. In this psalm, we see the Torah—the words of life in the law—as both preeminent and also central, more precious than any other part of God's creation.

◆ SEVENTH READING: The Seventh Reading, the last from the Old Testament, continues the theme of God's intimate interaction with a rebellious people, a people who "defiled" the gift of God "by their conduct and deeds" (Ezekiel 36:16). God inflicts great punishment upon Israel for its lack of faith and for choosing to worship idols: "I scattered them among the nations, dispersing them over foreign lands; according to their conduct and deeds I judged them" (Ezekiel 36:19). Nevertheless, the prophet Ezekiel is sent to announce that God will prove to Israel and all the nations that he is able to gather what he has scattered—he will forgive. Even more importantly, God is the source of real conversion: it is not that Israel turns back on its own, but God turns Israel back to himself. "I will give you a new heart and place a new spirit within you, taking from your bodies your stony hearts and giving you natural hearts" (Ezekiel 36:26). When the Church hears this reading in the context of "this night," it is reminded that our summons at Baptism is initiated by God. The spirit to turn back to God when we have wandered astray is, in fact, God's gift to us. God places within us the desire to return to him.

◆ PSALM 42: The Lectionary offers three possible Responsories to the Seventh Reading. The first, from Psalm 42, is sung whenever Baptism will be celebrated at the Vigil. The psalm asks God for the gift of God's light and fidelity, so that those who receive it may approach the dwelling place of God, specifically the altar of God. These verses eloquently prophesy the journey of the catechumens, who thirst for the waters of Baptism, and attain it through the light and fidelity that God extends to new believers through the covenant. Having been refreshed by the waters of Baptism, the neophytes come to the altar of God, where they participate in Holy Communion, the intimate union that makes them fully the Body of Christ, a dwelling place for God most high.

◆ CANTICLE: This canticle from Isaiah may be used if Baptisms are not celebrated.

◆ RESPONSORIAL PSALM 51: This psalm may also be used if Baptisms are not celebrated. This penitential psalm is one of the great laments in the entire Book of Psalms. Calling out to God, the psalmist asks for a clean heart—akin to the clean heart God promises in the reading from Ezekiel. The psalmist ask for restorative action by God; in turn, he will become someone who helps others to know God's ways and return to God. The greatest offering is not a burned offering, but the transformation of the self into someone who is both humble and contrite.

◆ EPISTLE: Just as the readings from the Old Testament were originally composed by the ancient Israelites to tell the story of how it came into being as a great nation, how God provides for the covenant,

and what mutual fidelity to that covenant will bring, so too does this reading from Paul's letter to the Romans serve as a benchmark description of who we are as followers of Christ. "Are you unaware that we who were baptized into Christ Jesus were baptized into his death?" (Romans 6:3). But that is not all: Baptism into Christ's Death is not simply a mark of our past but also constitutes our present life and our future glory: we are "dead to sin and living for God in Christ Jesus" (Romans 6:11). In terms of salvation history, redemption comes from adherence to the New Law, which is Christ himself, and Baptism is the sacramental key to this relationship. What better response to this cornerstone of salvation history than to sing out "Alleluia, Alleluia, Alleluia" with the three couplets of Psalm 118.

◆ RESPONSORIAL PSALM/GOSPEL ACCLAMATION: This hymn of victory would have been sung by the people upon entering the precincts of the Temple. Its glorious words reintroduce the Christian community to the cry of "Alleluia!" which they have not spoken since before the commencement of Lent. Through the victory that has been achieved, the people know that they, truly, are God's chosen ones. Likewise, the Christian community, knowing what has been achieved once and for all people in Christ, raise their voices to extol the fulfillment of God's promise.

◆ GOSPEL: The women see a large stone and wonder who will roll it back for them. Then the women are amazed to see a young man clothed in white. They hear the most important news that has ever been spoken: "[Jesus] has been raised; he is not here." They see the empty tomb. They receive the commission to report this good news. The young man instructs them to tell the disciples—and Peter. Apparently, Peter was

going to need a special message because of his misbehavior and his doubts, but also because of his leadership among those who would hear the word.

Third Part: Baptismal Liturgy

The Baptismal Liturgy begins after the homily. The rites take place at the baptismal font, so the priest goes there with the ministers, unless there is to be a procession to the font (see below). If, however, the font is in a location where it cannot be easily seen by the faithful, then a vessel with water is placed in the sanctuary. Notice the importance given to the participation of the entire assembly—it is crucial that they be able to see what is going on. This is in keeping with the main thrust of the renewal of the liturgy.

Next, the elect are called forward and presented by their godparents or, in the case of small children, are carried by their parents and godparents. It is admittedly odd that the Missal refers to them as catechumens when, in fact, the terminology used in the *Rite of Christian Initiation of Adults* refers to them as the elect. The Missal does not give any specific texts for this calling forward and presentation.

If there is to be a procession to the baptistery or to the font, it begins now, and the order of procession is clearly noted: a minister with the Paschal candle leads the procession, followed by those to be baptized and their godparents, then other ministers, the deacon, and lastly the priest. (Thus, if there is to be a procession to the font, the priest and the ministers do not immediately go there.) The Litany of the Saints, given in the Missal, is sung during the procession. Names of some saints may be added, especially the saint for whom the parish is named, and other patron saints, for example, of those to be baptized. Also, if there are candidates to be baptized, the priest adds a prayer at the end of the litany.

If there is no procession to the font, the priest addresses the assembly using the words given in the Missal, or words similar to them. The Missal provides a text not only for the case when Baptisms are to take place, but also for the case if no one is to be baptized, yet the font is still to be blessed.

There is a third possibility: that no one is to be baptized, and that no font is to be blessed. In that instance, there is no Litany of the Saints, and the Blessing of Water takes place at once.

After all have arrived at the font and the Litany ends, the priest blesses the baptismal water, with has hands extended during the prayer. The Missal gives the text of the prayer first with musical notation and then without, indicating a certain preference for singing the prayer. The prayer includes the gesture of lowering the Paschal candle into the water either once or three times and then holding the candle in the water for the remainder of the prayer, with an acclamation sung (or said) by the assembly as the candle is lifted out of the water. If no one is to be baptized and if the font is not to be blessed, there is a completely different introduction and blessing prayer for the priest to use.

When Baptisms are to take place, they take place immediately after the blessing of the baptismal water and the acclamation of the people. The Missal first directs the priest to the appropriate ritual (that is, either the *Rite of Christian Initiation of Adults* or *Rite of Baptism for Children*) for the prescribed questions and answers concerning the renunciation of sin. There is also a mention that if the anointing of adults with the oil of catechumens has not already taken place at some point before this (that is, as part of any earlier preparatory rites), then it is to occur now. This, however, conflicts with the *Rite of Christian Initiation of Adults*, 33.7, which states that in the United States, "the anointing with the oil of catechumens is reserved for use in the period of the catechumenate and in the period of purification and enlightenment and is not to be included in the preparation rites on Holy Saturday or in the celebration of initiation at the Easter Vigil or at another time." As of this writing, this point would seem to be in need of clarification.

Next the priest questions the adults, and the parents and godparents of children, about the faith, again as indicated in the respective rites. Interestingly, the Missal admits of an option that, should the number of those to be baptized be very large, the priest may, immediately after the response of those to be baptized and the parents and godparents of children, also ask for and receive the renewal of baptismal promises of the entire assembly. Presumably, this option is offered as a way of not unduly prolonging the ritual when the numbers are large.

After the professions of faith, the priest baptizes the elect and the children (here the Missal does refer to the adults as the elect!). While no mention is made of the manner of Baptism, it would be good to reflect on what the *Rite of Christian Initiation of Adults* and *Rite of Baptism for Children* ritual books say about the suitability of and preference for immersion.

After the Baptisms, the infants (children under the age of discretion) are anointed with Chrism (this is the anointing on the crown of the head, as described in the *Rite of Baptism for Children*). Next, white garments are given to all the newly baptized, adults and children, followed by the lighting of the baptismal candles from the Paschal candle. The Missal states that the Rite of Ephphetha is omitted for the infants.

The explanatory rites completed, there is a procession back to the sanctuary (unless, of course, these rites have occurred in the sanctuary), in the same order as before, and with the newly baptized carrying their lighted candles. The Missal suggests singing the baptismal canticle *Vidi aquam* during this procession, or some other appropriate song.

Finally, the Missal notes that once the procession has returned to the sanctuary, the adults are to immediately receive the Sacrament of Confirmation according to the proper ritual book. (Priests who baptize an adult or a child over the age of discretion have by law the faculty to confirm, and should do so.)

After the Rites of Baptism and of Confirmation are complete, or after the blessing of water if there have been no Baptisms, the renewal of baptismal promises for the assembly takes place. All in the assembly hold lighted candles (although it does not make sense for the newly baptized to participate in this, since they have just done so; it can be powerful for them to watch the "veteran" Catholics renew what they themselves just did for the first time). The introduction to the questions, which may be said by the priest using the exact words in the Missal or other similar words, makes reference both to the Paschal Mystery (the very meaning of what we are doing) and the fact that this celebration comes as the fruition of the Lenten observance; the reference to Lent serves to reinforce a sense of the "Ninety Days," so to speak, of Lent-Easter. Two forms of questions for the renunciation of sin are given, and then there are the traditional questions for the profession of faith, followed by a conclusion by the priest. The priest then sprinkles the assembly with the blessed water while an appropriate baptismal song is sung, perhaps the *Vidi aquam*.

A rubric indicates that during the sprinkling the newly baptized are led to their place among the faithful. In practice, the adults may need some time to put themselves together, especially if Baptism was done by immersion. Drying off, changing clothes, and getting ready to rejoin the assembly can take place in another location while the assembly renews their baptismal promises and are sprinkled, with the neophytes rejoining the assembly during or immediately after.

After the sprinkling, the priest returns to the chair and the Universal Prayer is prayed in the usual way; the Creed is omitted. The Missal makes specific mention that the newly baptized participate in the Universal Prayer for the first time; it's a significant moment for them as they exercise this important function of the priestly people of God—that of interceding for the needs of others and of the whole world—and its importance should not be lost on them or on the entire assembly.

Fourth Part: The Liturgy of the Eucharist

After the Universal Prayer, the Mass continues as usual with the beginning of the Liturgy of the Eucharist. The Missal makes specific mention of the desirability of having the bread and wine brought forward by the newly baptized adults and/or by the parents or godparents of newly baptized children. Thus is their participation in the offering of the sacrifice for the very first time duly highlighted. Needless to say, high priority should also be given to bringing forward and consecrating all the bread that will be needed for Holy Communion; it is fitting, given the newness of life that is central to this celebration, that any consecrated bread remaining from Good Friday has perhaps been consumed, or at least is not used for this Paschal celebration.

The Prayer over the Offerings makes yet another explicit reference to the "paschal mysteries," asking that the Lord accept our prayers along with these sacrificial offerings so that we might be brought "to the healing of eternity" through those mysteries.

Preface I of Easter is the Preface prescribed for this Mass, and the phrase "on this night" is used. The Preface succinctly announces the Paschal Mystery: "by dying he has destroyed our death, and by rising, restored our life."

There are special inserts that are to be used in the Eucharistic Prayer; be careful, as these can be tricky because the inserts are found in the Ritual Masses section toward the back of the Missal, under "I. For the Conferral of the Sacraments of Initiation; 3. For the Conferral of Baptism." Eucharistic Prayer IV would be excluded from use this night, because of its proper Preface, but Prayers I or III would be good choices (II would perhaps not be appropriate to the solemnity of the occasion, due to its brevity, although there is nothing to absolutely forbid it). Eucharistic Prayer I, the Roman Canon, has these three special inserts and proper forms: at the *Memento Domine* ("Remember, Lord, your servants"), found in the Ritual Masses section; a proper form of the *Communicantes*, used from the Mass of the Easter Vigil until the Second Sunday of Easter, and found right within the text of the Prayer; and a proper form of the *Hanc igitur* ("Therefore, Lord, we pray") with two variations: one variation is found right within the text of the prayer itself, used from the Mass of the Easter Vigil until the Second Sunday of Easter, and a second variation is found in the Ritual Masses section, with this second variation perhaps being a better choice for use this night if Baptisms have occurred. The inserts for Eucharistic Prayers II and

III are found in the Ritual Masses section and are inserted in the places as indicated in the rubrics (there is only one insert for each prayer).

The Missal reminds the priest that before the "Behold the Lamb of God . . ." he may briefly address the newly baptized "about receiving their first Communion and about the excellence of this great mystery, which is the climax of initiation and the center of the whole Christian life." Those words in and of themselves can be the basis for the priest's remarks, and one would think it most beneficial to take advantage of this opportunity to offer extemporaneous remarks to highlight this important moment in the lives of the newly initiated and of the entire community.

The appropriateness of the newly baptized along with their godparents, their Catholic parents, spouses, and the catechists, indeed the entire assembly, all receiving Communion under both kinds is highlighted, and it is hoped that this is a common practice of the parish.

The Communion Antiphon, taken from chapter 5 of 1 Corinthians, refers to Christ as "our Passover" and enjoins us, since he has been sacrificed, to "keep the feast with the unleavened bread of purity and truth." The Prayer after Communion asks God to pour out on us "the Spirit of your love" so that the nourishment of the Eucharist might make us "one in mind and heart." Once again, unity is emphasized as the goal of receiving Holy Communion.

The text for a Solemn Blessing is given and should be used. A rubric indicates that this Solemn Blessing may be replaced by the final blessing formula from the *Rite of Baptism of Adults or of Children*; interestingly, while such a formula is given in the rite for children, there is no such formula in the rite for adults. Use of the formula from the rite for children would make sense if only children were baptized this night; otherwise, stick with the text given in the Missal. Lastly, the dismissal is chanted, by the deacon or by the priest, with the double Alleluia. This solemn dismissal is used throughout the Octave of Easter—that is, also on Easter Sunday, on the weekdays of Easter Week (within the Octave of Easter), and on the Second Sunday of Easter. It is not used, however, on the other weekdays or Sundays of Easter Time, being used again only at Pentecost.

Other Ideas

Don't let the details of this liturgy be distracting. Enter fully the joy and the beauty of the mystery that is being celebrated. Pay attention to the music, the movements, the gestures, the rich language of the Church's symbols, and the faces of all those gathered, especially those of the newly baptized. Let the powerful Scripture readings find a home within you; don't worry about the length of the liturgy, simply enter its rhythm and its grace. If the parish hosts a reception after the liturgy for the newly baptized be sure to attend and make a point of speaking with them; welcome them to the community and tell them how happy you are for them.

(#42, or Gospel #41, or at an afternoon or evening Mass, Gospel #46)   white

☼ 21 Easter Sunday: Solemnity of the Resurrection of the Lord

About Easter Sunday

The celebration of the Resurrection of Jesus Christ continues into Easter Sunday morning. Easter Sunday marks the end of the Triduum and is the first day of the Easter Octave. The celebration of the Triduum concludes after Vespers, and the great fifty days begin. Forty days of fast yield to fifty days of feast.

On Easter Sunday, many of those who were present the night before return, especially the neophytes. In addition, there may be many people attending who have not been to church in a while. Have plenty of hospitality ministers to greet and seat them. Have enough seats and enough worship aids so all can participate. Insert words of welcome and a description of the parish into the worship aid or bulletin. Perhaps you will make them feel so welcome that they will return to church because of you.

It is not surprising that in many parishes some of those baptized at the Easter Vigil, those still "wet behind the ears," wake up on Easter Sunday morning and go to Mass. Their excitement cannot be contained. If this is the case, invite the neophytes to wear the white garment donned at the Easter Vigil to Easter Sunday Mass. Some parishes

celebrate the receptions into full communion and/or the completion of sacramental initiation at a Mass or Masses on Easter Sunday morning. Others schedule these events on Sundays during Easter Time. This laudable practice helps distinguish the baptized from the unbaptized at the Easter Vigil. Without the additional ceremonies, the Vigil is celebrated much more smoothly, and Easter Time, the great fifty days, then takes on the characteristic of being an extended time of initiation. Be sure to include the names of the neophytes in the Universal Prayer (Prayer of the Faithful) at the Sunday Masses on Easter Sunday and throughout Easter Time. If the parish celebrates Easter Evening Prayer, consider inviting the neophytes to that celebration.

The Lectionary for Mass

◆ FIRST READING: On Easter Sunday morning, the First Reading takes us to the home of Cornelius, a devout man who was also a Roman centurion. He has had a vision in which he has been instructed to send for Peter, who also has had a vision that calls into question the Jewish food purity rules about which animals are clean versus unclean. In this passage, we hear Peter recount the story of the life, Death, and Resurrection of Jesus Christ. While all he has accomplished has been witnessed to by the prophets, the redemption of the Risen Christ has been accomplished for all people, including the gentiles. Anyone who believes and bears witness to him will be forgiven.

◆ RESPONSORIAL PSALM 118: More verses of the song of victory, Psalm 118, are heard this morning. God's mercy is not a one-time reality; it endures across the ages. God will protect those who believe, who are rescued through his power. The final verses (22–23), in which the rejected stone is mentioned, are recited by Jesus in reference to himself in the Gospel accounts of Matthew, Mark, and Luke. They also appear in Acts, Ephesians, and 1 Peter. Jesus has not fit the blueprint expected for the rebuilding of God's house.

◆ SECOND READING: Both of these selections for the Second Reading exhort the followers of Jesus Christ to set aside the old self and old life in favor of the new life they have been given in Christ. In the letter to the community in Corinth, Paul utilizes the metaphor of leaven. The image of yeast, a small bit of which can raise a great deal of flour, is one of the predominant images for the role of the laity in the constitutions of Vatican II. Lay people are called, through their faith and holiness, to "work for the sanctification of the world from within as a leaven" (*Lumen gentium*, 31).

◆ SEQUENCE: The Easter sequence is sung today before the Gospel. Carefully select an arrangement that can be easily played so that the sequence leads into the Gospel Acclamation. The cantor should sing the sequence at the ambo. After finishing the text (which may also be congregational) the cantor moves to the cantor stand while instrumental music continues to be played. Once at the cantor stand, the music segues into the Gospel Acclamation. Two themes stand out in the Easter sequence, *Victimae paschali laudes*. The first is God's victory in Christ who redeems and reconciles humanity with God. The second is that of witness as it calls on Mary to proclaim the Resurrection by recounting her experience of the empty tomb. The song ends with the hopeful, joy-filled cry "Have mercy, victor King, ever reigning!" The Easter sequence may be sung each day of the Octave. It is required on Easter Sunday.

◆ GOSPEL: In Luke's account of the Gospel, the Emmaus incident forms a bridge between the enigmatic accounts of the empty tomb and Jesus' appearance in the midst of his disciples. At first we hear of two downhearted disciples retreating from Jerusalem who are unknowingly joined by Jesus. His question about their discussion stopped them in their tracks as they asked how he could not have heard about all that had happened from Jesus' ministry through the women's discovery of the vacant tomb. He then reveals what they could not see. Luke has subtly designed this whole account to mirror the Eucharistic liturgy where the community finds Christ in their midst. It begins with an account of the apparent victory of evil, uses Scripture to reveal God's presence in the signs of the times, and ends with Christ's presence manifested among them in the breaking of the bread.

The Roman Missal

The Gloria is used today, and of course, today is a day for great flourish and solemnity in the selection of musical settings.

The Penitential Act is prayed unless replaced by the rite of sprinkling. However, it is probably best to replace the Creed with the renewal of baptismal promises. The text for it is not given again at the Mass during the Day; the priest will need to refer to the text used at the Easter Vigil. If this is done, the sprinkling that follows does not replace the Penitential Act. The Penitential Act should take place as usual.

The Collect uses the important phrase "on this day." Our participation in the liturgy on this day is our participation in the salvation won for us and made present for us; therefore, it is on this day that God, through his only begotten Son, has "conquered death / and unlocked for us the path to eternity." Therefore, we pray that "we who keep the solemnity of the Lord's Resurrection" may rise to new life through the renewal brought by the Holy Spirit.

In the Prayer over the Offerings, we express that we are offering the sacrifice by which the Church "is wondrously reborn and nourished" filled with "paschal gladness." Preface I of Easter is again, as at the Vigil, the Preface assigned for today. Because of this, use of Eucharistic Prayer IV is again precluded, and perhaps Eucharistic Prayers I or III would be better choices than Eucharistic Prayer II, given the festivity of the day. The only inserts or special forms to worry about are the "In communion with those" and the "Therefore, Lord, we pray" as indicated within the text of Eucharistic Prayer I; there are no other special inserts.

The three-part Solemn Blessing from the Easter Vigil may be used again at this Mass, and the dismissal with the double Alleluia is used, preferably sung.

Other Ideas

This is the day to take seriously the cry of the psalmist: "This is the day the Lord has made; let us rejoice and be glad." Start the day off by participating in the earliest scheduled liturgy, a "sunrise" liturgy if there is one. Plan to enjoy the day with others, engaging in events, visits, and so on, that you might not otherwise do. Enjoy nature; discover the signs of new life in your neighborhood or go further afield. Bring some joy to others, those who are alone or in hospital; gather fresh flowers and give them to a stranger. Listen to uplifting music, like the Hallelujah chorus from Handel's *Messiah*. Invite children to make suggestions about happy things to do and at the end of the day give thanks to God for new life in the whole world.

RECEPTION OF THE HOLY OILS

Introduction

"The reception of the Holy Oils may take place in individual parishes either before the celebration of the Evening Mass of the Lord's Supper or at another time that seems more appropriate." (Roman Missal, Chrism Mass, no. 15)

In 1989, the Holy See confirmed a ritual text for the reception of the holy oils for optional use in the dioceses of the United States, allowing for the reception to take place during the procession of the gifts at the Holy Thursday Mass of the Lord's Supper or on another suitable day. *The Roman Missal*, Third Edition, implemented in 2011, introduces a new rubric at the conclusion of the Chrism Mass. The first option for the reception of the holy oils is before the Mass begins, but according to pastoral necessity and any guidelines of the diocesan Bishop, "another time that seems more appropriate" could also include the offertory procession (as in the original ritual) or perhaps before the Penitential Act.

The original text of the *Reception of the Holy Oils* is still in force as an optional rite in the United States. As indicated in its introduction, the text may be adapted as needed. Whether or not a formal reception of the oils is celebrated, the pastor may wish to acknowledge the presence of the newly received holy oils as a sign of unity with the Bishop and the diocesan Church.

Rubrics

1. It is appropriate that the Oil of the Sick, the Oil of Catechumens, and the holy Chrism, which are blessed by the Bishop during the Chrism Mass, be presented to and received by the local parish community.

2. The reception of the holy oils may take place at the Mass of the Lord's Supper on Holy Thursday or on another day after the celebration of the Chrism Mass.

3. The oils should be reserved in a suitable repository in the sanctuary or near the baptismal font.

4. The oils, in suitable vessels, are carried in the procession of the gifts, before the bread and wine, by members of the assembly.

5. The oils are received by the Priest and are then placed on a suitably prepared table in the sanctuary or in the repository where they will be reserved.

6. As each of the oils is presented, the following or other words may be used to explain the significance of the particular oil.

7. The people's response may be sung.

Reception of the Holy Oils

Presenter of the Oil of the Sick:

The Oil of the Sick.

Priest:

May the sick who are anointed with this oil experience the compassion of Christ and his saving love, in body and soul.

The people may respond:

Blessed be God for ever.

Presenter of the Oil of Catechumens:

The Oil of Catechumens.

Priest:

Through anointing with this oil, may our catechumens who are preparing to receive the saving waters of Baptism be strengthened by Christ to resist the power of Satan and reject evil in all its forms.

The people may respond:

Blessed be God for ever.

Presenter of the Holy Chrism:

The holy Chrism.

Priest:

Through anointing with this perfumed Chrism may children and adults, who are baptized and confirmed, and Priests, who are ordained, experience the gracious gift of the Holy Spirit.

The people may respond:

Blessed be God for ever.

The bread and wine for the Eucharist are then received and the Mass continues in the usual way.

EASTER TIME

The Liturgical Time

The Roman Missal / The Meaning

IN *Universal Norms on the Liturgical Year and the Calendar* we read: "The fifty days from the Sunday of the Resurrection to Pentecost Sunday are celebrated in joy and exultation as one feast day, indeed as one 'great Sunday'" (UNLY, 22). We find the texts for this season in *The Roman Missal* within "The Proper of Time: Easter Time/ Easter Sunday of the Resurrection of the Lord." Texts are provided for each of the eight Sundays of the season, beginning with the vigil Mass for Easter and concluding with Pentecost Sunday.

Each day of Easter week, beginning with Easter Sunday and concluding with the Second Sunday of Easter (or Sunday of Divine Mercy), is a solemnity and calls for the Gloria, Creed, and using Preface I of Easter with its appropriate wording: "on this night/on this day/in this time." Treat each day of the Octave as Easter day. From the Easter Vigil through the Second Sunday of Easter, inclusive, there are two options for the dismissal of the people: "Go forth, the Mass is ended, alleluia, alleluia," or "Go in peace, alleluia, alleluia." Unlike the rubrics in the former Sacramentary, this form of the dismissal is not used again until Pentecost. This change is still not followed by many priests and deacons, who continue to use the double alleluia dismissal every Sunday. Follow the directions in *The Roman Missal*, third edition.

Easter Time invites us to honor Christian initiation by using the blessing and sprinkling of water that the Order of Mass suggests from time to time, "especially in Easter Time" (footnote to the "Penitential Act"). The texts for this are found in "Appendix II: Rite for the Blessings and Sprinkling of Water." If you use fresh water each week, use the blessing as written. If the water blessed at the Vigil is used each week, adapt the text. For example, the beginning of the blessing could read: "Lord our God, / in your mercy be present to your people's prayers, / and, for us who recall the wondrous work of our creation / and the still greater work of our redemption, / accept our thanks for this blessed water. . . ." Since Easter Time is the preeminent season of the liturgical year, make use of all the signs and symbols that can emphasize its importance: sung Alleluias, sprinkling with blessed water, incense, sung presidential prayers, and anything that proclaims Christ is risen! For he is risen, indeed, Alleluia!

Each day of Easter Time has its own texts that are to be used unless a feast day takes precedence: St. Catherine of Siena, Memorial, (April 29); St. Joseph the Worker (May 1) has its own Preface; the feast of Sts. Philip and James (May 3) calls for the Gloria, as does the Feast of St. Matthias (May 14); May 2 gives us St. Athanasius; the Visitation of the Blessed Virgin Mary (May 31) calls for the Gloria; finally, among memorials and feasts during Easter Time is St. Justin, Martyr (June 1).

There are five Prefaces of Easter. Preface I is to be used from the Easter Vigil through the Second Sunday of Easter. Its focus on the Paschal Mystery provides a fitting and succinct summary of what we celebrate during this week and this season. Preface I reminds us about the proper *Communicantes* ("In communion with those") and *Hanc igitur* ("Therefore, Lord, we pray") in the Roman Canon, that are prayed when it is used. Preface II talks about how we, the children of light, "rise to eternal life / . . . / for his Death is our ransom from death, / and in his rising the life of all has risen." Preface III talks about Christ the sacrificial Victim and Lamb, who lives forever and pleads our cause. Preface IV highlights the restoration of the universe through Christ's Death and Resurrection. Preface V emphasizes Christ as

"Priest, the Altar, and the Lamb of sacrifice." It is most fitting in the final weeks of Easter Time, that focus on the promised coming of the Holy Spirit through the intercession of the Lamb and Priest, Jesus Christ. Either Preface I and II of the Ascension can be used on the Ascension, itself, and are options, along with the other Easter Prefaces, for the days between the Ascension and Pentecost "in all Masses that have no proper Preface" (Order of Mass, 50). The texts for the Ascension are found within the texts for the Sixth Week of Easter. Whether your province of the Church celebrates the Ascension on Thursday during the Sixth Week, that is, forty days after Easter, or on the Seventh Sunday of Easter, use the texts given during the Sixth Week of Easter. The directions about which texts to use are clear. You will find Solemn Blessings for Easter Time, the Ascension of the Lord, and the Holy Spirit in "The Order of Mass: Blessings at the End of Mass."

Easter Time concludes with the Solemnity of Pentecost (June 9). Texts are provided for celebrating the Vigil Mass in an extended form, which parallels the structure of the Easter Vigil. You will also find a "Simple Form." Either form may be celebrated "either before or after First Vespers (Evening Prayer I) of Pentecost Sunday." There are texts for use "At the Mass during the Day." The Pentecost Preface is found within the texts for Sunday. There is a proper form of the *Communicantes* ("In Communion with") for the Roman Canon. The Gloria and Creed are prayed. The Missal directs that, "With Easter Time now concluded, the paschal candle is extinguished. It is desirable to keep the paschal candle in the baptistery with due honor so that it is lit at the celebration of Baptism and the candles of those baptized are lit from it." The Easter Vigil, rubric 17, directs that the Paschal candle be given a place of honor near the ambo or in the middle of the sanctuary. Now it is extinguished and moved. Some communities choose to process with it at the end of Mass (or Evening Prayer if that is prayed as a parish). The Collect for Saturday of the Seventh Week of Easter, at the morning Mass, gives us our marching order for the season: "Grant, we pray, almighty God, / that we who have celebrated the paschal festivities, / may by your gift hold fast to them / in the way that we live our lives." Amen!

The Lectionary for Mass

WE HEAR FROM ACTS of the Apostles as the First Reading throughout Easter Time. Acts is the sequel to the Gospel according to Luke, and in it the evangelist shows how the life, Death, and Resurrection of Jesus Christ gradually reached beyond Jerusalem and environs to touch the whole of the known world. The precious message is carried in earthen vessels—in Peter, the rock who keeps changing his mind; in Paul, the persecutor of the Church who becomes her greatest preacher; and in countless others, named and unnamed, saints and sinners, all of them flawed and all of them chosen. In some places the word spreads like wildfire; in others it seems to drop like a stone. Little by little, the Church grows. The Acts of the Apostles is filled with Luke's absolute faith in the message of Jesus. Although Luke's account ends with Paul's arrest in Rome, awaiting trial, it ends in joy: for the Good News is reaching both Jews and Gentiles; nothing can stop the spread of the Gospel.

◆ RESPONSORIAL PSALMS: An optional communal response to every psalm of this season is "Alleluia," which could also summarize the message and mood of these psalms. The psalms are all hymns of thanksgiving and praise. God's promise has been fulfilled over and over again in the Old Testament, and the ultimate fulfillment of God's promise is found in Christ. On the last Sundays of Easter Time, the psalms also proclaim the kingship of the Lord, enthroned in heaven.

◆ SECOND READINGS: The Second Readings for Easter Time are taken from the Book of Revelation, which can be difficult to understand because of its complex symbolism. When reading and listening to these readings, however, it is good to remember that the main message of the Book of Revelation is that Jesus Christ is Lord! Christ has triumphed over all that could cause us to be separated from God. During Easter Time, the readings from Revelation present a portrait of the Risen Christ and are inspired by that vision.

◆ GOSPEL READINGS: The Gospel readings for Easter Time are all taken from the Gospel according to John, except for the Ascension, which is taken from Luke's account. During Easter Time, the Gospel readings follow a similar pattern for all three years of the Lectionary cycle of readings.

On Easter Sunday, we find the empty tomb; on the Second Sunday, we encounter doubting Thomas; and on the Fourth Sunday, we hear about the Good Shepherd. On the Third Sunday, Jesus feeds the disciples at the sea of Tiberias. On the Fifth, Sixth, and Seventh Sundays, we hear excerpts from Jesus' final discourse at the Last Supper. In dioceses that celebrate the Ascension on the Seventh Sunday of Easter, the readings are taken from the Solemnity of the Ascension and describe Jesus being taken up into heaven. These narratives include various instructions and commission for the disciples, for which they will be empowered by the coming of the Spirit at Pentecost.

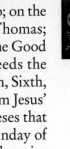

Children's Liturgy of the Word

ON EASTER SUNDAY, families should stay together for celebration of Mass. Additionally, the logistics of larger than usual numbers of children could create space issues in having children's Liturgy of the Word. However, if you can make it happen, inviting children to this experience may evangelize visiting families. The dismissal should be prefaced by a good explanation of what the children are going to do and an invitation to newcomers to try it.

The prayer environment for Easter Time should be well-lit with extra candles, flowers, white fabric and a large bowl of water, perhaps even banners with images of Easter joy, or a depiction of an empty tomb. A lively sung seasonal psalm, such as Psalm 118, is desirable. A joyful, but simple sung "Alleluia" should precede the Gospel.

If you have children's Liturgy of the Word on Easter Sunday, the important image is the empty tomb. A key theme for reflection is how to be witnesses for Jesus, even if you cannot see him.

Other themes of note during Easter Time: These Sundays show us the active community of early Christians. How are we acting for Christ today? What are we doing for him?

The Sundays in May present us with special appearances by Jesus in the Gospel accounts. On the third Sunday he eats with the disciples on the beach. On the fourth Sunday he introduces himself as the Good Shepherd. On the fifth Sunday he tells them he will soon be leaving. On the sixth

Sunday he reveals he will be going to the Father and promises to send the Holy Spirit.

If you are in a diocese that transfers the Ascension of the Lord to Sunday, your readings will be those for the Ascension of the Lord and not the Seventh Sunday of Easter. (If you don't know, check with your pastoral staff.) The First Reading shows us Jesus being assumed, body and spirit, into heaven to sit at the right hand of the Father. The disciples are left staring at the sky in wonder after he leaves, unsure what to do next. Help children understand that Jesus is now alive in heaven with his Father, and that he promised to send the Holy Spirit so we would not miss him so much.

If your parish celebrates Ascension on the Thursday before the seventh Sunday, you will use the readings for the Seventh Sunday, which begins with the witness and martyrdom of Stephen. The phrase Luke uses is "he fell asleep." With very young children, best to leave it at that. In the Gospel, Jesus prays for his disciples, that they may all be one. This is a great opportunity to present the idea of Christian unity.

Pentecost is on June 9. We have come to the end of our Easter journey. Replace the white cloths with red and invite the Holy Spirit in as we read about the descent of the Spirit upon the Apostles and the reappearance of Jesus, breathing the Spirit into them. Images of fire or doves could be added to the environment. Help children understand that the Spirit was sent to be their helper from God.

we begin Easter Time, gives ancient voice to our belief: this pilgrim Church is carried forward by the Church triumphant as well as by the Church here on earth.

The season begins with St. Catherine of Siena, Doctor of the Church, peacemaker and vigorous challenger and champion of the Church. Her memorial is followed by that of St. Athanasius, Bishop of Alexandria (called "Doctor of the Incarnation") who was a defender of the First Council of Nicaea, the first formal attempt of the Church to take stock of its members and articulate its teachings and its creed.

The Church in its infancy can be studied in the stories of the Apostles Philip, James, and Matthias, all celebrated during this season. All three were witnesses to Jesus' ministry and Resurrection, Sts. Philip and James as his early companions, while St. Matthias, was the Apostle selected to replace Judas. As with so many men and women of the early Church, all three were martyred. St. Justin, whose memorial comes later in the season, was another martyr whose earnest attempt to explain to his persecutors the practices of the Christian gathering gave us one of our earliest descriptions of the Mass.

Easter Time draws to a close with Pentecost Sunday. The lit Paschal candle can and should figure prominently in the Masses of Pentecost as Easter draws to a close—perhaps in a procession at the end of each Mass.

The Saints

Easter Time is about growth. The growth of the new Church that followed the Resurrection is recounted in the Scripture readings for this time; our neophytes grow in faith through the process of mystagogia that begins now; our own parishes and communities undergo physical and spiritual growth as we welcome the newly-baptized members around the eucharistic table. The saints of this season play an important part during these months of renewal. Those newly-baptized and confirmed may be forming an understanding of the role of the saints in their own lives, as they learn about the role these holy women and men played in the ongoing life of the Church. The litany of the Easter Vigil, so fresh in our memory as

The Liturgy of the Hours

An INTENTIONAL gathering of the parish for Morning or Evening Prayer during the Octave of Easter could continue the celebration and punctuate the season. Sometimes during the eight days after Easter there are several funerals that must be celebrated, since a funeral Mass is not allowed during the Triduum. If a funeral Mass occurs during the Octave of Easter, contact various parish groups via e-mail or the website and social media page, and ask them to gather for Evening Prayer on that day, remembering especially the deceased and the family of the deceased in the intercessions. What prayerful support for a grieving family, to know that the parish has gathered in their honor to pray Evening prayer in this holy season. Often, if a funeral Mass occurs midmorning, the family of the deceased has said goodbye to the mourners by dinner time. They may even return for intentional prayer, to fill the evening with praise and thanksgiving for redemption and the promise of salvation.

Remember to light the Paschal candle when you pray Morning or Evening Prayer, and bless yourself with holy water if you celebrate near the font. Invite all those who have meeting during the Easter season to begin in the church with Evening Prayer. Provide prayer cards or worship aids and simple instructions so that each group can "lead themselves" through this prayer. Recall that the whole community, not just the ordained, takes on the responsibility of bringing souls to Christ, and the season of Easter is a particular reminder with the presence of the neophytes. The Alleluia concludes most of the antiphons in the Hours during the Easter season, a joyful reminder that Christ has risen indeed.

The Solemnity of the Ascension, whether celebrated on Thursday, May 30, or transferred to the Seventh Sunday of Easter on June 2, is a special opportunity for Evening Prayer in the parish. Connect Evening Prayer with the continuing Paschal joy of the season, and engage the best musical leadership and accompaniment in the parish. Christ Jesus is alive among us, and present in this assembly. The alternative prayer in *Christian Prayer* sets the tone and reinforces the theology of the Ascension:

"Father in heaven, our minds were prepared for the coming of your kingdom, when you took Christ beyond our sight so that we might seek him in his glory. May we follow where he has led and find our hope in his glory, for he is Lord for ever."

The Office of Readings (celebrated as the first Hour of the day) for the Easter season includes additional selections that are precious gems of teaching and preaching, from the Fathers of the Church. These jewels for the Hours are often overlooked because they are "additional." Perhaps adding a homily could draw attention to these readings, as well as a parish mandate to select one of these readings to begin each meeting during the season of Easter.

The Rite of Christian Initiation of Adults

WHAT COULD BE more wonderful than fifty days of rejoicing? The Octave of Easter intends that we raise the double-Alleluia acclamation, sing *Victimae Paschali Laudes,* and thereby extend the Great Feast for a week. The neophytes are basking in the glow of the Easter Vigil, and returning each Sunday (many wear their white garments) to sit in a special place, receive Holy Communion, and worship with an understanding of what it means to become Catholic. The Paschal candle flickers intentionally near the ambo, and the period of postbaptismal catechesis ensues. Mystagogy insists: What happened to the newly baptized during the Easter Vigil? What is changed, since the Vigil? What did we smell, taste, feel, experience? All of these questions need intense, personal responses from the neophytes, guided into postbaptismal catechesis by those who have gifts for mystagogy. Each team should identify their mystagogues who help the neophytes see and feel the experience and implications of the Vigil.

Rather than inviting the newly baptized to participate in a ministry of the parish (they may have been participating in some way prior to this), it is more important to help them enter into discovery regarding "where is God in all of this?" just as the disciples asked after the Resurrection, recognizing Jesus finally when he appeared and showed them his hands and his side. What signs and wonders did the neophytes experience at the Vigil? Are they fearful of moving forward on the journey of faith, or can the mystagogue help them take the next step in discipleship? Breaking open the Word is more important than ever, as the parish continues to congratulate the neophytes, and as the parish staff keeps the season holy and festive—in homily, in environment, and in proclamation of the Word of God. To connect with the parish community on Sundays of the Easter season, the homilist must find ways to help the congregation recognize and celebrate the presence of the Risen Christ.

Invite the neophytes to one of the Masses of the Easter season at which the celebration of Reception into Full Communion takes place. Since those entering into full communion have already received the Sacrament of Penance, they begin their journey of faith in joyful renewal. There's something energizing and inspiring about being in right relationship with God. Remember that all postbaptismal catechesis should focus on the experience of receiving the Easter sacraments, rather than doctrine. The RCIA team focuses in a pastoral way during the Easter season: some engaged in mystagogy, some guiding those entering into full communion, some perhaps celebrating convalidations with couples, and others starting to focus once again on inquiry. How wondrous that the RCIA team can experience its own diaspora during this glorious season: evangelizing and being evangelized all over again by the expressions of faith around them.

Sacraments of Initiation

EASTER TIME IS, of course, the preferred time to celebrate sacraments of initiation. In many parishes this season is the time when First Communions are celebrated, as many still follow the school year model. A Sunday parish liturgy is the best time for the children of the parish to receive since the presence of the parish community emphasizes that this is a parish event, and that the Sunday gathering to celebrate the Eucharist is central to parish life. However, due to a variety of reasons, such as large numbers of children receiving or few Sunday Masses, many parishes may choose to celebrate on a Saturday. If there is a parish school, separate ceremonies, one for the faith formation children and another for the school children, should be avoided. A child should always receive their First Communion at Mass; unless an extreme situation, First Communion should not be given at a Sunday Celebration in the Absence of a Priest.

The beauty of celebrating First Communion during Easter is its connection to the Easter sacraments. The Church considers Eucharist the completion of initiation, but unless a diocese celebrates the restored order of initiation, most children will receive Communion first and then Confirmation at an older age. If a diocese does celebrate the restored order, Confirmation may be celebrated outside of Mass, since the children have not yet received Communion, or both sacraments could be celebrated at the same liturgy with the bishop.

May is a wonderful time to gather all the first communicants who have received during the year at a Sunday Mass to participate in a May crowning. Invite the children to wear their communion outfits and process with flowers to a statue of Our Lady, concluding with a crowning of the statue. This is a great witness to the parish as they all come together to honor the Mother of God.

Easter Time is also a popular time to celebrate Confirmation, but take care not to give the impression that this celebration is a "graduation" from faith formation. The newly confirmed should be encouraged to continue their faith formation and to join parish youth groups. If there are adult baptized Catholics who have not yet received Confirmation, the extended Vigil of Pentecost is a perfect time for them to receive this sacrament and complete their initiation.

Of course Baptism is a sacrament that is so closely related to Easter that this is a wonderful time to celebrate it, especially at a Sunday Mass. The sprinkling rite, which is not exclusive to Easter, reminds the assembly of their own Baptism and, when done in conjunction with an infant Baptism, reinforces the importance of the sacrament. If possible, use water that was blessed at the Easter Vigil for baptisms during this season. If water blessed at the Vigil is used during Eastertide, the blessing of the water used for Baptism is omitted from the rite.

The Rite of Penance

DURING HIS PONTIFICATE, Pope John Paul II designated the Second Sunday of Easter as the Sunday of Divine Mercy. Those parishes that advocate devotion to the Divine Mercy often schedule prayer services on this Sunday. The devotion includes the opportunity for individual confession which may require that additional confessors be available. The devotion is not part of the Sunday Eucharistic liturgy.

A common practice in many parishes during the weeks of Easter Time is the preparation of children for their First Communion. Part of their preparation may be the celebration of their first Reconciliation. Both celebrations should be a parish event. Parents who are the first teachers of their children in the way of faith should certainly be involved and the whole parish should be invited to participate as well.

Going to confession for the first time can be a daunting experience for a young child. (Author's note: There is much discussion around the issue of the appropriate age when a child can actually appreciate the purpose and meaning of confession.) However, a couple of practices can help the young person in this regard. First, the example of parents and catechists going to confession at the same celebration is a teaching moment. Another practice is for one or both parents to accompany their son or daughter to greet the confessor and to introduce them to the priest. This simple gesture recalls the moment in the *Rite of Baptism* when parents first "introduced" their child to the Church when they responded to the question: "What name do you give your child?"

Two other groups in the parish that might be celebrating the Sacrament of Reconciliation during these Easter weeks are the newly baptized and those students preparing for Confirmation. Even with a small number of neophytes, a communal celebration of the sacrament should be scheduled. Their sponsors, catechists, neophytes from previous years, and members of the parish could make up the assembly. This offers a visible reminder to the newly baptized that they truly belong to a community of faith and that they are not alone on their journey of faith.

A similar communal celebration of Reconciliation should be scheduled for those preparing for Confirmation. As with the celebration for first Reconciliation, the example of parents and catechists should be obvious. The students can be included in the liturgical ministries for this celebration, acting as readers, greeters, members of a choir, and might even be called on to offer a brief reflection on their understanding of the Sacrament of Confirmation.

The Order of Celebrating Matrimony

THE NUPTIAL BLESSING is the formal blessing given to the newly married couple after the Lord's Prayer during the Celebration of Matrimony within Mass, or at the conclusion of the Universal Prayer at the Celebration of Matrimony without Mass. This ancient blessing is never omitted.

If the optional ritual for the Blessing and Placing of the Lazo or the Veil is chosen, it is done before the Nuptial Blessing. The veil may be placed over the shoulders of the newly married couples by two family members or friends. This option, as well as the option of the Blessing and Giving of the Arras, earlier in the ritual, reflects a cultural adaptation popular among many Filipino and Latino families.

During the Nuptial Blessing, the bride and bridegroom either approach the altar or remain at their place and kneel. Then the priest, with hands extended over them, invokes God's blessing on them and asks that they be strengthened to remain faithful to the Marriage covenant they have just entered into. The focus is not so much on what the couple has done but rather on what God has done in consecrating the bond of Marriage, joining the husband and wife together and sending the Holy Spirit to strengthen them. The blessing also asks that the couple be blessed with children and be given strength to be good parents, although that section could be omitted if the couple is older. As is typical for formal liturgical prayers and blessings and with a nod to our focus on the second coming, the Nuptial Blessing ends with the exhortation that the couple attain the fullness of Christian life in the Kingdom of Heaven. There is a reference to the Sacrament of the Eucharist that could be omitted if either the bride or the groom will not be receiving Holy Communion. In the Order of Celebrating Matrimony without Mass, the Nuptial Blessing is given by the priest or deacon. It is even given in mixed marriages when either the bride or the bridegroom is not baptized, but with some alteration of the words. It could also be omitted and replaced with another prayer when one of the parties is unbaptized or is a catechumen. If the priest or deacon can sing well, it would be appropriate for them to chant the Nuptial Blessing with the musical notation provided in the Ritual.

Before the reforms of the Second Vatican Council, the Nuptial Blessing focused primarily on the bride. The origins of this, dating back to the early days of the Roman Empire, lie in the acknowledgment of the change in the bride's legal status. Our contemporary understanding of the mutuality and equality of both parties necessitated the change in the focus from the bride alone to both the bride and the groom.

The Pastoral Care of the Sick

As THE CHURCH CELEBRATES the joy and wonder of both spring and the Resurrection of the Lord, parish ministers can consider ways for those who are sick or living in long care residences to participate in that same joy and sense of new life.

As the parish celebrates sacramental events such as First Communion and Confirmation, invite those who are unable to join in the parish celebrations to keep the young people in prayer. Pastoral visitors could prepare cards to be signed by the people they visit and then present them to the newly confirmed and the first communicants. Consider assigning a Confirmation candidate to each pastoral care visitor to accompany them on one of their visits to a nursing home or other care residence as a way to introduce them to the work of being a disciple of the Lord.

If the parish has not hosted a communal celebration of the Anointing of the Sick in some time, then Easter Time is a good time to do so. In those areas where winter weather might have prevented such a celebration, the spring offers a better option. Many of the Scripture readings in the Lectionary for Easter offer good sources for homilies and intercessions for this celebration. Consider having a festive reception for all those who participate. This would give the other members of the parish an opportunity to meet and greet those who usually are unable to be at church.

This is a good time for pastoral care ministers to gather for their own renewal and reflection on their ministry. Sharing stories, keeping in mind the need for confidentiality, is a good way to encourage each other and to celebrate the gift of their respective ministry.

The Order of Christian Funerals

IT COULD BE SAID that the *Order of Christian Funerals* finds its liturgical home during Easter Time. The proclamation of Jesus Christ "who was handed over for our transgressions and was raised for our justification" (Romans 4:25) is at the center of the Church's life.

As the Church celebrates the power and grace of the Resurrection of Jesus Christ, especially in the Easter season, the liturgy of a Christian funeral is informed by the many references to the new life in Lord that permeates the readings and prayers of this season. Many of the Scripture passages in the *Order of Christian Funerals* have references to Baptism through which every believer enters into the life, Death, and Resurrection of the Lord. The Gospel texts speak of Jesus' promise that those who are faithful to his teaching will enjoy eternal life with the Father. The parable of the grain of wheat that dies in order to yield a rich harvest provides an appropriate reference for a funeral homily. The Gospel texts that recall Jesus' intervention in the lives those who mourn, such as the widow of Nain when her son has died and Mary and Martha when their brother Lazarus dies, can be integrated into homilies that present the redeeming love of God for those who are grieving the death of a loved one. In fact many of the readings for the weekday and Sunday Lectionary in the Easter season are included in the list of suggested texts for the funeral liturgy.

The Roman Missal includes a special Collect for the funeral Mass during the Easter season and the wording of the five Prefaces for Masses for the Dead places a clear emphasis on the theology of death and Resurrection.

The liturgical symbols of Easter, such as the baptismal water, the Paschal candle, and the Alleluia have obvious references for the funeral liturgy; their meaning in the life of the Christian can easily be incorporated into a homily. The opening rites of the funeral liturgy take place at the entrance to the church and in many churches the baptismal font is located in that area. The water for sprinkling the casket should be taken directly from the font. The placing of the pall recalls the baptismal garment and often family members are invited to arrange it on the casket. These symbols are powerful expressions of the Church's theology of death and resurrection that is rooted in St. Paul's letter to the Romans: "we were indeed buried with him through baptism into death, so that, just as Christ was raised from the dead by the glory of the Father, we too might live in newness of life" (Romans 6:4).

The Paschal candle remains at the ambo during this time and stands as a reminder of the glorious light into which we are called through our sharing in the Resurrection Christ our Light!

The Book of Blessings

EASTER TIME is spring time; the time of new birth in the Church and in the fields and hopefully in our hearts. The newly baptized are called neophytes—a term which means the "newly planted," a beautiful phrase that connects the spiritual life of the community and the potential life that will spring forth from the earth. The *Book of Blessings* gives a number of seasonal blessings for this wonderful time of new birth. Chapter 26 offers an Order of Blessing of Fields and Flocks. Chapter 27 offers the Order of Blessing of Seeds at Planting Time. Every time we invoke a blessing we also express thanksgiving. As these rites seek a blessing on the seeds to be planted in the fields and for the fruitfulness of the flocks, they express thanksgiving to God the creator for the land and its fertility and creatures.

In his public ministry Jesus used many references to the land and the harvest when he was teaching about the Word of God and the work of the Kingdom. The Scripture texts for these blessings are rich with imagery that resonates with the task of farmers and gardeners as they prepare for another year of planting, cultivation, and harvest.

One other blessing that can be used during Easter Time is the Blessing of Mothers on Mother's Day. The second Sunday of May is designated as Mother's Day and an order of blessing is found in Chapter 55. Its counterpart, the Order of Blessing of Fathers on Father's Day is found in Chapter 56. Father's Day is on the Third Sunday of June and falls in Ordinary Time.

The Liturgical Environment

SOMETIMES I WALK into churches during Easter Time and wonder if they used a confetti cannon to shoot Easter lilies into every inch of the sanctuary. The fifty glorious days of Easter are celebrated with joy and enthusiasm, but also with noble beauty. Rather than using your entire budget for Easter Sunday, craft a plan for unfolding the season. Like Christmas, Easter Masses will be crowded. Allow room in the nave and sanctuary for the extraordinary crowds to circulate. Greet parishioners and guests with lilies, blooming bulb flowers and splendid floral arrangements in the sanctuary as well as in spaces where overflow seating is arranged. While placing live plants in a cry room may be problematic, draping a wall with fabric or just suspending ribbon streamers from circulation vents brings these families more fully into the season. During the Octave, relocating the dispersed plants and flowers to the church proper will create a sense of continued newness for Divine Mercy Sunday.

The Paschal candle has an elevated position near the ambo throughout the season. White and gold ribbon woven through or around its base accents its symbolism. A sheer white fabric suspended over the assembly, from pillar to pillar, or simply draped behind the crucifix draws eyes upward. Silver or gold accents in ribbon, pot covers or fabrics pooled under groupings of plants contributes to the image of Resurrection. If your church has high ceilings, consider lining your outer aisles with portable stands supporting ribbon banners, using white, gold, and silver ribbons of varying widths and lengths.

As the lilies and tulips fade, replace them with baskets filled with potted ivy and potted flowers. Colorful calla lilies, azaleas, or begonias in pots will thrive for an extended time. Planning helps stretch your budget to bring in fresh floral arrangements when the others fade. Designate a garden on the parish property for planting the bulbs and lilies, or offer them to parishioners for their own gardens.

Easter Time is filled with special occasions: Baptisms, weddings, First Communions, and graduations abound during the season. As you plan for the season, take these into consideration. Timing refreshed flowers to coincide with special events will be appreciated by those involved. For parishes using the sprinkling rite throughout the season, create an aspergillum by wiring a bundle of boxwood or other greenery together and wrapping the stems with white and gold ribbon. The effect is aesthetically pleasing and symbolically robust as the greenery provides a more generous sprinkling than the traditional tool.

Dismantling the Easter environment to make way for Pentecost steps the environment down a bit as white and gold give way to the red of the Holy Spirit. Attach small bells to wire and suspend them in trees near church entrances to broadcast the solemnity. Display banners depicting symbols of the Spirit. Remove all of the Easter flowers, replacing them with ones testifying to our diverse Church led by the one Spirit: small quantities of anthurium, birds of paradise, bromeliad, crotons, and orchids create interest with their flame-colored blooms. While some of their blooms are short-lived, so is Pentecost, and their greenery can easily be integrated into Spring Ordinary Time.

The Liturgical Music

PASTORAL MUSICIANS should relish the eight weeks of Easter, because, in all actuality, each week is but one celebration. It is laudable that the sprinkling rite be utilized each week at each liturgy and that the same settings of the Gloria, Alleluia, and Eucharistic Prayer acclamations be retained. Utilize the rich hymn texts of Easter and employ the use of "Alleluia" throughout the entire season. It is important that we do everything we can to convey our Easter joy! Easter Time officially ends on Pentecost Sunday. As part of Easter Time, it is appropriate to utilize the same ritual music. Pentecost Sunday, like Easter Sunday, calls for the beautiful and powerful "golden sequence" or *Veni, Sancte Spiritus* to be heard after the Second Reading. In addition to the chant, other settings are available and range from strophic settings to choral settings to contemporary settings. It is interesting to note that the solemn dismissal with double Alleluia is used today, just like on Easter Sunday and throughout the Octave of Easter.

The Liturgical Ministers

THE FIRST READING for the Sundays of Easter Time is taken from the Acts of the Apostles. These readings recount the life of the early Church and how the fledgling community of believers took up the challenges of discipleship. This is a good time to draw attention to the ministry of the assembly. We expend good energy and resources to make sure that the various liturgical ministers like readers, greeters, servers, and so on are well formed and prepared for their ministry. But we sometimes overlook the primary ministry of every liturgy, that of the assembly, the congregation. It is their ministry that complements and completes all the other ministries. It is their participation that enlivens the liturgy and affirms their baptismal priesthood. Homilists might use these Sundays to catechize about the role of the assembly at liturgy. Bulletin inserts could reference various actions and gestures that the assembly does to participate actively and fully. The music ministry could spend a couple of minutes at each liturgy teaching new Mass settings and encouraging the assembly to enrich their experience of praying the liturgy by singing with full hearts and voices!

Other Prayers, Rites, and Devotions

EASTER TIME unfolds in the framework of fifty days of rejoicing and prayerful abundance: in sequence, in Scripture (Acts of the Apostles and Year C, the Gospel according to John with the exception of the Ascension), and in the worship space itself ("resurrection" draping of the main cross, abundant floral, the most joyful musical settings for Mass). *Catholic Household Blessings & Prayers* provides for a blessing of families during Easter Time, and interestingly, Regina Coeli replaces the Angelus at noontime, from Holy Saturday until Pentecost. Publish the Regina Coeli for the parish, and encourage catechists to share the beauty of these two prayers to the children in religious education. Learning these prayers for Catholic school students will open up another avenue for their own popular piety.

The Second Sunday of Easter is known as Divine Mercy Sunday (Pope St. John Paul II made this surprise announcement on April 30, 2000, at the canonization of St. Faustina) and carries with it a novena and the Chaplet of Divine Mercy. "Have mercy on us and on the whole world," is the Divine Mercy mantra, as the chaplet is prayed on rosary beads.

During Easter Time, the sprinkling rite may replace the Penitential Act at all Masses. With its rich baptismal symbolism, this sacramental act of sprinkling water on the congregation encompasses all generations in every parish. Some churches provide a small, bottled sample of the newly blessed baptismal water for people to use at home. And the month of May makes us mindful of the Blessed Mother, in many devotions that the Church encourages.

The *Directory on Popular Piety and the Liturgy* focuses strongly on devotions to Mary, and urges that these devotions harmonize with the season. It might be of interest to many that "prayerfully hearing the Word of God" can be a devotion to Mary, the Mother of God, who heard the Word of God in her heart. Throughout May, until around Pentecost, many parishes will hold a "May Crowning" with music and devotional prayer. The Order of Crowning an Image of the Blessed Virgin Mary was created by the United States bishops to guide the action and text of devotional prayer within Mass, within a celebration of Liturgy of the Word, and also in the context of Evening Prayer. Add appropriate music and the rite speaks for itself.

Evangelization

THE ROAD TO EMMAUS is a profound example for thinking about telling our stories through digital media. An interesting possibility for storytelling in our time is the use of blogs. Blogs are essentially online journaling platforms, which have been adapted for many different uses. Most compelling among these are blogs that tell a story or document a particular journey that the author is on: weight loss, persevering through illness, having a new baby, or taking a trip and narrating progress along the way. Such storytelling blogs are compelling because we enter into the journey with the author, draw hope from their successes, draw

inspiration from their perseverance, and can even become part of the journey with them through offering comments and support along the way. We can readily build on this dynamic for creating blogs that tell our stories of faith.

Sharing our faith journey through a blog can be like a digital Emmaus experience, where we walk with one another, share our story, and through mutual support and presence find our hearts more hopeful and enkindled along the way. To commit to blogging can be an especially beautiful experience if it is offered this way in the spirit of the Easter season.

Blogging can be difficult to start up because it can take a while for an authentic sense of community to gather around the story told. For this reason, it is important to think intentionally about who the audience might be and to reach out to them with an invitation to walk with our story. It is also important to think about the story itself—is it truly a journey that invites readers along? Does it offer joy, hope, and encouragement? Is it genuine and authentic in its tone? Does it invite the voice and participation of others? These elements can help gather community more readily along the digital road of the blog.

The journey of faith is lifelong, complex, and can be deeply personal at times. To choose to blog about it is a big decision that calls for reflection about the ways we can offer to others our gift of self through the sharing of our stories. At the same time, we are called by the Risen Lord to go and proclaim his Good News, and this often resonates most compellingly with people when it comes from our own authentic witness of life. The blog can be a place to offer our witness of the Risen Lord and invite others along the way to him.

The Parish and the Home

THE FIFTY DAYS of Easter Time are sometimes sadly neglected in parishes while there is a flurry of seemingly separate activity. Be sure to tie the celebrations of first sacraments to Easter Time. These are golden opportunities to express Easter joy as a parish, so try not to compartmentalize them from the rest of the parish. Ideally, Baptisms and First Communion are celebrated on weekends amidst the community that ordinarily gathers around the Eucharistic table. Separate celebrations confuse families into thinking these are about them and their child, instead of the community. Encourage families of those being baptized or receiving First Communion or Confirmation to see themselves as part of the parish community as much as is possible. With larger numbers, logistics may be difficult, but there should always be some connection to the weekend assembly.

This is also a time for parish dances, picnics, festivals, and other social celebrations. Sustaining Easter Time for fifty days after school is out for summer, when many families prioritize weekend sports over attending Mass, requires conscious effort and preparation. This is a time to help people find that being part of their Catholic community is a true source of joy and engagement. It is not time for parish staff to give people tacit permission to be elsewhere, so creativity is a must!

Because Pentecost is on June 9—a full month after most parish faith formation programs shut down for summer—invite families to a Pentecost gathering and parish picnic before they leave for the summer and remind them as it comes close. They are expected by the Holy Spirit, who will send them forth that day to live as missionary disciples—"fishers of men"—not just people who sun themselves on the beach!

Reflections through the Year

At the end, we will find ourselves face to face with the infinite beauty of God (cf. 1 Corinthians 13:12), and be able to read with admiration and happiness the mystery of the universe, which with us will share in unending plenitude. Even now we are journeying towards the sabbath of eternity, the new Jerusalem, towards our common home in heaven. Jesus says: "I make all things new" (Revelation 21:5). Eternal life will be a shared experience of awe, in which each creature, resplendently transfigured, will take its rightful place and have something to give those poor men and women who will have been liberated once and for hope. (LS, 244)

In the meantime, we come together to take charge of this home which has been entrusted to us, knowing that all the good which exists here will be taken up into the heavenly feast. In union with all creatures, we journey through this land seeking God, for "if the world has a beginning and if it has been created, we must inquire who gave it this beginning, and who was its Creator." Let us sing as we go. May our struggles and our concern for this planet never take away the joy of our hope. (LS, 244)

Mass Texts

◆ INTRODUCTION TO THE MASS

"Christ is risen! Christ is risen, indeed. Alleluia!" Through Christ's Death and Resurrection the old order is destroyed, all creation is renewed, and the promise of new life is restored. We have reason to rejoice as we gather to praise and thank God for the glory of the Resurrection. We turn to God in gratitude and in need of reconciliation and new life.

◆ SEASONAL ALTERNATE TROPES FOR PENITENTIAL ACT FORM C

Lord Jesus, you are our Resurrection and our life: Lord, have mercy.

Christ Jesus, by dying you destroyed our death: Christ, have mercy.

Lord Jesus, by rising you restored our life: Lord, have mercy.

◆ DISMISSAL FOR CHILDREN'S LITURGY OF THE WORD

Sisters and brothers, Jesus has made us children of light. Because Jesus' light shines on us, we need not be afraid of any darkness. This gift can make us very happy. Go, listen to the readings we hear as Church today. Listen carefully and let the words you hear fill your heart with love, light, and peace so that there is no more room for fear or darkness.

◆ DISMISSAL OF CATECHUMENS

Every day of our lives we can thank God for the gift of new life made available to us in the Death and Resurrection of Jesus and the waters of Baptism. Go and reflect on who the resurrected Christ is. Let the light of the Resurrection shine on any fear or darkness in your life. Ask the Risen Lord to free you from them. May your continuing union with Christ be a source of light and hope for us. Go in peace.

◆ Seasonal Universal Prayer (Prayer of the Faithful)

Invitation to Prayer

You breathed on your disciples that first Easter night and shared peace with them. Breathe on us in these prayers. Fill us with your peace. Empower us to breathe on one another with the gifts of peace, mercy, and hope that the Resurrection offers.

Intercessions

1. That the joy of the Resurrection may shine through the lives of Christians who proclaim the joy and peace you offer, we pray to the Lord:

2. That places in our world that are dead due to sin, violence, abuse, war, terrorism, and any darkness, may find light in world leaders who seek the wisdom the Holy Spirit offers, we pray to the Lord:

3. That anyone who is hardened by their life's journey may be softened by the witness of those who have found life in the face of death, hope in the face of despair, and forgiveness in the face of sin or hurt, we pray to the Lord:

4. That signs of new life which appear all around us, may bring a smile of hope to all who live in doubt or fear, we pray to the Lord:

5. That this faith community may witness the power of the Resurrection by the ways we attend to and care for all creation, we pray to the Lord:

6. That those who have died may be enjoying the Resurrection that we await, and that the face of the resurrected Christ may shine on those who are dying, we pray to the Lord:

Concluding Prayer

Life-giving God,
the celebration of the Resurrection of your Son,
    Jesus Christ,
reminds us that,
for your faithful people, life is changed, not ended.
Hear the prayers of this gathering of your
    faithful people.
Change us so that we live the joy we celebrate,
in the Resurrection of your Son, Jesus Christ,
who lives and reigns with you and the Holy Spirit,
one God, for ever and ever.
Amen.

April 2019
Month of the Holy Eucharist

Optional Memorials in Easter Time

The Missal commentaries below pertain to the seasonal weekdays or other obligatory observances. The *General Instruction of the Roman Missal* states that when celebrating optional memorials during Easter Time "one of the following may be chosen: either the Mass of the weekday, or the Mass of the Saint or of one of the Saints whose Memorial is observed, or the Mass of any Saint inscribed in the Martyrology for that day" (GIRM, 355b).

MON 22 (#261) white
Monday within the Octave of Easter
SOLEMNITY

The Lectionary for Mass

◆ FIRST READING: Today we begin our long sequence of readings from the Acts of the Apostles. Today's reading comes immediately following the account of the descent of the Holy Spirit upon the disciples on Pentecost. Peter stands before the people "with the Eleven," yet clearly their leader. During the past week, we have seen Peter's weakness; today we see his strength. With the confidence of an eyewitness, Peter tells his fellow Jews what has happened. The Messiah has been crucified, delivered up by his own people, but the power of God has raised him from the dead. Peter cites the Scriptures at length (Psalm 16, which is our Responsorial today) to demonstrate that the words of the prophets have been fulfilled. At the end of today's passage, Peter tells his hearers that something utterly new has happened. David died and was buried, "and his tomb is in our midst to this day." But this new king who sits on David's throne will never die. Death itself has been overthrown. Easter makes all the difference!

◆ RESPONSORIAL PSALM 16 is a song of trust in the Resurrection. God's faithful servant has no fear, even in the depths of the "nether world."

◆ EASTER SEQUENCE: The sequence may be sung each day of the Octave. Refer to page 175 for more details.

◆ GOSPEL: Two groups of witnesses to the Resurrection of Jesus Christ react in very different ways. The women hasten to tell the disciples what has happened. They are full of emotion — "fearful yet overjoyed." On the way, they encounter Jesus himself, who reassures them with the words he said so often during his ministry: "Do not be afraid." He gives them a commission: to carry a message to his "brothers," the disciples. The faith of the women is contrasted with the doubts of the guards who were stationed at the tomb, who also hasten away in fear. But their hearts are closed, and seeing does not make them believe. Instead, they allow themselves to be silenced by a bribe from the high priests, who invent their own version of the story. When it comes to the Resurrection, seeing does not necessarily mean believing. It takes an act of faith to understand that Jesus is truly risen from the dead.

The Roman Missal

Our long journey through the desert has brought us "into a land flowing with milk and honey" (Easter Entrance Antiphon)! We praise God who adds "new offspring" to the Church through Baptism, and we pray that all remain faithful to their Baptism throughout their lives (Collect) and "attain unending happiness" (Prayer over the Offerings). We pray for the abounding grace of the "paschal Sacrament" (Prayer after Communion) we receive on this Easter day. The Gloria is sung or said today, as it is every day within the Octave of Easter. Preface I

of Easter is assigned for today, and, as specified at the text for the Preface, the phrase "on this day" is used. If Eucharistic Prayer I, the Roman Canon, is used, the special inserts are used. Consider also using Eucharistic Prayer II. The solemn dismissal with the double Alleluia is sung or said today, as it is throughout the Octave of Easter. Since each day of the Octave is still considered part of Easter Sunday, you can pull out the stops for today's solemnity. Use incense, and a longer, more formal Gospel procession. If you don't usually have music at daily Mass, do so this week.

TUE 23 (#262) white
Tuesday within the Octave of Easter
SOLEMNITY

The Lectionary for Mass

◆ FIRST READING: Today's First Reading is a continuation of Peter's Pentecost speech. The hearts of many of those who heard Peter's proclamation of Jesus as Lord and Messiah were opened to repentance and the gift of faith. Some three thousand people were baptized.

◆ PSALM 33 reminds us that the Lord is not only upright and just, but kind.

◆ GOSPEL: All this week, we will read accounts of the first appearances of the Risen Lord to his disciples. Today we hear the wonderful story of Christ's appearance to Mary Magdalene in the garden. Peter and the beloved disciple have already come to see the tomb and have hastened away again; but Mary remains there weeping. While the beloved disciple "saw and believed," Mary responds differently. She weeps because, as she says, "I don't know where they laid him." But when he appears to her, it is not his physical appearance, but his voice, uttering her name, that she recognizes. The Risen Christ seems to touch each person in a unique way, calling each of us by name, calling us to faith in him.

The Roman Missal

God gives us "paschal remedies" that we may have "perfect freedom" and rejoice both on earth and in heaven in Christ's Resurrection (Collect). We pray that God may protect us (Prayer over the Offerings) and prepare us for eternal life (Prayer after Communion). The Gloria is once again sung or said today. Preface I of Easter is again assigned for today, and, as specified at the text for the Preface, the phrase "on this day" is used. If Eucharistic Prayer I is prayed, remember to use the special inserts. Consider also using Eucharistic Prayer III. The solemn dismissal with the double Alleluia is sung or said today, as it is throughout the Octave of Easter. Since each day of the Octave is still considered part of Easter Sunday, you can pull out the stops for today's solemnity. Use incense, and a longer, more formal Gospel procession. If you don't usually have music at daily Mass, do so this week.

WED 24 (#263) white
Wednesday within the Octave of Easter
SOLEMNITY

The Lectionary for Mass

◆ FIRST READING: The Resurrection of the Lord changed everything for the disciples, as we see clearly in the First Reading. Peter, who fled from his master when he was arrested, and trembled behind locked doors, has been transformed. He preached an amazing sermon on Pentecost, and now he shows what faith in Jesus Christ can do in the healing of the crippled man, begging at "the Beautiful Gate." The cure is complete: the man not only walks but "leaped up . . . walking and jumping and praising God." In the name of Jesus Christ,

there is forgiveness, healing—in a word, salvation.

◆ RESPONSORIAL PSALM 105 calls on the whole world to rejoice in God, who is faithful to his covenant forever.

◆ GOSPEL: The disciples are on their way away from Jerusalem. They seem blinded by their grief and disappointment, for when Jesus himself approaches, "their eyes were prevented from recognizing him." He asks them what they are "conversing and debating" about, and they pour out their story, which reveals both their love for Jesus—"a prophet mighty in deed and word"—and their pain: "we were hoping that he would be the one" (24:21). Jesus exclaims, "Oh, how foolish you are," and through the Scriptures he explains how it was "necessary that the Christ should suffer." How consoling those words must have been to the disciples who thought that with the death of Jesus on the Cross, everything was over. No wonder they invite this stranger to stay and eat with them. It is only in the breaking of the bread that the disciples recognize Jesus: then they realize that they knew him all along.

The Roman Missal

Each year the Church is gladdened by the celebration of Christ's Resurrection; we pray that we may experience the joys that Easter promises (Collect). We ask for "salvation of mind and body" (Prayer over the Offerings), that we may be cleansed of our former way of life and transformed into "a new creation" (Prayer after Communion). The Gloria is once again sung or said today. Preface I of Easter is again used today, as is the phrase "on this day." If Eucharistic Prayer I is used, the special inserts are also again used. Consider using also the Eucharistic Prayer for Various Needs and Occasions I. The solemn dismissal with the double Alleluia is

sung or said today, as it is throughout the Octave of Easter. Since each day of the Octave is still considered part of Easter Sunday, you can pull out the stops for today's solemnity. Use incense, and a longer, more formal Gospel procession. If you don't usually have music at daily Mass, do so this week.

THU 25 (#264) white
Thursday in the Octave of Easter
SOLEMNITY

The Lectionary for Mass

◆ FIRST READING: After the healing of the crippled beggar, there is a great hubbub in the Temple: everyone gathers around Peter and John in amazement. Peter responds with another address, inviting them to turn their amazement into faith. It is Jesus, the same Jesus whom they put to death, who healed this man, and "faith in his name" will heal them as well, bringing "times of refreshment" and the promised fulfillment of all things.

◆ RESPONSORIAL PSALM 8 is a hymn of praise to God, who gives to human beings a glorious destiny.

◆ GOSPEL: The disciples who so slowly and sadly walked the road to Emmaus hasten back again to Jerusalem and tell the disciples what has happened. Then, suddenly, Jesus is in their midst: not a ghost or a spirit, but Jesus himself. Jesus gives them a gift and a mission. He "opened their minds to understand the Scriptures," just as he explained the Scriptures to the disciples along the way. The scriptures are the key to understanding the Paschal Mystery. The mission is simple: to preach the name of the Christ "to all the nations, beginning from Jerusalem."

The Roman Missal

We continue to pray for the neophytes and for all the baptized, that we may be one in faith and in "the homage of their deeds," the praise they offer to God by the good work they do (Collect). We offer the sacrifice of the Mass for the newly baptized and for ourselves (Prayer over the Offerings). We pray that the "holy exchange" of the Eucharist may bring us present help and "eternal gladness" (Prayer after Communion). The Gloria is sung or said today, as it is every day within the Octave of Easter. Once again Preface I of Easter is the Preface to be used for today, and the phrase "on this day" is used. If the Roman Canon is used, be sure to use the special inserts. Consider using Eucharistic Prayer II. Since each day of the Octave is still considered part of Easter Sunday, you can pull out the stops for today's solemnity. Use incense, and a longer, more formal Gospel procession. If you don't usually have music at daily Mass, do so this week.

FRI 26 (#265) white
Friday within the Octave of Easter
SOLEMNITY

The Lectionary for Mass

◆ FIRST READING: Since Pentecost, Peter has preached and healed in the name of Jesus; now he begins to experience the persecution that the followers of Jesus must also expect to share. He and John are arrested for preaching on the Resurrection, and they are brought before the same people who condemned Jesus — Annas, Caiphas, and other members of the "high-priestly class." They demand to know by whose authority Peter and John healed the cripple. Peter — not daunted by this intimidating assembly — sets out to convert them as well, proudly proclaiming the name of Jesus, and citing the fulfillment of Scripture to these scholars of the law.

◆ OUR RESPONSORIAL IS PSALM 118, the same psalm Peter cites in his address to the chief priests. Jesus is "the stone which the builders rejected," who "has become the cornerstone" through the marvelous work of God.

◆ GOSPEL: We return to John's account of the appearances of the Risen Lord. Peter declares to the others, "I am going fishing." Has he given up? Is he returning to his former practice, now that his master is gone? However we read the passage, the expedition is fruitless, and when Jesus (whom, again, the disciples do not recognize at first) calls out to them, they have caught nothing. But when they follow his advice, they cannot even draw in the net for the number of fish. The beloved disciple recognizes the presence of the Lord, and Peter leaps in the water and swims to shore. The homely details of the 153 large fish, the charcoal fire, and the invitation to "come, have breakfast" have a deeper meaning as well. Again and again, these accounts of the appearances of the Risen Christ remind us of the Eucharist — the abiding presence of the Risen Lord in the midst of his people.

The Roman Missal

The Paschal Mystery is God's covenant with us, to reconcile us to himself. We pray that we may profess our faith in this great mystery, and express our faith in the way we live our lives (Collect). We pray that our offering may draw our minds from earth to heaven (Prayer over the Offerings). We ask God to redeem all he has saved through Christ's Passion, that they may rejoice in his Resurrection (Prayer after Communion). The Gloria is sung or said today. As with all the days this week, Preface I of Easter is assigned for today, and, as specified at the text for the Preface, the phrase "on this day" is used. If Eucharistic Prayer I, the Roman Canon, is used, the special inserts are used. The solemn dismissal with the double Alleluia is sung or said today, as it is throughout the Octave of Easter. Since each day of the Octave is still considered part of Easter Sunday, you can pull out the stops for today's solemnity. Use incense, and a longer, more formal Gospel procession. If you don't usually have music at daily Mass, do so this week.

SAT 27 (#266) white
Saturday within the Octave of Easter
SOLEMNITY

The Lectionary for Mass

◆ FIRST READING: The chief priests are astonished to hear these "uneducated, ordinary men" boldly speaking in their presence, even citing the Scriptures, and they are literally silenced — "they could say nothing in reply." The leaders forbid the disciples to speak in the name of Jesus, but Peter and John flatly refuse. They will obey God, not human beings. "It is impossible for us not to speak about what we have seen and heard," they declare, and there is nothing the authorities can do about it.

◆ RESPONSORIAL PSALM 118: We continue praying the great Easter psalm, Psalm 118, in which the psalmist boldly proclaims the Lord's deeds, even in the midst of trial and suffering.

◆ GOSPEL: During this Easter octave we have heard the accounts of the appearances of the Risen Lord according to Matthew, Luke, and John; today we hear from Mark, who with his usual brevity and power, gives us a series of three Resurrection stories. Mary Magdalene saw the Risen Christ, and told the disciples, but they did not believe her. Two disciples "walking along on their way to the country" — perhaps the same disciples who met Jesus on their way to Emmaus — also encountered the Risen Lord, but the Eleven did not believe them, either. When Jesus appears to the Eleven, he rebukes them for not believing these witnesses to his Resurrection, but he gives them a mission nevertheless: "Go into the whole world and proclaim the Gospel to every creature." Jesus uses human instruments to tell the Good News to the world.

The Roman Missal

In many of our parishes, we saw the newly baptized in white garments as they emerged from the waters of new life. In the Collect, we pray that those who have been reborn in Baptism may be clothed "with blessed immortality." The prayers echo the "delight" and "joy" of Easter Time (Prayer over the Offerings), as we pray that all who are renewed by the sacraments may share in the resurrection of the body (Prayer after Communion). The Gloria is sung or said today. Preface I of Easter is to be used today, although today is the last weekday for which it will be exclusively assigned. The phrase "on this day" is again used, as are the special inserts for Eucharistic Prayer I if that prayer is selected. Consider using Eucharistic Prayer III. Since each day of the Octave is still considered part of Easter Sunday, you can pull out the stops for today's solemnity. Use incense, and a longer, more formal Gospel procession. If you don't usually have music at daily Mass, do so this week.

(#45C) white

28 Second Sunday of Easter/Sunday of Divine Mercy

SOLEMNITY

About Divine Mercy Sunday

The Sunday of Divine Mercy is a day established by Pope John Paul II as "a perennial invitation to the Christian world to face with confidence in divine benevolence the difficulties and trials that humankind will experience in the years to come" (Congregation for Divine Worship and the Discipline of the Sacraments, May 23, 2000). In a way similar to Passion Sunday (Palm Sunday) or the Fourth Sunday of Easter (Good Shepherd Sunday), the Second Sunday of Easter bears the additional title of Sunday of Divine Mercy. This is not a new solemnity or feast, nor does it celebrate a new or separate mystery of redemption, but rather, it leads into the continuing celebration of God's mercy during Easter Time. As the Octave Day of Easter, the Lectionary readings and prayer texts highlight the mystery of divine compassion that underlies the Church's Easter faith.

The Lectionary for Mass

◆ FIRST READING: In Acts, Luke offers several descriptions of how the Risen Christ and the gifts of the Spirit given at Pentecost had transformed the followers of Jesus. The disciples, in the name of the Risen Christ, were able to perform many signs and wonders. People were awed, overwhelmed, and attracted all at the same time.

◆ RESPONSORIAL PSALM 118: The psalmist acclaims God's everlasting love and invites his hearers to give thanks. The rejected stone is now the cornerstone, and the psalmist experiences life, not death, on this day of salvation. Truly this was the experience of those who heard the Apostles' words and witnessed their marvelous works.

◆ SECOND READING: Easter's victory comes only after the Cross. So it was for Jesus, so it will be for John, who is imprisoned on the island of Patmos because of his witness to Jesus. His vision of the victorious Lord sustains and encourages him. His vision is likewise a call to make known what he sees and hears.

◆ GOSPEL: The Risen Christ comes into the midst of his fearful disciples, bringing them peace, gifting them with his Spirit, and sending them to bring forgiveness. Thomas, who was absent, does not believe the witness of the others. A week later, he is with the disciples gathered again behind locked doors. Jesus invites Thomas to see, to touch, and to believe; Jesus pronounces a blessing on all who will believe without seeing. We are among them.

The Roman Missal

This Sunday completes the Easter Octave, and the Missal texts continue to strongly emphasize the meaning and effects of sacramental initiation. Historically, this day was given the name Dominica in albis—the last day for the neophytes to wear their white baptismal garments.

Keep in mind, given the baptismal character of all of Easter Time, that the rite for the blessing and sprinkling of water is a good option to take advantage of. The rite may be used as a memorial of Baptism in place of the Penitential Act at the beginning of Mass on Sundays, and parishes and liturgy preparation groups would do well to do this on all the Sundays (and any other major celebrations) during Easter Time. The rite is found in appendix II at the back of the Missal. The priest and ministers enter as usual, and the priest greets the people as usual. Then, standing at the chair (or perhaps going to the baptismal font), with a vessel containing water to be blessed nearby, he calls the people to prayer and then blesses the water; be sure to use the third option, the prayer during Easter Time. Salt may be blessed and added to the water if that is the custom of the people.

After this, the priest sprinkles himself, the ministers, and the people, ideally moving throughout the church. One of the chants suggested in the Missal or some other appropriate song is sung during the sprinkling. After the sprinkling, the singing ends, and the priest returns to his chair and prays the closing to the rite. After this prayer, the Gloria is sung.

The splendid Collect is a prayer for the grace to recognize the Christ in whom we have been baptized, whose Spirit gives new life, and whose blood redeems us. The Prayer over the Offerings includes a special optional insert for the newly baptized. The Gloria and the Creed are sung or said today.

Preface I of Easter is assigned for today, although today will be the last Sunday for which it will be the only one to be used; the phrase "on this day" is again the proper phrase to be used among the possible choices. Consider chanting the introductory dialogue and the Preface today, and every Sunday during Easter Time; if this is not the regular practice of your community, this can be a way of powerfully drawing attention to the festivity of the liturgical time, and in particular if this was

the practice during Lent, this can be a way of highlighting the continuity of the liturgical times (but be sure to prepare and rehearse your assembly as needed, especially if your people are not familiar with the responses!). If Eucharistic Prayer I is selected, the proper forms of the "In communion with those" and the "Therefore, Lord, we pray" are still used, as it is the Octave of Easter.

The simple Prayer after Communion asks that the "paschal Sacrament" may have an ongoing effect on our hearts and minds.

If a Solemn Blessing is to be used, it is the Solemn Blessing for Easter Time, found at number 6 in the "Blessings at the End of Mass and Prayers over the People" section of the Missal immediately following the Order of Mass. Notice how the third section of the blessing continues the baptismal theme of Easter by its specific reference to that sacrament.

Finally, for the last time until Pentecost, the solemn double Alleluia dismissal is used.

Of course use festive music, incense, and a longer, more formal Gospel procession.

Other Ideas

This Sunday may be the first time that the newly baptized, the neophytes, are able to be present at the liturgy following the Easter Vigil. Consider recognizing them in some way so that the whole parish can welcome them. Many parishes schedule Baptisms on the Sundays of Easter Time. Consider celebrating the Sacrament of Baptism at one of the Sunday liturgies; perhaps rotating at different liturgies over the course of Easter Time. If Baptisms are scheduled on Sunday afternoon invite the parents and godparents to be present for the last scheduled liturgy and invite the assembly to join in a blessing over them. The focus of the entire Easter season is on what it means to be baptized in Jesus Christ; these suggestions can

help to maintain that focus for the whole community.

(#267) white

M O N **29** **Memorial of St. Catherine of Siena, Virgin and Doctor of the Church**

The Lectionary for Mass

◆ FIRST READING: In our ongoing reading from the Acts of the Apostles, Peter and John, set free by the chief priests, return home. The believers rejoice, praising God with the words of Psalm 2. At the end of today's reading, God seems to set the seal of approval on the assembly, as the whole building shakes and the people are again filled with the Holy Spirit, as on Pentecost.

◆ OUR RESPONSORIAL IS PSALM 2, the same prayer offered by the followers of Jesus on the return of Peter and John.

◆ GOSPEL: This week we hear passages of Jesus' words to Nicodemus from the third chapter of the Gospel according to John. Nicodemus, a Pharisee and a "ruler of the Jews," comes to listen to Jesus, but by night; he is still in spiritual darkness. In the dialogue that follows, Jesus gently leads Nicodemus into a new way of thinking. To "see the Kingdom of God" —to come out of the darkness— one must be "born from above": one's very being must be renewed through "water and Spirit." The final lines of the Gospel suggest that even though the spirit is a great mystery—"you do not know where it comes from or where it goes"—we are still able to perceive its presence around us.

The Roman Missal

The prayers for the memorial are found in the Proper of Saints. They speak of Catherine's "contemplation of the Lord's Passion" and her love for and service of the Church (Collect), and her extraordinary wisdom which continues to teach us (Prayer over the Offerings). The sacrament from which St. Catherine drew life is the same "heavenly table / at which we have been fed" (Prayer after Communion). Consider using Eucharistic Prayer II.

Today's Saint

St. Catherine of Siena (1347–1380) was a Dominican tertiary and mystic, the twenty-fourth of twenty-five children. In spite of family opposition, she dedicated herself to Christ at a very young age and at the age of sixteen, she withdrew from her family to lead a life of intense prayer. When she emerged, she began to dedicate herself to care of the sick and poor. Her joyful spirit attracted a number of followers. After a series of mystical experiences, Catherine felt compelled to write letters to those in secular and Church authority, which she dictated to her friend, the Dominican Raymond of Capua. Her influence became so great that papal legates consulted her. At this time, the popes had moved their residence from Rome to Avignon, France. Catherine begged Gregory XI to return to Rome, which he did in 1377. St. Catherine died in 1380 at the age of thirty-three, leaving behind her writings, the *Dialogue on Divine Providence*, letters, and prayers. She is represented in art holding a lily and wearing the habit of a Dominican tertiary, and is the patron saint of Europe and Italy. In 1970, Pope Paul VI made her a Doctor of the Church, one of the first women, along with Teresa of Avila, to be so honored.

30 (#268) white
T U E **Easter Weekday**

Optional Memorial of St. Pius V, Pope / white

The Lectionary for Mass

◆ THE FIRST READING gives us a picture of a Christian utopia. The community is "of one heart and mind," and they share all things in common. Those who are wealthy bring their money and put it at the feet of the apostles, who distribute it "to each according to need." Yesterday we read about "signs and wonders." The absolute trust and mutual love of this community was surely one of the greatest wonders the Holy Spirit worked in the early Church.

◆ IN RESPONSORIAL PSALM 93 our King "is robed in majesty."

◆ GOSPEL: Nicodemus speaks for all of us when he asks Jesus, "How can this happen?" How can a person be born again, of water and the spirit? Jesus' response seems difficult. "Just as Moses lifted up the serpent in the desert, so must the Son of Man be lifted up." Only in light of Easter can we understand Jesus' reply to Nicodemus. It is through the saving Passion of Christ, raised up on the Cross, that we participate in this new life, this life of the spirit.

The Roman Missal

On the weekdays of Easter Time, the Prayer over the Gifts and the Prayer after Communion are repeated week by week. Commentaries are included for these prayers on the Easter Sundays when they occur. Each day has its own unique Collect. The Collect for today reminds us that we, too, are called to that apostolic task, "to proclaim the power of the risen Lord." Consider using Eucharistic Prayer II.

Today's Saint

St. Pius V (1504–1572) was pope immediately following the Council of Trent (1545–1563). He was a reformer who saw the laxness that had overtaken the Church, and he fought to overcome it by paring down the papal court and enforcing the decrees of Trent. He is best remembered for promulgating the 1570 edition of *The Roman Missal*, which was used until the liturgical reforms of the Second Vatican Council, and for reforming the Liturgy of the Hours. He was a Dominican friar, and after he was elected to the papacy, he continued to wear his white habit. Since then, it has been customary for the pope to wear a white cassock.

May 2019
Month of Our Lady

1 (#269) white
W E D **Easter Weekday**

Optional Memorial of St. Joseph the Worker / white

The Lectionary for Mass

◆ FIRST READING: Wonders and signs continue to accompany the Apostles. Placed under arrest once again, they are set free by an angel, with defiant instructions: "Go and take your place in the temple area, and tell the people everything about this life." The Apostles obey and are promptly arrested again. But even their enemies handle them more gingerly this time, "because they were afraid of being stoned by the people." The Apostles are walking in the footsteps of their master.

◆ RESPONSORIAL PSALM 34, with its praise of God the deliverer, is a fitting response to the First Reading.

◆ GOSPEL: Today's Gospel is among the most famous passages in all of Scripture. Some translations of the Bible attribute these words to Jesus; but the Lectionary gives them to us in the voice of the evangelist. These words form a sort of concluding commentary to Jesus' dialogue with Nicodemus, who came to him under cover of night. Out of love, God sent his Son into the world, not as judge but as redeemer. Some remained in darkness, not because they could not see the light, but because they "preferred darkness to light." The choice, it seems, is in our hands.

The Roman Missal

Having just celebrated the Sunday of Divine Mercy, we are reminded of God's love and mercy: "may by his likeness to ourselves / bring us reconciliation" (Collect) and may we "be conformed to the mysteries of [his] mighty love" (Prayer over the Offerings). Consider using the Eucharistic Prayer for Reconciliation I.

Today's Saint

The optional Memorial of St. Joseph the Worker is a relatively new addition to the calendar. It was introduced by Pope Pius XII in 1955, as an alternative to secular May Day celebrations of the worker, which originated in Communist countries and which did more to promote Communist propaganda than to promote the worker. Pope Pius XII urged workers to look to St. Joseph the carpenter and to see the dignity inherent in human labor, which could become a source of holiness. The prayers for today from *The Roman Missal* call Joseph our "wise and faithful servant" who is our patron as we "complete the works [God] set us to do."

(#270) white

THU 2 Memorial of St. Athanasius, Bishop and Doctor of the Church

The Lectionary for Mass

◆ FIRST READING: Today the Apostles are again brought before the court to answer questions about Jesus. Again Peter speaks out boldly: "We must obey God rather than men." The Apostles cannot deny what they have heard and seen; they cannot deny the name of Jesus, even if it means they will be condemned to death as Jesus was.

◆ RESPONSORIAL PSALM 34: The psalmist praises the God who hears

the prayer of the just person in distress.

◆ GOSPEL: Today's short, dense Gospel brings together many of the themes we have heard in this week's readings. "There is a sharp distinction in this Gospel between above and below, light and darkness, belief and unbelief—and all of this centers on the person of Jesus" (*The Collegeville Bible Commentary*, p. 986). God has shared everything with the Son, through love, and, through love, the Son will share everything with us, for "he does not ration his gift of the Spirit."

The Roman Missal

The prayers for the memorial are drawn from the Proper of Saints. They recall that Athanasius championed Christ's divinity in a time when the Church was divided by heresies. We "profess, as he did, an unblemished faith" (Prayer over the Offerings) in "the true divinity of" Christ (Prayer after Communion). Consider using Eucharistic Prayer II.

Today's Saint

St. Athanasius (295–373), bishop of Alexandria and Doctor of the Church, contributed immensely to the development of doctrine and spirituality. He defended the teaching of the First Council of Nicaea (AD 325) that Jesus was both fully human and fully divine. The Arians, who taught that Jesus was not divine, unleashed a series of attacks upon Athanasius, resulting in exile not just once, but five times in his life, amounting to seventeen years out of the forty-five he was bishop. During one of these exiles, he wrote the influential biography of the renowned hermit and monk St. Anthony of Egypt. This spiritual classic, entitled *Life of Antony*, has been and continues to be read by people longing to remove worldly distractions that keep them from mystical union with God. He is also

noted for two other works: *On the Incarnation* and *Discourses against the Arians*. Many titles have been bestowed upon him, including defender of faith, champion of orthodoxy, mystical theologian, and spiritual master. Athanasius is venerated by Eastern as well as Western Christians, and is especially revered by the Coptic (Egyptian) Church.

(#561) red

FRI 3 Feast of Sts. Philip and James, Apostles

The Lectionary for Mass

◆ FIRST READING: Paul proclaims that the Paschal Mystery forms the heart of the Gospel. The Paschal Mystery is to be proclaimed and lived in the heart of the Church and is to be handed on as a living reality. The Lord Jesus was crucified, died, rose, and appeared to his Apostles. Jesus unites the Church to himself and shares with his Body the fruits of the new creation.

◆ RESPONSORIAL PSALM 19: On this feast, the psalm extols the Apostles' ministry in proclaiming the Good News to all the earth. It remains our mission as the apostolic Church.

◆ GOSPEL: Philip's desire to see the Father echoes the desire of all people who long for truth, beauty, and goodness. Philip's desire is met by Jesus' proclamation of his consubstantial (of "one being" or "essence") union with the Father, such that to know Jesus is to know the Father. As Jesus led Philip along a journey of faith, we too must not lose heart at the frailty of our faith, but we must allow Jesus to challenge and to accompany us to the fullness of faith in him.

The Roman Missal

The prayers for the feast are found in the Proper of Saints. One of the Prefaces of the Apostles is used. The Gloria is said or sung, and the Solemn Blessing of the Apostles may be used at the end of Mass. The Collect asks for "a share in the Passion and Resurrection" of Christ through the prayers of Philip and James. The Communion Antiphon is taken from Philip's words to Jesus, and the Lord's reply: "Lord, show us the Father, and that will be enough for us. / Whoever has seen me, Philip, has seen the Father also, alleluia." Consider using Eucharistic Prayer I.

Today's Saints

St. Philip (first century) was a native of Bethsaida, and was among John the Baptist's followers who saw John point out Jesus as the Lamb of God. He is most prominent in the Gospel according to John. It was Philip who asked Jesus to "show us the Father, and we will be satisfied," to which Jesus replied, "Whoever has seen me has seen the Father" (John 14:8–9). Legends of Philip have him preaching in Greece, Phrygia, and Syria along with Bartholomew. Philip enraged the proconsul by converting his wife to Christianity and was crucified upside-down in AD 54. A gnostic gospel found at Nag Hammadi is attributed to him, but there is no evidence that it was actually written by him. Philip is shown in art with two loaves or a basket filled with bread, because of his role in the story of the feeding of the five thousand (see John 6:5–7).

The St. James (first century) who is celebrated today is "James the Less," described in the Gospel as the "brother of the Lord," which at that time could also mean "cousin," and in Acts of the Apostles 15 as the leader of the Church at Jerusalem. He is usually thought to be the same person as James the son of Alpheus and James the Just. He was called to be a disciple along with his brother, Jude. James appears in the lists of the Apostles, but he becomes most prominent after the Ascension, when he was made

the first bishop of Jerusalem. He, along with Peter and John, authorized Paul's mission to the Gentiles. The Church historian, Eusebius, records that James was martyred by being stoned and then thrown from the highest point of the Temple in Jerusalem. Sts. Philip and James are celebrated on the same day in honor of the anniversary of the dedication of the church dedicated to them in Rome (now called the Church of the Twelve Apostles).

SAT 4 (#272) white
Easter Weekday

The Lectionary for Mass

◆ FIRST READING: Shortly after the flogging and release of the Apostles, trouble shakes within the community—a dispute arising from the age-old prejudice between Jews and Gentiles. The Gentile widows are getting less in the distribution of charity than the Jewish widows. The Apostles respond to this problem by getting help—they lay hands on "seven reputable men" who become the first deacons, commissioned with a ministry of service as the Apostles are ministers of the word. The grace of the Holy Spirit is not hoarded by a few; it is shared widely.

◆ RESPONSORIAL PSALM 33 is the prayer of renewed trust in God, and a plea for mercy.

◆ GOSPEL: After the feeding of the multitude comes another sign: Jesus walking on the water. Confusion, fear, and misunderstanding are side by side with recognition and love. Jesus' words urge the disciples to recognize him—"it is I"—not only as the Jesus they know, but as the incarnate God. In Greek, the words are "I am," the same words Jesus uses at key moments in the Gospel. "I am" is the very name of God. Jesus is leading his disciples deeper into the knowledge of his divine identity—only

with this understanding will they be able to receive the deeper meaning of the loaves and fishes.

The Roman Missal

There are two options for today's Collect. In the first, we beg God to "set aside . . . / the bond of sentence" written by our sins and cancel it through the Resurrection of Christ. In the second, we see "the gates of mercy" flung wide through the Paschal Mystery, and we pray that we may "never stray from the paths of life." Consider using Eucharistic Prayer II.

☀ 5 (#48C) white
Third Sunday of Easter

The Lectionary for Mass

◆ FIRST READING: In between the event described in last Sunday's reading and today's text, the Apostles have been arrested, imprisoned, and miraculously released to resume their proclamation of the Gospel. As today's reading begins, they are apprehended again. Always, there is the shadow of the Cross—Jesus', the disciples', and our own. Would that we, too, could rejoice in our sufferings for the sake of Jesus.

◆ RESPONSORIAL PSALM 30 is a song of praise celebrating God's deliverance of his people and, particularly in today's liturgy, of the Apostles. Surely the words of the psalmist sustained them, giving them courage and hope in all they would endure.

◆ SECOND READING: In a vision, John, the Christian prophet, sees God's heavenly throne surrounded by the elders, the living creatures, and countless angels. They sing praise to the victorious Lamb of God. All creatures in heaven and on earth join in the triumphal hymn.

◆ GOSPEL: The Apostles have returned to their former occupation as fishermen—in this instance, with little success. Jesus gifts them with a miraculous catch of fish, then nourishes them with food for body and spirit. The disciples know, without a doubt, that it is the Lord. The longer option includes Jesus' triple questioning of Peter's love for him (paralleling his earlier threefold denial). Peter likewise receives a threefold commission to shepherd Jesus' flock. Peter's destiny is the focus of the final verses. His martyrdom, like Jesus' own Death, would glorify God. Today's Gospel ends with the command and invitation to "Follow me." The way of the disciple can be none other than the way of Jesus.

The Roman Missal

It would be a good idea to again use the rite for the blessing and sprinkling of water. The rite is found in appendix II at the back of the Missal and it replaces the Penitential Act. The Gloria and the Creed are sung or said today. The Collect is full of joy—the joy of "the restored glory of our adoption" in Christ, the joy of "the day of resurrection," the joy of a new "youthfulness of spirit." The Prayer over the Offerings continues the joyful tone of the texts by describing the Church as "exultant" as we offer these gifts, again asking that the offerings will "bear fruit in perpetual happiness." Any one of the five Easter Prefaces may be selected for today; if Preface I is chosen, remember that the correct

wording is "in this time." Consider chanting the introductory dialogue and the Preface today, and every Sunday during Easter Time, in order to highlight the ongoing festivity of the season. Consider Eucharistic Prayer III. In the Prayer after Communion, we ask that all who share in the "eternal mysteries" may one day know the resurrection of the body. You might consider using the solemn blessing for Easter Time, found at number 6 in the "Blessings at the End of Mass and Prayers over the People" section of the Missal immediately following the Order of Mass. Remember that a regular formula for dismissal is used, not the solemn double Alleluia.

Other Ideas

Today's Gospel is an excellent passage for all liturgical ministers to use as a reflection on their ministry. It's about fishing "on the right side of the boat," a phrase that could lead to wondering if our ministry is really according to the Lord's example, or have we started to follow a personal agenda. The faithful disciple is the one who takes his or her direction from the Lord in all things. Easter Time fills us with great joy in our ministry; it should also fill us with a renewed commitment to look deeply in the waters of our life to see how the Lord is "catching" us up in his mission. What activity outside the liturgy is connected to ministry? For example, do readers find an opportunity to read to those who have poor eyesight? Do Communion ministers find ways to provide food for the hungry?

M O N 6 (#273) white
Easter Weekday

The Lectionary for Mass

◆ FIRST READING: In the Gospel, we see the disciples as frightened, weak, vacillating characters; but in the Acts of the Apostles, we are

again astonished at the absolute fearlessness of their witness to Christ. What a difference Pentecost made! Filled with the Holy Spirit, they have been transformed. Today, we begin reading the account of Stephen, the "protomartyr" or first martyr of the Church. The narrative echoes the account of the condemnation of Jesus point for point. Stephen, "filled with grace and power," is doing great things among the people. His enemies seek to debate with him, but they are no match for the "wisdom and the Spirit" of his words. False witnesses are hired, and Stephen is dragged before the Sanhedrin. He listens to the false testimony against him in silence, with a face "like the face of an angel." In accepting martyrdom for the sake of "the name," Stephen is not just imitating his master. He becomes a living witness of the Gospel and in his imitation of Christ.

◆ RESPONSORIAL PSALM 119 is the prayer of a fearless witness to the Lord, who prays for guidance and protection.

◆ GOSPEL: Following the feeding of the five thousand, the people wanted to make him king, so Jesus departs and goes to Capernaum. Now some of the people have caught up with him. Jesus urges them to "not work for food that perishes, but for the food that endures for eternal life." As in his dialogue with Nicodemus, Jesus urges the people to go deeper. Through the Eucharist, God will feed not only the body, but the soul.

The Roman Missal

We must leave behind the "old self with all its ways" and "live as Christ did." Our sharing in "the healing paschal remedies" is transformative, making us more like Christ (Collect). Any one of the five Easter Prefaces may be used today; the readings don't seem to necessarily suggest any one more appropriate than another, although perhaps Preface I, focusing in general on the Paschal Mystery, with its mention that "dying he has destroyed our death, / and by rising, restored our life," would resonate well with the orations. Consider using the Eucharistic Prayer for Various Needs and Occasions I.

TUE 7 (#274) white
Easter Weekday

The Lectionary for Mass

◆ FIRST READING: In today's First Reading, we hear the Holy Spirit speaking through Stephen. Using the words of Moses ("you stiff-necked people"), he reminds the authorities that throughout their history they have persecuted the prophets. Then, looking up to heaven, Stephen sees a vision of "Jesus standing at the right hand of God." But the people refuse to hear. They "covered their ears," shutting out the inspired words of Stephen, and they stone him on the outskirts of the city. Stephen is faithful to Jesus to the last, dying with Christ's own words on his lips.

◆ RESPONSORIAL PSALM: Today we echo the words of Jesus and of Stephen, their last profession of faith: "Into your hands, O Lord, I commend my spirit" (antiphon).

◆ GOSPEL: Jesus continues to address the crowd. He provides for their bodies in the multiplication of the loaves and the fishes. This is a sign of the far greater feast that is to come, when they will be fed with "the bread of God" that "gives life to the world." What is this bread? The Risen Christ himself. In the Eucharist, the Lord we worship gives his flesh and blood as food for his people.

The Roman Missal

Today's Collect continues Easter Time's overall emphasis on sacra-mental initiation with reference to "those reborn of water and the Holy Spirit," as it asks for "an increase of the grace you have bestowed"; this increase is available through the Eucharist, which is the culmination of and renews the life of grace begun at Baptism.

The Prayer over the Offerings, recently used this past Sunday, expresses the joy of the Church, a joy that originates in the new life given at Easter and finds fulfillment in the happiness of the Kingdom of God. The Prayer after Communion, also repeated from Sunday, asks that those who have been renewed by eternal mysteries—pointing to how every celebration of the Eucharist is our present participation in the Paschal Mystery—may "attain in their flesh / the incorruptible glory of the resurrection," thus, like the Prayer over the Offerings, reminding us of the eschatological fulfillment that awaits us. Any one of the five Easter Prefaces may be used today. Perhaps, in light of the First Reading, from Acts, which portrays Stephen's death as paralleling Jesus', we could find in Preface V of Easter, with its mention of Christ our Passover being sacrificed, its reference to the oblation of Christ's Body, and its mention of Christ "commending himself to you for our salvation," an echo of both Jesus and Stephen handing themselves over in death, that this exchange—this liturgical celebration—"may bring your help in this present life / and ensure for us eternal gladness." Consider using Eucharistic Prayer II.

WED 8 (#275) white
Easter Weekday

The Lectionary for Mass

◆ FIRST READING: After the martyrdom of Stephen, the Church in Jerusalem goes through a period of persecution, for a man named Saul "was trying to destroy the Church," hunting down the faithful and handing both men and women over to the authorities. The disciples are scattered, and Philip goes to Samaria, where he preaches "the Christ" and works great signs, casting out demons, and healing the people. The reading that began with "severe persecution" ends with "great joy."

◆ RESPONSORIAL PSALM 66: Our response today echoes the joy with which the First Reading ends—it is a song of praise of the God who delivers his beloved from all their enemies.

◆ GOSPEL: Jesus has invited the people to come to him, to feast on him. But although they see him, they do not believe. Faith is a gift from the Father. By faith alone we are able to answer Jesus' invitation, to share in his banquet, and to participate in his resurrected life.

The Roman Missal

Today's Collect emphasizes God's initiative in saving us, as it points to "those you have endowed with the grace of faith," and it again reminds us to look beyond our present participation in the Paschal Mystery toward our full participation as it asks that God give us "an eternal share in the Resurrection of your Only Begotten Son." The Prayer over the Offerings speaks of the ongoing power of the Paschal Mystery in our life, asking that "the renewal constantly at work within us / may be the cause of our unending joy." We should always remember that the effects of the Lord's Resurrection are ongoing in our lives, especially through the liturgy (in the words of the prayer, "these paschal mysteries"). In the Prayer after Communion we once again hear the felicitous phrase "holy exchange" as we pray that this exchange—this liturgical celebration—"may bring your help in this present life / and ensure for us eternal gladness."

Any one of the five Easter Prefaces may be selected for today; perhaps Preface II, with its theme of new life in Christ, would resonate well with what was said above concerning the orations. Consider using Eucharistic Prayer III.

THU 9 (#276) white
Easter Weekday

The Lectionary for Mass

◆ FIRST READING/RESPONSORIAL PSALM 66: We continue to follow the wonderful doings of Philip among the Gentiles. Yesterday he worked wonders in Samaria; today, under the guidance of the Holy Spirit, he encounters an Ethiopian eunuch on the desert road to Gaza. The eunuch is reading the prophet Isaiah, but he cannot understand what he reads. Philip explains to him that Jesus is the fulfillment of the prophecy of the suffering servant of the Lord. The eunuch believes, and immediately asks for Baptism. After the Baptism, Philip is caught up by the Holy Spirit, and the eunuch goes on his way rejoicing. This is the shortest RCIA process on record, but all the elements are there. The eunuch has already experienced God in some way, and he has sought him in the Scriptures. Philip, inspired by the Holy Spirit, leads him to faith by explaining the Scriptures. Baptism is both a culmination and a beginning, as is suggested by the pool of water on the side of the desert road — somewhere between his starting place and his destination. At the end of the reading, the eunuch "continued on his way rejoicing," and Responsorial Psalm 66, a song of praise and thanksgiving, gives us an insight into his joyful prayer.

◆ GOSPEL: In the Bread of Life discourse, Jesus gradually leads the people deeper and deeper into his new teaching. He and the Father are one, and through Jesus we have access to the Father. In a sense, all those who come to Jesus are prophets, for "they shall all be taught by God." At the end of today's reading, Jesus takes us to a new level. "I am the bread of life," he tells them again, but now he adds: "and the bread that I will give is my Flesh for the life of the world."

The Roman Missal

The Collect points to our ongoing celebration of the fifty days of Easter Time, and the mystery we focus on, as it asks that we experience God's "compassion more readily / during these days when, by your gift, / we have known it more fully." The mention of having been "freed from the darkness of error" can, of course, call to mind the illumination that occurred at Baptism, another theme that runs throughout Easter Time. The Prayer over the Offerings expresses how this "wonderful exchange" makes us partakers of the very life of God (that is, in the liturgy the very work of our redemption is accomplished). Being made sharers in the life of God, however, the prayer reminds us that we must "make it ours by a worthy way of life." The Prayer after Communion returns to the old way of life/new way of life motif, asking that we be led to the new way. Among the Easter Prefaces to be used today, perhaps either II, with its reference to "children of light" or IV, with its statement that "the old order [is] destroyed, / a universe cast down is renewed, / and integrity of life is restored to us in Christ" would continue the themes found in the orations. Consider using Eucharistic Prayer III.

FRI 10 (#277) white
Easter Weekday

Optional Memorial of St. Damien de Veuster, Priest / white

The Lectionary for Mass

◆ FIRST READING: The wonderful account of the conversion of Saul gives us a glimpse of the active presence of the Risen Christ in the Christian community. Saul is a determined persecutor of the disciples, who has already scattered the Church in Jerusalem, and is now seeking permission to extend his persecution to the outlying regions. Just outside Damascus, he is flung to the ground by a blinding light and a voice from heaven. In persecuting the followers of Christ, Saul has been persecuting Jesus Christ himself. Saul is utterly prostrated by the encounter — unable to see, to eat, or to drink. At the same time, Jesus speaks to Ananias and guides him to where Saul is staying in Damascus. To Ananais, not to Saul, Jesus reveals his plan: "this man is a chosen instrument of mine to carry my name before Gentiles, kings, and children of Israel" (Acts 9:15). Jesus uses human instruments, sometimes faulty ones. He sees potential in us that we cannot even imagine.

◆ RESPONSORIAL PSALM 117, the shortest of all the psalms, is the song of all apostles of the Lord: "Go out to all the world and tell the Good News"!

◆ GOSPEL: Jesus' words about the bread of life provoke immediate division. "How can this man give us his Flesh to eat?" they ask. Jesus answers in words that challenge them still further. Again and again he repeats the words flesh and blood, food and drink. It is only through participation in this meal that we will share in the life of the Risen Christ. Unlike manna, this food — the flesh and blood of Christ himself — brings eternal life.

The Roman Missal

The grace of Easter is not a moment in time, but a lifetime! We have already come to know "the grace of the Lord's Resurrection," yet we continue to pray that "through the love of the Spirit" we may "rise to newness of life" (Collect). The various references to living in newness of life, and the Gospel's reference to having life because of our feeding on the Bread of Life might make Easter Prefaces I or II likely candidates for use today. Consider using the Eucharistic Prayer for Reconciliation II.

Today's Saint

Joseph de Veuster (1840–1889) was born in Belgium and entered the Congregation of the Sacred Hearts of Jesus and Mary, where he took the name Damien. He professed his vows in 1860. Three years later, although not yet ordained, he was sent to Hawaii and was ordained in Honolulu in 1864. Once he realized that a large number of lepers had been exiled to Moloka'i, Damien asked for and received permission to live among them and minister to them. Moloka'i was a lawless place, and Damien found its residents living in squalor. He helped them build homes, and he provided whatever medical treatment fell within his capability. In 1885, after twelve years of this ministry, Damien realized that he himself had contracted the disease. In spite of this, he continued his work until he was too incapacitated to go on. Adherents of other churches criticized him and spread gossip about his morality, but the author Robert Louis Stevenson defended him in a famous 1890 essay. Damien was canonized by Pope Benedict XVI in 2009. He is the patron saint of victims of leprosy.

S
A 11 (#278) white
T **Easter Weekday**

The Lectionary for Mass

◆ FIRST READING: The followers of Jesus share in his life. Stephen's martyrdom showed how faithfully he walked in the footsteps of his master; today's reading reveals how the apostles, filled with the Holy Spirit, are able to work the same wonders that Jesus did. Peter heals Aeneas, saying, "Jesus Christ heals you. Get up and make your bed." He even raises the faithful disciple Tabitha from the dead, in a way that recalls Jesus' raising of Jairus' daughter. As with the miracles Jesus worked, these healings have a purpose: "This became known all over Joppa, and many came to believe in the Lord." Healings are signs, leading to a still greater miracle: faith.

◆ RESPONSORIAL PSALM 116 is a prayer of thanksgiving to God for all his mercies. As we pray these words, it is easy to hear in them the voice of Aeneas, of Tabitha, and of all the people touched by God's healing power in Jesus Christ.

◆ GOSPEL: Today's Gospel brings us to the end of the Bread of Life discourse. The disciples struggle with this teaching: "This saying is hard; who can accept it?" The Eucharist is a stumbling block, and "many of his disciples returned to their former way of life and no longer walked with him." But the Twelve remain. Peter's reply to Jesus' question, "Do you also want to leave" gets to the heart of the matter. Peter does not stay because he understands everything Jesus says. He stays because of his faith: "We have come to believe and are convinced that you are the Holy One of God."

The Roman Missal

Baptism is central to Easter Time and a theology of this sacrament is evident in today's prayers: "You have been buried with Christ in Baptism, / through which you also rose" (Entrance Antiphon); "in the font of Baptism / [God has] made new" (Collect); may we "attain the gifts that are eternal" (Offerings); and "keep safe . . . / those whom you have saved by your kindness" (Communion). Consider using Eucharistic Prayer I.

☀ 12 (#51C) white
Fourth Sunday of Easter

Good Shepherd Sunday

About Good Shepherd Sunday

The Fourth Sunday of Easter is traditionally referred to as Good Shepherd Sunday. Hearing the Shepherd's voice, followers recognize and know it is their God. Safe in the knowledge that they cannot be taken from the hand of the Shepherd, those who hear his voice follow as faithful believers willing to go where God calls and sends them. When all the clamor of false voices and seductive distractions threaten to overwhelm, we have only to listen carefully to be led to do the work of the Father.

The Lectionary for Mass

◆ FIRST READING: We witness the popularity of Paul and Barnabas, chosen by the Holy Spirit as missionaries of the Gospel. After an introductory verse, the reading skips over Paul's speech in the synagogue on their first Sabbath in Antioch and resumes with a description of its effect on many who heard them. Their popularity soon led to opposition from the Jews, and even persecution. Paul and Barnabas read this as a sign that they should go to the Gentiles.

◆ RESPONSORIAL PSALM 100: The first antiphon option is particularly apropos in light of both today's Second Reading (last line) and Gospel. Note also the reference to "flock" in the second stanza of this joyful hymn of praise.

◆ SECOND READING: Our reading from Revelation echoes the theme of persecution heard in today's text from Acts of the Apostles. Only here, the focus is the eternal reward enjoyed by those who are victorious. The Lamb who was sacrificed is at the same time the Shepherd of his people.

◆ GOSPEL: The reference to "follow" in today's Gospel harks back to today's First Reading (those who "followed" Paul and Barnabas). Those who heard these missionaries, in effect, heard the word of God which they spoke. In the Word of God proclaimed in the liturgy, we likewise hear the voice of the Lord our Shepherd.

The Roman Missal

On this Good Shepherd Sunday, the Missal texts are full of images of shepherds. Continue to use the Rite for the Blessing and Sprinkling of Water, as discussed for the Second Sunday of Easter, or, if you haven't been using it, consider beginning to do so. This rite, found in appendix II of the Missal, replaces the Penitential Act. The Gloria is sung today. The Creed is said. In the Collect, we pray that "the humble flock" may follow "the brave Shepherd" (Christ) to where he has gone — to the very "joys of heaven." The Prayer over the Offerings is one of "delight," "renewal," and "joy." While any one of the five Easter Prefaces may be selected for today, certainly Preface III with its reference to Christ as "the Lamb, once slain, who lives for ever," would be appropriate. Continue or begin chanting the introductory dialogue and the Preface today, in order to highlight the ongoing festivity of Easter Time. Consider using Eucharistic Prayer I or III. The Prayer after Communion, addressed to God, the "kind Shepherd," asks that the whole flock redeemed by Christ's Blood may come to "eternal pastures." You might consider using the solemn blessing for Easter Time, found at number 6 in the "Blessings at the End of Mass and Prayers over the People" section of the Missal. Remember that a regular formula for dismissal is used, not the solemn double Alleluia.

Other Ideas

This Sunday is often referred to as Good Shepherd Sunday since the Gospel passages for each cycle of the Lectionary all refer to Jesus as a shepherd. It used to be a Sunday for a homily on vocations to the priesthood. But Jesus is the model for all vocations. Consider what vocations are represented in your parish; it will be a very long list! Include an intercession for all those vocations and offer a blessing for those who shepherd others in faith. Some examples would be parents, teachers, catechists, sponsors of the catechumens, leaders of liturgies for children, youth group leaders, and many others. And of course, pastors. The mission of the Lord needs all of us.

MON 13 (#279) white
Easter Weekday

Optional Memorial of Our Lady of Fatima / white

The Lectionary for Mass

◆ FIRST READING: The first major issue to confront the followers of Jesus Christ was what to do with the Gentile believers. Were these converts to be required to follow the entirety of the old law or only the new law of Christ? In today's reading, Peter comes under attack because he ate with uncircumcised believers. He responds by describing a vision he had at Joppa, in which a heavenly voice declared all foods clean. Even as Peter was receiving this revelation, the Holy Spirit was guiding a family of non-Jews to Peter: he "will speak words to you by which you and all your household will be saved." Peter gives in, asking, "who was I to be able to hinder God?" The other disciples also glorify God whose gift of "life-giving repentance" is offered not only to the chosen people, but to all.

◆ RESPONSORIAL PSALM 42/43: In the Psalm, the psalmist yearns for the presence of God, and seeks guidance to the "holy mountain," the "dwelling-place" of God.

◆ GOSPEL: This week we read from the tenth chapter of the Gospel according to John. This passage in which Jesus describes himself as the good shepherd comes immediately following the story of the man born blind. In the Gospel according to John, we should take special notice whenever Jesus says, "I am," for we are sure to hear something about the Son's relationship with the Father. "I am the bread of life," "I am the light of the world," and now "I am the gate." Jesus knows us as a shepherd knows his sheep, and he invites us to know him: "the sheep follow him, because they recognize his voice." In the Gospel according to John, Jesus is at once utterly mysterious and totally accessible.

The Roman Missal

It is by God's gift that we celebrate the Paschal Mystery here on earth; we pray that we may "rejoice in the full measure of . . . grace / for ages unending" (Collect). Time intersects with eternity. Any one of the five Prefaces of Easter may be used today. Consider using the Eucharistic Prayer for Various Needs and Occasions III.

About Today's Optional Memorial

Today the Church honors Mary as Our Lady of Fatima. In 1917, in a tiny, rural town of Portugal, the Blessed Virgin Mary appeared to three shepherd children on the thirteenth day of six consecutive months, beginning on May 13. During these apparitions, the lady urged the children to pray for sinners and above all to pray the Rosary. On October 13, the last of the apparitions, the children were joined by a crowd of around 70,000 people, who witnessed what came to be called "The Miracle of the Sun." Today pilgrimage to the site of the apparitions continues all year round. The largest crowds gather on May 13 and October 13, when up to a million of the faithful come to pray and participate in processions, both during the day and at night, by the light of tens of thousands of candles. Our Lady of Fatima, pray for us.

T U E 14 (#564) red **Feast of St. Matthias, Apostle**

The Lectionary for Mass

◆ FIRST READING: Virtually all we know about Matthias is contained in this passage from the Acts of the Apostles. Peter calls on all the believers, both men and women, to choose another Apostle to replace Judas, so that the circle of the Twelve can be complete. The people choose two candidates, Matthias and Joseph. They pray earnestly; finally, they draw lots. The process is an informal one, but the ultimate choice is left to the Holy Spirit.

◆ RESPONSORIAL PSALM 113 praises the Lord, who sets the poor in the company of princes, just as Matthias was raised from among the people to the high calling of Apostle.

◆ GOSPEL: On this Feast of St. Matthias, we read a passage from the Last Supper discourses, which reminds us that the mission we receive from Jesus is pure gift: "It was not you who chose me, but I who chose you." The call comes from the Lord, who does not treat us as slaves, who obey because they must, but as friends, who share fully in the love of the Father.

The Roman Missal

The prayers for the feast are found in the Proper of Saints. The Gloria is said or sung today. One of the Prefaces of the Apostles is used. The Collect alludes to the fact that St. Matthias was chosen by lot to take the place of Judas among the Twelve. We pray that, through his intercession, we may "be numbered among the elect." Consider using Eucharistic Prayer I.

Today's Saint

Before the descent of the Holy Spirit at Pentecost, the eleven remaining Apostles had the task of replacing Judas Iscariot, who had committed suicide after his betrayal of Jesus. They cast lots, and Matthias (first century) was chosen from among the one hundred twenty disciples (Acts of the Apostles 1:18–26). He was selected as a candidate by the Apostles because he met the following two qualifications: (1) a disciple of Jesus from Jesus' baptism to his Ascension and (2) a witness to Jesus' Resurrection. Tradition has him preaching in Judea and then in Georgia in the Caucasus, where he was crucified. The apocryphal Acts of Andrew and Matthias speak of a mission to evangelize cannibals. Other traditions put him in Ethiopia and in Jerusalem, where he is supposed to have been stoned and beheaded. His symbol in art is an axe, from the legend of his beheading.

W E D 15 (#281) white **Easter Weekday**

Optional Memorial of St. Isidore / white

The Lectionary for Mass

◆ FIRST READING: The Holy Spirit continues to work in the Church at Antioch, and the faithful of Antioch are open to the Holy Spirit. "While they were worshiping the Lord and fasting," the Holy Spirit speaks to them, setting Saul and Barnabas apart for a special mission. The people, obedient to the Holy Spirit, "laid hands on them and sent them off." One would think the fledgling Church at Antioch would be afraid to lose these two great leaders and teachers of the faith. But their confidence in the Holy Spirit's guidance is absolute.

◆ RESPONSORIAL PSALM 67 is an appropriate response to the account of the widening circle of the Gospel we heard about in the First Reading.

◆ GOSPEL: Pressured to declare once and for all whether he is the Messiah, Jesus "cried out," urging the people to believe. His message is one of invitation, not condemnation: "I did not come to condemn the world but to save the world." Jesus' words are light, and if we listen to them, we too become light; and they lead us directly to the Father.

The Roman Missal

The "humble" and the "just" give glory to God (Collect) and we praise him, "among the nations" (Entrance Antiphon). He chose us and now we must "bear fruit" (Communion Antiphon) for we have been "imbued with heavenly mysteries" (Prayer after Communion). Consider using the Eucharistic Prayer for Reconciliation II.

Today's Saint

Today we honor St. Isidore the Farmer (c. 1080–1130), not St. Isidore of Seville, the Doctor of the Church whose memorial falls on April 4. Isidore the Farmer was born in Madrid to poor parents who sent him to work for a landowner. He was very devout and married a like-minded woman, Maria, who also became a saint. Isidore attended daily Mass and was often late arriving at the fields, but he managed to get his work done nonetheless. He shared the little he had with the poor. He is the patron saint of farmers; it is fitting to remember him in the Northern Hemisphere's agricultural season.

T H U 16 (#282) white
Easter Weekday

The Lectionary for Mass

◆ First Reading: Paul's mission brings him to Antioch in Pisidia (not to be confused with the Antioch near Seleucia, which he just left). He stands up in the synagogue and speaks to the Jewish people in language they will understand. He traces God's love for the chosen people from the time of Moses, to the anointing of David as king, to the coming of Jesus, heralded by John.

◆ Responsorial Psalm 89 recounts God's promise to David: to give him a throne that will last forever.

◆ Today's Gospel takes us to Holy Thursday. After washing the feet of his disciples, Jesus reminds them that they must do as he has done, for "no slave is greater than his master." Knowing that he is about to be handed over, Jesus reassures them so that they may keep believing, in spite of everything: "I am telling you before it happens, so that when it happens you may believe that I am." The disciples need to recognize that the suffering servant is also the Son of God.

The Roman Missal

Any one of the five Easter Prefaces may be selected. Consider using the Eucharistic Prayer for Reconciliation I.

F R I 17 (#283) white
Easter Weekday

The Lectionary for Mass

◆ First Reading: Paul continues his address to the people in the synagogue at Antioch. Jesus is the fulfillment of all that the prophets foretold, the prophets they hear proclaimed in the synagogue, "sabbath after sabbath." But Jesus has been raised from the dead: this is "good news."

◆ Our Responsorial today is Psalm 2, which Paul cites in his address at Antioch; it is a messianic psalm, which speaks of the coming of the "Son," "begotten" of God.

◆ Gospel: On the night before his Passion, Jesus speaks to his disciples. It is hard to imagine more reassuring words than those we hear in today's Gospel. Thomas speaks for many of us when we face grief, confusion, and doubt: "Master, we do not know where you are going; how can we know the way?" Jesus' reply reminds us that being a Christian is not an idea, but a relationship with a living person, Jesus Christ: "I am the way and the truth and the life."

The Roman Missal

In the Collect, we pray that all who have been redeemed by the blood of Christ may have life and protection from God, "author of our freedom and of our salvation." Any one of the five Easter Prefaces may be used today, although perhaps using Preface I, II, or IV, with their explicit mention of the life we share in Christ, would provide an echo of the Gospel reading. Consider using Eucharistic Prayer II.

S A T 18 (#284) white
Easter Weekday

Optional Memorial of St. John I, Pope and Martyr / red

The Lectionary for Mass

◆ First Reading: Word has spread about Paul's amazing address in the synagogue: a week later, "almost the whole city gathered to hear the word of the Lord." When the synagogue officials reject the message out of jealousy, Paul and Barnabas are not bitter or resentful; nor do they waste time in useless argument and debate. Instead, they turn to the Gentiles, who receive the Gospel with joy. When more severe persecutions drive them away, the apostles simply "shook the dust from their feet" as Jesus had told them to do, and moved on.

◆ Responsorial Psalm 98: We praise the God whose word has reached to the very ends of the earth.

◆ Gospel: We continue to read from the Last Supper discourse in the Gospel according to John. Jesus responds gently to Philip's prayer, "show us the Father." The disciples already have everything they need: they just need to open their eyes and recognize that in seeing Jesus, they have seen the Father. This passage gives us insight into the relationship Jesus has with his Father. It is a union so complete that when Jesus speaks, he does "not speak on

[his] own. The Father who dwells in me is doing his works." This relationship of mutual indwelling is the same relationship into which Jesus invites those who believe in him.

The Roman Missal

In the Collect, we pray that what we do today—"our present observance" of the Paschal Mystery of Christ—may benefit us for eternity. Consider using the Eucharistic Prayer for Various Needs and Occasions II.

Today's Saint

St. John I (+ 526) was a native of Tuscany and was elected pope when quite elderly. Despite his protests, he was sent by the Arian King Theodoric to Constantinople, where he was to convince Emperor Justin to moderate his decree against the Arians. Theodoric threatened reprisals against Orthodox Christians in the West if he failed. When John returned, Theodoric had him arrested on suspicion of conspiring with the emperor. He died in prison of ill treatment.

19 (#54C) white
Fifth Sunday of Easter

The Lectionary for Mass

◆ FIRST READING: Again and again in the stories of Acts of the Apostles we hear of the trials and sufferings endured by the first Christian missionaries because of their proclamation of Jesus. A perusal of chapters 13 and 14 of Acts of the Apostles reveals that such was the case in each of the cities named in today's reading. These first missionaries realized that hardship was an inevitable, indeed necessary, part of Christian discipleship. Such had been, after all, the way of their Lord and master. The Gentiles' faith in Jesus seems to have been one of the most unexpected happenings in these early days, despite numerous Old Testament texts which point to it. This, too, became cause for rejoicing and praising the Lord.

◆ RESPONSORIAL PSALM 145: This hymn of praise celebrates the goodness of the Lord to all. We hear this today with reference to the first Jewish Christian missionaries, who spoke of the glories of God's Kingdom not only to the Jews, but also to the Gentile "children of Adam."

◆ SECOND READING: Throughout Easter Time, we celebrate the passing away of the reign of death and the new creation of life eternal with God. The vision of John we hear today looks to fulfillment in the full realization of the new creation at the end of time when all is transformed and made new.

◆ GOSPEL: The first part of today's Gospel, spoken by Jesus to the disciples at table with him the night before he died, takes us back to the painful moment of Judas' betrayal and Jesus' imminent death on the Cross. In John, this is the moment of Jesus' glorification. This same reality must be lived out by his missioned disciples, as we heard in today's First Reading. It is interesting to hear the "love commandment," the second focus in today's Gospel, in these last days of Easter Time ("the little while") prior to Jesus' Ascension. To love one another as Jesus loved them is the parting command that the Risen Christ gives us today.

The Roman Missal

Even though we are at the Fifth Sunday of Easter, the season is still reverberating with the joy and enthusiasm of the sacramental initiation that occurred at the Easter Vigil: the Collect makes explicit reference to "those you [God] were pleased to make new in Holy Baptism." The prayer goes on to ask that those newly baptized will "bear much fruit / and come to the joys of life eternal." The meaning of Baptism continues to be center stage in the liturgical theology of Easter Time. We ask God to "constantly accomplish the Paschal Mystery within us," so that all the baptized may bear fruit and come to eternal life, which is not something that happened: it is something that is happening. It is a "wonderful exchange" indeed that has made us "partakers of the one supreme Godhead"! And yet, that is what we are through our sharing in the Eucharist (Prayer over the Offerings). Every day is Passover, in the sense that every day we are called "to pass from former ways to newness of life" (Prayer after Communion). Continue to use the rite for the blessing and sprinkling of water, as discussed for the Second Sunday of Easter, or, if you haven't been doing it, there's no reason why it cannot be used this week. This rite, found in appendix II of the Missal, replaces the Penitential Act. The Gloria is sung or said today, as is the Creed. Any of the five Easter Prefaces may be selected for today. Continue to chant the introductory dialogue and Preface in order to highlight the ongoing festivity of Easter Time, especially if it is not your practice to do so during Ordinary Time. Consider using Eucharistic Prayer III. Consider using the Solemn Blessing for Easter Time, found at number 6 in the "Blessings at the End of Mass and Prayers over the People" section of the Missal. Remember that a regular formula for dismissal is used, not the solemn double Alleluia.

Other Ideas

Don't forget to light the Paschal candle by the ambo at all Sunday liturgies. In your parish bulletin this week and next, be sure to let people know if the Solemnity of the Ascension will be on Sunday instead of Thursday. In the minds of many, the words Ascension and Thursday go together, even though the decision to change this was made by most dioceses over fifteen years ago.

There are three weeks until Pentecost. Prepare to involve parishioners representing various cultures and languages of the parish. If some of the readings are in different languages, prepare a worship aid that offers the texts in English. Say or sing the intercessions of the Prayer of the Faithful in several languages.

M O N 20 (#285) white
Easter Weekday

Optional Memorial of St. Bernardine of Siena, Priest / white

The Lectionary for Mass

◆ FIRST READING: We continue to hear about the missionary journey of Paul and Barnabas. They are driven by persecution out of Iconium as they had formerly been driven out of Antioch. Coming to Lystra, they encounter a crippled man, who listens to Paul's teaching. Paul sees something special in this man: "the faith to be healed." But the people misinterpret this wonderful healing, and, taking Paul and Barnabas for gods, prepare to offer them sacrifice. Paul and Barnabas react far more strongly to this attempt at worship than they did to the persecutions they received in other towns. They "tore their garments, . . . rushed out into the crowd, shouting." It is God, not they, who healed the cripple.

◆ RESPONSORIAL PSALM 115 is the perfect response to this reading: "Not to us, O Lord, not to us, / but to your name give glory."

◆ GOSPEL: Jesus continues to invite his disciples into the mutual love of the Father and the Son. If we love Jesus, we will keep his word. If we keep his word, then the Father will love us and dwell with us. The Holy Spirit is the teacher who will "remind you of all that I told you," helping us to understand and follow the Word of the Lord.

The Roman Missal

In the Collect, we pray for God's abiding presence, that his "right hand" might perpetually help us and defend us "from all wickedness." The Prayer over the Offerings makes it clear that what we offer is a participation in the sacrifice of the Eucharist. The Prayer after Communion asks that the fruits of the Eucharist we just celebrated will "increase in us" and be poured "into our hearts." Any of the five Easter Prefaces may be used. Consider using the Eucharistic Prayer for Various Needs and Occasions II.

Today's Saint

St. Bernardine of Siena (1380–1444) was an Italian Franciscan, a priest, and preacher. He was orphaned young and raised by a pious aunt. While still a student, he helped care for the sick during an outbreak of the bubonic plague, contracted the disease, and almost died. Bernardine joined a strict branch of the Franciscans, called the Observants, around 1402. Known as the "apostle of Italy," he preached devotion to the Holy Name of Jesus, popularizing the use of the monogram IHS and encouraging his hearers to burn unnecessary luxuries in "bonfires of vanities."

T U E 21 (#286) white
Easter Weekday

Optional Memorial of St. Christopher Magallanes, Priest, and Companions, Martyrs / red

The Lectionary for Mass

◆ FIRST READING: Today we read of the completion of the missionary journey of Paul and Barnabas. After nearly being worshiped, Paul is stoned and left for dead. But he simply gets up and keeps on going. After preaching the word in Derbe, Paul and Barnabas go back to the places where they had been persecuted—Lystra, Iconium, and Antioch—encouraging the believers, appointing presbyters, reminding them that they will have to suffer for the sake of the kingdom. They finally return to Antioch where they began and report all that God has done through them, "and how he had opened the door of faith to the Gentiles." This missionary journey would change the world forever.

◆ IN RESPONSORIAL PSALM 145, we recall the "friends" (antiphon) of God who proclaim to all people "the glorious splendor of your kingdom."

◆ GOSPEL: Jesus again tells his disciples that he is going away, but that they must not be "troubled or afraid." He gives them his peace, speaking with special emphasis and repetition that clues us in to how important this gift is: "Peace I leave with you; my peace I give to you. Not as the world gives do I give it to you." The Cross, Jesus hints at the end of today's passage, is not the victory of "the ruler of the world," but rather the victory of love: "the world must know that I love the Father."

The Roman Missal

We ask for "constancy in faith and hope," so that we may never doubt the promises of our faith (Collect).

Any one of the five Easter Prefaces may be used today. Consider using the Eucharistic Prayer for Various Needs and Occasions I.

Today's Saints

St. Christopher Magallanes was a Mexican priest whose years of ministry coincided with an extreme anticlerical era in Mexico. He was falsely accused of promoting rebellion and arrested while on his way to celebrate Mass. Christopher was killed without trial after absolving his executioners, saying, "I die innocent, and ask God that my blood may serve to unite my Mexican brethren." He and his companions died between 1915 and 1928. He was canonized by St. Pope John Paul II on May 21, 2000, along with twenty-one priests and three laymen, also martyred for resisting the anti-Catholic Mexican government of the 1920s.

WED 22 (#287) white — Easter Weekday

Optional Memorial of St. Rita of Cascia, Religious / white

The Lectionary for Mass

◆ FIRST READING: Having returned from their missionary journey, Paul and Barnabas set off for Jerusalem to speak with the apostles about a knotty question: should the Gentile believers be required to undergo circumcision, in keeping with the Mosaic law? This reading gives us a glimpse of a historic moment in the Church. It might be called the first synod or even the first council; when a problem confronts the Church, the "Apostles and presbyters" gather together in one place to hear the different points of view, and to listen to one another with prayer.

◆ RESPONSORIAL PSALM 122 is the prayer of pilgrims to Jerusalem, "built as a city / with compact unity."

◆ GOSPEL: Jesus uses many comparisons to help his disciples understand their relationship with him. In today's Gospel he tells them, "I am the vine, you are the branches." It is yet another comparison that helps us to understand the kind of relationship we must have with Jesus. We are intimately connected with him as our source of life; at the same time, he lives — that is, he bears fruit — through us.

The Roman Missal

Any one of the five Prefaces of Easter are equally appropriate for today, although if the priest celebrant wishes to emphasize the Johannine Gospel theme of the intimate union between Jesus and his followers (the vine and the branches), perhaps either Preface I or Preface III would provide this emphasis most fittingly. Consider using Eucharistic Prayer II.

Today's Saint

St. Rita of Cascia lived in Italy from 1377 to 1457. Against her wishes, her parents arranged for her to marry a man who ended up abusing her. She had two sons with him; both followed their father's bad example. Rita's husband converted toward the end of his life, but he was murdered by an old enemy. Her sons died soon after. Rita was refused entrance to an Augustinian monastery several times because she was a widow, but eventually she was admitted and lived there until her death. She is depicted with a wound in her forehead because she asked to suffer in union with Jesus and was given a wound from a thorn in his crown.

THU 23 (#288) white — Easter Weekday

The Lectionary for Mass

◆ FIRST READING: The debate on whether Gentile converts must be circumcised is of great significance for the Church: in hindsight, we can see that this is really a debate about whether Christianity will remain a sect of Judaism, or something entirely new. After much debate, Peter speaks, showing how requiring Gentiles to be circumcised would be putting God to the test— for hadn't God already shown his favor to them by giving them the Holy Spirit? After Peter speaks, Paul and Barnabas tell of the wonders they witnessed among the Gentiles. Finally James suggests that Gentiles be bound by only a few restrictions.

◆ RESPONSORIAL PSALM 96 is a call to praise God among all the nations.

◆ GOSPEL: Jesus invites us into a loving relationship. Love is not a thing one gives or does; it is more like a place where one lives with Jesus. Again and again Jesus uses that word, remain. If we keep the commandments we remain in the love of Jesus; and to remain in him is to find "complete" joy.

The Roman Missal

Any one of the five Prefaces of Easter might be used equally well today. Consider using Eucharistic Prayer III.

FRI 24 (#289) white — Easter Weekday

The Lectionary for Mass

◆ FIRST READING: The Apostles send a special group — Paul and Barnabas, along with two other disciples, Judas and Silas — to the Gentile believers with the decision. They are not to be bound by the whole law; in Christ, there is a new freedom. The people are "delighted" by the decision of this early council of the Church.

◆ IN RESPONSORIAL PSALM 57, we give thanks to God whose love reaches beyond the chosen people to all the nations.

◆ GOSPEL: We don't often get the same Gospel reading two days in a row, but we do this year. Jesus commands his disciples to "love one another as I love you." In the Gospel according to John, the words love and commandment are often side by side. To love God is to keep his commandments; God's commandments can be summarized in one word: love. Christ suffers on the Cross not for the sake of suffering—but to show his love.

The Roman Missal

Any one of the five Prefaces of Easter might be used equally well today. Consider using Eucharistic Prayer I.

SAT 25 (#290) white
Easter Weekday

Optional Memorials of St. Bede the Venerable, Priest and Doctor of the Church / white; St. Gregory VII, Pope / white; St. Mary Magdalene de'Pazzi, Virgin / white

The Lectionary for Mass

◆ FIRST READING: In today's passage from Acts, we see Paul on the move again. He returns to Derbe, Lystra, and Iconium, carrying with him "the decisions reached by the Apostles and presbyters in Jerusalem." He moves through Phrygia and Galatia, but when he tries to go into Asia and Bithynia, they are "prevented": it is not time to preach there yet. Instead, Paul is led by a vision to preach in Macedonia. The word continues to spread.

◆ RESPONSORIAL PSALM 100 is a joyful invitation to all the nations to sing to God, serve him, and learn his ways.

◆ GOSPEL: Throughout the Last Supper discourses, Jesus has reminded his disciples not to be afraid. In the reading for today, he tells them frankly what they have to expect. They will be treated as he has been treated: with persecution, hatred, and rejection. They will suffer, because "no slave is greater than his master."

The Roman Missal

Through Baptism, God gives us "heavenly life" and makes us "capable of immortality." We pray that we may "attain the fullness of glory" (Collect). Of the five Easter Prefaces that can be used today, it is Preface IV of Easter, with its mention of "the old order destroyed," that perhaps provides an echo of the Gospel reading of the day, in which Jesus talks to his disciples about being hated by the world. Consider using Eucharistic Prayer II.

Today's Saints

The Venerable Bede (673–735), an English Benedictine monk, wrote *The Ecclesiastical History of the English People*, which was his most famous work. Unlike historians who came before him, he did careful research and cited his references.

St. Gregory VII (c. 1021–1085) was a reformer pope best known for his disputes with the Holy Roman Emperor Henry IV. He fought to prevent the appointment of Church officials by secular authorities and died saying, "I have loved justice and hated iniquity; therefore, I die in exile."

St. Mary Magdalene de'Pazzi (1566–1607) was the daughter of a prominent family in Florence. She developed a love of prayer at an early age and began having mystical experiences. Her parents sent her to be educated in a convent but brought her home when they decided she should marry. Fortunately, Mary persuaded them that she had a vocation to be a Carmelite, and they allowed her to return. Her life was marked by prayer, penance, devotion to the Eucharist, and love for the poor.

26 (#57C) white
Sixth Sunday of Easter

The Lectionary for Mass

◆ FIRST READING: One of the most pressing issues for the earliest Christian community, and indeed the subject of the first church "council" as Acts of the Apostles tells the story, pertained to Gentile Christians. Jesus, his disciples and Apostles, and the first members of the Christian community were all Jewish. Now the new community has to decide: Must Gentiles who come to have faith in Jesus also become Jews (that is, be circumcised according to the law of Moses)? We hear today the decision of the Apostles and elders of the community: what is asked of Gentile believers is observance of dietary laws, avoidance of idolatry, and prohibition of Marriage within certain degrees of kinship, but not circumcision.

◆ RESPONSORIAL PSALM 67: This joyful hymn of praise acclaims God's salvation for all the nations (Gentiles) in each stanza and, indeed, in almost every line.

◆ SECOND READING: The universal theme is likewise found in the description of the glorious, heavenly Jerusalem, whose gates, marked with the names of the ancestors of Israel, open in every direction, toward all peoples. The walls of the city are inscribed with the names of the Apostles. Jesus, who brought salvation to all, is the fulfillment of the promises first made to Israel. The city gleamed with the glory of God who was its light, and the Lamb, who was its lamp.

◆ GOSPEL: The strong connection, almost identification, between loving Jesus and keeping his word is stressed. Jesus and his Father come to us in and through this loving obedience and dwell within us. Jesus tells his disciples here, the night before he dies, that the Father will send the Holy Spirit, an Advocate on their behalf, just as he had sent Jesus. The Holy Spirit will teach them and help them to remember all that Jesus told them. Jesus' farewell gift to them is a deep and abiding peace. His return to the Father should be a source of great joy. He has accomplished the mission for which he was sent. They will not be left alone.

The Roman Missal

Continue to use the rite for the blessing and sprinkling of water, as discussed for the Second Sunday of Easter. If you haven't been doing it, there's no reason not to use it this week. This rite, found in appendix II of the Missal, replaces the Penitential Act.

The Gloria is sung or said today, as is the Creed. We pray that we may not only celebrate Easter, but live it, so that "what we relive in remembrance / we may always hold to in what we do" (Collect). In the Prayer over the Offerings, we pray that our prayers may rise up with our offerings, so that we may be transformed as they are, "conformed to the mysteries of your mighty love." Any one of the five Easter Prefaces may be used equally appropriately today. Continue to chant the introductory dialogue and Preface in order to highlight the ongoing festivity of the season, especially if it is not your practice to do so during Ordinary Time. Consider using

Eucharistic Prayer III. In the Prayer after Communion, we ask for an increase in the fruits of the Eucharist, which is the "paschal Sacrament." Consider using the Solemn Blessing for Easter Time, found at number 6 in the "Blessings at the End of Mass and Prayers over the People" section of the Missal. Remember that a regular formula for dismissal is used, and not the solemn double Alleluia.

Other Ideas

Jesus gives us a "new commandment" in the Gospel text for today: "love one another." This could provide a context for a wonderful photo collage in the gathering area of the church, or in some other space that would attract the attention of the parishioners. Ask the children of the parish to display art work showing love in action; or gather some photos from parish events that exhibit the many ways that love is expressed throughout the parish at any time of the year. Seeing what others do in the name of love can encourage us to do loving things ourselves, and we come to realize that we are not alone trying to bring the love of the Lord to the world around us. Send a "love note," or call someone whom you haven't seen or spoken to in a long time. Keeping in touch lifts our spirits and brightens our day.

MON 27 (#291) white
Easter Weekday

Optional Memorial of St. Augustine of Canterbury, Bishop / white

The Lectionary for Mass

◆ FIRST READING: Today's reading from the Acts of the Apostles suddenly switches from third person into first person. Does this mean that the author of the Acts of the Apostles was actually with Paul on his sea journey to Philippi? Probably not, Scripture scholars tell us; it was a convention in Greek literature to use the first person to

describe sea voyages, to make the narrative more vivid. Paul arrives at Philippi where he preaches the word, and encounters a woman named Lydia. She is a working woman, "a dealer in purple cloth," and listens attentively to the message. She believes, and her entire household is baptized. She immediately puts her Baptism into practice, inviting Paul and those with him into her home, and they accept her hospitality.

◆ RESPONSORIAL PSALM 149 praises the God who "takes delight in his people," and who loves to be in their midst.

◆ GOSPEL: Today's Gospel combines comfort and challenge. The comfort is the promise of the "Advocate," the "Spirit of truth," who will come from the Father and "testify" to Christ. The challenge comes next. The persecution will be intense, so much so that "the hour is coming when everyone who kills you will think he is offering worship to God." Through these persecutions, the Holy Spirit will be with the followers of Jesus Christ to strengthen them.

The Roman Missal

We ask for "the fruit produced by the paschal observances," that Easter may have an effect in our lives (Collect). Consider using Eucharistic Prayer II.

Today's Saint

St. Augustine, born in the first third of the sixth century, was a Benedictine monk and was named the first archbishop of Canterbury in 598. He was prior of a monastery in Rome when St. Gregory the Great, after seeing blonde Saxon slaves in the market, chose him to lead a mission to England. Augustine worked in Kent in the south of England, and once he converted King Æthelberht, the rest of Kent followed. He died in 604 and was buried in the abbey church at Canterbury, which became a place of pilgrimage. The shrine was destroyed and the relics were lost during the English Reformation.

TUE 28 (#292) white
Easter Weekday

The Lectionary for Mass

◆ FIRST READING: For the second time in the Acts of the Apostles we see that prison bars cannot contain the disciples of Jesus. Paul and Silas, beaten by the authorities and flung into prison, are "praying and singing hymns to God," when an earthquake loosens their chains and flings open all the doors of the prison. The guard is about to kill himself—so terrified is he of the consequences of the escape of the prisoners on his watch—when Paul and Silas call out. They have not taken advantage of the earthquake to depart. The man is amazed. He brings Paul and Silas to his home, cleans their wounds, then he and his entire family receive Baptism with great rejoicing.

◆ IN RESPONSORIAL PSALM 138, we can hear the prayer of thanksgiving offered by the apostles on their deliverance from prison: "Your right hand saves me, O Lord."

◆ GOSPEL: As we draw near the end of Easter Time, the Gospel focuses more and more on the Holy Spirit. Today, Jesus reassures his disciples that it is good for him to depart—for unless he does, "the Advocate will not come to you."

The Roman Missal

The Collect is a simple prayer for a share in the Resurrection of Christ. The Prayer over the Offerings asks that "we might always find delight in these paschal mysteries" which will "ensure for us eternal gladness" (Prayer after Communion). Consider using Eucharistic Prayer III.

WED 29 (#293) white
Easter Weekday

The Lectionary for Mass

◆ FIRST READING: Paul comes to Athens, one of the greatest cities in the ancient world. His address to the Athenians in the Areopagus gives us insight into how this great missionary worked. He first walked through the city, observing the various temples. Having learned about their way of life, he is able to meet the Athenians where they are. "I see that in every respect you are very religious," he tells them, not rejecting their beliefs, but leading them from faith in an "Unknown God" to belief in the God of Jesus Christ. He quotes their poets, speaking to them in language they can understand. And though the Resurrection proves a stumbling block, they are intrigued. "We should like to hear you on this some other time."

◆ RESPONSORIAL PSALM 148: Paul urged the Athenians to see God's presence in creation; Psalm 148 calls on all of creation to praise the Lord.

◆ GOSPEL: Jesus tells his disciples that he has much more to teach them, but they "cannot bear it now." The Holy Spirit he will send to them will continue their teaching. Through the Holy Spirit, Jesus Christ continues to teach us in every age and every place.

The Roman Missal

If tomorrow is celebrated as the Ascension, this Mass is celebrated in the morning. The evening Masses should be for the Vigil of the Ascension.

◆ FOR THE MORNING MASS: The Collect today reminds us how every celebration of the Eucharist unites us with the Communion of Saints: we participate in the fruits of Jesus' Resurrection now, through our liturgical celebration of the

mysteries, while the saints already share in the fullness of the Resurrection in the Kingdom. In the Prayer over the Offerings we again hear of "the wonderful exchange effected in this sacrifice," which should become the pattern for every aspect of our life; growing in that conformity to the life of Christ is the goal of liturgical celebration. The Prayer after Communion presents the effects of our participating in the "heavenly mysteries" as passing "from former ways to newness of life." Consider using Eucharistic Prayer III.

THU 30 (#58C) white
Solemnity of the Ascension of the Lord

Holyday of Obligation

About Today's Solemnity

The distinct celebration of the Ascension of the Lord was unknown in the first three and a half centuries. The chronology of dating the Ascension to forty days after Easter exists only in the Acts of the Apostles. In the Gospel according to Luke, the Ascension appears to have taken place much earlier, even on Easter Day. The original ending to Mark's account of the Gospel did not include the Ascension at all, and it can only be inferred from Matthew's conclusion. When fourth-century Egeria mentions a celebration forty days after Easter in Bethlehem, it may have been for the Holy Innocents. But by the fifth century the observance seems to be universally accepted. In the dioceses where today is celebrated as the Ascension, it is a Holyday of Obligation.

The Lectionary for Mass

◆ FIRST READING: In his introduction to the second volume of his work, Luke again begins by addressing the man who sponsored his work. He then picks up where his Gospel account left off, only with a slightly different chronology concerning Jesus' return to the heavenly realm. In Acts of the Apostles, this takes place after "forty days," that Biblically significant number. His point: the Apostles experienced the presence of the Risen Christ with them over an extended period of time. His parting words to them: "wait" for the promised Holy Spirit, later described as "power" (the Greek word is *dynamis*). The Holy Spirit is the "power" they will need to be his witnesses, not only to the Jews, but to the Gentiles as well.

◆ RESPONSORIAL PSALM 47: Returning to heaven, Jesus is enthroned at the right hand of his heavenly Father. Today's Psalm breaks forth in a joyful hymn of praise.

◆ SECOND READING: The Letter to the Hebrews speaks of Jesus' passage through death into life and his return to the heavenly realm as his entrance, as supreme high priest, into the heavenly tabernacle. Throughout the letter, Hebrews develops the theme of Jesus' sacrificial offering of himself and of his priesthood as fulfilling, and indeed far surpassing, the priesthood and sacrificial rites of the Law of Moses. Jesus' self-sacrifice is a once-and-for-all sacrifice. What this means for us is confidence and hope, a point especially emphasized in the second part of the reading. We can and should be confident: Christ has opened the way for us.

◆ GOSPEL: In his Gospel, Luke situates the Ascension on Easter evening, shortly after he appeared to the disciples and shared a meal with them. He interprets the Scriptures for them, showing that his Death and Resurrection have fulfilled them. He commissions them, but instructs them to wait until they receive the "power from high," that is his Holy Spirit. His final act toward them is blessing; theirs to him, adoration.

The Roman Missal

Two sets of Mass formularies are given for the solemnity, one for the Vigil Mass and one for the Mass during the Day. A rubric before the texts for the Vigil Mass explains that where the Solemnity of the Ascension is not observed as a Holyday of Obligation, it is observed on the Seventh Sunday of Easter.

◆ AT THE VIGIL MASS: Remember that the Creed is said today as is the Gloria. The Preface assigned for this Mass is either Preface I or Preface II of the Ascension. Preface I makes explicit that the purpose of Christ's Ascension was "not to distance himself from our lowly state," but rather so that we "might be confident of following where he, our Head and Founder, has gone before." Preface II states the same thing in a slightly different way, noting that the purpose of the Ascension was so that "he might make us sharers in his divinity." As with the Sundays of Easter Time, it would be a good idea to chant the introductory dialogue and Preface today. If the Roman Canon is used as the Eucharistic Prayer for this celebration, remember that there is a proper form of the *Communicantes* ("In communion with those . . ."); it is found within the prayer itself, on the page that lists the several different forms of the *Communicantes*. There is a special Solemn Blessing specifically for the Ascension of the

Lord that can be used for the final blessing at the end of Mass, and it would be good to make use of it. We're not at Pentecost yet, however, so the solemn double Alleluia dismissal is not yet used. Stick with one of the usual dismissal formulas. Of course use festive music with full choir, banners in the entrance procession, incense, and a longer, more formal Gospel procession.

◆ AT THE MASS DURING THE DAY: There is no reason not to use the Rite for the Blessing and Sprinkling of Water, especially if it has been used on the Sundays throughout Easter Time. Baptism into the Paschal Mystery means immersion in the fullness of the mystery, which includes Christ's ascended glory. The rite is found in appendix II of the Missal and replaces the Penitential Act. The Gloria is sung today. The Creed is said. The priest celebrant has a choice from among two Collects for today. The first option sets a tone of gladness and joy as it notes that "the Ascension of Christ your Son / is our exaltation" because we, his Body, are "called to follow in hope" where he, our Head, has gone. The reality that liturgy is at its core a celebration of our participation in the mysteries of Christ cannot be stated emphatically enough, and this prayer is yet another example of how this truth is basic to the meaning of liturgical celebration. The second prayer asks that, since we "believe that your Only Begotten Son, our Redeemer, / ascended this day to the heavens," we may be granted to even now dwell in spirit "in heavenly realms." Notice too the important assertion of "this day," an important reference to the salvific reality being made present in our own time and space. The Creed is said today. See the comments about the Vigil Mass for some thoughts about the two options for the Preface, which are the same for the Mass during the Day, and for the proper insert if Eucharistic Prayer I is used. As with the Vigil Mass, it would be good to use the special Solemn Blessing specifically for the Ascension of the Lord as the final blessing at the end of Mass. Since we're not at Pentecost yet, one of the usual dismissal formulas, not the solemn double Alleluia dismissal, is used. Of course use festive music with full choir, banners in the entrance procession, incense, and a longer, more formal Gospel procession.

Other Ideas

The month of June was often considered prime time for weddings. It might be appropriate to call attention to some issues surrounding the celebration of parish weddings. The universal Church recently received a revised *Order of Celebrating Matrimony.* Consider publishing a series of bulletin articles on the revised rite with special focus on the role of the couple in making choices for their ceremony. Some aspects of the rite could be used for reflections for all married couples. If the parish has particular guidelines for weddings then these could be published as well. Invite all engaged couples to be present for a Sunday liturgy on a weekend in June and provide the blessing for engaged couples. The revised rite includes these two blessings in the appendix.

THU **30** (#294) white
Easter Weekday

The Lectionary for Mass

◆ First Reading: Paul comes to a turning point in his preaching of the word. Up to this point, he has preached to both Jews and Gentiles. But after his reception by the Jews at Corinth, Paul gives up: he decides to devote himself exclusively to the non-Jews. This reading is full of names of disciples, both Jews and Gentiles, who became followers of Christ: Priscilla, Aquila, Titus

Justus, Crispus. By their faith, they became part of the Christian story.

◆ Responsorial Psalm 98 is a song of praise of the God who is over all the nations. It is our response of praise to Paul's announcement of his mission to the Gentiles.

◆ Gospel: The Passion of Jesus is near. As he prepares his disciples for the violent separation they are to undergo, the brutal execution of their beloved teacher, he uses gentle language, not mentioning death at all. He only says, "you will not see me . . . you will see me." Even as his Passion approaches, Jesus' focus is on his disciples, and on the joy which is still to come.

The Roman Missal

If the Ascension is celebrated in your diocese on Sunday, then today's prayers are from Thursday after the Sixth Sunday of Easter in the Proper of Seasons. Consider using the Eucharistic Prayer for Various Needs and Occasions I.

FRI **31** (#572) white
Feast of the Visitation of the Blessed Virgin Mary

About Today's Feast

When the angel brought Mary the amazing message that she would be the mother of God's Son, he also brought her some family news: her elderly cousin, Elizabeth, was going to have a baby as well. Immediately, Mary set out to visit her cousin and help her at what must have been a challenging time. When Mary arrived, something amazing happened: the child in Elizabeth's womb leapt up in recognition, and Elizabeth, too, was filled with the Holy Spirit and realized that Mary was carrying God's Son. Even before his birth, John the Baptist was pointing the way to Christ!

We echo Elizabeth's joyful exclamation every time we pray the Hail Mary: "Blessed are you

among women, and blessed is the fruit of your womb!" And we echo Mary's response to her cousin, her Magnificat, in the Office of Evening Prayer.

The Lectionary for Mass

◆ First Reading, Option 1: The passage from Zephaniah is full of joy in the Lord, whose presence casts out fear from the community of Israel, removes their judgment, and thwarts their enemies. On such Scriptures as these, Elizabeth and Mary were nourished. It was through God's word that they first came to know the Lord whose Word became flesh in Mary's womb.

◆ First Reading, Option 2: The second option is St. Paul's simple guide to Christian living from the end of the letter to the Romans. We see all these patterns of the disciple's life reflected in the Gospel account of Mary and Elizabeth: mutual affection, respect, service, hospitality, joy.

◆ Canticle: The keynote is well expressed in the antiphon: "Among you is the great and Holy One of Israel." God is in our midst.

◆ Gospel: Immediately after the angel departs, Mary sets out to visit her cousin Elizabeth. The passage consists largely of the words of Elizabeth and the prayer of Mary. Both have become enduring parts of the prayer of the Church. We echo Elizabeth every time we pray the Hail Mary; we pray Mary's Magnificat every day at Evening Prayer. The reading is all about the presence of God. At the sound of Mary's greeting, the unborn John the Baptist in Elizabeth's womb leaps for joy, and then his mother is filled with the Spirit and proclaims Mary blessed, "the mother of my Lord." The presence of the God-made-flesh in Mary's womb brings Elizabeth recognition and awareness; and Mary responds with a prayer of thanksgiving, filled with praise of the God who works such wonders. The Visitation is at once the feast of Mary's faith and of Jesus' work of grace, which begins from the moment of his conception.

The Roman Missal

The Entrance Antiphon from Psalm 66 perfectly captures the joy of Mary and Elizabeth, who both speak words of faith at their holy meeting: "Come and hear . . . / I will tell what the Lord did for my soul." The Gloria is said or sung on this feast. The Collect is full of echoes of the Gospel account of the Visitation. Just as Mary visited her cousin in response to the Spirit's urging, we pray that we may be "faithful to the promptings of the Spirit." Just as Mary praised God in her Magnificat, we pray that we may "magnify [God's] greatness / with the Virgin Mary." We ask God to receive what we offer, just as he received "the charity" of Mary (Prayer over the Offerings). Preface II of the Blessed Virgin Mary is used. The Prayer after Communion echoes the language of Mary's Magnificat: "May your Church proclaim your greatness, O God, / for you have done great things for your faithful." We pray that we may be like John the Baptist in his mother's womb, aware of "the hidden presence of Christ," and rejoice to receive him in the Sacrament of his Body and Blood. Consider using Eucharistic Prayer III.

June 2019
Month of the Sacred Heart

S A T 1
(#296) red
Memorial of St. Justin, Martyr

The Lectionary for Mass

◆ FIRST READING: In Acts, the disciples encounter a new situation. Apollos is a Jew, a scholar, who has come to believe in Jesus, "although he knew only the baptism of John." In Ephesus, he is speaking boldly and publicly of "the Way of the Lord" in the synagogues. How to handle this unaffiliated prophet? Priscilla and Aquila "took him aside" and spoke to him privately. Then Apollos, like Paul before him, is welcomed into the community. This early Christian community was so attuned to the Holy Spirit that they immediately recognized the Holy Spirit's presence in others — even in outsiders.

◆ RESPONSORIAL PSALM 47: Throughout the Easter Season, the insistent refrain of our psalms has been praise of God's love which reaches beyond all boundaries to embrace the whole world. In Psalm 47, we rejoice in the God who reigns over all nations.

◆ TODAY'S GOSPEL is full of wonderful promises. God loves the Son so much that "whatever you ask the Father in my name he will give you." In time, Jesus will no longer speak to them in "figures of speech," but directly. For the sake of his Son, God loves us and listens to our prayers. Jesus leads his disciples little by little to a deeper understanding of the gift of the Holy Spirit, who will live in us, teaching us, uniting our prayer with that of the Father and the Son.

The Roman Missal

Full texts for today's memorial are found in the Proper of Saints at June 1. Use Preface I or II of Holy Martyrs. Consider using the Eucharistic Prayer for Various Needs and Occasions II.

Today's Saint

St. Justin, also called Justin Martyr (c. 100–165), was born in Judea and raised pagan by parents who were probably Greek or Roman. He studied philosophy, converted to Christianity, and spent his life teaching and writing. Justin is best known for his *Apologies* and for his *Dialogue with Trypho*. He fought against the heresy of Marcion, who rejected the Old Testament. Justin's life ended in Rome, where he was martyred under Marcus Aurelius. He is one of the first Christian apologists, and he was one of the first to employ philosophy as a tool toward greater understanding of revelation.

2
(#61C) white
Seventh Sunday of Easter / Solemnity of the Ascension of the Lord

In some dioceses, the Solemnity of the Ascension of the Lord is transferred to the Seventh Sunday of Easter. If this is the case in your diocese, use the readings and prayer texts from the Ascension. See page 210 in this Sourcebook for commentary.

The Lectionary for Mass

◆ FIRST READING: Today's First Reading from Acts of the Apostles recounts the death of Stephen, the first martyr in the Church. It is an interesting choice for this second to last Sunday of Easter Time. Perhaps Stephen's vision of God's glory prompted its choice since Jesus prays in today's Gospel that his followers will see the glory which the Father has given him. This is precisely what Stephen sees in his vision. Stephen's death and Jesus' reception of his spirit, marks the completion of his journey to his heavenly home. So it will be for us.

◆ RESPONSORIAL PSALM 97: Today's Psalm celebrates God's kingship. Although kingship is not specifically mentioned in today's First Reading, it is implied: that is, Jesus, standing at the right hand of God. The language evokes the prophet Daniel's vision of the exaltation of the Son of Man.

◆ SECOND READING: The verses chosen for today's reading come from the end of Revelation, a book filled with descriptions of heaven and of the rewards given to those who are judged righteous after their death. Note the names given to Jesus, especially Alpha and Omega: these very words are used in the preparation of the Paschal candle at the Easter Vigil. Note also the prominence of the word "come." Jesus promises to come soon. The Church prays, "come, Lord Jesus." How deep is our longing, our prayer, for his coming?

◆ GOSPEL: Today's Gospel is set in the context of Jesus' last words to his disciples the night before he died. Here Jesus is speaking not only to the disciples, but to the heavenly Father. In his prayer, Jesus asks that his followers be united as one, more specifically, as he and the Father are one. The unity of his followers will give witness to the world that the Jesus in whom they believe, and whose teachings they follow, was indeed sent by the Father. The unity of the Father and the Son, the love between the Father and the Son—this is the same unity

and love that Jesus prays will be the experience and the witness of all who believe in him.

The Roman Missal

If you are in a region that observes the Solemnity of the Ascension today, refer to the comments on page 210 for the celebration of Mass today. What follows is for the Seventh Sunday of Easter. Continue to use the Rite for the Blessing and Sprinkling of Water, as has been done, it is hoped, on all the Sundays of Easter Time. If this has not been the case, it can nonetheless still be used today if desired. Remember that this rite, found in appendix II of the Missal, replaces the Penitential Act. The Gloria and the Creed are sung or said. We believe that Christ has risen and ascended to his Father; in the Collect, we pray that we may experience his abiding presence in our midst. We pray that the "acts of devotedness" we bring to God in the celebration of the Eucharist may help us to "pass over to the glory of heaven" (Prayer over the Offerings). The Ascension is a fact, and a promise of future glory, because we believe that "what has already come to pass in Christ," the Head of the Church, "will be accomplished in the body of the whole Church" (Prayer after Communion). Although the choice of the Preface may be taken from among the five Easter Prefaces or the two Ascension Prefaces, it would seem to be pastorally advantageous to use one of the two Prefaces of the Ascension. Continue to chant the introductory dialogue and Preface. Consider using Eucharistic Prayer III. Use the solemn blessing for Easter Time, found at number 6 in the "Blessings at the End of Mass and Prayers over the People" section of the Missal, and one of the regular formulas for dismissal is used.

Other Ideas

The nine days between Ascension and Pentecost are the original novena, a time set apart by Jesus himself: "he enjoined them not to depart from Jerusalem," we hear in today's reading from the Acts of the Apostles, "but to wait for 'the promise of the Father'" (Acts 1:4). The novena begins the day after "Ascension Thursday." If you are observing the Pentecost novena, do so with special solemnity on this in-between Sunday. You might highlight this time of watchful prayer by doing something a little different with the Prayer of the Faithful, incorporating a moment of silent prayer for the gifts of the Holy Spirit.

(#297) red

MON 3 Memorial of St. Charles Lwanga and Companions, Martyrs

The Lectionary for Mass

◆ FIRST READING: Paul travels to Ephesus, where Apollos had been preaching. He finds some believers there, who, like Apollos, have not yet heard the whole of the Gospel. They do not know about the Holy Spirit and have only received John's baptism, a "baptism of repentance." Paul, great missionary that he is, gently meets them where they are. He teaches them, baptizes them, and lays hands on them.

◆ RESPONSORIAL PSALM 68: We praise God who "gives a home to the forsaken," leading them to safe havens.

◆ GOSPEL: On the night before his death, Jesus encourages his disciples with words of tenderness, unity, and love. Jesus warns them that the moment is drawing near when they will be scattered, when they will abandon him. With the absolute confidence and foreknowledge he constantly displays in the Gospel according to John, Jesus says, "but I am not alone, because the Father is with me." He then tells them to "take courage, I have conquered the world."

The Roman Missal

All of the prayers are proper to the memorial. Use one of the two Prefaces for Holy Martyrs. Consider using Eucharistic Prayer II.

Today's Saints

St. Charles Lwanga (+ 1886) was a Ugandan catechist who served as a page in the court of King Mwanga II. King Mwanga felt threatened by the presence of missionaries in his country, and he insisted that Christians renounce their faith. After a massacre of Anglicans in 1885, the head page, Joseph Mukasa, reproached the king, who had him beheaded and arrested his followers. Charles baptized those who were still catechumens, and he and twenty-one others were burnt alive. Although they were not canonized, Paul VI recognized the martyrdom of the Anglican Christians when he canonized Charles and his companions.

T U E **4** (#298) white
Easter Weekday

The Lectionary for Mass

◆ FIRST READING: Through most of the Easter Season, our readings from Acts and our readings from John have not been closely linked with each other, except in their common concern for the working of the Holy Spirit. Today's readings are an exception. Both contain solemn farewells, and both show us faithful servants of God who face the future without fear. In the First Reading, Paul speaks to all the presbyters of the Church in Ephesus. He is being called to Jerusalem, not by human beings, but "compelled by the Spirit." He does not know what will happen to him there, but he does know that he will never see these friends again. He tells them

solemnly that he has taught them everything, "the entire plan of God," holding nothing back.

◆ RESPONSORIAL PSALM 68 praises the God who "bears our burdens," just as God sustained Paul through imprisonments, dangers, and trials of every kind.

◆ THE GOSPEL marks the beginning of Jesus' great prayer to the Father. Jesus has accomplished all of the great work the Father gave to him. He has taught his disciples everything, bringing them into union with himself. Now he is ready to return to the Father.

The Roman Missal

Although the choice of the Preface may be taken from among the five Easter Prefaces or the two Ascension Prefaces, strongly consider using one of the two Prefaces of the Ascension as a way of highlighting the unique liturgical time in which we find ourselves, in between Ascension and Pentecost in days that pray for the coming of the Spirit. Consider using the Eucharistic Prayer for Various Needs and Occasions II.

W E D **5** (#299) red
Memorial of St. Boniface, Bishop and Martyr

The Lectionary for Mass

◆ FIRST READING: We continue to read the farewell discourses of Paul and of Jesus. Paul gives the presbyters of Ephesus some practical advice: "Be vigilant." Watch out for false teachers, "savage wolves," who will seek to scatter the flock. He reminds them of how he himself worked to support himself when he was among them—"In every way I have shown you that by hard work of that sort we must help the weak." Most importantly, Paul prays for them and commends them to "that gracious word" of God which "can build you up."

They part with prayers and tears, and the people of Ephesus stay close to Paul, walking with him all the way to the ship that will bear him to Jerusalem.

◆ RESPONSORIAL PSALM 68: We continue to pray Psalm 68, praising the God whose love reaches to all the earth.

◆ GOSPEL: Jesus prays for his disciples. He prays that "they may be one," with the same unity shared by the Father and the Son. He prays that they may be kept from "the Evil One": not by being taken out of harm's way, but by God's protection. He prays that they may "share my joy," and he prays that God will "consecrate them in the truth." Jesus prays that his disciples may share, not partially but fully, in the life he shares with his Father.

The Roman Missal

The Collect is drawn from the Proper of Saints, with the remaining prayers taken from the Common of Martyrs: For One Martyr or of Pastors: For Missionaries. The Preface of Holy Martyrs or of Holy Pastors may be used. Consider using Eucharistic Prayer I.

Today's Saint

St. Boniface (c. 675–754) was an Anglo-Saxon Benedictine monk. He was first sent as a missionary to Frisia, which is in the vicinity of the Netherlands, but he failed because of wars between the local tribes and the Frankish king Charles Martel. Boniface then went to Rome and was commissioned by the pope to evangelize in Germany. He started by chopping down an oak tree dedicated to Thor, and when he was not immediately struck down, the people believed and became Christians. Boniface returned to evangelize the Frisians but was killed by them in AD 754. He is buried in the cathedral in Fulda.

THU 6 (#300) white
Easter Weekday

Optional Memorial of St. Norbert, Bishop / white

The Lectionary for Mass

◆ FIRST READING: Paul arrives in Jerusalem and is immediately embroiled in controversy. Aware of the divisions among the Jewish leaders, he tells the Sanhedrin that he is not on trial for professing the name of Jesus, but for "hope in the resurrection of the dead." As Paul anticipated, the Pharisees and Sadducees on the Sanhedrin are divided and begin to debate among themselves. When they are unable to resolve the issue, Paul is taken into custody by the Roman troops. At the end of today's reading, the Lord reassures Paul that this is how it was meant to be. "Just as you have borne witness to my cause in Jerusalem, so you must also bear witness in Rome."

◆ RESPONSORIAL PSALM 16 is the prayer of God's faithful servant, who is confident in God's power to save even in the midst of unimaginable dangers.

◆ GOSPEL: Today we hear the conclusion of Jesus' prayer for unity. The disciples must be united with the unity that binds the Father and the Son, so that "the world may believe that you sent me." Jesus has already given them everything they need in order to be at unity, to be "brought to perfection as one." Again and again in these Last Supper discourses, Jesus tells us that he has given everything to us—he has kept nothing back. The glory, the truth, and the love he received from his Father he longs to share with us.

The Roman Missal

The choices for the Preface today include any one of the five Prefaces of Easter or the two Prefaces of the Ascension. It would seem most beneficial to highlight the unique nature of these days as time in between the Ascension and Pentecost by using one of the Ascension Prefaces. Consider using Eucharistic Prayer II.

Today's Saint

St. Norbert was born into a noble German family, leading a life of ease. He later entered a Benedictine monastery and was ordained. Narrowly escaping death (he was struck by lightning), Norbert experienced a profound conversion. He thus embarked on a reform movement, founding a community of Augustinian cannons, which came to be known as the Norbertines or Premonstratensians.

FRI 7 (#301) white
Easter Weekday

The Lectionary for Mass

◆ FIRST READING: Scripture scholars point out that Luke's account of Paul's trial and condemnation in the Acts of the Apostles has marked parallels with the account of the trial and condemnation of Jesus in Luke's account of the Gospel. Today, we have a long speech by Festus to King Agrippa, who has come to Caesarea. Again we see the interplay between sacred and secular authorities; again we have a Roman ruler, Festus, seeking to gain favor with the Jews by holding Paul captive. Festus is a politician, and the religious debates of the Jews have little meaning for him—"they had some issues with him about their own religion and about a certain Jesus who had died but who Paul claimed was alive." As Paul said to the Sanhedrin in Jerusalem, he is on trial for his belief in the Resurrection of Jesus Christ from the dead.

◆ RESPONSORIAL PSALM 103 praises the God of kindness, the God who forgives our transgressions. This psalm anticipates the story of forgiveness we hear in today's Gospel reading.

◆ GOSPEL: Throughout Easter, we have heard John's account of the Gospel of Jesus Christ; during these last two weekdays of the Easter season, we hear the conclusion of John's account. Today, we read the moving encounter of Peter with the risen Jesus. It was by the shores of a lake that Peter first saw Jesus and answered his call to discipleship. Now, on another shore, Jesus calls Peter again. "Do you love me? . . . Feed my sheep." Peter receives a new call: to love God, to shepherd the flock, and to suffer as Jesus did.

The Roman Missal

Through Christ's Resurrection and the Spirit's light, "the gates of eternity" stand open before us. We pray that our sharing in God's great gifts may deepen our devotion and strengthen our faith. The choices for the Preface today include any one of the five Prefaces of Easter or the two Prefaces of the Ascension. Consider using Eucharistic Prayer I.

SAT 8 (#302) white
Easter Weekday

The Lectionary for Mass

◆ FIRST READING: Today, as the Easter season draws to a close, we hear the endings of the Acts of the Apostles and of the Gospel according to John. But these endings are more like beginnings. Paul arrives in Rome, under arrest and in chains. We know that he will eventually be condemned and executed; nevertheless, for two years, "with complete assurance," he proclaims the Kingdom of God and teaches about Jesus.

◆ RESPONSORIAL PSALM 11: Today's short Responsorial, Psalm 11, echoes that sense of anticipation we get in the First Reading: "The just will gaze on your face, O Lord."

◆ GOSPEL: Peter knows now what his own task, and his fate, will be; but Jesus has not said anything to the beloved disciple. "Lord, what about him?" Peter asks. Jesus gives him no clear reply, instead reiterating his call to Peter: "What concern is it of yours? You follow me." We do not know when Jesus will come again. We must wait, not in idleness and speculation, but in confident labor, just as Paul and Peter did. From beginning to end, the Gospel according to John has focused on the testimony of witnesses, and it is fitting that it ends with a reassertion that the writer is trustworthy: "we know that his testimony is true." But the final lines emphasize that the Gospel is incomplete. No book can contain all that Jesus did. We are invited to look beyond the pages of the Gospel, to see the continuation of the story in the action of the Holy Spirit in our lives. Amen!

The Roman Missal

Notice how the Missal's designation of "At the Morning Mass" clearly distinguishes this Mass from the Vigil of Pentecost, which will be celebrated later the same day, in the evening. The Collect, perhaps somewhat curiously, does not specifically mention the Holy Spirit (except in the Doxology, of course), but it does convey a sense of completion or coming to a close with its phrase about "we who have celebrated the Paschal festivities" — throughout these fifty days. The prayer goes on to ask that we may "hold fast to them in the way that we live our lives," thus affirming the goal of all liturgical celebration — that what we celebrate in ritual (dying and rising; offering ourselves in union with Christ) may be lived out in daily life. The Prayer over the Offerings does explicitly mention, in a way that connotes a sense of anticipation and excitement, that the Holy Spirit is indeed "coming near," as

it asks that the event "prepare our minds for the divine Sacrament, since the Spirit himself is the remission of all sins." The notion of our being prepared fits well with this point in the liturgy at the Prayer over the Offerings as part of the Preparation of the Gifts; the mention of the remission of sins reminds us of one of the fruits of participation in the Eucharist, namely, forgiveness. The Prayer after Communion uses the old/new motif that we have heard so often throughout Easter Time, as it begs that "as we have been brought from things of the past to new mysteries [both in this Eucharistic celebration and throughout the whole fifty days of Easter Time, which are coming to a close today], so, with former ways left behind, we may be made new in holiness of mind [the concrete transformation to be brought about through our participation in the mysteries]." The choices for the Preface today include any one of the five Prefaces of Easter or the two Prefaces of the Ascension. Consider using Eucharistic Prayer II.

(#62C , #63C) red
9 Solemnity of Pentecost

About Today's Solemnity

The Greek word for Pentecost (*pentekoste*) means "fiftieth," and in early Christianity it referred to the entire fifty days of Easter. The roots of Pentecost can be found in the

Jewish festival of Weeks (Shavuot), the fifty-day celebration following Passover (Exodus 23:16). It was a harvest festival in which the first fruits of the harvest were offered to God in gratitude. It eventually became associated with the giving of the Torah on Mount Sinai. Early Christians reinterpreted the Jewish festival as a commemoration of the coming of the Holy Spirit, since Acts records that the Holy Spirit came to the disciples when the festival of Pentecost was fulfilled (see Acts 2:1–11). The celebration of Pentecost may begin on Saturday afternoon or evening with the Vigil. By the end of the fourth century in the West, Pentecost became a time for the initiation of those not baptized at Easter. Thus, a night vigil was added like the Easter Vigil for this purpose. With this early history in mind, this is a most appropriate time to initiate those who were not ready at the Easter Vigil, or (not and) to celebrate the Reception of Baptized Christians into the Full Communion of the Catholic Church (see RCIA, 473).

The Lectionary for Mass: Vigil Mass

◆ FIRST READING, OPTION 1: This ancient story of Babel is thought by many scholars to be an etiology which explains the many languages found throughout the world. It is also a story of humanity's relationship with God: the people build the city with the tower to "make a name for ourselves," implying that they do so separate and apart from God. As such, it is a continuation of the story of the garden. The Lord responds not by destroying the city or tower but by scattering them throughout the earth.

◆ FIRST READING, OPTION 2: In this encounter between Moses, the Israelites, and God, the people assent to listen to God's voice and heed it, establishing a covenant between God and the people of Israel. God is presented as both near (the people will be his special possession) and powerful (the theophany on the mountain). Moses is designated as the leader who goes up to the mountain on behalf of the people.

◆ FIRST READING, OPTION 3: The vision of dry bones being brought to life by God in Ezekiel presents the hope of new life and restored relationship with God following the long exile of the people. It is a statement of the power of the promise of God to take what seems lost and to make it new: the Lord's spirit will be placed within the people, they will be settled into their land, and will therefore know the Lord.

◆ FIRST READING, OPTION 4: In this vision from the prophet Joel, the Lord pours his spirit upon all, equally. Young and old, male and female, even upon servants and handmaids, the spirit is given to all who call upon the name of the Lord, and they will see visions and dream dreams. God will work great wonders and signs on the day of the Lord. Those who call upon God's name comprise a remnant of faithful ones, survivors whom the Lord shall call.

◆ RESPONSORIAL PSALM 104: This psalm of praise declares the majesty and glory of God as a response to any or all of the designated readings, linking these stories of God's love and the spirit of God with the Second Reading and Gospel that follow. Through our proclamation of this song, we ask God to renew the outpouring of the Spirit upon us, and upon the earth. All of creation is a sign of God's greatness; the spirit of the Lord brings life and renewal.

◆ SECOND READING: In his letter to the Romans, Paul depicts the present and the future of our life in Christ. We have received the Holy Spirit and yet wait for the redemption of our bodies in the initiation into eternal life. Hope for something already seen is not true hope; we wait with endurance for the fulfillment of the promise of union with God through the Spirit. Yet in our present, incomplete life in Christ, the Spirit is with us in our weakness, strengthening and interceding for us.

◆ GOSPEL: This passage is set on the last day of the feast of Tabernacles, a weeklong harvest celebration that included remembrance of the Exodus water miracle. Water was taken daily from the pool of Siloam to the Temple and poured over the altar with prayers for winter rain. In this context, Jesus says that we are to come to him, through whom living water will come. He says this in reference to the Spirit who has not yet descended upon the disciples.

Responsorial Psalms and Collects at the Extended Vigil

The Roman Missal provides additional psalms and Collects for an extended Vigil. The full texts of the psalms are in the new *Lectionary for Mass: Supplement* (2017). The following is an outline for the sequence of readings, psalms, and Collects.

◆ Genesis 11:1–9. Sing Psalm 33:10–15. Use the prayer for Wednesday of the Seventh Week of Easter.

◆ Exodus 19:3–8a, 16–20b. Sing the canticle of Daniel 3:52 – 56. Use the prayer for Tuesday of the Seventh Week of Easter.

◆ Ezekiel 37:1–14. Sing Psalm 107:2–9. Use the prayer for Friday of the Seventh Week of Easter.

◆ Joel 3:1– 5. Sing Psalm 104, as on Pentecost Sunday. Use the prayer for Monday of the Seventh Week of Easter. Following this prayer, sing the Gloria. Then pray the Collect Prayer of the Vigil of Pentecost. The reading from Romans follows and Mass proceeds as usual.

The Lectionary for Mass: Mass during the Day

◆ FIRST READING: The First Reading is the same each year: the account of Pentecost from the Acts of the Apostles. It begins with unity: "they were all in one place together" (Acts 2:1). The Holy Spirit comes in powerful signs—"a noise like a strong driving wind," "tongues as of fire." Immediately, amazing things happen: filled with the Holy Spirit, they begin to speak in different languages. Jews from every nation, gathered in Jerusalem for the feast, are astounded—not by the mighty rushing wind, or the tongues of fire—but by the simple fact that they understand each other.

◆ RESPONSORIAL PSALM 104 is sung every year on Pentecost. It is a song of praise to God, who created all things, but who continually renews his creation. "If you take away their breath, they perish / . . . When you send forth your spirit, they are created." God is actively engaged in the world he has made; he is not finished yet.

◆ SECOND READING: Paul makes a sharp contrast between living according to the flesh (by worldly standards) and living according to the Spirit, the gift of God's presence, life, and power within us, received at Baptism. Note that this is the same Spirit, the same Power, that raised Jesus from the dead. That's powerful power! The Spirit within us also prays within us, as it gently leads us back to our God. The Aramaic word *Abba* is best rendered as "Daddy." How intimately God has united us to himself.

◆ PENTECOST SEQUENCE: Following the Second Reading, the Pentecost sequence is sung or spoken. Called the "Golden Sequence" because of the great beauty of the words and their accompanying chant, *Veni Sancte Spiritus* is a thirteenth-century prayer for the Holy Spirit's presence. In this prayer, we call on the Holy Spirit as "Father of the poor," as source, comforter, guest; as refreshment, rest, coolness, solace, light. We ask the Holy Spirit to fill us, heal us, strengthen us, wash us, bend us, melt us, warm us, guide us.

◆ GOSPEL: Twice in today's Gospel, the Holy Spirit is referred to as an "Advocate," meaning "one who intercedes or acts for the good of another." In other words, God's Holy Spirit continues Jesus' work on our behalf, the work of bringing us the fullness of life. Our job is to listen to the words spoken by God and obey them.

The Roman Missal: Extended Vigil

The Missal gives rubrics and texts to be used for the extended celebration of a Pentecost Vigil, and it is hoped that every parish will take advantage of such a celebration for its parishioners. Instructions are even given if a parish wishes to celebrate First Vespers (Evening Prayer I) in common. This might be something for communities to consider as a way of highlighting the Liturgy of the Hours as something that is meant to be prayed by every baptized Christian, not just the clergy.

If Evening Prayer I is not to be celebrated communally and Mass is to begin in the usual way, then all is done as usual for the beginning of Mass, including the Kyrie (Lord have mercy), after which the priest prays the Collect of the Mass. This would be an ideal occasion to use the Rite for the Blessing and Sprinkling of Water, found in appendix II at the back of the Missal, especially if your parish has been doing this on all of the Sundays of Easter Time. Even if you have not been making use of this rite, today is a perfect occasion to do so as it brings together the themes of Paschal Mystery, Easter Time, Baptism, and the Holy Spirit, and its use allows the enactment of the

ritual to convey the sense of fullness and completion so appropriate for this solemnity. Remember that this rite takes the place of the Penitential Act. It's important to note, however, that in this extended Vigil, the Collect would be prayed by the priest immediately after the concluding prayer, "May almighty God cleanse us of our sins . . . ," not the Gloria, which comes later (see below).

After the Collect, an address is given to the people, using the exact words in the Missal or words similar to them. The address asks the people to follow the example of Mary, the Apostles, and the disciples who persevered in prayer and who awaited the Spirit as promised by the Lord. We follow that example by listening "with quiet hearts to the Word of God," meditating "on how many great deeds God in times past did for his people" and praying "that the Holy Spirit, whom the Father sent as the first fruits for those who believe, may bring to perfection his work in the world."

After this follows an extended Liturgy of the Word modeled on the Liturgy of the Word at the Easter Vigil. The Missal refers us to the readings proposed as options in the Lectionary, with a Responsorial Psalm and a prayer corresponding to the reading following each one. (It is possible to have a period of sacred silence in place of any of the Responsorial Psalms.) The Missal then goes on to give the texts for prayers that correspond to each of the readings and their subsequent psalms. It is then after the Fourth Reading that the Gloria is sung.

When the Gloria is completed, the priest then prays the Collect in the usual way; this time, the Collect used is the text found as the first one given as the Collect for the Simple Form of the Vigil Mass, the "Almighty, ever-living God, who willed the Paschal Mystery . . ."

After this, the reader proclaims the Epistle, Romans 8:22–27, and everything continues in the usual way. The texts for the remainder of the Extended Form of the Vigil Mass are taken from the Simple Form of the Vigil Mass, which follows in the Missal. Commentary on those texts is provided below.

Simple Vigil: If the Extended Form of the Vigil is not being celebrated, then all occurs as usual at Mass; however, there are still proper texts that must be used for the Vigil Mass, distinct from the Mass during the Day.

As with the extended form of the Vigil Mass, the simple form would be an ideal occasion to use the Rite for the Blessing and Sprinkling of Water, found in appendix II at the back of the Missal, especially if your parish has been doing this on all of the Sundays of Easter Time. Even if you have not been making use of this rite, consider doing so now. Remember that this rite takes the place of the Penitential Act. The Gloria immediately follows the prayer the priest prays as the conclusion to the Rite for Blessing and Sprinkling of Water.

In the simple form of the Vigil, either one of the two Collects given in the Missal may be used. The second prayer was discussed above, under the extended form. The Preface assigned for today is the Preface of Pentecost, the text for which (both with and without musical notation) is given along with the texts for the Mass during the Day, two pages further along (this might be a little confusing; the priest celebrant should be sure to check this ahead of time). Given the festivity of the day, it would be a good idea to sing the introductory dialogue and the Preface, especially if this has been the custom on Sundays throughout Easter Time. Note that if Eucharistic Prayer I, the Roman Canon, is used, there is a proper form of the *Communicantes*

("In communion with those . . ."), which mentions the traditional image of the Holy Spirit as tongues of fire.

A formula for Solemn Blessing is suggested, the formula titled "The Holy Spirit" (number 8 under "Blessings at the End of Mass and Prayers over the People"), and it would be good to use this formula. Since it is Pentecost, the solemn dismissal with the double Alleluia returns for use one last time before Easter Time next year.

Of course use festive music with full choir, banners in the entrance procession, incense, and a longer, more formal Gospel procession.

The Roman Missal: Mass during the Day

As with either the extended form or the simple form of the Vigil Mass, the Mass during the Day provides an ideal occasion to use the Rite for the Blessing and Sprinkling of Water, found in appendix II at the back of the Missal, especially if your parish has been doing this on all of the Sundays of Easter Time, and strong consideration should be given to this. Remember that this rite takes the place of the Penitential Act. The Gloria immediately follows the prayer said by the priest at the end of the rite.

The text for the Preface, both with and without musical notation, is proper for today and is given right there at the place in the Missal along with the other texts for the Mass during the Day. See above for commentary on the Preface, as well as for notes concerning the proper insert if Eucharistic Prayer I is used.

The formula titled "The Holy Spirit" (number 8 under "Blessings at the End of Mass and Prayers over the People") is suggested for use as the final blessing, and it would be good to do so. Remember that since it is Pentecost, the solemn dismissal with the double Alleluia is used today, one last time before Easter Time next year.

Of course use festive music with full choir, banners in the entrance procession, incense, and a longer, more formal Gospel procession.

Other Ideas

One of the familiar and memorable texts for this Sunday is the reading from the Acts of the Apostles. This passage recounts the great gathering of people who were speaking in their native languages about "the mighty acts of God." Today almost every parish will have members representing more than one native language. Consider proclaiming the readings from Scripture in two or more of those languages. If the language used in the liturgy is usually English, then translations of the readings could be provided for those who do not understand the other languages. The readers and cantors could be invited to wear a native costume to add to the sense of diversity that makes up the people of God in every local community of faith. Consider inviting members of the parish to wear native dress for today's liturgy (or simply red clothing).

In Psalm 104 we pray that the Lord will send us his spirit to "renew the face of the earth." Today is a good day to explore as a parish what the Catholic Church teaches about the environment. Include petitions in the Universal Prayer for enlightened minds, compassionate hearts, and a call to action to protect our common home. Pope Francis ends his encyclical *Laudato si'* with a beautiful prayer. Since the prayer is quite lengthy, print excerpts in the parish bulletin and post on social media. Here is an excerpt that you might use:

> God of love, show us our place in this world
> as channels of your love
> for all the creatures of this earth,
> for not one of them is forgotten in your sight.
> Enlighten those who possess power and money
> that they may avoid the sin of indifference,
> that they may love the common good, advance the weak,
> and care for this world in which we live.
> The poor and the earth are crying out.
> O Lord, seize us with your power and light,
> help us to protect all life,
> to prepare for a better future,
> for the coming of your Kingdom of justice, peace, love and beauty.
> Praise be to you!
> Amen.

ORDINARY TIME DURING SUMMER AND FALL

The Roman Missal / The Meaning

WE RETURN TO ORDINARY TIME on the Monday after Pentecost, June 10, and it concludes on the Saturday of the Thirty-Fourth Week of the year, November 30. Advent begins the following day, December 1. The weekdays from Monday, June 10, through Saturday, June 15, use the texts for the Tenth Sunday in Ordinary Time. As noted in the winter Ordinary Time section, "any of the thirty-four Masses may be used, provided the pastoral needs of the faithful are taken into consideration" (Ordinary Time, rubric 3b).

If a particular day is a solemnity, feast, or obligatory memorial with its own proper texts, they are to be used. The "Ordinary Time" section follows the "Easter Time" in *The Roman Missal*. Each Sunday provides an Entrance Antiphon, Collect, Prayer over the Offerings, Communion Antiphons, and Prayer after Communion. There are eight Prefaces for the Sundays in Ordinary Time and six Common Prefaces for the weekdays. Six Solemn Blessings are provided for Ordinary Time in the section "The Order of Mass: Solemn Blessings," along with Solemn Blessings for the Blessed Virgin Mary (#15), Sts. Peter and Paul (#16), the Apostles (#17), All Saints (#18), the Dedication of a Church (#19) and Celebrations of the Dead (#20). Become familiar with these, especially since they apply to a number of solemnities and feasts during this time of the liturgical year. Some of these may be of particular interest to your parish life and history.

Choose texts wisely in light of the readings we hear during summer and fall. Let the Gospel according to Luke guide you as you hear it during Ordinary Time. This can be a good time to explore the four Eucharistic Prayers for Use in Masses for Various Needs (EPVN), each of which proclaims that God loves the human race and always walks with us on the journey of life. EPVN II prays that "as we walk your ways with faith and hope, / we may strive to bring joy and trust into the world." EPVN III asks: "Keep us attentive to the needs of all / that, sharing their grief and pain, / their joy and hope, / we may faithfully bring them the good news of salvation / and go forward with them / along the way of your Kingdom." EPVN IV asks God: "Open our eyes / to the needs of our brothers and sisters; / inspire in us words and actions / to comfort those who labor and are burdened. / Make us serve them truly, / after the example of Christ and at his command." These themes reaffirm emphases that we find in Luke's account of the Gospel.

Explore the section "For the Holy Church." With prayers for the laity, spiritual or pastoral gatherings, ministers of the Church, and the evangelization of peoples, this section can be a rich resource for calling and commissioning ministers, starting of committee and council meetings, and the beginning of the school and religious education year. The prayers for priests, religious, Marriage, and the family can be used to celebrate anniversaries that can occur during this time of year. The prayers for persecuted Christians are needed in our day and time. With Independence Day (US) and Labor Day celebrated during the summer and elections celebrated in the fall, the section "For Civil Needs" offers timely prayers that set these celebrations within the context of our faith. Pray with and reflect on these prayers and make use of them where appropriate. *The Roman Missal* is a rich resource that has yet to be mined for what it offers our liturgical life and pastoral settings.

Make note of some major solemnities and feasts during this time of year: the Holy Trinity is celebrated on the Sunday after Pentecost (June 16), the Solemnity of the Most Holy Body and Blood of Christ is celebrated on the Sunday after that (June 23), the Most Sacred Heart of Jesus is celebrated on the Friday after the Second Sunday after Pentecost (June 28), Sts. Peter and Paul (June 29), St. Mary Magdalene (July 22), St. James, (July 25), Sts. Joachim and Anne (a "Liturgical Grandparents Day," July 26; bless them at Mass), the Transfiguration (August 6), the Assumption of the Blessed Virgin Mary (August 15), St. Bartholomew (August 24), St. Augustine (August 28), the Passion of St. John the Baptist (August 29), the Exaltation of the Holy Cross (September 14), St. Matthew (September 21), St. Francis of Assisi (October 4, many places bless animals this day), St. Luke (October 18), Sts. Simon and Jude (October 28), All Saints (November 1), the Commemoration of all the Faithful Departed, All Souls (November 2), the Dedication of the Lateran Basilica (November 9), St. Andrew (November 30), Thanksgiving Day (November 28). A number of founders of religious communities fall during this time, too. You will probably have feasts and memorials that are important to your worshiping communities.

Ordinary Time during summer and fall covers a lengthy period. While parish life can be more relaxed during summer and pick up with a passion during fall, make use of this time to live the words of Common Preface I: "In him you have been pleased to renew all things, / giving us all a share in his fullness."

The Lectionary for Mass

WITH OUR RETURN to Ordinary Time, the readings follow the same structure as those from Ordinary Time in the fall and winter. The First Reading, taken from the Old Testament, was selected to mirror the Gospel for the day.

The Second Reading is a semicontinuous reading from one of the New Testament letters. The Gospel reading in Ordinary Time Year C is primarily taken from the Gospel according to Luke. Throughout the summer, with Luke as our guide, we will hear about the demands of discipleship and accompany the Lord on the public journey to Jerusalem. As the liturgical year comes to a close with the Solemnity of Our Lord Jesus Christ, King of the Universe, the readings call us to rejoice that Jesus is anointed to shepherd us in the lineage of David who was anointed to shepherd God's people, Israel. With the criminal next to Jesus, we ask our king to remember us in his Kingdom of paradise. Having faithfully journeyed through the liturgical year from the First Sunday of Advent to the Solemnity of Christ the King, we prepare ourselves through the Lectionary readings of the final weeks of Ordinary Time to celebrate our king and to "increase our faith" (Luke 17:5) once again as we sense the beginning of a new liturgical year around the corner.

◆ First Readings: During the summer, we will hear from various Old Testament books in no particular order. Remember, the First Reading is chosen to correspond with the Gospel. The readings address the qualities of faithfulness, obedience, humility, and commitment, all qualities of discipleship. We hear from the historical books of Samuel and Kings; the prophets Zechariah, Isaiah, and Jeremiah; and the wisdom literature of Ecclesiastes, Wisdom, and Sirach. As summer changes to fall, the poetic readings from Wisdom and Sirach will be interspersed with readings from the Pentateuch, historical books, and the minor prophets, Amos, Habakkuk, and Malachi. The First Readings provide examples from Israel's history about how the people were stubborn and the prophets called them to change. As a whole, the First Readings encourage us to repentance and stress the Lord's own mercy and justice, which will bring healing even in the face of a lack of repentance by his people.

◆ Responsorial Psalms: As we have seen before in Ordinary Time, each Sunday is assigned a psalm and the proclamation of that psalm is an important part of the Liturgy of the Word. The seasonal psalms for Ordinary Time may also be substituted.

Because of its lyrical nature, the psalm is best proclaimed in song. The simple refrains of the psalms make them easy to learn and remember. As part of the Liturgy of the Word, the Responsorial Psalm is our prayerful assent to the Word proclaimed in the liturgy. The psalms assigned for each Sunday were chosen to reflect the content of the readings of the day, particularly the Old Testament and Gospel readings.

◆ Second Readings: In the summer, the continuous readings of the New Testament are taken from the letters to the Galatians, the Colossians, and the Hebrews. In Galatians, Paul is emphasizing that faith in Christ justifies us more than simple observance of the law. In Colossians, Paul presents what is known as a "high Christology"—Christ is the firstborn of creation and the firstborn of the dead, and we who are joined to him will share in his exaltation. In Hebrews, the author reminds us of our need for faith, encourages us to persevere in times of trouble and hardship, and invites us to participate once and for all in the final covenant established by Jesus through the shedding of his blood. In the fall, we will hear primarily from the pastoral letters of 1 and 2 Timothy. The Second Reading for the Twenty-Third Sunday in Ordinary Time is the Sunday Lectionary's only selection from Philemon, a very short letter on the institution of slavery, which was considered acceptable in Paul's time, and the spirit of equality in Christ that characterized the Christian community. Philemon was written by Paul from prison and was addressed to three specific individuals.

On the three Sundays prior to the Solemnity of Christ the King, the Second Reading comes from 2 Thessalonians, also known to be written by Paul. In this letter, Paul writes to the Christian community at Thessalonica about remaining faithful to the Gospel despite the deceptive teachings they are hearing about the Parousia from false teachers.

The final Second Reading for Year C of the Lectionary cycle of readings comes from Colossians. It serves as a fitting conclusion to the liturgical year, as it incorporates one of the early Christian liturgical hymns of praise and gratitude to Jesus Christ, redeemer of the human race and head of the Church, Savior and King.

◆ Gospel Readings: Throughout the Gospel according to Luke, the theme of discipleship is prominent. In Luke, the disciples are called to identify with the mind and spirit of Jesus, whose first concern is for the poor, the lowly, the outcast, the prisoner, the afflicted, and the sinner. In identifying with Jesus' ministry, the disciples must embrace Jesus' concerns.

During the summer Sundays, we hear a recounting of Jesus' public ministry through his teaching of both the disciples and those he encounters on his journey to Jerusalem. Despite criticisms and misunderstandings on the part of those who are being served, the disciple is called to persevere. Jesus predicts his own suffering and his followers should expect likewise. Discipleship is a call to love all, even those who are not very lovable and those who scorn the disciple. Overall, in Jesus' preaching and ministry and in his interaction with others, he emphasizes that his followers are to be aware of their need to pray in order to accomplish the ministry to which they have been called. From the Twelfth Sunday in Ordinary Time, we hear Jesus asking the question: "Who do the crowds say that I am?" (Luke 9:20). We now enter into the second half of the Gospel according to Luke and the journey to Jerusalem. Along the way, Jesus does not shrink from strong statements and challenging questions to his followers.

Children's Liturgy of the Word

BY NOW, summer activities are in full swing, school is out, and numbers for Children's Liturgy of the Word may be smaller. Respond by making attendance at your celebrations worthwhile. We should not take time off from Mass, so don't encourage it by discontinuing the children's session. Faith is not on a school-year model. You may want to recruit a separate summer team, to relieve those who have sustained this ministry through the school year.

The Sundays of Ordinary Time resume with two dogmatic celebrations: the Solemnities of the Most Holy Trinity (June 16) and the Most Holy Body and Blood of Christ (June 23). The color for these days is white rather than Ordinary Time green.

Throughout these Sundays in Ordinary Time in the summer we will hear the narrative of Jesus' life, hearing that he his homeless and has nowhere to lay his head, about the sending of the seventy-two, the parable of the Good Samaritan, the story of Mary and Martha and the dinner preparations, the gift of the Lord's Prayer, and more. These Gospel accounts present beautiful stories that help us understand what Jesus taught and who he was. The idea is to keep steady and to keep the children's eyes on Jesus.

The medium green of these summer days in Ordinary Time can be evocative of the growth of leaves and grasses in the natural world. Keep the environment simple. Add a few green plants. Continue to sing the psalm and the Gospel acclamation.

For most people, an autumnal mindset begins after Labor Day, this year, September 2. Schools are back in session. Volunteers and families who have been away for the summer return, and our sessions take on a different character. Change out the summer green for a slightly darker shade. Add elements from the natural world—first fruits of the harvest, and after the first frost, colored leaves, nuts, and other signs of the season. As the year ends, add more harvest symbols. The gathering of sheaves of wheat mirrors the time when our souls will be harvested.

The readings begin to shift to a darker tone as we approach the end of the liturgical year. Jesus asks much of his followers—renunciation of possessions, not serving both God and money, not being an unprofitable servant, or bragging about being better than others. We hear about the prodigal son, about Lazarus and the insensitivity of the rich man, the gratitude of one of nine lepers, the persistence of a faithful widow, Jesus eating at the house of Zacchaeus, what it will be like for the children of this age when they are in heaven, and about the end of all things. By the last Sunday of the year, the Solemnity of Our Lord Jesus Christ, King of the Universe, we are in full-on end-time mode.

The wise prayer leader stays grounded in hope and positivity and is not focused on stories of those who failed. Focus instead on those who succeeded and who at the end of time will be with the Lord. On Christ the King we will hear Jesus promise the good thief on the cross "Amen, I say to you, today you will be with me in Paradise."

This is the place of darkness from which we will light the small tentative light of the first candle on the Advent wreath as we cross into the new liturgical year of 2020. In the end is the beginning, because, as we proclaim when we bless the Paschal Candle, "Christ yesterday and today / the Beginning and the End / the Alpha / and the Omega / All time belongs to him / and all the ages / To him be glory and power / through every age for ever. Amen."

The Liturgy of the Hours

IF your parish ministers consider this long stretch of time as ordinary or usual, it's time to reconsider Ordinary Time as an opportunity for growth and evangelization. In the northern hemisphere, most of the weeks between Pentecost and the Solemnity of Our Lord Jesus Christ, King of the Universe, provide visual experiences of growth and harvest. Ordinary Time proposes a richness of Scripture story, opportunity for service to others, and becoming strong and sturdy in faith. Prayer is one way to enter into this season as it stretches before us. Honed in the fire of Pentecost, we step up our efforts at daily prayer and communal prayer. How many times have we heard from the ambo, "you don't take a vacation from God" in the summer? Clearly, we are challenged to do more, to pray more, and to develop more consistent habits of prayer during Ordinary Time. The Liturgy of the Hours as prayed by the parish has a wonderful chance of taking root in the summer and through the fall. Extra hours of daylight provide secular time for liturgical time: Morning and Evening Prayer can be accomplished in the cool of the morning or the waning sunshine of the evening. We greet the day a bit earlier, and often retire somewhat later in the evening during this long stretch of Ordinary Time.

Shift the prayer before parish meetings to Evening Prayer, and look for electronic or web-based resources for easy and "green" access: this coordinates nicely with the wisdom of Pope Francis in *Laudato si'*, concerning the environment. Spread the Kingdom of God with Morning Prayer, perhaps among a small group committed to arriving early in the workplace two days a week. Reflect with care and sincerity on what God has done for us, if only in observance of the sixty-six feasts and memorials of this season (not including the Solemnity of the Assumption and the Solemnity of All Saints).

In Ordinary Time, the Liturgy of the Hours invites us to consecrate time with daily prayer, and serves as "an excellent preparation for the celebration of the eucharist itself, for it inspires and deepens in a fitting way the dispositions necessary for the fruitful celebration of the eucharist: faith, hope, love, devotion, and the spirit of self-denial" (GILOH, 12). Encourage the use of Evening Prayer when youth and young adult groups meet, and when youth groups go to camp and retreats. Remember and reflect with renewed intensity that "faith is deepened for those who take part and their minds are lifted up to God," (GILOH, 14) especially for our youth, teens, and young adults. The Liturgy of the Hours can be an essential part of vacation Bible school in parishes because it can be nicely adapted to the age group being served. In addition, younger children especially love to sing their prayers.

In encouraging adaptation of Morning and Midday Prayer, we can challenge ourselves to pray an Hour with those who come early to work at the parish festival or those who attend the parish picnic (particularly when Mass is not feasible due to weather and difficult set-up). Following a parish outing or large-scale gathering, a form of Evening Prayer would be most appropriate. Above all, strive to pray the Liturgy of the Hours in a way that invites consistency and encourages love of the psalms. These psalms express our pain, our hope, our desperation, our gratitude and our joy today as much as they did with those who prayed them many centuries ago.

The Rite of Christian Initiation of Adults

PERHAPS IT'S TIME to get ready for the Signing of the Senses as the RCIA team celebrates the Rite of Acceptance into the Order of Catechumens with candidates who seek Baptism. This long stretch of liturgical time is definitely not ordinary or usual: it is a length of counted, ordinal time that allows us to grow, and to answer some pretty important questions: to what do we give our lives? To whom should we show mercy and be reconciled? What matters to me, as a Catholic Christian, and what should I be concerned about?

Each time that the Rite of Acceptance takes place, we must remember that it needs to happen in the context of a community of faith. The RCIA reminds that "It is desirable that the entire Christian community or some of part of it, consisting of friends and acquaintances, catechists and priests, take an active part in the celebration" (45) and "after the celebration of the rite of acceptance, the names of the catechumens are to be duly inscribed in the register of catechumens" (46). The importance of being called and named is emphasized. Ordinary Time is about contemplating the richness of the entire rite, renewing and refreshing the team leaders and catechists, and continuing the hospitable invitations to "taste and see" what the Church, and the parish community of faith, has to offer. The Church holds catechumens in high esteem, as viewed through the lens of the RCIA (47):

> From this time on the Church embraces the catechumens as its own with a mother's love and concern. Joined to the Church, the catechumens are now part of the household of Christ, since the Church nourishes them with the word of God and sustains them by means of liturgical celebrations.

The Sacraments of Initiation

THINGS ARE SLOWING DOWN in parishes during the summer months of Ordinary Time. In most parishes, First Communion and Confirmation season is over as many school and faith formation programs are finished for summer recess. There is no prohibition against celebrating First Communion or Confirmation during the summer. Perhaps a child was ill during the time the parish celebrated First Communion, a child might be home schooled and deemed ready to receive Communion, or the parish offers a summer faith formation program with First Communion celebrated at the end of the summer. The solemnities at the beginning of Ordinary Time, especially the Most Holy Body and Blood of Christ, are wonderful times to celebrate First Communion. Even if First Communion is not celebrated on Corpus Christi, it is a powerful witness to have the First Communicants participate in a Corpus Christi procession.

A celebration of Confirmation with young people may be less likely due to the difficulty of gathering all the candidates during the summer months, but there might be a possibility that an adult Catholic is ready to receive the sacrament at a Sunday Mass. The priest will need to receive the faculty to confirm a baptized Catholic.

Baptism of course is celebrated year round, and often there can be a spike in the number of children being baptized, especially in areas where it is cold in the winter. It is important to make young parents and their guests feel welcome and to use Baptism as a means of evangelizing by putting our best foot forward in celebrating the Sacrament. With summer being a time of visiting priests, make sure they know how the parish celebrates Baptisms, and introduce them to Baptism assistants if there are any, who may proclaim the readings, welcome the families, and assist in other ways.

This period of Ordinary Time is a good opportunity for those responsible for preparing the celebrations of these sacraments to come together for reflection and evaluation of the celebrations of the past year. Reviewing the rites and diocesan guidelines are always helpful tools of evaluation. Gathering with the pastor and associate pastors, liturgy committee, music director, catechetical leader, and school principal if there is a parish school, to discuss make the celebration of the liturgy is important.

Ordinary Time in the fall is when things in the parish start up again. It is a time when bishops again begin to schedule parish Confirmations. Ritual Masses cannot be celebrated on All Souls' Day, but All Saints Day is a wonderful time to celebrate Confirmation if the parish has a choice, and the readings for this solemnity are quite appropriate for Confirmation.

The beginning of the school year is also a good time to celebrate prayer services with First Communion or Confirmation families, along with the godparents and sponsors, as a way of showing their commitment to preparing well for these sacraments. Such services could focus on their Baptism as a way of connecting the sacraments of initiation. Any opportunity to gather for prayer with children, young people, and their parents will only help them to better prepare to receive these sacraments. You might consider scheduling an evening that includes Eucharistic adoration as many young people and their parents have never experienced this devotion. Of course their participation at Sunday liturgy is indispensable as a preparation for the sacraments, and parishes should work hard to prepare Sunday celebrations that are inviting and engaging.

No matter what time of year the sacraments of initiation are celebrated, know that each and every celebration of these sacraments is helping our young people to grow in their Christian life and to receive the great grace that God chooses to bestow on them and their families.

The Rite of Penance

COMMUNAL celebrations of the Sacrament of Penance are usually connected to a particular season, as noted in this *Sourcebook* in the seasonal overviews for Advent and Lent. But, why not connect such a celebration of Reconciliation to a feast day in the liturgical calendar? One such feast is the Exaltation of the Holy Cross (September 14). This celebration could accomplish two purposes. First, it is a good way to start off the "new year" in the life of the parish that is often associated with the end of the summer and beginning of the fall. This is especially true if there is a parish school. Second, it draws attention to the theological relationship between God's redeeming power through the Death of Jesus on the Cross and the sacrament itself. The Entrance Antiphon of the Mass for this feast makes this connection: "We should glory in the cross of our Lord Jesus Christ, in whom is our salvation, life and resurrection, through whom we are saved and delivered."

Another reason to focus on Reconciliation is the general state of unrest and antagonism that always seems to have a presence in our local communities, in our country, and in so many regions around the world.

As I write this article the city of Chicago is experiencing record numbers of shootings and murders in its streets for this year (2016). The need for the healing of tremendous suffering and brokenness is evident almost daily. Other communities, hopefully, are not so violent, yet there are still occasions when we might well gather for prayer. The *Rite of Penance* offers a wonderful list of texts and prayers that can be used in nonsacramental celebrations of Reconciliation (see chapter IV: Various Texts used in the Celebration of Reconciliation). In appendix II a sample outline is offered titled "Penance Prepares for a Fuller Sharing in the Paschal Mystery of Christ for the Salvation of the World." Another outline for a service on such an occasion is given in section III, Common Penitential Celebrations no. III: The Beatitudes. These words from the pastoral notes underline the importance of both prayer and actions that bring reconciliation to bear on the world around us (RP, 5):

People frequently join together to commit injustice. But it is also true that they help each other in doing penance; freed from sin by the grace of Christ, they become, with all persons of good will, agents of peace and justice in the world.

The Order of Celebrating Matrimony

THE CONCLUSION of the wedding liturgy is rather simple. A threefold blessing over the couple is followed by the final blessing. Curiously there are no specific words of dismissal. At the celebration within Mass it would be appropriate to use one of the four formularies provided in the Roman Missal. It has been customary for many presiders take this opportunity to formally announce the newly married couple to the assembly before sending them forth. The dismissal should be simple and brief.

The *Order of Celebrating Matrimony* states "It is a praiseworthy practice to end the celebration with a suitable chant" (107). Curiously, this is specifically mentioned only in form II of the rite: The Order of Celebrating Matrimony without Mass. Since most assemblies sing a hymn at the conclusion of Mass and during celebrations of the other sacraments, it would be appropriate to sing a hymn at the conclusion of the wedding, regardless of whether it takes place in the context of a Mass or not.

Instrumental music may accompany the procession of the bride and groom, the bridal party, and the liturgical ministers. The "traditional" recessional, "Wedding March" by Felix Mendelssohn, is from incidental music for Shakespeare's *A Midsummer Night's Dream*. Since this comedy makes a mockery of Marriage, its use during the Celebration of Matrimony is inappropriate. There are a number of festive instrumental pieces that are more appropriate here.

The ritual notes that the witnesses and the priest may sign the Marriage record either in the vesting room or in the presence of the people, but it is not done on the altar. Most often this is done without fanfare in the sacristy.

Many couples will choose to have a receiving line so that they may receive their guests at the end of the wedding liturgy. Rather than imposing the devotional element of bringing flowers to Blessed Mother during the liturgy, the newly married couple might take a quiet moment of prayer before the statue or image of the Blessed Mother before heading off to take pictures and enjoy their reception.

The Pastoral Care of the Sick

THE MANY WEEKS of Ordinary Time in the summer and fall offer many opportunities to interact with those who are sick. Because of the broad range of medical conditions, not all events or liturgical celebrations fit everyone. Those who are more mobile might be encouraged to spend some time outdoors. Pastoral visitors could arrange for their participation in any parish summer fest, like a parish picnic or an outdoor Mass. This is a good opportunity to involve volunteers from the parish who are not directly involved in a particular ministry. Some health care centers sponsor their own outdoor activities. Pastoral ministers could offer their assistance with such events.

September is a good month to have a day of reflection for all those who are engaged in care of the sick. Consider inviting family members who have someone being cared for at home. Invite any professional care givers and those who provide support for the sick. A good day for this gathering is on or near the Feast of the Exaltation of the Holy Cross (September 14). The Feast of Our Lady of Sorrows (September 15) is also an appropriate date. Reflections on the meaning of suffering, the grace of Christ's Death on the Cross, and the comfort of Mary in her suffering offer rich insights for reflection, for spiritual health, and for Christian hope.

During the month of November, the Church remembers those who have died and commends them in prayer. Those who are ill often think of their own dying and can receive much comfort from being present with them and assuring them of the Church's prayers and simply letting them know that we care. For those whose illness is terminal the Rite for the Pastoral Care of the Sick offers the liturgy of Viaticum (see chapter 5) as well as Prayers for the Dying (see chapter 6). Viaticum can be given within Mass or outside Mass. The latter rite can be led by a lay pastoral minister. The readings and prayers for both these rites bring great comfort to the person who is sick as well as to family members and care givers who accompany the sick person.

The "end of life" issue has become a common topic of discussion these days. It can be a difficult conversation and there are certainly a variety of opinions among professionals and family members. The parish might consider sponsoring a forum to explore the various issues and to present the teaching of the Church as it applies to this matter. Pastoral care of the dying is a responsibility of the whole Church, and all those who surround the dying person should do so with a deep appreciation for the sacredness of life as well as trusting in the Lord's promise of eternal life.

The Order of Christian Funerals

ORDINARY TIME has been described as the continual unfolding of the Paschal Mystery over the numerous Sundays of the liturgical year that are not included in a particular season. The Gospel texts for these Sundays recall the many encounters between Jesus and those who gather around him to listen to his teachings and his ongoing instruction to the disciples. As in the Easter season, some of these texts are offered as options in the Order of Christian Funerals.

Jesus frequently used the cycles of nature, such as the planting, cultivating, and harvesting of crops as analogies for his teaching on the Kingdom of God. These references are very much at home in the lives of those who live in the many rural parishes of the country. They are especially appropriate for the funeral liturgy. As the time of harvest arrives in the last few weeks of this section of the liturgical year everyone is aware of the changes in nature. The amount of daylight diminishes; the foliage of our gardens and fields begins to change colors and eventually dies; the fruits of the harvest are gathered into pantries; and the changing weather patterns remind us that life also changes from season to season, year to year.

The texts of the Sunday Lectionary speak of the end times, of judgment and the importance of being faithful to way of the Lord. Such thoughts can find their way into the prayers and music of the funeral liturgy. But the tone is not, of course, all doom and gloom. The Church constantly celebrates the astonishing grace and mercy of God. We are called into the glory of the Kingdom, as Paul reminds us: "If, then, we have died with Christ, we believe that we shall also live with him" (Romans 6:8).

When we pray the words of Eucharistic Prayer III, "for all our departed brothers and sisters and for all who were pleasing to God in their passing from this life," we continue the ancient tradition of the Church in praying for the dead.

During the month of November the Church remembers in a particular way those who have died. The Solemnity of All Saints (November 1) and the Commemoration of All the Faithful Departed (November 2) are opportunities for every faith community to remember those members who have died in the past year. Many dioceses schedule liturgies of commemoration in Catholic cemeteries during November as a reminder that during our earthly journey we are spiritually connected to those called into the communion of saints.

The Roman Missal provides texts for these liturgies in Masses for the Dead / Various Commemorations.

Latino communities erect *altarsitos* in their homes and often in the parish church. Pictures and mementos of those who have died are placed on these small altars. Many Filipino communities visit gravesites and leave food offerings for the deceased, an ancient Christian custom.

Many parishes keep a *Book of the Names of the Dead* in a prominent place during November. (LTP has a beautiful book available for this purpose.) This is a reminder for everyone to pray for those brothers and sisters in faith who have died and now rest with the communion of saints.

The Book of Blessings

THERE ARE SEVERAL opportunities to make use of blessings during these many weeks of Ordinary Time. As noted above, the blessing of Fathers on Father's Day is found in chapter 56. At the beginning of the summer months the Blessing of Travelers is appropriate. One of the intercessions that are listed (BB, 629) could be adapted and included in the Prayer of the Faithful on the

chosen Sunday. The shorter rite (BB, 635) could be used at the end of Mass.

When the school year begins at the end of the summer there is an Order of Blessing of Students and Teachers (BB, chapter 5). This blessing could be part of the initial assembly of the school community within the context of a celebration of the Word of God, or as part of a Mass for the beginning of a new school year. The *Book of Blessings* offers both options.

The Memorial of St. Francis on October 4 is a popular day for the Blessing of Animals. If the memorial falls on a weekday the parish likely schedules the blessing for the following Saturday or Sunday. The Order of Blessing of Animals is found in chapter 25. The rubrics presume a liturgy outside of Mass. A priest, deacon, or lay minister can lead this blessing.

Just as there is a blessing for the beginning of the planting season there is one for the time of harvest. The Order of Blessing on the Occasion of Thanksgiving for the Harvest can be used at any appropriate time during the months of autumn (BB, chapter 28). For the Church in Canada it would be associated with the day of Thanksgiving which is the second Monday of October. For the Church in the United States it would be the celebration of Thanksgiving, the fourth Thursday in November. Since Thanksgiving is a festive and important time for family gatherings, the parish could provide a copy of the blessing prayers as an insert in the Sunday bulletin.

In many dioceses and parishes it is a custom to celebrate a liturgy in the Catholic cemetery on November 2, the Commemoration of All the Faithful Departed. A Liturgy of the Word is found in chapter 57. The order can also be within Mass. In those situations where a communal liturgy is not scheduled in the cemetery, individuals may choose to visit the cemetery on their own. A copy of the prayers, readings, and the Litany of Saints could be made available to members of the parish for their personal use.

The Saints

THE SECOND PORTION of Ordinary Time begins after Pentecost and is much longer than the first, lasting through the final day before Advent. The Solemnity of the Most Holy Body and Blood of Christ, toward the very beginning of the season, is marked with a procession; perhaps in bulletins and homilies, connections can be drawn between this procession and the one that may have just taken place on Pentecost, with the Paschal candle.

Placed as it is after the events of the Christ's Passion, Resurrection, and Ascension, Ordinary Time in summer and fall is focused on the Age of the Church—the age we are living in now, as we prepare for the second coming of Christ and the Kingdom of God. As we progress from Easter toward Advent once more, moving through the Exaltation of the Holy Cross, the Transfiguration, and many other feasts and memorials that celebrate the "unveiling of things unseen," we encounter in the memorials of the saints opportunities to be transfigured ourselves as once more we ponder the mystery of Christ in all its aspects. Like these saints, we are called to "renew the face of the earth"; through them, we find strength and inspiration to do so (Psalm 104; antiphon for Pentecost).

The saints of the season run the gamut: missionary martyrs (the North American martyrs, the Korean martyrs: St. Maximilian Kolbe) to musicians (St. Cecilia); soldiers (St. Ignatius of Loyola, St. Martin of Tours) to teachers and caretakers of the poor (St. Francis Cabrini, St. Vincent de Paul); model parents (Sts. Joachim and Anne; St. Monica) to biblical scholars (St. Jerome, St. Bonaventure). Beloved friends of Jesus during his life are celebrated during this time: St. Mary Magdalene and St. Martha, St. Andrew, St. James, Sts. Simon and Jude, St. John the Baptist. Evangelists St. Luke and St. Matthew have their feast days during Ordinary Time. So do founders of renowned orders— St. Benedict, St. Dominic, St. Francis of Assisi— and great bishops—St. Augustine, St. Alphonsus Ligouri, St. Ignatius of Antioch.

As their backgrounds and vocations varied greatly, so too did their faith journey. Some seemed never to waver, while others required more convincing. St. Thomas is famous for his moment of doubt, changing to conviction when faced with the risen Lord. And St. Augustine is said to have prayed, "Lord, make me holy, but not too soon." Ordinary men and women may be comforted and edified by this witness of the struggle of discipleship in all its aspects; its moments of confusion and fear, as well as its moments of exaltation.

This season offers a myriad of opportunities for parishes to create devotional niches and other displays dedicated to these saints. Statues or images, set in a place that will not impede or overshadow the importance of the community's liturgy, can be changed according to the day and include candles, seasonal flowers or greenery, and prayer cards. Remember the various cultures, represented by the saints of this season, that may also form sizable communities within your parishes— Korean, Basque, Italian, and so on—and recognize with what traditions they may honor these saints. As well, community efforts focused on the particular charism of each saint should be considered. Besides the obvious projects like soup kitchens and other drives and sponsorships for the poor, parishes could recognize St. Francis of Assisi by holding a neighborhood cleanup, collecting money for an environmental cause, and of course by blessing animals at a special liturgy. A parish dinner in honor of the hospitality of St. Martha, or a fundraiser for seminarians to honor St. Charles Borromeo, are other possibilities. This is a fruitful time for a creative look at the focus of the saints in light of the current needs of the local Church.

Of course, the Marian observances require particular attention. Many parishes have statues of Our Lady in their sanctuaries, or in grottoes or parish gardens; these should be decorated and tended especially for each celebration of Mary. Outdoor displays offer unique witness to the community outside the sanctuary walls. The Solemnity of the Assumption is a Holyday of Obligation; parish bulletins, social media pages, and announcements should make note of that early in the month.

Another Holyday of Obligation, the Solemnity of All Saints, should be a joyful celebration. Parish schools often have students dress as their favorite saint; after Mass, families can gather to learn about these heroes of the faith.

The Church understands the wisdom of incorporating belief: As Catholics, we use oil, fire, water, bread, and wine in our sacraments. We chant and burn incense; we embody our prayer as we stand, kneel, bow, and prostrate. Similarly, during this season, as the faithful light candles and ask the saints for intercession, as they decorate altars and place fragrant flowers in front of statues, they absorb the stories of the holy men and women the Church recognizes as saints. Candle by candle, prayer by prayer, they make those stories a part of their story, and move toward a sainthood of their own.

The Liturgical Environment

Summer Ordinary Time begins immediately after Pentecost. After the marathon of Lent, Triduum, and Easter, changing to the lengthy season of Ordinary Time can be a relief. Taking your cue from nature, choose a trio of greens as the canvas for your environment: a spring green to start the season, moving to a deep green in late summer, and shifting to a yellow-green during the fall months. As you change fabric colors, consider changing the placement of the fabric or the shape. Begin with simple vertical fabric, then change to a draped placement or a series of smaller widths hung together on a single large rod. Experiment with textures: fabrics with a sheen, those with a discreet woven pattern or a small print.

Obtaining sturdy green plants that will thrive well in your church is good stewardship. Peace lilies, palm plants, schefflera, and ivy plants are common choices. Establish a stationary framework to which you can add interest in the form of succulents, ferns, flowering cacti, woven bamboo or native grasses as the season progresses. Rearranging the plants periodically is good for their growth and adds variety.

Summer Ordinary Time begins with two solemnities: Trinity Sunday and the Body and Blood of Christ (Corpus Christi). The color for these Sundays is white; place white fabric on the ambo these weeks and integrate Trinitarian symbols, wheat, and grapes into your plant groupings to highlight the feasts. The Nativity of St. John the Baptist is also a solemnity; in many cultures, it is celebrated with water games. Consider placing large clear vases of water among your plants to mark the occasion.

The Assumption, celebrated August 15, provides an opportunity to feature the fruits of local gardens. The German custom of blessing fruits and herbs on the Assumption made its way into the 1964 Roman Ritual; whether your parish offers this blessing or not, baskets overflowing with ripe eggplants, tomatoes, cauliflower and corn underscore the connection between the fertility of the Blessed Virgin and harvest. Pots filled with pungent basil, dill, and lavender entice the senses. Leave these in place for a week, removing them after the Queenship of Mary. The blessing of the harvest is found in the *Book of Blessings*.

As summer fades, interspersing tall vases with dried grasses among the plants is an attractive way to incorporate nature's changes. Alternately, fill clear glass cylinders with varieties of harvested grains. Update your plants with branches of twisted willow. Alter the look of the pots by setting them inside larger pottery urns or durable baskets.

The Archangels are honored on September 29, and the Guardian Angels on October 2. Within this week, you might add images of these angels to your narthex or a devotional chapel. The Feast of St. Luke on October 18 can be marked by placing an oversized *Book of the Gospels* on a pedestal among plants near the ambo.

November is the month of All Souls, beginning with All Saints and All Souls' days. As the Scriptures speak on the end times and we remember those who have died in faith, convert your environment to reflect nature's glory. Use Styrofoam blocks inside large pots or use bowl tape to create a grid across the container's opening to support branches of colorful leaves, repurposing dried grasses as filler. Before bringing harvested squash (acorn, cucuzza, and star varieties are especially interesting) or pumpkins indoors, clean them with a solution of water and bleach to slow deterioration. Chrysanthemums, often used in *ofrendas* for *Día de los Muertos*, add seasonal color to the mix.

The liturgical year ends with the Solemnity of Our Lord Jesus Christ, King of the Universe. Give this solemnity the attention it merits by adding white and gold elements to the existing decor. Dignified fresh floral arrangements amidst the earthy arrangements give special emphasis as autumn ends and Advent approaches.

The Liturgical Music

DUE TO WIDE and legitimate reasons, many choral ensembles go on a summer hiatus come Corpus Christi. While this may be necessary in some places, the music should never come to a complete halt! We cannot authentically catechize those in the music ministry and model for our colleagues on the parish staff the importance of music's contribution to the liturgy if we ourselves are so willing and eager to shut off the organ, or close the piano lid, from mid-June to September. At the very least, a combination of an organist (or other instrumentalist) and cantor should be present to lead, support, and encourage the assembly in their sung prayer. Perhaps, instead of having the entire choral ensemble take off for the summer, you may experiment with having a quartet, men's schola, women's schola, or some other varied combination drawn from the various ensemble to be present throughout the summer. This may take some effort in terms of scheduling but doing so will speak volumes as to the degree and importance of music's unique service to the liturgy. We are not just Church musicians September through June but rather pastoral musicians 365 days of the year. Establishing smaller choral ensembles and thinking outside the box will serve your communities well and even serve your musicians well by affording them the opportunity to continue music study and further develop their talents and craft.

This time of year also provides a good opportunity to introduce new hymns and ritual music. If introducing a new hymn to the core repertoire, consider using the tune as a prelude or postlude for a few weeks before introducing it to the assembly. Once you do introduce it, try to use it for a few weeks so that the assembly gets the chance to truly know the piece and can sing it with full enthusiasm. The same for any new ritual music: use whatever it is throughout the summer and into the fall. Ritual music typically takes longer for the assembly to own than a hymn. Be sure to get some well-deserved rest in order to recharge yourself for the busy fall. Try to get as much preparation done over the summer as you can. This may seem like a lot of work but tackling it during a quieter time of year will reduce the stress you will face if trying to prepare in the fall when everything starts up once again.

The fall months also bring about the annual push for new recruits. Ask your current choristers to invite someone they may know, or hear in church, to come to choir. Consider having an open rehearsal in order to provide prospective choristers a glimpse into the workings of the choir. Develop well worded and interesting press releases for your bulletin and local newspaper. Use social media sites to help get the word out to the community that you are looking for additional singers. Contact your local AGO and NPM chapter. Does your parish community have a parochial school or local community school? Communication with the music teacher may yield additional singers for the various choral ensembles. Advertise in all of these varied sources a few weeks before the start of your choral season. I do advise colleagues not to be shy or hesitant about having an audition and interview for all prospective choristers. An audition, as long as it's realistic, is an indispensable way for directors to meet incoming choristers and to assess musical strengths, weakness, areas needing improvement, and determine proper placement within the choir. It also communicates that the music ministry is an important part of parish life. As St. Paul taught "For as in one body we have many parts, and all the parts do not have the same function, so we, though many, are one body in Chris" (Romans 12:4). While auditions may not allow each potential chorister entry into the music ministry, it just may allow us the opportunity to communicate with our colleagues on the parish staff in determining people to serve in other areas of ministry.

The Liturgical Ministers

PERHAPS ONE of the most challenging issues for liturgy coordinators during this time is managing ministry schedules. In the early weeks of this period of Ordinary Time, vacation time can play havoc with the usual scheduling. When the fall weeks arrive it becomes a matter of getting everyone back in sync with the many parish responsibilities, especially those that depend on volunteers. A word to liturgical ministers: even if you are not scheduled but you are available, it's a nice gesture if you check when you arrive for liturgy to see if you might be needed to fill in for someone who has canceled or failed to show at the last minute. And, a further word to those who are scheduled, either find someone to replace you or let the Mass coordinator know if you cannot be present. It's not about being a slave to a schedule as much as it is about making sure that the liturgy for the assembly is well served by ministers who are present and well prepared. Some parishes schedule a retreat day for all ministers near the end of the summer; this can be a good way to welcome new participants, to renew friendships and to share a renewed enthusiasm for this most wonderful work in and for the Church.

Other Prayers, Rites, and Devotions

ORDINARY TIME unfolds in summer and fall, and suggests to us that popular piety might be food for thought for parishes during this long stretch of time. On June 28, the celebration of the Solemnity of the Sacred Heart of Jesus suggests that the parish bulletin not only accentuate the celebration of that day's Mass, but provide an opportunity to publish information about the promises that Jesus made to St. Margaret Mary Alacoque in an apparition. Expound a bit on the nine first Fridays as a devotion to the Sacred Heart, helping people understand something about how a devotion can mean something in their lives.

Additional food for thought could occur during vacation Bible school, a summer concept that continues to grow across the United States and attract many children for catechesis and fun. Using your parish music ministers, teach the children to sing the Lord's Prayer, a Marian song or two, and possibly the Salve Regina (they can sing Latin if they understand what the prayer is about). Music is one of the treasures of the Church, and there are many new settings of Marian music especially (plus more than a few Te Deums in many languages) that form a habit of "sung devotion" in our children. Expressions of popular piety, in every generation, can contribute to spreading the new evangelization in our Church communities. Encourage children and adults to share their devotions that are attached to music, particular in planning vacation Bible school at your parish.

October is traditionally the Month of the Holy Rosary: teach the Rosary, learn new mysteries, share the Rosary before meetings and after Mass, pray a contemplative Rosary with an ad hoc Rosary group, formed intentionally for the month of October. Introduce a bi- or multilingual Rosary observance, bringing together some of the different cultures of the parish.

Evangelization

ORDINARY Time through the summer and fall invites us to celebrate the life and ministry of Jesus: to walk with him and his disciples along the roads of Galilee, to listen to his teaching, to witness his miracles, to learn from his outreach to those where God is least expected. Far from the mundane, Ordinary Time is a time for us to grow in discipleship—to learn to follow the Lord, to listen to his voice, to become conformed to him more and more.

When it comes to social media, connecting the idea of discipleship to our digital presence can be an especially fruitful practice during the long season of ordinary time. If discipleship means to follow the Lord as our teacher, a good question to ask is what we can learn from him about communicating with others, and how we can emulate his communication through what we do on social media.

In some sense we can say that Jesus Christ was an act of God's communication—he is after all the Word of God incarnate. But more specifically, we can also recognize some distinctive elements of his communication, and learn from these for our digital lives. When thinking about Jesus Christ the communicator, we can say that his words gave life, his words built relationships, his words were offered in a way that people could understand, and his words revealed the Father. These four elements can begin to shape our ordinary presence on social media and become a sort of rubric for thinking about digital discipleship.

Jesus' words gave life: through his words life returned to Lazarus, to Jairus' daughter, to the widow's son at Nain. Do our words give life to others? Are we building people up, giving them hope, encouragement, and a sense of possibility? Do our words reveal a glimmer of life lived to the fullest?

Jesus' words built relationships: he reached out to people, accepted invitations, talked with those no one wanted to talk with, and invited people to follow him toward living a fuller live. Are we willing to enter into conversations on social media with those who are different than us? Do our words forge dialogue and build bridges? Do we communicate respect for those whose dignity is easy to forget?

Jesus spoke in ways that people could understand: he used images, metaphors, and stories that resonated with his time and audience. Are we sharing our faith in ways that people can understand? Can those who have never heard the Good News or have become desensitized to it hear it from us as relevant, true, and life-giving in this day and age? Are we connecting faith and life in genuine and effective ways?

Jesus' words revealed the Father: he was the Father's Word spoken to humankind. Are our words pointing to us or pointing to God? Are we self-promoting and enjoy chasing the attention social media can bring us or are we self-giving and strive above all to direct attention to God's truth, goodness, and beauty?

While these four ways do not exhaust all that we can learn from Jesus, it is a beginning for shaping the way we can communicate as his disciples.

The Parish and the Home

THE SUMMER months should be a time when the community lives its faith, commissioned and sent by the Holy Spirit, yet too often there are few opportunities during June, July, and August for gathering, and those who organize things during the year are on vacation. Why not make it different during the summer months this year? Recruit a different team of volunteers to gather the parish for a procession for the Solemnity of the Most Holy Body and Blood of Christ (Corpus Christi), followed by a picnic. Offer field trips and service projects for teens and adults. Gather helpers to weed and repair the church grounds, or better yet, offer such assistance to elderly or disabled neighbors. Organize a bus trip to a baseball game. (What about the altar servers and their families?) Gather parish council and commission members for a picnic and evening of visioning for the future of the parish.

On the Solemnity of the Assumption of the Blessed Virgin Mary (August 15), offer an evening Mass followed by a light dinner and lessons on Rosary making, or a showing of a Marian video. As fall sets in, welcome back those who have been away by offering refreshments and social interaction after weekend Mass.

Before October 31 and November 1, plan an intergenerational Halloween/All Saints event, allowing parents as well as children to dress as favorite saints. During refreshment time, invite people to talk about their saints at their tables.

During November, have parish members who have lost a loved one that year write the names in a *Book of the Names of the Dead*, displayed near an "altar of the dead," featuring photos of the departed. Make All Souls' Day Mass memorable by having people carry a lighted candle after the homily in procession, placing it next to the photo of their loved one. Send home instructions for families to make a home "altar of the dead." If your parish includes Latino families, incorporate and explain to others traditions associated with the Day of the Dead celebration.

For Thanksgiving, a food drive, ecumenical service, or a parish Mass on the night before are all appropriate ways to celebrate this American holiday. Afterward, provide opportunities for people of all ages to offer thanks and praise to God in their own way through music, drama, art, and other talents at a parish talent show. The end of another liturgical year is a perfect time to celebrate who we are and who we can be.

Reflections through the Year

Saint Francis, faithful to Scripture, invites us to see nature as a magnificent book in which God speaks to us and grants us a glimpse of his infinite beauty and goodness. "Through the greatness and the beauty of creatures one comes to know by analogy their maker" (Wisdom 13:5); indeed, "his eternal power and divinity have been made known through his works since the creation of the world" (Romans 1:20). For this reason, Francis asked that part of the friary garden always be left untouched, so that wild flowers and herbs could grow there, and those who saw them could raise their minds to God, the Creator of such beauty. Rather than a problem to be solved, the world is a joyful mystery to be contemplated with gladness and praise. (LI, 12)

The urgent challenge to protect our common home includes a concern to bring the whole human family together to seek a sustainable and integral development, for we know that things can change. The Creator does not abandon us; he never forsakes his loving plan or repents of having created us. Humanity still has the ability to work together in building our common home. Here I want to recognize, encourage and thank all those striving in countless ways to guarantee the protection of the home which we share. Particular appreciation is owed to those who tirelessly seek to resolve the tragic effects of environmental degradation on the lives of the world's poorest. Young people demand change. They wonder how anyone can claim to be building a better future without thinking of the environmental crisis and the sufferings of the excluded. (LI, 13)

Mass Texts

◆ Introduction to the Mass

One of the Prefaces to the Eucharistic Prayer prays: "In you we live and move and have our being." This is true for every season of the year and every season of our lives. Our celebration helps to deepen our relationship with Jesus so that we can live, move, and be in him more fully, each and every day. Knowing that we do not always live Jesus as clearly as we could, we turn to him grateful for and in need of mercy.

◆ Seasonal Alternate Tropes for Penitential Act Form C

Lord Jesus, you teach us by your words and deeds: Lord, have mercy.

Christ Jesus, you feed us with your Body and Blood: Christ, have mercy.

Lord Jesus, you free us by your death and resurrection: Lord, have mercy.

◆ Dismissal for Children's Liturgy of the Word

Jesus taught us to pray, to listen for his voice and talk with him about our lives. When we pray we come to know Jesus better and we learn how to show people that we want to live like him. As you go to listen to today's readings, hear him speaking to you. Discover how he is asking you to live like him more clearly. And when you return to us, you can show us how to follow Jesus more closely in our lives, too. Go in peace.

◆ Dismissal of Catechumens

Throughout our readings these months, Jesus is on a journey to Jerusalem, the place of his suffering and Death, which leads to his Resurrection and new life. You are on a journey to new life that comes from growing closer to Jesus and discovering where his Spirit is asking you to go. Listen to the Word of God today. Reflect on how you can live the Word more clearly. Ask the Holy Spirit to guide you as you continue your journey of faith. Go in peace.

◆ Seasonal Universal Prayer (Prayer of the Faithful)

Invitation to Prayer

God has created the human race to know, love, and serve God by following Jesus Christ. Jesus taught us to pray, and so we follow him by turning to our loving God through these prayers.

Intercessions

1. That our Church leaders guide us on our journey of faith so that we live the love we promised to live in Baptism, we pray to the Lord:

2. That women and men who lead nations, countries, cities, and states, seek the wisdom that comes from God alone, we pray to the Lord:

3. That our eyes be open to the needs of all, to share their joys, hopes, pains, and sorrows, by walking with them life's journey, we pray to the Lord:

4. That the violence, terror, and abuse so prevalent in our world be transformed into ways of peace, support, and care, we pray to the Lord:

5. That we take time to pray and listen for the voice of God to direct us to be who we are, and be that well, for God's glory, we pray to the Lord:

6. That our beloved dead and all who have died may find the face of God welcoming them to eternal life when they end this life's journey, we pray to the Lord:

Concluding Prayer

Ever-loving and ever-living God,
you have no need of our praise,
yet our thanksgiving is itself your gift.
We make these prayers,
seeking the wisdom of your Spirit,
because we need you to help us live your command
    to love as Jesus loved.
Free us to live Jesus, each day,
through the power of your Spirit,
for with them you are one God,
for ever and ever.
Amen.

June 2019
Month of the Sacred Heart

Weekdays during Ordinary Time

Except for the days of the First and Thirty-Fourth Weeks in Ordinary Time, *The Roman Missal* does not provide prayer texts for the weekdays in Ordinary Time. Instead, priest celebrants and those who prepare the liturgy may select from among the prayers provided for the Sundays in Ordinary Time.

Optional Memorials during Ordinary Time

On all Saturdays during Ordinary Time that do not have an obligatory memorial, a memorial to the Blessed Virgin Mary may be celebrated. The prayers may be selected from the Common of the Blessed Virgin Mary. Commentary below is only provided for Sundays, solemnities, feasts, and obligatory memorials. The following should be consulted for celebrating optional memorials during Ordinary Time: for the celebration of other optional memorials, "on weekdays in Ordinary Time, there may be chosen either the Mass of the weekday, or the Mass of an Optional Memorial which happens to occur on that day, or the Mass of any Saint inscribed in the Martyrology for that day, or a Mass for Various Needs, or a Votive Mass" (GIRM, 355c).

MON 10 (#359) green
Weekday

Tenth Week in Ordinary Time

The Lectionary for Mass

◆ FIRST READING: St. Paul's greeting to the community at Corinth begins with traditional praise of God the Father of Jesus Christ. The theme of compassion and encouragement fills the opening verses for Paul's second letter to the Corinthians. Just as they share in the sufferings of Christ, so too, they find their encouragement and salvation in him. Paul and Timothy will never give up their hope in the Corinthians. Neither do we give up our hope in each other. As people of faith, we encourage each other to follow the path of Christ.

◆ RESPONSORIAL PSALM 34: In the words of the psalmist, we give thanks for the Lord's goodness. For the many ways the Lord accompanies us in the midst of life's sufferings, we bless the Lord, glorify the Lord, and continue to look to the Lord for guidance. We taste the goodness of the Lord. In the Lord's goodness we find encouragement.

◆ GOSPEL: Better words of encouragement for the living as disciples of Jesus one will never find than the Beatitudes of Matthew's account of the Gospel. Blessedness belongs to those who are "poor in spirit," who mourn, who are meek— to those who "hunger and thirst for righteousness," to the merciful and clean of heart, to the peacemakers, and even to those who are persecuted and insulted. The joy of God's Kingdom belongs to them!

TUE 11 (#580; Gospel #360) red
Memorial of St. Barnabas, Bishop and Martyr

The Lectionary for Mass

◆ FIRST READING: This short reading gives us a lot of information about Barnabas' role as an Apostle. Some sources say that his name was really Joseph, but he got the nickname "Barnabas" or "son of encouragement." We might let that remind us that the real meaning of evangelization is to share good news. In honor of this Apostle, may we all be sources of encouragement.

◆ RESPONSORIAL PSALM 98: As we sing that the Lord's saving power has been revealed to the whole world, we remember that revelation comes about only through the dedication of "Apostles." We are called daily to reveal God's justice and kindness.

◆ GOSPEL: In this familiar passage, Jesus uses images of salt and light to express how his disciples are to be in the world. Like salt, which gives flavor to food, or a lamp, which "gives light to all in the house," their presence must be felt. We become salt and light not by speaking more loudly than others, but by the "good deeds" we perform. We are not, of course, calling attention to ourselves. Rather, our actions should always point to the one who inspires them in us: God.

The Roman Missal

All the orations are proper for today and can be found in the Proper of Saints at June 11. The Collect recognizes the saint for his preaching of the Gospel to the nations, calling him "a man filled with faith and the Holy Spirit." The prayer goes on to ask that the Gospel may continue to "be faithfully proclaimed by word and by deed" even down to our own day. The Prayer over the Offerings asks that the offerings we make transform us to do that work of spreading the Gospel in the same way St. Barnabas did: "set us on fire" with the same "flame of your love, / by which Saint Barnabas brought the light of the Gospel to the nations." Either Preface I or Preface II of the Apostles is the Preface to be used today. The Prayer after Communion points to the Kingdom that is revealed and anticipated in the celebration of the Eucharist, a Kingdom we hope to arrive at fully one day, as it asks that "what we celebrate in sacramental signs . . . we may one day behold unveiled." Consider using Eucharistic Prayer I.

Today's Saint

Even though St. Barnabas (first century) was not one of the original Twelve Apostles, he was given the title of "apostle" by St. Luke and the early Church fathers due to his apostolic endeavors on behalf of Christianity. His original name was Joseph, but the Apostles gave him the surname Barnabas, meaning "son of encouragement." Together with St. Paul, he extended the missionary efforts of the Church beyond Jerusalem to Antioch, and after much success moved on to other places throughout Asia Minor. After parting ways with St. Paul over issues regarding circumcision and the Mosaic law, St. Barnabas embarked on further missionary journeys with John and Mark (see Acts of the Apostles 15:36–40).

W E D 12 (#361) green
Weekday

The Lectionary for Mass

◆ FIRST READING: Paul's confidence in his mission to the Corinthians and other fledgling communities comes from God. He directly attests to this in today's reading. He knows he can neither take credit for his ministerial qualifications nor for the words he preaches. God in Christ is the author of his ministry of death and Resurrection.

◆ RESPONSORIAL PSALM 99: Throughout the ages, priests and prophets have extolled the Lord's name. They have recognized God's holiness and followed his laws. When they sinned, God forgave them. For the forgiveness God offers us and in recognition of God as our Lord, we acclaim his holiness in the words of this enthronement hymn.

◆ GOSPEL: Jesus comes to fulfill, not abolish the law. The least are those who choose not to follow his commandments, and the greatest, those who not only follow his commandments, but also teach them to others.

T H U 13 (#362) white
Memorial of St. Anthony of Padua, Priest and Doctor of the Church

The Lectionary for Mass

◆ FIRST READING: Paul does not preach himself, but preaches Jesus Christ crucified and raised as the Lord. Those who believe in Jesus will see the veil of darkness removed and will witness God's glory. God will transform them into the image of glory. Those who choose not to believe and go forward themselves to preach the Gospel will perish.

◆ RESPONSORIAL PSALM 85: The psalm refrain expresses the people's confidence that the Lord's glory will reside in their land. The verses proclaim hope in the Lord's promise that kindness, truth, justice, and peace might reign. As we pray the words of Psalm 85, we voice our own hope that the Lord will make known these gifts to us and our land.

◆ GOSPEL: Jesus instructs his disciples that in order for them to enter the Kingdom of heaven, their righteousness must exceed that of the hypocritical righteousness of the scribes and Pharisees. The disciples must reconcile with their opponents. Before bringing their gift to the altar, they must seek unity with those with whom they experience discord. Forgiveness is a hallmark of a disciple's life, for the God of Jesus Christ is a forgiving God.

The Roman Missal

The proper Collect for the day, found at June 13 in the Proper of Saints section of the Missal, recognizes St. Anthony of Padua "as an outstanding preacher / and an intercessor in their need." The prayer goes on to ask God that, with the saint's assistance, "we may know your help in every trial." (Thus, we can turn to St. Anthony not only when we have lost some item, but when we have lost strength and resolve in the face of struggle and difficulty.) The Prayer over the Offerings and the Prayer after Communion come from either the Common of Pastors: For One Pastor, or from the Common of Doctors of the Church, or from the Common of Holy Men and Women: For Religious. The same variety exists for the choice of the Preface today: Preface I or II of Saints, the Preface of Holy Pastors, or the Preface of Holy Virgins and Religious. Consider using Eucharistic Prayer I.

Today's Saint

St. Anthony of Padua (1195–1231), a member of a noble Portuguese family, joined the Canons Regular of St. Augustine at a young age, but later joined the Franciscans to engage in missionary work. Although his missionary dreams were halted due to illness, he received public acclaim for his preaching style, which led to the conversion of many from heresy, earning him the title "the Hammer of the Heretics." He had the privilege of meeting St. Francis of Assisi in person and was later elected provincial of Northern Italy. His writing is extensive, especially in the area of sermons; therefore, he was named a Doctor of the Church. People invoke his name when trying to find lost items. This comes from the story in the saint's biography when a young novice took Anthony's Psalter, but returned it in a hurry when the angry saint appeared to him in a vision!

FRI 14 (#363) green
Weekday

The Lectionary for Mass

◆ FIRST READING: Paul's mission was never easy. He faced persecution and suffered much, as did the Corinthians as their community of faith developed. Competing factions wanted to pull them away from Christ. Paul encourages the Corinthians on their journey of faith by letting them know that while suffering and death are present, they too, will share in Christ's Resurrection. The power of God evident in the Resurrection of Jesus Christ is a treasure!

◆ RESPONSORIAL PSALM 116 is one of many thanksgiving psalms in which the psalmist thanks and praises God for his presence during times of need. In return for the freedom God provided, the psalmist accepts his role as a servant of God. To God, the psalmist offers a sacrifice of praise and declares his vows.

◆ GOSPEL: Jesus references the Old Testament teaching on adultery and divorce. His teaching calls the disciples and us to consider how we sin and break relationships with one another and God by failing to treat each other with respect and love. As disciples, we have an obligation to recognize when we choose death over life in our relationships.

SAT 15 (#364) green
Weekday

Optional Memorial of the Blessed Virgin Mary / white

The Lectionary for Mass

◆ FIRST READING: In Christ, everything is new! The old things no longer have hold over us. This is Paul's message to the Corinthians. We are reconciled to God in Christ. We are "ambassadors for Christ." Each day, we recognize the areas in our lives where we continually need to be reconciled to God. And, each day, too, we proclaim the message of reconciliation to our family, neighbors, and indeed all the peoples of the world.

◆ RESPONSORIAL PSALM 103: We sing Psalm 103 in praise of God for the mercy he offers to us individually and to all of his people. The refrain reminds us how kind and merciful God is. The verses give us words to acknowledge the forgiveness and healing that comes from God, and the limitless bounds of God's love.

◆ GOSPEL: As we continue to proclaim from Matthew 5, perhaps we might wonder if the disciples would have been retreating under the weight of the demands of following Jesus. In today's brief five verses, Jesus instructs the disciples not to take false oaths, but to dedicate themselves solely to the Lord. By themselves, the disciples can do nothing, but when they give their yes completely to the Lord, all things will be possible.

16 (#166C) white
Solemnity of the Most Holy Trinity

About Today's Solemnity

The Solemnity of the Most Holy Trinity, observed on the Sunday after the Solemnity of Pentecost, dates to the seventh century; it has been on the Church's universal calendar for nearly seven hundred years. "The mystery of the Most Holy Trinity is the central mystery of Christian faith and life," the Catechism tells us. "It is the mystery of God in himself. It is therefore the source of all the other mysteries of faith, the light that enlightens them" (*Catechism of the Catholic Church*, 234). As Christians, we believe in one God, in three Persons: Father, Son, and Holy Spirit.

Through the centuries, saints and artists have helped us to understand the Holy Trinity through images and comparisons. St. Patrick is said to have explained the Trinity to the people of Ireland by showing them a shamrock, with its three leaves on one stem. St. Ignatius Loyola compared the Trinity to a chord played on an instrument: three distinct notes forming one sound. The early iconographers of the Church in the East depicted the Trinity with imagery from the Old Testament story of Abraham's angelic visitors. A familiar symbol of the Trinity is a triangle with rays radiating from it, and in the middle of the triangle an open eye, representing the all-seeing Providence of God.

The Lectionary for Mass

◆ FIRST READING: The passage from Proverbs describes how Wisdom was present with the Lord from before creation. When the Lord created the heavens and the earth, Wisdom was near the Lord. Wisdom played before the Lord in joy. Wisdom played on the earth the Lord created. Wisdom appreciated humanity.

◆ RESPONSORIAL PSALM 8 gives us the words to express our wonderment at the splendor of God's creation. From the heavens to the earth, and in recognition of all the earth's creatures, we praise the name of the Lord. We also acknowledge with humility, our place—the place of humanity—within creation.

◆ SECOND READING: In the opening verses of Romans 5, Paul speaks of the triad of faith, hope, and love, and in the context of the three, provides a reference to God, the Lord Jesus Christ, and the Holy Spirit. A few centuries later the Church would cite references like these to develop its doctrine of the Trinity.

◆ GOSPEL: Jesus speaks of his departure to the disciples and assures them that the Spirit of truth will be present with them after he leaves. The Spirit will serve as a guide to the disciples, leading them to the truth. All that Jesus shares in from the Father, the Spirit will give to the disciples so that they, too, might participate in the Father's glory.

The Roman Missal

The texts for this solemnity are found after the texts for the Thirty-Fourth Week in Ordinary Time, toward the end of the "Ordinary Time" section of the Missal, and several pages before the "Order of Mass" section begins. The Gloria and the Creed are sung or said today. The Collect expresses for us the meaning of this solemnity not in terms of some dry theological doctrine but rather in terms of the active, dynamic power of the triune God: the Father sends into the world the Word of truth and the Spirit of sanctification and, in so doing, reveals to the human race his own "wondrous mystery." The prayer affirms that through the Trinity we know the very life of God himself.

The Prayer over the Offerings makes the important liturgical point that as we make the offering of our lives at this liturgy—"this oblation of our service"—its ultimate purpose is that by it we might be made "an eternal offering to you." The prayer expresses how in the liturgy we are swept up into the life of the Trinity so that our entire life might be lived with the same

self-emptying, self-giving love as exists between the divine Persons. The Preface, "The Mystery of the Most Holy Trinity," is proper for today and its text is given along with the other texts for the Mass; there is both a text with and without musical notation. The text reiterates the theological meaning of God being "one God, one Lord: / not in the unity of a single person, / but in a Trinity of one substance, equal in majesty." The Prayer after Communion also gives voice to the basic statement about the Trinity nonetheless being "undivided Unity." Consider using Eucharistic Prayer III.

Since there should be a certain emphasis given to how the life of the Christian should be a reflection of and a participation in the life of the Trinity, perhaps the formula "Go in peace, glorifying the Lord by your life" would be an appropriate choice for the dismissal today.

Of course use festive music with full choir, banners in the entrance procession, incense, and a longer, more formal Gospel procession.

Other Ideas

Throughout the celebration of the Sunday liturgy we invoke the Trinity several times; from the opening blessing to the dismissal at the end of Mass. There is also the gesture of blessing ourselves with holy water as we enter and leave the church. Make a mental note of all the times the Father, Son, and Holy Spirit are mentioned within the liturgy. What does it mean to make the gesture of blessing on ourselves and to receive the blessing from the priest? Consider the blessing over the *Book of the Gospels* and over the elements for Eucharist. What does it mean to bless these items? Does it make a difference in how we regard them and how we use them? Think of the times that we bless ourselves and those times when we can offer a blessing to others in our daily life.

MON 17 (#365) green
weekday

Eleventh Week in Ordinary Time

The Lectionary for Mass

◆ FIRST READING: Paul cites Isaiah 49:8 as he appeals to the Corinthians not to accept God's grace in vain. The message he preaches is true. His intent is not to deceive anyone, but lead everyone to the grace of God in Jesus Christ. Now *is* the day of salvation. Would that the Corinthians—would that we—accept this message from those who have been sent to us as God's ministers.

◆ RESPONSORIAL PSALM 98 draws our attention to the salvation the Lord has already made known. This psalm connects with Paul's proclamation to the Corinthians in the First Reading that now is the time of salvation. Together with all peoples and all lands, we joyfully sing to the Lord for his boundless gifts.

◆ GOSPEL: The Old Testament teaching that an eye should be taken for an eye and a tooth for a tooth, no longer holds authority in Jesus. Jesus teaches his disciples that revenge is not the way. Rather, generosity and service characterize disciples. When he instructs his disciples to turn the other cheek, Jesus is not teaching them to open themselves to violence, but rather metaphorically coaching them to replace the paradigm of retaliation with one of forgiveness.

TUE 18 (#366) green
Weekday

The Lectionary for Mass

◆ FIRST READING: Paul speaks about the collection for Jerusalem and references the generosity of the Macedonians despite the suffering and poverty they endured. He invites the Corinthians to take part of the "gracious act" of giving to symbolize the unity of the Church. Their support of the larger Christian community reflects their knowledge of the gracious act performed by Jesus Christ who became poor for their sakes so they might experience his richness.

◆ RESPONSORIAL PSALM 146: This hymn of praise exudes the joy of one who has found richness in the Lord. Healing, justice, and new life abound when one keeps faith in the Lord. The only fitting response is to praise the Lord with one's soul.

◆ GOSPEL: Hate, even toward an enemy, has no place in a disciple's heart. While the Old Testament did speak of hating one's enemy, love of neighbor was limited to those in one's country or general geographical area. Jesus requires that anyone who follows him love all people. In love, is the perfection of the heavenly Father.

W
E
19 (#367) green
D **Weekday**

Optional Memorial of St. Romuald, Abbot / white

The Lectionary for Mass

◆ FIRST READING: Paul continues to expand on the theme of generosity. Give joyfully, he advises the Corinthians. Do not hold back when giving and do not give simply out of obligation. When we give generously, God will multiply exponentially our gift as he has produced abundant grace in Jesus Christ.

◆ RESPONSORIAL PSALM 112: How blessed we are when we have faith in the Lord and follow the Lord's commands! The Lord will provide riches to our house. Light will pierce the darkness. Such are the impacts of God's amazing generosity. May we be blessed for standing in awe of our generous God.

◆ GOSPEL: Jesus' words to his disciples remind us to not let our

performance of righteous deeds and our almsgiving be for our own self-glorification as it was for the hypocrites. Our prayer and fasting should foster our relationship with the Father so that he can continue to magnify our generosity toward others. Our repayment will come. This we know in faith.

Today's Saint

St. Romuald (c. 950–1027) was born in Ravenna and led a self-indulgent life as a young man, but when he saw his father kill an opponent in a duel, he fled to a monastery. Romuald yearned for a stricter life than he found there, and so he withdrew to become a hermit. Eventually, he founded the Camaldolese branch of the Benedictine family, integrating community life with the solitary life. His monks live and work in individual hermitages but come together to celebrate Eucharist and the Liturgy of the Hours.

T
H **20** (#368) green
U **Weekday**

The Lectionary for Mass

◆ FIRST READING: Paul fills his self-reflection on his mission to the Corinthians with deep affection for them. His worries about them turning from their faith in the God of Jesus Christ and pledging allegiance to another gospel are real and heartfelt. Paul gave so intensely and freely of himself (asking nothing in return) when he preached the "foolishness" of the Cross to the Corinthians, that he again wants them to know the truth of the knowledge he brought to them.

◆ RESPONSORIAL PSALM 111: God's works throughout the history of the Israelite people manifest God's mercy and love for them. For these mighty and powerful works of justice and truth, the psalmist gives thanks with his whole heart. We join our voices in thanksgiving and praise with the psalmist today

as we acclaim the God of justice and truth who is eternally faithful.

◆ GOSPEL: The verses from Matthew 6 fall between the two sections of yesterday's Gospel reading. In the passage, Jesus teaches his disciples how they are to pray. The Matthean version of the Lord's Prayer forms the centerpiece of this passage and is sandwiched between Jesus' instructions to his disciples not to pray verbosely like those who do not believe and his teaching to forgive others' sins.

F
R **21** (#369) white
I **Memorial of St. Aloysius Gonzaga, Religious**

The Lectionary for Mass

◆ FIRST READING: Paul recounts the suffering and persecution he has experienced. Yet in spite of the ills he has faced, he still dares to boast of the foolishness of the Cross. His anxiety for the Churches he has founded is palpable. Surely, everyone who is in a leadership position in ministry can relate to Paul's anxiety. How authentic and sincere must a leader's faith in the Resurrection be in the face of suffering.

◆ RESPONSORIAL PSALM 34 is a common psalm for Ordinary Time. Note how today's refrain from verse 18b connects to the emphasis in the First Reading on God's presence with the faithful during times of suffering. God's abiding faithfulness for those who live their faith never ceases. Nothing compares to this goodness we can taste and see.

◆ GOSPEL: Following his teaching on prayer and fasting, Jesus advises his disciples not to accumulate treasures on earth. Destruction easily comes to material possessions, but nothing can destroy heavenly treasures. We should align our hearts with the treasure we desire and our eyes should reflect the light of faith lest darkness take over our lives.

The Roman Missal

The Mass prayers, all of which are proper for the day, can be found at June 21 in the Proper of Saints section of the Missal. The Collect describes St. Aloysius' life as one of penitence joined "to a wonderful innocence of life," applying that to our own journey by asking "that, though we have failed to follow him in innocence, / we may imitate him in penitence." The Prayer over the Offerings again uses the imagery of innocence associated with this saint by asking that "we may take our place at the heavenly banquet, / clothed always in our wedding garment." The banquet imagery is appropriate as we participate in the Liturgy of the Eucharist. The Prayer after Communion announces that we have been fed "with the food of Angels," and goes on to ask that we serve the Lord "in purity of life" and that "we persevere in constant thanksgiving." Although either one of the two Prefaces of Saints could be used today, perhaps the Preface of Holy Virgins and Religious would be a better choice. Consider using the Eucharistic Prayer for Various Needs and Occasions IV.

Today's Saint

St. Aloysius Gonzaga (1568–1591) was born to a noble family in Italy who destined him for the military. While recovering from an illness, he read the lives of the saints and spent time in prayer. As a result, Aloysius decided to dedicate himself to God as a Jesuit. Most of his family was against it, but he joined anyway, making his vows in 1587. In 1591, the plague broke out in Rome. Aloysius volunteered to care for the victims and became sick himself. He recovered, but his health was broken, and he died within a few months. Many schools are named for him because he is the patron saint of Catholic youth.

SAT **22** (#370) green
Weekday

Optional Memorials of St. Paulinus of Nola, Bishop / white; Sts. John Fisher, Bishop and Thomas More, Martyrs / red; Blessed Virgin Mary / white

The Lectionary for Mass

◆ FIRST READING: God's grace is enough for Paul. Since Paul experienced the sufficiency of God's grace for himself in the adversities that came his way as he preached the Gospel, he wanted the Corinthians to know that God's grace is also enough for them in the trials their community of faith experiences. In weakness, we are strong in Christ.

◆ RESPONSORIAL PSALM 34: Today's verses continue where yesterday's left off. In conjunction with the First Reading, the verses emphasize the Lord's care for those who find refuge in him. Those who see the Lord's goodness and trust in it for their own lives will never fail to know it.

◆ GOSPEL: God will feed us as he feeds the birds of the sky. God provides for us as he makes the flowers to bloom and the fields to yield abundant harvests. Anxiety is not for those who devote themselves to God rather than serving wealth. God knows the needs of disciples and so, not needing to provide for their own needs, the work of disciples remains the work of seeking the Kingdom.

Today's Saints

St. Paulinus of Nola (c. 354–431) was raised in a family of wealthy politicians in Bordeaux. His interests were varied: everything from practicing law to writing poetry, from traveling to governing. After the death of a newly born son, he and his wife, Therasia, gave away the family fortune to the poor and to the Church. St. Paulinus and Therasia moved to Italy where they began to live, along with some other friends, a life of prayer and service. They lived in a two-story building in which the first floor provided a place of rest for the wayward and the lost, and the second floor was their place of residence based on the rhythms of monasticism. Gaining a reputation for holiness, St. Paulinus was ordained a priest and was eventually made a bishop of Nola.

St. John Fisher (1469–1535) and St. Thomas More (1478–1535) lived during a time of great upheaval and reformation. Both were friends and consultants to King Henry VIII, and both were executed because they would not declare the king's supremacy over the Church. St. John Fisher, born in Yorkshire, was an astute scholar recognized for his profound insight into the complex questions of life. He held many positions of esteem, including a tutor to the young Henry VIII, Chancellor of Cambridge University, and bishop of Rochester.

St. Thomas More, born in London, was a family man characterized by a deep affection for his wife and three daughters. He, too, held many powerful positions in the Church and in society; in particular, a Parliament lawyer, Speaker of the House of Commons, and Chancellor of England.

(#169C) white

☀ 23 Solemnity of the Most Holy Body and Blood of Christ

About Today's Solemnity

This Eucharistic day, observed with such solemnity throughout the world, began in a quiet Belgian convent in the thirteenth century, with the vision of a holy nun, St. Juliana. In her vision, she saw the moon, full and bright. It was glorious, except that one part of its disk was in shadow. The meaning of the vision was then revealed to her: the moon represented the liturgical year; the shadow, a missing feast in honor of the Blessed Sacrament. Juliana spoke to her confessor about what she had seen. Amazingly, within thirty-five years, Pope Urban IV had established the Feast of Corpus Christi, the Body of Christ, in the Church's universal calendar. Hundreds of years later, in 1849, Pope Pius IX added the Feast of the Precious Blood celebrated on July 1. Following the Second Vatican Council, the two liturgies became one solemnity in honor of the Most Holy Body and Blood of Christ. Of course, we already had a day honoring the Eucharist: the Evening Mass of the Lord's Supper on Holy Thursday, which even includes a procession with the Blessed Sacrament. But the purpose and the mood of the two processions are strikingly different.

On Holy Thursday, we walk with Jesus to the Mount of Olives, to keep watch with him on the night of his betrayal. The sacrament is carried in the ciborium, covered with the humeral veil: and Christ's glory, too, is veiled as he undergoes his Passion. On Corpus Christi, we walk in the afterglow of Easter Time, in company with the Risen Lord. This time, the Blessed Sacrament is exposed in a monstrance: the Lord's glory is not hidden, but visible to all. Corpus Christi is one of the most Catholic of days, an expression of our faith in the Real Presence of Christ in the Blessed Sacrament. And yet, this celebration is also outward looking, carrying the liturgy out of the church and into the streets. We come together in all our diversity and we celebrate our unity.

The Lectionary for Mass

◆ FIRST READING: The king of Salem and priest, Melchizedek, blessed bread and wine, and offered a blessing upon Abram in celebration of his victory over Chedorlaomer and the other kings on his side. In return, Abram provided Melchizedek one-tenth of everything he had. And, though in the verses that follow today's passage, the king of Sodom commands Abram to give him the people that are the Lord's, Abram refuses remaining faithful to the Lord.

◆ RESPONSORIAL PSALM 110: Today's psalm is a royal psalm that celebrates the Lord's power in the person of the king. Those who follow as priests in the line of Melchizedek, who blessed Abram (a reference to the First Reading), will share in the eternal priesthood.

◆ SECOND READING: The Second Reading from Paul's first letter to the Corinthians was also the Second Reading on Holy Thursday for the Evening Mass of the Lord's Supper. This brief passage is the earliest

account of the institution of the Eucharist. We see its pattern of taking bread, giving thanks, breaking bread, and proclaiming the bread is Jesus' Body given for us and repeating it with the cup in the Church's Eucharistic Prayer. Every time we celebrate the Eucharist, we do so in remembrance of Jesus as the early Christian community did.

◆ SEQUENCE: This Sunday, the Church may sing one of the four sequences—ancient, poetic songs that precede the singing of the Gospel Acclamation. The sequence for the Most Holy Body and Blood of Christ, *Lauda Sion*, is ascribed to St. Thomas Aquinas. The sixth stanza of the sequence reminds us of the history of the Eucharistic feast. Today's sequence is optional. A musical arrangement by Richard Proulx and Alan J. Hommerding is available from World Library Publications. The composition is based on Tantum Ergo. A sample PDF is available here: www.wlp .jspaluch.com/download/008739 .pdf. The sequence should be sung from the ambo; however, the assembly may be invited to take part. A worship aid with the music should be provided. Accomplished musicians should segue from the sequence into the Gospel Acclamation, allowing time for the cantor to move from the ambo to the cantor stand.

◆ GOSPEL: With five thousand men (we do not know the total number in the crowd because Luke does not tell us how many women and children were present) to feed, all the Twelve have are five loaves and two fish. Jesus asks the Twelve to divide the masses into groups of fifty, and without arguing about whether or not there would be enough food, the Twelve follow his instructions. Jesus took, blessed, and broke the provisions, and the disciples share them. Everyone ate. Everyone was satisfied. Even more could have shared in the meal Jesus provided. Such is how Jesus feeds us in the Eucharist today. There is always enough of Jesus for others to join the assembly.

The Roman Missal

Of course use festive music with full choir, banners in the entrance procession, incense, and a longer, more formal Gospel procession today. In Sacrament of the Eucharist, God has "left us a memorial of your Passion." The prayer goes on to ask that because of our revering of "the sacred mysteries of your Body and Blood," we may "always experience in ourselves / the fruits of your redemption." As this prayer speaks of the fruits of being redeemed, we must always remember that those fruits are expressed in a life of self-emptying love. Therefore, the focus is not so much on a passive contemplation of the Real Presence in the Eucharist, but, as with all liturgical celebration, how our participation in the mystery is a means of being transformed by God to live out the mystery that is being celebrated. The Gloria and the Creed are sung or said.

The Prayer over the Offerings reinforces the idea that worship of the Eucharist must be expressed in the practical living out of our lives. This prayer reinforces that one of the chief results of Eucharistic celebration must be unity: as the one bread and one cup are prayed over at the one altar around which is gathered the one Body of Christ, we see in those signs the mystery of what we are to become—"one body, one spirit in Christ," in the words of Eucharistic Prayer III. The Preface that is given along with the other formularies for this Mass is Preface II of the Most Holy Eucharist; only the text with music is given, indicating a certain preference for chanting the introductory dialogue and the Preface itself. However, a rubric indicates that Preface I of the

Most Holy Eucharist, which can be found along with the texts of other Prefaces further along in the Missal, may also be used. The Prayer after Communion points to the important but often overlooked eschatological dimension of the Eucharist, as it reminds us that the reception of the Body and Blood of the Lord in the present age is a foreshadowing of sharing in God's divine life for all eternity. Consider using Eucharistic Prayer I.

◆ PROCESSION: Noting that it is desirable for a Eucharistic procession to take place after Mass, the Missal gives instructions on how this is to be carried out. The host that will be carried in the procession should be a host that has been consecrated at this Mass; thus it is made clear how worship of the Eucharist outside Mass is an extension of the grace of the offering of the sacrifice. If such a procession is to take place after Mass, the host to be carried in procession is placed in the monstrance when the Communion of the faithful is over, and that monstrance is set on the altar. The Prayer after Communion is then prayed, but the Concluding Rite is omitted. Instead, the procession forms immediately after the Prayer after Communion. The Missal gives no further rubrics concerning the procession; liturgy preparers should consult the ritual, *Holy Communion and Worship of the Eucharist outside Mass* for specific instructions. The Missal does note, however, that the procession need not take place immediately after Mass, but may instead follow after a public and lengthy period of adoration coming at the end of Mass.

Consult LTP's new resource, *Guide for Celebrating® Worship of the Eucharist outside of Mass.* As part of the *Preparing Parish Worship*™ series, this resource provides detailed instructions for the procession on Corpus Christi.

Other Ideas

Although we focus on the mystery and sacrament of the Eucharist every Sunday, on this Sunday we are called to be even more aware and grateful for this astonishing gift of the Lord. At each of the liturgies this weekend bestow a blessing on those who are extraordinary ministers of Holy Communion. If you are an extraordinary minister of Holy Communion take a moment to reflect on the significance of your ministry. What a great joy to be able to offer to others the Body and Blood of Christ. As a communicant, reflect on your attitude as you approach the altar, on your posture as you receive Communion, on your attentiveness to the words of the Communion minister, and on the meaning of the journey as you approach and leave the altar, the Lord's Table. What does it mean to receive "food for the journey" every Sunday?

(#586/#587) white

MON 24
Solemnity of the Nativity of St. John the Baptist

About Today's Solemnity

John the Baptist was the great prophet and herald of Jesus the Messiah. He prepared the way of the Lord and revealed Jesus to others as both the Messiah and the Lamb of God. St. John exemplifies the Christian life as one who proclaims the Gospel message of healing and repentance while he points out Christ to others and shows them the way to become united with God. This is an ancient solemnity, reaching back to the fourth century, though the date of the celebration varied in East and West. In the East, the birth of the forerunner was celebrated on the day after Epiphany, January 7, because of the association of that feast with the Baptism of the Lord. In the West, it was celebrated on June 24, in keeping with Luke 1:36, which notes that

Elizabeth was six months pregnant at the time of the Annunciation of the Lord.

Lectionary for Mass: Vigil Mass

◆ FIRST READING: The Lord called Jeremiah to be a prophet even before the Lord formed him in his mother's womb. Accepting one's prophetic call is not easy. Jeremiah attempts to excuse himself from the call because he is too young, but the Lord refuses to accept this reason. The Lord places the divine Word in Jeremiah's mouth and sends him forth to proclaim words of change: destruction of sinful ways and the planting of God's justice.

◆ RESPONSORIAL PSALM 71: The psalm refrain, taken from Psalm 71:6, connects to God's words in the First Reading that speak of his call of Jeremiah even before the prophet was in the womb. Even in his mother's womb, the psalmist found strength in the Lord. The Lord now is the psalmist's refuge and hope. From his birth through his youth, until the present time, the Lord delivers him.

◆ SECOND READING: Prophets have testified about the grace of salvation that is ours. They embraced their mission because the Spirit of Christ lived within them and showed them that Christ's sufferings would lead to glory. The prophets, including John the Baptist whose birth we celebrate today, were not self-serving. Rather, they served God by proclaiming the Good News about the grace that is ours.

◆ GOSPEL: The Gospel reading comes from the opening chapter of Luke and is the annunciation of the Nativity of John the Baptist. One day, the lot fell to the elderly Zechariah to enter the sanctuary to perform his priestly duties. With the assembly at prayer outside the sanctuary, the Lord's angel appeared to Zechariah and announced to him that a son to be named "John" would be born to his wife, Elizabeth. In the tradition of the prophets who came before him, John would prepare the way for the Lord's coming. Surely, the Holy Spirit worked overtime to calm the fears of Elizabeth and Zechariah at this news!

The Lectionary for Mass: Mass during the Day

◆ FIRST READING: The Lord called the prophet Isaiah from within his mother's womb and destined him from birth to be a servant who showed the Lord's glory. Isaiah was a light to the nations, a prophet who proclaimed the Lord's salvation so that it might extend to the far reaches of the known world. John the Baptist follows in the line of the great prophets such as Isaiah.

◆ RESPONSORIAL PSALM 139: The psalmist's words of self-reflection capture God's omniscience in regard to his own life and journey of faith. God knows every one of the psalmist's actions. Like God formed the prophet Isaiah in the womb, so too, God has formed the very being of the psalmist in his mother's womb. For this tender and personal knowledge, the psalmist gives thanks.

◆ SECOND READING: Paul sees John the Baptist's prophetic announcement of a baptism of repentance to the people of Israel in line with all those who followed upon King David. In his address to the people in the synagogue at Antioch in Pisidia, Paul recognizes that John proclaimed that there is one who would come after him who would bring salvation. Christians recognize Jesus as the Savior whom John the Baptist heralded.

◆ GOSPEL: Elizabeth and Zechariah's neighbors and relatives wanted their son to be named Zechariah after his father, but Elizabeth knew better. She rebutted their request saying her son's name would be "John." The mute Zechariah supported his wife's decision by writing John's name on his tablet and freedom comes to Zechariah as the Lord restores the elderly father's voice. The circumcised son of Elizabeth and Zechariah, now part of a long line of Israel's prophets, will prepare the way for the coming of the Lord's salvation in Jesus!

The Roman Missal: Vigil Mass

The Gloria and the Creed are sung or said today. The Collect uses the interesting appellation "the Precursor" to refer to St. John, a title somewhat unfamiliar to us but one which certainly defines his role in salvation history. The prayer asks that we may come safely to the One foretold by John. The Prayer over the Offerings once again makes a connection between liturgy and life, petitioning God "that what we celebrate in mystery / we may follow with deeds of devoted service." The Preface is proper for today, "The Mission of the Precursor," and the text, with and without musical notation, is located among the texts for the Mass during the Day, two pages over from the Vigil Mass texts. The Preface recalls the events associated with St. John the Baptist's life and echoes the Scripture passages associated with him: how he was consecrated "for a singular honor / among those born of women"; how "His birth brought great rejoicing"; how he leapt for joy in the womb; how "He alone of all the prophets / pointed out the Lamb of redemption"; how "he baptized the very author of Baptism"; and how he gave witness to Christ by the shedding of his blood. The Prayer after Communion emphasizes the Communion of Saints as it asks that "the prayer of Saint John the

Baptist / accompany us who have eaten our fill / at this sacrificial feast." There is also a plea for forgiveness through the intercession of the saint: since he was the one to proclaim Jesus as the Lamb who would take away our sins, we ask that "he implore now for us your favor." Consider using Eucharistic Prayer III.

Since today is a daily Mass, it may be difficult to have a heightened celebration due to people's work schedules. However, do your best to emphasize the importance of today. If you don't usually have music at daily Mass, do so today (even just a cantor and accompanist will add solemnity!). Schedule liturgical ministers, add incense and a Gospel procession.

The Roman Missal: Mass during the Day

Please note that since today is a solemnity, the Masses for this evening's Saturday night Mass, unless otherwise noted by your local bishop, are for the Solemnity of the Nativity of St. John the Baptist and not for the Sunday. This means you should use the prayers and readings from the Mass for St. John the Baptist and not the readings and prayer texts for Sunday, the Twelfth Sunday in Ordinary Time. The Gloria and the Creed are sung or said today. The Collect speaks about the preparatory role of the Baptist as one who was raised up "to make ready a nation fit for Christ the Lord." This prayer prays that we may be directed "into the way of salvation and peace." The Prayer over the Offerings expresses why it is fitting to celebrate the nativity of St. John: it is because he "both foretold the coming of the world's Savior / and pointed him out when he came." The text for the proper Preface used today is located immediately following the Prayer over the Offerings. See the commentary above under the Vigil Mass. The

Prayer after Communion uses the imagery of the Lamb so closely associated with John the Baptist's announcement of Jesus, and in so doing the prayer gives voice to a rich Eucharistic theology with its phrase "Having feasted at the banquet of the heavenly Lamb . . ." Consider using Eucharistic Prayer I. Since today is a daily Mass, it may be difficult to have a heightened celebration due to people's work schedules. However, do your best to emphasize the importance of today. If you don't usually have music at daily Mass, do so today (even just a cantor and accompanist will add solemnity!). Schedule liturgical ministers, add incense and a Gospel procession.

T U E 25 (#372) green
Weekday

Twelfth Week in Ordinary Time

The Lectionary for Mass

◆ First Reading: Lot and Abram, kinsmen though they were, agreed to go separate ways on the land. Lot chose to go eastward to the Jordan Plain near Sodom and its wicked inhabitants, while Abram stayed in Canaan. With Lot having departed, the Lord promises progeny and land to Abram. In response, Abram builds an altar around which he would worship the Lord.

◆ Responsorial Psalm 15: The question from the opening verse of Psalm 15, which serves as the refrain for the Responsorial Psalm, is one an Israelite who desired to be let into the Temple court would have asked an official. The verses provide the answer as to who could enter. The requirements seem demanding: do justice, live truth, walk without blame, do not speak insults, do no harm, do not lend money and charge interest, and do not accept a bribe. Those who act accordingly will live with the Lord on the holy mountain.

◆ Gospel: Three sayings of Jesus form today's Gospel. In the first, Jesus teaches his disciples to not spend their energy giving what is holy to those who will not accept it. Should the disciples do so, they themselves will face persecution from those who reject their message. The second saying is the "Golden Rule" to do unto others what we would want them to do to us. And, in the third saying, Jesus speaks of the narrow gate that leads to the Kingdom. With words that the disciples could have construed as discouraging, if not at least challenging, Jesus tells them not many will find this gate.

W E D 26 (#373) green
Weekday

The Lectionary for Mass

◆ First Reading: Abram has a vision in which the Lord tells Abram he will have a great reward. But Abram questions how this could happen since he has no heir except for Eliezer, the steward of his house. The Lord simply invites Abram to look up at the sky to know that his descendants will be as numerous as the stars. Abram and his descendants will also know the gift of the land, which they will possess.

◆ Responsorial Psalm 105: Just as Abram came to trust that the Lord would uphold his covenant, we acknowledge the Lord's faithfulness in the psalm refrain. In a direct connection to the First Reading, verse 6 notes the descendants of Abraham.

◆ Gospel: Jesus uses the metaphor of a tree producing good fruit or bad fruit to show his disciples that the fruit we produce will be how we will be known. With stern words, he lets the disciples know that should they not produce good fruit, they will be thrown into the fire as a rotten tree is cut down and destroyed. Twice Jesus tells them,

"By their fruits you will know them." What are our fruits?

THU 27 (#374) green
Weekday

Optional Memorial of St. Cyril of Alexandria, Bishop and Doctor of the Church / white

The Lectionary for Mass

◆ FIRST READING: There is an option to use a long form or short form for today's First Reading, which recounts the story of Abram's servant, Hagar, giving birth to his son, Ishmael. Sarai, who could not get pregnant, offered Hagar to Abram to be his concubine. Yet when Hagar became pregnant, jealousy and envy mightily arose and Sarai began to abuse Hagar.

◆ RESPONSORIAL PSALM 106: A psalm of thanksgiving follows upon the First Reading and reflects our gratitude for the Lord's mighty deeds. Abram will know prosperity. Yet it is also important to hear the psalm's emphasis on the Lord's mercy given the circumstances surrounding the birth of Ishmael.

◆ GOSPEL: Our continuous reading of Matthew 7 finds Jesus teaching again about who will enter the Kingdom of heaven. We already know few will enter the narrow gate. Those few will be those who do the Father's will. They will be the ones who truly listen to Jesus' words and act consistently with the words they heard. Others, whose actions do not follow upon the words they claim to have heard and internalized, will see their house collapse as if it was built on sand.

Today's Saint

As the patriarch of Alexandria, St. Cyril of Alexandria (376–444) was an avid defender of the faith; therefore, he was no stranger to conflict. He found himself at odds with Nestorius, the archbishop of Constantinople, who taught that the Blessed Virgin is the mother of Christ (Christotokos) not the Mother of God (Theotokos). St. Cyril presided over the First Council of Ephesus (431), which condemned this particular belief, known as Nestorianism, as heresy and proclaimed Mary as the Mother of God. The Council of Chalcedon (451) based its teachings regarding the two natures of Christ on the thought of St. Cyril. Due to the breadth of his writing on the Incarnation and the dignity of the human person, he was declared a Doctor of the Church.

FRI 28 (#172) white
Solemnity of the Most Sacred Heart of Jesus

About Today's Solemnity

The Solemnity of the Sacred Heart of Jesus is celebrated on the Friday after the Most Holy Body and Blood of Christ. This devotion has a life outside of the liturgy as well: the nine Fridays and the twelve promises made by Jesus to St. Margaret Mary Alacoque are still familiar to many Catholics. Help people to understand and grow in love of this devotion by providing catechesis. Even something as simple as placing a printed prayer near your church's image of the Sacred Heart can help people understand how the devotion relates to their lives.

The Lectionary for Mass

◆ FIRST READING: The Word the Lord speaks through the prophet Ezekiel follows upon the Lord's rebuke of the shepherds of Israel who failed to lead the people as God would lead. The shepherds have put themselves first instead of caring for their people and left the people for dead. In contrast, the Lord will shepherd the people by bringing them home from the places to which they scattered. The Lord will give them rest and heal their sick. Those leaders who have become strong at the expense of their people, the Lord will destroy.

◆ RESPONSORIAL PSALM 23: The beloved Psalm 23 echoes the theme of the Lord as the shepherd of the people. In the Lord, there is nothing for which the psalmist will remain in want. So much hope exists in the psalmist's words as he speaks of the lush pastures, the table the Lord will spread, and his overflowing cup. The psalm culminates in verse 6, as the psalmist confesses his belief that "only goodness and kindness" will go with him during his lifetime and he will dwell in the Lord's house forever.

◆ SECOND READING: Paul teaches us that the love of God through the Holy Spirit has come into our hearts. Christ himself died for not only the just, but the "ungodly." In doing so, he justified us with his blood. We are reconciled to God in Jesus Christ. Because of this reconciliation, our hearts now can speak to God's heart through the heart of Jesus Christ.

◆ GOSPEL: The context in Luke for the parable of the lost sheep is the Pharisees and scribes complaining about how Jesus welcomes sinners and eats with them. This parable reveals just how different Jesus' mission is from that of the Pharisees and scribes. Jesus cares for even one, individual person who has lost his or her way as a shepherd goes in search of one of his hundred sheep who has also lost its way. Jesus' heart opens wide for repentant sinners inviting them into his joy.

The Roman Missal

The orations are found in the Proper of Time. There are two options for the Collect. In the Prayer over the Offerings, we ask God to look at his Son's love for us in his heart—and to let our offering be "an expiation of our offenses." The proper Preface is subtitled "The Boundless Charity of Christ." In Christ, raised high on the Cross, pierced by the soldier's lance, we behold "the wellspring of the Church's Sacraments," a fountain of salvation open to all. Christ's Sacred Heart is an "open heart," offering love and life to every person. In the Prayer after Communion, we pray that we may also be "fervent with the fire of holy love," and be so drawn to Christ that "we may learn to see him in our neighbor." The Gloria and the Creed are sung or said. Consider using Eucharistic Prayer III.

(#590/#591) red

29 SAT
Solemnity of Sts. Peter and Paul, Apostles

About Today's Solemnity

Today we commemorate Sts. Peter and Paul, martyred around the year AD 64 during Nero's persecution following the Great Fire of Rome. Tradition says that Peter fled Rome to avoid arrest and saw Jesus on the road. "Where are you going?" Peter asked. Jesus replied, "I am going to Rome to be crucified again." Peter turned back and was crucified upside down because he felt unworthy to meet his death the same way as Christ. Paul was arrested in Jerusalem and was sent to Rome, where he was placed under house arrest. He was slain by beheading, because as a Roman citizen he could not be subjected to the indignity of crucifixion.

The Lectionary for Mass: Vigil Mass

◆ FIRST READING: The story of the crippled beggar lying at the gate of the Temple who receives the gift of healing in the name of the Lord Jesus from the hands of Peter and not the alms he expected is the subject of today's First Reading. What better way to give God praise than fully using that which is restored to full health! The man walks and jumps with joy, giving God praise.

◆ RESPONSORIAL PSALM 19 declares the "glory of God" as spoken by creation. In the light of today's First Reading, "their" refers not to creation, but to the voice of the Apostles.

◆ SECOND READING: Paul speaks to the Galatians of his encounter with the Risen Jesus, a "revelation" that changed his life. Paul turned from persecutor to missionary of the Gospel, sent by the Risen Lord to the Gentiles.

◆ GOSPEL: The Risen Christ commissions Peter, entrusting to him with the care of the sheep of his flock. Jesus also speaks of how Peter will one day follow him, led by another to death, and ultimately to glory.

The Lectionary for Mass: Mass during the Day

◆ FIRST READING: Herod Agrippa, the grandson of Herod the Great, has Peter arrested and condemned to death for proclaiming faith in Jesus as messiah and Lord. There are many similarities here between Jesus' condemnation and Peter's. As the community prays for Peter, an angel of the Lord miraculously rescues him from prison. Peter thinks it a vision. Once he realizes its reality, he acknowledges that the Lord is directing not only the events of his life but also those of the entire people of God. In faith, we too trust that the Lord is present and engaged in our daily living, directing and guiding us through the Spirit, into deeper relationships with one another and with God.

◆ RESPONSORIAL PSALM 34: This thanksgiving psalm acknowledges that the Lord does listen when the poor ones cry out and does respond and save them from all fears and distress. The refrain picks up on Acts of the Apostles by emphasizing that the angel of the Lord rescues those who fear the

Lord, namely those who have awe, reverence, and respect for God's power and majesty. Two rich images end the psalm. One has the Lord's angel encamped around all who fear the Lord to rescue them from all distress. The other asks us to taste and see the goodness of the Lord, who nourishes us with great love and compassion.

◆ SECOND READING: The author of 2 Timothy asks us to consider what Paul must have been thinking as he faced his imprisonment and death. Using sports imagery, the author asserts that Paul has competed well and finished the race. All that awaits him is the merited crown that God will bestow on him for having proclaimed God's Word to the Gentiles. Paul experienced all sorts of dangers in his ministry but the Lord was ever with him, rescuing him from harm, in order that his mission to the Gentiles might be completed. Like Peter, Paul acknowledges that it is all the Lord's doing, as he awaits final and total union with God.

◆ GOSPEL: At Caesarea-Philippi, Peter declares Jesus to be "the Christ, the Son of the Living God." This affirmation, a gift of faith from God to Peter, leads Jesus to establish Peter as the rock upon which Jesus will build his Church, here understood not as a building but as an assembly of believers. In other words, Peter is to lead others as they strive to be faithful disciples. Jesus asserts Peter's leadership in the community and assures that the powers of evil will never overwhelm them. Along with the other readings, we believe that God directs, guides, and sustains the community of believers, as we strive to live as the Lord's faithful disciples.

The Roman Missal: Vigil Mass

The Collect continues to honor Peter and Paul together as it affirms that "through them you gave your Church / the foundations of her heavenly office"; the prayer goes on to ask that through them the Church may be assisted on her way to eternal salvation. Remember that the Creed is said at this Vigil Mass.

The Prayer over the Offerings speaks of hopefulness and encouragement: it tells us that "the more we doubt our own merits, / the more we may rejoice that we are to be saved / by your loving kindness." We offer this Eucharist in union with the Apostles Peter and Paul who themselves, as the Scriptures so clearly tell us, were men who sinned and had their faults and weaknesses. The Preface is proper for today, and it is found among the prayers for the Mass during the Day, a page turn away from the Vigil prayers. A text is given both with music and without; since it is a solemnity, strongly consider singing the introductory dialogue and the Preface. The Preface mentions in tandem the attributes that are the reasons we commemorate these two Apostles: Peter is "foremost in confessing the faith" and is the one "who established the early Church from the remnant of Israel"; Paul is the faith's "outstanding preacher . . . master and teacher of the Gentiles." Thus is the mission of the Church both within Israel and beyond her to the whole world avowed. The Prayer after Communion entreats that as we have been "enlightened with the teaching of the Apostles," so may we be strengthened by "this heavenly Sacrament." Consider using Eucharistic Prayer III.

The Solemn Blessing for Sts. Peter and Paul, Apostles (#16 under "Blessings at the End of Mass and Prayers over the People") is suggested, and should be used today. It refers to Peter's "saving confession" and uses the image of the solid rock, and to "the tireless preaching of Saint Paul." It then brings the two together by highlighting "the keys of St. Peter and the words of St. Paul."

Since today is a daily Mass, it may be difficult to have a heightened celebration due to people's work schedules. However, do your best to emphasize the importance of today. If you don't usually have music at daily Mass, do so today (even just a cantor and accompanist will add solemnity!). Schedule liturgical ministers, add incense and a Gospel procession.

The Roman Missal: Mass during the Day

The Collect for this Mass during the Day reminds us that the Church's faith came through the Apostles Peter and Paul; it was through them that the Church "received / the beginnings of right religion." Remember that, because it is a solemnity, the Creed is said today.

The Prayer over the Offerings asks for the powerful intercession of these two Apostles, praying that their prayer may "accompany the sacrificial gift / that we present to your name for consecration." Again we are reminded that every Eucharist is celebrated in communion with all the saints who have gone before us. The Preface is proper for today; see the commentary for it above, under the Vigil Mass. Although the Prayer after Communion does not mention Peter and Paul by name, it does pray that we might persevere "in the breaking of the Bread / and in the teaching of the Apostles"—notice the reference to the Eucharist and to Tradition, without which the Church does not exist—and so live as Church as "one heart and one soul." The unity of the Church founded on the Apostles Peter and Paul is strengthened and nourished through sacrament and through authentic teaching. Consider using Eucharistic Prayer I.

As at the Vigil Mass, the Solemn Blessing for Sts. Peter and Paul, Apostles (#16 under "Blessings at the End of Mass and Prayers over the People") is suggested for today, and should be used. The blessing mentions Peter's "saving confession" and the image of the solid rock, and Paul's "tireless preaching," also noting "the keys of St. Peter and the words of St. Paul."

Since today is a daily Mass, it may be difficult to have a heightened celebration due to people's work schedules. However, do your best to emphasize the importance of today. If you don't usually have music at daily Mass, do so today (even just a cantor and accompanist will add solemnity!). Schedule liturgical ministers, add incense and a Gospel procession.

(#99C) green

30 Thirteenth Sunday in Ordinary Time

The Lectionary for Mass

◆ FIRST READING: At the Lord's word, Elijah invites Elisha to join him in his prophetic mission. Elisha will eventually be the prophet who succeeds Elijah. Elijah called Elisha as he was performing a farmer's ordinary task of plowing. Elisha asks Elijah if he can first say goodbye to his parents before setting out on mission with Elijah. The experienced prophet sends Elisha back to say his farewells, but Elisha does not go back to his family empty-handed. He would bring provisions for his family to eat while he was away. This was symbolic for how prophets feed people with the Lord's word.

◆ RESPONSORIAL PSALM 16: God's presence will bring life to all who follow him. God will show us the way for our life and in God our joy will overflow. Only in this God, and not in others, will we find our inheritance. Elisha probably realized this for himself as he left his family behind in the First Reading to accompany Elijah and begin a prophetic mission.

◆ SECOND READING: We can use the freedom God gives us for the flesh or for love. The choice is ours, but the commandment to love our neighbors as ourselves is clear. Paul needed to lay this choice out to the Galatians for the community struggled how to see everyone—male and female—rich and poor—Jew and Gentile—as children of the same God. In God, no one is opposed to one another. We live in freedom to love every neighbor equally in God.

◆ GOSPEL: Jesus' demand for those who want to be his disciples to follow him unconditionally to Jerusalem seems to stand in contrast to Elijah permitting Elisha to go back to bid farewell to his family in the First Reading. Like Jesus, his followers must set their face directly on Jerusalem. He does not promise an easy journey, but the journey is the way to the Kingdom of God.

The Roman Missal

The Collect contrasts light and darkness. God has chosen us as "children of light." We pray that we may not be wrapped in the darkness of error," but remain in the "bright light of truth." We pray that our "deeds" may be worthy of the "sacred gifts" we receive in this sacrifice (Prayer over the Offerings). We pray that the "divine sacrifice" we have received may so "fill us with life" that we

may "bear fruit that lasts forever" (Prayer after Communion). The Gloria and the Creed are sung or said today. Consider using the Eucharistic Prayer II.

Other Ideas

Once the school year is over many parishioners will be traveling to other parishes during the summer. Place a large map on a board in the gathering area and invite people to use colored pins to mark the places where they will be visiting. And, since there will be visitors to your parish from other places, have a second set of colored pins for visitors to indicate where they have come from. Be sure to express hospitality to all visitors. Some parishes extend a general welcome at the beginning of Mass. Be sure to ask those who are greeters to pay special attention to anyone who is visiting your parish. Don't forget to welcome home those students of the parish who have been away during the academic year. Consider having a reception for them after the liturgies on this weekend.

July 2019
Month of the Most Precious Blood

M O N 1 (#377) green
Weekday

Optional Memorial of Bl. Junípero Serra, Priest / white

The Lectionary for Mass

◆ FIRST READING: En route with the men who had visited him near the Terebinth of Mamre, Abraham bargains with the Lord on behalf of the people of Sodom and Gomorrah. Should the Lord find ten innocent people without grave sin, the Lord will not destroy the city. While the story ends at the number of ten innocent people, we get the sense that surely the Lord

would spare the city if the Lord only found one innocent person. God's mercy abounds!

◆ RESPONSORIAL PSALM 103 speaks eloquently of the Lord's kindness and mercy. The Lord will pardon all our sins. As Abraham found in the First Reading, so we find in the psalmist's words how much the Lord's mercy abounds. Sin does not have the last word. God's redeeming kindness does.

◆ GOSPEL: As Jesus crosses to the other shore, a scribe expresses willingness to follow him wherever he goes, but it is one of Jesus' own disciples who asks first to bury his father before following. Jesus' stern command to his disciples to follow without condition leaves us once again to ponder the demands of discipleship.

Today's Saint

Bl. Junípero Serra (1713–1784) was a Spanish Franciscan friar, best known for founding the string of twenty-one missions that stretch from San Diego to Sonoma, California. Junípero was born in Majorca and at the age of sixteen entered the Franciscans. After completing his theological studies, he served as professor of philosophy at Majorca before volunteering for the missions in the New World. Upon arrival, he went to Mexico City to dedicate his mission at the shrine of Our Lady of Guadalupe. Serra founded his first mission at San Diego in 1769, and worked his way up the coast along El Camino Real, making converts as he went. In spite of a leg injury he suffered at the beginning of his ministry, he traveled on foot whenever possible, eventually covering twenty-four thousand miles. The chapel at Mission San Juan Capistrano is believed to be oldest standing building in California, and it is the only mission left where Serra is known to have celebrated the liturgy.

T U E **2** (#378) green
Weekday

The Lectionary for Mass

◆ FIRST READING: The Lord extends mercy to Lot and his family as the Lord instructs them to leave Sodom and Gomorrah and never look back. When Lot hesitated to leave, the Lord's men personally led them to safety. Yet Lot's wife looked back to Sodom and Gomorrah, and the entire plain the Lord destroyed. She had not completely embraced new life in the Lord and so she suffered the consequence.

◆ RESPONSORIAL PSALM 26 replicates the theme of the Lord's mercy found in Psalm 103 from yesterday. The refrain helps us see how the mercy of God rests immediately before our very eyes just as it was before Lot and his family as they left Sodom and Gomorrah. When we walk in faith and "integrity" as the psalmist's word say, we can honestly ask for God's redemption and mercy.

◆ GOSPEL: The wife of Lot fell short on faith as she turned back to the wicked cities. The disciples who accompanied Jesus in a boat similarly struggled with their faith when a severe storm rocked the boat. While Jesus' response to their request for him to save them, questions the quantity—perhaps even quality—of the disciples' faith, he calms the storm. The disciples did address Jesus as "Lord" when they asked him to save them, but clearly their faith is forming as they respond with amazement at the power he has over the wind and the sea.

W E D **3** (#593) red
Feast of St. Thomas, Apostle

The Liturgy of the Word

◆ FIRST READING: The author of Ephesians tells the early Christian believers that they are members of God's household with the holy ones who have gone before them. On this Feast of St. Thomas, we acknowledge in the author's words that the Apostles and prophets laid the foundation for God's household and Christ Jesus is the cornerstone. How fortunate are we that in Jesus and the Holy Spirit, we are being built together into a place where God dwells.

◆ RESPONSORIAL PSALM 117: The two verses that compose Psalm 117 make it the shortest of the hymns in the psalter. The opening verse calls us to praise and glorify the Lord, while the second verse declares the constancy of God's kindness and faithfulness. Today's refrain comes from Jesus' commission of the remaining eleven disciples at the conclusion of Mark and reflects the disciples' mission to proclaim the Good News to the entire world.

◆ GOSPEL: On the Feast of St. Thomas, we appropriately proclaim the Gospel passage from John that relates the Apostle's post-Resurrection encounter with Jesus. Thomas doubted the disciples who said to him they had seen the Lord and told them he would not believe until he had seen the actual nail marks in Jesus' hands. A week after Thomas stated this to the disciples, Jesus came through locked doors and offered peace. To Thomas, he extended his hands and invited him to put his finger into the nail marks of crucifixion. Thomas believed, and perhaps Thomas acknowledged, too, the reality that disciples would share in Jesus' suffering but ultimately also share in his Resurrection.

The Roman Missal

The Gloria is sung or said today, since it is a feast. The Collect points to the Apostle Thomas' acknowledgment of the Lord as read in the Scriptures. The Prayer over the Offerings again refers to St. Thomas' confession, asking that the gifts God has given us—the gifts of faith—be kept safe. The Prayer after Communion again echoes the Gospel as the prayer asks that, in receiving the Sacrament of the Eucharist, "we may recognize him / with the Apostle Thomas by faith / as our Lord and our God." This recognition of the Lord, however, cannot be a passive gazing; rather, as a result of sacramental Communion, we must go on to "proclaim him by our deeds and by our life." The Preface, proper for today, is one of the two Prefaces of the Apostles. Also, the Solemn Blessing formula titled "The Apostles" (#17 of the "Blessings at the End of Mass and Prayers over the People") is fittingly used as the final blessing at the end of Mass today. Consider using Eucharistic Prayer I.

Today's Saint

St. Thomas (first century), also called "Didymus" or "the Twin" (John 11:16) was one of the Twelve Apostles. He is remembered for doubting the Resurrection of Christ: "Unless I see the mark of the nails in his hands, and put my finger in the mark of the nails and my hand in his side, I will not believe." The following week, Thomas was with the Twelve, when Jesus appeared and chided him for his lack of faith: "Have you believed because you have seen me? Blessed are those who have not seen and yet have come to believe" (John 20:25–29). After seeing the Risen Christ alive, Thomas exclaimed "My Lord and my God!" (John 20:28). According to tradition, Thomas is the only Apostle who went outside the borders of the Roman Empire to evangelize. Although there is a Gospel account attributed to him, it is not accepted in the canon of Scripture, and is, in fact, of Gnostic origin. The people of Kerala in South India fervently believe that it was Thomas who evangelized them. He is represented in art with a spear, the instrument of his martyrdom.

THU 4 (#380) green
Weekday

Optional proper Mass for Independence Day / white

The Lectionary for Mass

◆ FIRST READING: Abraham's willingness to sacrifice his son, Isaac, stands as a lasting testament to us of just how strong the faith of this father was. The Lord will never rescind his covenantal promises to Abraham as we hear again the Lord's promises to provide Abraham with countless descendants and land. Abraham's obedience to the Lord signifies how Abraham himself will uphold his part of the covenant.

◆ RESPONSORIAL PSALM 115: Abraham walked in obedience to the Lord in the First Reading. The refrain from Psalm 113:9 echoes this theme as the psalmist states how he will walk in the Lord's presence and knows by doing so, he will walk among the living. Trust and faith in the Lord bring life, not death.

◆ GOSPEL: Jesus continues his travels at sea and arrives at his hometown where people bring him a paralytic. The Gospel reading does not tell us what the people expect of Jesus. But Jesus sees faith in the people merely because they had the courage to approach him with the paralytic. With words of forgiveness for the paralytic's sins, Jesus heals the child and further perturbs the scribes who are present. They question his authority, but the crowds glorify God.

The Roman Missal: Independence Day

For the optional Mass for Independence Day, the Gloria is said or sung. Two complete sets of prayers are provided in the Proper of Saints. The first option for the Collect is a prayer that God's "peace may rule in our hearts" and God's "justice guide our lives." The second option gives thanks for all that has been accomplished, and calls on us to share the blessings we have received "with all the peoples of the earth." The first option for the Prayer over the Offerings asks God to lead us to "true justice and lasting peace" through the Gospel. The second echoes the familiar motto, *E pluribus unum* (from many, one): God has "molded into one our nation, drawn from the people of many lands." Just as the "grains of wheat become one bread," and "the many grapes one cup," we pray that we may, as one, be "instruments of . . . peace."

The first option for the Preface speaks of Christ's message of peace as the beginning of "the vision of our founding fathers," a message that "lives on in our midst," both today and tomorrow. The second focuses on Christ's love for all peoples, "his witness of justice and truth." We are "reborn in the Spirit," and like the Spirit we are to be "filled with love for all people." The first option for the Prayer after Communion is a prayer for unity, that together we may "build the city of lasting peace." The second is a prayer that as a nation we may trust in God, and do God's will. A proper Solemn Blessing is provided, which focuses on harmony, wisdom, love, and unity. Consider using the Eucharistic Prayer for Various Needs and Occasions III.

FRI 5 (#381) green
Weelday

Optional Memorials of St. Anthony Zaccaria, Priest / white; St. Elizabeth of Portugal / white

◆ FIRST READING: Abraham's wife Sarah passes away in the land of Canaan, and Abraham faithfully lays her to rest on the land he procured after a transaction with the Hittites. After Sarah's burial, the reading continues with a lengthy conversation between Abraham and his servant about how the servant will assist Isaac in finding a wife. After the sadness of death, the Lord brings joy in the love between Isaac and Rebekah.

◆ RESPONSORIAL PSALM 106: The fitting response to the joy the Lord brings into our lives is thanks. The psalmist notes the blessedness of those who observe the Lord's commands, as Abraham did. We pray with the psalmist the Lord remember us with his favor and come to us with his "saving help." As we pray this psalm, we fill our words with trust, that the Lord indeed is good, mirroring the confidence of the psalmist who wrote generations before us.

◆ GOSPEL: Jesus calls Matthew as he sits working at his job as a tax collector. Matthew follows Jesus without asking any questions or putting up any resistance. While they were at table, other tax collectors and sinners joined them. The Pharisees must have been in the house, too, because they question Jesus' disciples about why he would eat with sinners. Jesus overhears the questions and replies in a short parable-like statement of how the sick (sinners) need a physician, but those who are well do not. Would the Pharisees understand the connection to their own self-righteous attitude?

Today's Saints

St. Anthony Mary Zaccaria (1502–1539) was from Cremona, Italy. He was born into a noble family, and dedicated himself to the Lord from a young age. He studied philosophy, went to study medicine at the University of Padua, and practiced for three years before deciding to become a priest. Anthony had already done so much study that he was ordained quickly, in 1528. He founded three religious orders:

the Barnabites or Clerics Regular of St. Paul—the first order named for St. Paul—the Angelic Sisters of St. Paul for nuns, and a lay community. The three groups worked together to reform society. Because of the implied criticism of abuses in the Church, Anthony was investigated for heresy twice, but was acquitted both times. In addition to founding the Barnabites, he popularized the forty-hour devotion of exposition of the Eucharist. In 1539, he became ill with a fever, and because his health had been undermined by his penitential practices, he died at the age of 37. Anthony is the patron of his order, the Barnabites, and is represented in art wearing a cassock and with a lily, a cross, or a symbol of the Eucharist. Today the Barnabites can be found in sixteen countries, including Italy, the United States, Brazil, and Afghanistan.

St. Elizabeth of Portugal (1271–1336) was the grandniece of St. Elizabeth of Hungary and is known by the Spanish version of her name, Isabel. When very young, she was married to the King of Portugal. Elizabeth had been raised to be devout, but at her husband's court, she found much corruption and immorality. In spite of this, she managed to continue her life of prayer, penance, and devotion to the care of the sick. This caused resentment in the court, which Elizabeth bore quietly. After her husband, the king, died, she went to live in a convent of Poor Clares that she had founded, and she took the habit of a Third Order Franciscan. Throughout her life she was well known for her peacemaking skills, most importantly when she prevented a war between Portugal and Castile in 1336. The exertion weakened her health, and she died soon after and is buried at Coimbra. Elizabeth of Portugal is a patron saint of Franciscan Tertiaries.

S A T **6** (#382) green
Weekday

Optional Memorials of St. Maria Goretti, Virgin and Martyr / red; Blessed Virgin Mary / white

The Lectionary for Mass

◆ FIRST READING: Rebekah helps her younger son, Jacob, to deceive his father, Isaac, and receive the blessing intended by tradition for the oldest son. Even though Isaac questions whether Jacob really is Esau, in the end, Isaac imparts the blessings on Jacob. The blessing includes the abundance of the earth's riches and the homage of the nations. Jacob will now be in charge of his brothers. We know the sin of deception will not have the final word.

◆ RESPONSORIAL PSALM 135 is a psalm of praise. The Lord truly is good. The Lord's goodness will overpower any sin, including the sin of deception and the human desire to lord power over others. God works good even through sin. The psalmist reminds us of this as he records how the Lord took Jacob to himself and Israel as his own, despite their penchant for sin.

◆ GOSPEL: It is not the Pharisees who question Jesus in today's Gospel reading, but the disciples of John. They want to know from Jesus why they and the Pharisees fast, but his disciples do not. Jesus uses a wedding metaphor to teach them that so long as he (the bridegroom) is with the disciples (the wedding guests) they will not fast. When Jesus leaves his disciples, they will fast, but it will be a new fast for new wine only goes into new wineskins.

Today's Saint

St. Maria Goretti (1890–1902) is one of the youngest saints to be canonized. She died of stab wounds after she resisted a rapist. Maria came from a poor Italian family. They lost their farm and a few years later, her father died of malaria. In spite of their hard existence as farm laborers, the family was close-knit and devout. By 1902, the family was sharing a building with another family of farm workers, one of whom was Alessandro Serenelli, who made it a habit to sexually harass Maria. One day, finding her alone, he threatened to kill her if she did not submit to him. Maria protested that what he asked was a mortal sin. Alessandro choked and then stabbed her, leaving her bleeding to death. She was taken to the hospital, but she could not be saved and died forgiving her murderer. Shortly after Maria died, Alessandro was arrested, charged with her murder, and sentenced to twenty years in prison. He remained unrepentant until Maria appeared to him in a dream. Upon his release, he went to Maria's mother and asked for forgiveness. Eventually he became a Capuchin lay brother and was present at Maria's canonization in 1950, as was her mother. Maria Goretti is the patron saint of rape victims and teenage girls and is shown in art dressed as a peasant farmer, holding lilies. Her story has prompted thought on the broader meaning of chastity, integrating sexual purity with personal integrity, and self-determination.

7 (#102C) green
Fourteenth Sunday in Ordinary Time

The Lectionary for Mass

◆ FIRST READING: The Lord communicates to Isaiah a vision for a new Israel in which all who love her can be glad. Israel will prosper and her people will find comfort in the Lord. God will comfort his people as a mother comforts her child. The Lord's power is in his care for his people. How joyful our hearts will be when we experience this!

◆ RESPONSORIAL PSALM 66: The psalmist cries out in joy in response to Isaiah's joyful vision of a new and restored people. We gladly shout in the psalmist's words declaring the wonders of God's deeds.

◆ SECOND READING: Paul shares in the sufferings of Jesus and the marks on his body provide evidence of this. Only in the Cross can Paul and others who follow Christ boast. Nothing else the world gives us or religions require of us, including circumcision, holds meaning. Followers of Jesus, regardless of their background, find meaning in aligning themselves with his Cross.

◆ GOSPEL: The second episode of Jesus sending his followers on a mission is today's Gospel reading. In the first episode in Luke, Jesus commissions the Twelve (9:1–6), whereas in this episode, occurring a chapter later in Luke, Jesus sends forth seventy-two of his followers to go out in pairs to carry out his mission. The longer form of the reading includes Jesus' advice to the newly sent to shake off the dust of any resistance they encounter. It also includes the report the seventy-two give Jesus upon their return and describes their amazing joy at the power of Jesus at work in them.

The Roman Missal

The Collect uses imagery of high and low: Christ became low in "abasement" that "a fallen world" might be "raised up." We who have been rescued from "slavery to sin" ask for the "holy joy" of the redeemed. In the Prayer over the Offerings we pray that by the power of this sacrifice, our daily lives may reflect the "life of heaven." In the Prayer after Communion, we pray that, "replenished" by the Eucharist, we may attain to salvation, and praise God without ceasing. Sing or say the Gloria and the Creed. Consider Eucharistic Prayer III.

Other Ideas

The focus on hospitality noted in last Sunday's reference continues today. Jesus tells his disciples to rely on the hospitality that is offered to them as they spread the Gospel. This is a good time to review the various ways that the parish offers hospitality both to visitors and to its own members throughout the year. Are new recruits needed as greeters? Invite entire families to do this. One parish asks families of first communicants to act as greeters; another parish invites the families of those being confirmed to be ministers of hospitality. Be sure to invite those who come to church on their own; those who are widows or widowers are often the ones who know many parishioners. Often a more direct appeal works better than a generic invitation in the bulletin.

8 (#383) green
Weekday

The Lectionary for Mass

◆ FIRST READING: A resting stone for Jacob as he slept becomes a memorial stone to God's goodness in response to the blessings the Lord promises Jacob in a dream. Jacob vows his faithfulness to God should God accompany him on the journey and return him home safely to his father's house. The Lord, who promises Jacob the land on which he slept and blessing for all his descendants, Jacob will take as his God. Forever will God live with his people and on his land.

◆ RESPONSORIAL PSALM 91, the psalm on which the beloved song "On Eagle's Wings" is based, helps us reflect today on the trust we place in God. The psalmist speaks from experience as he writes how God will rescue us from danger and take us under God's wings. At all times in the journey of faith, God will be with us. Even in times of distress, when it is difficult to know God's presence, the psalmist tells us we only need to call upon God and God will answer.

◆ GOSPEL: Matthew sandwiches the healing of the woman with a twelve-year hemorrhage in between the official's request for Jesus to raise his daughter and Jesus' arrival at the official's house where Jesus finds the official's daughter not dead, but asleep. In a very personal healing, Jesus commands the crowd to leave the house, and then, clasping the girl's hand, he helps her to rise. Of course, this news spreads rapidly!

TUE 9 (#384) green
Weekday

Optional Memorial of St. Augustine Zhao Rong, Priest, and Companions, Martyrs / red

The Lectionary for Mass

◆ FIRST READING: Jacob takes his wives, servants, children, and possessions across the stream of the Jabbok. Alone, Jacob encounters a man with whom he wrestles until dawn. Jacob requests of the man to bless him before Jacob lets him go, and the man responds with a question to Jacob about his identity. In the man, Jacob sees the face of God, as the stranger changes Jacob's name to Israel.

◆ RESPONSORIAL PSALM 17: The psalmist laments his unjust attack, but still he professes his faith that God's justice will prevail. Like yesterday's reference in Psalm 91 to God wings of protection, verse 8b also includes this common imagery. Would that our trust in God's justice lead us to see God face to face one day.

◆ GOSPEL: Jesus continues to perform healings and exorcisms that leave the crowds amazed, but the Pharisees confused and perturbed. After Jesus restores the speech of a mute man by driving out a demon, the Pharisees remark that Jesus was able to do this because he called upon the "prince of demons." Their remark did not deter Jesus as the Gospel writer, Matthew, informs us that Jesus continued his mission of proclaiming the Kingdom of God in word and deed. Few others will take up this mission in light of the abundant harvest God provides.

Today's Saints

Between 1648 and 1930, eighty-seven Chinese Catholics and thirty-three Western missionaries, some of whom were Dominicans, Franciscans, Salesians, Jesuits, and Vincentians, were martyred for their ministry or for refusing to renounce their Christian faith. Many of the Chinese converts were killed during the Boxer Rebellion, a xenophobic uprising during which many foreigners were slaughtered by angry peasants. St. Augustine Zhao Rong was a Chinese diocesan priest who was tortured and killed in 1815, after the Emperor Kia-Kin issued decrees banning Catholicism. St. Augustine Zhao Rong and the other Chinese martyrs were canonized in 2000 by Pope John Paul II.

WED 10 (#385) green
Weekday

The Lectionary for Mass

◆ FIRST READING: We move ahead in Genesis to a narrative in which Joseph's brothers come to him to procure provisions in order to survive the famine that has beset the land. Joseph recognizes his brothers, but they do not recognize him. After three days of confinement, Joseph instructs all but one to return home with provisions and bring back their youngest brother. The brothers know why they are being punished and argue among themselves, but Joseph keeps his sadness to himself.

◆ RESPONSORIAL Psalm 33: God's word of justice is everything to us! God will prevail over all the manipulative and evil plans that people can concoct. All that God asks of his people is for us to trust in him and to pray in hope for his mercy and kindness. In a direct connection to the First Reading, verse 19 attests that God will ensure his people survive in spite of famine.

◆ GOSPEL: Jesus now passes on his authority to drive out demons and heal the sick to the Twelve. Matthew lists the names of the Twelve giving Peter's first. Jesus sends the Twelve not to pagan territories or Samaritan towns, but to those people of Israel who have yet to hear the message of the nearness of heaven's Kingdom. In Matthew, the limiting of the Twelve's mission was consistent with Jesus' own mission as the evangelist's primary Jewish audience struggled with if and how Gentiles should be welcomed into the early Christian community.

THU 11 (#386) white
Memorial of St. Benedict, Abbot

The Lectionary for Mass

◆ FIRST READING: Joseph reveals his identity to his brothers. His resentment for his brother's having sold him into slavery in Egypt falls away as he tells his brothers that God sent him ahead of them to Egypt in order to save lives. Joseph's proclamation of faith shows how God's mercy triumphs in the face of evil.

◆ RESPONSORIAL PSALM 105 recounts how God worked through the evil of Joseph's brothers when they sold him to the Egyptian Pharaoh as a slave. God is faithful despite their sin, for eventually the king released Joseph and made him ruler of the king's house. The Lord's word of freedom triumphed—then as it does now. For this we remember the Lord's saving marvels in the words of the psalm's refrain.

◆ GOSPEL: Jesus sends the Apostles to proclaim the presence of the Kingdom of heaven hear and now. They do not need to take anything with them to carry out their mission of healing the sick, exorcising demons, raising the dead, and cleansing lepers. Peace is their gift to the homes they enter whose residents welcome them. Those who do not welcome their words will face the fate of Sodom and Gomorrah.

The Roman Missal

The prayers are found in the Proper of Saints. The prayers for today are full of references to the teachings of St. Benedict. He was "an outstanding master in the school of divine service" (Collect), and we pray that we may be "attentive" to his teaching (Prayer after Communion) and, following his example, seek the Lord (Prayer over the Offerings). Consider using Eucharistic Prayer II.

Today's Saint

Saddened by the immoral state of society, St. Benedict of Nursia (480–553/7) left the city to live as a hermit at Subiaco. In time, more and more men were attracted to his charismatic personality as well as to his way of life. He eventually moved a group of monks to Monte Cassino, near Naples, where he completed the final version of his rule, now known as *The Rule of St. Benedict*, on the fundamentals of monastic life, including the day-to-day operation of a monastery. The rule asserts that the primary occupation of the monk is to pray the Divine Office in tandem with a vowed life of stability, obedience, and conversion. The whole of the monastic vocation can be summarized in the opening line of his rule, "Listen carefully." St. Benedict is considered the father of Western monasticism.

FRI 12 (#387) green
Weelday

The Lectionary for Mass

◆ FIRST READING: In another vision, God uses Israel's original name, Jacob, and commissions him to go to Egypt. Jacob is to take everything he has with him—both his family and his possessions. God will make Jacob a great nation there. Jacob follows God's word and reunites with Joseph, his son, in Goshen. Having seen Joseph alive, Israel's mission is now complete and he can rest in peace.

◆ RESPONSORIAL PSALM 37: Today's refrain proclaims the Lord is the author of the salvation of the just. The verses repeat the themes of our trust in the Lord and the Lord's protection of his people that we have seen in the psalms over the past weeks. Even when the wicked find refuge in the Lord, the Lord will save them. The Lord's mercy is truly expansive.

◆ GOSPEL: Jesus' commission of the Twelve is much lengthier in Matthew than in the other synoptics. In a continuous reading from yesterday's Gospel passage, today we hear Jesus issue words of warning to the Apostles about those who will persecute and imprison them. The Apostles should not worry about what they will say in response to the courts, for the Spirit of the Lord will speak through them. The Son of Man will return before they complete their mission. In him, the mission of the Kingdom will be wholly fulfilled.

SAT 13 Weekday (#388) green
Weekday

Optional Memorials of St. Henry / white; Blessed Virgin Mary / white

The Lectionary for Mass

◆ FIRST READING: Before Jacob dies, he requests of his sons to bury him with the other faithful ancestors—Abraham and Sarah, Isaac and Rebekah, and Leah. After Jacob's death, Joseph's brothers approach him asking for forgiveness and expressing their willingness to be his slaves. Joseph recognizes he cannot take God's place so he reiterates his belief that God turned their evil action into good. Once Joseph dies, his brothers must fulfill the oath they made to him to not bury him in Egypt but in the land of the ancestors.

◆ RESPONSORIAL PSALM 105: Today's refrain comes from Psalm 69:33 and invites us to have glad hearts for all the Lord has done. The verses are the same as those appointed for Wednesday in the Easter Octave and on June 26. In light of the First Reading, the reference in verse 6 to the people of Israel (and us today) as Abraham's descendants and sons of Jacob is especially appropriate.

◆ GOSPEL: Jesus' lengthy discourse to his disciples continues and its intensity increases as the evangelist sets up a clear choice between following Jesus or not. Jesus the Great Teacher advises them not to be afraid of the master of the evil house, Beelzebul, nor those who belong to his house. The Father will take care of the Apostles as he cares for the tiniest of birds, the sparrow, and counts the hairs on our heads. The Apostles will speak their words in the light of faith, but those who do not accept their words Jesus will not present to the Father.

Today's Saint

St. Henry II (972–1024) was a German king and Holy Roman Emperor, the only German king to be canonized. Henry had considered becoming a priest, but when his father died, he inherited his father's title of Duke of Bavaria. He became King of Germany in 1002 and married Cunegunda, who is also a saint. He had a reputation for being learned and pious, and was a positive influence in Church-state relations. At that time, secular authorities appointed bishops and often selected their political allies. Henry appointed bishops who would be good pastors, and supported them in their work. Although he waged many wars, he was not the aggressor but fought only to protect his borders and preserve peace. Henry is a patron saint of Benedictine oblates and is invoked against infertility, for he and his wife were childless.

14 (#105C) green
Fifteenth Sunday in Ordinary Time

The Lectionary for Mass

◆ FIRST READING: Moses addresses the people and lets them know the Lord's commandments written in the book of the law are not far from the people. They are neither abstract statutes nor mysterious decrees that the people would need to search out in the sky or the sea. Rather, the Lord's word is close to them. They already know it. They have already taken it in. Their challenge at this moment is to live the word in their daily lives. Our challenge is the same.

◆ RESPONSORIAL PSALM 69: The lament of Psalm 69 explains the struggle of the hymn writer who prays for the Lord to offer his saving help. In return, the writer will praise and glory God's name. The latter stanzas expand the focus from the personal help the psalmist requests to the assistance the Lord provides the poor and the salvation the Lord will bring to Zion. The refrain helps us remember that our responsibility is to turn to the Lord when we are in need, for when we do, we will live!

Those who prepare the liturgy should note that they also have the option of singing Psalm 19 (verses 8, 9, 10, and 11).

◆ SECOND READING: Christ Jesus holds everything together, the author of Colossians writes in the early Christian hymn from the letter's opening chapter. It is in the beautiful, poetic language of these verses that the author identifies Christ Jesus as the head of the body, the Church. Here the author also intimates a comparison between Christ Jesus and Wisdom in the Old Testament. Both were present at creation and all things were created through them.

◆ GOSPEL: Two questions from a legal scholar shape today's Gospel reading. At the outset, the legal scholar asks Jesus what he must do to inherit eternal life. Jesus' question back to him logically points him to what he finds in the law, to which the scholar cites the commandment of love—love of God and love of neighbor as yourself. Jesus is satisfied with his response and tells him to follow the law to receive life. But the scholar pushes forward with a clarifying question about who his neighbor is. In response, Jesus tells what we have come to cherish as the parable of the Good Samaritan. No doubt the scholar did not anticipate the parable that teaches us to equitably extend God's boundless mercy to everyone as an answer to his question.

The Roman Missal

The Gloria and the Creed are sung or said today. The Collect addresses the living of the Christian life, as it reminds us that God shows the light of truth "to those who go astray," praying that "they may return to the right path." However, we must always remember that we are all among those who could at any time go astray; hence, the prayer goes on to ask that all who "are accounted Christian" may be given "the grace to reject whatever is contrary to the name of Christ." Being converted to the Gospel is an ongoing journey for us all, one that is never complete. The Prayer over the Offerings speaks to the effects of participating in the sacred meal of the Eucharist, noting that the ultimate end of the offerings (of bread and wine) is that of being consumed "by those who believe." Thus, the prayer asks that those offerings "may bring ever greater holiness" to those who consume them. The Prayer after Communion directly picks up on this by its opening reference to the action that has just taken place: "Having consumed these gifts, we pray, O Lord . . ." Notice how participation in Eucharistic liturgy is highlighted here by the sacred actions of offering and of eating and drinking. It is only participating in the sacred actions that we can in any way hope that the "saving effects upon us may grow." Any one of the eight Prefaces of the Sundays in Ordinary Time could rightly be used to equal pastoral advantage today. Consider using Eucharistic Prayer II.

Other Ideas

The parable of the Good Samaritan gives a good context for a reflection today. But the parable is more than a good thought, it is about good actions. In what ways does the parish reach out to others in the larger community throughout the year? Make a list of the various social actions and initiatives that the parish sponsors and supports. The work of the St. Vincent de Paul society is one example. But there are many others, such as collections of food items at Thanksgiving, collections for mission projects, and pastoral visitations to those who are confined to hospitals or their own homes. Do you know of persons who are being left out? Are there additional ways for the whole parish to be a Good Samaritan? Are there Good Samaritans who provide rides to and from church? Should there be?

15 Memorial of St. Bonaventure, Bishop and Doctor of the Church

MON

(#389) white

The Lectionary for Mass

◆ FIRST READING: The oppression of the people of Israel begins as a new king in Egypt recognizes how numerous God's people have become. Taskmasters forced the people of Israel to build cities for Pharaoh, but yet the more they tried to subjugate God's people, the more their numbers grew. Slavery, then, became their life as Pharaoh and his subjects attempted by every means possible to reduce the population of God's people.

◆ RESPONSORIAL PSALM 124: The psalm writer remembers how, if it were not for the Lord's presence among his people, they surely would not have survived. The fury of their enemies would have overtaken them. They would have perished in the torrent of rising waters. Yet, the Lord, the Creator of heaven and earth, rescued them. The faithful ones recognize their help comes from the Lord.

◆ GOSPEL: In the ultimate paradox, Jesus tells the Apostles that he has not come to bring peace, but the sword. Even family members will choose sides against one another based on the message of the Kingdom of heaven. Jesus' disciples will take up their cross and find their life in him when they lose their worldly life. Discipleship comes with a cost, but its reward goes unmatched.

The Roman Missal

The Collect is found in the Proper of Saints, with the remaining prayers taken from the Common of Pastors: For a Bishop or the Common of Doctors of the Church. Consider using Eucharistic Prayer II.

Today's Saint

St. Bonaventure (1221–1274), scholastic theologian and philosopher, was born in Italy and joined the Franciscans in 1243. He studied theology at Paris with his great contemporary, Thomas Aquinas. After teaching for a time, he was chosen minister general of the Franciscans in 1257, at a time when the order suffered from divisions, which he was able to do much to heal. Later, he was named cardinal bishop of Albano. Bonaventure was declared a Doctor of the Church in 1588 by Pope Sixtus V and is called the "Seraphic Doctor" because his love of God is so evident, even in his philosophical writings. When the Council of Lyons was called to bring the Greek and Latin churches back together, Bonaventure went at the request of Pope Gregory X, but he died before the Council's work was finished, receiving the Sacrament of the Sick from the pope himself. St. Bonaventure is shown in art dressed in a Franciscan habit and wearing a cardinal's hat.

16 Weekday

TUE

(#390) green

Optional Memorial of Our Lady of Mt. Carmel / white

The Lectionary for Mass

◆ FIRST READING: The First Reading from Exodus 2 presents us with the well-known story of Moses' birth to a Levite woman and his placement along the banks of the river as a mere three-month-old. Pharaoh's daughter finds him in the basket and gets a Hebrew maiden to nurse him. Eventually Pharaoh's daughter adopts Moses, who will stand up for his kinspeople in response to Egyptian oppression. Strong bonds of faith and kinship exist among God's people.

◆ RESPONSORIAL PSALM 69 is a lament in which the psalmist recounts his suffering, but also expresses hope in the Lord's saving kindness. At a time when people did not believe in the resurrection of the dead or an afterlife, their trust that God would bring justice meant that God would triumph over their enemies in this life. When they turned to the Lord as the refrain from verse 33 states, they would live. Faithfulness to God brings life from him.

◆ GOSPEL: Jesus' harsh words to the unbelieving people of Chorazin, Bethsaida, and Capernaum should have unsettled anyone who heard them. The people of the pagan towns of Tyre and Sidon would have repented of their evil if Jesus performed his mighty deeds in their midst. Even the inhabitants of the city of Sodom, known for their immoral ways, would have penitent hearts if Jesus healed the sick and exorcised demons in their corrupt city. How much more does Jesus expect a life of faithful discipleship from those who have witnessed his amazing deeds and recognized the presence of the Kingdom of heaven in him.

About Today's Optional Memorial

Mount Carmel is part of a mountain range in northern Israel, significant to Christians for its biblical association with the prophet Elijah (see 1 Kings 18). In the twelfth century, the Carmelites were founded at a site that is supposed to have been Elijah's cave and soon built a monastery there. For this reason, the Carmelites honor the Blessed Virgin Mary under the title Our Lady of Mount Carmel. The English Carmelite, St. Simon Stock (feast day, May 16), is believed to have been given the brown scapular by Our Lady, and those who wear it believe they can be sure of her help at the hour of their death.

W E D 17 (#391) green
Weekday

The Lectionary for Mass

◆ FIRST READING: Moses encounters the Lord in a burning bush near Horeb, the mountain of God. Drawn to the burning bush that was not consumed by the flames, Moses approaches the bush only to a certain point. At that point, God calls Moses, who responds to the Lord, "Here I am." Moses will accept his call to lead the children of Israel out of slavery to the Promised Land. God's presence in the fire that spared the bush stands as a sign that God will accompany Moses in his mission.

◆ RESPONSORIAL PSALM 103: Verse 7 mentions God revealed his ways to Moses and performed divine deeds for Israel's children. This verse links with God's call of Moses in the First Reading to lead the chosen people out of slavery in Egypt. The refrain attests to the Lord's kindness and mercy. For the Lord's forgiveness and healing, our souls bless God's holy name as the psalmist himself blessed God.

◆ GOSPEL: In a manner such as the evangelist John would have written decades later, Matthew has Jesus speak words of praise to the Father. Jesus' words emphasize the mutual knowledge of the Father and the Son, and reveal Jesus' identity as the Son of God. Jesus will choose those to whom he will disclose the Father. Presumably, Jesus will make known the Father to those who have accepted the nearness of the Kingdom of heaven.

T H U 18 (#392) green
Weekday

Optional Memorial of St. Camillus de Lellis, Priest / white

The Lectionary for Mass

◆ FIRST READING: In Moses' encounter with the Lord in the burning bush, the Lord gives a lengthy response to Moses' question about what he is to tell the Israelites should they ask him for the Lord's name. "I AM" is the Lord's name and "I AM" has commissioned Moses to lead the Lord's people out of Egypt to the bountiful land flowing with milk and honey. The king of Egypt will resist the three-day journey in the desert upon which Moses and the Israel's elders will embark in order to worship the Lord, but the Lord will prevail through marvelous deeds on behalf of the Israelites and in opposition to the dominant powers of Egypt.

◆ RESPONSORIAL PSALM 105: The Lord always remembers the covenant made with Abraham and his descendants. One of the many ways the Lord fulfills the covenant is by sending servants to guide his people. Among these servants, the psalm references Moses and Aaron. For the Lord's servant-leaders, then and now, we give thanks for God makes known his wondrous deeds through them.

◆ GOSPEL: Jesus invites those among the crowds who labor and find themselves burdened, to come to him. The Apostles heard how challenging their mission is to be, but yet Jesus tells the crowds his "yoke is easy" and his "burden light." If we yoke ourselves to Jesus, he will guide us along the way. His meekness and humility will lead us into the Kingdom of heaven. Would that we do come to him.

Today's Saint

Laying aside a life of violence and gambling, St. Camillus de Lellis (1550–1614) was ordained a priest and later founded the Order of Clerks Regular Ministers to the Sick (the Camillians), a religious order dedicated to the sick, especially those afflicted with the plague. Whether they were ministering in a hospital or tending to the wounded on the battlefield, the Camillians were easily identified by their black habit with a large red cross on the breast. St. Camillus implemented many innovative approaches to hospital care, including proper ventilation, suitable diets, and isolation of people with infectious diseases. He is also credited with inventing field ambulances and military hospitals. Along with St. John of God, he is patron saint of hospitals, nurses, and the sick.

F R I 19 (#393) green
Weelday

The Lectionary for Mass

◆ FIRST READING: Pharaoh was stubborn, if not tenacious, and refused to free the children of Israel. Yet the ruler's obstinacy is no match for the Lord. On the night of Passover, the Lord's people would go unharmed because of the lamb's blood on their doorposts, but the first born of the Egyptians would know death. Forever this night now stands as a memorial of God's care for his people and the freedom he offers them.

◆ RESPONSORIAL PSALM 116: The opening verse asks the question about how the psalmist can repay the Lord for all the good the Lord has done. In the ensuing verse, the psalmist answers his own question. He must first take up the cup of salvation and then call on the Lord's name. Together with the psalmist, we recognize our need to offer continuously a sacrifice of thanksgiving to the Lord. Our faithfulness to do so is our vow to the Lord.

◆ GOSPEL: We know from the opening lines of the Gospel reading that undoubtedly Jesus is in for another conflict with the Pharisees. His disciples were harvesting grain on the Sabbath, a day on which, according to the law (the Pharisaic interpretation of it), no one was to work. Wise sage that Jesus is, he responds to the Pharisees repudiation of the disciples' work by reminding them of how David and his companions entered God's house and ate the offering bread which legally only priest could consume. Mercy is Jesus' way, not sacrifice. He makes the Sabbath new.

S A T 20 (#394) green **Weekday**

Optional Memorial of St. Apollinaris, Bishop and Martyr / red; Blessed Virgin Mary / white

The Lectionary for Mass

◆ FIRST READING: The people of Israel leave Egpyt in a rush and without time to prepare food for their journey. On this holy vigil night the Lord frees his people from the bonds of slavery which they had endured for generations. From this night forward, generation upon generation will keep vigil in remembrance of the gift of freedom the Lord gave his people.

◆ RESPONSORIAL PSALM 136: We praise the Lord for his mercy endures forever. The testimony to the endurance of the Lord's mercy repeats itself over and over in the psalm refrain and as the latter half of each verse. Would that we always remember how the Lord's mercy has been present generation upon generation, and in particular in the freeing of the people of Israel from the bondage of slavery in Egypt.

◆ GOSPEL: We find the Pharisees at this point so distraught with Jesus that as the Gospel reading opens we find them plotting to put him to death. Heeding the advice he gave previously to the Apostles about leaving the homes where the people do not welcome them, Jesus moves on to a different location. Numerous people followed him and yet, facing the possibility of death at the hands of the Pharisees, Jesus still heals the sick. Quoting what we know as the first of the servant songs in Isaiah, Jesus sees himself as the fulfillment of the prophet's words. Jesus' justice will reign despite the suffering he will endure.

Today's Saint

Not much is known about St. Apollinaris (dates unknown) except that he was from Antioch, a Syrian, and the first bishop of Ravenna. Tradition says he was appointed bishop by St. Peter himself. Apollinaris was exiled with his people during the persecution of Emperor Vespasian. As he left the city, he was pointed out as the leader of the Christians. He was tortured and executed with a sword. St. Apollinaris is a patron saint of those suffering from epilepsy or gout and is shown in art with a sword, the instrument of his martyrdom.

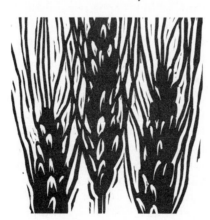

☀ 21 (#108C) green **Sixteenth Sunday in Ordinary Time**

The Lectionary for Mass

◆ FIRST READING: Abraham and Sarah extend hospitality to the three men who appear near their tent. The two provide water for bathing, the shade of a nearby tree, and food in abundance. As the encounter with the men comes to a close, Abraham's and Sarah's hospitality returns to them in kind. One of the men promises to return in a year and when he returns, the elderly Sarah will have a son. Certainly, the Lord was present in the three men: conceivably the Lord was also present in Abraham and Sarah, for their hospitality mirrored God's own.

◆ RESPONSORIAL PSALM 15: The opening verse of Psalm 15, which is not included in our Responsorial Psalm, sets the context for the rest of the Psalm. In Psalm 15:1, the person who wants to be admitted into the Temple of God's house asks who might dwell in the Lord's tent and on his holy mountain. The rest of the psalm answers this question declaring doing justice leads one to live in the Lord's presence.

◆ SECOND READING: Paul speaks about his apostolic ministry to the Colossians. As he does so, he tells them he rejoices in the sufferings he has endured not for his own sake, but for theirs. His ministry is to proclaim Christ to them. As believers, their ministry is also to proclaim Christ and to teach others of the wisdom they have found in him.

◆ GOSPEL: Martha is all about comparison. She wants to make sure the Lord judges her and her sister fairly, and it seems that the Lord finds himself more concerned about Martha's anxiety than about the fact that she is doing the hard labor of serving while Mary simply listened to the Lord talk. The point of Jesus' words that Mary has chosen the "better part" is not to hierarchically judge the sisters for their different choices, but to teach Martha to root herself in the Lord's Word and rather than to worry herself over many, many things. Then she will have abundant energy to serve in the Lord's name.

The Roman Missal

The Gloria and the Creed are sung or said today. The Collect, in asking God to "mercifully increase the gifts of your grace," can be seen as setting a tone for hearing the parables in today's Gospel. The Prayer over the Offerings reminds us that Christ's "one perfect sacrifice" completed all prior offerings of the law and asks that our sacrifice, like Abel's, will be made holy; the communal aspect of our worship is highlighted as the prayer gives the reason we ask the sacrifice to be made holy: "so that what each has offered to the honor of your majesty / may benefit the salvation of all." The Prayer after Communion is a prayer used frequently in Easter Time; it asks that we "pass from former ways to newness of life" as a result of our having been "imbued with heavenly mysteries." The passage of the Paschal Mystery focused on so intently during Easter Time is, of course, at the heart of every celebration of the Eucharist. Any one of the eight Prefaces of the Sundays in Ordinary Time may be selected for today. Using Eucharistic Prayer I, the Roman Canon, with its mention of "Abel the just" could provide a connection with today's Prayer over the Offerings. You might also consider using Euchairstic Prayer III.

Other Ideas

The story of Mary and Martha in today's Gospel is a wonderful description of family dynamics! Use the opportunity on this Sunday to have a good discussion as a family about the importance of everyone's responsibility for the happiness of family life. Maybe it's a good time to review the various family chores. The conversation needs to be respectful and honest, no judgmental remarks or hurtful innuendoes.

The family of faith, both in church and in the home is a sign of Christ's presence in the world. Praying together as a family, as Mary contemplated the teaching of Jesus, and working together as a family, like Martha who desired to serve others, can be complementary ways that enrich the spiritual life of young and old alike. Would you consider yourself a Mary or a Martha, or a combination of both?

MON 22 (#603) white
Feast of St. Mary Magdalene

The Lectionary for Mass

◆ FIRST READING, OPTION 1: In the first option from Song of Songs, the writer uses the metaphor of a bride and groom to refer to the love between God and his people. The bride is desperate in her longings; just as we are desperate to be in relatiosnhip with God.

◆ FIRST READING, OPTION 2: The death of Christ has given birth to a new creation, a new reality, a new covenant of reconciliation between God and humankind. The love of Christ drives Paul—both Christ's love for Paul and Paul's love for Christ—to be an ambassador for God in his apostolic ministry. What love God has shown us in the Incarnation, Death, and Resurrection of Christ!

◆ RESPONSORIAL PSALM 63: In the psalm, the author longs deeply for God to the point that his soul thirsts for him. The psalmist's confidence in the Lord's kindness and care is evident. Like us, the author has gazed upon the Lord in the sanctuary and known the riches of the banquet. The Lord who provides is also the Lord to whom we cling when others scorn us.

◆ GOSPEL: Our Gospel reading is proper for today's feast of St. Mary Magdalene. Mary Magdalene discovers the empty tomb and express-

es her concern to Simon Peter and the disciple Jesus loved that someone has taken Jesus' body from the tomb and hid him. The disciples return home, but Mary remains outside the tomb in tears where she encounters two angels who inquire as to the reason for her weeping and then sees, but does not recognize Jesus. How near the Risen Lord was to her and is to us if we choose to recognize him.

The Roman Missal

The prayers are found in the Proper of Saints. The Collect speaks of Mary as the one "entrusted . . . before all others" with the Good News of the Resurrection. We are to follow her example and "proclaim the living Christ" (Collect). We ask God to receive our offerings, as Christ received the "homage of charity" of St. Mary Magdalene, an allusion to Luke 7:36–38, when a penitent woman, traditionally associated with Mary Magdalene, anoints Jesus' feet with her tears, and dries them with her hair (Prayer over the Offerings). The Preface of Holy Men and Women is used. After his Resurrection, Mary clung to Jesus, her Master. We pray that we may be filled with that same "persevering love" (Prayer after Communion). Consider using the Eucharistic Prayer for Reconciliation I.

Today's Saint

St. Mary Magdalene (first century) was one of the followers of Jesus and one of the few witnesses of his Crucifixion and burial. At dawn on the third day, she went to anoint the body and was the first to see the empty tomb. She immediately ran to tell Peter and John (see John 20:1–2)—for this reason, she has been called the "apostle to the Apostles" by St. Bernard of Clairvaux, among others. One tradition puts her in Ephesus after the Ascension, but the French believe she sailed to Marseilles in a small boat, accompanied by her brother Lazarus, and lived in a cave doing penance for the rest of her life.

T U E 23 (#396) green **Weekday**

Optional Memorial of St. Bridget, Religious / white

The Lectionary for Mass

◆ FIRST READING: God's magnificent power is evident in the parting of the Red Sea. We need also to see from the story of God providing safe passage for the people of Israel through the Red Sea how God manifests his power in Moses. The great leader follows God's command to stretch out his hand over the sea both at night and at dawn so that the sea could part and flow back to its usual level. God's power is active in his people today as it was in Moses' time.

◆ CANTICLE: The Responsorial Psalm comes from the song Moses and the Israelites sang to the Lord in praise of his saving work. Today's verses focus on the Lord's destruction of evil that had presented itself in Pharaoh and his armies.

◆ GOSPEL: If you are a disciple, you are a relative of Jesus and belong to his immediate family. Doing the will of God is the requirement for being a member of Jesus' family. Throughout our reading of the Gospel according to Matthew, we have seen how Jesus schools the disciples in their mission to proclaim the Kingdom of heaven in their words and actions. We have also learned how difficult this mission is. Today's Gospel reading provides us the opportunity to reflect on the extent of our willingness to embrace a disciple's mission and belong to Jesus' family.

Today's Saint

St. Bridget was a mystic and the founder of the Bridgettines. She was happily married to a Swedish lord and had eight children, one of whom was St. Catherine of Sweden. The couple went on pilgrimage to Santiago de Compostela in the early 1340s, and Bridget's husband died soon after their return. St. Bridget is a patron saint of Europe and of widows, and is shown in art bearing a pilgrim's staff and bag, or wearing a crown.

W E D 24 (#397) green **Weekday**

Optional Memorial of St. Sharbel Makhlūf, Priest / white

The Lectionary for Mass

◆ FIRST READING: We move ahead one chapter in Exodus from the Israelites responding joyfully in praise of God for the freedom God brought them from the Egyptians to hear the Israelites grumbling to Moses and Aaron in the desert. In Egypt, they had their fill. Now in the desert, they face hunger, even famine. The Lord once again graciously responds to his people, raining down bread from heaven for them to eat.

◆ RESPONSORIAL PSALM 78 references the manna and the quail the Lord provided to the Israelites for their nourishment in the desert. The psalmist also acknowledges how the Lord can bring nourishment to his people, but also his wrath against them should they choose not to obey him.

◆ GOSPEL: Today's Gospel reading from Matthew 13 is the first in a series of nature parables contained in that chapter. Jesus uses these parables to instruct not only his disciples whom he had previously taught, but also the large crowds gathered around him. At the end of today's parable of the sower, Jesus

advises those with ears to hear and internalize their commitment to plant themselves in rich soil and produce fruit. We will hear this advice repeated at the end of other parables.

Today's Saint

St. Sharbel Makhlūf (1828–1898) was a Maronite Catholic monk and priest in Lebanon. He joined the monastery of St. Maron at 23, and after living in community became a hermit from 1875 to his death. His reputation for holiness drew visitors who sought a word of wisdom or blessing. Sharbel observed a strict fast and had great devotion to the Eucharist. Although dedicated to his life as a hermit, he always willingly went out to perform priestly ministry in local villages when requested. Sharbel died on Christmas Eve 1898, after becoming ill while celebrating Eucharist. He was canonized in 1977.

T H U 25 (#605) red **Feast of St. James, Apostle**

The Lectionary for Mass

◆ FIRST READING: St. Paul presents the beauty of the treasure of faith that believers hold to the Corinthians. The power of life always comes from God, not from us. When we face trials and persecution, when we face death, when we chose sin, our treasure is the true faith that lives in God. We believe that God will raise us with Jesus. In this hope, our thanks to God overflows.

◆ RESPONSORIAL PSALM 126: The psalmist's lament helps us understand how God's people newly returned from exile realistically knew that the life that lay ahead of them would not always be easy. But, their faith led them to believe that when they did "sow in tears" they would reap in joy. The Lord would always restore their fortunes. He would never withhold life from them.

◆ GOSPEL: Greatness comes from service not from the human desire to lord authority over others. The Apostles learn this after Jesus responds to the desire of the mother of Zebedee's sons to have them sit on Jesus' left and right in the Kingdom. While Jesus tells her that the Father, not he, will judge, those who will be in the Kingdom must be willing to drink from the same cup of suffering as he will. Even the Apostles quarrel among themselves when Zebedee's sons agree they can drink from Jesus' chalice. The life of an Apostle is not a comfortable life without demands.

The Roman Missal

The Gloria is sung or said today, since it is a feast. The Collect acknowledges the martyrdom of St. James as it notes that God "consecrated the first fruits of your Apostles / by the blood of Saint James." The Prayer over the Offerings continues this recognition by referring to the saint as "the first among the Apostles / to drink of Christ's chalice of suffering." As the prayer goes on to ask that "we may offer a sacrifice pleasing to you," we cannot help but be challenged to know that such sacrifice involves our willingness to participate in that same chalice of suffering. The Prayer after Communion proclaims that we receive the holy gift of the Eucharist with joy on this feast day. The Preface, proper for today, is one of the two Prefaces of the Apostles. Consider using Eucharistic Prayer I. Also, the Solemn Blessing formula titled "The Apostles," number 17 of the "Blessings at the End of Mass and Prayers over the People," may be used as the final blessing.

Today's Saint

The St. James we honor today is the brother of the Apostle John, one of the "Sons of Thunder" (Mark 3:17) who were privileged witness-

es of some of Jesus' greatest signs: the raising of the daughter of Jairus from the dead, the Transfiguration, and the agony in the garden. James was the first Apostle to suffer martyrdom and the only one to have his death recorded in the Acts of the Apostles. According to legend, his friends carried his remains away in a rudderless boat that drifted all the way to Spain. Many centuries later, they were discovered, and a great cathedral was built over the spot (Santiago de Compostela), which became one of the most popular pilgrimage destinations of the Middle Ages. To this day, hundreds of thousands of pilgrims make their way to that remote corner of Spain to venerate the relics of St. James. He is depicted in art dressed as a pilgrim with a scallop shell on his hat, the way pilgrims to Compostella dress. He is venerated as the patron saint of Spain, Nicaragua, and Guatemala.

(#399) white
Memorial of Sts. Joachim and Anne, Parents of the Blessed Virgin Mary
FRI 26

The Lectionary for Mass

◆ FIRST READING: In the Exodus account, God gives Moses and the Israelites the commandments after Moses comes down from the top of Mount Sinai. After God delivers the commandments, the people witness thunder and lightning and smoke rising from the mountain. Fear overtook them, yet they will learn that the command of the Lord brings life. Their obedience to the commandments will draw them close to the Lord.

◆ RESPONSORIAL PSALM 19: The psalm refrain comes from John 6:68 and is Peter's response to Jesus' question to the Twelve whether or not they too wanted to desert him. Peter professes his belief that Jesus, whom he addresses as "Lord," has the "words of eternal life." The

Apostles have nowhere else to go. The verses come from Psalm 19 and attest to the perfect sweetness of the law of the Lord, and thus, directly connect to the wisdom found in the commandments given to the Israelites.

◆ GOSPEL: In between the parable of the sower and Jesus' explanation of the parable, which is today's Gospel reading, the disciples inquire about why Jesus speaks in parables. Jesus informs them that only disciples know the mysteries of heaven. The crowds have yet to see and understand. Jesus' explanation of the parable of the sower intends to direct the crowds to see the best choice is to plant themselves in the rich soil of God's word lest their hearts turn to evil or their roots not be strong enough to withstand persecution.

The Roman Missal

All the orations are proper for today, and are to be found in the Proper of Saints at July 26. The Collect asks Sts. Joachim and Anne to pray that we may attain salvation. The Prayer over the Offerings gives an implicit acknowledgment of the two saints' role in salvation history by asking that "we may merit a share in the same blessing / which you promised to Abraham and his descendants." Either Preface I or Preface II of Saints would be the proper choice for today, with perhaps Preface I being the better choice of the two. The Prayer after Communion reminds us of the divine exchange as it notes that God's Only Begotten Son was "born from among humanity" so that "humanity might be born again from you." The prayer goes on to ask that those who have been fed with the heavenly Bread of the Eucharist might be sanctified "by the spirit of adoption." Thus, the role of Sts. Joachim and Anne as parents of the Blessed Virgin Mary continues to be a theme underlying the texts for today. Consider using Eucharistic Prayer II.

Today's Saints

The tradition of Sts. Joachim and Anne (first century) is not scriptural but comes mostly from the apocryphal Protoevangelium of James. It became popular in the thirteenth century when Jacobus de Voragine retold the story in his *Golden Legend*, which was very popular in the Middle Ages. The story of the conception of Mary echoes that of Samuel (see 1 Samuel 1:20): Joachim and Ann are a childless couple who pray to have children and promise to dedicate their child to God. Each is told by an angel that they will conceive, and afterward they meet at a gate of Jerusalem and embrace in joy. This event has been depicted in art by artists such as Dürer and Giotto.

SAT 27 (#400) green Weekday

Optional Memorial of the Blesssed Virgin Mary / white

The Lectionary for Mass

◆ FIRST READING: Much as we do in the Liturgy of the Word, Moses took the book of the covenant and read it to the people. They responded in affirmation stating that what the Lord has said they would follow and enact in their lives. Performing the ritual of sprinkling the people with sacrificial blood from animals, Moses seals the covenant. The Lord and his people are forever united in covenant.

◆ RESPONSORIAL PSALM 50 follows on the sealing of the covenant by ritual sacrifice detailed in the First Reading, by reflecting a similar covenantal theme. The psalmist, however, writes that the sacrifice God desires from his people who now live in covenant with him is a sacrifice of praise. God wants his people to affirm the redeeming

justice he offers and respond by glorifying his name.

◆ GOSPEL: Jesus uses another nature parable, that of the weeds among the wheat, to teach the crowds that weeds and wheat, those who hear the message of the Kingdom of heaven and those who do not, will live together until the harvest. Then, at the time of God's judgment, God will take the wheat to himself, but the weeds he will burn. From this parable that is only found in Matthew, disciples learn that the final judgment is left to God. We cannot even begin to imagine how to separate weeds and wheat in our lifetime.

☼ 28 (#111C) green Seventeenth Sunday in Ordinary Time

The Lectionary for Mass

◆ FIRST READING: In the reading, Abraham's visitors proceed on toward Sodom, but the Lord still stands before Abraham. The two enter into a back and forth conversation about how many innocent people the Lord must find in Sodom before he relents on destroying the city. Abraham's bargaining skills coupled with the generosity of the Lord's mercy lead to the Lord saying he would spare the city if he found ten innocent people.

◆ RESPONSORIAL PSALM 138: We sing a song of thanksgiving as our response to God's willingness

to extend his gracious mercy to us as exemplified in the First Reading. With the grateful heart of the psalmist whom God rescued, we acknowledge how God answers our call for help. We exalt God for he preserves us when we experience distress. In faith, we express our confidence that God's mercy does indeed endure forever.

◆ SECOND READING: Plunging into the baptismal waters, we die with Christ. As we arise from the waters, we rise with him. God's power—the same power that raised Christ from the dead—enables us through faith to participate in Christ's death and Resurrection. All the debt we owe to God for our sin, no longer exists. God, through the power of his mercy, wipes the slate clean with his forgiveness.

◆ GOSPEL: Upon observing Jesus at prayer, one of his disciples asks him to teach them how to pray. In response, Jesus teaches them what Christians for centuries have known as the Our Father. In Luke's account of the Gospel, Jesus follows the words of prayer he teaches his disciples with a parable about a friend in need of bread for a hungry visitor who has arrived at midnight. Disciples will answer the call to friendship by giving bread to those in need. Or, in other words, disciples lives the prayer to the Father in their daily life.

The Roman Missal

The Gloria and the Creed are sung or said today. The Collect speaks eloquently of God as the firm foundation of our lives; with that foundation, we can "use the good things that pass / in such a way as to hold fast even now / to those that ever endure." The sense of the imminent-yet-not-fully-realized Kingdom of God that underlies this Collect connects well with the Gospel parables today. The Prayer over the Offerings continues to acknowledge the need to progress in the life of the Kingdom, which is both here and yet-to-come: we bring our offerings from the abundance of God's gifts (the already of the Kingdom), and we pray that "these most sacred mysteries may sanctify our present way of life / and lead us to eternal gladness" (growing in grace toward a future fulfillment). Any one of the eight Prefaces of the Sundays in Ordinary Time may be selected for today. The dismissal formula "Go in peace, glorifying the Lord by your life" would reinforce the need for us to live life in a way whereby we grow in the ways of the Kingdom. The Prayer after Communion highlights the nature of every Eucharistic celebration as anamnesis—the "perpetual memorial of the Passion of your Son." Consider usin the Eucharistic Prayer for Reconciliation I.

Other Ideas

The theme of hospitality continues in today's Gospel. But first Jesus teaches the disciples a prayer that we know and love, the Our Father. Besides praying the Our Father at the Sunday Eucharist, when do you pray the Our Father? You might be surprised at the number of occasions when the Our Father is prayed. Some examples come to mind: during the Rosary, when celebrating the Sacrament of the Anointing the Sick, at a Vigil service for someone who has died, at parish meetings, as an evening prayer with children, in school classrooms, when a pastoral visitor takes communion to someone who is ill. As you pray the Our Father take time to reflect on each phrase. Ask, which words do you fine most moving? Which words might be difficult to live by? Which words bring you the most comfort?

MON 29 (#401; #607, Gospel) white
Memorial of St. Martha

The Lectionary for Mass

◆ FIRST READING: Moses came down the mountain only to find the people worshipping a golden calf. The Scripture account does not tell us why or how Aaron led the people to turn away from God and worship the calf. Aaron provides Moses the excuse that people simply are prone to evil. Moses confronts the people with their grave sin and takes it upon himself to approach the Lord for forgiveness. In due time, the Lord will punish the people who have sinned and their names alone will the Lord remove from the book of the elect.

◆ RESPONSORIAL PSALM 106: Today's refrain focuses on the people's responsibility to give thanks to the Lord for his goodness. The reference in the opening stanza to the calf coincides with the First Reading. How soon the people forgot how the Lord had saved them. Would that the Lord extend his the goodness of his mercy to bring them back to the roots of their faith.

◆ GOSPEL, OPTION 1: On this Memorial of St. Martha, the Gospel Reading describes how deeply Martha cared for her brother Lazarus who now was dead. Martha's statement to Jesus when he came to her home portrays her confidence in his power. She addresses him as "Lord" and asserts that if Jesus had been present, Lazarus would not have died. In the personal conversation between Martha and Jesus, Jesus tells Martha Lazarus will rise. Martha clearly expresses her faith in the resurrection on the last day, but in an "I am" statement Jesus communicates to her that he is the resurrection. Her response is pure, unconditional belief in Jesus as the Christ.

◆ GOSPEL, OPTION 2: This passage, unique to Luke, narrates the hospitality offered Jesus by Martha and Mary. For Martha, hospitality is best expressed by attentiveness to details while for Mary hospitality is best expressed by attentiveness to the person. Martha even asks Jesus to tell Mary to help her with the details of hospitality. Jesus responds with the confusing statement that Mary has chosen the better part. The story has generated many different interpretations. However, what is clear is that hospitality demands attentiveness to the person first, from which the details of service will flow. Both are essential in offering hospitality with attentiveness to the person flowing into the best ways to be of service. Martha and Mary are two sides of the same coin of ministry and discipleship. Let us learn to minister well by being attentive to the needs of each person we encounter.

The Roman Missal

The prayers, found in the Proper of Saints, are full of allusions to the Gospel accounts of Martha, who welcomed Christ to her home, and who believed in him as the Son of God. Martha welcomed Christ as a guest. We pray that we may so serve Christ in our brothers and sisters, that God may welcome us to "the halls of heaven" (Collect). Martha's "homage of love" was pleasing to the Lord. We pray that "our dutiful service" may likewise "find favor" in God's sight (Prayer over the Offerings). Earth and heaven are contrasted. We pray that we may turn away from the things of earth to the things of heaven. At the same time, we must follow the example of St. Martha, growing in sincere love for Christ on earth so that we may behold him in heaven (Prayer after Communion). Consider using Eucharistic Prayer II.

Today's Saint

St. Martha was the sister of Lazarus and Mary, friends of Jesus. She appears to have been a practical-minded woman, for she seems to have organized the dinner in Luke 10:38–42, and she protests when Jesus commands that the stone be rolled from the entrance to her brother's tomb after he'd been dead for three days. At the same time, however, she is one of the few in the Gospel to profess her faith in Jesus as the Messiah: "Yes, Lord, I believe that you are the Messiah, the Son of God, the one coming into the world" (John 11:27). The Golden Legend records the tradition that Martha, with her sister, Mary, and brother, Lazarus, fled Judea after the death of Jesus and landed at Marseilles. Martha is supposed to have traveled to Avignon, where she converted many to Christianity. St. Martha is shown in art bearing the tools of a housekeeper—keys or a broom—and is a patron saint of domestic servants, homemakers, cooks, and single laywomen.

T U E 30 (#402) green Weekday

Optional Memorial of St. Peter Chrysologus, Bishop and Doctor of the Church / white

The Lectionary for Mass

◆ First Reading: Through a personal relationship with the Lord, Moses had the opportunity to speak with God face to face. In these conversations, Moses came to know the Lord as a "merciful and gracious God," who would not anger quickly and who would extend loving kindness to generation upon generation. Moses would worship this one, true God and invite him to accompany the Israelites on their journey despite their stubbornness and propensity to sin. For forty days and nights, Moses remained with the Lord near the meeting tent inscribing the word of the covenant on the tablets.

◆ Responsorial Psalm 103 echoes the theme of God's mercy and kindness found in the First Reading. The psalmist has had a personal experience of God's love and justice and applies his experience to everyone. God's mercy extends to all people. It is universal in nature.

◆ Gospel: Jesus dismisses the crowds to whom he told the parable of weeds and offers its explanation only to the disciples who have inquired of him to clarify its meaning. Jesus explains to them that the significance of the parable lies in whether they will be the righteous children of the Kingdom or children of the Evil One. Their fate at the end of the age depends on it. Thus, in closing, Jesus reminds them once again, that those of us with ears ought to hear.

Today's Saint

Not much is known about St. Peter, who lived from approximately 380 to 450. He was bishop of Ravenna from about the year 433. Of his homilies, 176 survive, brief and to the point, in which he explains the Incarnation, the Creed, and the major heresies of his day. He was given the name Chrysologus, or "golden-worded," for his eloquent preaching.

W E D 31 (#403) white Memorial of St. Ignatius of Loyola, Priest

The Lectionary for Mass

◆ First Reading: The radiance of Moses's face after he meets face-to-face with God appears too bright for the children of Israel to look at. God had spoken to him on the mountain and had sent him back to the people to convey all that God imparted to him. Having communicated the Lord's message to the people, Moses put a veil over his face, but would remove it when he went back to speak with the Lord. This pattern would repeat itself multiple times as Moses bore God's presence to the people in the Word the Lord spoke.

◆ Responsorial Psalm 99: The Lord's holiness the psalm speaks of is evident in the radiant glow of Moses's face after he encounters the Lord. The psalmist recognizes the kingship of God and that Moses and Aaron were some of those who reverenced the Lord and conversed with him to learn his ways. On the Lord's holy mountain, Moses and Aaron worshipped him. Our worship carries on this day.

◆ Gospel: In the three short verses of today's Gospel reading, Jesus uses two parables to teach his disciples that the Kingdom is priceless in monetary terms. We must be all in for the Kingdom with our entire lives.

The Roman Missal

All the orations, located at July 31 in the Proper of Saints, are proper for this obligatory memorial. The Collect reflects aspects often associated with Ignatian spirituality with its references to the greater glory of God's name and fighting the good fight on earth. The Prayer over the Offerings describes the sacred mysteries we are celebrating as "the fount of all holiness." In view of this, perhaps it would be good to use Eucharistic Prayer II today, with its mention of the Lord as "the fount of all holiness." Preface I or Preface II of Saints or the Preface of Holy Pastors are all appropriate choices for today's Preface. The Prayer after Communion asks that the "sacrifice of praise" we have offered here on earth may bring us to the joys of eternity where we will "exalt your majesty without end." Consider using Eucharistic Prayer II.

Today's Saint

St. Ignatius of Loyola (1491–1556) was the founder and first Father General of the Society of Jesus, or Jesuits, and author of the *Spiritual Exercises*. Born in the Basque region of Spain, he joined the army and was severely wounded in battle. While recovering, he read a life of Christ and lives of the saints, and decided to emulate them. He laid his military equipment before a statue of Mary at the Benedictine Abbey of Montserrat, and spent several months in a cave near Manresa. After making a pilgrimage to the Holy Land, he enrolled at the University of Paris, and he gathered six companions who would become the first Jesuits.

August 2019
Month of the Immaculate Heart of Mary

(#404) white

T H U 1
Memorial of St. Alphonsus Liguori, Bishop and Doctor of the Church

The Lectionary for Mass

◆ FIRST READING: Moses follows the Lord's instructions as he builds a dwelling place for the Ark of the Covenant. The Lord revealed his presence when the cloud covered the meeting tent. Then, the Lord's glory was within the dwelling place. The children of Israel knew they could go forward in their journey when the cloud lifted from the dwelling place. How do we know God's presence with us on the journey of faith?

◆ RESPONSORIAL PSALM 84 is a hymn sung by the Israelites on their pilgrimages to Jerusalem. It is also an option for the Responsorial Psalm for the funeral liturgy. The refrain from Psalm 84:2 exclaims how lovely the Lord's dwelling place truly is. The verses tap into the people's deep desire and longing for God and the hope that they will dwell in God's house.

◆ GOSPEL: After Jesus relays the final in the series of parables to his disciples, the disciples agree that they understand that at the end of the age God's angels will separate the righteous from the wicked. In the parable, the wide net of the Kingdom of heaven catches good fish and bad fish; the latter, of course, the fishers need to discard. The disciples, in particular the Twelve, will now continue Jesus' mission of teaching, integrating the words of the Torah's law with Jesus' new message as Jesus moves on to face rejection in his hometown.

The Roman Missal

The proper orations for this obligatory memorial are taken from August 1. The Collect points to St. Alphonsus as an example of virtue and it notes his "zeal for souls." The Prayer over the Offerings makes reference to the Holy Spirit, asking God "to enkindle our hearts / with the celestial fire your Spirit," so that we might make a holy offering of ourselves just as St. Alphonsus offered himself. Preface I or Preface II of Saints, or the Common of Holy Pastors, are the choices from which to select the Preface for today. Pointing to the stewardship and preaching of St. Alphonsus, the Prayer after Communion asks that we too, in receiving "this great mystery," may praise God without end. Consider using Eucharistic Prayer II.

Today's Saint

Following a successful career as a lawyer, St. Alphonsus Mary Ligouri (1696–1787) lost a legal case. He believed this to be a sign from God that he should change his life and study for the priesthood. At the suggestion of a bishop friend, he founded the Congregation of the Most Holy Redeemer, also known as the Redemptorists, a community of priests dedicated to preaching, hearing confessions, and administering the sacraments. One of his most important contributions to the Church is his prolific writing in the area of moral theology. Also included among his writings are many devotional works regarding Mary and the saints. He influenced the Church not only through his writings, but also through his leadership as a bishop. Due to his many accomplishments, he was declared a Doctor of the Church and is recognized as one of the greatest moral theologians in Church history.

F R I 2
(#405) green
Weekday

Optional Memorials of St. Eusebius of Vercelli, Bishop / white; St. Peter Julian Eymard, Priest / white

The Lectionary for Mass

◆ FIRST READING: Among the festivals the Lord instructs Moses that children of Israel shall observe are the Passover of the Lord together with the feast of Unleavened Bread on the day following. The Day of Atonement and the feast of Booths are two other feasts the people are to mark annually. Each year, these celebrations will acknowledge how God was present and continues to be present with his people throughout their history.

◆ RESPONSORIAL PSALM 81: The people sang Psalm 81 at one of their annual pilgrimage feasts. The psalmist's words reflect how multiple instruments praise the Lord and announce the feast that God's word decreed the people would celebrate. Faithfulness to God requires the people to not worship idols, for God freed them from slavery in Egypt.

◆ GOSPEL: Jesus arrives in Nazareth to teach the people of his hometown in the synagogue. As crowds previously were amazed at Jesus' words and actions, aston-

ishment now fills the citizens of Nazareth present in the synagogue. But their astonishment leads them not to follow Jesus, but to question his identity and take umbrage with him. Jesus recognized their lack of faith and moved on from this place whose people refused to welcome him, as he had told the disciples to do when they experienced rejection.

Today's Saints

St. Eusebius (+ 371) was born in Sardinia. He was made the first bishop of Vercelli, probably in the 340s, and formed his clergy into a monastic community. At the 355 Synod of Milan, he refused to condemn Athanasius for opposing the Arian heresy, which undermined belief in the full divinity of Christ. As a result, he was exiled to Syria, to Cappadocia, and later to Egypt. When he was finally allowed to return from exile, he joined Athanasius at a synod that affirmed the divinity of the Holy Spirit and urged merciful treatment of repentant bishops who had signed Arian creeds. Once he returned to Vercelli, he joined Hilary of Poitiers to defeat the Arian heresy in the West. He died in 371 but was probably not martyred.

St. Peter Julian Eymard (1811–1868) was a French Catholic priest, who founded two religious orders, the Congregation of the Blessed Sacrament and, for women, the Servants of the Blessed Sacrament. Originally rejected as a candidate for the priesthood because of poor health, he was eventually ordained for the Diocese of Grenoble and later joined the Marist Fathers. Peter Julian Eymard worked tirelessly to encourage frequent reception of Holy Communion and has been called the "apostle of the Eucharist." He was a friend of his contemporaries, St. Peter Chanel and St. John Vianney, and advised the sculptor Auguste Rodin not to give up art to become a lay brother in his Congregation.

**S
A 3 (#406) green
T Weekday**

Optional Memorial of the Blessed Virgin Mary / white

The Lectionary for Mass

◆ FIRST READING: We move ahead a few chapters in Leviticus to find the Lord still instructing Moses on Mount Sinai. The Lord's instructions in Leviticus 25 deal with the observance of a sabbatical year every seven years and a jubilee year in the fiftieth year, the year after seven sets of seven years. In the jubilee year, everyone will return to their own property which they will purchase from their neighbor to whom they have previously sold the land. The Lord directs everyone to deal justly with each other in the buying and selling of the land.

◆ RESPONSORIAL PSALM 67: We sing a joyful song of thanksgiving for a bountiful harvest on this day when the First Reading speaks of the year of jubilee. May we exult with all the nations in praise of God for the fruits of the earth that God provides and for the justice with which God rules and guides the earth's peoples.

◆ GOSPEL: Herod's confusion leads him to believe that Jesus, on the basis of the mighty power at work in him, is John the Baptist raised from the dead. Herod had previously arrested and beheaded John because he worried that John's proclamation of repentance would motivate the people to rise up against him (Herod). Today's Gospel narrates the arrest and beheading of John as a prelude to Jesus' own suffering and death at the hands of the authorities. In Herod's thinking that John had risen, we see a glimpse of Jesus' own Resurrection.

**(#114C) green
Eighteenth
Sunday in
Ordinary Time**

The Lectionary for Mass

◆ FIRST READING: Most of us have had a day or two when we could relate to Qoheleth's feeling of emptiness that he expresses in the Hebrew phrases translated as "Vanity of vanities!" It is human nature to want our work to be productive. Our human nature also leads us to yearn for a sense of fulfillment and purpose in life. Some days leave us wanting and sorrow and grief find their way into our life. Yet, for people of faith, worldly wisdom is insufficient.

◆ RESPONSORIAL PSALM 90 helps us to recognize the passing nature of our days on earth. We will return to the dust out of which God created us. We could respond to these truths with the hopelessness of Qoheleth in the First Reading, or we could make the psalmist's words of hope our own and ask the Lord to fill us with his kindness when day breaks so that we may shout with "joy and gladness all our days."

◆ SECOND READING: The author of Colossians encourages his audience to "seek what is above," rather than "what is on earth." He provides a list of vices that Christians needs to put to death since our old selves have died in Baptism and we have put on a new self. Our relationships with one another must embody our new selves. They must honor the truth that no divisions exist in Christ.

◆ GOSPEL: The Gospel reading directly responds to Qoheleth's emptiness as we learn from the parable of the rich fool that earthly wealth does not matter to God. What matters is the direction of one's life. Have we renounced greed? Is our life headed in the direction of the Kingdom of God? Does our life include the riches of Jesus' teaching? Are we utterly dependent on God? Conceivably, Jesus' parable led the disciples and the person in the crowd who boldly asked Jesus to tell his brother to share his inheritance with him [the person in the crowd] to reflect on questions such as these.

The Roman Missal

The Collect points to how God constantly gives life to his creation: he creates, and he also restores what he creates and keeps safe what he restores. This is the reason we glory in God as our "Creator and guide." The Prayer over the Offerings highlights the theme of offering, which is central to every celebration of the Eucharist, as it petitions that we may be made an eternal offering to God. The Prayer after Communion returns to the theme of protection heard in the Collect, asking that those renewed with the heavenly gifts of the Eucharist might be worthy of eternal redemption. Of the eight Prefaces of the Sundays in Ordinary Time that could be used today, Preface III echoes the idea of God's protection and restoration as it speaks of God coming to our aid with his divinity. Preface VI speaks about the daily effects of God's care. The Gloria and the Creed are sung or said today. Consider using Eucharistic Prayer III.

Other Ideas

There are times in our life when we are a little bit selfish. Our parents taught us when we are very young to share, a valuable lesson for the rest of our lives. The rich man in today's Gospel is very selfish; he simply doesn't have enough room for all the stuff he has and wants to keep for himself. What can we do without? Maybe these quieter days of summer would be a good time to sort through our cupboards and closets and give away what we no longer need. Or, stage a sidewalk sale and give the proceeds to a local charity or to St. Vincent de Paul society. It has been said that when we own too much stuff, the stuff starts to own us. Even nations are guilty of hoarding resources while others suffer scarcity. How can you bring attention to this inequity?

MON 5 (#407) green
Weekday

Optional Memorial of the Dedication of the Basilica of St. Mary Major / white

The Lectionary for Mass

◆ FIRST READING: The children of Israel complain that all they have to eat in the desert is manna. They have neither meat, nor any of the other delicacies they had when they were in Egypt. Moses feels the burden of the Lord's people upon him and it is more than he can bear. He knows he is not the one who gave birth to the people and thereby reasons that he should not have to act as their father. Moses would rather die than carry the people by himself.

◆ RESPONSORIAL PSALM 81: We continue on in Psalm 81 for today's Responsorial Psalm from where we left off this past Friday. The psalmist writes today's verses in the voice of a leader who recounts that his people did not listen to the Word of God he spoke. Their hearts hardened, but God would feed Israel when they would remain faithful to him.

◆ GOSPEL: Wanting to be alone after he had heard of the death of John the Baptist, Jesus went away by boat to a deserted place. He could not find solitude as a large crowd awaited him as he disembarked. The disciples wanted Jesus to send the crowd away to find their own food. But, Jesus had another idea. He would feed them on the five loaves and two fish they had. He fed them and there was more than enough for all, and they came to know Jesus as their food for life.

About Today's Optional Memorial

Today the Church celebrates the dedication of the Basilica of St. Mary Major, *Santa Maria Maggiore*, in Rome, the oldest church in the West dedicated to the Blessed Virgin Mary. At the Council of Ephesus in 431, Mary was acclaimed not only as the mother of Jesus, but as the Mother of God. Following the Council, Pope Sixtus III dedicated this basilica to the honor of Mary, Mother of God. This great church houses the oldest image of the Virgin and Child in Rome, known as the *Salus Populi Romani*, "Salvation of the people of Rome." Perhaps the most-visited place in the basilica is the crypt of the Nativity, where the faithful venerate the relics of the manger in which Mary laid the infant Jesus.

TUE 6 (#614) white
Feast of the Transfiguration of the Lord

About Today's Feast

The Feast of the Transfiguration of the Lord reminds us about the depth of mystery that surrounded Jesus Christ—mystery in the sense that we can never exhaust who he really is or categorize him in any way. Fully human, he may indeed have needed a tent or a place to camp on the mountain, like Peter asked. But just when the Apostles may have been getting really comfortable with their understanding of Jesus as friend and teacher, they catch a glimpse of his heavenly glory, challenging them to remain open to Christ communicating to them who he is as Son of God. We have moments like the Apostles each time we encounter and grapple with a new and challenging image of God in the Scriptures. Remaining humble and open to the revelatory action of God's Word and Spirit is a way to enter ever more deeply into the mystery of who God is for us in Jesus Christ.

The Lectionary for Mass

◆ FIRST READING: In Daniel's apocalyptic vision, the kingdoms of this world will fall to the Kingdom of "One like a Son of Man" who comes on heaven's clouds. Christians see Daniel's vision fulfilled in Jesus Christ whose kingship will last forever. Just as the "One like a Son of man" received power, glory, and kingship from the Ancient One, so too, Jesus received the same from the Father.

◆ RESPONSORIAL PSALM 97: Beginning with its opening words, Psalm 97 acclaims the Lord's kingship. The Lord reveals his power by coming in a storm, a customary manner in which the power of a god showed forth at the time. Mountains and heavens proclaim God's kingship, and the peoples witness God's glory. We join in acclaiming that the Lord is exalted above all gods on this Feast of the Transfiguration.

◆ SECOND READING: The author of 2 Peter reminds his audience that he did not fabricate the truth about the coming of Jesus Christ because they had the testimony of the Apostles who were eyewitnesses to draw upon. In recounting Jesus' Transfiguration, the author highlights the glory Jesus received from the Father who identified him as his beloved Son. Christians, thus, should listen to the message about

Jesus' glory and live in his light until the Parousia.

◆ GOSPEL: Luke places the narrative of Jesus' Transfiguration after Peter's confession of Jesus as the Messiah, Jesus' first prediction of his Passion, Death, and Resurrection, and Jesus' instruction to the disciples that they, too, must take up their cross. Luke's is the only account of the Transfiguration that finds the disciples asleep after their journey up the mountain with Jesus. But, they awake in time to see Jesus' glory and wish to rest forever in it on the mountain. Yet, their journey of the cross is the journey down the mountain to Jerusalem with Jesus. His glory remains always within and around him, available for the disciples to share.

The Roman Missal

The orations for this feast are all proper for the feast today, and are located in the Proper of Saints section of the Missal at August 6.

The Gloria and the Creed are sung or said today. The Collect places the meaning of the Transfiguration not as some event that took place in the past, but rather as something that serves as an invitation to explore ever more deeply the reality of who God reveals himself to be. Thus, in the Collect we are enjoined to listen to the voice of God's beloved Son, that is, now, in the present, so that "we may merit to become co-heirs with him." We must recall that all liturgical celebration is about our entrance in the present into the mystery that is being made manifest and present through the ritual actions and the anamnesis of the Church.

The Prayer over the Offerings employs imagery of the Transfiguration by referring to the "radiant splendor" of the Son. The Preface, "The Mystery of the Transfiguration," is proper for today, and is given in the pages along with the other Mass texts. Music is provided, so perhaps

today would be a good day to sing the introductory dialogue and the Preface. This Preface reminds us, as with so many of the mysteries of our faith, that the reality we celebrate about Christ is a reality we are called to also experience— we are all called to be transfigured with Christ, as his Transfiguration shows us "how in the Body of the whole Church is to be fulfilled / what so wonderfully shone forth first in its Head." The Prayer after Communion, which also uses the imagery of radiance and splendor, picks up the theme of transformation: we pray that the "heavenly nourishment" we have received will "transform us into the likeness of your Son." We are reminded that our reception of Holy Communion is never simply a passive reception, but it is always to be an active participation in being transformed into what we receive. Consider using Eucharistic Prayer II.

WED 7 (#409) green
Weekday

Optional Memorials of St. Sixtus II, Pope, and Companions, Martyrs / red; St. Cajetan, Priest / white

The Lectionary for Mass

◆ FIRST READING: Moses sent people in advance to the land the Lord gave the children of Israel to investigate its bounty. The explorers found the land flowing with milk and honey, but also inhabited by ferocious people against whom the Israelites could struggle mightily. When the Israelites heard this news, they once again grumbled. The Lord will punish those who scorned the Promised Land.

◆ RESPONSORIAL PSALM 106 parallels the First Reading from Numbers. The psalmist describes how the Israelites sinned and forgot the wonders the Lord had done for them. God's people turned to grumbling in the desert and failed to remember how the Lord saved them. They pray that the Lord remember them and rescind his wish to destroy them.

◆ GOSPEL: A Canaanite woman desires Jesus' healing touch for her daughter possessed by a demon. The disciples immediately want to send the woman away, and Jesus himself states that he was sent only to Israel's lost sheep. But the faith of the Canaanite woman moves Jesus to heal her daughter and shows how indeed Jesus' mission extends to beyond the people of Israel to Gentiles.

Today's Saints

St. Sixtus II was pope for less than a year, from August 30, 257, to August 6, 258. He restored relations with the African and Eastern churches, which had been broken off over the question of heretical Baptism. Pope Sixtus, along with several deacons, was one of the first victims of the persecution begun by the emperor Valerian in 258. He is referred to by name in Eucharistic Prayer I.

St. Cajetan—not to be confused with Thomas Cardinal Cajetan—was born in 1480 and founded the Order of the Clerics Regular, or Theatines, which was canonically erected by Clement VII in 1524. The idea behind the Order was to combine the spirit of monasticism with active ministry. He died in 1547. He is a patron saint of workers, gamblers, and the unemployed, and is especially venerated in Argentina.

T H U 8 (#410) white
Memorial of St. Dominic, Priest

The Lectionary for Mass

◆ FIRST READING: The people now find themselves without water and, in response to their situation, this time they convene a council against Moses and Aaron. Having listened to the people of Israel

express their frustrations to the point of their boiling over, the two leaders find themselves prostrate in front of the meeting tent. As Moses follows the Lord's command, water issues forth from out of the rock. And, not just a trickle of water flows forth, but an abundance of water. The people of Israel will never thirst again in the Lord.

◆ RESPONSORIAL PSALM 95: The direct connection with the First Reading is found in the reference to Meribah in verse 8. It was there that the people of Israel argued with the Lord for water and the Lord abundantly provided for them making his holiness known.

◆ GOSPEL: Jesus seems initially interested in whom others say he is, but his real interest lies in who the disciples say he is. Peter is the first and the only of the disciples whom Matthew records as responding to Jesus' question. Peter's response identifies Jesus as the Christ, and in return, Jesus states that he will build his Church on the rock of Peter's confession. Faith in Jesus as the Christ is and always will be the bedrock of the Church.

The Roman Missal

The orations are all to be found at August 8 in the Proper of Saints. The Collect not surprisingly underscores Dominic's reputation as an outstanding preacher. The Prayer over the Offerings prays for protection, "through the great power of this sacrifice," for "those who champion the faith," thus reminding us that we are called to be preachers of the truth, like St. Dominic. The Prayer after Communion again highlights St. Dominic's preaching: since the Church flourished by means of his preaching, we also ask that we might be "helped through his intercession." In view of St. Dominic's life and preaching, the Preface of Holy Pastors would appear to be the most apt choice for

today, although Preface I or II of Saints could also be used. Consider using Eucharistic Prayer II.

Today's Saint

St. Dominic (c. 1170–1221), a contemporary of St. Francis of Assisi, founded a mendicant order of men (those who rely on the charity of others), called the Order of Preachers or Dominicans, to preach against theological error. One of the pressing issues facing the newly established Order was the Albigensian heresy, claiming that matter, specifically the body, is evil. In order to fight against this heretical thinking, the Black Friars, as they were commonly known because of the color of the cape they wore over their white habit, went from town to town preaching the goodness of the body. In order to preach sound doctrine with clarity, St. Dominic exhorted his sons to engage in rigorous academic study. He eventually started a contemplative female branch of the Dominicans to support the apostolate of the men through prayer.

F R I 9 (#411) green
Weelday

Optional Memorial of St. Teresa Benedicta of the Cross, Virgin and Martyr / red

The Lectionary for Mass

◆ FIRST READING: Moses addresses the people of Israel in a profoundly moving reflection on the personal relationship between God and his people. Using rhetorical questions, Moses leads the people to ponder how unique the Creator's connection is to those whom he created and how God continues to enter into relationship with them, speaking to them, and guiding them in their journey. Moses concludes by informing the people that their responsibility in return for all God does for them is to keep the commandments Moses presents to them on this day.

◆ RESPONSORIAL PSALM 77: Our Responsorial Psalm comes from the second part of Psalm 77 in which the psalmist narrates his own personal remembrance of all God has done for his people. The psalmist recounts God's wonderful deeds, including how God led his people under the guidance of Moses and Aaron. As a response to the first half of the psalm, the psalmist cries out about distress he experiences and asks if God's love has ended.

◆ GOSPEL: Jesus presents the Cross as the heart of a disciple's life in today's Gospel. A disciple who follows Jesus must take up his or her cross. A disciple must lose his or her life for Jesus. A disciple will then find everything he or she desires in the Kingdom. Who is ready, then, to live as a true disciple of Jesus?

Today's Saint

St. Teresa Benedicta of the Cross was born Edith Stein at Breslau in 1891 into an observant Jewish family, but by the time she reached her teens, she had become an atheist. She went on to study philosophy and received her doctorate at Freiburg under the philosopher Edmund Husserl but left her university career to teach at a girls' school when Husserl did not support her further studies. Influenced by her study of scholastic theology and spirituality, she became a Catholic in 1922. In 1932, she became a lecturer at Munster, but anti-Semitic laws passed by the Nazis forced her to resign, and she entered the Carmel at Cologne in 1933. In an attempt to protect her from the Nazis, she was transferred to a Carmel in the Netherlands, but when the Dutch

bishops condemned Nazi racism, the Nazis retaliated by arresting Jewish converts. Edith, along with her sister Rosa, who had also become a Catholic, was deported to Auschwitz and died in the gas chamber on August 9, 1942.

SAT 10 — (#618) red
Feast of St. Lawrence, Deacon and Martyr

The Lectionary for Mass

◆ FIRST READING: Paul encourages the Corinthians to give to the Church at Jerusalem by following the Macedonians who have generously given out of their need. Today's passage, from 2 Corinthians 9:6–10 might be part of another letter Paul originally wrote to the Corinthians. In these verses Paul coaches the Corinthians to model their giving on God's abundant generosity. Paul cites Psalm 112:9 to show how God calls us to extend generosity to the poor. In return, we will receive the blessing of eternal righteousness from God. God will never leave the Corinthians or us wanting, so let our cheerful giving begin!

◆ RESPONSORIAL PSALM 112: After Paul's citation of Psalm 112 in the First Reading, how appropriate it is that the Lectionary appoints this Psalm as our Responsorial Psalm. Psalm 112 speaks of the blessings the gracious person will receive from the Lord. The Lord will bless the generous with children and riches and remember us forever.

◆ GOSPEL: On this Feast of St. Lawrence, the Gospel reading from John comes immediately after Jesus had entered Jerusalem. In this passage, Jesus' solemn teaching includes three sayings. The first, a

brief parable, instructs the disciples that in death much fruit is produced. The second informs them that their life can be preserved eternally so long as they do not hang on to it too strongly in this world. The third speaks of the connection between serving and following Jesus. The disciples must follow Jesus to his death. Such is the life of taking up the Cross. Jesus teaches the disciples in these three sayings that his glory will come at the hour of his death.

The Roman Missal

The prayers for the feast are found in the Proper of Saints for August 10. The Gloria is said or sung. The simple petition in the Collect might be spoken of any saint: "grant that we may love what he loved / and put into practice what he taught." Use the Preface I or II for Holy Martyrs. Consider using Eucharistic Prayer I.

Today's Saint

St. Lawrence (+ 258) was one of seven deacons of ancient Rome martyred under Emperor Valerian in 258. Tradition says that he was deacon to Pope St. Sixtus II. According to St. Ambrose, Lawrence met the pope being taken to execution and is supposed to have said, "Where are you going without your deacon?" Sixtus prophesied that he would follow in three days. Lawrence is said to have been martyred by being cooked alive on a grill. He is portrayed in art holding a gridiron, the instrument of his martyrdom, and wearing a dalmatic, the vestment of a deacon. St. Lawrence is a patron saint of the city of Rome and of comedians because of the quip he is reputed to have made to his executioners: "Turn me over; I'm done on one side."

(#117C) green

☀11 Nineteenth Sunday in Ordinary Time

The Lectionary for Mass

◆ FIRST READING: God's care for his people was evident on the night of the Passover when he spared the first-born of the Israelites and accompanied them in their journey to freedom from slavery. The Egyptians, on the other hand, received the fate that was due them for their oppressive actions. The Israelites' faith stands as an example to us to this day.

◆ RESPONSORIAL PSALM 33 reminds us our blessedness comes from the Lord. Those whom God has chosen will find their inheritance in him. We wait in hope for this day. Here and now we pray the Lord's kindness rest upon us so that we might extend it to others and, with God's help, support them in times of need.

◆ SECOND READING: Everything Abraham did, he did "by faith." This two-word phrase is repeated three times for emphasis in the passage from Hebrews, and a fourth time in the longer form of the Second Reading. God fulfilled his promise to Abraham to bless him with descendants as numerous as the stars, but these descendants also die. In the longer former of the reading, the author of Hebrews goes back to Abraham's story and sees in his willingness to offer his only son, Isaac, as a sacrifice, faith that God was able to raise the dead.

◆ GOSPEL: The shorter form of the Gospel reading includes Jesus' instructions to his disciples to prepare themselves for the coming of the Son of Man. The longer form begins with Jesus advising the disciples to devoid themselves of earthly belongings and give alms as they work to align their hearts with their true treasure. In addition, after the parable about the master whose house was broken into, the longer form includes Peter's question to Jesus about whom the parable was intended for. Jesus responds indirectly, continuing in the language of the parable to show Peter that much will be required of those who know the Master's will.

The Roman Missal

The Gloria and the Creed are sung or said today. The Collect echoes St. Paul's words in Galatians 4:6: "As proof that you are children, God sent the spirit of his Son into our hearts, crying out, 'Abba, Father!'" We are "taught by the Holy Spirit" and "dare to call [God] our Father." We ask God to bring to perfection within us this "spirit of adoption," that we may come to our promised inheritance. We ask God to receive the offerings of his Church, the gifts he himself has given and will transform for us, for our salvation (Prayer over the Offerings). We ask God to save us and teach us through the sacrament we have received (Prayer after Communion). Consider using Eucharistic Prayer I.

Other Ideas

Today's Gospel continues Jesus' teaching about possessing worldly goods. He says that it is more important to have heavenly riches than the things of the world. Continuing the thought from last week, consider inviting some others to join you in gathering goods that can be given to agencies that assist others who are less fortunate. Maybe you could organize a parish-wide sale of previously enjoyed items with all the proceeds going to a mission project. On a personal note, what are the spiritual treasures that you think are most important in your life? Do you pray on a regular basis? Have you ever considered a weekend retreat? Perhaps you could begin planning to gather a few fellow parishioners to join a small group to pray the Sunday Scriptures. Consider doing that once the summer is over.

(413) green

M O N 12 Weekday

Optional Memorial of St. Jane Frances de Chanal / white

The Lectionary for Mass

◆ FIRST READING: As part of a persuasive discourse to the people, Moses speaks about what the Lord asks of Israel. The theme of keeping the Lord's commandments appears central once again. God also asks that his people temper their stubbornness and change their hearts to live a life of justice and love in service to the Lord and others. Think of the impact on the world the numerous descendants of Abraham will have as they live faithfully in response to their God.

◆ RESPONSORIAL PSALM 147: God has redeemed Jerusalem through his Word and brought life to her people through the commandments. The very brief refrain from Psalm 147:12a helps us see the only suitable response to God is to offer praise. Life and peace have come through God's law and for this we glorify God.

◆ GOSPEL: Jesus predicts his Passion and death for the second time in Matthew's account of the Gospel (see 16:21–23). The disciples are aggrieved and clearly fixated on the first part of the prediction that informs them their teacher will die. Perhaps Jesus' prediction of his own Resurrection after three days confused them for they had no prior experience on which to understand it. Faithful disciples look forward to life in the Kingdom of heaven with Jesus and thus have no obligation to pay the Temple tax, although Jesus does not want those bound by payment to take offense.

Today's Saint

Under the influence of her spiritual director St. Francis de Sales, St. Jane (1572–1641), a wealthy widow and mother from France, founded the Congregation of the Visitation of the Virgin Mary. Unusual in its time, this new community of cloistered nuns welcomed individuals with frailties due to health and age, and who were often refused admittance by other cloistered orders. She was no stranger to pain, from the death of her husband and some of her children, to the death of her dear friend St. Francis, but she transformed the experiences of sorrow into moments of transformation and service to the sick.

T U E 13 (#414) green Weekday

Optional Memorial of Sts. Pontian, Pope, and Hippolytus, Priest, Martyrs / red

The Lectionary for Mass

◆ FIRST READING: Moses, now a hundred and twenty years old, passes leadership of the Lord's chosen people to Joshua. Bravery, persistence, and faithfulness must mark Joshua's tenure as he leads the people into the land the Lord promised to them. But, Joshua will not lead alone: the Lord will accompany him every step of the way—both before him and with him.

◆ CANTICLE: Today is a canticle instead of a psalm. The text comes from the Song of Moses in the Book of Deuteronomy. Moses sings of God's greatness to his people and how the Lord has led his people, despite the times they had chosen the sin of infidelity to the Lord. In his old age and with his death approaching, Moses gives these words to the people so that when they choose to turn from God's ways, they will take pause and remember God's faithfulness to them throughout the generations.

◆ GOSPEL: The greatest in the Kingdom of heaven has the humility of a child: so Jesus surprisingly responds to the disciples' question about who is the greatest. What does this mean for life as a disciple on earth? It means we must welcome the humble and become humble ourselves. The mercy we extend to one who has lost his or her way out of a hundred people exemplifies our Kingdom discipleship.

Today's Saints

Little is known about St. Pontian (c. + 236), save that he was pope from 198 or 199 to 236. After the schism of St. Hippolytus ended, Emperor Maximinus exiled Pontian to the Sardinian mines, where he died.

St. Hippolytus (c. 170–c. 236) was a prolific writer and probably a disciple of Irenaeus. He wrote the *Refutation of All Heresies* and exegeses of the Song of Songs and Daniel, but he is best known as a possible author of the *Apostolic Tradition*, an invaluable source of information on customs and liturgy during the first centuries of the Church. Ironically, Hippolytus shares this day with Pope Pontian, against whom he led a schism.

W E D 14 (#415) red Memorial of St. Maximilian Mary Kolbe, Priest and Martyr

The Lectionary for Mass

◆ FIRST READING: Moses receives a beautiful view of the Promised Land from the Lord before he dies. After the prescribed thirty-day ritual mourning, the leadership of God's people transitions smoothly to Joshua, for the spirit of wisdom resides in him. Moses had previously laid hands upon him, a ritual act we carry forward to today to symbolize the gift of the Holy Spirit and the conferral of the call to leadership.

◆ RESPONSORIAL PSALM 66: The refrain and the final stanza of the Responsorial Palm taken from Psalm 66 are written in the first person. They reflect the psalmist's personal experience of how God acted in his life to save him. In contrast, the first two stanzas (see verses 1–3a, and 8) are directed to the community to praise God for his wondrous deeds.

◆ GOSPEL: Jesus offers his disciples guidance on the process of forgiveness and reconciliation, and the role of the Church in this process. The disciples have the power to bind and loose and what they have bound and loosened on earth will remain so in heaven. Jesus' solemn teaching in this passage concludes with a statement on the power of the prayer in community and his presence within a community even only of two or three.

The Roman Missal

The Collect, the Prayer over the Offerings, and the Prayer after Communion are all proper for today and are taken from August 14. The Collect recognizes the saint for his "zeal for souls and love of neighbor" as well as his Marian devotion. The Prayer over the Offerings asks that through the oblations we present at this celebration, "we may learn / from the example of St. Maximilian / to offer our very lives to you." Indeed, the offering of our lives is the heart of our participation in the Eucharistic celebration. One of the two Prefaces of Holy Martyrs would probably be most appropriate today, although the Preface of Holy Pastors or even one of the two Prefaces of Saints could also be considered. The Prayer after Communion reminds us of our communion with the saints in the Eucharist, as it asks that through the Eucharist "we may be inflamed with the same fire of charity / that St. Maximilian received from this holy banquet." Consider using Eucharistic Prayer for Reconciliation II. Evening Masses are for the Vigil of the Assumption of the Blessed Virgin Mary (see below).

Today's Saint

St. Maximilian Maria Kolbe (1894–1941) was a Polish Franciscan who volunteered to die in place of a stranger in Auschwitz. From an early age, Maximilian had a strong devotion to the Virgin Mary, and in 1907, he entered the Conventual Franciscans, along with his brother. He was sent to study at the Pontifical Gregorian University in Rome, and seeing anti-Catholic demonstrations, he decided to form the Militia Immaculata. He was innovative in his use of modern media, especially printing technology and radio, for catechesis, publishing first a monthly magazine, and then a daily newspaper that soon had the widest circulation in Poland. During the 1930s, he started a mission in Japan and built a monastery in Nagasaki that was one of the few buildings left undamaged by the atomic bomb dropped at the end of World War II. Because he hid Jews from the Nazis in his

monastery in Poland, the Gestapo arrested Maximilian, and eventually he was transferred to Auschwitz. When three prisoners escaped, the camp commandant selected ten men to die by starvation. One of the men cried out, "My wife! My children!" and Maximilian volunteered to take his place in the bunker. He survived for two weeks, outliving the others, dying only when the guards injected him with carbolic acid. St. Maximilian Kolbe was canonized by Pope John Paul II in 1982. He is a patron saint of journalists, amateur radio operators, and of prisoners, and he is often depicted wearing the striped uniform of a death-camp inmate.

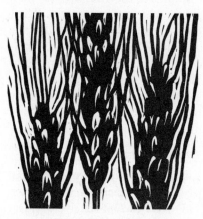

(#621/#622) white

THU 15 Solemnity of the Assumption of the Blessed Virgin Mary

Holyday of Obligation

About Today's Solemnity

The dogma of the Assumption of the Blessed Virgin Mary was proclaimed in 1950, but this observance has been celebrated on this day from the middle of the fifth century. On this solemnity, we profess our belief that Mary has gone before us, body and soul, into heaven. For her, the resurrection of the dead has taken place already. And thus the Assumption is technically an "Easter feast." God invites us to eternal life, to enjoy the glorious new creation of his Son in body, soul, and spirit. Our final hope is

the resurrection of our own bodies at the end of time to exist forever in this new order of creation. The Solemnity of the Assumption is our great celebration of this final hope. Mary is a pioneer for us in faith. She was the first among us to accept Jesus Christ into her life. In her bodily Assumption, she is also the first fully to enjoy eternal life at the side of her risen son in the glory of heaven. Where she has gone, we hope to follow. We rejoice in the fulfillment of God's promise in her, as we turn to her to guide us to the side of her risen son who reigns in heaven.

The Lectionary for Mass: Vigil Mass

◆ FIRST READING: To the people of Israel, God's presence resided in the Ark of the Covenant. The procession with the Ark of the Covenant takes place as David assembled all Israel in Jerusalem. Once the Ark was inside the tent David set up for it, he offered burnt offerings and peace offerings to God and blessed the people. Throughout the ages, the Church has recognized Mary, the Mother of God, as the Ark of the new covenant for she bore Jesus. Because of his sacrifice on the Cross no other offerings are necessary.

◆ RESPONSORIAL PSALM 132 was traditionally a processional hymn sung as the people carried the Ark of the Covenant into its location in the Temple. The psalmist asks God that his priests wear the garment of justice and that both God and the people remain faithful to the covenant made with David.

◆ SECOND READING: Paul culminates his presentation about the centrality of Jesus' Resurrection with a rhetorical question based on Hosea 13:14. In Jesus' Resurrection, death and sin no longer have power. God through Jesus Christ has won victory.

◆ GOSPEL: A woman's cry acclaims the blessedness of Jesus' mother. Jesus responds to her with what seems at first to be a denial of her statement. His words, however, are not that. Rather, Jesus attempts to turn our focus to the faithfulness of his mother—for Mary is the model of one who hears and observes the Word of God.

The Lectionary for Mass: Mass during the Day

◆ FIRST READING: Christians see the vision from Revelation that describes the pregnant woman who gave birth to a male child as referring to Mary, the Mother of God. In the birth of the male child, Jesus, salvation comes. In Jesus, the Kingdom of God is realized. God has prepared Mary a place in heaven into which she was assumed body and soul where God will forever protect her and those with her from persecution as, in the vision, God protected the woman in the desert.

◆ RESPONSORIAL PSALM 45 is a wedding song for the marriage between a king and queen. Roman Catholics see in the reference to the splendor of the queen, the beauty of Mary, Queen of Heaven. As the queen stands at the king's right hand adorned in gold, so Mary lives forever with God in heaven.

◆ SECOND READING: Paul uses the harvest image of the "firstfruits" to show the Corinthians that Christ's Resurrection came first, but that when he comes again, those of us who have remained faithful to him will also rise with him. Death is now forever subject to Christ and the victory he won over it.

◆ GOSPEL: Elizabeth acclaims Mary and Jesus blessed as she greets her pregnant cousin. The Church has for centuries prayed Elizabeth's words as part of the Hail Mary /Ave Maria. The scene of the visitation is the occasion for Mary to respond with her song of praise to God, which we know as the Magnificat.

The Roman Missal: Vigil Mass

The Prayers and Preface for the solemnity are found in the Proper of Saints. The Gloria and the Creed are said or sung today. Please note that there are two full sets of prayers. Those of the Vigil can be used on the afternoon or evening of August 14, with those of the Day reserved for August 15. The Collect echoes Mary's Magnificat. God looked "on the lowliness of the Blessed Virgin Mary, / [and] raised her to this grace." We pray that, with the help of her prayers, we, too, may be saved and "exalted . . . on high." The sacrifice we offer today is "the sacrifice of conciliation and praise." We pray that we may both know God's "pardon" and rejoice "in perpetual thanksgiving" (Prayer over the Offerings). The Prayer after Communion is a simple prayer for protection as we honor Mary's Assumption into heaven. Consider using Eucharistic Prayer III. The Solemn Blessing of the Blessed Virgin Mary may be used.

The Roman Missal: Mass during the Day

Mary has gone "body and soul into heavenly glory." We pray that we may keep our eyes fixed where she has gone, "attentive to the things that are above," and come one day to share her glory (Collect). Through Mary's intercession, we pray that our hearts may be "aflame with the fire of love" and longing for God (Prayer over the Offerings). God would not allow decay to touch Mary's body, because from her body Christ, "the Author of all life," was born. In Mary's Assumption, we glimpse our own destiny—"the beginning and image / of your Church's coming to perfection / and a sign of sure hope and comfort to your pilgrim people" (Preface). We ask Mary's intercession, that "we may be brought to the glory of the resurrection" (Prayer after Communion). The Solemnity of the Assumption flows from the Resurrection of Christ, in which Mary already shares, body and soul. The Gloria and the Creed are said or sung today. Consider using Eucharistic Prayer III. Of course use festive music with full choir, banners in the entrance procession, incense, and a longer, more formal Gospel procession.

Other Ideas

As the universal Church celebrates this solemnity of Mary there are a number of ways for individuals to honor Mary in her role as Mother of God and Mother of the Church. Her Assumption into heaven, known as her Dormition (falling asleep) in the Eastern Church, recognizes her singular relationship with Christ. Both individuals and families could recite the Rosary sometime today. The Glorious Mysteries, with the fourth being the Assumption, are used. If there is a Marian shrine in your parish church then gather there for the Rosary. If you are able to visit someone from the parish who is in a hospital, or who is in a health care residence, then they might very well appreciate praying with you. You can find short meditations on the mysteries by going online and searching under "Mysteries of the Rosary."

FRI 16 (#417) green
Weekday

Optional Memorial of St. Stephen of Hungary / white

The Lectionary for Mass

◆ FIRST READING: Today and tomorrow the First Reading comes from the final chapter of the Book of Joshua. Joshua is already advanced in age and nearing death as he speaks to the tribes of Israel at Shechem. In today's passage, Joshua recounts the Lord's saving history and how the Lord has worked through the ancestors in faith whom he appointed to lead them. The passage concludes with Joshua reminding the people how the Lord gave them undeveloped land and cities and they have eaten of vineyards and olive trees they themselves did not root down.

◆ RESPONSORIAL PSALM 136: The refrain in which we acclaim the eternal endurance of the Lord's mercy repeats after every line in the psalm. The people originally could have repeated this refrain antiphonally, much as we do today. There is a joyful energy, momentum, and rhythm to this psalm that we can capture as we acclaim God's saving deeds that continue to this day and will do so forever.

◆ GOSPEL: The Pharisees attempt to put Jesus to the test by asking him a question about the legality of a man divorcing his wife regardless of the reason. Jesus, however, does not fall into their trap of wanting him to take sides on the issue of divorce. In response, he cites Genesis in order to show the Pharisees what they do not know but they really should. God joins people together in relationships, but sometimes our hard and stubborn hearts get in the way. We are human and, therefore, always in need of God's mercy, especially when our relationships fall short of the ideal standard of the heavenly Kingdom.

Today's Saint

St. Stephen (+ 1038) is thought of as the founder of the kingdom of Hungary, was its first king, and established Christianity there. According to legend, he was baptized by St. Adalbert of Prague. Hungarians believe that Pope Silvester II sent Stephen a jeweled gold crown, along with a letter recognizing him as king. This crown is venerated by the people

of Hungary, although the Crown of St. Stephen that we have today probably dates from the twelfth century. St. Stephen discouraged the practice of pagan customs, brought priests in to serve as missionaries, and founded several dioceses. He had hoped to retire and lead a life of prayer and contemplation after handing the kingdom to his son, Emeric, but Emeric died young, breaking his father's heart. Stephen ruled until his death in 1038 on August 15, the celebration of the Assumption of the Blessed Virgin Mary. As he died, he asked Mary to look after the people of Hungary as their queen. Stephen was the first canonized "confessor king," a new category, and is venerated as the patron saint of Hungary. He is also the patron saint of kings, masons, and children who are dying.

SAT 17 (#418) green Weekday

Optional Memorial of the Blessed Virgin Mary / white

The Lectionary for Mass

◆ FIRST READING: In today's First Reading, Joshua continues his speech to the tribes of Israel at Shechem. Joshua lays before the people and their leaders a choice: will they and their households serve the Lord or will they choose to serve other gods? This is our choice as well as it was theirs. Will we remember how God acts to reveal his love to us day after day and year after year? Will we enter into covenant with God as Joshua did with the people that day before he died a youthful one hundred and ten years old?

◆ RESPONSORIAL PSALM 16 follows up the ritualization of the covenant Joshua made with the people as they agreed to follow the Lord. The psalmist prays to the Lord to keep him safe. He recognizes the guidance the Lord will give him for his life. He chooses, as the tribes of

Israel did in the First Reading to acknowledge the Lord as his "inheritance" (Psalm 16:5a) over other gods.

◆ GOSPEL: In today's brief, three-verse passage from the following chapter in Matthew, we find people bringing children to Jesus so that he might lay hands on them and pray with them. The disciples obviously missed the point of Jesus' teaching the first time, because they reprimanded him. In response, Jesus simply repeats a second time that the heavenly Kingdom belongs to those like children. Perchance the disciples needed to grow in their own humility.

☀ 18 (#120C) green Twentieth Sunday in Ordinary Time

The Lectionary for Mass

◆ FIRST READING: Princes who were unhappy with the prophet Jeremiah's teaching throw him in the cistern after King Zedekiah relinquishes any power he had and informs the princes that they have control over the prophet. Jeremiah would certainly have faced death as he sank deeper and deeper in the cistern's mud. But a court official pleads with the king to allow him to remove the prophet from the cistern before he dies of hunger. We do not know why, but Zedekiah ordered the prophet's rescue from sure death.

◆ RESPONSORIAL PSALM 40: The theme of rescue from destruction found in Psalm 40 directly links to the rescue of Jeremiah from the cistern in the First Reading. In the refrain, we cry out for the Lord to come to our aid. In the first stanza (40:2), we wait with the psalmist for the Lord to come. The second stanza describes how the Lord rescues the psalmist (40:3), while the third and fourth stanzas (40:4 and 18) reflect the psalmist's response of thanksgiving and faith for his rescue. We, too, sing a new song for the times God rescues us!

◆ SECOND READING: The journey of faith might be long and arduous, but the author of Hebrews reminds us that we have a great "cloud of witnesses" who have gone before us. We need only let their perseverance buoy us when we struggle to continue. Moreover, Jesus provides us the example par excellence of continuing the journey. He endured the suffering of the Cross because he trusted in the joy that lay ahead. Think of the joy that will be ours when we resist sin with all our might.

◆ GOSPEL: The intensity of Jesus' teaching to his disciples increases as he tells them he has come to set the earth on fire. His death will do this, for people will come to see that his death is not the end of the story. He follows this teaching with a question to the disciples about whether or not he has come to bring peace. One would think the disciples would be a little leery to respond to this question, even though it is a rhetorical one. Perhaps they already thought no would be the correct answer, which it is. Jesus does respond to his own question and elaborates on how divisions will occur within households based on his teaching—a teaching that turns worldly wisdom upside down and offers a seismic paradigm shift away from ordinary human wisdom.

The Roman Missal

The Gloria and the Creed are sung or said today. The Collect speaks to the need to keep God as the highest priority in our lives as it asks that we might love him "in all things and above all things." Ultimately, it is God alone who can fulfill us since what he promises surpasses every human desire. The Prayer over the Offerings reminds us once again that the celebration of the Eucharist is a "glorious exchange"—we offer what God has first given to us, and, in receiving those offerings back, we receive God's very self. The Prayer after Communion expresses how partaking of the Eucharist transforms us now as it conforms us to Christ's image on earth, and then goes on to ask that "we may merit also to be his coheirs in heaven." The transformation begun through sacramental communion reaches its fulfillment in union with Christ in heaven. Consider using Eucharistic Prayer IV today; use of this prayer means you also must use its proper Preface, not one of the Prefaces of Sundays in Ordinary Time.

Other Ideas

As the summer draws to a close many parishioners, including those in various ministries will return home from their travels. Consider a "welcome back to ministry" gathering. This might take the form of an evening reflection and some social time to renew acquaintances and enthusiasm for their respective ministries. There are several blessings that would be appropriate for this gathering; see the *Book of Blessings*, Part VI. The Order of Blessing those who Exercise Pastoral Service (BB, chapter 60) works well as a general blessing for everyone in ministry. On a Sunday later in September consider some form of recognition for each liturgical ministry. Schedule a "ministry fair" so parishioners can meet those in ministry and have an opportunity to sign up for a particular ministry.

MON 19 (#419) green
Weekday

Optional Memorial of St. John Eudes, Priest / white

The Lectionary for Mass

◆ FIRST READING: Unfaithfulness took root in the children of Israel as they turned to worship other gods rather than the God of their ancestors. In our First Reading from Judges 2, we hear how the people suffered consequences for their infidelity at the hands of the Lord as he had warned them. Even the judges whom the Lord brought before the people could not turn them from their idol worship.

◆ RESPONSORIAL PSALM 106: The Responsorial Psalm is taken from the latter portion of Psalm 106 in which the psalmist recounts how the Lord's people became entrapped in their service to idol gods. Time after time, the Lord extended mercy to his people, and yet often they sinned again. The psalm refrain comes from much earlier in the hymn (see Psalm 106:4a) and expresses the people's prayer to the Lord to remember them for they know deeply in their hearts that God will never abandon them despite their sin.

◆ GOSPEL: Life in Jesus comes from not only following the commandments, but from giving of one's entire being to follow Jesus. It comes from living as a disciple in relation to others, especially the poor. It means following Jesus without bringing along the material possessions we have. The young man in today's Gospel hears Jesus respond to his question about what he must do to gain eternal life with these requirements. It was not the answer this young man with many worldly possessions wanted to hear.

Today's Saint

St. John Eudes (1601–1680), a successful preacher in France, cared for plague victims on both a physical and spiritual level. In light of the Protestant Reformation, he felt that the academic and spiritual training of priests needed to be strengthened; therefore, he established a society of diocesan priests: the Congregation of Jesus and Mary, commonly called the Eudists. Their sole purpose was directed toward the foundation of new seminaries where future priests would be equipped with the necessary tools to respond pastorally to the turbulent times. He eventually established a religious community of women, the Congregation of Our Lady of Charity of the Refuge, dedicated to the rehabilitation of prostitutes.

(#420) white
TUE 20 Memorial of St. Bernard, Abbot and Doctor of the Church

The Lectionary for Mass

◆ FIRST READING: The Lord calls Gideon, the least in his family which itself is in the lowest class of families in Manasseh, to lead Israel from out of the oppression they suffer at the hands of the Midians. Gideon does not know how he will be able to achieve this, yet he wants to have confidence in the Lord's call so he asks for a sign. The Lord appears in a fire that comes from a rock. Fire, a traditional sign of the Lord's presence, reveals the authenticity of the Lord's presence in the angel who spoke to him.

◆ RESPONSORIAL PSALM 85: The verses taken from this psalm of lament express confidence that the Lord will bring justice and peace to his people. The psalmist attests that he will hear God's proclamation of peace, much as Gideon in accepting the Lord's call trusted that the Lord would prevail over the Midians. When we sing the refrain, we too, acknowledge the peace the Lord speaks of to us.

◆ GOSPEL: The disciples are again perplexed as they hear Jesus solemnly teach them how difficult it will be for someone who is rich to enter the Kingdom of heaven. One might think after the disciples have already heard Jesus reverse worldly wisdom multiple times, that now they would not react with astonishment. They have yet to fully grasp that it is God who saves. There is nothing they or we can do to merit a place in the heavenly Kingdom.

The Roman Missal

All three of the orations are proper for today, found in the Proper of Saints at August 20. The Collect describes St. Bernard with bright and energetic terms such as "zeal for your house," "a light shining and burning in your Church" and asks that "we may be on fire with the same spirit / and walk always as children of the light." Such phrases point to the remarkable influence St. Bernard had on the people of his time. The Prayer over the Offerings continues to extol St. Bernard as a role model as it refers to him as "a man outstanding in word and deed, who strove to bring order and concord to your Church." Such concord is appropriate in this prayer as it names the sacrament we offer at this celebration as "the Sacrament of unity and peace." We can never forget that unity, concord, and peace must be the fruits that result from Eucharistic celebration. The Prayer after Communion prays that the Eucharist we receive truly have an effect on our life. Preface I or II of Saints or the Preface of Holy Virgins and Religious are appropriate choices today. Consider using the Eucharistic Prayer for Reconciliation II.

Today's Saint

St. Bernard (1090–1153) joined the Cistercian Abbey at Cîteaux, known for its strict and austere way of life. Within a short time he was noticed for his leadership; hence, he was appointed abbot of a new monastery at Clairvaux. His monastic vision at Clairvaux led to the foundation of several monasteries throughout France, Britain, and Ireland. In solitude he wrote numerous theological and spiritual classics, including his treatise *On Loving God*, eighty-six sermons on the Song of Songs, and a major work *On Consideration*, a reflection on papal spirituality. St. Bernard had a special devotion to Mary, earning him the titles "Our Lady's faithful chaplain" and "Mary's harper." Due to his abundant writing and influence upon the Church, he was declared a Doctor of the Church.

(#421) white
WED 21 Memorial of St. Pius X, Pope

The Lectionary for Mass

◆ FIRST READING: The citizens of Shechem and Beth-millo appoint Abimelech king, but Jotham, the youngest son of Jerubaal, took issue with the appointment of his brother. Jotham address the people from the top of Mount Gerizim. He disputes the appointment of his brother in a metaphorical and personified conversation in which a variety of trees ask another tree to reign. The point of the passage: the Lord can truly reign over his people.

◆ RESPONSORIAL PSALM 21: In this royal psalm, the psalmist communicates to us how the people's king finds his strength only in the Lord. The king, commissioned by the Lord through the rituals of crowning and anointing, serves the people in the Lord's name. Any victories he brings, are the Lord's victories and the king's joy reflects the Lord's own gladness.

◆ GOSPEL: In another parable about the Kingdom of heaven, Jesus teaches his disciples that God's generosity reverses the way of the world's generosity. Hourly pay is not the standard for God. Generosity is. Just as the landowner's workers are paid beginning with those who started the latest in the day and ending with those who started the earliest, so the last will be first and the first, last in the Kingdom. How difficult it is for us to grasp the equality of God's generosity!

The Roman Missal

Texts for today can be found at August 21. The Collect acknowledges the saint's desire to "restore all things in Christ" as it recognizes his intelligence and great accomplishments. The Prayer over the Offerings reminds us of the reverence with which we must always celebrate the divine mysteries, and the Prayer after Communion asks that "the power of this heavenly table" may make us "constant in the faith." The Preface of Holy Pastors would be a good choice for today since St. Pius X was a pope. You may also use the prayers found in the Common of Pastors: For a Pope. Consider using the Eucharistic Prayer for Various Needs and Occasions I.

Today's Saint

St. Pius X (1835–1914) was born Giuseppe Sarto in Riese, Italy. He grew up poor but was able to attend seminary on a scholarship. As pope he was a reformer but at the same time conservative in matters of theology. He published the first Code of Canon Law, which gathered the laws of the Church into one volume. His early pastoral experience influenced him to encourage frequent reception of Communion, his lasting legacy. He reformed the liturgy, especially the breviary (Liturgy of the Hours) and encouraged the use of Gregorian chant, replacing

the ornate Baroque and Classical compositions that were commonly used. Pius X lowered the age of reason from twelve to seven, making it possible for younger children to receive the Eucharist. It is said that the onset of World War I caused him so much distress that he died in 1914, as the war began. Pius X is a patron saint of first communicants for his role in lowering the age of first Holy Communion.

(#422) white

THU 22 Memorial of the Queenship of the Blessed Virgin Mary

About Today's Memorial

Today's Memorial of the Queenship of the Blessed Virgin Mary is a relatively new one on the Catholic calendar, established by Pope Pius XII in 1954. But its roots reach deep into our Catholic tradition. The early Church Fathers recognized that the Mother of Christ, the King, is herself a Queen. Through the centuries, artists have loved to paint the humble Virgin crowned by the Holy Trinity amid the glories of heaven. In the Litany of Loreto, we call upon Mary as Queen of angels, Queen of all saints, Queen conceived without sin, Queen assumed into heaven, Queen of the Rosary, Queen of peace. Mary is our Queen, but she is also our Mother. And in the words of St. Thérèse, the Little Flower, "She is more Mother than Queen."

The Lectionary for Mass

◆ FIRST READING: The Lord blesses Jephthah with the Spirit so that he might fight against the Ammonites and achieve victory through the Lord's power. Before going to battle, Jephthah promised to the Lord that should he defeat the Ammonites, upon his return he would offer whoever came through the door of his house to the Lord. Jephthah's daughter and only child is the first to greet him when he arrived victorious. Her own faith-

fulness to the Lord reinforces her father's commitment to follow through on his vow.

◆ RESPONSORIAL PSALM 40: The refrain for today's Responsorial Psalm emphasizes the response of a faithful servant to the Lord's call. In the words of the psalmist, we present ourselves to the Lord to do the Lord's will. We take delight in the Lord for we know how the Lord's true desire is our faithfulness, rather than burnt or sin offerings.

◆ GOSPEL: We move ahead to chapter 22 in a semicontinuous reading of Matthew's account of the Gospel. We find Jesus—already in Jerusalem and having cleansed the Temple and spoken a few other parables which have led the chief priests and elders to question his authority—set to teach the about who are welcome at God's feast in the Kingdom of heaven. The implication of the parable of the wedding feast that those who come clothed in inappropriate attire God will surely not be welcome in the Kingdom will not sit well with the authorities. They are invited to the banquet, but will they be chosen?

The Roman Missal

All the orations for this obligatory memorial are proper for today and are located in the Proper of Saints at August 22. The Collect acknowledges the Blessed Virgin Mary as our Mother and our Queen. The Prayer over the Offerings makes explicit the connection between the offering we make and Christ's offering on the Cross, while the Prayer after Communion points to eschatological fulfillment as it asks that through this Eucharist we "may merit to be partakers at your eternal banquet." The Preface is one of the two Prefaces of the Blessed Virgin Mary; if Preface I is used, the correct phrase to use is "on the feast day." Consider using Eucharistic Prayer II.

FRI 23 (#423) green
Weekday

Optional Memorial of St. Rose of Lima, Virgin / white

The Lectionary for Mass

◆ FIRST READING: The story of Ruth and Naomi from the time of the judges when there was a famine in the land demonstrates the bond of faithfulness between God's people and their God. Ruth responds to Naomi's request for her to follow her sister-in-law back to her people and god in a beautiful, poetic statement of faith. Ruth will remain with Naomi and take Ruth's people and God as her own.

◆ RESPONSORIAL PSALM 146: The psalmist, like Ruth, knows that the God of Jacob and the other ancestors in faith, is the only God who is faithful to his people. The true God who upholds the blind, the stranger, the fatherless, and the widow is the God deserving of our praise. From the depths of our soul, we praise the Lord for we cannot support one another without him.

◆ GOSPEL: As we skip forward in Matthew 22, today's Gospel begins by noting how Jesus silenced the Sadducees. Jesus left the Sadducees speechless when he responded to them about their ill-intentioned question about to whom of the seven brothers will a woman be married at the resurrection. One of the Pharisees—even knowing Jesus had quieted the Sadducees—still dares to ask him to identify the greatest commandment. Love of God and love of neighbor are the two greatest commandments. No separation exists between the two. This presents an obstacle for those who pretend to be people of faith like the Pharisees.

Today's Saint

During St. Rose of Lima's (1586–1617) brief life, people noticed her physical beauty, declaring her *como una rosa* ("like a rose"), but the beauty of her soul far surpassed her physical appearance. St. Rose longed to live solely for God, so she renounced the institution of Marriage by claiming Christ as her spouse. Basing her life upon St. Catherine of Siena, she lived a penitential life, setting up an infirmary in the family home to care for impoverished children and the sick. She gained popularity due to her selfless service to the needy. As the first canonized saint of the Americas, she is the patron saint of South and Central America, the Philippines, and the West Indies.

SAT 24 (#629) red
Feast of St. Bartholomew, Apostle

The Lectionary for Mass

◆ FIRST READING: In a vision of Jerusalem, the heavenly city, an angel reveals to John that the names of the Twelve Apostles of the Lamb are inscribed on the foundational stones of the city's wall. The Twelve Apostles stand in line with the twelve tribes of the children of Israel whose names are also on the wall. Much of the imagery from this passage has its roots in the latter chapters of Ezekiel where the prophet puts the Lord's vision for a new Israel.

◆ RESPONSORIAL PSALM 145: The verses from the middle of Psalm 145 focus on how the works of the Lord show forth the Lord's kingship. Those who are the Lord's friends make known the wonders of his enduring Kingdom. We are among those, like the Apostles in Jesus' time, who join our voices to proclaim the Lord's kingdom throughout the earth.

◆ GOSPEL: Duplicity would be the fault of the scribes and Pharisees, and Israel throughout its history had also struggled with this sin, but not so for Nathanael. Jesus knew this from the first time when he saw him under the fig tree. In Jesus' time the fig tree stood as a symbol of peace the Messiah would bring. Nathanael confirms Jesus' statement about him in his confession of Jesus as the Son of God and King of Israel.

The Roman Missal

The prayers for the feast are found in the Proper of Saints. The Gloria is said or sung today. The Preface of the Apostles is used. We pray that God may strengthen us in the faith to which the Apostle Bartholomew "clung wholeheartedly" (Collect) and that through his prayers we may know God's help (Prayer over the Offerings). Consider using Eucharistic Prayer I.

Today's Saint

Not much is known about St. Bartholomew (first century) other than the fact that he was one of the Twelve Apostles. He is also mentioned in the Acts of the Apostles as one of the disciples waiting for the descent of the Holy Spirit. According to a second-century Alexandrian teacher Pantaenus, an early Christian community in India claims St. Bartholomew as its founder. Tradition states that he preached throughout Persia, Mesopotamia, Lycaonia, and Phrygia. It is believed that he was skinned alive and beheaded at Albanopolis, on the west coast of the Caspian Sea. He is patron saint of tanners due to the loss of his skin during his martyrdom.

(#123C) green

☀ 25 Twenty-First Sunday in Ordinary Time

The Liturgy of the Word

◆ FIRST READING: Today's passage from a few verses later in the same and final chapter of Isaiah speaks of God gathering the nations from distant lands together on his holy mountain in Jerusalem. All will acclaim the Lord's glory and live together in the Lord's house where the Lord will care for them as a mother cares for her children.

◆ RESPONSORIAL PSALM 117: In light of today's First Reading, the refrain from Jesus' great commission to the remaining eleven disciples coincides with the journey of the nations to Jerusalem in the First Reading. All shall know the glory of the Lord! Let our praise in the two verses of the briefest of the hymns in the psalter be heard throughout our assemblies and beyond.

◆ SECOND READING: Using a citation with Old Testament roots in Deuteronomy and Proverbs, the author of Hebrews encourages his audience to remain firm in their commitment to the way of faith. Christians are to take the Lord's discipline as a sign of his fatherly love for them. In the end, an unwavering commitment of faith in word and in deed will lead one to share in the peace righteousness brings.

◆ GOSPEL: An unidentified person whom Jesus met as he journeyed to Jerusalem asked him the question that many today still wonder about: Will only a few people be saved? As is often the case, Jesus responds indirectly with a short metaphorical statement and parable. From the first, we learn that many will attempt to enter through the narrow gate, but will not have enough strength to do so. From the second, we learn that our actions toward others matter in relation to our future. Will we chose to be first or last according to Jesus' wisdom?

The Roman Missal

The Gloria and the Creed are sung or said. The Collect asks that we might love what God commands and desire what God promises. The Prayer over the Offerings reminds us that we have been gathered by God to become one people "through the one sacrifice offered once for all," and therefore we pray for "the gifts of unity and peace in your Church." The Prayer after Communion asks for completion of the works of God's mercy, thereby implying that those works have begun in our sacramental communion. Preface I of the Sundays in Ordinary Time describes how we have been summoned "to the glory of being now called / a chosen race, a royal priesthood, a holy nation, a people for your own possession, to proclaim everywhere your mighty works"; this would certainly pick up on a theme heard in the Prayer over the Offerings. Similarly, so would Preface VIII, which speaks about the people gathered and formed as one, made the Body of Christ, and now manifest as the Church. One of those two Prefaces might be a good choice for today. Consider using Eucharistic Prayer II.

Other Ideas

Most parochial schools will begin another academic year this coming week. This weekend is a good time to offer a blessing to students, teachers, catechists, and those in administrative positions. All these folks make a great contribution to the education of young people and they should know that the whole community prays for them and supports them. The *Book of Blessings* includes a blessing for catechists (BB, chapter 4), and one for the blessing of teachers and students (BB, chapter 5). Representatives from the parish school could be present at each Sunday liturgy to offer a few words of appreciation to the whole parish for their ongoing support. Remember to include all the students and volunteer catechists who are responsible for the faith formation classes.

MON 26 (#425) green Weekday

The Lectionary for Mass

◆ FIRST READING: The greeting and thanksgiving from the opening chapter of the earliest of Paul's letters emphasizes the enduring faith of the Thessalonians. Their conversion to "the living and true God" of Jesus Christ remains a lasting example for others. As we continue to await the Second Coming of God's Son, we buoy our faith with the example of the Christian community at Thessalonica.

◆ RESPONSORIAL PSALM 149: A hymn of praise invites us to celebrate with joy how the Lord delights in his people. With song and dance the people praise the Lord. With a myriad of instruments, the assembly makes a joyful noise to the Lord. May we glory in the Lord's name as the Lord glories in the faithful.

◆ GOSPEL: Jesus instructed his disciples and the crowds to heed the commandments of Moses as the Pharisees do, but not to follow their example (see Matthew 23:4). His instruction precedes seven woes addressed directly to the scribes and Pharisees, three of which we find in today's Gospel. The scribes and Pharisees are like "blind guides" attempting to lead people with their inconsistency and hypocrisy.

TUE 27 (#426) white
Memorial of St. Monica

The Lectionary for Mass

◆ FIRST READING: Paul and his companions shared with the Thessalonians the Gospel and their very own being as they grew in relationship and love for God's people at Thessalonica. Even though they were Apostles, Paul and those who accompanied him were neither arrogant nor intimidating. They cared for the Thessalonians with the gentleness of a mother. Their example of missionary work shows us how we can proclaim the Gospel to those who need to hear its Word of Life today.

◆ RESPONSORIAL PSALM 139: The psalmist addresses God about God's profound and intimate knowledge of him. God knows the psalmist inside and out—the steps the psalmist will take on his journey of faith and the words he will speak. Such was God's knowledge of Paul. Such is God's knowledge of all those of us who speak the Gospel in God's name. How wonderfully freeing is his omniscience.

◆ GOSPEL: Today's Gospel covers Jesus' fourth and fifth woes to the scribes and Pharisees. In both, Jesus chastises them for paying attention to outward deeds of the law—tithing and cleansing—while neglecting the inward deeds—judgment, mercy, and faithfulness—and cleansing the heart of selfish pleasures. Until they

change their ways, Jesus' description of the scribes and Pharisees as "blind guides" remains accurate.

The Roman Missal

The proper Collect for today, found in the Proper of Saints at August 27, describes St. Monica as one who wept "motherly tears . . . for the conversion of her son Augustine." The Prayer over the Offerings and the Prayer after Communion are taken from the Common of Holy Men and Women: For Holy Women, and either Preface I or Preface II of Saints is the Preface to be used for today. Consider using Eucharistic Prayer II.

Today's Saint

St. Monica (c. 331–387) knew the pain of disappointment, an unfaithful husband named Patricius who drank too much, and a promiscuous son, St. Augustine of Hippo, who lived an immoral youth. Through patience and love, her husband had a change of heart, choosing to become a Christian. St. Augustine's conversion was a much more difficult task. St. Monica prayed constantly and fasted daily, but nothing seemed to work, so she consulted St. Ambrose, bishop of Milan, for guidance. Through the intervention of God the two of them managed to lead St. Augustine to the waters of Baptism. St. Monica exemplifies that unconditional love and persistence are portals for God's saving grace.

WED 28 (#427) white
Memorial of St. Augustine, Bishop and Doctor of the Church

The Lectionary for Mass

◆ FIRST READING: As read continuously from 1 Thessalonians 2, we hear Paul reflecting to the Christian community how tirelessly he and his companions worked so they did not need to burden the

community by having to provide for them. In today's passage, Paul reminds the Thessalonians how fatherly he treated them after noting yesterday how his ministry was characterized with the gentleness of a mother. His fatherly encouragement intended to help lead the Thessalonians toward God and his "Kingdom," a term infrequently used in the Pauline epistles.

◆ RESPONSORIAL PSALM 139: Today's Responsorial Psalm is a continuous reading from Psalm 139 from yesterday. The refrain remains the same. Verse 7 begins the first stanza and poses two questions about where the psalmist can go and not be in the presence of God and his Spirit. The remaining verses contain many conditional statements in which the psalmist places himself in different locations, yet still knows the Lord accompanies him and knows him.

◆ GOSPEL: The final two of the seven woes Jesus addresses to the scribes and Pharisees compose today's Gospel reading. In these woes, Jesus continues to focus his rebuke on the hypocrisy of the scribes and the Pharisees. Their outward and inward selves do not correspond to each other. They might appear beautiful on the outside, but inside they are dead. And, though the hypocritical scribes and Pharisees have built lavish tombs to honor the prophets, they themselves actually bear a resemblance to those who killed the prophets. One is left wondering whether seven woes will be enough for the scribes and Pharisees to understand Jesus' point and realign their outward and inward selves.

The Roman Missal

The Prayer over the Offerings and the Prayer after Communion are all proper for today, located at August 28. In the Collect we pray for the same spirit as that which inspired St. Augustine to thirst for "the sole fount of true wisdom." The Prayer over the Offerings prays that this Eucharist may be for us "the sign of unity / and the bond of charity"; we can recall how that was a major theme of St. Augustine's preaching about the Eucharist. The Prayer after Communion echoes Augustinian preaching on the Eucharist once again as it asks that "being made members of his Body, / we may become what we have received." The Preface of Holy Pastors would be a most apt choice for today, although either Preface I or II of Saints would be acceptable. Consider using Eucharistic Prayer II.

Today's Saint

St. Augustine of Hippo (354–430) is one of the four great Latin Fathers of the Church. Augustine was born in North Africa in present-day Algeria. His mother was St. Monica and his father, Patricius, a pagan. Augustine showed early promise as a scholar, but he disappointed his mother by espousing Manicheism (gnostic religion) and leading a hedonistic life (a life devoted solely to pleasure), even living with a mistress with whom he had a child. Eventually, due to Monica's prayers, he decided to become a Christian and was baptized by St. Ambrose in Milan. He became a priest and, later, the bishop of Hippo. Augustine was a prolific writer and is credited with writing one of the first autobiographies, his *Confessions*. His books, homilies, and letters are a rich source of theological insight still mined today by students of every Christian denomination or ecclesial community.

(#428; #634, Gospel) red

THU 29 Memorial of the Passion of St. John the Baptist

About Today's Memorial

"I tell you, among those born of women, no one is greater than John," Jesus told the crowds (Luke 7:28). John the Baptist, the forerunner, came to prepare the way of the Lord, and he did that from the first moments of his life. In his mother's womb, he leapt for joy at the nearness of the Lord. He preached repentance to the people, preparing them for the coming of the Kingdom, and baptizing them with water so that they might be prepared to receive baptism "with the Holy Spirit and with fire." Even in his death, John prepared the way for the Lord. He boldly told Herod that he was violating the Law in taking his brother's widow as his wife, and Herod had him arrested and imprisoned and then executed. Even in his martyrdom, he prepared the way of the Lord, pointing to the way of the Cross.

The Lectionary for Mass

◆ FIRST READING: Paul vacillates between feeling joy for the Thessalonians because of their faith and worry for them because of the struggles they will face. His prayer to see the Thessalonians in person never ceases. Paul's lengthy thanksgiving finally concludes with his request of God to unite the Apostle and his missionary team with the Thessalonians to strengthen them in the interim before Jesus comes again.

◆ RESPONSORIAL PSALM 90: Despite the struggles the community faces, the people still turn to the Lord and pray for the Lord to fill them with his love. The people want to do the Lord's work. They want to align the way they live each

day with the Lord. They want to sing for joy! Would that our prayer as the Lord's people be similar.

◆ GOSPEL: Today we hear Mark's account of the death of John the Baptist. Herod had mixed reactions toward John the Baptist. The king feared John because he was righteous, but Herod also found himself both curious and confused at John's words. The king's fear and confusion got the better of him as he fulfills the wish of Herodias' daughter to receive the head of John the Baptist as her birthday gift. In a prelude to how Joseph of Arimathea would care for Jesus' body, John's disciples tend to his body.

The Roman Missal

The texts for the memorial are to be found in the Proper of Saints at August 29. The Collect reminds us that St. John the Baptist was a forerunner (precursor) of the Lord not only in his birth, but also in his death. We pray in this prayer that "we, too, may fight hard / for the confession" of what God teaches. The Prayer over the Offerings employs imagery and phrases closely associated with the Baptist ("make straight your paths"; "that voice crying in the desert") in the way it asks that the offerings have an effect in our lives. The text for the Preface, "The mission of the Precursor," is given along with the other texts for this Mass, and it is the same Preface as used on the Nativity of St. John the Baptist in June (the text with music can be found there if the Preface is to be sung). The Prayer after Communion prays that we recognize both what the sacrament signifies and what it effects in us. Consider using Eucharistic Prayer I.

FRI 30 (#429) green
Weekday

The Lectionary for Mass

◆ FIRST READING: Paul teaches the Thessalonians that God calls them to holiness in their relationships. Immorality holds no place in the life of one who follows the will of God. For people of faith, the connection between honoring a human being and honor God could not be stronger.

◆ RESPONSORIAL PSALM 97: The third stanza, which is the single verse from Psalm 97:10, provides an obvious connection to the First Reading. In this verse, the psalmist speaks of how God's loves those who despise evil and protects the faithful. In the other verses from this hymn, we acclaim the Lord as king who rules over all. Justice characterizes the Lord and those who follow him.

◆ GOSPEL: As we progress to Chapter 25 in Matthew, the parables begin to focus more on the disciples' preparation for the end times and the Lord's coming in judgment. Our consideration today turns to Jesus' parable about the ten virgins—five foolish and five wise. We are left to ponder our own readiness for the unknown day and hour when the Lord will come. Will he count us among the wise he knows or the foolish he does not recognize?

SAT 31 (#430) green
Weekday

Optional Memorial of the Blessed Virgin Mary / white

The Lectionary for Mass

◆ FIRST READING: We can always do more to deepen the love we have for one another, for God himself has taught us how to love. Progressing in the life of faith means progressing in our love for one another. The way we care for others in love and charity should characterize the way we live in the time before Christ returns.

◆ RESPONSORIAL PSALM 98: Today's refrain from Psalm 98:9 affirms our belief that the Lord comes to govern with justice. The verses attests to the new song we sing together with all of creation for the marvels the Lord has done and the justice and equity with which the Lord rules.

◆ GOSPEL: Like the parable of the ten virgins Jesus told his disciples in yesterday's Gospel reading, today's parable of the talents leaves us to contemplate a similar question. Will the Lord find us to be good and faithful servants or will he find us among the lazy servants? Surely, as his disciples we would hope that he would extend an invitation to us to share in the master's joy. As his disciples, then, we learn from the parable of the talents, that he expects much of us in our earthly life as we accept our responsibility to proclaim the nearness of God's Kingdom and our hope that it is still yet to come.

September 2019
Month of Our Lady of Sorrows

(#126C) green
1 Twenty-Second Sunday in Ordinary Time

The Lectionary for Mass

◆ FIRST READING: We might think of today's readings as consisting of several independent sayings. The first is concerned with humility. Sirach's wisdom is rooted in life experience: no one likes to be around an arrogant person who is into self-exaltation. Verse 20 has to do with knowing one's place in the larger scheme of things and coming to a sense of awe, mystery, and humble reverence. Verse 27 encourages an active search for wisdom with the help of sages and proverbs. Verse 29 makes an interesting parallel between water putting out a fire and almsgiving atoning for sin.

◆ RESPONSORIAL PSALM 68: Today's antiphon with its focus on the poor picks up on the last line of the First Reading (alms). Psalm 68 is a hymn of praise (see the first stanza of today's response). The second stanza focuses on God's providential care for the poor. The "needy" of the last stanza refers to all God's people ("your flock").

◆ SECOND READING: Today's text from Hebrews contrasts Israel's experience of God on Mount Sinai with our experience of God on Mount Zion in the heavenly Jerusalem (now). The reading invites us to think about when and how we approach the heavenly Mount Zion. Take note of all those gathered there with God and Jesus.

◆ GOSPEL: Today's First Reading and Gospel are nice complements to one another: the warning against self-exaltation, the exhortation to concern for the poor, and the mention of seeking wisdom through the advice of the Wise Person (Jesus). The reference to the resurrection of the righteous provides a nice link to the Second Reading, specifically, to God the judge and the spirits of the just (righteous). Jesus is very clear on what is expected of those who want to enter into the new covenant and be counted among the righteous.

The Roman Missal

The Gloria and the Creed are sung or said today. The Collect reminds us of our absolute dependence on God as we turn to him beseeching that he "nurture in us what is good" and keep safe what he has nurtured; thus are we reminded of the constant care God offers us. The Prayer over the Offerings in effect points to the sacramental principle and the efficacy of symbols in liturgical celebration as it asks that this offering may "accomplish in power . . . what it celebrates in mystery." The Prayer after Communion calls the Eucharist "the food of charity," thus reminding us that the Eucharist should bear fruit in us by stirring us up to serve God in our neighbor. Consider using Eucharistic Prayer III.

Other Ideas

This Labor Day weekend we can reflect on and give thanks for "the work of human hands," to borrow a phrase from the liturgy. In fact

the word *liturgy* comes from two ancient words that mean "the work of the people." Consider the works of the many people that are needed to make the liturgy possible: the authors who wrote the prayers, the composers who give us music, the writers who recorded the Word of God, the book binders, the artists who inscribed the Lectionary and the Missal, the furniture makers and candle makers, the farmers who planted and harvested the grain, and the vine growers who crushed the grapes. The list goes on and on. And then there are all the liturgical ministers whose gifts shape the work they do and the holy work of the whole assembly! Give thanks today for the work of human hands.

M O N 2 (#431) green
Weekday

Proper Mass for Labor Day

The Lectionary for Mass

◆ FIRST READING: Today's text addresses the sorrow and grief the Thessalonians experience at the death of their loved ones. They are assured that they and their loved ones will be together again with the Lord when he comes in glory.

◆ RESPONSORIAL PSALM 96: Once again, the theme of the Lord's judgment is heard in the Responsorial Psalm. The Lord will come as judge. All creation rejoices in his presence.

◆ GOSPEL: This text is a sort of programmatic statement for the whole of Jesus' ministry and teaching. Empowered by God's spirit, he is sent in particular to those who are poor or imprisoned, physically disabled, or in need of consolation from the Lord. Note that Jesus is in the synagogue in his hometown of Nazareth, and he gets mixed reviews. Jesus, well-versed in the Scriptures, knows that it is often the lot of prophets to be rejected by their own. On this day, those who

could not receive his word were so enraged that they tried to kill him. This is a hint of what will happen later in the Gospel.

The Roman Missal: Labor Day

The Mass "For the Sanctification of Human Labor" (Masses for Various Needs and Occasions, #26) may be used on this Labor Day, with the Preface for Independence Day and Other Civic Observances, I or II.

T U E 3 (#432) white
Memorial of St. Gregory the Great, Pope and Doctor of the Church

The Lectionary for Mass

◆ FIRST READING: The Thessalonians are exhorted to be watchful for the coming of the Lord, for he will come when least expected. They must continue to live as children of light and support and encourage one another.

◆ RESPONSORIAL PSALM 27: Today's Responsorial song of confidence can easily be understood in terms of the age to come, although in its original context, its reference was this life. We long to dwell in the heavenly house of the Lord forever.

◆ GOSPEL: Today's Gospel is an account of Jesus' healing of the man with an unclean spirit. Jesus' word has power over the evil spirits and is capable of restoring the man to health.

The Roman Missal

All the orations, proper for the day, are found in the Proper of Saints at September 3. The Collect points to the way St. Gregory was exemplary in his shepherding role in the Church as pope. The Prayer over the Offerings recalls the forgiveness that comes to us through the Eucharist, since it notes how "through its offering" God has "loosed the offenses of all the world." The Prayer after Communion uses the image of

Christ the teacher to ask that those who have been fed with the living bread may learn God's truth, and express it in works of charity." The appropriate Preface to use for today would be either the Preface of Holy Pastors or Preface I or II of the Saints. The Mass "For the Sanctification of Human Labor" (Masses for Various Needs and Occasions, #26) may be used on this Labor Day with Preface V of the Sundays in Ordinary Time. Consider using Eucharistic Prayer II.

Today's Saint

St. Gregory the Great (540–604) was a mayor, a monk, a pope, and a writer. Unhappy with his life as mayor of Rome, St. Gregory allocated half of his fortune to the poor and the other half to the foundation of seven monasteries. After joining a monastery in pursuit of a simple life, he was elected to the papacy. As pope, he cared for the poor, implemented reforms to improve Church governance and clerical behavior, promoted the monastic vocation, and renewed the liturgy. His name is often associated with Gregorian chant (plainsong) and Eucharistic Prayer II (along with St. Hippolytus). A prolific writer and Doctor of the Church, St. Gregory composed numerous theological texts and is cited 374 times in St. Thomas Aquinas' *Summa Theologiae.*

WED 4 (#433) green
Weekday

The Lectionary for Mass

◆ FIRST READING: Paul is filled with thanksgiving for this community that has faithfully received the word of the Gospel from Epaphras. His testimony about the community's Christian life is encouragement and consolation to Paul and Timothy, his traveling companion.

◆ RESPONSORIAL PSALM 52: The image of the green olive tree suggests life, growth, and fruit—which is what the First Reading says about the Gospel. Our faith in the Lord is first and foremost his gift, received through the ministry of others. May we always be thankful for what God has done and proclaim his goodness to others.

◆ GOSPEL: Jesus heals the mother of Peter's wife. Word of his healing activity spreads quickly, and many bring their loved ones to him. Jesus must have continued his healing work throughout the night, for at daybreak we see him seeking solitude. In what little time he has to commune alone with God, he comes more and more in touch with his mission to proclaim the Kingdom of God.

THU 5 (#434) green
Weekday

The Lectionary for Mass

◆ FIRST READING: What a beautiful and consoling message it is to hear that someone is praying for us, and that is exactly what Paul tells the Colossians. The words of his prayers are ones we can easily pray; they ask for the wisdom and knowledge to live in a manner worthy of the Lord, bearing the fruit of good works, and growing in the knowledge of God. Those who belong to Christ belong to the kingdom of light.

◆ RESPONSORIAL PSALM 98: The Lord has made known his salvation through the word of the Gospel which the Colossians have believed. Today's song of praise, prayed by Israel centuries ago, anticipated the inclusion of the Gentiles in God's plan of salvation.

◆ GOSPEL: Jesus is a man who speaks the Word of God. His message and his authority attract people. Simon must have likewise been attracted by Jesus' word: he willingly offers his boat to facilitate Jesus' teaching of the crowd, and he obeys Jesus' command even though it is at odds with his own experience (they have caught nothing all night). Seeing what Jesus' word can accomplish, Peter and his companions leave all to follow him and work on his behalf.

FRI 6 (#435) green
Weekday

The Lectionary for Mass

◆ FIRST READING: Today's text highlights Jesus' preexistence as God, his role in creation, and his work of sustaining it and holding it together. He who is the image of God became visible to us when he became flesh and reconciled all things to God.

◆ RESPONSORIAL PSALM 100: Once again we hear the call to all the nations to join in the joyful praise of God, our Creator, Shepherd, and Savior.

◆ GOSPEL: It must have been difficult for the people to understand why Jesus' disciples seemingly acted so differently from both the followers of John the Baptist and the Pharisees. On one occasion when he was questioned about this, Jesus answers by comparing himself to a Bridegroom, thus drawing on an image of God in the biblical tradition (see Isaiah 54:6).

SAT 7 (#436) green
Weekday

Optional Memorial of the Blessed Virgin Mary / white

The Lectionary for Mass

◆ FIRST READING: Today's reading focuses on God's reconciling work accomplished in Christ. It is hard to comprehend the tremendous change in our very being that happens in Baptism when God shares his very life with us. Yes, something of the divine is within us. May we always live faithfully, mindful of the gift we have received.

◆ RESPONSORIAL PSALM 54: God himself is our helper in every aspect of our lives. Without him, we are and can do nothing. How can we not offer a sacrifice of praise in thanksgiving?

◆ GOSPEL: Too literal, too legal a mindset can block the recognition of the ultimate meaning and significance of the Law, and even more, the underlying mercy of God for all his creatures. The person and authority of Jesus has priority over the letter of the Law. If exceptions are allowed even in the Old Testament for the man who was king (David), how much more so for the one who is the Son of Man and Lord?

(#129C) green

☀8 Twenty-Third Sunday in Ordinary Time

The Lectionary for Mass

◆ FIRST READING: Wisdom's author is in touch with the uncertainties and anxieties of human existence. If we are unable to understand the ways of life on earth, how can we begin to fathom heavenly things? Only through God's gift of wisdom and his divine Spirit is this possible.

◆ RESPONSORIAL PSALM 90: The transitoriness and fragility of the human creature are the focus of the first two stanzas of this Psalm's realistic appraisal of human life. The psalmist is indeed a wise man, recognizing his dependence on God and his need for God's guidance, teaching, and mercy. We pray for God's blessing on all the days of our lives and on the work of our hands.

◆ SECOND READING: Paul writes these words from prison, where he was on more than one occasion because of his proclamation of the Gospel, or more precisely, because of the turmoil and unrest it created. Paul was no stranger to the difficulties of being faithful to the Lord's call. Even prison, however, could not impede his proclamation of the Word. Onesimus, a runaway slave, hears and believes. Paul beseeches Philemon, Onesimus' master, to receive him as Paul's child of faith and as a brother in Christ.

◆ GOSPEL: The First Reading puts into perspective Jesus' hard sayings in today's Gospel. Only in the wisdom of God and through the power of God's spirit can we hear, not to mention, do, what Jesus asks. To become his disciple, one must first accede to Jesus' demand to renounce all possessions, and indeed one's very self. Only then can we be as available and open as God requires.

The Roman Missal

The Gloria and the Creed are sung or said today. The Collect gives a description of those gathered to enact worship: they are redeemed, adopted by God, and are therefore "beloved sons and daughters." We pray that in belonging and in believing in Christ, we "may receive true freedom / and an everlasting inheritance." The Prayer over the Offerings designates two fruits we are hoping for as a result of making the offering this day: that it might allow us to "do fitting homage" to God's "divine majesty," and that it may unite us with one another in

mind and heart. The Prayer after Communion acknowledges that the celebration of the Eucharist nourishes us with both "Word and heavenly Sacrament"; we should never forget the inherent unity of the Liturgy of the Word and the Liturgy of the Eucharist, the two parts of the Mass that are so intimately connected that they form one act of worship. Consider using the Eucharistic Prayer for Reconciliation II.

Other Ideas

In today's Gospel, Jesus says that we are to carry our cross in order to be his disciple. In this sense our cross is not a physical thing as it was for Jesus and on which he died. Reflect on what your cross or crosses in life might be. I once asked a group of senior residents what their cross in life was for them. One said "the thing I'm sitting in," pointing to his wheelchair; another said that "she couldn't hold her grandchild on her knee any more" because of her walker. Crosses come in many shapes and sizes and weights. And they can be different for each person, but all of them remind us of the cross of Christ. Consider how you can help others carry their cross. After all, the Cross of Christ was about love, and our cross can lead us to love him as his Cross was about his love for us.

MON9 (#437) white Memorial of St. Peter Claver, Priest

The Lectionary for Mass

◆ FIRST READING: Paul's words today encourage us to see our own suffering, offered for the sake of the Church. It is not that Christ did not do enough—but rather, that the Church is still in the process of becoming. Sufferings offered as a prayer or sacrifice for another can give pain meaning and purpose. Such is the example of Christ. Note that the word "mystery" occurs three times in today's reading. God and his plan of salvation for us, the subject of his Word to us in the Scriptures, is so much more than anything we can ask or imagine.

◆ RESPONSORIAL PSALM 62: So much in life is mystery, especially the ultimate things. Only in God will we find the answers, the way, and peace. Psalm 62 is a song of confidence in God alone.

◆ GOSPEL: The details in today's Gospel are interesting. Was the man right-handed? If so, that would be a serious impairment. The Pharisees and the scribes are watching closely to see what Jesus would do. Jesus questions them on their interpretation of Sabbath observance and acts in accord with the mercy and loving kindness of the Lord.

The Roman Missal

St. Peter Claver called himself "the slave of the slaves for ever." The Collect echoes his words, speaking of Peter as the "slave of slaves," a man of "wonderful charity and patience." We pray that we may imitate him in "seeking the things of Jesus Christ" and loving "our neighbor in deeds and in truth." The remaining prayers are drawn from the Common of Pastors or the Common of Holy Men and Women. Consider using the Eucharistic Prayer for Various Needs and Occasions IV.

Today's Saint

St. Peter Claver (1581–1654), a Spanish Jesuit priest, spent his life tending to the needs of African slaves in Colombia. While serving as a missionary, he ministered to the slaves by providing them with food and medicine, washing their wounds, preparing them for Baptism, and witnessing their marriages. He actively pursued lawyers to plead the cases of imprisoned slaves and prepared criminals for death. He also preached missions to plantation owners and sailors.

TUE 10 (#438) green Weekday

The Lectionary for Mass

◆ FIRST READING: The first part of today's reading refers to a Christian's manner of life, as the words "walk" and "philosophy" indicate. Pay particular attention to the verbs in the second part of the reading, which stress what has happened to us as a result of Christ's saving Death and Resurrection in which we share in Baptism.

◆ RESPONSORIAL PSALM 145: Today's Psalm is fittingly one of praise. Surely it was the Lord's compassion for all that he made that led to such marvelous gifts as described in the First Reading. We, like the Colossians Paul addresses, are to be people of thanksgiving.

◆ GOSPEL: It is interesting to note how many times in the Gospel Jesus goes off by himself to spend time with his heavenly Father in prayer, particularly before important decisions or moments in his life. As a result of prayer, he named his disciples. Through prayer, he knew of his mission to heal and he experienced God's power working through him.

WED 11 (#439) green Weekday

The Lectionary for Mass

◆ FIRST READING: Through Baptism, the reality of our life has been changed because of what Christ has done for us. We must live accordingly. The second part of the reading details what our manner of life should be like.

◆ RESPONSORIAL PSALM 145: Today's response is the same as yesterday, only the last stanzas are different. Our lives should be such that we make known God's kingdom in word and deed.

◆ GOSPEL: Luke's version of the Beatitudes differs slightly from Matthew's. We see here, for example, his concern for the poor and those who are in need of any kind. These are the ones who are acclaimed blessed and promised that their needs will one day be met. Correspondingly, those who have great possessions now risk woe and doom if they neglect the needs of others.

THU 12 (#440) green Weekday

Optional Memorial of the Most Holy Name of Mary / white

The Lectionary for Mass

◆ FIRST READING: The instructions on a Christian manner of life continue. This chapter from Colossians makes an excellent examination of conscience. How do we measure up in fulfilling what Paul prescribes?

◆ RESPONSORIAL PSALM 150: Today's response is from the great hymn of praise which closes the entire Psalter and which flows naturally from the last line of today's reading. May all that we do and say praise the Lord.

◆ GOSPEL: Today's Gospel is a series of sayings that stress loving those who mistreat us and giving selflessly regardless of cost. Above all, believers must be merciful, for this is one of God's main attributes. What we do to others will be done to us.

About Today's Optional Memorial

◆ THE MOST HOLY NAME OF MARY is the counterpart to the optional Memorial of the Most Holy Name of Jesus celebrated on January 3. Both of these optional memorials had been removed from the general calendar after the reform of the liturgical calendar in 1969. The memorials were restored with the promulgation of the third edition of *The Roman Missal*.

(#441) white
FRI 13 Memorial of St. John Chrysostom, Bishop and Doctor of the Church

The Lectionary for Mass

◆ FIRST READING: We begin a series of readings from 1 Timothy. After the characteristic greeting, Paul tells his own story. He was once "a blasphemer and a persecutor and an arrogant man" (1 Timothy 1:13), but now, through the mercy of God, he has become a trustworthy minister of the Gospel. Paul uses his own story to help Timothy, a young bishop, understand that God chooses his ministers not because they have earned the office, but simply because of his freely given grace.

◆ RESPONSORIAL PSALM 16: Indeed, the Lord was Paul's inheritance and all that mattered to him in life. Today's Psalm expresses confidence in God. Within the context of today's liturgy, we can easily understand this as a reference to Jesus. See how the words of the stanzas are borne out in Paul's life.

◆ GOSPEL: Jesus' words call for clear-sighted vision of one's self, particularly of weaknesses and sinfulness. How easy it is to focus myopically on the speck in the other's eye and miss the beam in our own!

The Roman Missal

The prayers for today's memorial are proper and found in the Proper of Saints. Consider using Eucharistic Prayer II.

Today's Saint

After a short stint as a monk, St. John Chrysostom (c. 350–407), whose surname means "golden mouth," returned to Antioch, where he was ordained a priest and became a noted preacher. During his free time he wrote commentaries on the Pauline letters as well as the Gospel according to Matthew and according to John. Due to his reputation for preaching and writing, he was appointed bishop of Constantinople. As bishop he initiated a program of reform that challenged clerical abuses and the extravagant lifestyle of the upper class. His reforms were not always received well, especially on the part of Empress Eudoxia; therefore, he was exiled from the city for a period of time. St. John Chrysostom bears two distinctive titles in the Church: Father of the Church and Doctor of the Church.

(#638) red
SAT 14 Feast of the Exaltation of the Holy Cross

About Today's Feast

Today's Feast of the Exaltation of the Holy Cross began as a commemoration of a unique event: the miraculous finding of the True Cross by St. Helena, the mother of Emperor Constantine. Helena journeyed to the Holy Land to see the place of the Lord's Crucifixion. She found the spot and tore down a temple she found there honoring the Greek goddess Aphrodite, and she began to build a new basilica in honor of Christ. As they began to lay the foundations, the remains of three crosses were discovered, but they did not know which was the true Cross. The Cross of Christ was eventually revealed when a dying woman was healed after touching one of the crosses. The basilica was completed, and the Church in both East and West observes this feast in honor of the Cross on the anniversary of dedication.

The Lectionary for Mass

◆ FIRST READING: A tired and discouraged Israel let itself slip into a rebellious attitude toward God and his servant Moses. God punished the Israelites through the bites of poisonous serpents. Only then did they acknowledge their sin. God, in his mercy, allowed those bitten by the snake to be healed simply by looking at a bronze replica of the serpent, raised up on a pole at his command.

◆ RESPONSORIAL PSALM 78: The source of difficulties described in the First Reading was precisely that Israel forgot the works of the Lord. The psalmist has learned from Israel's experience and calls on all who hear him to do likewise.

◆ SECOND READING: This early Christian hymn acclaims the self-emptying of Christ, who relinquishing his heavenly glory, became one of us that he might show us the way to God through his obedience, Passion, and Resurrection.

◆ GOSPEL: Jesus' words to Nicodemus recall the incident in today's First Reading. The Greek verb translated as "lifted up" means both to raise up as on a staff or a cross and to exalt. The "lifted up" Son of Man is now the source of salvation and life for all the world.

The Roman Missal

All the texts are taken from September 14 in the Proper of Saints. The Gloria is sung or said today. The Creed is not said at this Mass, since the feast falls on a Thursday. The Preface is proper for today, "The victory of the glorious Cross," and the text, with and without musical notation, is located right there amid the other texts for the day. This Preface puts forth a very positive theology of the Cross, not focused on Christ's sufferings, but rather on the new life that flows from his sacrifice. Consider using the Eucharistic Prayer for Reconciliation II.

(#132C) green

☀ 15 Twenty-Fourth Sunday in Ordinary Time

The Lectionary for Mass

◆ FIRST READING: How quickly the Israelites turned away from the God who had revealed himself to them and created their own god! How quickly they forsook the covenant so recently made. They are, as the Lord described them, a "stiff-necked" people. God's anger is understandable, his threatened punishment, justifiable. Today we witness both the power of Moses' intercession and God's merciful fidelity to the covenant.

◆ RESPONSORIAL PSALM 51: Although today's antiphon is taken from the Gospel, it is nonetheless a fitting response from a stiff-necked people. The verses are from Psalm 51, a prayer of repentance.

◆ SECOND READING: Paul's words acknowledge his previous ignorance regarding his treatment of Christians before his own personal experience of the 13. The saying he quotes about Jesus coming into the world to save sinners is amply illustrated by today's Gospel.

◆ GOSPEL: The parables in chapter 15 are unique to Luke's account of the Gospel. Note, first, the setting: the tax collectors and sinners, people considered as outcasts by the official religious establishment, are receptive to Jesus' word. He, in turn, is receptive to them, even sharing meals—a sign of acceptance and fellowship—with them. Two options are given. The longer includes the parable of the prodigal son (the merciful father? the stiff-necked and unforgiving elder brother?). All three focus on the joy in heaven over the repentance of sinners.

The Roman Missal

We pray that we may "serve [God] with all our heart" and so "feel the working" of his mercy in our lives (Collect). We pray that the offering of each of us "may serve the salvation of all." We are one Body in Christ: the love and faith, the needs and hopes we each bring to our prayer touches others in ways we cannot imagine (Prayer over the Offerings). We pray that the "heavenly gift" we have received may so work in us that God's will may prevail over our own desires (Prayer after Communion). The Gloria and the Creed are sung or said today. Consider using the Eucharistic Prayer for Reconciliation II.

Other Ideas

Have you ever lost something, like your wallet, your glasses, your keys, or your cell phone? And do you recall what joy and relief you felt when you found them? In the parables of the lost coin, the lost sheep, and the Prodigal Son, Jesus says that the joy of the woman, the shepherd and the father is only a fraction of the joy that God knows when a sinner repents. Are you anxious about confessing your sins? Are you afraid that God withholds forgiveness? Have you ever refused to forgive someone who said they were sorry? Reread this Gospel from Luke and reflect on the profound message of mercy that is in each of the parables and then see if your answer to these questions isn't different from before. Would you invite the neighbors over to celebrate your forgiveness? Maybe not, but the Lord shares in your joy!

(#443) red

M O N 16 Memorial of Sts. Cornelius, Pope, and Cyprian, Bishop, Martyrs

The Lectionary for Mass

◆ FIRST READING: In the early days of the Church—as in some countries in our world today—Christians were not always and everywhere accepted or welcomed; thus, the importance of intercessory prayer, especially for rulers and civil officials. The intent is that Christians might be able to practice their faith and live in peace. Their example is likewise to speak of the goodness and truth of their way of life and bear testimony to Jesus.

◆ RESPONSORIAL PSALM 28: Today's Psalm echoes the gesture of prayer mentioned in today's First Reading: the lifting up of hands. The antiphon is a prayer of thanksgiving (a theme likewise found in the First Reading). The stanzas speak of confident trust in God's care for his people.

◆ GOSPEL: A Roman centurion, a Gentile, believing in what he had heard about Jesus as a healer, asks some of the Jewish elders to ask Jesus to come and heal his dying slave. (Note the good word the elders put in for the centurion, obviously a benefactor of the local synagogue and perhaps himself a God-fearer.) Jesus sets out to do so, only to be met by friends of the centurion who had been sent to tell Jesus not to inconvenience himself by coming to the house, but only to say a word of healing. The centurion believes in the power of Jesus' word. Jesus not only heals the slave, he pronounces the Gentile centurion a model of faith to his Jewish contemporaries.

The Roman Missal

The prayers for the memorial are found in the Proper of Saints. The Collect speaks of these saints as "diligent shepherds and valiant Martyrs." We pray that we may "spend ourselves without reserve / for the unity of the Church" (Collect), be "steadfast in all trials" as they were (Prayer over the Offerings), and be strengthened by the Spirit so that we may "witness to the truth of the Gospel" (Prayer after Communion). Consider using Eucharistic Prayer I.

Today's Saints

St. Cornelius (+ 253) and St. Cyprian (+ 258) lived during the persecution by the Emperor Decius. St. Cornelius, the pope, faced the issue of whether or not Christians who renounced their faith during the persecutions should be welcomed back into the Church. With great compassion he publicly declared that these individuals may return to the Church after a period of penance. St. Cyprian, bishop of Carthage, spent much of his life in hiding due to the persecutions, but this did not stop him from offering pastoral guidance and dispensing wisdom to the people of his diocese. Through letters he urged the people to remain faithful to their Christian call. Both Sts. Cornelius and Cyprian shared the same fate—a martyr's death.

T U E **17** (#444) green **Weekday**

Optional Memorial of St. Robert Bellarmine, Bishop and Doctor of the Church / white

The Lectionary for Mass

◆ FIRST READING: Paul sets forth the criteria for those chosen as bishops and deacons. The qualifications reveal a life-situation in the early Church different from our own.

◆ RESPONSORIAL PSALM 101: Today's Psalm echoes the qualities set forth in today's First Reading. How important that those who minister and serve in the Church

be people of blamelessness and integrity of heart.

◆ GOSPEL: Perhaps it is the mother who is the focus in today's Gospel, rather than the son. She is a widow and now has lost her only son. In the society of her time she would be totally helpless, with no means of financial support. When Jesus saw her, he was moved with pity for her. Raising her dead son to life, he gives him to her. What needs do we have that the Lord looks on in his mercy? What gifts does the Lord give us to meet these needs?

Today's Saint

St. Robert Bellarmine (1542–1621), bishop and Doctor of the Church, was an astute scholar with a knack for diplomatically responding to the controversies of his day. As a Jesuit priest embroiled in the Protestant Reformation, he sensitively communicated through word and writing the Catholic perspective, especially regarding the relationship between Church and state. One of his most important contributions to the Church is a three-volume work, *Disputations on the Controversies of the Christian Faith*, which explained Catholic fundamentals in a nondefensive, systematic way. St. Robert, a devotee of St. Francis of Assisi, demonstrated heroic virtue by praying for his opponents, living simply, and embracing spiritual discipline.

W E D **18** (#445) green **Weekday**

The Lectionary for Mass

◆ FIRST READING: Throughout this letter, Paul is concerned with the behavior of Christians, members of the household of God. He likewise continually reiterates the centrality of Jesus, who dwelt among us and now reigns in heavenly glory.

◆ RESPONSORIAL PSALM 111: The antiphon is an acclamation of praise for the great works of God. Juxtaposed with the First Reading, it points to Jesus and his saving Gospel. The Psalm, appropriately, is one of thanksgiving for all that God has done for his people. Pray it bearing in mind what God has done for us in Christ.

◆ GOSPEL: Jesus speaks of his contemporaries (those who hear his preaching and those who heard John the Baptist) as children, in this instance, as children dissatisfied with what is offered them. Jesus calls this generation to be children of wisdom instead, open to his teaching and to his work.

T H U **19** (#446) green **Weekday**

Optional Memorial of St. Januarius, Bishop and Martyr / red

The Lectionary for Mass

◆ FIRST READING: Given his young age, Timothy must have been an exceptionally gifted individual to hold the position and ministry he did in the Church. His youth, says Paul, should not be an obstacle for himself or for others. He was to persevere diligently in the task with which he was charged; his was the ministry of salvation.

◆ RESPONSORIAL PSALM 111: What Timothy received, like all that had been given to God's people throughout the ages, was the gift and work of the Lord. Preeminent among these is the gift of salvation. Praise and thanksgiving are fitting response.

◆ GOSPEL: Jesus paints quite a contrast between Simon the righteous Pharisee and the unnamed sinner who washes the feet of his guest with her tears and anoints them with oil. Though Simon invited Jesus to his home for dinner, it is the woman who welcomed and received him into her heart. She was the one who received salvation and forgiveness because of her great love.

Today's Saint

St. Januarius (c. † 305) was bishop of Benevento in Italy during the Diocletian persecutions. After suffering the fate of a martyr—being thrown to wild beasts and then beheaded—his relics were transported to Naples where it is said that a vial of his blood liquefies on three feast days related to his life: today, the day he supposedly prevented an eruption of Mount Vesuvius in 1631 (December 16), and the Saturday before the first Sunday in May, commemorating the transfer of his relics.

(#447) red
FRI 20 Memorial of Sts. Andrew Kim Tae-gŏn, Priest, and Paul Chŏng Ha-sang, and Companions, Martyrs

The Lectionary for Mass

◆ FIRST READING: Sound teaching is a prominent concern in the pastoral epistles (1 and 2 Timothy, and Titus), as the Church at the time was particularly threatened by heresies. False teachings only lead to corruption and division in the Church. So, too, do discontent and the love of money. Paul's words call us to examine the desires and motivations of our hearts.

◆ RESPONSORIAL PSALM 49: Today's psalm refrain comes from the Gospel according to Matthew, addressing the poverty of spirit as described in today's First Reading (contentment with having what is needed; disinterest in amassing wealth). The verses of today's Psalm associate fleeting wealth and riches with those who are at enmity with God. True riches are found in the salvation God gives.

◆ GOSPEL: Today's Gospel focuses on the many women among Jesus' disciples who journey with him from Galilee to Jerusalem, and are present—albeit from a distance—at the Cross. Note that the only thing said about Mary Magdalene is that she had been healed of evil spirits and infirmities. She is not to be confused with the sinful woman in yesterday's Gospel.

The Roman Missal

All the orations for this memorial of the martyrs of Korea are proper for today, and can be found in the Proper of Saints at September 20. The Collect acknowledges the blood of these martyrs as the seed that bears fruit. The Prayer over the Offerings reminds us that in celebrating the Eucharist, we are to offer ourselves, both at the liturgy and in all of life, as it asks that through the intercession of these martyrs "we ourselves may become / a sacrifice acceptable to you / for the salvation of all the world." The Prayer after Communion labels the Eucharistic food as "the food of the valiant," thus designating it as the nourishment that strengthens us to cling faithfully to Christ and to "labor in the Church for the salvation of all." Either Preface I or Preface II of Holy Martyrs would be the appropriate choice for today. Consider using Eucharistic Prayer II.

Today's Saints

During the eighteenth and nineteenth centuries, approximately eight thousand adherents to the Catholic faith in Korea were martyred (from 1839 to 1867); 103 of them were canonized by Pope John Paul II in 1988. The canonized martyrs were victims of a particularly heinous series of persecutions happening between 1839 and 1867. During this time, Korea was ruled by an anti-Christian dynasty that did everything possible to eliminate Catholic ideology and influence,

including maliciously murdering Christian missionaries and their followers. Two of the more notable martyrs are St. Andrew Kim Tae-gŏn, priest and martyr; and St. Paul Chŏng Ha-sang, a layman, both of whom were dedicated to the revitalization of the Church in Korea.

(#643) red
SAT 21 Feast of St. Matthew, Apostle and Evangelist

The Lectionary for Mass

◆ FIRST READING: Everyone in the community is gifted by God's grace. Everyone! This is God's Word to us. Each has received and continually receives the gift of God's grace. There are various gifts in the community, but all are necessary. Everyone has a responsibility to "build up" the community which long ago was built on the foundational work of the Apostles.

◆ RESPONSORIAL PSALM 19: How far away our land is from that where Jesus and his Apostles lived. We give thanks that the Apostles proclaimed his message "through all the earth" and that it has reached us.

◆ GOSPEL: Tax collectors were looked down upon in Jesus' day. They were agents of a foreign (Gentile) government and they supplemented their income with what they superimposed on the taxes of others. Through table fellowship with tax collectors, Jesus showed his acceptance of them. This was not to approve of their wrongdoing but to offer them the opportunity to convert and be healed. This can happen only in the face of love and acceptance.

The Roman Missal

The prayers for the feast are found in the Proper of Saints. The Gloria is said or sung today. The Preface of the Apostles is used. The Collect emphasizes the "untold mercy" of God, who chose Matthew "the tax collector" to be both Apostle and Evangelist. We pray that we may imitate him, and "hold firm in following" the Lord. The Prayer after Communion echoes the Gospel account of the call of St. Matthew: Jesus is glad to dine with this tax collector, because he "did not come to call the righteous but sinners" (Matthew 9:13). Just as Matthew rejoiced to welcome "the Savior as a guest in his home," so we rejoice to welcome Christ who has come to dwell with us through the sacrament we share. The Solemn Blessing of the Apostles may be used. Consider using Eucharistic Prayer I.

Today's Saint

St. Matthew (first century), referred to as the "tax collector," is one of the Twelve Apostles and the Evangelist who authored the first of the four accounts of the Gospel. His account has a twofold purpose: one, to announce that Jesus is the eternal king of all creation; and two, to encourage faith in the face of doubt, especially regarding persecution. We have very little information about him, other than he invited Jesus to his home to dine with societal outcasts (see Matthew 9:9–13), and that he preached the Good News after the Resurrection. Tradition says he began preaching in Judea, then moved on to Ethiopia, Persia, Syria, Macedonia, and possibly Ireland. He is venerated as a martyr, even though history does not tell us how or where he died.

(#135C) green

22 Twenty-Fifth Sunday in Ordinary Time

The Lectionary for Mass

◆ FIRST READING: God's words are justly severe to those who with full forethought defraud the poor, all the while observing, at least outwardly, the ritual celebrations as prescribed in the law. God's word is strong: he will never forget this injustice. One day, God's people will pay for their sins of iniquity.

◆ RESPONSORIAL PSALM 113: It is the poor, taken advantage of by the wicked depicted in the words of Amos, who are the recipients of God's blessing and deliverance. Today's song of praise can seem jarring when it is juxtaposed with Amos' words; indeed, it would be for the wicked. For the oppressed poor, the Psalm's message is a word of Good News: God will raise them up.

◆ SECOND READING: Paul stresses the importance of prayer for all civil leaders that through their government, religious tolerance and peace abound for all people. Such is the will of Christ Jesus who wants all people to be saved and to know the truth revealed in the Gospel.

◆ GOSPEL: There is a certain irony in today's Gospel depiction of the steward who loses his position because of his wasteful management of the master's property and who, prior to leaving his job, ensures his own well-being by drastically writing off the debts owed to his master, thus incurring additional losses for his master. When the master became aware of his actions, he praised him for his astuteness. (We aren't told whether or not he received his job back!) Described in the parable as a "child of this world," he stands in contrast to "the children of light" and of God. Several sayings attributed to Jesus, all concerning wealth, follow the parable. All call us to examine our attitude toward, and use of, money.

The Roman Missal

The Gloria and the Creed are sung or said today. The Collect notes how all the commands of God's sacred Law are grounded in one foundation: the unity of love of God and love of neighbor. The Prayer over the Offerings prays that we may truly possess what we "profess with devotion and faith"; since the context for this possession is asking God to receive our offerings, then it is the offering of ourselves in union with Christ that we are professing, and it is the offering of ourselves in union with Christ that we pray will become more and more a reality through our participation in the offering of the Eucharist. Any one of the eight Prefaces of the Sundays in Ordinary Time are appropriate for today. The Prayer after Communion also makes an important connection between liturgical celebration and everyday life: it asks that redemption might be ours "both in mystery [liturgical celebration] and in the manner of our life." Consider using Eucharistic Prayer III.

Other Ideas

Paul urges Timothy and the early Christians to offer "supplications, prayers, petitions and thanksgivings for everyone." The Prayer of the Faithful that we offer every

Sunday is likened to this exhortation by Paul. Listen carefully to the intercessions; can you recall who was prayed for and what was asked for in the petition? Sometimes it is easy to pray for the people we like and not so easy to pray for those we dislike or with whom we disagree. Paul mentions offering prayers for those in authority. Often people in authority can be the most difficult to pray for because of their positions over us or their policies that we don't agree with. Praying for someone is not agreeing with them but asking God to take care of them; it is a way for us to acknowledge God understands even when we don't.

MON 23 (#449) white
Memorial of St. Pius of Pietrelcina, Priest

The Lectionary for Mass

◆ FIRST READING: Due to the victory of Cyrus of Persia over the Babylonians, the Jews in exile in Babylon were allowed to return to Jerusalem. Among their first tasks was to rebuild God's Temple that had been destroyed by the Babylonians. Note that the biblical author interprets this as the charge God gave (inspired) Cyrus. The Jews receive gifts from their Babylonian neighbors to help rebuild the Temple.

◆ RESPONSORIAL PSALM 126 celebrates the end of the Babylonian exile, a dream come true for Israel. What marvels the Lord had done for them; what joy marked their return to their homeland.

◆ GOSPEL: "Take care . . . how you hear" (Luke 8:18, emphasis added). In one ear and out the other? Or, do we listen with the ear of the heart and shine forth with the light of love for God and others?

The Roman Missal

The Collect for the memorial is found in the Proper of Saints. The Collect speaks of the "singular grace" by which the saint was given "a share in the Cross." We pray that we, too, in our own way, may be "united constantly to the sufferings of Christ." The remaining prayers are drawn from the Common of Pastors: For One Pastor or of Holy Men and Women: For Religious. Consider using Eucharistic Prayer II.

Today's Saint

Early in life St. "Padre" Pio of Pietrelcina (1887–1968), a Capuchin priest from Italy, demonstrated an unquenchable thirst for God. While praying one day before a crucifix, he received the visible wounds of crucifixion that Christ bore in his Passion and Death, known as the stigmata. After an examination by a doctor, it was determined that there was no natural explanation for the wounds. Along with the stigmata, he experienced other mystical phenomena, including bilocation, the ability to be in two places at the same time, and reading the hearts of those who sought counsel and forgiveness in the Sacrament of Reconciliation. These two miraculous gifts enabled him to lead both the sinner and devout closer to God. Upon his death the stigmata were no longer visible.

TUE 24 (#450) green
Weekday

The Lectionary for Mass

◆ FIRST READING: Ezra's account of the rebuilding of the Temple and the support of the Persian kings continues. The dedication of the Temple was celebrated with great joy. How special that first celebration of Passover back in their homeland and in their Temple must have been, as they continued to witness God's marvelous deeds for them.

◆ RESPONSORIAL PSALM 122 is a hymn that pilgrims sang as they joyfully made their way to the temple in Jerusalem. It is a fitting response to the account of the Temple's rebuilding and dedication.

◆ GOSPEL: Hearing and doing the word of God puts one in a relationship with Jesus that is tighter than the bonds of natural family ties.

WED 25 (#451) green
Weekday

The Lectionary for Mass

◆ FIRST READING: In the midst of the joy and the hope of a new beginning for Israel, we find Ezra's honest acknowledgment of the guilt of his people and the deserved punishment of their servitude in Babylon. Confession of our sinfulness makes us even more aware of the gifts and graces God gives us.

◆ CANTICLE: Today's prayer is a hymn found not in the Psalter but in the Book of Tobit. It acclaims God's deliverance of his people among the Gentiles (non-Jews), an example of which is described in the First Reading.

◆ GOSPEL: The Apostles sent in Jesus' name are empowered by him in their mission of healing and proclamation of the Gospel. He asks for radical trust and contentment with what is offered them by those who receive them. If rejected, they must testify against those who would not receive them.

THU 26 (#452) green
Weekday

Optional Memorial of Sts. Cosmas and Damian, Martyrs / red

The Lectionary for Mass

◆ FIRST READING: Today, we backtrack a bit in history with the prophet Haggai to the time before the Temple was rebuilt. Here it seems that the people did not first set about rebuilding the Temple upon their return; rather, they started constructing houses for themselves. They are called to repentance and to begin building a house for the Lord.

◆ RESPONSORIAL PSALM 149: The Lord takes pleasure in his people, a sentiment echoed at the end of the First Reading and in today's antiphon. The verses speak of joyful praise of God in a liturgical assembly with song and dance.

◆ GOSPEL: The question of Jesus' identity pervades the Gospel accounts. In today's text, it is Herod the tetrarch who is perplexed about him.

Today's Saints

Sts. Cosmas and Damian (c. †287) were brothers, possibly twins, who practiced medicine without accepting money for their services. They became known in the East as the *anargyroi*, meaning "moneyless ones" or "moneyless healers." As vibrant witnesses to the Christian faith, they were arrested during the Diocletian persecutions. When they refused to renounce their faith and engage in idolatrous worship, they were beheaded and cast into the sea. They are patron saints of twins, confectioners, the sightless, and many medical professions (for example, physicians, nurses, and dentists). Their names are included in Eucharistic Prayer I.

FRI (#453) white
27
Memorial of St. Vincent de Paul, Priest

The Lectionary for Mass

◆ FIRST READING: For those who remembered the splendor of Solomon's Temple, the sight of the post-Exilic Temple paled in comparison. The prophet speaks a word of hope and encouragement with the promise that in days to come,

the glory of the Temple would exceed even that of Solomon's time.

◆ RESPONSORIAL PSALM 43: The Psalm encourages hope in the Lord's promise, for he is our Savior. The stanzas progress from the experience of being threatened by the deceitful and impious to the confident hope of one day offering a joyful sacrifice of thanksgiving for God's deliverance.

◆ GOSPEL: No doubt the people of Jesus' day had never met anyone quite like him. Who is this? they asked. In today's Gospel—and note the context, prayer—Jesus asks his disciples what people were saying about him. He asks them as well: What do you say? Peter confesses that Jesus is the Christ, the messiah. Lest his disciples misunderstood the nature of his messiahship, Jesus is quick to tell them that he will suffer and be killed, but also that he will be raised on the third day.

The Roman Missal

All the orations are found in the Proper of Saints at September 27. The Collect, not surprisingly, recognizes the saint for his "apostolic virtues" in working for the relief of the poor and, as is sometimes overlooked, for the formation of the clergy. The Prayer over the Offerings describes how St. Vincent imitated "what he celebrated in these divine mysteries"; therefore, we ask that we too may imitate them and become what we receive, that is, "be transformed into an oblation acceptable to you." The Prayer after Communion asks that in being renewed by this heavenly sacrament, we may both be prompted by the example of St. Vincent and be sustained by his prayers. Either the Preface of Holy Pastors or one of the two Prefaces of Saints would be appropriate for today. Consider using the Eucharistic Prayer for Various Needs and Occasions IV.

Today's Saint

St. Vincent de Paul (1581–1660), a French priest, gradually became aware of the growing disparity between the rich and poor; therefore, he laid the framework for the Servants of the Poor, which provided for the physical needs of the poor. Recognizing the call to care for not only their physical needs, but also their spiritual needs, he established a society of priests, the Congregation of the Mission (Vincentians), dedicated to preaching to peasants, catechezing the marginalized, and performing other charitable works. In collaboration with St. Louise Montfort de Marillac, he founded the Daughters of Charity, a new community of sisters not bound by traditional vows or enclosure who are devoted to the sick, orphaned, and imprisoned. St. Vincent is the patron saint of charitable societies. Many day care centers, hospitals, thrift stores, and soup kitchens are named in his honor.

SAT (#454) green
28
Weekday

Optional Memorials of St. Wenceslaus, Martyr / red; St. Lawrence Ruiz and Companions, Martyrs / red; Blessed Virgin Mary / white

The Lectionary for Mass

◆ FIRST READING: The word of the prophet assures God's people of a future day of glory for Jerusalem, God dwelling in her midst. What is more, the Gentile nations will join themselves to Israel and together they will praise the Lord.

◆ CANTICLE: Today's canticle, from the Book of Jeremiah, speaks of the return of God's people to Jerusalem. God is imaged as the shepherd who gathers his flock and redeems them from the hand of the conqueror. Zion is another name for Jerusalem.

◆ GOSPEL: Jesus keeps telling his disciples what kind of messiah he will be. Right now they are full of amazement at his mighty deeds; but Jesus says, "Pay attention to what I am telling you" (Luke 9:44): the Passion is coming. But the disciples do not understand; in fact, they are afraid to understand.

Today's Saints

Most people are familiar with St. Wenceslaus (c. 907–929), due to the popular Christmas carol "Good King Wenceslaus." Although this ancient carol is not based on historical events, it illustrates the fame King Wenceslaus received because of his heroic life. As a Christian king in Bohemia, a primarily pagan country, he worked fervently to Christianize his people. His attempt to evangelize the Bohemians was not received well by some, including his brother who eventually murdered him. As he was dying, he prayed that God would forgive his brother. Shortly following his death, people proclaimed him a martyr.

St. Lawrence Ruiz (1600–1637), a married man with three children, fled to Japan from Manila to escape an unjust charge. Upon arrival, he was greeted with hostility, due to a recent edict that banned Christianity. When he and fifteen other companions would not adhere to the state religion and trample on religious images associated with the Catholic faith, they were executed. St. Lawrence and his companions join 231 other Catholics martyred in Japan between the sixteenth and seventeenth centuries.

(#138C) green

☀ 29 Twenty-Sixth Sunday in Ordinary Time

The Lectionary for Mass

◆ FIRST READING: God's special concern for the poor and helpless is evident throughout the Scriptures. God's law ordains that those who have earthly goods should be mindful of those who do not. But Israel did not always heed God's word. In today's text from the prophet Amos, God's word of judgment is spoken against those who ignore the poor.

◆ RESPONSORIAL PSALM 146 is a song of praise to God who shows tremendous care and concern for the poor, the oppressed, the powerless, and those in any need.

◆ SECOND READING: Paul's exhortation to Timothy is applicable to us all. We are all men and women of God. Let us live now, striving to love and serve God and others, as we await the coming of our Lord.

◆ GOSPEL: Jesus' parable points to God's loving concern for those who are in need now and to the abundance and consolation they will receive in the age to come. Similarly, those who refuse to show mercy to those in need will be punished forever.

The Roman Missal

The Mass texts for today are found in the "Ordinary Time" section of the Proper of Time. The Gloria and the Creed are sung or said today. In choosing the Preface for today, you might consider Preface II of the Sundays in Ordinary Time, with its mention of Christ responding with compassion to "the waywardness that is ours"; Preface IV, with its emphasis on Christ bringing renewal, on his canceling out our sins, and on his opening the way to eternal life; or Preface VII, as it mentions our disobedience, which has been overturned by Christ's obedience. Consider using Eucharistic Prayer III.

Other Ideas

The story of the rich man and the poor man Lazarus always bothers our conscience. We ask ourselves: When did I ignore the needs of another person? Was it the guy at the traffic lights looking for a handout? Was it the homeless person on the sidewalk looking for money to buy some food? It can be so easy to be dismissive of their pleas, and justify our lack of response. Have you ever thought what it would be like to be in their shoes? To be so destitute that you would need to beg for survival? At every Mass, just after the Our Father we ask the Lord to save us from "all distress." What might we do to assist others in their distress? Consider putting some coins or dollar bills within easy reach in your car and the next time you see a brother or sister looking for help, smile and hand over a little bit of love to them.

(#455) white

MON 30 Memorial of St. Jerome, Priest and Doctor of the Church

The Lectionary for Mass

◆ FIRST READING: We hear words of promise for Jerusalem about the return of her citizens after their exile in Babylon. The Lord will again dwell within the Temple in Jerusalem. Even if this seems impossible to the people, nothing is impossible for God.

◆ RESPONSORIAL PSALM 102: The antiphon reiterates the Lord's promise of the restoration of Jerusalem. The verses come from the end of this song of lament, perhaps from the time of the exile, and state confidently that the Lord will answer the people's cry for deliverance and restore Jerusalem. All nations (Gentiles) will come to know the Lord and revere him.

◆ GOSPEL: Perhaps it may seem strange to think of Jesus' disciples arguing among themselves, but that is exactly what is happening in today's Gospel reading. To make matters worse, they are arguing about who is the greatest in the presence of him who came to serve. They have really missed the point of Jesus' teaching. The disciples should not be concerned with greatness, but rather, with lowliness. Jesus is dead set against any kind of elitism.

The Roman Missal

The prayers for the memorial are found in the Proper of Saints. They speak of St. Jerome's great love for the Word of God, his "living and tender love for Sacred Scripture" (Collect). We pray that we may find in God's word "the fount of life" (Collect), and that our meditation on the Scriptures may fill us with eagerness to offer "the sacrifice of salvation" (Prayer over the Offerings). Consider using Eucharistic Prayer II.

Today's Saint

St. Jerome (345–420) is the patron saint of scholars and librarians. With a great love of learning and books, as priest he developed a passion for the interpretation of Sacred Scripture. With a comprehensive knowledge of classical languages, St. Jerome produced a Latin text of the entire Bible eventually known as the Vulgate. He wrote numerous

commentaries on several books of the Bible, including a highly reputable work on the Gospel according to Matthew. St. Jerome joins three other saints (Ambrose, Augustine, and Gregory the Great) as the first Doctors of the Church.

October 2019
Month of the Most Holy Rosary

(#456) white
Memorial of St. Thérèse of the Child Jesus, Virgin and Doctor of the Church

TUE 1

The Lectionary for Mass

◆ FIRST READING: What a vivid picture is presented in these words from Zechariah. Gentile peoples have become missionaries to one another, announcing that God is with his people and leading one another to Jerusalem.

◆ RESPONSORIAL PSALM 87: The psalm celebrates the glory of Jerusalem, particularly her motherhood. She has become home to people from countless nations.

◆ GOSPEL: Jesus' journey to Jerusalem—and his Passion and Death—would take firm and resolute determination. There was antagonism between the Samaritans and the Jews stemming from the time of the Babylonian Exile. The issue here, however, is not so much this antagonism but the disciples' desire to seek revenge for the Samaritans' lack of hospitality. Jesus rebukes his disciples for their violent thoughts.

The Roman Missal

All the orations are proper for today, as found in the Proper of Saints at October 1. The Collect explicitly mentions the "Little Way" of St. Thérèse, noting how God's Kingdom is open "to those who are humble and to little ones."

The Preface of Holy Virgins and Religious would seem to be the most appropriate choice for a Preface today, although certainly Preface I or II of Saints could also be used. Consider using Eucharistic Prayer II.

Today's Saint

St. Thérèse of the Child Jesus (1873–1897), also known as the "Little Flower," was the youngest of Sts. Zélie and Louis Martin's five daughters. Zélie died of breast cancer when Thérèse was only four years old, a blow from which Thérèse took years to recover. The family moved to Lisieux, to be closer to Zélie's brother and his family. After their mother's death, Thérèse became very close to her sister, Pauline, but five years later, Pauline entered the Carmel of Lisieux. Eventually, all five sisters would become nuns, four of them at the Lisieux Carmel. Because she was so young, Thérèse had to obtain permission from the diocesan bishop to join the Carmel, and she was able to at age fifteen. As a Carmelite nun, she overcame the narrow, negative spirituality prevalent in nineteenth-century France, and focused on love—her love of God and God's love for her. She called her path of holiness the "Little Way," referring to her belief that every act, no matter how small, brings us as close to God as do heroic acts performed by spiritual giants such as St. Ignatius of Loyola or St. Teresa of Avila. She developed tuberculosis when she was only twenty-four and was unable to join a Carmel in the missionary territory of Vietnam. A year later, when only twenty-five, she died of the disease, after suffering through a period in which she doubted the existence of heaven. Thérèse left behind a memoir, *L'histoire d'une âme* (*The Story of a Soul*), which she wrote under obedience to her sister, Pauline, who had become prioress. It was published posthumously, after heavy editing by her sisters to bring it into conformity with their idea of piety, but recent editions have restored the original material. Translated into over fifty languages, it has inspired faith in skeptics and strengthened the souls of believers. Because of her missionary spirit, Thérèse of Lisieux is the patron saint of the missions. Pope John Paul II declared her a Doctor of the Church in 1997, one of only three women so honored, along with Teresa of Avila and Catherine of Siena.

WED 2 (#457; Gospel, #650) white
Memorial of the Holy Guardian Angels

The Lectionary for Mass

◆ FIRST READING: The book of Nehemiah offers yet another perspective on the rebuilding of the city of Jerusalem after the Babylonian Exile. Nehemiah was a servant in the court of the Persian king. He received official approbation and support to go and help rebuild the walls of the city of Jerusalem. Nehemiah interpreted the king's favor toward him as an indication of the favor of God upon him.

◆ RESPONSORIAL PSALM 137, prayed by the Jews exiled in Babylon, laments their misery in not being at home in Jerusalem, as well as the destruction of the city and its Temple. Nehemiah, in today's First Reading, exemplifies one who has not forgotten the city and seeks to restore it as soon as possible.

◆ GOSPEL: The Gospel text draws upon the Jewish tradition that every nation has an angel in heaven. Here, each person has a guardian angel. Most of the text focuses on the child and the necessity of becoming like a child—simple, open, and trusting.

The Roman Missal

The orations are proper again for today, and these are found at October 2. The Collect pleads that God always have the holy angels guard and defend us. The Prayer over the Offerings also asks for the protection of our guardian angels, so that "we may be delivered from present dangers / and brought happily to life eternal." The proper Preface, "God glorified through the Angels," is given right there along with the other texts for this memorial. This Preface describes how the honor we pay to angels results in God being glorified; to venerate the angels is to praise God. The Prayer after Communion reminds us that the nourishment we receive in the Eucharist is nourishment for eternal life; we therefore ask this day that the angels guide us into that life. Consider using Eucharistic Prayer I.

Today's Angels

While not a defined teaching of the Church, the belief that each person has a guardian angel has roots deep in antiquity among Christians and non-Christians. The ancient Babylonians and Assyrians believed in angels, and they are mentioned in the Old Testament as well, beginning in the Book of Genesis, where they deliver God's punishment on the cities of the plain and rescue Lot and his family from the destruction (see Genesis 28–29). Perhaps one of the best and most touching examples of the activity of angels is found in the Book of Tobit, where the archangel Raphael leads and advises Tobiah on his journey (see Tobit 6–12). In the New Testament, Jesus himself seems to indicate that each of us is assigned a guardian angel when he says, "Take care that you do not despise one of these little ones; for, I tell you, in heaven their angels continually see the face of my Father in heaven" (Matthew 18:10).

THU 3 (#458) green
Weekday

The Lectionary for Mass

◆ FIRST READING: When the walls of the city of Jerusalem had been rebuilt, Ezra the priest gathered all the people for a public reading of the Law of God. In fact, the description of the event suggests a liturgical assembly. We might think of it as comparable to our own Liturgy of the Word. Note, too, that there is instruction based on the Law (perhaps like our homily?). People of all ages, even children, were part of the assembly. Did the weeping reflect the people's sadness in realizing how far they were from being faithful to the Lord? Even this realization can lead the people to joyful thanksgiving for all that God has done for them—and for us, despite our infidelities.

◆ RESPONSORIAL PSALM 19 acclaims God's Law as a source of joy, as indeed it was in today's First Reading. The stanzas highlight all that the Lord can do for us and all that he should mean to us.

◆ GOSPEL: Jesus sends some of his followers out to proclaim the Good News of the Kingdom, to bring peace, and to heal. The harvest is great.

FRI 4 (#459) white
Memorial of St. Francis of Assisi

The Lectionary for Mass

◆ FIRST READING: We return to the Babylonian captivity. The prophets, and in today's First Reading, the people as well, clearly perceived it as a time of punishment for Israel's infidelities.

◆ RESPONSORIAL PSALM 79: The people pray for the deliverance that they know they do not deserve. They appeal to God's glory, that it might be manifest among them, and among the nations too.

◆ GOSPEL: In this chapter on the mission of the disciples, Jesus speaks of both the reception and the rejection of their message. Acts of power and healing should lead to repentance. The rejection of the Gospel by the contemporaries of Jesus is far worse than the sins of Tyre and Sidon.

The Roman Missal

Once again all the orations are proper for the day; these are found at October 4 in the Proper of Saints. The Collect, as we might expect, gives special recognition to the poverty and humility of St. Francis, praying that by walking in the footsteps of the saint we might also follow Christ. The Prayer over the Offerings observes how St. Francis "ardently embraced" the mystery of the Cross, the mystery that is celebrated in the Eucharist. The Prayer after Communion prays that the holy gifts of the Eucharist may transform us to imitate "the charity and apostolic zeal of St. Francis" and thus speak God's love everywhere. Preface I or II of Saints would be good choices for today's Preface. Consider using Eucharistic Prayer III.

Other Ideas

The blessing of animals has become a popular event given St. Francis' love of animals and all of God's creation. This blessing could be celebrated on the day of the memorial, or the Sunday before, if that is more convenient for those who work. A simple prayer service might include the beautiful hymn, "All Creatures of Our God and King" or the "Canticle of the Sun." The *Book of Blessings* includes an order of service (chapter 25) that can be adapted to the situation. Provide refreshments for the people and the pets! If animals will be blessed individually with holy water, be careful that they don't become spooked. Encourage pet guardians to bring animals on leashes and/or in carriers to prevent squabbles and animals getting loose.

Today's Saint

The son of a wealthy merchant, St. Francis of Assisi (1182–1226) seemed destined for grand castles, exquisite clothing, and fine food. After a conversion experience, he relinquished the trappings of this world to minister to the leper and preach to the spiritually hungry. His home became the earth; his clothing, humility; and his identity, an impoverished beggar seeking God. Many young men joined St. Francis in this new way of life, leading to the foundation of the *frati minori* ("lesser brothers"), which eventually became known as the Friars Minor. He is perhaps one of the most popular saints in Church history due to his love of creation as exemplified in his famous "Canticle of the Sun." Pope Pius XI described St. Francis as an *alter Christus*, which means "another Christ."

SAT 5 (#460) green Weekday

Optional Memorials of Bl. Francis Xavier Seelos, Priest / white; Blessed Virgin Mary / white

The Lectionary for Mass

◆ FIRST READING: Comforting words of hope and promise addressed to the Israelites in captivity in Babylon are heard in today's First Reading. Israel's sins are acknowledged and she is encouraged to repent and return to God. As Israel's Savior, God will bring the Israelites back to their homeland.

◆ RESPONSORIAL PSALM 69: The theme of returning to the Lord (i.e., seeking the Lord) recurs in the first stanza of today's Psalm, with the promise that the Lord hears the prayer of those who are in need. We hear again God's promise to rebuild Jerusalem and the cities that were destroyed. The exiled people will be restored to their homeland.

◆ GOSPEL: Jesus instructs his disciples to rejoice, not so much in the acts of power they perform but, rather, in the fact that their names are written in heaven. Jesus' prayer in the second part of the Gospel stresses that the revelation the disciples have received is a gift from the Lord and a source of blessing for them.

Today's Saint

St. Francis Xavier Seelos was a German a member of the Congregation of the Most Holy Redeemer (Redemptorists). He came to the United States of America in 1843 to minister to German immigrants. The following year he was ordained a priest in the Church of St. James in Baltimore, Maryland. He was known to be very kind, pastoral, and concerned for the poor. Many sought his help as confessor and spiritual advisor. Although he was proposed as Bishop of Pittsburgh, he instead became a missionary throughout the United States traveling to New Jersey, New York, Ohio, Pennsylvania, Connecticut, Rhode Island, Illinois, Michigan, Missouri, Wisconsin, and Louisiana. It was in Louisiana that he became ill with yellow fever and died in 1867. He was only forty-eight years old. If you are celebrating this optional memorial, the approved texts for this Mass can be found on the USCCB website: www.usccb.org /about/divine-worship/liturgical -calendar/blessed-francis-xavier -seelos.cfm.

(#141C) green

☀ 6 Twenty-Seventh Sunday in Ordinary Time

The Lectionary for Mass

◆ FIRST READING: It takes great faith not to lose hope in God in times of deep suffering and affliction. Habakkuk, in today's First Reading, exhorts his hearers to faith and hope. We may think of the word "vision" (which occurs twice) as all God has promised, all that hope encompasses. This hope has its time—it will come to fruition. The promises will be fulfilled. We must only have faith.

◆ RESPONSORIAL PSALM 95: Hear the word of the Lord and receive it—in your heart. Psalm 95 calls us to humble obedience to the God in whom we find strength.

◆ SECOND READING: Bear your hardships, encourages Paul, fan into even stronger flames the fervor of your zeal for the Gospel. Embrace in your heart the rich deposit of faith the Church teaches.

◆ GOSPEL: Today's Gospel consists of two rather independent sayings or teachings. The first begins with a request or prayer: "Increase our faith." Jesus' response points out the strength and power of even a little faith. The second part of the Gospel is the parable of a servant. How easy it is to think only of what we shall receive in return for whatever we do. Before the Lord, however, we are servants and whatever we do is only what we have been commanded.

The Roman Missal

The Gloria and Creed are sung or said today. The Collect recalls that God's love and grace are superabundant and overflowing; that is the basis for our asking God "to pardon what conscience dreads / and to give what prayer does not dare to ask." God will always surpass our expectations and fill us with life and love, despite our unworthiness. The Prayer over the Offerings recalls that the sacrifice we celebrate today was instituted by divine command, and its purpose is to continue the sanctifying work by which we are redeemed (in the liturgy, the work of our redemption is actually being accomplished). Any one of the eight Prefaces of the Sundays in Ordinary Time is equally appropriate today. The Prayer after Communion speaks of the important action of transformation: we are to "be transformed into what we consume." Consider using Eucharistic Prayer I.

Other Ideas

Faith is an interesting word. Yet *faith* is so much more than just a word. Jesus compares faith to the tiny mustard seed. Only a little bit of faith can cause amazing things to happen in our life. That gives us an important insight: faith leads to action. What we believe shapes how we live. Name some of the people who have passed on faith to you. Ask yourself, was it their words or their actions that rang true for you? As a Christian believer what actions in your life, at work or at home, in relationships or in private gestures, are based on your faith? The Creed that we say at Mass lists what we believe in. Take a few moments and write down an action creed; begin with "because I believe, this what I do, or how I act, or I resolve to . . ." and include those things you do that arise from your faith.

MON 7 (#461) white Memorial of Our Lady of the Rosary

About Today's Memorial

Pope John Paul II called the Rosary "the school of Mary," a special devotion that teaches us about the profoundly close relationship Mary shared with her Son, Jesus Christ. More than this, praying the Rosary invites us into this relationship, nurturing our faith and deepening our understanding of who Jesus Christ was for the world. The Church celebrates Our Lady of the Rosary in order to honor Mary's example and guidance to her Son. May we learn in her school how to open our lives to her Son Jesus, and how to imitate his example of sharing God's love with the world.

The Lectionary for Mass

◆ FIRST READING: Today we begin the story of the prophet Jonah, a delightful and somewhat humorous story with a very strong message! Perhaps we can identify with Jonah's desire to flee from what the Lord was asking of him— at least at one time or another in our lives! As Jonah soon discovered, there is no running away from the Lord. In today's reading, we hear of the Lord's care for this rebellious prophet who resisted his call.

◆ CANTICLE: Today's canticle is Jonah's prayer from the belly of a fish. Remember that the sea is a symbol of chaos and destruction. We know from the last line of the First Reading that the Lord heard Jonah's prayer.

◆ GOSPEL: What must I do? Tell me exactly. We all want certitude regarding what we have been asked to do, especially when it is a matter of eternal life. There are several surprising elements in the parable in today's Gospel. Why did the official religious personnel pass by the man in need? If he were dead, contact with a corpse would have rendered them defiled and therefore unfit for Temple worship. But even more surprising is the way in which the question changes from "Who is my neighbor?" to "Which of these . . . was neighbor?" Jesus couches the command in a new way: Be neighbor by showing mercy.

The Roman Missal

The prayers for the memorial are found in the Proper of Saints. We have heard the Good News of the Incarnation of Christ; we pray that we may follow him in his Passion and Cross, and so come to "the glory of his Resurrection." It is an appropriate prayer as we honor Mary as Our Lady of the Rosary, for in the Rosary, through the Joyful, Luminous, Sorrowful, and Glorious Mysteries, we follow Christ from the Incarnation to the glory of heaven. Consider using Eucharistic Prayer II.

TUE 8 (#462) green Weekday

The Lectionary for Mass

◆ FIRST READING: The Lord tries again with Jonah, commissioning him to preach repentance to the Ninevites in the country of Assyria. In contrast to Jonah, the Ninevites are immediately obedient to the Lord's command. Both humans and animals underwent a period of fasting and repentance. Seeing this, the Lord relents—has a change of heart—and does not inflict the punishment that was threatened.

◆ RESPONSORIAL PSALM 130: This song of repentance is most apropos given the reading's account of the repentance of the Ninevites. Acknowledging their sins, repenting in sack cloth and ashes, fasting from food and drink, the Ninevites

waited for—and received—merciful deliverance from the Lord.

◆ GOSPEL: What an interesting study in personalities is set before us today. Both Martha and Mary have great love for Jesus. Martha seems to be the manager of the home; Mary is the more quiet one. Martha's perhaps understandable reaction is: "Tell her to help me" (Luke 10:40). Her reaction reminds us how easy it is to get caught up in anxieties. In listening to Jesus, Mary has chosen the better part.

WED 9 (#463) green Weekday

Optional Memorials of Sts. Denis, Bishop, and Companions, Martyrs / red; St. John Leonardi, Priest / white

The Lectionary for Mass

◆ FIRST READING: Perhaps we are surprised at Jonah's reaction when he witnesses God's merciful response to the Ninevites. Does Jonah's anger and resentment come from a bit of self-righteousness? Jonah is more concerned with himself than with the people to whom he was sent. But God is concerned with the Ninevites and looks on them with mercy.

◆ RESPONSORIAL PSALM 86: The Lord is indeed merciful and gracious as the First Reading proclaims, echoing words that God himself spoke to Moses at Mount Sinai. Today's Psalm is a prayer of confident trust in the mercy of God.

◆ GOSPEL: What a beautiful image! The disciples want to pray in the same manner that they see Jesus praying. The prayer that Jesus teaches them is what we know as the Our Father. God is Father, source of life and provider of our needs. He loves us so much! To the Father we are more important than the wrong we do, but we must turn to him for forgiveness.

Today's Saints

St. Denis of Paris († 258) was the bishop of Paris during the third century, martyred during the persecution by the emperor Decius. It's possible that Denis came from Italy to convert Gaul, settling in Paris on the Île de la Cité in the River Seine. According to Gregory of Tours, he was beheaded with a sword on Montmartre, the highest hill in Paris, which may have been a Druidic holy place, and local tradition holds that the martyrdom of St. Denis gave the hill its name. After his death, his body and those of his companions, Sts. Eleutherius and Rusticus, were recovered by the Christian community and buried. Later, St. Geneviève started the construction of a basilica on the spot. St. Denis of Paris is often confused with Dionysus the Areopagite, who was converted by St. Paul in Athens (Acts of the Apostles 17:34), and with Pseudo-Dionysius the Areopagite, a sixth-century theologian who's best known for describing the ranks of angels in the *Celestial Hierarchy*. Because he was martyred by beheading, St. Denis is portrayed decapitated, dressed in bishop's vestments, and holding his own head. He is a patron saint of France, the city of Paris, and is one of the Fourteen Holy Helpers, invoked against headaches, rabies, and demonic possession.

St. John Leonardi (c. 1541–1609) was an Italian priest who founded the Confraternity of Christian Doctrine. Born in Diecimo, his father sent him to pharmacy school when he was seventeen, and John plied this trade for ten years before realizing that he had a vocation to the priesthood. He was ordained in 1572 and developed an apostolate among young people with the Confraternity of Christian Doctrine. In 1574, he founded a community of priests, the Order of Clerks Regular of the Mother of God. After Paul V approved his new order, John moved to Rome, where he cofounded the seminary of the Propagation of the Faith. He died during an influenza epidemic, after caring for his stricken brothers. St. John is the patron saint of pharmacists.

THU 10 (#464) green Weekday

The Lectionary for Mass

◆ FIRST READING: "What's the use?" Haven't we all felt that way at one time or another? In today's reading, the Israelites, who have been engaged in penitential practices that are seemingly to no avail, ask this same question. The Lord did not seem to respond. To the contrary, though, the Lord did see and hear—and noted those who reverenced him and trusted in him. Their prayers would be heard, and they would be spared on the day of judgment.

◆ RESPONSORIAL PSALM 1: Today's Psalm proclaims the blessedness of all who trust in the Lord. They are like a fruitful tree planted near running waters.

◆ GOSPEL: Jesus encourages his disciples to be persistent in prayer through the parable of the persistent friend. If human parents demonstrate such watchful care for their children, how much more attentive will the heavenly Father be, who gifts all who believe in Jesus with his Holy Spirit.

FRI 11 (#465) green Weekday

Optional Memorial of St. John XXIII, Pope / white

The Lectionary for Mass

◆ FIRST READING: The prophet Joel warns of an imminent day of the Lord—a day of judgment and destruction. All are to prepare for it through repentance and prayer.

◆ RESPONSORIAL PSALM 9: The theme of the Lord's judgment is echoed in today's antiphon. Surprisingly, perhaps, the first stanza speaks of thanksgiving, but so it should. Those who trust in the Lord have no reason to fear. They will witness God's judgment against the wicked.

◆ GOSPEL: What is the source of Jesus' power over evil? It can only be from God. The two parables at the end of the Gospel remind us that we must be ever watchful of the strength of the evil one who strives to separate us from God.

Today's Saint

Known for his modesty and pastoral concern, "Good Pope John" dedicated his ministry to placing the Church at the service of the needs of the world. As supreme pontiff, John XXIII refused to be a prisoner of the Vatican, and instead modeled his papacy on the Good Shepherd, visiting the prisons of Rome, reaching out to the sick, and welcoming visitors of every faith and nation. He surprised the world by announcing the Second Vatican Council on January 25, 1959. His hope was that the Council would signal a new style for the Church and its authority.

SAT 12 (#466) green Weekday

Optional Memorial of the Blessed Virgin Mary / white

The Lectionary for Mass

◆ FIRST READING: Joel's words announce the imminence of the day of the Lord, a time marked by signs in the heavens and on the earth, when all the nations who have done violence against God's chosen people in Judah will be judged. On that day, God, who dwells in Zion, will be a refuge for his people and they will be vindicated.

◆ RESPONSORIAL PSALM 97: Today's Psalm celebrates God's kingship and just judgments. Note the repetition of the cosmic elements mentioned in today's First Reading. On the day of judgment, God's people have every reason to rejoice. For them, it is a day of deliverance and reward, a day of thanksgiving.

◆ GOSPEL: Faith in Jesus establishes new relationships, transcending even natural family ties. Note the emphasis on hearing the Word, and even more importantly, on doing it.

13 (#144C) green Twenty-Eighth Sunday in Ordinary Time

The Lectionary for Mass

◆ FIRST READING: Today's reading begins midway through the story of Naaman, whose skepticism in the face of the prophet's command, among other details of the story, is omitted. The focus is rather on the moment of healing. Elisha's selflessness in the face of Naaman's gratitude reminds us of the servant's response in last Sunday's Gospel reading. He was only doing what was required. Overwhelmed by the power of God at work in his life, Naaman, the Gentile, promises to worship him alone.

◆ RESPONSORIAL PSALM 98: Both the First Reading and the

Gospel show God's power at work in the lives of Gentiles through the hands of Israelite intermediaries. As a result, people from all the nations sing the praises of God.

◆ SECOND READING: Never forget, writes Paul to Timothy, that Jesus Christ rose from the dead. One wonders, how could we? This belief is the cornerstone of his Christian faith. It spurs Paul on in his ministry even though it meant imprisonment; it is the source of his endurance. Paul knows that we can depend on the promises of Christ.

◆ GOSPEL: What faith these lepers had—first in approaching Jesus, believing he could cure them, and then obediently doing what he told them. A priest would have to declare them clean before they could reenter the Israelite community. Realizing that he had been healed, one returned to thank Jesus before going to the priest.

The Roman Missal

We ask that God's grace may be with us always, going before and following after us, and that we may be "determined / to carry out good works" (Collect). It is the perfect formula for a holy life! We ask God to accept our prayers together with the "sacrificial offerings" we present, that we may "pass over to the glory of heaven" (Prayer over the Offerings). The Gloria and the Creed are sung or said today. Consider using the Eucharistic Prayer for Reconciliation I.

Other Ideas

This weekend Canadians celebrate Thanksgiving, and the Gospel story of the grateful Samaritan offers a good context for reflections on being thankful. Of course Thanksgiving in the United States comes later in November, but being thankful is never out of season. The word *Eucharist* comes from the Greek word that means "thanks-

giving." Every Eucharist is an act of thanksgiving for all that the Lord has done for us. Sometimes we participate in Eucharist wondering what we get out of it or what we need to do in order for it to be a meaningful celebration. What if we changed our approach to one of asking what will I be most thankful for at this liturgy. An attitude of gratitude instead of a presumption of entitlement can make a big difference in how we celebrate Eucharist.

MON 14 (#467) green
Weekday

Optional Memorial of St. Callistus I, Pope and Martyr / red

The Lectionary for Mass

◆ FIRST READING: Today we begin Paul's letter to the Romans. Paul begins his letters with a salutation which often names his coworkers and stresses some aspect of his ministry. In the Letter to the Romans, Paul stresses his call to be an apostle of Jesus, who is the fulfillment of all that was prophesied in the Scriptures. In particular, Paul is an apostle to the Gentiles (non-Jews). Paul also speaks of the Romans' vocation to belong to Jesus and to be holy.

◆ RESPONSORIAL PSALM 98: How fitting is today's responsorial antiphon! The Lord has indeed made known his salvation to both the Gentiles (the "nations" in the second stanza, the "ends of the earth" and the "lands" in the third) and the Jews (Israel, second stanza). We sing God's praise for all his marvelous deeds.

◆ GOSPEL: Jesus speaks to the crowd, drawing upon the heritage of the Old Testament to demonstrate that he is greater than Jonah, who preached repentance to Nineveh, and greater than Solomon, whose reputation for wisdom drew people from distant lands.

Today's Saint

Following a life of slavery and hard labor, St. Callistus I (+ 222) was appointed deacon in charge of the Christian cemetery on the Appian Way, now called the catacomb of San Callisto. Recognized for his abounding wisdom and natural bent for leadership, he was eventually elected pope. He had many critics, due to his liberal stance regarding the forgiveness of those who had apostatized during times of persecution. St. Callistus, heeding the commands of Christ, believed the repentant should be forgiven and welcomed back into the Church. Tradition maintains that he began the ember days, periods of fast and abstinence, which were replaced by days of prayer and penance determined by each diocese. He is commemorated as a martyr; he was probably killed during a public disturbance.

TUE 15 (#468) white
Memorial of St. Teresa of Jesus, Virgin and Doctor of the Church

The Lectionary for Mass

◆ FIRST READING: The Jews believed that they were righteous, that is, in the right relationship with God through observance of the Law. Paul, drawing on the words of the prophet Habakkuk asserts that righteousness comes through faith (2:4). In subsequent verses, Paul attests to the revelation of God manifest in creation. As a result, those (Gentiles) who worshipped idols rather than God are not to be excused. They received the punishment they deserved. We may fittingly ask ourselves what idols we worship.

◆ RESPONSORIAL PSALM 19, a song of praise, reiterates the theme of today's First Reading: all of creation bears witness to the glory of the Creator God.

◆ GOSPEL: Jesus is once again at a meal, sharing table fellowship with his Pharisee host, a strict adherent to the law. Though welcoming his guest, the Pharisee at the same time judges him. Jesus confronts him for his hypocrisy. What matters is not what is on the outside, but what is within, particularly as expressed in loving concern for the poor through almsgiving.

The Roman Missal

All the orations are proper for this obligatory memorial, and they can be found in the Proper of Saints at October 15. It would seem that the Preface of Holy Virgins and Religious would be the most logical choice for the Preface today. Consider using Eucharistic Prayer II.

Today's Saint

St. Teresa of Jesus (1515–1582), more commonly known as St. Teresa of Avila, joined the Carmelite Convent of the Incarnation at the age of 21. Disheartened by the laxness of its observance of the Carmelite Rule, in particular its opulent nature and overly social atmosphere, she began a reform movement laying the framework for the Discalced Carmelites. This new branch of Carmelites modeled themselves on the poor and crucified Christ, adopting a life of poverty and abstinence. In collaboration with St. John of the Cross, she helped bring this new way of life to the male Carmelite communities. Although their reforms were met with great resistance, they moved forward with faith and persistence. Among her many writings, she is well known for two classics: *The Way of Perfection* and *The Interior Castle*.

WED 16 (#469) green
Weekday

Optional Memorial of St. Hedwig, Religious / white; St. Margaret Mary Alacoque, Virgin / white

The Lectionary for Mass

◆ FIRST READING: Paul's words express an uncomfortable and disturbing message to all who pass judgment on other people without recognizing their own sin and hypocrisy. Paul voices an urgent call to repentance. We must not presume on the mercy of our impartial God at the time of judgment. All will be repaid according to their works.

◆ RESPONSORIAL PSALM 62: The Psalm is one of confidence and trust in God. Only one who is truly just can face God's judgment with confidence and peace.

◆ GOSPEL: Controversy between Jesus and the scribes and Pharisees pervades the Gospel accounts. While observing the letter of the law, they miss the deeper call to love, to be righteous, and to be open to God's love and mercy. Self-justification is always dangerous.

Today's Saints

St. Hedwig of Silesia (1174–1243) was Duchess of Silesia and of Poland and an aunt of St. Elizabeth of Hungary. When only twelve, she was married to Henry I of Silesia. They lived a devout life, performed penitential practices, and together supported the founding of many religious communities in Silesia. When Henry died in 1238, Hedwig went to live in the Cistercian convent her husband had founded at her request. Hedwig was canonized in 1267 and is a patron saint of orphaned children.

St. Margaret Mary Alacoque (1647–1690) was a French Visitation nun and mystic, whose visions of Jesus led her to promote devotion to the Most Sacred Heart as we know it today. Margaret was a pious child and practiced prayer and penance. She entered the Visitation convent in Paray-le-Monial in 1671. Unfortunately, the nuns there were suspicious of her, and Margaret Mary found her vocation tried, especially by the delay of her profession. The following year, she began having the visions that revealed the devotion to the Sacred Heart and its practices such as communion on First Fridays, and the holy hour of Eucharistic adoration on Thursdays. She was discouraged from spreading this devotion until the convent's Jesuit confessor, St. Claude la Colombière, declared that her visions were genuine. St. Margaret Mary died in 1690, but after her death, the Jesuits spread the devotion to the Sacred Heart. She is a patron saint of polio sufferers, orphans, and those devoted to the Sacred Heart.

THU 17 (#470) red
Memorial of St. Ignatius of Antioch, Bishop and Martyr

The Lectionary for Mass

◆ FIRST READING: Our reading picks up on a theme from the beginning of Paul's letter: we are made righteous through faith in Jesus. There is no longer any distinction between Jews and Gentiles; all are sinners, all can be justified through faith in Jesus.

◆ RESPONSORIAL PSALM 130: The antiphon acclaims God as the source of mercy and redemption. Psalm 130 is a prayer of lament, voiced by one who is conscious of sin and confidently prays for forgiveness.

◆ GOSPEL: Jesus continues his harsh condemnation of the scribes and Pharisees. They give honor to the prophets of the past, but fail to recognize the prophet who is in their midst. They seek to control access to knowledge: without striving after wisdom themselves, they try to prevent others from learning the ways of God.

The Roman Missal

All the orations, found at October 17, are proper for today. The Collect highlights the "glorious passion of St. Ignatius of Antioch." The Prayer over the Offerings includes a wonderful reference to the saint's proclamation before his martyrdom that he was the wheat of Christ, to be ground by the teeth of beasts (a statement that is used as today's Communion Antiphon); the prayer asks that just as St. Ignatius was accepted as the wheat of Christ, so may our oblation be pleasing to God. In other words, may we too be wheat and bread, transformed into an offering acceptable to God as this gift of bread will be transformed. The Prayer after Communion connects with this thought in asking that the heavenly bread we receive this day renew us "and make us Christians in name and in deed"— the deed perhaps including martyrdom, following the example of St. Ignatius. Given the emphasis on martyrdom in the orations, the most likely choice for the Preface would be one of the Prefaces of Holy Martyrs, although the Preface of Holy Pastors or even one of the two Prefaces of Saints could not be excluded as possibilities. Consider using Eucharistic Prayer I.

Today's Saint

St. Ignatius of Antioch (c. 37–107), an apostolic father and possible disciple of John the Evangelist, served the community of Antioch as bishop. Living during the anti-Christian reign of the Roman emperor Trajan, he was sentenced to be fed to animals in the Roman Colosseum because he would not engage in idol worship. His journey to Rome was marked by extensive writing in which he composed

seven letters. These letters, directed to various churches, emphasized the humanity and divinity of Christ, the centrality of Eucharist, and the importance of Church unity.

FRI 18 (#661) red
Feast of St. Luke, Evangelist

The Lectionary for Mass

◆ First Reading: Paul always ends his letters with very personal notes, and today we hear of Luke's loyalty and fidelity in remaining with Paul even though others have deserted him. It is this mention of Luke that results in today's text as the First Reading. We can surmise that it is through the presence of Luke that Paul experienced the strength of the Lord, enabling him to continue his proclamation of the Gospel to the Gentiles.

◆ Responsorial Psalm 145: Today's responsorial verse calls to mind Jesus' reference to the disciples in John's account of the Gospel as his "friends." Certainly, in writing the Gospel accounts and Acts of the Apostles, Luke makes known the glorious splendor of God's kingdom. The first two stanzas of today's Psalm could well be a description of what a Gospel "does."

◆ Gospel: We hear of Jesus' sending out seventy two disciples ahead of his own intended visit to various towns and places. Clearly they are to prepare his way. They are to be unencumbered by possessions, realistic about meeting opposition, people of peace, healers of the sick, and proclaimers of God's kingdom.

The Roman Missal

The texts for this Mass, all proper for the feast today, are located in the Proper of Saints section of the Missal at October 18. The Gloria is sung or said today, since it is a feast. The Collect employs

themes typically associated with St. Luke's Gospel account: God's love for the poor, and the universality of the Gospel as it goes out to all nations. The Prayer over the Offerings prays that the food of this Eucharist may bring us freedom of heart to serve God, in addition to healing and glory. The Prayer after Communion asks for strength from the Eucharist so that we might continue to be strong "in the faith of the Gospel which St. Luke proclaimed." The proper Preface designated for today is Preface II of the Apostles. Consider using the Eucharistic Prayer for Various Needs and Occasions II.

Today's Saint

St. Luke the Evangelist (first century) is traditionally known as the author of the Gospel that bears his name as well as of the Acts of the Apostles. He is also identified with the "beloved physician" referred to by St. Paul (Colossians 4:14). Luke was a Gentile from Antioch in Syria, and his roots show both in his writing style and in his sympathetic treatment of Gentiles in the Gospel that bears his name. According to Acts of the Apostles, he accompanied St. Paul on some of his evangelizing journeys, and he stays with Paul when he is imprisoned in Rome. Some sources claim he was martyred, but it is thought that he died an old man of natural causes. A tradition states that he was the first icon painter, and the Black Madonna of Częstochowa is attributed to him. His symbol is an ox or bull because the Lucan Gospel begins with Zechariah, the father of John the Baptist, offering a sacrifice in the Temple. St. Luke is patron saint of artists and physicians.

(#472) red

Memorial of Sts. John de Brébeuf and Isaac Jogues, Priests, and Companions, Martyrs

S A T **19**

The Lectionary for Mass

◆ FIRST READING: Paul holds up Abraham as an example of one who was in right relationship with God because of his faith.

◆ RESPONSORIAL PSALM 105: The history of Israel is recounted in today's verses which also focus on God's covenant with Abraham and Isaac his son. The last stanza actually refers to the exodus event, but we can hear it in today's liturgy as God leading forth his people throughout history in the joy of salvation.

◆ GOSPEL: Jesus promises a heavenly reward to those who acknowledge him before others. This is the witness to which we are called. But woe to those who are closed to the workings and movements of God's Holy Spirit.

The Roman Missal

The Collect for the memorial is found in the Proper of Saints, with the remaining prayers drawn from the Common of Martyrs: For Missionary Martyrs. Consider using the Eucharistic Prayer for Various Needs and Occasions IV.

Today's Saints

On this day the Church honors the saints who gave their lives to spread the Catholic faith in North America: two Jesuit priests, St. Isaac Jogues (1607–1646) and St. John de Brébeuf (1593–1649), and their companions. St. Isaac was captured and tortured for his preaching of the Gospel. He escaped and returned to Europe, but only to seek permission to offer Mass with his scarred and mutilated hands. The pope granted his wish, and St. Isaac returned to the New World where he was put to death in 1646. Jean de Brébeuf dedicated himself to preaching the Gospel among the Huron peoples in what is now upstate New York and Canada. He translated the Catechism into the Huron language and wrote a series of "Instructions for Missionaries" that mingled divine and practical counsels: "Love the Hurons as brothers," he urged, "and bear with their shortcomings. Never keep them waiting, and learn to get into a canoe without carrying sand or water with you. Eat first thing in the morning, because that's what the Indians do. Work as they do, and serve them in whatever way you can." Jean de Brébeuf knew that only by understanding the Indians could missionaries hope to help them understand the Gospel. North American martyrs, pray for us.

(#147C) green

Twenty-Ninth Sunday in Ordinary Time

20

The Lectionary for Mass

◆ FIRST READING: The lifting up of arms and hands in the air is an ancient gesture of prayer, one that the priest still uses today at Mass. In our First Reading, Moses raises his hands in prayer, interceding with God for Israel's success in battle. Today's text teaches us to persevere and to support one another in prayer.

◆ RESPONSORIAL PSALM 121: The Israelites prayed today's psalm as they journeyed on pilgrimage to the Temple in Jerusalem. Note that the Psalm speaks of lifting up the eyes in prayer. We should pray this song often as we make our way through life, since it both asks for and assures God's protection on the journey.

◆ SECOND READING: Earlier in this letter, Paul specifically names Timothy's mother Eunice and grandmother Lois as his teachers. Paul encourages Timothy to be faithful to the Scriptures that he learned in his youth and to persevere in proclaiming and teaching the Word at all costs.

◆ GOSPEL: What a comparison Jesus makes between the dishonest judge and God! We all know the feeling of being ready to do almost anything if it will mean someone will stop bothering us! How much more will God, who loves us, hear our prayers. The point of the parable is given at the outset: persevere in prayer.

The Roman Missal

The Gloria and the Creed are sung or said today. The Collect prays that we might always conform our will to God's will, and serve him in sincerity of heart. This petition might in some way be seen as connecting with the Gospel for today, in that discernment of God's will is important in figuring out how we are to live as both citizens of heaven and citizens of the civil society in which we find ourselves. That kind of discernment demands that we constantly seek to purify our actions and our motives, to be focused on the values of the kingdom, and so the Prayer over the Offerings appropriately prays for that purification through our participation in this celebration: that "we may be cleansed by the very mysteries we serve." We need to look at everything through the lens of the Paschal Mystery, celebrated in the Eucharist, in order to properly discern. The Prayer after Communion also assists us in this discernment as it describes how, from our participation in heavenly things (that is, this Eucharist), "we may be helped by what you give in this present age and prepared for the gifts that are eternal." In choosing a Preface for today, consider how Preface I of the Sundays in Ordinary Time describes for us how we are to live in the world, namely, as a chosen race, a holy nation, and a people belonging to God who proclaim everywhere his mighty works. Also consider using Eucharistic Prayer IV this week, with its own proper Preface; the sweeping résumé of salvation history it gives sets our notions of civil society in its proper perspective before God's majesty. Consider using Eucharistic Prayer III.

Other Ideas

A few Sundays ago we heard the Gospel reading in which Jesus shares a prayer with his disciples, the prayer we know as the Our Father. Today he tells them to "pray always." Since the early days of the Church saying prayers was a way of keeping time. Out of this practice came the Liturgy of the Hours, an ancient form of prayer that is done at certain times of the day and night. It is prevalent in monastic communities to this day. But recently it has become a common practice in many parishes, usually done only twice in a day, at morning and evening. If your parish has this practice consider joining with those who pray at these times. If you are not able to join with others you can find short forms of the Liturgy of the Hours for your personal use. There are many ways to "pray always," this is one of the best. Refer to the seasonal overviews in this *Sourcebook*

for more ideas about celebrating the Hours in your parish.

MON 21 (#473) green
Weekday

The Lectionary for Mass

◆ FIRST READING: Once again, Abraham is held up as a model of faith. Despite the fact his barren wife Sarah was well beyond childbearing age, Abraham believed against all odds that God's promise of an heir would be realized (see Genesis 15:3–6). It was truly an act of faith—Abraham was "empowered" by it. Because of this faith, he was deemed righteous. Believers of every race and time are also deemed righteous because of their faith in Jesus Christ, risen from the dead.

◆ CANTICLE: Today's response is from a canticle in the New Testament, Zechariah's hymn of praise when his son, John (the Baptist), was born. The child's birth was the fulfillment of a promise God made to Zechariah that he and his wife Elizabeth would have a child despite their old age (see Luke 1:5–25). We can also hear the words of today's canticle as ultimately fulfilled in Jesus.

◆ GOSPEL: Sadly, the situation at the beginning of today's Gospel is all too familiar. Jesus' parable touches deeply into the truth regarding riches. Ultimately earthly wealth doesn't matter, since we can't take it with us into the next life. Let us labor, instead, for riches in what matters to God.

TUE 22 (#474) green
Weekday

Optional Memorial of St. John Paul II, Pope / white

The Lectionary for Mass

◆ FIRST READING: Beginning in Romans 5:12, Paul contrasts Christ with Adam, the first human

creature. Through Adam, sin came into the world, through Christ, justification and life; through Adam, death; through Christ, everlasting life. How very much more has Christ done for us! His grace overflows into the lives of all who believe.

◆ RESPONSORIAL PSALM 40: Today's responsorial verse is a concise summary of the life and death of Christ: Here am I, Father, I came to earth to do your will. Christ's obedience was the perfect sacrifice, acceptable to God and accomplishing salvation.

◆ GOSPEL: We are called to be vigilant no matter how long into the night we must wait for the Master, for the coming of the Lord. The heavenly reward envisaged in this parable is a banquet served by the Master become servant himself.

Today's Saint

In the early years, Catholics and non-Catholics alike were attracted to the athletic man who sneaked out of his villa to ski and reached out to the young at World Youth Days. People of many faiths prayed for him when he was shot in St. Peter's Square and were awed with the mercy he granted his assailant. None escaped the poignancy of a feeble John Paul II praying at the Western Wall in Israel, leaving a prayer inside the wall. Even a scant follower of the pope knew that the man who forgave his assailant, traveled the world to evangelize, and sought healing in relations with the Jewish people looked to the Blessed Virgin as a model of faith. For Mass, use the texts from the Common of Pastors: For a Pope.

WED 23 (#475) green
Weekday

Optional Memorial of St. John of Capistrano, Priest / white

The Lectionary for Mass

◆ FIRST READING: Paul's mission to the Gentiles has gone well; he deserves the title Apostle to the Gentiles. He boldly states that they are coheirs of the salvation of God; indeed they are members of the same body as all the others who have heard the Good News of Jesus Christ. But Paul assures his readers that he became "a minister by the gift of God's grace" and what has happened was in the plan of God whose "eternal purpose" has now been made known to the Church.

◆ RESPONSORIAL PSALM: Psalm 124 celebrates the Lord's deliverance of Israel out of Egypt. Christ's Paschal Death and Resurrection have made our passage from death to life possible. We share in this new life this through the saving waters of Baptism. Our help, our salvation, is in the name of the Lord Jesus, risen from the dead.

◆ GOSPEL: Chapter 12 of Luke contains several parables of vigilance. We hear another one today. Does our Master's (Lord's) delay in returning (to the earth at the end of time) result in our being careless? Perhaps even abusing people and things? We must be prepared to render an account. We know not the time of our Master's coming.

Today's Saint

St. John of Capistrano (1386–1456) was an Italian Franciscan priest. He was born in the Kingdom of Naples and studied law at Perugia, got married, and became a magistrate. During a war, he was sent as a peace ambassador but was thrown in prison, and during this time realized that he was called to be a priest. He and his wife had never consummated their marriage, so they separated, and John entered the Franciscans. He applied himself to a life of extreme asceticism and developed a reputation as a powerful preacher, in Italy as well as in countries such as Germany and Poland. So great were the crowds who came to hear him that no church could hold them, and he had to preach outdoors. In addition to preaching, John fought heresy through his writing and led an army against an invasion of Turks. He survived the battle but died of bubonic plague in 1456. St. John of Capistrano is a patron saint of those in the legal profession. The famous Mission San Juan Capistrano in southern California is named for him.

THU 24 (#476) green
Weekday

Optional Memorial of St. Anthony Mary Claret, Bishop / white

The Lectionary for Mass

◆ FIRST READING: It seems that the Romans were struggling to break with their prebaptismal patterns of life. Paul encourages them to live their life for God in Christ, no longer as slaves to sin. Sin leads to death; God's gift, to eternal life.

◆ RESPONSORIAL PSALM 1: Today's antiphon is Psalm 40:5, from the same Psalm that we had on Tuesday. If we look at the verse in its entirety, we see that the Psalmist contrasts the blessed one who hopes in the Lord with the person who is idolatrous or strays after falsehood, which is exactly what Paul says to the Romans. The stanzas of today's response are from Psalm 1, which likewise contrasts the just person who delights in the law of the Lord with the wicked.

◆ GOSPEL: Sadly, commitment to the Lord can sometimes result in family divisions. This was a reality in Luke's community and is still the case today. Let us pray for our families and for perseverance for those who face opposition in their commitment to the Lord.

Today's Saint

As a successful weaver and skilled printer in Spain, St. Anthony Mary Claret (1807–1870) felt called to be ordained a priest and preach parish missions. He eventually gathered young men together in community to preach missions, which led to the foundation of a new religious congregation called the Claretians. Later in life he was appointed archbishop of Santiago, Cuba, a huge diocese with many problems, including racism, slavery, and anti-Christian persecution. His Christian response to the problems (for example, establishing credit unions to loan money to the poor) resulted in fifteen assassination attempts upon his life. Following his tenure as bishop, he served as confessor to Queen Isabella II and was able to exert his influence in the court to implement new projects, such as starting a natural history museum and schools of music and languages.

FRI 25 (#477) green
Weekday

The Lectionary for Mass

◆ FIRST READING: Paul acknowledges that all people, himself included, struggle against sin. It takes real effort to live a Christian life and to avoid evil. Good intentions are not enough. Christ has already accomplished the victory and he is ready to help us. As long as we are in this mortal body, we must fight against sin and seek the help of God's grace and life within us.

◆ RESPONSORIAL PSALM 119, like Psalm 1, acclaims the Law of the Lord as the source of life. In the light of the Christ event, we can pray this Psalm to the Lord Jesus, the teacher of the new Law. In our struggle against sin, we need his compassion, his kindness, his saving help.

◆ GOSPEL: Jesus chides the crowds; they are capable of interpreting the signs of nature, but can't discern the sign of the present moment marked by his presence among them. The saying at the end of the Gospel encourages Jesus' listeners to work out their differences and to seek reconciliation among themselves rather than resort to law courts, which will only result in punishment.

S A T 26 (#478) green
Weekday

Optional Memorial of the Blessed Virgin Mary / white

The Lectionary for Mass

◆ FIRST READING: "If the Spirit of the one who raised Jesus from the dead dwells in you"—what powerful words at the conclusion of today's reading! And let there be no doubt—the Spirit of the One who raised Jesus from the dead does indeed dwell in us through Baptism. Yes, we live in mortal bodies, we struggle against the flesh (Paul's word for anything which stands in opposition to the Spirit of God), but we are victorious in the spirit of Christ. He is our life now and will raise us to eternal life in the age to come.

◆ RESPONSORIAL PSALM 24: Today's Psalm speaks of the deep human longing to see the face of God. Psalm 24 is a processional Psalm used in the Temple liturgy. The second stanza calls our attention to what is required of the one who would be in the presence of the Lord. Is not our life a "procession" to the heavenly Temple where we will be in the presence and see the face of the living God?

◆ GOSPEL: A tragic incident involving loss of life is reported to Jesus. According to the popular mentality, this was punishment for sin. Jesus warns that a worse fate awaits those who refuse to take his words to heart and turn from evil.

☀ 27 (#150C) green
Thirtieth Sunday in Ordinary Time

The Lectionary for Mass

◆ FIRST READING: Though not "unduly partial," God does show special care for the poor, the oppressed, and the helpless—those with no one to provide for their needs. This is clear not only from God's actions in the history of Israel, but also in the commands of his law (see, for example, Exodus 22:21). The Lord hears and answers their cries for help.

◆ RESPONSORIAL PSALM 34: What we might call God's preferential option for the poor and helpless is evident in today's Responsorial Psalm as well, a hymn of praise confessing God's justice and deliverance of those who are oppressed. The psalmist's confession of what God has done is meant as a witness and incentive to hope for others (end of first stanza).

◆ SECOND READING: What Paul says about himself to Timothy conveys the image of one who serves God willingly. Paul uses both the

cultic language of sacrifice and images from athletic competition (the race, the crown) in speaking of his own discipleship. As in both the First Reading and the Responsorial Psalm, Paul likewise attests to his experience of the Lord's deliverance from all that threatened him.

◆ GOSPEL: The introduction to today's parable warns about being overly convinced of our own righteousness. The Pharisees took great pride in their observance of the Law and so considered themselves to be in right relationship with God because of it. Note, however, that the Pharisee prayed not to God, but to himself (Luke 18:11). The tax collector is the one who prayed to God willingly in humility and repentance. By doing so, this outcast and reputed sinner is the one who receives mercy and justification from God.

The Roman Missal

The Mass texts for today are found in the "Ordinary Time" section of the Proper of Time. The Gloria and the Creed are sung or said today. The prayers for today ask God to "increase our faith, hope, and charity," so that we may do as he commanded—to "love." Consider using Eucharistic Prayer III or IV.

Other Ideas

Today's Gospel reading is the account of the Pharisee and the tax collector who both go up to the Temple to pray. The difference in their prayer is striking. Reread this passage and note the differences not only in their words but in their attitudes. The prayer of the tax collector is every believer's prayer: "O God, be merciful to me a sinner." It is an act of faith because only God knows how best to deal with sinners. It is an act of honesty since we know what is in our hearts. And it is an act of humility since it recognizes that it is God, and not ourselves, who can make us whole again. It is this prayer that leads us to the Sacrament of Reconciliation. Perhaps this would be a good time to celebrate that sacrament and know again the wonderful healing of God's love for us.

MON 28 (#666) red Feast of Sts. Simon and Jude, Apostles

The Lectionary for Mass

◆ FIRST READING: Our unity in Christ abolishes all distinctions between us. Through our common faith, we are united to Christ and to one another: as brothers and sisters in the family of God, fellow citizens of God's holy city, the household of God, a temple or dwelling place of God. On this feast of Sts. Simon and Jude, are we aware of how our faith today has been built on the foundation of the Apostles' witness centuries ago?

◆ RESPONSORIAL PSALM 19: In its original context, today's psalm spoke of the witness of the heavens to the glory of the Creator God. On this feast of Sts. Simon and Jude, we celebrate the witness of the Apostles who brought the Gospel message throughout all the earth.

◆ GOSPEL: Little is known about the Apostles whose feast we celebrate today. Simon is identified as a zealot, someone zealous to re-establish the nation of Israel and be rid of Roman domination. We might even go so far as to think of him as somewhat of a revolutionary. Of Jude, we know only that he is the son of James. Jesus chose these and the other Apostles after spending a night in prayer.

The Roman Missal

The prayers on this feast of the two Apostles are found in the Proper of Saints. The Gloria is said or sung, and one of the Prefaces of the Apostles is used. Simon and Jude are mentioned in Eucharistic Prayer 1.

Today's Saints

Today we honor two Apostles about whom we know very little. Tradition maintains that St. Simon the Zealot preached missions throughout Persia and Egypt. St. Jude, not to be confused with Judas Iscariot, is the patron of hopeless causes and is called Thaddeus in the Gospel according to Matthew and the Gospel according to Mark. It is believed that he engaged in missionary work in Mesopotamia and Persia. Both Apostles are thought to have been martyred in Persia, and their relics were transferred to St. Peter's Basilica in Rome sometime during the seventh or eighth century.

TUE 29 (#480) green Weekday

The Lectionary for Mass

◆ FIRST READING: All creation—nature and humankind—is being transformed. Creation is in labor like a mother giving birth, as we come to be in the new life God has ordained for us. The Spirit is within us, pushing us on to this new life. All that we must suffer now pales in comparison with the life that is coming to be.

◆ RESPONSORIAL PSALM 126: In its original context, Psalm 126 celebrated Israel's deliverance from exile in Babylonia. Christian tradition has long viewed our life on earth as a sort of exile from our heavenly homeland. The Psalm speaks of joy in light of what the Lord has done and prays for full restoration. The juxtaposition of weeping and sadness with joy is yet another link with the First Reading.

◆ GOSPEL: There are two images for the kingdom of God in today's Gospel, and Jesus' Palestinian listeners would be familiar with both from everyday life: a mustard seed and grains of yeast. Though small at first, they eventually have tremendous effects. The tiny mustard seed grows into a large bush, which provides shelter and a home for the birds of the air. The small grains of yeast cause flour to expand and become bread for human nourishment. And so it is with the kingdom of God.

WED 30 (#481) green Weekday

The Lectionary for Mass

◆ FIRST READING: Much of Romans 8 has to do with the powerful presence of God's Spirit in our lives. Today's text focuses on the help that the Spirit gives us in our weakness and in our prayer. Do we recognize what is available to us? Do we draw on it? Do we truly believe that with the Spirit's help and power, all things in our life can work together for good?

◆ RESPONSORIAL PSALM 13: Today's psalm is a cry for help against the threat of enemies. The psalmist is confident in God's mercy and help. When it is received and the enemy is overcome, the psalmist will sing God's praise with thanksgiving.

◆ GOSPEL: Entering the Kingdom of God demands the spiritual strength that comes from faithful adherence to the words and commands of the Lord. Many who are self-assured by virtue of their religious practices may not be as secure in the eyes of the Lord as they are in their own. Similarly, some of those deemed unfit for the kingdom by self-appointed judges may, in fact, be worthy of a higher place.

T
H
U
31
(#482) green
Weekday

The Lectionary for Mass

◆ FIRST READING: Paul is all too familiar with opposition and suffering in his life, especially from those who did not receive his message about Jesus Christ. No matter how great the difficulties experienced, no matter how overwhelming the suffering, Paul is convinced that the love of Christ Jesus the Lord remains with us. Nothing, absolutely nothing, can separate us from that love.

◆ RESPONSORIAL PSALM 109: Today's psalm is a prayer that cries out for God's mercy and deliverance in times of distress. If we look at the psalm in its entirety, we discover that the psalmist identifies the suffering as a result of false accusation. The psalmist has fasted in prayer for God's deliverance and promises to thank God publicly for his help.

◆ GOSPEL: Like today's psalmist and like other prophets before him, Jesus knew false accusation and opposition. Herod, in particular, is mentioned in today's text. Jesus senses the imminence and inevitability of his death. Yet, in fidelity to the call he has received he must continue on his journey to Jerusalem. In today's text, Jesus employs the image of a mother hen carefully gathering and protecting her chicks under her wing to speak of his longing to gather Jerusalem's children into the fullness of life and salvation. Though acclaimed the messenger of salvation as he enters Jerusalem, he is ultimately rejected and put to death.

November 2019

Month of All Saints

F
R
I
1
(#667) white
Solemnity of All Saints

Holyday of Obligation

About Today's Solemnity

On this day, the Church honors all the saints, those who have finished the race and now rejoice in God's presence. We honor the towering figures like Sts. Peter, Paul, Augustine, Francis, and Thérèse of the Child Jesus, and we honor the humble saints as well, those whose names are known to few or to none: the grandparents and ancestors, the friends and teachers who lived their faith to the full and inspired faith in others. This is a day to celebrate them all.

An observance in honor of all the saints has been celebrated on November 1 since at least the seventh century, and it originated even earlier, with a feast in honor of all martyrs in the year 359. "Why should our praise and glorification, or even the celebration of this feast day mean anything to the saints?" asked St. Bernard of Clairvaux in a homily on All Saints' Day. "Clearly, if we venerate their memory, it serves us, not them. But I tell you, when I think of them, I feel myself inflamed with a tremendous yearning. Calling the saints to mind inspires, or rather arouses in

us, above all else, a longing to enjoy their company. . . . We long to share in the citizenship of heaven to dwell with the spirits of the blessed. . . . In short, we long to be united in happiness with all the saints" (Office of Readings, Volume IV, p. 1526). All holy men and women, saints of God, pray for us.

The Lectionary for Mass

◆ FIRST READING: John recounts his visions of two groups of people who are gathered in heaven in the presence of the victorious Lamb of God and the enthroned God. The 144,000 evokes the fullness of the twelve tribes of Israel whose faithfulness is rewarded. The universal scope of salvation includes every nation, race, and people. All have been faithful. All have been victorious, having endured a time of great distress.

◆ RESPONSORIAL PSALM 24: Today's antiphon perhaps best describes us as we wait to enter our heavenly home and be counted among those in the presence of God. The second stanza directs our thoughts to what is required of those who would dwell in the Lord's presence.

◆ SECOND READING: We are already children of God in the here and now, says John. But his words also touch on the unfathomable mystery of what we have yet to become: we shall be like God and we shall see God as he is.

◆ GOSPEL: In today's Gospel reading we hear the Beatitudes from Matthew's account of the Gospel. Notice that there are nine in today's text, the last one being a reference to those who are persecuted—also a link with today's First Reading. The first and eighth Beatitudes speak of the blessedness, or happiness, of those who are poor in spirit (who know their need for and dependence upon God) or who suffer because of their righteous conduct. It is an inner happiness that God alone can give, and it is the realization of life in God's kingdom. The other Beatitudes speak of the heavenly reward that is yet to be realized. Suffering and sorrow are inevitable on the way to the kingdom. Meekness, mercy, integrity, and "making peace" must all be manifest in the one who would dwell on God's mountain.

The Roman Missal

The Gloria and the Creed are sung or said today. The Collect reminds us of the great cloud of witnesses by which we are surrounded as it tells of how in this one celebration we venerate the merits of all the saints. Thus, we can take comfort in asking for the reconciliation with God "for which we earnestly long" because we can count on the intercession of so many saints.

The Prayer over the Offerings reiterates that we live our lives, and offer this Eucharist, in the Communion of Saints, and therefore they celebrate with us. We can experience their solidarity with and concern for us because they are assured of immortality in the Lord.

The Preface, titled "The glory of Jerusalem, our mother," is given, with and without musical notation, right there among the pages for all the other texts for this Mass. The Preface points to Jerusalem as our mother and the heavenly city where our brothers and sisters who have gone before us give God eternal praise. The key point to be emphasized is that we as pilgrims seek to advance to the heavenly Jerusalem as well, and our hope of arriving there is not unfounded since we have the strength and good example of the saints to assist us. This reminds us that the liturgical celebration of All Saints is not only about those faithful upon whom the Church has designated the title of sanctity, but it is also about our call to that same sanctity.

Eucharistic Prayer I, the Roman Canon, with its two listing of saints' names, might be considered an appropriate choice for use at this solemnity.

The Prayer after Communion reminds us that the holiness of the saints is only possible because it is rooted in God's holiness, God who alone is holy. In addition, although not explicitly so, the image of the heavenly Jerusalem — the eschatological aspect inherent in every Eucharist — is once again invoked as the prayer asks that "we may pass from this pilgrim table to the banquet of our heavenly homeland."

The Solemn Blessing formula for All Saints, found in the section of the Missal "Blessings at the End of Mass and Prayers over the People," is suggested for today, and would be well used. Also, in light of the call to sanctity that is given to us all as we strive to imitate and be in communion with the saints, perhaps the dismissal formula "Go in peace, glorifying the Lord by your life" would be the most appropriate form of dismissal for today.

Of course use festive music with full choir, banners in the entrance procession, incense, and a longer, more formal Gospel procession.

Other Ideas

Today's solemnity is a celebration of the whole Church. It honors all those who are listed as saints in our liturgical calendar, and all those whom God has called to be holy, that would be us. In the Beatitudes, Jesus names those who seem to be the most unlikely of saints: the poor, the meek, the sorrowful, and the persecuted. Yet these attributes marked the lives of many saints. Have you ever thought that you were a saint? Maybe not, but God calls us to be holy and it is God who names us as blessed. Today's solemnity is a good opportunity to involve and to catechize the children of the parish.

S A T **2** (#668) white or violet or black
The Commemoration of All the Faithful Departed
ALL SOULS' DAY

Today's Commemoration

On the day after All Saints comes All Souls' Day, the Commemoration of the Faithful Departed, in which the Church prays for all who have died. As Catholics, we believe in Purgatory. Not everyone necessarily has to pass through purgatory. Today, we pray for them, trusting that God will hear and answer our prayers that they know eternal light, happiness, and peace.

As we remember and pray for our loved ones who have died, the reality that we ourselves must one day die is also brought home to us as a gentle, insistent reminder. In Mexico, the Day of the Dead (Día de Muertos) is a way of praying for our ancestors, remembering and celebrating them, and making friends with death. As St. Ambrose wrote, "Death is then no cause for mourning, for it is the cause of mankind's salvation. Death is not something to be avoided, for the Son of God did not think it beneath his dignity, nor did he seek to escape it" (Office of Readings, Volume IV, p. 1539). May the souls of all the faithful departed through the mercy of God rest in peace.

The Lectionary for Mass

Please note that a wide selection of readings is offered in Lectionary #668. What follows are the author's suggestions.

◆ FIRST READING (Wisdom 3:1–9): In appearance, death can seem to be the absolute end of life, beyond which there is nothing more, as the first lines of this reading suggest. This is far from the truth, as the first-century author of the Book of Wisdom realized. There is hope of immortality and everlasting blessing. What beautiful images for death: God "took one" to himself

(Wisdom 3:6); God's faithful people "abide with him in love" (Wisdom 3:9). Note also the references to shining and darting about like sparks (Wisdom 3:7). This is an image of the transformation that the just will undergo in the age to come; they will be like the angels who are described with similar imagery in the Scriptures.

◆ RESPONSORIAL PSALM 23 is a much loved prayer of confidence, whose image of the dark valley represents all our fears and unknowns regarding death. But there is no need to fear; we are led by the Lord to a place of rest and joyful fullness of life in the house of the Lord.

◆ SECOND READING (Philippians 3:20–21): God's word assures us that our weak and lowly bodies will be transformed to conform to the image of the glorious Risen Christ. Our eyes have yet to see what is in store for us in the age to come.

◆ GOSPEL (John 14:1–6): What Jesus has to say to the disciples at the Last Supper reflects his awareness of the imminence of his own death. Perhaps what can speak to us the most on All Souls' Day is the image, repeated here yet again, of Jesus coming to take us to himself at the time of death (see John 14:3). He is the way to the Father, the way to our heavenly home.

The Roman Missal

All the texts are taken from November 2 in the Proper of Saints. Any one of the three sets of formularies may be chosen, at the discretion of the priest celebrant or, as appropriate, the parish's liturgy preparation/worship team. All the texts proclaim the centrality of the Paschal Mystery in understanding the meaning of Christian death: because of Jesus' Death and Resurrection, death leads to new life for all those united to Christ. Therefore, because of our faith in the Risen Christ, we can find hope in death. Some of the Mass prayers (the Prayer over the Offerings in formulary set 2; the Prayer after Communion in formulary set 3) explicitly mention Baptism; thus, calling to mind the baptismal symbols used in the funeral Mass (sprinkling with holy water, Paschal candle, white garment). Any one of the five Prefaces for the Dead may be used today, again at the discretion of the priest celebrant or according to the preparations made by a parish committee. Also, the Solemn Blessing formula "In Celebration for the Dead" (number 20 under "Blessings at the End of Mass and Prayers over the People") is suggested and should be used for all Masses today. The Gloria is not sung or said on All Souls' Day. Consider using Eucharistic Prayer I.

Other Ideas

It was widely held in folklore throughout the world that the souls of the dead return to earth on All Souls' Day. In many countries, it is customary to visit the graves of loved ones, and to even have a festive meal in the graveyard. In Mexico, this day–Día de Muertos–is particularly festive. Parishioners can also remember those that have passed by setting out photos along with candles in their homes.

3 (#153C) green
Thirty-First Sunday in Ordinary Time

The Lectionary for Mass

◆ FIRST READING: Our text from the Book of Wisdom focuses on God the creator, not in terms of his power, but in terms of his mercy and love for what he has created. What a tender God! Our loving and merciful God knows our sinfulness and failures, and takes the initiative in leading us back to himself.

◆ RESPONSORIAL PSALM 145: What response can we make to our God for his goodness and loving mercy other than praise and thanksgiving, as is voiced throughout today's Psalm. The Lord our God is faithful, and in his mercy, he lifts up all who fall.

◆ SECOND READING: Acknowledging God's power at work in them, Paul prays for the Thessalonians, that they may be worthy of the calling they have received. What a beautiful wish: that the Lord Jesus be glorified in them, and they in him. Would that it also be realized in us! We, like the Thessalonians, must be firmly grounded in our faith.

◆ GOSPEL: In Jesus' day, tax collectors were a despised lot. They worked for the Romans, the Gentile power who ruled their land. Tax collectors commonly supplemented their income with a surcharge. It was with this despised man who was so eager to see Jesus that he climbed a tree for a better look, and it was at this man's home that Jesus chose to stay. What a change in Zacchaeus as a result! How are we changed by Jesus' presence with us?

The Roman Missal

Even to praise God is God's gift. We pray that "we may hasten without stumbling" to the promises of God (Collect). We pray that our "sacrificial offerings" to God may be pure and bring us "a holy outpouring" of God's mercy (Prayer over the Offerings). We pray that God's power might be at work in us, so that the gift we receive in the Eucharist may prepare us to receive what it promises: eternal life (Prayer after Communion). The Gloria and the Creed are sung or said today. Consider using Eucharistic Prayer IV.

Other Ideas

Who among us doesn't love the story of Zacchaeus? We easily identify with this little guy who wants to see someone important passing through his neighborhood. But the crowd presents a problem for someone so short of stature. Young children in church could easily identify with him as they often find it difficult to see what's happening during the liturgy. As adults we identify with Zacchaeus on another level. We would like to "see" Jesus; in other words we would like to feel close to him in our life.

Here's a suggestion: imagine that Jesus actually showed up at your house for dinner. How would that change the table talk? Would you feel guilty or excited or both? And, like Zacchaeus, what might you decide to change in your life after this amazing encounter?

MON **4** (#485) white
Memorial of St. Charles Borromeo, Bishop

The Lectionary for Mass

◆ FIRST READING: Paul comes close to making the claim that the mission to the Gentiles resulted from the Jews' rejection of the Gospel. It is a point that serves his argument well. Only in the experience of our disobedience and sin can we know (personally experience) the mercy of God. God's plan, God's ways are mysterious—but in him, in them, we find life. "To God be glory forever!"

◆ RESPONSORIAL PSALM 69: The psalmist's prayer arises from an experience of distress and cries out for God's salvation. Is this not our experience when we are aware of our sinfulness? God is not deaf to the cries of those who are his own.

◆ GOSPEL: The theme of selfless love and concern for the needs of others is likewise heard in today's Gospel. We should reach out to the less fortunate who have no means to repay us rather than to those who can and do repay us.

The Roman Missal

All the orations are proper for this obligatory memorial and are found in the Proper of Saints at November 4. The Collect asks that the Church in our time might be constantly renewed with the same spirit that filled bishop St. Charles Borromeo, thus, identifying the saint as someone noted for reforming the Church in his time. The prayer articulates that the Church is ever in need of being more deeply conformed to the likeness of Christ. The Prayer over the Offerings prays for the specific fruits and good works we are requesting to result from this offering, namely, good fruit and works that embody the same virtues as St. Charles that made him such an attentive pastor. We pray for today's Eucharist to have concrete

---

effect in our lives in the Prayer after Communion also, this time praying for the same determination, "which made St. Charles faithful in ministry / and fervent in charity." The Preface of Holy Pastors could be considered the preferred choice for a Preface today, although Preface I or II of Saints could be used as well. Consider using Eucharistic Prayer II.

Today's Saint

St. Charles Borromeo (1538–1584), a doctor of civil and canon law, was a great champion of the Church redefining itself in light of the Protestant Reformation. As Archbishop of Milan, he promulgated the reforms of the Council of Trent, giving special attention to liturgical and clerical renewal. Other significant contributions he made to the Church include the establishment of new seminaries for the education of the clergy, defining a code of moral conduct for clergy, and founding the Oblates of St. Ambrose, a society of diocesan priests, to enforce the reforms of Trent. St. Charles adopted a simple life in which he responded to the needs of the poor and sick by providing monetary and spiritual support.

TUE **5** (#486) green
Weekday

The Lectionary for Mass

◆ FIRST READING: Paul uses the analogy of a human body with its varied and interrelated parts to describe the Body of Christ, the Church, with its varied and interrelated—and necessary—gifts. Paul encourages all Christians to use the gifts they have received for service to others. The second part of the reading consists of a series of exhortations on the practicalities of living a Christian life, both in relation to the Lord and to one another.

◆ RESPONSORIAL PSALM 131: Today's response is the prayer of one who has emptied himself or herself in order to be filled with, and focused on, the Lord who alone is the source of our peace. The peaceful image of a child resting on its mother's breast describes the psalmist's experience of inner peace, rooted in the Lord.

◆ GOSPEL: Today's text is a continuation of Gospel passages heard over the past several days. It begins with a saying looking forward to the heavenly banquet. The parable illustrates the relationship between our responses to God's invitation and our participation in the banquet. Are we among those who find excuses not to come? The Master desires that his banquet be filled. Those present may be the very ones we least expect or perhaps even shun (the blind, the sick, the widowed, the outcast, etc.), but who nonetheless responded to God's call.

W E D 6 (#487) green
Weekday

The Lectionary for Mass

◆ FIRST READING: Paul's practical exhortations continue, today focusing exclusively on our relationship with our neighbor. The whole law is fulfilled when the commandment to love one's neighbor as oneself is observed.

◆ RESPONSORIAL PSALM 112: The blessedness spoken of in today's antiphon is a deep happiness that is the Lord's blessing and the reward of the one who is faithful. The stanzas of the Psalm give the criteria by which one is deemed worthy to receive the Lord's blessing.

◆ GOSPEL: If we would embrace discipleship, we must first consider the cost; specifically, we must be truly willing to put our relationship with the Lord before all other relationships and possessions.

T H U 7 (#488) green
Weekday

The Lectionary for Mass

◆ FIRST READING: Romans 14 is primarily concerned with the attitudes—and judgments—that members of the community have toward one another when there are differences of opinion about religious practices and customs (see Romans 14:1–5). Paul commands the honoring, not the judging, of the other's view. In Christian community we are brothers and sisters of one another. The various customs and practices are to be observed for the Lord, to whom we all belong, for whom we live, for whom we die. It is the Lord who judges.

◆ RESPONSORIAL PSALM 27: In its original context, the Psalm referred to the good things of the Lord in this life, despite threats from opponents. Juxtaposed with our reading from Romans, we easily think of the heavenly land of the living. The psalmist's longing is for God's dwelling place in the Temple in Jerusalem; for us, it is for God's heavenly dwelling place. For this we wait with confidence, courage, and longing.

◆ GOSPEL: To sit at table together and share a meal signified the acceptance and welcome of the other person(s). Such was Jesus' attitude toward sinners. The two parables he tells in today's Gospel convey the joy of the heavenly Father when a sinner, found by Jesus, finds salvation in him.

F R I 8 (#489) green
Weekday

The Lectionary for Mass

◆ FIRST READING: We have come to the concluding sections of St. Paul's letter to the Romans. Paul summarizes what he has taught them. He reassures them that

though he has written "boldly" (Romans 15:15), with much counsel and teaching, he finds them to be "full of goodness, filled with all knowledge, and able to admonish one another" (Romans 15:14). He speaks of his own call, which is not to preach to those among whom the faith is already established, but rather to those who have never heard the name of Christ.

◆ RESPONSORIAL PSALM 98 echoes the universality of the Apostle's mission—the power of the Lord will be revealed to every nation.

◆ GOSPEL: Today's parable of the steward who squandered his master's property stands in stark contrast with the example of Paul who was such a faithful servant of the Gospel with which he was entrusted! Commentators on this parable point out the necessity of understanding Palestinian business practices of the time. The steward was the owner's representative in financial matters and would normally add on his own commission to the debt. Accordingly, by reducing the debts, the steward was foregoing his own commission. In this was the prudence for which he was commended.

S A T 9 (#671) white
Feast of the Dedication of the Lateran Basilica

About Today's Feast

Today the Church throughout the world celebrates a feast in honor of a church in Rome: the Basilica of St. John Lateran. St. John Lateran is not just any church: it is the cathedral of the Bishop of Rome, who is, of course, the pope.

"Lateran" was the name of a Roman family whose lands were seized by Emperor Constantine in the fourth century. He proceeded to build a great basilica dedicated in honor of St. John the Baptist, but the name of the family that had once owned the land remained associated with it, and the church is called San Giovanni in Laterano, or "St. John in the Lateran." For centuries, the old Lateran palace was the residence of the popes. It was only when the popes returned to Rome following the Avignon exile in the fourteenth century that they moved their residence to the Vatican Hill, which they considered to be a healthier part of the city. St. John Lateran continues to serve as the pope's cathedral and is as a sign of our unity as a Church under the leadership of the Holy Father. As we recall the dedication of this important church, the "mother church" of all the churches of the world, we should look inward as well.

The Lectionary for Mass

◆ First Reading: Today's First Reading is Ezekiel's vision of the life-giving waters that flow from the dwelling place of God. What a vision of hope this must have been for the people exiled from their homeland. All creatures flourish in these waters of life whose source is God. Their fruits provide nourishment and healing.

◆ Responsorial Psalm 46: Our antiphon and the second stanza of the Psalm echo the theme of the life-giving waters flowing from God's holy Temple. This psalm is one of confidence as it acknowledges God's presence and strength in times that shake us.

◆ Second Reading: What a profound image is given us in this reading, especially in light of the First Reading and Responsorial Psalm. We are God's building. We are God's holy place. God's life-giving water flows in us.

◆ Gospel: Jesus' body is the true dwelling place of God, the true Temple. "Destroy it," he tells his adversaries, "and it will be raised" (author's paraphrasing). His actions, in driving out those who were making God's house a place for their own financial profit, challenge us to ask ourselves what is going on in our hearts, since through Baptism, God now dwells in us.

The Roman Missal

The texts for this Mass are all found in the Proper of Saints section of the Missal, at November 9. The Gloria is sung or said today, since it is a feast. Since today is Saturday, the Creed is not sung or said today. There is a choice between two options for the Collect today. The first option uses the imagery of living stones to refer to the dwelling place of God, and thus asks for an increase of the spirit of grace in the Church. When the prayer goes on to ask that God's faithful people build up the heavenly Jerusalem by "new growth," it is presumably by a growth in holiness and grace, although certainly growth by the incorporation of new living stones (new members) could also be understood as well. The second option for the Collect uses the imagery of the Church as the Bride of Christ and has a little more of an eschatological focus as it specifically asks that the people of God may be led to attain God's promises in heaven.

Consider using the Eucharistic Prayer for Various Needs and Occasions II. The Prayer over the Offerings, in asking God to accept the offering being made, also asks that those who make that offering may receive "in this place / the power of the Sacraments / and the answer to their prayers." We can note an emphasis intended by inclusion of the phrase "in this place," thus, highlighting the Church both as the living stones and as a people who gather in a sacred space to enact the Divine Liturgy. The text for today's proper Preface is given right along with the other texts for this Mass, and it is given both with and without musical notation. The Preface, titled "The mystery of the Church, the Bride of Christ and the Temple of the Spirit," reiterates the imagery of the people as the Temple of the Spirit who make the Church resplendent through their living lives acceptable to God. The visible buildings that make up the Church are foreshadows of her heavenly glory.

The Prayer after Communion continues this eschatological theme of foreshadowing by addressing God as the one "who chose to foreshadow for us / the heavenly Jerusalem / through the sign of your Church on earth." Thus, the prayer goes on to ask that by our partaking of the Eucharist, "we may be made the temple of your grace / and may enter the dwelling place of your glory." Indeed, we can be reminded that it is only by celebrating the Eucharist that the Church can be Church; without Eucharist, the Church does not exist.

(#156C) green

10 Thirty-Second Sunday in Ordinary Time

The Lectionary for Mass

◆ First Reading: This is the account of eight Jewish martyrs, a mother and her seven sons, who attest to their belief in the resurrection of the dead. Their martyrdom took place at the time of Greek rule over Palestine. These brave martyrs chose death rather than to disobey the law of the Lord. Encouraged by their mother, the brothers confessed their belief in being raised up by God after their death.

◆ RESPONSORIAL PSALM 17: One who is upright and faithful in keeping God's law cries out for deliverance in today's Psalm. Notice the reference to "waking" in the last line of the third stanza. Juxtaposed with today's First Reading, we can hear it as a reference to living in the presence of the Lord after the sleep of death.

◆ SECOND READING: The first part of this reading is actually a prayer for the Thessalonians to be strengthened in what they say and do. In the second, Paul asks the Thessalonians to pray for him and his companions in the ministry of evangelization (note the specific mention of deliverance which echoes today's Responsorial Psalm). The last part of the reading expresses confidence that the Lord will strengthen and protect the community.

◆ GOSPEL: Today's Gospel, like our First Reading, looks to the resurrection in the age to come. The Sadducees were a sect within Judaism who, unlike the Pharisees, did not believe in resurrection. The Sadducees held only to what was revealed in the Law of Moses, and resurrection was a later development in understanding. Our resurrected life will be completely other than what we know now in this life. In the age to come, we will be gloriously transformed like the Risen Christ.

The Roman Missal

We ask God to "keep from us all adversity," not so that we may carry out our own plans, but so that "we may pursue in freedom of heart / the things that are" God's (Collect). In the Mass, we celebrate "in mystery" the Passion of Christ. We pray that we may always honor this great mystery with "loving devotion" (Prayer over the Offerings). We ask

"the grace of integrity" for all those who have received God's "heavenly power" through sharing in the "sacred gift" of the Eucharist (Prayer after Communion). The Gloria and the Creed are sung or said today. Consider using Eucharistic Prayer III.

Other Ideas

What is heaven like? How many times we have asked that question, as children and as adults. Our curiosity as children evolves into a more serious question when we confront the death of someone we love in adult life. What happens in heaven? What will we look like? Will the others we knew on earth be there? This is the concern of the Sadducees in the Gospel reading today. Jesus' answer doesn't explain this mystery; it just says that life in heaven is different than life on earth. So maybe the question is can we live with that mystery? Can we trust God's love enough? If children ask about heaven it's OK to say you don't know what it's really like, but it must be good because God wants us to be there. If they ask if their pets go to heaven when they die, you can quote Pope Paul VI who said they do. (Refer to this helpful article in *America* magazine about animals and salvation: www.americamagazine.org/content/all-things/heaven-open-animals).

MON 11 (#491) white
Memorial of St. Martin of Tours, Bishop

The Lectionary for Mass

◆ FIRST READING: The Book of Wisdom begins with an exhortation to seek the Lord in integrity of heart, in goodness and righteousness. We are assured that he will manifest himself to us. However, the Spirit of the Lord shuns deceit and evil. The Spirit of God knows

what is in the human heart. Let us never forget this.

◆ RESPONSORIAL PSALM 139: Our antiphon is a prayer for God's guidance. Psalm 139 acknowledges God as one who knows every aspect of human existence, our thoughts, our speech, our actions. We should be mindful of his all-knowing presence.

◆ GOSPEL: Today's Gospel reading includes: a warning against being a cause of scandal; an exhortation to forgiveness regardless of the number of times we are wronged; and a teaching on the power of faith. How do the images of the millstone and the mustard seed help us to understand Jesus' message?

The Roman Missal

The prayers for this memorial are found in the Proper of Saints. We pray that we may be united with Christ in life and in death (Collect), "in tribulation" and "in prosperity" (Prayer over the Offerings), as St. Martin was. Consider using Eucharistic Prayer I.

Today's Saint

St. Martin of Tours (316–397) was forced by his father, a pagan officer in the Roman army, to join the military. While serving in the military, he had a life-changing event in which he cut his cloak in half to clothe a freezing beggar. Following this encounter he had a vision of Christ wrapped in the cloak. As a result of this experience, St. Martin chose to be baptized and declared himself a soldier of peace for Christ, refusing to participate in any act of violence. He took up the life of a hermit, thereby introducing monasticism into Gaul. Following his election as bishop of Tours he continued living as a monk, but made numerous trips to visit his people and establish new monasteries. The people of Gaul converted to Christianity due to his example.

(#492) red

T U E **12** Memorial of St. Josaphat, Bishop and Martyr

The Lectionary for Mass

◆ FIRST READING: God created human beings in his own image to be immortal, but death came into the world through Satan—an allusion to the story of the sin of Adam and Eve in Genesis 3. God, however, does not abandon those whom he intended for immortality. The author of Wisdom speaks at length regarding the fate of the souls of the just who have died: they are in God's hand; they are in peace. Verse 7 speaks of their "visitation," that is, the time of divine judgment. They shall be gloriously transformed; they shall shine like sparks. The imagery is also used in other biblical and extrabiblical literature of the time to describe heavenly angelic beings. The souls of the just are destined for a glorious heavenly reward with the Lord.

◆ RESPONSORIAL PSALM 34: Today's psalm is a hymn of praise voiced by the just who cried out for deliverance from their distress and who experienced the Lord's salvation.

◆ GOSPEL: Does it seem like a lot is being asked of servants? We must do all that we have been commanded by the Lord, especially to love and serve one another.

The Roman Missal

All the orations are proper today, and are taken from November 12. Given the emphasis in the orations today, one of the two Prefaces of Holy Martyrs would seem to be the most logical choice for a Preface; the Preface of Holy Pastors or one of the two Prefaces of Saints could also be considered. Consider using Eucharistic Prayer II.

Today's Saint

As a young man St. Josaphat (c. 1580–1623) was excited about the possibility of the Orthodox metropolitan city of Kiev, comprising Belarussians and Ukrainians, reuniting with the Church of Rome. When he was elected archbishop of Polotsk, Lithuania, he worked tirelessly to continue the efforts to bring the Orthodox communities of Kiev in full communion with the Catholic Church. Many people were strongly opposed to this reunion; therefore, they established a rival hierarchy and set up groups to defame his name. While preaching in a particularly hostile city, he was murdered. His commitment to ecumenical relations was eventually realized in the Byzantine Rite of Catholicism. St. Josaphat, the martyr, is the first Eastern saint to be formally canonized.

(#493) white

W E D **13** Memorial of St. Frances Xavier Cabrini, Virgin

The Lectionary for Mass

◆ FIRST READING: Wisdom voices a foreboding warning to the kings and rulers of the earth, reminding them that they are accountable to God the Most High for all of their judgments. What is more, they will be subject to a perhaps more rigorous scrutiny than the poor and lowly. Those in power should seek the Lord's instruction manifest in his words and in his law.

◆ RESPONSORIAL PSALM 82: Our responsorial antiphon, a prayer for God to come and judge the earth, is the last verse of Psalm 82. In the preceding verses, God addresses those who judge unjustly and admonishes them about what they should be doing as people in power (first stanza today). They must remember that they, too, will be subject to death and judgment (second stanza).

◆ GOSPEL: Lepers were among the outcasts in Israel because of their physical defilement (see Leviticus 13) and the fear of contagion. Thus, they stand at a distance from Jesus. Jesus' healing acts are another example of the kindness and love of the Lord. Note that the leper shunned both because of his physical affliction and ethnic origin (he was a Samaritan) is the one who returns to give thanks.

The Roman Missal

The Collect is the only proper for today, and it is found at November 13. The prayer describes how the saint was called from Italy to serve the immigrants of America, and then goes on to ask that we might be taught to have the same concern for the stranger and all those in need. The Prayer over the Offerings and the Prayer after Communion are taken from either the Common of Virgins: For One Virgin, or from the Common of Holy Men and Women: For Those Who Practiced Works of Mercy. An appropriate Preface for this celebration would be either the Preface of Holy Virgins and Religious or Preface I or II of Saints. Consider using the Eucharistic Prayer for Various Needs and Occasions II.

Today's Saint

St. Frances Xavier Cabrini (1850–1917), also known as Mother Cabrini, was an Italian immigrant to the United States. She was the first American citizen to be canonized. As a girl, Frances dreamed of sailing to China as a missionary. In 1880, she founded the Missionary Sisters of the Sacred Heart of Jesus, and her community's work drew the attention of Pope Leo XIII. She hoped that he would send her to China, but he instead sent her to New York City in 1889 to minister to Italian immigrants, saying "Not to the East, but to the West." She founded sixty-seven institutions throughout the United States, Europe, and South America. After her death, her sisters fulfilled her dream of working in China. St. Frances Cabrini is the patron saint of immigrants.

THU 14 (#494) green Weekday

The Lectionary for Mass

◆ FIRST READING: Today's reading offers a beautiful description of the attributes of divine wisdom. Note that the feminine pronoun is used for Wisdom as the word is feminine in gender in Greek (the book was written in Greek). Wisdom's work among humankind is timeless, "passing into holy souls from age to age she produces friends of God and prophets" (Wisdom 7:27). May we be found among them.

◆ RESPONSORIAL PSALM 119, the longest Psalm in Scripture, acclaims the wisdom and value of the Law of the Lord. With but one or two exceptions, each verse contains some reference to the Law, under a variety of different names. What attributes of God's word—God's Law, are named today? How does it affect our lives?

◆ GOSPEL: The coming of the Kingdom cannot be observed. It is already present in the person of Jesus and in the lives of believers. We await the coming of the Son of Man at the end of time when God's kingdom will be fully manifest.

FRI 15 (#495) green Weekday

Optional Memorial of St. Albert the Great, Bishop and Doctor of the Church / white

The Lectionary for Mass

◆ FIRST READING: The greatness and beauty of creation bear witness to the existence of God, yet sadly, not all people have recognized it. Instead, they reckoned one or another creature as god. How could they not find God in the marvelous things he has made? May we not be among those who fail to recognize the Creator in the work of his hands.

◆ RESPONSORIAL PSALM 19: In this hymn of praise, creation speaks the praises of God through its very existence. Its message extends throughout the world, indeed, throughout the universe.

◆ GOSPEL: Today's First Reading and Responsorial Psalm can be heard as a call to mindfulness. Today's Gospel, on the other hand, draws on the stories of Noah and Lot and their contemporaries to warn about inattentiveness and its consequences. Let us not take God's call, God's commands, and the judgment to come for granted.

Today's Saint

To the great disappointment of his father, St. Albert the Great (1206–1280), known as "the universal doctor," entered the Dominican order, where he was recognized for his acumen. Ahead of his time, he believed that learning did not take place in a vacuum; one must be an interdisciplinary learner. He loved the world of academia, anywhere from studying the natural sciences to unearthing the connection between reason and experience to learning the geography of the earth. As a prestigious teacher, he had the privilege of instructing and mentoring St. Thomas Aquinas, author of the *Summa Theologiae*. Toward the end of his life he began to experience memory loss and dementia, which led to his gradual demise. He was declared a Doctor of the Church by Pope Pius XI.

SAT 16 (#496) green Weekday

Optional Memorials of St. Margaret of Scotland / white; St. Gertrude, Virgin / white; Blessed Virgin Mary / white

The Lectionary for Mass

◆ FIRST READING: Wisdom's words speak of the night of the first Passover, when God's angel came down to the earth. The first-born of the Egyptians who had oppressed God's people died while the Israelites were spared and subsequently passed through the waters of the sea into freedom. The author of Wisdom describes the Israelites as frolicking with joy in praise of their Creator.

◆ RESPONSORIAL PSALM 105 recounts the history of Israel. The verses chosen for today fittingly pertain to the Passover-Exodus event. Note the joy and celebration in the last line of the last stanza!

◆ GOSPEL: Perseverance in prayer is the instruction Jesus' disciples receive in today's Gospel. The parable serves to illustrate the fact that if even a mortal judge yields to the persistent pleas of the widow, the immortal God will certainly respond to the pleas of his chosen ones.

Today's Saints

St. Margaret of Scotland (c. 1045–1093), the wife of King Malcolm III of Scotland, managed to raise eight children while promoting Church reform, especially in the area of liturgical practice. As a woman of great faith, she founded and restored monasteries, provided hospitality to pilgrims, spoke out on behalf of the falsely accused, and fed the poor from her own dining table. All of her charitable activity was grounded in a strong prayer life.

St. Gertrude the Great (1256–1302) was a nun at the Benedictine monastery of Helfta, the abbey where two other great female spiritual writers lived: Mechtilde of Magdeburg and St. Mechtilde (Matilda von Hackeborn-Wippra). Through prayer she was graced with many mystical and ecstatic experiences, which are recorded in a five-volume work titled *Legatus divinae pietatis*, commonly called *The Life and Revelations of St. Gertrude the Great*. Her spirituality focused on the humanity of Christ and was characterized by a strong devotion to the Sacred Heart of Jesus. According to many scholars, St. Gertrude's writings should be on the same shelf with other influential mystics, such as St. Teresa of Avila.

(#159C) green

☀ 17 Thirty-Third Sunday in Ordinary Time

The Lectionary for Mass

◆ FIRST READING: The day of the Lord will be a day of judgment and vindication: judgment against Israel's enemies and Israelites who were unfaithful, and vindication for all who were faithful. It will be a time of healing and wholeness. That day is coming soon, says the prophet Malachi.

◆ RESPONSORIAL PSALM 98: The coming of the Lord who brings justice and judgment is reason for all the earth to break forth into joy-filled songs of praise.

◆ SECOND READING: The Thessalonians are to imitate Paul's example

in working for their livelihood to avoid being a burden on anyone. They are to be focused on the Lord Jesus and the work that is theirs, not dissipated in their thoughts and actions.

◆ GOSPEL: Speculation about the end-time has been around for a long time. When will it happen? What signs will precede it? People have always wanted certainty about it. In today's Gospel, Jesus warns his listeners against false prophets and mistaken signs. With foreboding words, he tells his disciples that before the end comes, they will suffer and be persecuted because of his name—even by members of their own families. He assures the disciples of his presence with them and promises that through perseverance they will save their lives.

The Roman Missal

The Gloria and the Creed are sung or said today. The Collect identifies for us where the source of "constant gladness" and "full and lasting happiness" is to be found: it is to be found in serving "with constancy / the author of all that is good." This Collect asks that we make sure we are using all our gifts and resources to serve God well; it is only by doing so that we can hope to share in the fullness of the joy of the kingdom. We must also stay alert and sober so we can serve with constancy. The Prayer over the Offerings has an eschatological focus, appropriate for this penultimate Sunday of the liturgical year, as it asks that what we offer at this Eucharist may "gain us the prize of everlasting happiness." The Prayer after Communion, however, is focused more on the present as it implores that, having partaken of "the gifts of this sacred mystery," we may be given "a growth in charity." Any one of the eight Prefaces of the Sundays in Ordinary Time are appropriate options for today, but perhaps Preface V might

be considered the best choice with its emphasis on God setting humanity "over the whole world in all its wonder"; the text could serve to reinforce the theme of taking responsibility for using the gifts God has given us and building the Kingdom of God. Consider using Eucharistic Prayer III.

Other Ideas

Both the liturgy we celebrate and the nature that surrounds us have signs of death and dying during these days of November. But they also show signs of resurrection and new life. During this month we remember those who have died, those from our parish and from our family and friends. If your parish enshrines a *Book of the Names of the Dead* in a prominent place be sure to inscribe the names of your loved ones there. If you have young children in your family talk to them about praying for those who have died.

(#497) green

ᴹᴼᴺ 18 Weekday

Optional Memorials of the Dedication of the Basilicas of Sts. Peter and Paul, Apostles (679) / white; St. Rose Philippine Duchesne, Virgin / white

The Lectionary for Mass

◆ FIRST READING: We begin reading from the books of Maccabees which recount events during the time of the Greek rule of Palestine beginning in the fourth century before Christ. By the second century, it had become a time of "terrible affliction" for the Jews. The Greek influence was so strong that some of the Jewish people abandoned the ways of their ancestors and became more and more acculturated and sympathetic to the Gentile way of life. At one point, King Antiochus Epiphanes promulgated a decree that all the citizens should adopt his religious practices and even went so far as to erect an altar of Zeus (the chief god of the Greeks) in the Temple precincts, an "abomination" of the holy place. Scrolls of the Law were destroyed; those who observed Jewish laws and customs were put to death. Many willingly chose death, rather than disobey God's Law.

◆ RESPONSORIAL PSALM: Psalm 119 acclaims the Law of the Lord as a way of—and to—life. The verses which are the stanzas of today's response focus on the oppression experienced by those who strive to be faithful.

◆ GOSPEL: The man in today's Gospel might have been blind, but he knew who Jesus was and what he could do. He relentlessly calls out for mercy. Jesus restores his sight not only on the physical level, but in the depth of his being. He then follows Jesus as a disciple.

About Today's Optional Memorial

There are four major basilicas in Rome, and each of them has an observance on the Church's universal calendar: St. Mary Major on August 5, St. John Lateran on November 9, and now the Basilicas of St. Peter and St. Paul. It is not so much the church buildings we are honoring, of course, as the saints to whom they are dedicated. The proper readings for today's memorial focus our attention on the special grace God gave all believers through two imperfect, impetuous, but exceptional men: Peter and Paul.

Today's Saint

Beginning her life as a nun in the Order of the Visitation in France, St. Rose Philippine Duchesne (1769–1852) eventually joined the Society of the Sacred Heart, founded by St. Madeleine Sophie Barat. Due to her missionary zeal, she was sent, along with five other sisters, to St. Louis, Missouri, to care for the poor and educate Native

Americans. Under her leadership, the sisters established numerous schools and orphanages. She is remembered for her remarkable work, including evangelization and catechesis with Native Americans, particularly the Potawatomi people. Recognizing her extraordinary ministry, amazing ability to navigate difficulties, and profound spirituality, a contemporary said, "She was the St. Francis of Assisi of the Society."

T U E 19 (#498) green
Weekday

The Lectionary for Mass

◆ FIRST READING: Eleazar, a ninety-year-old Jewish man, chooses death rather than dishonor and disobey the Law of the Lord. He was very much aware of the example that he could be for those who were young, showing them "how to die willingly and generously for the revered and holy laws." He was a martyr who suffered joyfully for the sake of God's covenant.

◆ RESPONSORIAL PSALM 3: The Lord is acclaimed as the source of strength and endurance for those who strive to be faithful to God's Law. The psalmist expresses confidence in God's deliverance despite the mockeries of his oppressors.

◆ GOSPEL: Zacchaeus is certainly an enterprising man in more ways than one. Like Elezar, Zacchaeus offers us an example of one who is firm in his convictions and acts on them. Zaccheus' behavior after his encounter with Jesus evokes the description of the just person in today's Psalm.

W E D 20 (#499) green
Weekday

The Lectionary for Mass

◆ FIRST READING: This is the account of eight Jewish martyrs, a

mother and her seven sons, who attest to their belief in the resurrection of the dead. Today's text focuses on the mother, her courage and fidelity in exhorting her sons to choose death—and thus life—rather than disobey the Law of the Lord.

◆ RESPONSORIAL PSALM 17: Today's Psalm is a prayer for deliverance. The psalmist asserts his fidelity and expresses confidence in God's vindication. Notice the word "waking" in the last line of the third stanza. Juxtaposed with today's First Reading, we can hear the reference to living in the presence of the Lord after the "sleep" of death.

◆ GOSPEL: Jesus makes his way to Jerusalem where death awaits him. He is the nobleman of the parable who is despised by his own people who face imminent destruction. Those servants who remain faithful will be rewarded abundantly. The negligent, idle, or fearful ones will lose what they have.

T H U 21 (#500) white
Memorial of the Presentation of the Blessed Virgin Mary

About Today's Memorial

The Gospel accounts tell of the Presentation of the Lord Jesus in the Temple but do not speak of the Presentation of Mary. Nevertheless, Christians in the East and the West have observed a day in honor of Mary's Presentation for centuries. Many artists have depicted the scene: a tiny girl (Mary is said to have been three or four years old when she was presented in the Temple), climbing the steps to go into the Temple to offer herself to God. This memorial speaks of Mary's total openness to God. God kept her free from sin from the moment of her conception, so that she, whose presentation in the Temple we commemorate today, would become a Temple of the Holy Spirit.

The Lectionary for Mass

◆ FIRST READING: We meet Mattathias, a leader and respected man in the city of Modein, who refuses bribes from the king's officers. They want him to comply with the king's command and thus disobey the Law of the Lord. Mattathias and his sons, leaving all possessions behind, flee to the mountains, and his supporters to the desert, so they can live faithfully according to the Law of the Lord.

◆ RESPONSORIAL PSALM 50: Those who live righteously will experience the saving power of the Lord in their lives! Psalm 50 depicts God gathering all peoples for judgment. The verses chosen for today are addressed to those who are just and faithful, and exhort them to offer sacrifices of praise and to honor their vows to the Lord.

◆ GOSPEL: Jesus weeps for Jerusalem. The people have failed to recognize the presence of the one sent by God or accept his message. Destruction, not peace, awaits them. The Romans destroyed Jerusalem in the year AD 70.

The Roman Missal

The proper Collect is found at November 21 in the Proper of Saints. The prayer asks for the intercession of the Blessed Virgin Mary as we venerate her on this day. The Prayer over the Offerings and the Prayer after Communion are to be taken from the Common of the Blessed Virgin Mary, with the Preface being either Preface I or Preface II of the Blessed Virgin Mary; use "on the feast day" as the choice of phrasing in Preface I. Consider using Eucharistic Prayer II.

F R I 22

(#501) red

Memorial of St. Cecilia, Virgin and Martyr

The Lectionary for Mass

◆ FIRST READING: The Lectionary omits the account of the death of Mattathias and the succession of his son, Judas, called Maccabeus, as the leader of the people. Judas' victories in war against the Gentiles are also omitted. Following their victories, Judas and his followers turned their attention to the purification and rededication of the Temple after its abomination by the Gentiles. Today's reading tells of the celebration of this event. We know it today as the Jewish Festival of Hanukkah.

◆ CANTICLE: Today's response is a hymn of praise from the first book of Chronicles, originally sung on the occasion of King David entrusting his son Solomon with the precious metals and stones to be used in the construction of God's Temple. It is a fitting response to the account of the Temple's rededication.

◆ GOSPEL: The first thing Jesus does upon entering Jerusalem, at least as Luke tells it, is to go to the Temple, that most sacred site for Jews, the place where God is invisibly present among his people. Sacrifices are offered regularly. Accordingly, there are numerous sellers of animals for sacrifice and money-changers for the convenience of those traveling at a distance. Profit, however, has superseded service and Jesus drives them out. We also hear in today's text about the growing animosity of Jewish religious leaders toward Jesus.

The Roman Missal

The Collect for the memorial, the only prayer proper for today, is found at November 22. The Collect asks that we might imitate the example of the saint, one of the most famous and revered of the early Roman martyrs. The Prayer over the Offerings and the Prayer after Communion come from either the Common of Martyrs: For a Virgin Martyr, or from the Common of Virgins: For One Virgin. One of the Prefaces of Holy Martyrs would be an apt choice for today, and consider using Eucharistic Prayer I, the Roman Canon, since St. Cecilia's name is mentioned in it.

Today's Saint

According to legend, St. Cecilia (c. third century) was beheaded because she would not forsake her vow of virginity and would not make sacrifices to the gods.

S A T 23

(#502) green

Weekday

Optional Memorials of St. Clement I, Pope and Martyr / red; St. Columban, Abbot / white; Bl. Miguel Agustín Pro, Priest and Martyr / red; Blessed Virgin Mary / white

The Lectionary for Mass

◆ FIRST READING: Today's reading recounts King Antiochus' reaction upon hearing of the defeat of his armies in Palestine and of the rebuilding of the Temple in Jerusalem. Things were not going well for the king at this point. His attempt to capture the Persian city of Elymais to obtain its wealth as booty had failed as well. He became sick with grief, even to the point of death. According to the biblical author, Antiochus recognized that his failures were punishment for his actions in Jerusalem.

◆ RESPONSORIAL PSALM 9: Today's song of thanksgiving for victory in battle could well have been sung by God's people after the defeat of the Gentiles and the rebuilding of the Temple. Note how the third stanza echoes what Antiochus realized about his armies in the First Reading: their own actions had brought destruction upon themselves.

Nevertheless, God does not abandon those who are his own.

◆ GOSPEL: The Sadducees were a sect within Judaism who, unlike the Pharisees, did not believe in resurrection. The Sadducees held only to what was revealed in the law of Moses, and resurrection was a later development in understanding. What is most important in today's text is what is said about the nature of our resurrected life: we will be gloriously transformed like the angels.

Today's Saints

St. Clement I (c. † 100) was pope during a rather tumultuous time, when the early Christian communities were experiencing growing pains. He is most remembered for a letter referred to as 1 Clement, which was written to the Christian community at Corinth. His letter addressed division within the community, urging its members to live in charity and unity. An unverified tradition, but one accepted by the early Church historian Tertullian and St. Jerome, claims that St. Clement was consecrated by St. Peter as his immediate successor. He is venerated as a martyr but the manner of his death is unknown.

St. Columban (Columbanus) (c. 543–615) was an Irish monk and missionary who established many religious houses in France and Italy. Through word and example, he urged the Church (and especially the clergy) to ever greater holiness.

Bl. Miguel Agustín Pro (1891–1927), a Jesuit priest and martyr, lived under an anticlerical and anti-Christian political regime in Mexico. He was executed by a firing squad because he would not abandon his clerical call to care for the oppressed.

(#162C) white

Solemnity of Our Lord Jesus Christ, King of the Universe

24

About Today's Solemnity

Today is the Thirty-Fourth or Last Sunday in Ordinary Time and the Solemnity of Our Lord Jesus Christ, King of the Universe. This solemnity was established by Pope Pius XI in 1925, an observance celebrating an aspect of Jesus' identity rather than of his life. Conventional understandings of kingship and power are transformed. Rather than calling up images of Jesus Christ dressed in kingly robes, the Gospel proclaims him as king by the sign over his head on the throne of a wooden cross (I.N.R.I.—*Iesus nazarenus rex Iudaeorum*—Jesus of Nazareth, King of the Jews). Paradoxically, it is the thief who recognized in Christ the Lord and Messiah.

The Lectionary for Mass

◆ FIRST READING: In today's reading, all the tribes of Israel acclaim David as King, thus unifying the country. When God chooses David as king, he is shepherding his father Jesse's flocks. As king, he is to shepherd God's people. Mention is also made of David's military prowess during the reign of Saul.

◆ RESPONSORIAL PSALM 122: Today's psalm acclaims Jerusalem as the home of all the Israelites and a sign of their unity. David and his

house, or descendants, receive special mention in the last stanza. In its original context, Psalm 122 was a hymn sung by pilgrims as they made their way to the Temple for worship.

◆ SECOND READING: Today's text is part of Paul's prayer for the Colossians in the first chapter of the letter. It is likewise an exhortation to them: they are to be thankful that as believers they belong to the Kingdom of God's beloved Son, in whom and through whom they are redeemed and reconciled to God. Verses 15 to 20 are from an early Christian hymn which acclaims Jesus as the image of God and the one in and through whom all things were created. He is the firstborn from the dead in a new creation, and head of his Body the Church, to which the Colossians belong.

◆ GOSPEL: When he was crucified, Jesus was mocked as "King of the Jews" by those who failed to recognize him as the promised Messiah, the Christ or anointed one. One of the criminals crucified with Jesus recognized his innocence and begged to be remembered when he entered his Kingdom. His prayer was answered when Jesus assured him that he would be with him in Paradise that very day.

The Roman Missal

On the Solemnity of Our Lord Jesus Christ, King of the Universe, we honor the unique kingship of Christ. His Kingdom is not here: his Kingdom is with his Father, and yet it is being mysteriously built in our very midst. His is "an eternal and universal kingdom, / a kingdom of truth and life, / a kingdom of holiness and grace, / a kingdom of justice, love and peace" (Preface of Christ, King of the Universe).

The Gloria and the Creed are sung or said today. In the Collect, we call on all of creation to serve and to praise God. In the Prayer over the Offerings, we pray that Christ may grant to all the nations his unity and peace. And in the Prayer after Communion we pray that all who follow Christ, the King of the Universe, may come to eternal life in the Kingdom of heaven. The beautiful Preface, which is proper, praises God, who anointed Christ as eternal Priest and King, to save us and lead us to a new kind of kingdom: "a kingdom of truth and life, / a kingdom of holiness and grace, / a kingdom of justice, love, and peace." It is found with the other prayers in the Proper of Time. Consider using Eucharistic Prayer I.

Of course use festive music with full choir, banners in the entrance procession, incense, and a longer, more formal Gospel procession.

Other Ideas

Today marks the last Sunday of Ordinary Time, the last Sunday of the liturgical year. With Thanksgiving a few days away and the beginning of Advent next Sunday there is much to occupy our reflection today. This might be a good opportunity to review this past year of our spiritual journey. How was my relationship with the Lord? What might I change in the new year that begins next week? Does my answer include being more charitable and more grateful? If so, then Thanksgiving offers an excellent opportunity to do that. Many parishes collect food items on Thanksgiving; be extra generous this year. If the parish doesn't do this then find an agency in your community that has a food pantry and ask what they need. Starting off a new year by doing good is always a good idea!

MON 25 (#503) green Weekday

Thirty-Fourth or Last Week in Ordinary Time

Optional Memorial of St. Catherine of Alexandria, Virgin and Martyr / red

The Lectionary for Mass

◆ FIRST READING: We begin the Book of Daniel, our readings for this last week of Ordinary Time. With the destruction of Jerusalem, many Israelites were taken to Babylon in captivity. Among them were the nobility who had professional training or special expertise in various crafts and skills. Today we are introduced to Daniel and his companions, four young Jewish men determined to remain faithful to the laws of Israel despite their privileged status as those destined for the king's service. God rewarded them for their fidelity with good health, knowledge of literature and science, and more wisdom than their peers. Daniel, in addition, had the gift of interpreting dreams.

◆ CANTICLE: Today's response, from the Book of Daniel, is the hymn of praise sung by the Daniel's companions from the midst of the fiery furnace. Today's verses focus on God, enthroned in heavenly glory.

◆ GOSPEL: Today's Gospel is the beautiful story of the widow whose offering to the Temple treasury came from the very little she had to live on. Needy herself, she freely gave of what she had to God.

Today's Saint

This fourth-century Christian woman lived in Alexandria, Egypt, during the reign of the Roman emperor Maxentius. Legend says that Catherine bravely confronted the emperor about his pagan beliefs. Maxentius gathered fifty pagan philosophers and challenged her to a debate. Her arguments were so convincing that many of the philosophers converted to Christianity. He then threatened to kill her unless she married him and renounced her faith. She refused and was condemned to death on a spiked wheel but the wheel fell apart when she touched it. She was then beheaded, and legend says that angels carried her to Mount Sinai. She has been venerated since the tenth century.

TUE 26 (#504) green Weekday

The Lectionary for Mass

◆ FIRST READING: The Babylonian King Nebuchadnezzar had a dream which greatly disturbed him. He sought an interpretation from the wise men of his kingdom, but was unwilling to tell them the dream first, lest they make up an interpretation. If they were truly men of wisdom, he thought, they would know what he had dreamt and he could be sure of the validity of their interpretation. He threatened them with death if they failed. None, of course, succeeded. When the king's death order was to be carried out, Daniel and his companions were to be among those killed. When Daniel found out why, he begged the king to give him time to interpret the dream. Daniel succeeded, with the help of the God of Israel. Today's reading recounts both the dream and Daniel's interpretation.

◆ CANTICLE: Our response is again from the hymn of praise in Daniel. Today's stanzas call on various creatures and elements of nature to praise the Lord.

◆ GOSPEL: There are two foci in today's Gospel. The first is the destruction of the Temple, which took place in the year AD 70. The second is the terrifying signs that will precede the end time.

WED 27 (#505) green — Weekday

The Lectionary for Mass

◆ FIRST READING: The account of Daniel's remarkable gift of interpretation continues, but during the reign of another king. This time the challenge for Daniel is to interpret a mysterious event that happened during a banquet when the sacred vessels from the Temple in Jerusalem were being used by the Babylonians as ordinary drinking cups and thus profaned. As Daniel so wisely points out, the mysterious hand and the writing on the wall are God's judgment against the king.

◆ CANTICLE: More elements of creation are called upon to praise the Lord in these verses from the canticle of Daniel 3. This praise of God the Creator stands in stark contrast with the Babylonians' worship of their idols mentioned in the First Reading.

◆ GOSPEL: Today's Gospel speaks of afflictions Jesus' followers will endure, such as betrayal by family and friends and civil persecution, all because of their belief in Jesus' name. Jesus assures his followers of his continuing presence and protection.

THU 28 (#506) green — Weekday

Proper Mass for Thanksgiving Day (#943–947) / white

The Lectionary for Mass

◆ FIRST READING: Today's reading begins with Daniel 6:12, so a reading of the first 11 verses of this chapter would be most helpful in understanding the context. During the reign of King Darius, Daniel had attained a very high position in the kingdom, and his reputation for wisdom was unequaled. As a result, he was envied by his colleagues and subordinates who contrived a scheme to be rid of him. They had the king issue a decree prohibiting the petitioning of any god or any human being other than the king for a period of thirty days. Quite easily, they caught the pious Daniel at prayer—a clear violation of the king's decree—and here the reading begins. Despite the king's desire to save Daniel from the fate of the lions' den, he was bound to carry out the punishment. We hear today how God preserved Daniel's life. As a result, the king proclaimed that Daniel's God was to be reverenced.

◆ CANTICLE: Still more of creation is called upon to give praise to God in these verses from the canticle in Daniel 3.

◆ GOSPEL: In an apocalyptic tone, Luke describes the destruction of Jerusalem by the Romans. God's people must wait for the end time when cosmic signs will herald the coming of the Son of Man. Believers should not fear these signs, for they announce the time of their redemption. Victorious in their struggle, they have every reason to stand up straight (a posture of freedom) when facing the judgment at the end time.

The Roman Missal: Thanksgiving Day

There is a complete set of prayers for Thanksgiving Day, including a Preface, found at the end of November in the Proper of Saints. On this national holiday, we give thanks to God for his countless gifts of love and his infinite goodness, and we pray that our hearts may be open "to have concern / for every man, woman, and child" (Collect). With the gifts God has given comes a "responsibility and commitment" to advance the dignity of others (Preface), and to "share with them / the good things of time and eternity" (Prayer after Communion). Consider using the Eucharistic Prayer for Various Needs and Occasions II.

FRI 29 (#507) green — Weekday

The Lectionary for Mass

◆ FIRST READING: Today's reading from Daniel has special significance since it gives us important Old Testament background for the figure of the Son of Man, a title used in the Gospel accounts with reference to Jesus. This section of Daniel belongs to a genre of writing known as "apocalyptic." (The word means "revelation.") Apocalyptic literature consists of highly symbolic revelations about the end of time. Today's text recounts a nighttime vision given to Daniel. The four beasts represent different kingdoms that are ultimately conquered when brought to judgment before the "Ancient One" (God). Perhaps readers will recognize imagery evoking other descriptions of God's heavenly throne (see, for example, Isaiah 6:2.4; Ezekiel 1; Revelation 4:1–6). The one "like" a son of man, is one like a human being (see Psalm 8:5). In Daniel's vision, this Son of Man is exalted by God and given dominion, power, and glory. In New Testament traditions, this points to the exaltation of the risen and glorified Lord.

◆ CANTICLE: Still more verses from the canticle of praise in Daniel 3. The juxtaposition of verses with references to the sea and the animals which praise the Lord stand in stark contrast with the arrogant beasts of Daniel's vision!

◆ GOSPEL: Today's Gospel is a continuation of Jesus' discourse on the end time. He speaks of signs that will warn people that the end time, the coming of the kingdom of God in all its fullness, is near. Luke's audience, like other Christians of their day, believed that the end time would be within their lifetime.

S
A **30** (#684) red
T **Feast of St. Andrew, Apostle**

The Lectionary for Mass

◆ FIRST READING: A twofold emphasis is heard in today's reading. The first is on the importance of professing faith in Jesus as Lord (God) and as raised from the dead, if one is to be saved. The second is on the necessity of someone preaching the Gospel so that others may hear and believe. Without hearing, there can be no faith. Today, we celebrate the feast of the Apostle Saint Andrew, one of the first to go out to all the earth to proclaim the Gospel.

◆ RESPONSORIAL PSALM 19: There is a choice for the antiphon: a verse from the Psalm, which celebrates the righteousness of God's judgments, particularly as made known in the law, which the body of the Psalm acclaims; or a verse from John's account of the Gospel which acclaims the word of the Lord as the source of life.

◆ GOSPEL: Today's Gospel is the call of Andrew, the fisherman, whose mission will be to make a catch for the Lord through the proclamation of the Gospel. Notice the immediacy of the response of Andrew and the others to Jesus' call.

The Roman Missal

Today we turn to the Proper of Saints for the prayer texts for St. Andrew. All of the texts are proper. The Gloria is sung or said today. There is no Creed. Use one of the Prefaces of the Apostles. Consider using Eucharistic Prayer I.

Today's Saint

St. Andrew (first century) was the first of the Twelve to meet Jesus. Tradition says that he may have preached in parts of Asia Minor and Greece before being crucified on an X-shaped cross.